The Holy Qur'ân

English Translation
With Original 'Arabic Text

By
Abdullah Yusuf Ali

ISLAMIC BOOK SERVICE

The Holy Qur'ân

Revised edition: 2002

ISBN: 81-7231-388-8

Published by *Abdul Naeem* for
Islamic Book Service
2241, Kucha Chelan, Darya Ganj, New Delhi-110 002
Ph.: 3253514, 3265380, 3286551, Fax: 3277913
e-mail: ibsdelhi@del2.vsnl.net.in
        ibsdelhi@mantraonline.com
website: http//www.islamic-india.com

OUR ASSOCIATES
Islamic Book Service Inc.
136, Charlotte Ave., Hicksville, N.Y. 11801.
Ph.: 516-8700-IBS (427), Fax: 516-8700-429,
Toll Free # 866-2424-IBS
E-mail: sales@islamicbookservices.com
        ibsny@conversent.net

Al Munna Book Shop Ltd.
P.O. Box-3449, Sharjah (U.A.E.), Tel.: 06-561-5483, 06-561-4650
E-mail: nusrat@emirates.net.ae
Branch: Dubai, Tel.: 04-3529294

Zainab Foundation
Al-Baraka House,18-20, Park Street, Slough
SLI IPD, England, Tel.: 01753-533-511

Sartaj Company
P.O. Box-48535, Qualbert-4078, Durban,South Africa, Tel.: 305-3025
E-mail: sartaj@mweb.co.za

Printed at: **Noida Printing Press,** C-31, Sector-7, Noida (Ghaziabad) U.P.

CONTENTS

LIST OF PARTS

Part No.	Name of Parts	Pages

FROM THE PREFACE TO FIRST EDITION,
1934

. . . It may be asked: Is there any need for a fresh English translation? To those who ask this question I commend a careful consideration of the facts which I have set out in my Note on Translation. After they have read it, I would invite them to take any particular passage, say 2: 74 or 2: 102, or 2: 164 and compare it with any previous version they choose. If they find that I have helped them even the least bit further in understanding its meanings, or appreciating its beauty or catching something of the grandeur of the original, I would claim that my humble attempt is justified.

It is the duty of every Muslim, man, woman, or child, to read the Qur-ān and understand it according to his own capacity. If any one of us attains to some knowledge or understanding of it by study, contemplation, and the test of life, both outward and inward, it is his duty, according to his capacity, to instruct others, and share with them the joy and peace which result from contact with the spiritual world. The Qur-ān—indeed every religious book—has to be read, not only with the tongue and voice and eyes, but with the best light that our intellect can supply, and even more, with the truest and purest light which our heart and conscience can give us. It is in this spirit that I would have my readers approach the Qur-ān.

It was between the age of four and five that I first learned to read its Arabic words, to revel in its rhythm and music and wonder at its meaning. I have a dim recollection of the *Khatm* ceremony which closed that stage. It was called "completion": it really just *began* a spiritual awakening that has gone on ever since. My revered father taught me Arabic, but I must have imbibed from him into my innermost being something more,—something which told me that all the world's thoughts, all the world's most beautiful languages and literatures, are but vehicles for that ineffable message which comes to the heart in rare moments of ecstasy. The soul of mysticism and ecstasy is in the Qur-ān, as well as that plain guidance for the plain man which a world in a hurry affects to consider as sufficient. It is good to make this personal confession, to an age in which it is in the highest degree unfashionable to speak of religion or spiritual peace or consolation, an age in which words like these draw forth only derision, pity, or contempt.

I have explored Western lands, Western manners, and the depths of Western thought and Western learning to an extent which has rarely fallen to the lot of an Eastern mortal. But I have never lost touch with my Eastern heritage. Through all my successes and failures I have learned to rely more and more upon the one true thing in all life—the voice that speaks in a tongue above that of mortal man. For me the embodiment of that voice has been in the noble words of the Arabic Qur-ān, which I have tried to translate for myself and apply to my experience again and again. The service of the Qur-ān has been the pride and the privilege of many Muslims. I felt that with such life-experience as has fallen to my lot, my service to the Qur-ān should be to present it in a fitting garb in English. That ambition I have cherished in my mind for more than forty years. I have collected books and materials for it. I have visited places, undertaken journeys, taken notes, sought the society of men, and tried to explore their thoughts and hearts, in order to equip myself for the task. Sometimes I have considered it too stupendous for me,—the double task of understanding the original, and reproducing its nobility, its beauty, its poetry, its grandeur, and its sweet, practical, reasonable application to everyday experience. Then I have blamed myself for lack of courage,—the spiritual courage of men who dared all in the Cause which was so dear to them.

Two sets of apparently accidental circumstances at last decided me. A man's life is subject to inner storms far more devastating than those in the physical world around him. In such a storm, in the bitter anguish of a personal sorrow which nearly unseated my reason and made life seem meaningless, a new hope was born out of a systematic pursuit of my long-cherished project. Watered by tears, my manuscript began to grow in depth and earnestness if not in bulk. I guarded it like a secret treasure. Wanderer that I am, I carried it about, thousands of miles, to all sorts of countries and among all sorts of people. At length, in the city of Lahore, I happened to mention the matter to some young people who held me in respect and affection. They showed an enthusiasm and an eagerness which surprised me. They almost took the matter out of my hands. They asked for immediate publication. I had various bits ready, but not even one complete Sīpāra. They made me promise to complete at least one Sīpāra before I left Lahore. As if by magic, a publisher, a kātib (calligraphist, to write the Arabic Text), an engraver of blocks for such text, and a printer were found, all equally anxious to push forward the scheme. Blessed be youth, for its energy and determination! "Where others flinch, rash youth will dare!"

Gentle and discerning reader! what I wish to present to you is an English Interpretation, side by side with the Arabic Text. The English shall be, not a mere substitution of one word for another, but the best expression I can give to the fullest meaning which I can understand from the Arabic Text. The rhythm, music, and exalted tone of the original should be reflected in the

English Interpretation. It may be but a faint reflection, but such beauty and power as my pen commands shall be brought to its service. I want to make English itself an Islamic language, if such a person as I can do it. And I must give you all the necessary aid which I can....

The Text in English is printed . . . in parallel columns with the Arabic Text. Each *Sûra* and the verse of each *Sûra* is separately numbered, and the numbers are shown page by page. The system of numbering the verses has not been uniform in previous translations. European editors and translators have allowed their numbering to diverge considerably from that accepted in the East. This causes confusion in giving and verifying references. The different *Qirâats* sometimes differ as to the punctuation stops and the numbering of the verses. This is not a vital matter, but it causes confusion in references. It is important that at least in Islamic countries one system of numbering should be adopted. I have adopted mainly that of the Egyptian edition published under the authority of the King of Egypt. This will probably be accepted in Egypt and in Arabic-speaking countries, as those countries generally look up to Egypt in matters of literature. I am glad to see that the text . . . published by the Anjuman-i-Himayat-i-Islam of Lahore is following the same system of numbering. I recommend to other publishers . . . the same good example. If once this is done, we shall have a uniform system of numbering. I have retained the numbering of Sections as it is universally used in the Arabic copies, and marks a logical division of the *Sûras*. I have supplied a further aid to the reader in indicating sub-division of the Sections into paragraphs. They are not numbered, but are distinguished by the use of a flowery initial letter ....

. . . Every earnest and reverent student of the Qur-ân, as he proceeds with his study, will find, with an inward joy difficult to describe, how this general meaning also enlarges as his own capacity for understanding increases. It is like a traveller climbing a mountain; the higher he goes, the farther he sees. From a literary point of view the poet Keats has described his feeling when he discovered Chapman's Homer:

> Then felt I like some watcher of the skies
> When a new planet swims into his ken,
> Or like stout Cortez when with eagle eyes,
> He stared at the Pacific,—and all his men
> Looked at each other with a wild surmise,—
> Silent, upon a peak in Darien.

How much greater is the joy and sense of wonder and miracle when the Qur-ân opens our spiritual eyes ! The meaning which we thought we had grasped expands. New words are opened out. As we progress, still newer.

and again newer worlds "swim into our ken". The miracle deepens and deepens, and almost completely absorbs us. And yet we know that the "face of God"—our final goal—has not yet been reached. We are in the *mulk* of Sulaiman (Q. 2: 102), which the evil ones denied, belied, and even turned into blasphemy. But we can ignore blasphemy, ridicule and contempt, for we are in the threshold of Realities and a little perfume from the garden of the Holy One has already gladdened our nostrils . . .

The Arabic Text I have had printed from photographic blocks, made for me by Master Muhammad Sharif. The calligraphy is from the pen of Pir 'Abdul Hamid, with whom I have been in touch and who has complied with my desire for a bold round hand, with the words clearly separated, the vowel points accurately placed over or under the letter to which they relate, and the verses duly numbered and placed in juxtaposition with their English equivalents. Calligraphy occupies an important place in Muslim Art, and it is my desire that my version should not in any way be deficient in this respect.

I have been fortunate in securing the co-operation of Professor Zafar Iqbal in looking over the proofs of the Arabic Text. In connection with the Anjuman's edition of the Arabic Qur-ān he has devoted much time and thought to the correct punctuation of the Text, and he has also investigated its history and problems. I hope he will some day publish these valuable notes. I have been privileged to see the Anjuman's Text before its formal publication. I consider it the most carefully prepared Text of any produced in India and I have generally followed it in punctuation and the numbering of verses,—the only points on which my difficulties are likely to arise on the Qur'anic Text....

One final word to my readers. Read, study and digest the Holy Book. Read slowly, and let it sink into your heart and soul. Such study will, like virtue, be its own reward. If you find anything in this volume to criticise, please let it not spoil your enjoyment of the rest. If you write to me, quoting chapter and verse, I shall be glad to consider your criticism, but let it not vex you if I exercise my own judgment in deciding for myself. Any corrections accepted will be gratefully acknowledged. On the other hand, if there is something that specially pleases you or helps you, please do not hesitate to write to me. I have given up other interests to help you. It will be a pleasure to know that my labour has not been in vain. If you address me care of my Publisher at his Lahore address, he will always forward the letters to me.

LAHORE   **A. YUSUF 'ALI**
4th April, 1934
= 18th of the month of Pilgrimage 1352 H.

LIST OF SÛRAS (CHAPTERS)

TRANSLITERATION OF ARABIC WORDS AND NAMES

ا	⎰consonantal⎱ sound	a	ط	ṭ
ء			ظ	ẓ
آ	Long vowel *	ā	ع	' (inverted apostrophe)
ب	. . . .	b	غ	g
ت	. . . .	t	ف	f
ث	. . . .	<u>th</u>	ق	q
ج	. . . .	j	ك	k
ح	. . . .	ḥ	ل	l
خ	. . . .	<u>kh</u>	م	m
د	. . . .	d	ن	n
ذ	. . . .	ẓ	ه	h
ر	. . . .	r	و	consonant w
ز	. . . .	z	و	long vowel * û
س	. . . .	s	و	diphthong au
ش	. . . .	sh	ي	consonant y
ص	. . . .	ṣ	ي	long vowel * î
ض	. . . .	<u>dh</u>	ي	diphthong ai

Short vowels: ﹷ (*fatḥa*) a

ﹻ (*kasra*) i

ﹹ (*dhamma*) u

1. For the *hamzā* (ء) I have used no distinctive sign. An apostrophe for it and an inverted apostrophe for the *'ain* (ع), or *vice versa*, is confusing to English readers. As a moved consonant, it is sufficiently shown in English by the long or short vowel which moves it, e.g. *ab, Raûf*.

---

* Where it is really *pronounced* long. Hence <u>kh</u>alaqnā-kum but <u>kh</u>alaqnal-insān; Abû Sufyān but Abul-Qāsim; fin-nār but fî-hi.

Where it is a hiatus preceded by a *fatha*, I have shown it by a second *a* : thus, *Iqraa*, the cave of *Hiraa*. In other cases it has not been possible to show it without using a distinctive sign. The name of the Holy Book is usually written Qurān; but I prefer to write Qur-ān. However a few words like juz have an apostrophe indicating Hamza.

2. The final *h* preceded by the short *a* is scarcely pronounced, and I have left it out. Hence Sûra, Fātiha, Hijra, etc., where the Arabic spelling would require Sûrah, Fātihah, Hijrah, etc.

3. In internationalised words and names I have used the spelling ordinarily current in English; e.g. Mecca, Medina, Maulvi, Urdu, Islam, Israel, Abraham, Jacob. Here the boundary is thin and rather ill-defined, and possibly my practice and that of my proof-readers have not been absolutely uniform. But in place of Mecca and Madina, the more accurate form of Makkah and Madinah is adopted.

بسم الله الرحمن الرحيم

SÛRA–I
AL-FĀTIḤA
(INTRODUCTION)

First comes that beautiful Sûra, The Opening Chapter of Seven Verses, rightly called the Essence of the Book. It teaches us the perfect Prayer. For if we can pray aright, it means that we have some knowledge of Allah and His attributes, of His relations to us and His creation, which includes ourselves; that we glimpse the source from which we come, and that final goal which is our spiritual destiny under Allah's true judgement: then we offer oursleves to Allah and seek His light.

Prayer is the heart of Religion and Faith: but how shall we pray ? What words shall convey the yearnings of our miserable, ignorant hearts to the Knower of all ? Is it worth of Him or of our spiritual nature to ask for vanities, or even for such physical needs as our daily bread ? The Inspired One taught us a Prayer that sums up our faith, our hope, and our aspiration in things that matter. We think in devotion of Allah's name and His Nature; we praise Him for His creation and His cherishing care; we call to mind the Realities, seen and unseen; we offer Him worship and ask for His guidance; and we know the straight from the crooked path by the light of His grace that illumines the righteous.

Al-Fātiḥa, or the Opening Chapter

1. In the name of Allah, Most Gracious, Most Merciful.

بِسْمِ اللهِ الرَّحْمٰنِ الرَّحِيْمِ ۝

2. Praise be to Allah, the Cherisher and Sustainer of the Worlds:

اَلْحَمْدُ لِلّٰهِ رَبِّ الْعٰلَمِيْنَ ۝

3. Most Gracious, Most Merciful;

الرَّحْمٰنِ الرَّحِيْمِ ۝

4. Master of the Day of Judgment.

مٰلِكِ يَوْمِ الدِّيْنِ ۝

5. Thee do we worship, and Thine aid we seek.

اِيَّاكَ نَعْبُدُ وَاِيَّاكَ نَسْتَعِيْنُ ۝

6. Show us the straight way,

اِهْدِنَا الصِّرَاطَ الْمُسْتَقِيْمَ ۝

7. The way of those on whom Thou has bestowed Thy Grace, those whose (portion) is not wrath. And who go not astray.

صِرَاطَ الَّذِيْنَ اَنْعَمْتَ عَلَيْهِمْ غَيْرِ الْمَغْضُوْبِ عَلَيْهِمْ وَلَا الضَّآلِّيْنَ ۝

SÛRA-2
AL-BAQARAH
(INTRODUCTION)

As the Opening Sûra sums up in seven beautiful verses the essence of the Qur-ān, so this Sûra sums up in 286 verses the whole teaching of the Qur-ān. It is a closely reasoned argument.

This is the longest Sûra of the Qur-ān and in it occurs the longest verse (2: 282). The name of the Sûra is from the Parable of the Heifer in 2: 67-71, which illustrates the insufficiency of carping obedience. When faith is lost, people put off obedience with various excuses: even when at last they obey in the letter, they fail in the spirit, which means that they get fossilised, and their self-sufficiency prevents them from seeing that spiritually they are not alive but dead. For life is movement, activity, striving, fighting, against baser things. And this is the burden of the Sûra.

This is in the main an early Madinah Sûra.

Al-Baqarah,
or the Heifer (The Cow)

In the name of Allah, Most Gracious, Most Merciful.

1. A. L. M.

2. This is the Book; in it is guidance sure, without doubt, to those who fear Allah;

3. Who believe in the Unseen, are steadfast in prayer, and spend out of what We have provided for them;

4. And who believe in the Revelation sent to thee, and sent before thy time, and (in their hearts) have the assurance of the Hereafter.

5. They are on (true guidance), from their Lord, and it is these who will prosper.

6. As to those who reject Faith, it is the same to them whether thou warn them or do not warn them; they will not believe.

7. Allah hath set a seal on their hearts and on their hearing. And on their eyes is a veil; great is the chastisement they (incur).

8. Of the people there are some who say: "We believe in Allah and the Last day:" but they do not (really) believe.

9. Fain would they deceive Allah and those who believe, but they only deceive themselves, and realize (it) not !

10. In their hearts is a disease; and Allah has increased their disease: and grievous is the chastisement they (incur), because they lied (to themselves).

11. When it is said to them: "Make not mischief on the earth," they say: "We are only ones that put things right."

12. Of a surety, they are the ones who make mischief, but they realize (it) not.

13. When it is said to them: "Believe as the others believe:" they say: "Shall we believe as the fools believe?"—Nay, of a surety they are the fools, but they do not know.

14. When they meet those who believe. they say: "We believe;" but when they are alone with their evil ones, they say: "We are really with you; we (were) only jesting."

15. Allah will throw back their mockery on them, and give them rope in their trespasses; so they will wander like blind ones (to and fro).

16. These are they who have bartered guidance for error: but their traffic is profitless, and they have lost true direction,

17. Their similitude is that of a man who kindled a fire; when it lighted all around him, Allah took away their light and left them in utter darkness. so they could not see.

18. Deaf, dumb, and blind, they will not return (to the path).

19. Or (another similitude) is that of a rain-laden cloud from the sky: in it are zones of darkness, and thunder and lightning: they press their fingers in their ears to keep out the stunning thunder-clap, the while they are in terror of death. But Allah is ever

round the rejecters of Faith !

20. The lightning all but snatches away their sight: every time the light (helps) them, they walk therein, and when the darkness grows on them, they stand still, and if Allah willed, He could take away their faculty of hearing and seeing; for Allah hath power over all things.

21. O ye people ! worship your Guardian Lord, Who created you and those who came before you, that ye may become righteous,

22. Who has made the earth your couch, and the heavens your canopy; and sent down rain from the heavens; and brought forth therewith fruits for your sustenance; then set not up rivals unto Allah when ye know (the truth).

23. And if ye are in doubt as to what We have revealed from time to time to Our servant, then produce a Sûra like thereunto; and call your witnesses or helpers (if there are any) besides Allah, if ye are truthful.

24. But if ye cannot— and of a surety ye cannot—then fear the Fire whose fuel is Men and Stones,—which is prepared for those who reject Faith.

25. But give glad tidings to those who believe and work righteousness, that their portion is Gardens, beneath which rivers flow. Every time they are fed with fruits therefrom, they say: "Why, this is what we were fed with before," for they are given things in similitude; and they have therein spouses purified; and they abide therein (for ever).

26. Allah disdains not to use the similitude of things, even of a gnat as well as anything above it. Those who believe know that it is the truth from their Lord; but those who reject Faith say: "What means Allah by this similitude?" By it He causes many to stray, and many He leads into the right path; but He causes not to stray, except those who forsake (the path),—

27. Those who break Allah's Covenant after it is ratified, and who sunder what Allah has ordered to be joined, and do mischief on earth: these cause loss (only) to themselves.

28. How can ye reject the faith in Allah?— seeing that ye were without life, and He gave you life; then will He cause you to die, and will again bring you to life; and again to Him will ye return.

29. It is He Who hath created for you all things that are on earth; then He turned to the heaven and made them into seven firmaments; and of all things He hath perfect knowledge.

30. Behold, thy Lord said to the angels: "I will create a vicegerent on earth." They said: "Wilt Thou place therein one who will make mischief therein and shed blood?— whilst we do celebrate Thy praises and glorify Thy holy (name)?" He said: "I know what ye know not".

31. And He taught Adam the names of all things; then He placed them before the angels, and said: "Tell Me the names of these if ye are right."

32. They said: "Glory to Thee: of knowledge we have none. save what Thou

nast taught us: in truth it is Thou Who art perfect in knowledge and wisdom."

33. He said: "O Adam ! tell them their names." When he had told them their names, Allah said: "Did I not tell you that I know the   secrets of heaven and earth, and I know what ye reveal and what ye conceal?"

34. And behold, We said to the angels: "Bow down to Adam:" and they bowed down: not so Iblis: he refused and was haughty: he was of those who reject Faith.

35. And We said: "O Adam! dwell thou and thy wife in the Garden; and eat of the bountiful things therein as (where and when) ye will; but approach not this tree, or ye run into harm and transgression."

36. Then did Satan make them slip from the (Garden), and get them out of the state (of felicity) in which they had been. And We said: "Get ye down, all (ye people), with enmity between yourselves. On earth will be your dwelling place and your means of livelihood— for a time".

37. Then learnt Adam from his Lord certain words and his Lord turned towards him; for He is Oft-Returning, Most Merciful.

38. We said: "Get ye down all from here; and if, as is sure, there comes to you guidance from Me, whosoever follows My guidance, on them shall be no fear, nor shall they grieve.

39. "But those who reject Faith and belie Our Signs, they shall be Companions of the Fire; they shall abide therein."

40. O Children of Israel! call to mind the (special) favour which I bestowed upon you, and fulfil your Covenant with Me and I shall

fulfil My Covenant with you, and fear none but Me.

بِعَهْدِى أُوفِ بِعَهْدِكُمْ وَإِيَّايَ فَارْهَبُونِ ۝

41. And believe in what I reveal, confirming the revelation which is with you, and be not the first to reject Faith therein, nor sell My Signs for a small price; and fear Me, and Me alone.

وَءَامِنُوا بِمَا أَنْزَلْتُ مُصَدِّقًا لِّمَا مَعَكُمْ وَلَا تَكُونُوا أَوَّلَ كَافِرٍ بِهِ وَلَا تَشْتَرُوا بِـَٔايَتِى ثَمَنًا قَلِيلًا وَإِيَّايَ فَاتَّقُونِ ۝

42. And cover not Truth with falsehood, nor conceal the Truth when ye know (what it is).

وَلَا تَلْبِسُوا الْحَقَّ بِالْبَاطِلِ وَتَكْتُمُوا الْحَقَّ وَأَنْتُمْ تَعْلَمُونَ ۝

43. And be steadfast in prayer; give Zakat, and bow down your heads with those who bow down (in worship).

وَأَقِيمُوا الصَّلَوٰةَ وَءَاتُوا الزَّكَوٰةَ وَارْكَعُوا مَعَ الرَّٰكِعِينَ ۝

44. Do ye enjoin right conduct on the people, and forget (to practise it) yourselves, and yet ye study the Scripture? Will ye not understand?

أَتَأْمُرُونَ النَّاسَ بِالْبِرِّ وَتَنْسَوْنَ أَنْفُسَكُمْ وَأَنْتُمْ تَتْلُونَ الْكِتَٰبَ أَفَلَا تَعْقِلُونَ ۝

45. Nay, seek (Allah's) help with patient perseverance and prayer: it is indeed hard, except to those who are humble.

وَاسْتَعِينُوا بِالصَّبْرِ وَالصَّلَوٰةِ وَإِنَّهَا لَكَبِيرَةٌ إِلَّا عَلَى الْخَٰشِعِينَ ۝

46. Who bear in mind the certainty that they are to meet their Lord, and that they are to return to Him.

الَّذِينَ يَظُنُّونَ أَنَّهُم مُّلَٰقُوا رَبِّهِمْ وَأَنَّهُمْ إِلَيْهِ رَٰجِعُونَ ۝

47. O Children of Israel! call to mind the (special) favour which I bestowed upon you, and that I preferred you to all others.

يَٰبَنِى إِسْرَٰءِيلَ اذْكُرُوا نِعْمَتِىَ الَّتِى أَنْعَمْتُ عَلَيْكُمْ وَأَنِّى فَضَّلْتُكُمْ عَلَى الْعَٰلَمِينَ ۝

48. Then guard yourselves against a day when one soul shall not avail another nor shall intercession be accepted for her, nor shall compensation be taken from her, nor shall anyone be helped (from outside).

وَاتَّقُوا يَوْمًا لَّا تَجْزِى نَفْسٌ عَن نَّفْسٍ شَيْـًٔا وَلَا يُقْبَلُ مِنْهَا شَفَٰعَةٌ وَلَا يُؤْخَذُ مِنْهَا عَدْلٌ وَلَا هُمْ يُنصَرُونَ ۝

49. And remember, We delivered you from the people of Pharaoh: they set you hard tasks and chastisement, slaughtered your sons and let your women-folk live; therein

وَإِذْ نَجَّيْنَٰكُم مِّنْ ءَالِ فِرْعَوْنَ يَسُومُونَكُمْ سُوٓءَ الْعَذَابِ يُذَبِّحُونَ أَبْنَآءَكُمْ وَيَسْتَحْيُونَ نِسَآءَكُمْ

was a tremendous trial from your Lord.

50. And remember We divided the Sea for you and saved you and drowned Pharaoh's people within your very sight.

51. And remember We appointed forty nights for Moses, and in his absence ye took the calf (for worship), and ye did grievous wrong.

52. Even then We did forgive you, there was a chance for you to be grateful.

53. And remember We gave Moses the Scripture and the Criterion (between right and wrong), there was a chance for you to be guided aright.

54. And remember Moses said to his people: "O my people! ye have indeed wronged yourselves by your worship of the calf: so turn (in repentance) to your Maker, and slay yourselves (the wrong-doers); that will be better for you in the sight of your Maker." Then He turned towards you (in forgiveness): for He is Oft-Returning, Most Merciful.

55. And remember ye said: "O Moses! we shall never believe in thee until we see Allah manifestly," thereupon thunderbolt seized you.

56. Then We raised you up after your death; ye had the chance to be grateful.

57. And We gave you the shade of clouds and sent down to you Manna and quails, saying: "Eat of the good things We have provided for you:" (but they rebelled); to Us they did no harm, but they harmed their own selves.

58. And remember We said: "Enter this town, and eat of the plenty therein as ye

wish; and enter the gate prostrating, and say: Forgive (us) We shall forgive you your faults and increase (the portion of) those who do good."

59. But the transgressors changed the word from that which had been given them; so We sent on the transgressors a plague from heaven, for that they infringed (Our command) repeatedly.

60. And remember Moses prayed for water for his people; We said: "Strike the rock with thy staff." Then gushed forth therefrom twelve springs. Each group knew its own place for water. So eat and drink of the sustenance provided by Allah, and do no evil nor mischief on the (face of the) earth.

61. And remember ye said: "O Moses! we cannot endure one kind of food (always); so beseech thy Lord for us to produce for us of what the earth groweth,—its pot-herbs, and cucumbers, its garlic, lentils, and onions." He said: "Will ye exchange the better for the worse ? Go ye down to any town, and ye shall find what ye want!" They were covered with humiliation and misery: they drew on themselves the wrath of Allah. This because they went on rejecting the Signs of Allah and slaying His Messengers without just cause. This because they rebelled and went on transgressing.

62. Those who believe (in the Qur'an), and those who follow the Jewish

(scriptures), and the Christians and the Sabians,— any who believe in Allah and the Last Day, and work righteousness, shall have their reward with their Lord on them shall be no fear, nor shall they grieve.

63. And remember We took your Covenant and We raised above you the Mount (Sinai) (saying): "Hold firmly to what We have given you and bring (ever) to remembrance what is therein: perchance ye may fear Allah."

64. But ye turned back thereafter: had it not been for the Grace and Mercy of Allah to you, ye had surely been among the lost.

65. And well ye knew those amongst you who transgressed in the matter of the Sabbath: We said to them: "Be ye apes, despised and rejected."

66. So We made it an example to their own time and to their posterity, and a lesson to those who fear Allah.

67. And remember Moses said to his people: "Allah commands that ye sacrifice a heifer." They said: "Makest thou a laughing-stock of us?" He said: "Allah save me from being an ignorant (fool)!"

68. They said: "Beseech on our behalf thy Lord to make plain to us What (heifer) it is!" He said: "He says: the heifer should be neither too old nor too young, but of middling age: now do what ye are commanded !"

69. They said: "Beseech on our behalf thy Lord to make plain to us her colour." He said: "He says: a fawn-coloured heifer. pure and rich in tone. the

admiration of beholders!"

70. They said: "Beseech on our behalf thy Lord to make plain to us what she is: to us are all heifers alike: we wish indeed for guidance, if Allah wills."

71. He said: "He says: a heifer not trained to till the soil or water the fields; sound and without blemish." They said: "Now hast thou brought the truth." Then they offered her in sacrifice, and they scarcely did it.

72. Remember ye slew a man and fell into a dispute among yourselves as to the crime: but Allah was to bring forth what ye did hide.

73. So We said: "Strike the (body) with a piece of the (heifer)." Thus Allah brin-geth the dead to life and showeth you His Signs: perchance ye may understand.

74. Thenceforth were your hearts hardened: they became like a rock and even worse in hardness. For among rocks there are some from which rivers gush forth; others there are which when split asunder send forth water: and others which sink for fear of Allah, and Allah is not unmindful of what ye do.

75. Can ye (O ye men of Faith) entertain the hope that they will believe in you ?— seeing that a party of them heard the Word of Allah, and perverted it knowingly after they understood it.

76. Behold! when they meet the men of Faith, they say: "We believe": but when they meet each other in private, they say: "Shall you tell them what Allah hath revealed

to you, that they may engage you in argument about it before your Lord?"—Do ye not understand (their aim)?

77. Know they not that Allah knoweth what they conceal and what they reveal ?

78. And there are among them illiterates, who know not the Book, but (see therein their own) desires, and they do nothing but conjecture.

79. Then woe to those who write the Book with their own hands, and then say: "This is from Allah," to traffic with it for a miserable price !— Woe to them for what their hands do write, and for the gain they make thereby.

80. And they say: "The Fire shall not touch us but for a few numbered days:" say: "Have ye taken a promise from Allah, for He never breaks His promise? Or is it that ye say of Allah what ye do not know?"

81. Nay, those who seek gain in Evil, and are girt round by their sins,—they are Companions of the Fire: therein shall they abide (for ever).

82. But those who have faith and work righteousness, they are Companions of the Garden: therein shall they abide (for ever).

83. And remember We took a Covenant from the Children of Israel (to this effect): worship none but Allah; treat with kindness your parents and kindred, and orphans and those in need; speak fair to the people; be steadfast in prayer; and give Zakat, then did ye turn back, except a few among you, and ye backslide (even now).

84. And remember We took your Covenant (to this effect): Shed no blood amongst you, nor turn out your own people from your homes: and this ye solemnly ratified. And to this ye were witness.

85. After this it is ye, the same people, who slay among yourselves, and banish a party of you from their homes; assist (their enemies) against them, in guilt and transgression; and if they come to you as captives, ye ransom them, though it was not lawful for you to banish them. Then is it only a part of the Book that ye believe in, and do ye reject the rest ? But what is the reward for those among you who behave like this but disgrace in this life?—And on the Day of Judgment they shall be consigned to the most grievous chastisement for Allah is not unmindful of what ye do.

86. These are the people who buy the life of this world at the price of the Hereafter: their chastisement shall not be lightened, nor shall they be helped.

87. We gave Moses the Book and followed him up with a succession of Messengers; We gave Jesus the son of Mary clear (Signs) and strengthened him with the holy spirit. Is it that whenever there comes to you a Messenger with what ye yourselves desire not, ye are puffed up with pride ? — Some ye called impostors, and others ye slay !

88. They say, "Our hearts are the wrappings (which preserve Allah's Word: we need no more)" nay, Allah's curse is on them for their blasphemy: little is it they believe.

89. And when there comes; to them a Book from Allah, confirming what is with them,—

although from of old they had prayed for victory against those without Faith,— when there comes to them that which they (should) have recognized, they refuse to believe in it, but the curse of Allah is on those without Faith.

90. Miserable is the price for which they have sold their souls, in that they deny (the revelation) which Allah has sent down, in insolent envy that Allah of His Grace should send it to any of His servants He pleases: thus have they drawn on themselves Wrath upon Wrath. And humiliating is the Chastisement of those who reject Faith.

91. When it is said to them, "Believe in what Allah hath sent down," they say, "We believe in what was sent down to us": yet they reject all besides, even if it be Truth confirming what is with them. Say: "Why then have ye slain the prophets of Allah in times gone by, if ye did indeed believe?"

92. There came to you Moses with clear (Signs); yet ye worshipped the Calf (even) after that, and ye did behave wrongfully.

93. And remember We took your Covenant and We raised above you the mount (Sinai): (saying): "Hold firmly to what We have given you, and hearken (to the Law)" they said: "We hear, and we disobey": and their hearts were filled (with the love) of the Calf because of their Faithlessness. Say: "Vile indeed are the behests of your Faith if ye have any faith!"

94. Say: "If the last Home, with Allah, be for you specially. and not for anyone else, then seek ye for death, if ye

are sincere."

95. But they shall never seek for death, on account of the (sins) which their hands have sent on before them. And Allah is well-acquainted with the wrong-doers.

96. Thou wilt indeed find them, of all people, most greedy of life,—even more than the idolaters: each one of them wishes he could be given a life of a thousand years: but the grant of such life will not save him from (due) chastisement, for Allah sees well all that they do.

97. Say: Whoever is an enemy to Gabriel—for he brings down the (revelation) to thy heart by Allah's will, a confirmation of what went before, and guidance and glad tidings for those who believe,—

98. Whoever is an enemy to Allah and His angels and prophets, to Gabriel and Michael,— lo ! Allah is an enemy to those who reject Faith.

99. We have sent down to thee manifest Signs (*āyāt*); and none reject them but those who are perverse.

100. Is it not (the case) that every time they make a Covenant, some party among them throw it aside?— Nay, most of them are faithless.

101. And when there came to them a Messenger from Allah, confirming what was with them, a party of the People of the Book threw away the Book of Allah behind their backs, as if (it had been something) they did not know :

102. They followed what the Satans recited over Solomon's Kingdom. Solomon did not disbelieve but Satans disbelieved, teaching men, magic, and such things as came down at Babylon to the angels Hārūt and Mārūt. But neither of these taught anyone (such

things) without saying: "We are only for trial; so do not blaspheme." They learned from them the means to sow discord between man and wife. But they could not thus harm anyone except by Allah's permission. And they learned what harmed them, not what profited them. And they knew that the buyers of (magic) would have no share in the happiness of the Hereafter. And vile was the price for which they did sell their souls, if they but knew !

103. If they had kept their Faith and guarded themselves from evil, far better had been the reward from Allah, if they but knew!

104. O ye of Faith ! say not (to the Prophet) Ra'ina, but say, 'Unzurna and hearken (to him): to those without Faith is a grievous punishment.

105. It is never the wish of those without Faith among the People of the Book nor of the polytheists. That anything good should come down to you from your Lord. But Allah will choose for His special Mercy whom He will—for Allah is Lord of grace abounding.

106. None of Our revelations do We abrogate or cause to be forgotten, but We substitute something better or similar: knowest thou not that Allah hath power over all things ?

107. Knowest thou not that to Allah belongeth the dominion of the heavens and the earth ? And besides Him ye have neither patron nor helper.

108. Would ye question your Messenger

as Moses was questioned of old ? But whoever changeth from Faith to Unbelief. hath strayed without doubt from the even way.

109. Quite a number of the People of the Book wish they could turn you (people) back to infidelity after ye have believed. from selfish envy, after the Truth hath become manifest unto them: but forgive and overlook, till Allah brings about His command; for Allah hath power over all things.

110. And be steadfast in prayer and give Zakat: and whatever good ye send forth for your souls before you. ye shall find it with Allah: for Allah sees well all that ye do.

111. And they say: "None shall enter Paradise unless he be a Jew or a Christian" those are their (vain) desires. Say: "Produce your proof if ye are truthful."

112. Nay,—whoever submits his whole self to Allah and is a doer of good,—he will get his reward with his Lord; on such shall be no fear, nor shall they grieve.

113. The Jews say: "The Christians have naught (to stand) upon; and the Christians say: "The Jews have naught (to stand) upon." Yet they (profess to) study the (same) Book. Like unto their word is what those say who know not; but Allah will judge between them in their quarrel on the Day of

Judgment.

114. And who is more unjust than he who forbids that in places for the worship of Allah, His name should be celebrated ?—whose zeal is (in fact) to ruin them ? It was not fitting that such should themselves enter them except in fear. For them there is nothing but disgrace in this world, and in the world to come, an exceeding torment.

115. To Allah belong the East and the West: whithersoever ye turn, there is Allah's Face. For Allah is All-Embracing, All-Knowing.

116. They say: "Allah hath begotten a son": Glory be to Him.—Nay, to Him belongs all that is in the heavens and on earth: everything renders worship to Him.

117. The Originator of the heavens and the earth: when He decreeth a matter, He saith to it: "Be," and it is.

118. Say those without knowledge: "Why speaketh not Allah unto us ? Or why cometh not unto us a Sign ? So said the people before them words of similar import. Their hearts are alike. We have indeed made clear the Signs unto any people who hold firmly to Faith (in their hearts).

119. Verily We have sent thee in truth as a bearer of glad tidings and a warner: but of thee no question shall be asked of the Companions of the Blazing Fire.

120. Never will the Jews or the Christians be satisfied with thee unless thou follow their form of religion. Say: "The Guidance of Allah,–that is the (only) Guidance." Wert

thou to follow their desires after the knowledge which hath reached thee, then wouldst thou find neither Protector nor Helper against Allah.

121. Those to whom We have given the Book study it as it should be studied: they are the ones that believe therein: those who reject faith therein,—the loss is their own.

122. O Children of Israel ! call to mind the special favour which I bestowed upon you, and that I preferred you to all others.

123. Then guard yourselves against a Day when one soul shall not avail another, nor shall compensation be accepted from her nor shall intercession profit her nor shall anyone be helped (from outside).

124. And remember that Abraham was tried by his Lord with certain Commands, which he fulfilled: He said: "I will make thee an Imām to the people. He pleaded: "And also (Imāms) from my offspring!" He answered: "But My Promise is not within the reach of evil-doers."

125. Remember We made the House a place of assembly for men and a place of safety; and take ye the Station of Abraham as a place of prayer; and We covenanted with Abraham and Ismā'il, that they should sanctify My House for those who compass it round, or use it as a retreat. or bow, or prostrate themselves (therein in prayer).

126. And remember Abraham said: "My Lord, make this a City of Peace, and feed its People with fruits,– such of them as

believe in Allah and the Last Day." He said:
"(Yea), and such as reject Faith,–for a while
will I grant them their pleasure, but will
soon drive them to the torment of Fire,– an
evil destination (indeed) !"

127. And remember Abraham and Ismā'il
raised the foundations of the House (with
this prayer): "Our Lord ! accept (this service)
from us: for Thou art the All-Hearing, the
All-Knowing.

128. "Our Lord! make of us Muslims, bowing
to Thy (Will), and of our progeny a people
Muslim, bowing to Thy (Will); and show us
our places for the celebration of (due) rites;
and turn unto us (in Mercy); for Thou art the
Oft-Relenting Most Merciful.

129. "Our Lord ! send amongst them a
Messenger of their own, who shall rehearse
Thy Signs to them and instruct them in
Scripture and Wisdom, and purify them: for
Thou art the Exalted in Might, the Wise."

130. And who turns away from the religion
of Abraham but such as debase their souls
with folly? Him We chose and rendered
pure in this world: and he will be in the
Hereafter in the ranks of the Righteous.

131. Behold! his Lord said to him: Submit
(thy will to Me):" He said: "I submit (my will)
to the Lord and Cherisher of the Universe."

132. And Abraham enjoined upon his sons
and so did Jacob; "Oh my sons! Allah hath
chosen the Faith for you; then die not except
in the state of submission (to Me).

133. Were ye witnesses when Death
appeared before Jacob? Behold, he said to

his sons: "What will ye worship after me?"
They said: "We shall worship thy God and
the God of thy fathers,—of Abraham, Ismā'il,
and Isaac,—the One (True) God; to Him do
we submit."

134. That was a People that hath passed
away. They shall reap the fruit of what they
did, and ye of what ye do! Ye shall not be
asked about what they did.

135. They say: "Become Jews or Christians
if ye would be guided (to salvation)." Say
thou: "Nay! (I would rather) the Religion of
Abraham the True, and he joined not gods
with Allah."

136. Say ye: "We believe in Allah, and the
revelation given to us, and to Abraham,
Ismā'il, Isaac, Jacob, and the Tribes, and
that given to Moses and Jesus, and that
given to (all) Prophets from their Lord: we
make no difference between one and
another of them: and we submit to Allah.

137. So if they believe as ye believe, they
are indeed on the right path; but if they turn
back, it is they who are in schism; but Allah
will suffice thee as against them, and He is
the All-Hearing, the All-Knowing.

138. (Our religion) takes its hue from
Allah and who can give a better hue

than Allah. It is He Whom we worship.

مِنَ اللّٰهِ صِبْغَةً ۚ وَنَحْنُ لَهٗ عٰبِدُوْنَ ۞

139. Say: Will ye dispute with us about Allah, seeing that He is our Lord and your Lord; that we are responsible for our doings and ye for yours; and that we are sincere (in our faith) in Him?

قُلْ اَتُحَآجُّوْنَنَا فِى اللّٰهِ وَهُوَ رَبُّنَا وَرَبُّكُمْ ۚ وَلَنَآ اَعْمَالُنَا وَلَكُمْ اَعْمَالُكُمْ ۚ وَنَحْنُ لَهٗ مُخْلِصُوْنَ ۞

140. Or do ye say that Abraham, Isma'il, Isaac, Jacob and the Tribes were Jews or Christians? Say: Do ye know better than Allah? Ah! who is more unjust than those who conceal the testimony they have from Allah? But Allah is not unmindful of what ye do!

اَمْ تَقُوْلُوْنَ اِنَّ اِبْرٰهٖمَ وَاِسْمٰعِيْلَ وَاِسْحٰقَ وَيَعْقُوْبَ وَالْاَسْبَاطَ كَانُوْا هُوْدًا اَوْ نَصٰرٰى ۗ قُلْ ءَاَنْتُمْ اَعْلَمُ اَمِ اللّٰهُ ۗ وَمَنْ اَظْلَمُ مِمَّنْ كَتَمَ شَهَادَةً عِنْدَهٗ مِنَ اللّٰهِ ۗ وَمَا اللّٰهُ بِغَافِلٍ عَمَّا تَعْمَلُوْنَ ۞

141. That was a people that hath passed away. They shall reap the fruit of what they did, and ye of what ye do! Ye shall not be asked!—about what they did.

تِلْكَ اُمَّةٌ قَدْ خَلَتْ ۚ لَهَا مَا كَسَبَتْ وَلَكُمْ مَّا كَسَبْتُمْ ۚ وَلَا تُسْـَٔلُوْنَ عَمَّا كَانُوْا يَعْمَلُوْنَ ۞

142. The Fools among the people will say: "What hath turned them from the *Qibla* to which they were used?" Say: to Allah belong both East and West: He guideth whom He will to a Way that is straight.

سَيَقُوْلُ السُّفَهَآءُ مِنَ النَّاسِ مَا وَلّٰىهُمْ عَنْ قِبْلَتِهِمُ الَّتِيْ كَانُوْا عَلَيْهَا ۗ قُلْ لِّلّٰهِ الْمَشْرِقُ وَالْمَغْرِبُ ۚ يَهْدِيْ مَنْ يَّشَآءُ اِلٰى صِرَاطٍ مُّسْتَقِيْمٍ ۞

143. Thus have We made of you an *Ummat* justly balanced. That ye might be witnesses over the nations, and the Messenger a witness over yourselves; and We appointed the *Qibla* to which thou wast used, only to test those who followed the Messenger from those who would turn on their heels (from the Faith). Indeed it was (a change) momentous, except to those guided by Allah. And never would Allah ake your faith of no effect. For Allah is to all people most

وَكَذٰلِكَ جَعَلْنٰكُمْ اُمَّةً وَّسَطًا لِّتَكُوْنُوْا شُهَدَآءَ عَلَى النَّاسِ وَيَكُوْنَ الرَّسُوْلُ عَلَيْكُمْ شَهِيْدًا ۗ وَمَا جَعَلْنَا الْقِبْلَةَ الَّتِيْ كُنْتَ عَلَيْهَآ اِلَّا لِنَعْلَمَ مَنْ يَّتَّبِعُ الرَّسُوْلَ مِمَّنْ يَّنْقَلِبُ عَلٰى عَقِبَيْهِ ۗ وَاِنْ كَانَتْ لَكَبِيْرَةً اِلَّا عَلَى الَّذِيْنَ هَدَى اللّٰهُ ۗ

surely full of Kindness, Most Merciful.

وَمَا كَانَ اللّٰهُ لِيُضِيعَ اِيْمَانَكُمْ ۗ

اِنَّ اللّٰهَ بِالنَّاسِ لَرَءُوْفٌ رَّحِيْمٌ ۝

144. We see the turning of thy face (for guidance) to the heavens: now shall We turn thee to a *Qibla* that shall please thee. Turn then thy face in the direction of the Sacred Mosque: wherever ye are, turn your faces in that direction. The people of the Book know well that that is the truth from their Lord, nor is Allah unmindful of what they do.

قَدْ نَرٰى تَقَلُّبَ وَجْهِكَ فِى

السَّمَآءِ ۚ فَلَنُوَلِّيَنَّكَ قِبْلَةً

تَرْضٰىهَا ۖ فَوَلِّ وَجْهَكَ شَطْرَ

الْمَسْجِدِ الْحَرَامِ ۗ وَحَيْثُ مَا كُنْتُمْ

فَوَلُّوْا وُجُوْهَكُمْ شَطْرَهٗ ۗ وَاِنَّ

الَّذِيْنَ اُوْتُوا الْكِتٰبَ لَيَعْلَمُوْنَ

اَنَّهُ الْحَقُّ مِنْ رَّبِّهِمْ ۗ وَمَا اللّٰهُ

بِغَافِلٍ عَمَّا يَعْمَلُوْنَ ۝

145. Even if thou wert to bring to the people of the Book all the Signs (together), they would not follow thy *Qibla*; nor art thou going to follow their *Qibla*; nor indeed will they follow each other's *Qibla*. If thou after the knowledge hath reached thee, wert to follow their (vain) desires,—then wert thou indeed (clearly) in the wrong.

وَلَئِنْ اَتَيْتَ الَّذِيْنَ اُوْتُوا الْكِتٰبَ

بِكُلِّ اٰيَةٍ مَّا تَبِعُوْا قِبْلَتَكَ ۚ وَمَا

اَنْتَ بِتَابِعٍ قِبْلَتَهُمْ ۚ وَمَا بَعْضُهُمْ

بِتَابِعٍ قِبْلَةَ بَعْضٍ ۚ وَلَئِنِ اتَّبَعْتَ

اَهْوَآءَهُمْ مِّنْ بَعْدِ مَا جَآءَكَ

مِنَ الْعِلْمِ ۙ اِنَّكَ اِذًا لَّمِنَ

الظّٰلِمِيْنَ ۝

146. The people of the Book know this as they know their own sons; but some of them conceal the truth which they themselves know.

اَلَّذِيْنَ اٰتَيْنٰهُمُ الْكِتٰبَ يَعْرِفُوْنَهٗ

كَمَا يَعْرِفُوْنَ اَبْنَآءَهُمْ ۗ وَاِنَّ

فَرِيْقًا مِّنْهُمْ لَيَكْتُمُوْنَ الْحَقَّ

وَهُمْ يَعْلَمُوْنَ ۝

147. The Truth is from thy Lord; so be not at all in doubt.

اَلْحَقُّ مِنْ رَّبِّكَ فَلَا تَكُوْنَنَّ

مِنَ الْمُمْتَرِيْنَ ۝

148. To each is a goal to which Allah turns him; then strive together (as in a race) towards all that is good. Wheresoever ye are, Allah will bring you together. For Allah hath power over all things.

وَلِكُلٍّ وِّجْهَةٌ هُوَ مُوَلِّيْهَا ۖ

فَاسْتَبِقُوا الْخَيْرٰتِ ۚ اَيْنَ مَا

تَكُوْنُوْا يَاْتِ بِكُمُ اللّٰهُ جَمِيْعًا ۗ

اِنَّ اللّٰهَ عَلٰى كُلِّ شَيْءٍ قَدِيْرٌ ۝

149. From whencesoever thou startest forth, turn thy face in the direction of the Sacred Mosque; that is indeed the truth from thy Lord. And Allah is not unmindful of what ye do.

وَمِنْ حَيْثُ خَرَجْتَ فَوَلِّ وَجْهَكَ شَطْرَ الْمَسْجِدِ الْحَرَامِ ۖ وَإِنَّهُ لَلْحَقُّ مِن رَّبِّكَ ۗ وَمَا اللّٰهُ بِغَافِلٍ عَمَّا تَعْمَلُونَ ﴿﴾

150. So from whencesoever thou startest forth, turn thy face in the direction of the Sacred Mosque; and wheresoever ye are, turn your face thither: that there be no ground of dispute against you among the people. Except those of them that are bent on wickedness; so fear them not, but fear Me; and that I may complete My favours on you, and ye may (consent to) be guided;

وَمِنْ حَيْثُ خَرَجْتَ فَوَلِّ وَجْهَكَ شَطْرَ الْمَسْجِدِ الْحَرَامِ ۚ وَحَيْثُ مَا كُنتُمْ فَوَلُّوا وُجُوهَكُمْ شَطْرَهُ لِئَلَّا يَكُونَ لِلنَّاسِ عَلَيْكُمْ حُجَّةٌ إِلَّا الَّذِينَ ظَلَمُوا مِنْهُمْ فَلَا تَخْشَوْهُمْ وَاخْشَوْنِي وَلِأُتِمَّ نِعْمَتِي عَلَيْكُمْ وَلَعَلَّكُمْ تَهْتَدُونَ ﴿﴾

151. A similar (favour have ye already received) in that We have sent among you a Messenger of your own, rehearsing to you Our Signs, and purifying you, and instructing you in Scripture and Wisdom, and in new Knowledge.

كَمَا أَرْسَلْنَا فِيكُمْ رَسُولًا مِّنكُمْ يَتْلُوا عَلَيْكُمْ آيَاتِنَا وَيُزَكِّيكُمْ وَيُعَلِّمُكُمُ الْكِتَابَ وَالْحِكْمَةَ وَيُعَلِّمُكُم مَّا لَمْ تَكُونُوا تَعْلَمُونَ ﴿﴾

152. Then do ye remember Me; I will remember you. Be grateful to Me, and reject not Faith.

فَاذْكُرُونِي أَذْكُرْكُمْ وَاشْكُرُوا لِي وَلَا تَكْفُرُونِ ﴿﴾

153. O ye who believe! seek help with patient Perseverance and Prayer: for God is with those who patiently persevere.

يَا أَيُّهَا الَّذِينَ آمَنُوا اسْتَعِينُوا بِالصَّبْرِ وَالصَّلَاةِ ۚ إِنَّ اللّٰهَ مَعَ الصَّابِرِينَ ﴿﴾

154. And say not of those who are slain in the way of Allah: "They are dead." Nay, they are living, though ye perceive (it) not.

وَلَا تَقُولُوا لِمَن يُقْتَلُ فِي سَبِيلِ اللّٰهِ أَمْوَاتٌ ۚ بَلْ أَحْيَاءٌ وَلَٰكِن لَّا تَشْعُرُونَ ﴿﴾

155. Be sure We shall test you with something of fear and hunger, some loss in goods, lives and the fruits (of your toil), but give glad tidings to those who patiently persevere,—

وَلَنَبْلُوَنَّكُم بِشَيْءٍ مِّنَ الْخَوْفِ وَالْجُوعِ وَنَقْصٍ مِّنَ الْأَمْوَالِ وَالْأَنفُسِ وَالثَّمَرَاتِ ۗ وَبَشِّرِ الصَّابِرِينَ ﴿﴾

156. Who say, when afflicted with calamity:

الَّذِينَ إِذَا أَصَابَتْهُم مُّصِيبَةٌ

"To Allah we belong, and to Him is our return":—

157. They are those on whom (Descend) blessings from their Lord, and Mercy. And they are the ones that receive guidance.

158. Behold ! Safa and Marwa are among the Symbols of Allah. So if those who visit the House in the Season or at other times, should compass them round, it is no sin in them. And if anyone obeyeth his own impulse to Good,— be sure that Allah is He Who recogniseth and knoweth.

159. Those who conceal the clear (Signs) We have sent down, and the Guidance, after We have made it clear for the People in the Book,—on them shall be Allah's curse, and the curse of those entitled to curse.—

160. Except those who repent and make amends and openly declare (the Truth): to them I turn; for I am Oft-Returning, Most Merciful.

161. Those who reject Faith. And die rejecting,—on them is Allah's curse, and the curse of angels, and of all mankind;

162. They will abide therein: their penalty will not be lightened, nor will respite be their (lot).

163. And your God is One God: there is no god but He, Most Gracious, Most Merciful.

164. Behold ! In the creation of the heavens and the earth; in the alternation of the Night and the Day; in the sailing of the ships through the Ocean for the profit of mankind;

in the rain which Allah sends down from the skies, and the life which He gives therewith to an earth that is dead; in the beasts of all kinds that He scatters through the earth; in the change of the winds, and the clouds which they trail like their slaves between the sky and the earth;—(here) indeed are Signs for a people that are wise.

165. Yet there are men who take (for worship) others besides Allah, as equal (with Allah): they love them as they should love Allah. But those of Faith are overflowing in their love for Allah. If only the unrighteous could see, behold, they would see the Punishment: that to Allah belongs all power, and Allah will strongly enforce the Punishment.

166. Then would those who are followed clear themselves of those who follow (them): they would see the Chastisement and all relations between them would be cut off.

167. And those who followed would say: "If only we had one more chance, we would clear ourselves of them, as they have cleared themselves of us." Thus will Allah show them (the fruits of) their deeds as (nothing but) regrets. Nor will there be a way for them out of the Fire.

168. O ye people ! eat of what is on earth, lawful and good; and do not follow the footsteps of Satan for he is to you an avowed enemy.

169. For he commands you what is evil and shameful, and that ye should say of Allah that of which ye have no knowledge.

170. When it is said to them: "Follow what Allah hath revealed:" they say: "Nay ! we shall follow the ways of our fathers." What ! even though their fathers were void of

wisdom and guidance?

لَا يَعْقِلُونَ شَيْئًا قَ لَا
يَهْتَدُونَ ۞

171. The parable of those who reject Faith is as if one were to shout like a goat-herd, to things that listen to nothing but calls and cries: deaf, dumb, and blind. They are void of wisdom.

وَمَثَلُ الَّذِينَ كَفَرُوا كَمَثَلِ
الَّذِي يَنْعِقُ بِمَا لَا يَسْمَعُ إِلَّا دُعَاءً
وَنِدَاءً صُمٌّ بُكْمٌ عُمْيٌ
فَهُمْ لَا يَعْقِلُونَ ۞

172. O ye who believe ! eat of the good things that We have provided for you. And be grateful to Allah, if it is Him ye worship.

يَا أَيُّهَا الَّذِينَ آمَنُوا كُلُوا مِنْ
طَيِّبَاتِ مَا رَزَقْنَاكُمْ وَاشْكُرُوا لِلَّهِ
إِنْ كُنْتُمْ إِيَّاهُ تَعْبُدُونَ ۞

173. He hath only forbidden you dead meat, and blood, and the flesh of swine, and that on which any other name hath been invoked besides that of Allah. But if one is forced by necessity, without wilful disobedience, nor transgressing due limits,—then is he guiltless. For Allah is Oft-Forgiving Most Merciful.

إِنَّمَا حَرَّمَ عَلَيْكُمُ الْمَيْتَةَ وَالدَّمَ
وَلَحْمَ الْخِنْزِيرِ وَمَا أُهِلَّ بِهِ
لِغَيْرِ اللَّهِ فَمَنِ اضْطُرَّ غَيْرَ بَاغٍ
وَلَا عَادٍ فَلَا إِثْمَ عَلَيْهِ إِنَّ اللَّهَ
غَفُورٌ رَحِيمٌ ۞

174. Those who conceal Allah's revelations in the Book, and purchase for them a miserable profit,—They swallow into themselves naught but Fire; Allah will not address them on the Day of Resurrection, nor purify them: grievous will be their Chastisement.

إِنَّ الَّذِينَ يَكْتُمُونَ مَا أَنْزَلَ اللَّهُ
مِنَ الْكِتَابِ وَيَشْتَرُونَ بِهِ ثَمَنًا
قَلِيلًا أُولَئِكَ مَا يَأْكُلُونَ فِي
بُطُونِهِمْ إِلَّا النَّارَ وَلَا يُكَلِّمُهُمُ
اللَّهُ يَوْمَ الْقِيَامَةِ وَلَا يُزَكِّيهِمْ
وَلَهُمْ عَذَابٌ أَلِيمٌ ۞

175. They are the ones who buy Error in place of Guidance and Torment in place of Forgiveness. Ah ! what boldness (they show) for the Fire!

أُولَئِكَ الَّذِينَ اشْتَرَوُا الضَّلَالَةَ
بِالْهُدَى وَالْعَذَابَ بِالْمَغْفِرَةِ
فَمَا أَصْبَرَهُمْ عَلَى النَّارِ ۞

176. (Their doom is) because Allah sent down the Book in truth but those who seek causes of dispute in the Book are in a schism far (from the purpose).

ذَلِكَ بِأَنَّ اللَّهَ نَزَّلَ الْكِتَابَ
بِالْحَقِّ وَإِنَّ الَّذِينَ اخْتَلَفُوا
فِي الْكِتَابِ لَفِي شِقَاقٍ بَعِيدٍ ۞

177. It is not righteousness that ye turn

لَيْسَ الْبِرَّ أَنْ تُوَلُّوا وُجُوهَكُمْ

your faces towards East or West; but it is righteousness—to believe in Allah and the Last Day, and the Angels, and the Book, and the Messengers; to spend of your substance, out of love for Him, for your kin, for orphans, for the needy, for the wayfarer, for those who ask, and for the ransom of slaves; to be steadfast in prayer, and give Zakat, to fulfil the contracts which ye have made; and to be firm and patient, in pain (or suffering) and adversity, and throughout all periods of panic. Such are the people of truth, the God-fearing.

178. O ye who believe ! the law of equality is prescribed to you in cases of murder: the free for the free, the slave for the slave, the woman for the woman. But if any remission is made by the brother of the slain, then grant any reasonable demand, and compensate him with handsome gratitude. This is a concession and a Mercy from your Lord. After this whoever exceeds the limits shall be in grave chastisement.

179. In the Law of Equality there is (saving of) Life to you. O ye men of understanding; that ye may restrain yourselves.

180. It is prescribed, when death approaches any of you, if he leave any goods, that he make a bequest to parents and next of kin. According to reasonable usage; this is due from the God-fearing.

181. If anyone changes the bequest after hearing it, the guilt shall be on those who

make the change. For Allah hears and knows (all things).

182. But if anyone fears partiality or wrong-doing on the part of the testator. And brings about a settlement among (the parties concerned), there is no wrong in him: for Allah is Oft-Forgiving, Most Merciful.

183. O ye who believe ! fasting is prescribed to you as it was prescribed to those before you, that ye may (learn) self-restraint.—

184. (Fasting) for a fixed number of days; but if any of you is ill, or on a journey, the prescribed number (should be made up) from days later. For those who can do it (with hardship), is a ransom, the feeding of one that is indigent. But he that will give more, of his own free- will,—it is better for him. And it is better for you that ye fast, if ye only knew.

185. Ramadhān is the (month) in which was sent down the Qur'an, as a guide to mankind, also clear (Signs) for guidance and judgment (between right and wrong). So everyone of you who is present (at his home) during that month should spent it in fasting, but if anyone is ill, or on a journey, the prescribed period (should be made up) by days later. Allah intends every facility for you; He does not want to put you to difficulties. (He wants you) to complete the prescribed period, and to glorify Him in that He has guided you; and perchance ye shall be grateful.

186. When My servants ask thee concerning Me, I am indeed close (to them): I respond to the prayer of every suppliant

إِثْمَهُ عَلَى الَّذِينَ يُبَدِّلُونَهُ ۚ إِنَّ اللَّهَ سَمِيعٌ عَلِيمٌ ۞

فَمَنْ خَافَ مِنْ مُوصٍ جَنَفًا أَوْ إِثْمًا فَأَصْلَحَ بَيْنَهُمْ فَلَا إِثْمَ عَلَيْهِ ۚ إِنَّ اللَّهَ غَفُورٌ رَّحِيمٌ ۞

يَا أَيُّهَا الَّذِينَ آمَنُوا كُتِبَ عَلَيْكُمُ الصِّيَامُ كَمَا كُتِبَ عَلَى الَّذِينَ مِنْ قَبْلِكُمْ لَعَلَّكُمْ تَتَّقُونَ ۞

أَيَّامًا مَّعْدُودَاتٍ ۚ فَمَنْ كَانَ مِنْكُمْ مَّرِيضًا أَوْ عَلَى سَفَرٍ فَعِدَّةٌ مِّنْ أَيَّامٍ أُخَرَ ۚ وَعَلَى الَّذِينَ يُطِيقُونَهُ فِدْيَةٌ طَعَامُ مِسْكِينٍ ۖ فَمَنْ تَطَوَّعَ خَيْرًا فَهُوَ خَيْرٌ لَّهُ ۚ وَأَنْ تَصُومُوا خَيْرٌ لَّكُمْ إِنْ كُنْتُمْ تَعْلَمُونَ ۞

شَهْرُ رَمَضَانَ الَّذِي أُنْزِلَ فِيهِ الْقُرْآنُ هُدًى لِّلنَّاسِ وَبَيِّنَاتٍ مِّنَ الْهُدَىٰ وَالْفُرْقَانِ ۚ فَمَنْ شَهِدَ مِنْكُمُ الشَّهْرَ فَلْيَصُمْهُ ۖ وَمَنْ كَانَ مَرِيضًا أَوْ عَلَى سَفَرٍ فَعِدَّةٌ مِّنْ أَيَّامٍ أُخَرَ ۗ يُرِيدُ اللَّهُ بِكُمُ الْيُسْرَ وَلَا يُرِيدُ بِكُمُ الْعُسْرَ وَلِتُكْمِلُوا الْعِدَّةَ وَلِتُكَبِّرُوا اللَّهَ عَلَىٰ مَا هَدَاكُمْ وَلَعَلَّكُمْ تَشْكُرُونَ ۞

وَإِذَا سَأَلَكَ عِبَادِي عَنِّي فَإِنِّي قَرِيبٌ ۖ أُجِيبُ دَعْوَةَ الدَّاعِ إِذَا

when he calleth on Me: let them also, with a will, listen to My call, and believe in Me: that they may walk in the right way.

دَعَانِ ۖ فَلْيَسْتَجِيبُوْا لِىْ
وَلْيُؤْمِنُوْا بِىْ لَعَلَّهُمْ
يَرْشُدُوْنَ ۞

187. Permitted to you on the night of the fasts, is the approach to your wives. They are your garments and ye are their garments. Allah knoweth what ye used to do secretly among yourselves: but He turned to you and forgave you; so now associate with them, and seek what Allah hath ordained for you, and eat and drink, until the white thread of dawn appear to you distinct from its black thread; then complete your fast till the night appears; but do not associate with your wives while ye are in retreat in the mosques. Those are limits (set by) Allah: approach not night thereto. Thus doth Allah make clear His Signs to men: that they may learn self-restraint.

أُحِلَّ لَكُمْ لَيْلَةَ الصِّيَامِ الرَّفَثُ
إِلَىٰ نِسَآئِكُمْ ۚ هُنَّ لِبَاسٌ لَّكُمْ
وَأَنْتُمْ لِبَاسٌ لَّهُنَّ ۗ عَلِمَ اللّٰهُ أَنَّكُمْ
كُنْتُمْ تَخْتَانُوْنَ أَنْفُسَكُمْ فَتَابَ
عَلَيْكُمْ وَعَفَا عَنْكُمْ ۖ فَالْـٰٔنَ
بَاشِرُوْهُنَّ وَابْتَغُوْا مَا كَتَبَ اللّٰهُ
لَكُمْ ۚ وَكُلُوْا وَاشْرَبُوْا حَتّٰى يَتَبَيَّنَ
لَكُمُ الْخَيْطُ الْأَبْيَضُ مِنَ الْخَيْطِ
الْأَسْوَدِ مِنَ الْفَجْرِ ۖ ثُمَّ أَتِمُّوا
الصِّيَامَ إِلَى الَّيْلِ ۚ وَلَا تُبَاشِرُوْهُنَّ
وَأَنْتُمْ عَاكِفُوْنَ ۙ فِى الْمَسَاجِدِ ۗ
تِلْكَ حُدُوْدُ اللّٰهِ فَلَا تَقْرَبُوْهَا ۗ
كَذٰلِكَ يُبَيِّنُ اللّٰهُ اٰيٰتِهٖ لِلنَّاسِ
لَعَلَّهُمْ يَتَّقُوْنَ ۞

188. And do not eat up your property among yourselves for vanities, nor use it as bait for the judges, with intent that ye may eat up wrongfully and knowingly a little of (other) people's property.

وَلَا تَأْكُلُوْا أَمْوَالَكُمْ بَيْنَكُمْ
بِالْبَاطِلِ وَتُدْلُوْا بِهَا إِلَى الْحُكَّامِ
لِتَأْكُلُوْا فَرِيْقًا مِّنْ أَمْوَالِ
النَّاسِ بِالْإِثْمِ وَأَنْتُمْ تَعْلَمُوْنَ ۞

189. They ask thee concerning the New Moons. Say: They are but signs to mark fixed periods of time in (the affairs of) men, and for Pilgrimage. It is no virtue if ye enter your houses from the back: it is virtue if ye fear Allah. Enter houses through the proper

يَسْئَلُوْنَكَ عَنِ الْأَهِلَّةِ ۖ قُلْ هِىَ
مَوَاقِيْتُ لِلنَّاسِ وَالْحَجِّ ۗ وَلَيْسَ
الْبِرُّ بِأَنْ تَأْتُوا الْبُيُوْتَ مِنْ
ظُهُوْرِهَا وَلٰكِنَّ الْبِرَّ مَنِ
اتَّقٰى ۚ وَأْتُوا الْبُيُوْتَ مِنْ
أَبْوَابِهَا ۚ وَاتَّقُوا اللّٰهَ لَعَلَّكُمْ

doors: and fear Allah: that ye may prosper.

190. Fight in the cause of Allah those who fight you, but do not transgress limits; for Allah loveth not transgressors.

191. And slay them wherever ye catch them, and turn them out from where they have turned you out; for Persecution is worse than slaughter; but fight them not at the Sacred Mosque, unless they (first) fight you there; but if they fight you, slay them. Such is the reward of those who reject Faith.

192. But if they cease, Allah is Oft-Forgiving, Most Merciful.

193. And fight them on until there is no more Persecution and the religion becomes Allah's. But if they cease, let there be no hostility except to those who practise oppression.

194. The prohibited month for the prohibited month, —and so for all things prohibited,— there is the law of equality. If then anyone transgresses the prohibition against you, transgress ye likewise against him. But fear Allah, and know that Allah is with those who restrain themselves.

195. And spend of your substance in the cause of Allah, and make not your own hands contribute to (your) destruction; but do good; for Allah loveth those who do good.

196. And complete the *Hajj* or *'Umra* in the service of Allah, but if ye are prevented (from completing it), send an offering for sacrifice, such as ye may find, and do not shave your heads until the offering reaches

the place of sacrifice. And if any of you is ill, or has an ailment in his scalp, (necessitating shaving), (he should) in compensation either fast, or feed the poor, or offer sacrifice; and when ye are in peaceful conditions (again), if anyone wishes to continue the *'Umra* on to the *Hajj*, he must make an offering such as he can afford, but if he cannot afford it, he should fast three days during the *Hajj*. And seven days on his return, making ten days in all. This is for those whose household is not in (the precincts of) the Sacred Mosque. And fear Allah, and know that Allah is strict in punishment.

197. For *Hajj* are the months well known. If any one undertakes that duty therein, let there be no obscenity, nor wickedness, nor wrangling in the *Hajj*. And whatever good ye do, (be sure) Allah knoweth it. And take a provision (with you) for the journey, but the best of provisions is right conduct. So fear Me, O ye that are wise.

198. It is no crime in you if ye seek of the bounty of your Lord (during pilgrimage). Then when ye pour down from (Mount) 'Arafat, celebrate the praises of Allah at the Sacred Monument, and celebrate His praises as He has directed you, even though, before this, ye went astray.

199. Then return from the place whence it is usual for the multitude so to do, and ask for Allah's forgiveness. For Allah is Oft-Forgiving, Most Merciful.

200. So when ye have accomplished your rites, celebrate the praises of Allah, as ye used to celebrate the praises of your

fathers,—yea, with far more heart and soul. There are men who say: "Our Lord! Give us (Thy bounties) in this world!" But they will have no portion in the Hereafter.

201. And there are men who say: "Our Lord! Give us good in this world and good in the Hereafter. And save us from the torment of the Fire !"

202. To these will be allotted what they have earned; and Allah is quick in account.

203. Remember Allah during the Appointed Days, but if anyone hastens to leave in two days, there is no blame on him, and if anyone stays on, there is no blame on him, if his aim is to do right. Then fear Allah, and know that ye will surely be gathered unto Him.

204. There is the type of man whose speech about this world's life may dazzle thee, and he calls Allah to witness about what is in his heart; yet is he the most contentious of enemies.

205. When he turns his back, his aim everywhere is to spread mischief through the earth and destroy crops and progeny but Allah loveth not mischief.

206. When it is said to him, "Fear Allah," he is led by arrogance to (more) crime. Enough for him is Hell;—an evil bed indeed (to lie on)!

207. And there is the type of man who gives his life to earn the pleasure of Allah; and Allah is full of kindness to (His) devotees.

208. O ye who believe ! enter into Islam whole-heartedly; and follow not the

footsteps of the Satan for he is to you an avowed enemy.

209. If ye backslide after the clear (Signs) have come to you, then know that Allah is Exalted in Power, Wise.

210. Will they wait until Allah comes to them in canopies of clouds, with angels (in His train) and the question is (thus) settled ? But to Allah do all questions go back (for decision).

211. Ask the Children of Israel how many clear (Signs) We have sent them. But if anyone, after Allah's favour has come to him, substitutes (something else), Allah is strict in punishment.

212. The life of this world is alluring to those who reject faith, and they scoff at those who believe. But the righteous will be above them on the Day of Resurrection; for Allah bestows His abundance without measure on whom He will.

213. Mankind was one single nation. And Allah sent Messengers with glad tidings and warnings; and with them He sent the Book in truth, to judge between people in matters wherein they differed; but the People of the Book, after the clear Signs came to them, did not differ among themselves, except through selfish contumacy. Allah by His Grace guided the Believers to the Truth, concerning that wherein they differed. For Allah guides whom He will to a path that is straight.

214. Or do ye think that ye shall enter the Garden (of Bliss) without such (trials) as came to those who passed away before you ? They encountered suffering and adversity, and were so shaken in spirit that even the Messenger and those of faith who were with him cried: "When (will come) the help of Allah ?" Ah ! verily, the help of Allah is (always) near !

215. They ask thee what they should spend (in charity). Say: Whatever wealth ye spend that is good, is for parents and kindred and orphans and those in want and for wayfarers. And whatever ye do that is good,—Allah knoweth it well.

216. Fighting is prescribed upon you, and ye dislike it. But it is possible that ye dislike a thing which is good for you, and that ye love a thing which is bad for you. But Allah knoweth, and ye know not.

217. They ask thee concerning fighting in the Prohibited Month. Say: "Fighting therein is a grave (offence); but graver is it in the sight of Allah to prevent access to the path of Allah, to deny Him, to prevent access to the Sacred Mosque, and drive out its members." Tumult and oppression are worse than slaughter. Nor will they cease fighting you until they turn you back from your faith if they can. And if any of you turn back from their faith and die in unbelief,

their works will bear no fruit in this life and in the Hereafter: they will be companions of the Fire and will abide therein.

218. Those who believed and those who suffered exile and fought (and strove and struggled) in the path of Allah,—they have the hope of the Mercy of Allah: and Allah is Oft-Forgiving, Most Merciful.

219. They ask thee concerning wine and gambling. Say: "In them is great sin, and some profit, for men; but the sin is greater than the profit." They ask thee how much they are to spend; say: "What is beyond your needs." Thus doth Allah make clear to you His Signs: in order that ye may consider—

220. (Their bearings) on this life and the Hereafter. They ask thee concerning orphans. Say: "The best thing to do is what is for their good; if ye mix their affairs with yours, they are your brethren; but Allah knows the man who means mischief from the man who means good. And if Allah had wished, He could have put you into difficulties: He is indeed exalted in Power, Wise."

221. Do not marry unbelieving woman until they believe: a slave woman who believes is better than an unbelieving woman, even though she allure you. Nor marry (your girls) to unbelievers until they believe: a man slave who believes is better than an unbeliever, even though he allure you. Unbelievers do (but) beckon you to the Fire.

اسْتَطَاعُوْا وَمَنْ يَّرْتَدِدْ مِنْكُمْ عَنْ دِيْنِهِ فَيَمُتْ وَهُوَ كَافِرٌ فَأُولَٰئِكَ حَبِطَتْ أَعْمَالُهُمْ فِى الدُّنْيَا وَالْآخِرَةِ وَأُولَٰئِكَ أَصْحَابُ النَّارِ هُمْ فِيْهَا خَالِدُوْنَ ۝

إِنَّ الَّذِيْنَ اٰمَنُوْا وَالَّذِيْنَ هَاجَرُوْا وَجَاهَدُوْا فِىْ سَبِيْلِ اللّٰهِ أُولَٰئِكَ يَرْجُوْنَ رَحْمَتَ اللّٰهِ وَاللّٰهُ غَفُوْرٌ رَّحِيْمٌ ۝

يَسْئَلُوْنَكَ عَنِ الْخَمْرِ وَالْمَيْسِرِ قُلْ فِيْهِمَا إِثْمٌ كَبِيْرٌ وَّمَنَافِعُ لِلنَّاسِ وَإِثْمُهُمَا أَكْبَرُ مِنْ نَّفْعِهِمَا وَيَسْئَلُوْنَكَ مَا ذَا يُنْفِقُوْنَ ە قُلِ الْعَفْوَ كَذَٰلِكَ يُبَيِّنُ اللّٰهُ لَكُمُ الْاٰيٰتِ لَعَلَّكُمْ تَتَفَكَّرُوْنَ ۝

فِى الدُّنْيَا وَالْآخِرَةِ وَيَسْئَلُوْنَكَ عَنِ الْيَتٰمٰى قُلْ إِصْلَاحٌ لَّهُمْ خَيْرٌ وَإِنْ تُخَالِطُوْهُمْ فَإِخْوَانُكُمْ وَاللّٰهُ يَعْلَمُ الْمُفْسِدَ مِنَ الْمُصْلِحِ وَلَوْ شَاءَ اللّٰهُ لَأَعْنَتَكُمْ إِنَّ اللّٰهَ عَزِيْزٌ حَكِيْمٌ ۝

وَلَا تَنْكِحُوا الْمُشْرِكٰتِ حَتّٰى يُؤْمِنَّ وَلَأَمَةٌ مُّؤْمِنَةٌ خَيْرٌ مِّنْ مُّشْرِكَةٍ وَّلَوْ أَعْجَبَتْكُمْ وَلَا تُنْكِحُوا الْمُشْرِكِيْنَ حَتّٰى يُؤْمِنُوْا وَلَعَبْدٌ مُّؤْمِنٌ خَيْرٌ مِّنْ مُّشْرِكٍ وَّلَوْ أَعْجَبَكُمْ أُولَٰئِكَ يَدْعُوْنَ إِلَى

But Allah beckons by His Grace to the Garden (of Bliss) and forgiveness. And makes His Signs clear to mankind: that they may receive admonition.

222. They ask thee concerning women's courses. Say: They are a hurt and a pollution: so keep away from women in their courses, and do not approach them until they are clean. But when they have purified themselves, ye may approach them as ordained for you by Allah for Allah loves those who turn to Him constantly and He loves those who keep themselves pure and clean.

223. Your wives are as a tilth unto you, so approach your tilth when or how ye will; but do some good act for your souls beforehand; and fear Allah, and know that ye are to meet Him (in the Hereafter), and give (these) good tidings to those who believe.

224. And make not Allah's (name) an excuse in your oaths against doing good, or acting rightly, or making peace between persons; for Allah is one Who heareth and knoweth all things.

225. Allah will not call you to account for thoughtlessness in your oaths, but for the intention in your hearts, and He is Oft-Forgiving Most Forbearing.

226. For those who take an oath for abstention from their wives, a waiting for four months is ordained; if then they return, Allah is Oft-Forgiving, Most Merciful.

227. But if their intention is firm for divorce, Allah heareth and knoweth all things.

228. Divorced women shall wait concerning themselves for three monthly periods. And

it is not lawful for them to hide what Allah hath created in their wombs, if they have faith in Allah and the Last Day. And their husbands have the better right to take them back in that period, if they wish for reconciliation. And women shall have rights similar to the rights against them, according to what is equitable, but men have a degree over them and Allah is Exalted in Power, Wise.

229. A divorce is only permissible twice; after that, the parties should either hold together on equitable terms, or separate with kindness. It is not lawful for you, (men), to take back any of your gifts (from your wives), except when both parties fear that they would be unable to keep the limits ordained by Allah if ye (judges) do indeed fear that they would be unable to keep the limits ordained by Allah, there is no blame on either of them if she give something for her freedom, these are the limits ordained by Allah; so do not transgress them if any do transgress the limits ordained by Allah, such persons wrong (themselves as well as others).

230. So if a husband divorces his wife (irrevocably), he cannot, after that, re-marry her until after she has married another husband and he has divorced her. In that case there is no blame on either of them if they re-unite, provided they feel that they can keep the limits ordained by Allah. Such are the limits ordained by Allah, which He makes plain to those who know.

231. When ye divorce women, and they (are about to) fulfil the term of their (*'Iddat*), either take them back on equitable terms or set them free on equitable terms: but do not

take them back to injure them, (or) to take
undue advantage; if anyone does that, he
wrongs his own soul. Do not treat Allah's
Signs as a jest, but solemnly rehearse
Allah's favours on you, and the fact that He
sent down to you the Book and Wisdom, for
your instruction. And fear Allah, and know
that Allah is well acquainted with all things.

232. When ye divorce women, and they
fulfil the term of their ('Iddat), do not prevent
them from marrying their (former) husbands,
if they mutually agree on equitable terms.
This instruction is for all amongst you, who
believe in Allah and the Last Day That is
(the course making for) most virtue and
purity amongst you. And Allah knows, and
ye know not.

233. The mothers shall give suck to their
offspring for two whole years, for him who
desires to complete the term. But he shall
bear the cost of their food and clothing on
equitable terms. No soul shall have a burden
laid on it greater than it can bear. No mother
shall be treated unfairly on account of her
child. Nor father on account of his child, an
heir shall be chargeable in the same way, if
they both decide on weaning, by mutual
consent, and after due consultation, there
is no blame on them. If ye decide on a
foster-mother for your offspring there is no
blame on you, provided ye pay (the foster
mother) what ye offered, on equitable terms.
But fear Allah and know that Allah sees

well what ye do.

234. If any of you die and leave widows behind; they shall wait concerning themselves four months and ten days when they have fulfilled their term, there is no blame on you if they dispose of themselves in a just and reasonable manner. And Allah is well acquainted with what ye do.

235. There is no blame on you if ye make an indirect offer of betrothal or hold it in your hearts. Allah knows that ye cherish them in your hearts: but do not make a secret contract with them except that you speak to them in terms honourable, nor resolve on the tie of marriage till the term prescribed is fulfilled. And know that Allah knoweth what is in your hearts, and take heed of Him; and know that Allah is Oft-Forgiving. Most Forbearing.

236. There is no blame on you if ye divorce women before consummation or the fixation of their dower; but bestow on them (a suitable gift), the wealthy according to his means, and the poor according to his means;—a gift of a reasonable amount is due from those who wish to do the right thing.

237. And if ye divorce them before consummation, but after the fixation of a dower for them, then the half of the dower (is due to them), unless they remit it or (the man's half) is remitted by him in whose

hands is the marriage tie; and the remission (of the man's half) if the nearest to righteousness. And do not forget liberality between yourselves. For Allah sees well all that ye do.

بِيَدِهِ عُقْدَةُ النِّكَاحِ ۚ وَاَنْ تَعْفُوْٓا اَقْرَبُ لِلتَّقْوٰى ۚ وَلَا تَنْسَوُا الْفَضْلَ بَيْنَكُمْ ۚ اِنَّ اللّٰهَ بِمَا تَعْمَلُوْنَ بَصِيْرٌ ۝

238. Guard strictly your (habit of) prayers. Especially the Middle Prayer; and stand before Allah in a devout (frame of mind).

حَافِظُوْا عَلَى الصَّلَوٰتِ وَالصَّلٰوةِ الْوُسْطٰى ۗ وَقُوْمُوْا لِلّٰهِ قٰنِتِيْنَ ۝

239. If ye fear (an enemy), pray on foot, or riding, (as may be most convenient), but when ye are in security, celebrate Allah's praises in the manner He has taught you, which ye knew not (before).

فَاِنْ خِفْتُمْ فَرِجَالًا اَوْ رُكْبَانًا ۚ فَاِذَآ اَمِنْتُمْ فَاذْكُرُوا اللّٰهَ كَمَا عَلَّمَكُمْ مَّا لَمْ تَكُوْنُوْا تَعْلَمُوْنَ ۝

240. Those of you who die and leave widows should bequeath for their widows a year's maintenance without expulsion; but if they leave (the residence), there is no blame on you for what they do with themselves, provided it is reasonable. And Allah is Exalted in Power, Wise.

وَالَّذِيْنَ يُتَوَفَّوْنَ مِنْكُمْ وَيَذَرُوْنَ اَزْوَاجًا ۚ وَصِيَّةً لِّاَزْوَاجِهِمْ مَّتَاعًا اِلَى الْحَوْلِ غَيْرَ اِخْرَاجٍ ۚ فَاِنْ خَرَجْنَ فَلَا جُنَاحَ عَلَيْكُمْ فِيْ مَا فَعَلْنَ فِيْٓ اَنْفُسِهِنَّ مِنْ مَّعْرُوْفٍ ۗ وَاللّٰهُ عَزِيْزٌ حَكِيْمٌ ۝

241. For divorced women is a suitable Gift this is a duty on the righteous.

وَلِلْمُطَلَّقٰتِ مَتَاعٌۢ بِالْمَعْرُوْفِ ۗ حَقًّا عَلَى الْمُتَّقِيْنَ ۝

242. Thus doth Allah make clear His Signs to you: in order that ye may understand.

كَذٰلِكَ يُبَيِّنُ اللّٰهُ لَكُمْ اٰيٰتِهٖ لَعَلَّكُمْ تَعْقِلُوْنَ ۝

243. Didst thou not turn thy vision to those who abandoned their homes, though they were thousands (in number), for fear of death? Allah said to them: "Die". Then He restored them to life. For Allah is full of bounty to mankind, but most of them are ungrateful.

اَلَمْ تَرَ اِلَى الَّذِيْنَ خَرَجُوْا مِنْ دِيَارِهِمْ وَهُمْ اُلُوْفٌ حَذَرَ الْمَوْتِ ۖ فَقَالَ لَهُمُ اللّٰهُ مُوْتُوْا ۖ ثُمَّ اَحْيَاهُمْ ۗ اِنَّ اللّٰهَ لَذُوْ فَضْلٍ عَلَى النَّاسِ وَلٰكِنَّ اَكْثَرَ النَّاسِ لَا يَشْكُرُوْنَ ۝

244. Then fight in the cause of Allah, and know that Allah heareth and knoweth all

وَقَاتِلُوْا فِيْ سَبِيْلِ اللّٰهِ وَاعْلَمُوْٓا

things.

245. Who is he that will loan to Allah a beautiful loan, which Allah will double unto his credit and multiply many times ? It is Allah that giveth (you) Want or Plenty. And to Him shall be your return.

246. Has thou not turned thy vision to the Chiefs of the Children of Israel after (the time of) Moses? They said to a Prophet (that was) among them: "Appoint for us a King, that we may fight in the cause of Allah." He said; "Is it not possible, if ye were commanded to fight, that ye will not fight ?" They said: "How could we refuse to fight in the cause of Allah, seeing that we were turned out of our homes and our families?" But when they were commanded to fight, they turned back, except a small band among them. But Allah has full knowledge of those who do wrong.

247. Their Prophet said to them; "Allah hath appointed Tālūt as king over you." They said: "How can he exercise authority over us when we are better fitted than he to exercise authority, and he is not even gifted, with wealth in abundance?" He said: "Allah hath chosen him above you, and hath gifted him abundantly with knowledge and bodily prowess: Allah granteth His authority to whom he pleaseth: Allah is All-Embracing, and He knoweth all things."

248. And (further) their Prophet said to them: "A Sign of his authority is that there shall come to you the Ark of the Covenant, with (an assurance) therein of security from your Lord, and the relics left by the family of

Moses and the family of Aaron, carried by angels. In this is a Symbol for you if ye indeed have faith."

249. When Tālūt set forth with the armies, he said: "Allah will test you at the stream; if any drinks of its water, he goes not with my army: only those who taste not of it go with me: a mere sip out of the hand is excused." But they drank of it, except a few. When they crossed the river,—he and the faithful ones with him,—they said: "This day we cannot cope with Goliath and his forces." But those who were convinced that they must meet Allah, said: "How oft, by Allah's will, hath a small force vanquished a big one ? Allah is with those who steadfastly persevere."

250. When they advanced to meet Goliath and his forces, they prayed: "Our Lord ! pour out constancy on us and make our steps firm: help us against those that reject faith."

251. By Allah's will, they routed them; and David slew Goliath; and Allah gave him power and wisdom and taught him whatever (else) He willed. And did not Allah check one set of people by means of another, the earth would indeed be full of mischief: but Allah is full of bounty to all the worlds.

252. These are the Signs of Allah: we rehearse them to thee in truth: verily thou art one of the Messengers.

مُوسَىٰ وَءَالُ هَٰرُونَ تَحۡمِلُهُ ٱلۡمَلَٰٓئِكَةُ
إِنَّ فِى ذَٰلِكَ لَءَايَةً لَّكُمۡ إِن كُنتُم
مُّؤۡمِنِينَ ۝

فَلَمَّا فَصَلَ طَالُوتُ بِٱلۡجُنُودِ قَالَ
إِنَّ ٱللَّهَ مُبۡتَلِيكُم بِنَهَرٍ فَمَن
شَرِبَ مِنۡهُ فَلَيۡسَ مِنِّى وَمَن
لَّمۡ يَطۡعَمۡهُ فَإِنَّهُ مِنِّىٓ إِلَّا مَنِ
ٱغۡتَرَفَ غُرۡفَةَۢ بِيَدِهِۦ فَشَرِبُوا۟
مِنۡهُ إِلَّا قَلِيلًا مِّنۡهُمۡ فَلَمَّا
جَاوَزَهُ هُوَ وَٱلَّذِينَ ءَامَنُوا۟ مَعَهُۥ
قَالُوا۟ لَا طَاقَةَ لَنَا ٱلۡيَوۡمَ بِجَالُوتَ
وَجُنُودِهِۦ ۚ قَالَ ٱلَّذِينَ يَظُنُّونَ
أَنَّهُم مُّلَٰقُوا۟ ٱللَّهِ كَم مِّن
فِئَةٍ قَلِيلَةٍ غَلَبَتۡ فِئَةً كَثِيرَةَۢ
بِإِذۡنِ ٱللَّهِ ۗ وَٱللَّهُ مَعَ ٱلصَّٰبِرِينَ ۝
وَلَمَّا بَرَزُوا۟ لِجَالُوتَ وَجُنُودِهِۦ قَالُوا۟
رَبَّنَآ أَفۡرِغۡ عَلَيۡنَا صَبۡرًا وَثَبِّتۡ
أَقۡدَامَنَا وَٱنصُرۡنَا عَلَى ٱلۡقَوۡمِ ٱلۡكَٰفِرِينَ ۝
فَهَزَمُوهُم بِإِذۡنِ ٱللَّهِ وَقَتَلَ
دَاوُۥدُ جَالُوتَ وَءَاتَىٰهُ ٱللَّهُ ٱلۡمُلۡكَ
وَٱلۡحِكۡمَةَ وَعَلَّمَهُۥ مِمَّا يَشَآءُ ۗ
وَلَوۡلَا دَفۡعُ ٱللَّهِ ٱلنَّاسَ بَعۡضَهُم
بِبَعۡضٍ لَّفَسَدَتِ ٱلۡأَرۡضُ وَلَٰكِنَّ
ٱللَّهَ ذُو فَضۡلٍ عَلَى ٱلۡعَٰلَمِينَ ۝
تِلۡكَ ءَايَٰتُ ٱللَّهِ نَتۡلُوهَا عَلَيۡكَ
بِٱلۡحَقِّ ۚ وَإِنَّكَ لَمِنَ ٱلۡمُرۡسَلِينَ ۝

253. Those Messengers We endowed with gifts, some above others: to some of them Allah spoke; others He raised to degrees (of honour); to Jesus the son of Mary We gave Clear (Signs), and strengthened him with the Holy Spirit. If Allah had so willed, succeeding generations would not have fought among each other, after Clear (Signs) had come to them, but they (chose) to wrangle, some believing and others rejecting. If Allah had so willed, they would not have fought each other; but Allah does what He wills.

254. O ye who believe ! spend out of (the bounties) We have provided for you, before the Day comes when no bargaining (will avail), nor friendship nor intercession. Those who reject Faith—they are the wrong-doers.

255. Allah ! There is no god but He,—the Living, the Self-subsisting, Supporter of all, no slumber can seize Him nor sleep. His are all things in the heavens and on earth. Who is thee can intercede in His presence except as He permitteth? He knoweth what (appeareth to His creatures as) Before or After or Behind them. Nor shall they compass aught of His knowledge except as He willeth. His Throne doth extend over the heavens and the earth, and He feeleth no fatigue in guarding and preserving them: for He is the Most High, the Supreme (in glory).

256. Let there be no compulsion in religion: Truth stands out clear from Error: whoever

rejects Tagut and believes in Allah hath grasped the most trustworthy hand-hold, that never breaks. And Allah heareth and knoweth all things.

257. Allah is the Protector of those who have faith: from the depths of darkness He leads them forth into light. Of those who reject faith the patrons are the Tagut from light they will lead them forth into the depths of darkness. They will be Companions of the Fire, to dwell therein (for ever).

258. Hast thou not turned thy thought to one who disputed with Abraham about his Lord, because Allah had granted him power? Abraham said: "My Lord is He Who giveth life and death." He said: "I give life and death." Said Abraham: "But it is Allah that causeth the sun to rise from the East: do thou then cause it to rise from the West." Thus was he confounded who (in arrogance) rejected Faith. Nor doth Allah give guidance to a people unjust.

259. Or (take) the similitude of one who passed by a hamlet, all in ruins to its roots. He said: "Oh! how shall Allah bring it (ever) to life, after (this) its death ?" But Allah caused him to die for a hundred years, then raised him up (again). He said: "How long didst thou tarry (thus) ?" He said: "(Perhaps) a day or part of a day." He said: "Nay, thou hast tarried thus a hundred years: but look at thy food and thy drink; they show no signs of age: and look at thy donkey: and that We may make of thee a Sign unto the people. Look further at the bones, how We bring them together and clothe them with flesh." When this was shown clearly to him,

he said: "I know that Allah hath power over all things."

كَيْفَ نُنْشِزُهَا ثُمَّ نَكْسُوهَا لَحْمًا فَلَمَّا تَبَيَّنَ لَهُ قَالَ أَعْلَمُ أَنَّ اللّٰهَ عَلَى كُلِّ شَيْءٍ قَدِيرٌ ۝

260. Behold! Abraham said: "My Lord! show me how Thou givest life to the dead.". He said: "Dost thou not then believe?" He said: "Yea! but to satisfy my own heart." He said: "Take four birds; tie them (cut them into pieces), then put a portion of them: on every hill, and call to them: they will come to thee (flying) with speed. Then know that Allah is Exalted in Power, Wise."

وَإِذْ قَالَ إِبْرٰهِ‍ٖمُ رَبِّ أَرِنِى كَيْفَ تُحْىِ الْمَوْتٰى قَالَ أَوَلَمْ تُؤْمِنْ قَالَ بَلٰى وَلٰكِنْ لِيَطْمَئِنَّ قَلْبِى قَالَ فَخُذْ أَرْبَعَةً مِّنَ الطَّيْرِ فَصُرْهُنَّ إِلَيْكَ ثُمَّ اجْعَلْ عَلٰى كُلِّ جَبَلٍ مِّنْهُنَّ جُزْءًا ثُمَّ ادْعُهُنَّ يَأْتِينَكَ سَعْيًا وَاعْلَمْ أَنَّ اللّٰهَ عَزِيزٌ حَكِيمٌ ۝

261. The parable of those who spend their wealth in the way of Allah is that of a grain of corn: it groweth seven ears, and each ear hath a hundred grains. Allah giveth manifold increase to whom He pleaseth: and Allah careth for all and He knoweth all things.

مَثَلُ الَّذِينَ يُنْفِقُونَ أَمْوَالَهُمْ فِى سَبِيلِ اللّٰهِ كَمَثَلِ حَبَّةٍ أَنْبَتَتْ سَبْعَ سَنَابِلَ فِى كُلِّ سُنْبُلَةٍ مِّائَةُ حَبَّةٍ وَاللّٰهُ يُضَاعِفُ لِمَنْ يَشَاءُ وَاللّٰهُ وَاسِعٌ عَلِيمٌ ۝

262. Those who spend their wealth in the cause of Allah, and follow not up their gifts with reminders of their generosity or with injury,—for them their reward is with their Lord: on them shall be no fear, nor shall they grieve.

الَّذِينَ يُنْفِقُونَ أَمْوَالَهُمْ فِى سَبِيلِ اللّٰهِ ثُمَّ لَا يُتْبِعُونَ مَا أَنْفَقُوا مَنًّا وَلَا أَذًى لَهُمْ أَجْرُهُمْ عِنْدَ رَبِّهِمْ وَلَا خَوْفٌ عَلَيْهِمْ وَلَا هُمْ يَحْزَنُونَ ۝

263. Kind words and covering of faults are better than charity followed by injury. Allah is Free of all wants, and He is Most Forbearing.

قَوْلٌ مَّعْرُوفٌ وَمَغْفِرَةٌ خَيْرٌ مِّنْ صَدَقَةٍ يَتْبَعُهَا أَذًى وَاللّٰهُ غَنِىٌّ حَلِيمٌ ۝

264. O ye who believe! cancel not your charity by reminders of your generosity or by injury—like those who spend their wealth

يَا أَيُّهَا الَّذِينَ آمَنُوا لَا تُبْطِلُوا صَدَقَاتِكُمْ بِالْمَنِّ وَالْأَذٰى كَالَّذِى

to be seen of men, but believe neither in Allah nor in the Last Day. They are in Parable like a hard, barren rock, on which is a little soil: on it falls heavy rain, which leaves it (just) a bare stone. They will be able to do nothing with aught they have earned. And Allah guideth not those who reject faith.

265. And the likeness of those who spend their wealth seeking to please Allah and to strengthen their souls, is as a garden, high and fertile: heavy rain falls on it but makes it yield a double increase of harvest, and if it receives not heavy rain, light moisture Sufficeth it. Allah seeth well whatever ye do.

266. Does any of you wish that he should have a garden with date-palms and vines and streams flowing underneath, and all kinds of fruit, while he is stricken with old age, and his children are not strong (enough to look after themselves)—that it should be caught in a whirlwind, with fire therein, and be burnt up ? Thus doth Allah make clear to you (His) Signs; that ye may consider.

267. O ye who believe ! give of the good things which ye have (honourably) earned, and of the fruits of the earth which We have produced for you, and do not aim at anything which is bad, out of it ye may give away something, when ye yourselves would not receive it except with closed eyes. And know that Allah is Free of all wants, and

Worthy of all praise.

268. Satan threatens you with poverty and bids you to conduct unseemly. Allah promiseth you His forgiveness and bounties. And Allah careth for all and He knoweth all things.

269. He granteth wisdom to whom He pleaseth; and he to whom wisdom is granted receiveth indeed a benefit overflowing; but none will receive admonition but men of understanding.

270. And whatever ye spend in charity or whatever vow you make, be sure Allah knows it all. But the wrong-doers have no helpers.

271. If ye disclose (acts of) charity, even so it is well, but if ye conceal them, and make them reach those (really) in need, that is best for you: it will remove from you some of your (stains of) evil. And Allah is well acquainted with what ye do.

272. It is not for you to guide them to the right path. But Allah guides to the right path whom He pleaseth. Whatever of good ye give benefits your own souls, and ye shall only do so seeking the "Face" of Allah. Whatever good ye give, shall be rendered back to you, and ye shall not be dealt with unjustly.

273. (Charity is) for those in need, who, in Allah's cause, are restricted (from travel). And cannot move about in the land, seeking (for trade or work): the ignorant man thinks, because of their modesty, that they are free from want. Thou shalt know them by their (unfailing) mark: they beg not importunately from all and sundry. And whatever of good ye give, be assured Allah

knoweth it well.

274. Those who (in charity) spend of their goods by night and by day, in secret and in public, have their reward with their Lord: on them shall be no fear, nor shall they grieve.

275. Those who devour usury will not stand except as stands one whom the Satan by his touch hath driven to madness. That is because they say: "Trade is like usury," but Allah hath permitted trade and forbidden usury. Those who after receiving admonition from their Lord, desist, shall be pardoned for the past; their case is for Allah (to judge); but those who repeat (the offence) are Companions of the Fire: they will abide therein (for ever).

276. Allah will deprive usury of all blessing, but will give increase for deeds of charity: for He loveth not any ungrateful sinner.

277. Those who believe, and do deeds of righteousness, and establish regular prayers and give Zakat, will have their reward with their Lord: on them shall be no fear, nor shall they grieve.

278. O ye who believe ! fear Allah, and give up What remains of your demand for usury, if ye are indeed believers.

279. If ye do it not, take notice of war from Allah and His Messenger: but if ye repent ye shall have your capital sums: deal not unjustly, and ye shall not be dealt with unjustly.

280. If the debtor is in a difficulty, grant him time till it is easy for him to repay. But it ye

remit it by way of charity, that is best for you if ye only knew.

281. And fear the Day when ye shall be brought back to Allah. Then shall every soul be paid what it earned, and none shall be dealt with unjustly.

282. O ye who believe ! when ye deal with each other, in transactions involving future obligations in a fixed period of time, reduce them to writing. Let a scribe write down faithfully as between the parties: let not the scribe refuse to write: as Allah has taught him, so let him write. Let him who incurs the liability dictate, but let him fear Allah, his Lord and not diminish aught of what he owes. If the party liable is mentally deficient, or weak, or unable himself to dictate, let his guardian dictate faithfully. And get two witnesses, out of your own men. And if there are not two men, then a man and two women, such as ye choose, for witnesses, so that if one of them errs, the other can remind her. The witnesses should not refuse when they are called on (for evidence). Disdain not to reduce to writing (your contract) for a future period, whether it be small or big; it is juster in the sight of Allah, more suitable as evidence, and more convenient to prevent doubts among yourselves, but if it be a transaction which ye carry out on the spot among yourselves, there is no blame on you if ye reduce it not to writing. But take witnesses whenever ye make a commercial contract; and let neither scribe nor witness suffer harm. if ye do (such harm), it would be wickedness in

you. So fear Allah; for it is Allah that teaches you. And Allah is well acquainted with all things.

عَلَيْكُمْ جُنَاحٌ اَلَّا تَكْتُبُوهَا ۗ
وَاَشْهِدُوٓا اِذَا تَبَايَعْتُمْ ۖ وَلَا
يُضَآرَّ كَاتِبٌ وَّلَا شَهِيدٌ ۚ وَاِنْ
تَفْعَلُوْا فَاِنَّهُ فُسُوقٌ بِكُمْ ۗ
وَاتَّقُوا اللّٰهَ ۗ وَيُعَلِّمُكُمُ اللّٰهُ ۗ
وَاللّٰهُ بِكُلِّ شَيْءٍ عَلِيمٌ ۝

283. If ye are on a journey, and cannot find a scribe, a pledge with possession (may serve the purpose). And if one of you deposits a thing on trust with another, let the trustee (faithfully) discharge his trust, and let him fear Allah his Lord. Conceal not evidence; for whoever conceals it,—his heart is tainted with sin. And Allah knoweth all that ye do.

وَاِنْ كُنْتُمْ عَلٰى سَفَرٍ وَّلَمْ تَجِدُوْا
كَاتِبًا فَرِهٰنٌ مَّقْبُوْضَةٌ ۖ فَاِنْ
اَمِنَ بَعْضُكُمْ بَعْضًا فَلْيُؤَدِّ
الَّذِى اؤْتُمِنَ اَمَانَتَهُ وَلْيَتَّقِ
اللّٰهَ رَبَّهُ ۗ وَلَا تَكْتُمُوا الشَّهَادَةَ ۗ
وَمَنْ يَّكْتُمْهَا فَاِنَّهُ اٰثِمٌ قَلْبُهُ ۗ
وَاللّٰهُ بِمَا تَعْمَلُوْنَ عَلِيمٌ ۝

284. To Allah belongeth all that is in the heavens and on earth. Whether ye show what is in your minds or conceal it, Allah calleth you to account for it. He forgiveth whom He pleaseth, and punisheth whom He pleaseth. For Allah hath power over all things.

لِلّٰهِ مَا فِى السَّمٰوٰتِ وَمَا فِى الْاَرْضِ ۗ
وَاِنْ تُبْدُوْا مَا فِىٓ اَنْفُسِكُمْ اَوْ
تُخْفُوْهُ يُحَاسِبْكُمْ بِهِ اللّٰهُ ۖ فَيَغْفِرُ
لِمَنْ يَّشَآءُ وَيُعَذِّبُ مَنْ يَّشَآءُ ۗ
وَاللّٰهُ عَلٰى كُلِّ شَيْءٍ قَدِيْرٌ ۝

285. The Messenger believeth in what hath been revealed to him from his Lord, as do the men of faith, each one (of them) believeth in Allah, His angels, His books, and His Messengers. "We make no distinction (they say) between one and another of his Messengers." And they say: "We hear, and we obey: (we seek) Thy forgiveness, our Lord, and to Thee is the end of all journeys."

اٰمَنَ الرَّسُوْلُ بِمَآ اُنْزِلَ اِلَيْهِ
مِنْ رَّبِّهٖ وَالْمُؤْمِنُوْنَ ۗ كُلٌّ
اٰمَنَ بِاللّٰهِ وَمَلٰٓئِكَتِهٖ وَكُتُبِهٖ
وَرُسُلِهٖ ۗ لَا نُفَرِّقُ بَيْنَ اَحَدٍ
مِّنْ رُّسُلِهٖ ۚ وَقَالُوْا سَمِعْنَا
وَاَطَعْنَا ۖ غُفْرَانَكَ رَبَّنَا وَاِلَيْكَ
الْمَصِيْرُ ۝

286. On no soul doth Allah place a burden greater than it can bear. It gets every good that it earns, and it suffers

لَا يُكَلِّفُ اللّٰهُ نَفْسًا اِلَّا وُسْعَهَا ۗ
لَهَا مَا كَسَبَتْ وَعَلَيْهَا مَا اكْتَسَبَتْ ۗ

SÛRA–3
ÃL-I-'IMRÃN
(INTRODUCTION)

This Sûra is cognate to Sûra 2, but the matter is here treated from a different point of view. The references to Badr (Ramadhãn, H. 2) and Uḥud (Shawwãl, H. 3) give a clue to the dates of those passages.

Like Sûra 2, it takes a general view of the religious history of mankind, with special reference to the People of the Book, proceeds to explain the birth of the new People of Islam and their ordinances, insists on the need of struggle and fighting in the cause of Truth, and exhorts those who have been blessed with Islam to remain constant in Faith, pray for guidance, and maintain their spiritual hope for the Future.

The new points of view developed are: (1) The emphasis is here laid on the duty of the Christians to accept the new light; the Christians are here specially appealed to as the jews were specially appealed to in the last Sûra; (2) the lessons of the battles of Badr and Uḥud are set out for the Muslim community; and (3) the responsibilities of that community are insisted on both internally and in their relations to those outside.

every ill that it earns. (Pray:) "Our Lord ! condemn us not if we forget or fall into error; our Lord ! lay not on us a burden like that which Thou didst lay on those before us; our Lord ! lay not on us a burden greater than we have strength to bear. Blot out our sins, and grant us forgiveness. Have mercy on us. Thou art our Protector; grant us victory over the unbelievers.

رَبَّنَا لَا تُؤَاخِذْنَا إِنْ نَسِيْنَا أَوْ اَخْطَأْنَا ۚ رَبَّنَا وَلَا تَحْمِلْ عَلَيْنَا اِصْرًا كَمَا حَمَلْتَهٗ عَلَى الَّذِيْنَ مِنْ قَبْلِنَا ۚ رَبَّنَا وَلَا تُحَمِّلْنَا مَا لَا طَاقَةَ لَنَا بِهٖ ۚ وَاعْفُ عَنَّا ۗ وَاغْفِرْ لَنَا ۗ وَارْحَمْنَا ۚ أَنْتَ مَوْلَىٰنَا فَانْصُرْنَا عَلَى الْقَوْمِ الْكٰفِرِيْنَ ۝

Āl-i-'Imrān, or the
Family of 'Imrān

In the name of Allah, Most Gracious, Most Merciful.

1.   A. L. M.

2.   Allah ! There is no god but He,—the Living, the Self-Subsisting, the Supporter of all.

3.   It is He Who sent down to thee (step by step), in truth, the Book, confirming what went before it; and He sent down the Torah (of Moses) and the Gospel (of Jesus).

4.   Before this, as a guide to mankind, and He sent down the Criterion (of judgment between right and wrong). Then those who reject Faith in the Signs of Allah will suffer the severest chastisement and Allah is Exalted in Might, Lord of Retribution.

5.   From Allah, verily nothing is hidden on earth or in the heavens.

6.   He it is Who shapes you in the wombs as He pleases. There is no god but He, the Exalted in Might, the Wise.

7.   He it is Who has sent down to thee the Book: in it are verses basic or fundamental clear (in meaning); they are the foundation

سُوْرَةُ اٰلِ عِمْرَانَ مَدَنِيَّةٌ وَهِيَ مِائَتَانِ وَثَمَانُوْنَ اٰيَةً

بِسْمِ اللّٰهِ الرَّحْمٰنِ الرَّحِيْمِ ۝
الٓمّٓ ۝ اللّٰهُ لَا إِلٰهَ إِلَّا هُوَ الْحَيُّ الْقَيُّوْمُ ۝ نَزَّلَ عَلَيْكَ الْكِتٰبَ بِالْحَقِّ مُصَدِّقًا لِّمَا بَيْنَ يَدَيْهِ وَ اَنْزَلَ التَّوْرٰىةَ وَالْاِنْجِيْلَ ۝ مِنْ قَبْلُ هُدًى لِّلنَّاسِ وَ اَنْزَلَ الْفُرْقَانَ ۗ إِنَّ الَّذِيْنَ كَفَرُوْا بِاٰيٰتِ اللّٰهِ لَهُمْ عَذَابٌ شَدِيْدٌ ۗ وَاللّٰهُ عَزِيْزٌ ذُوانْتِقَامٍ ۝ إِنَّ اللّٰهَ لَا يَخْفٰى عَلَيْهِ شَيْءٌ فِى الْاَرْضِ وَلَا فِى السَّمَاءِ ۝ هُوَ الَّذِيْ يُصَوِّرُكُمْ فِى الْاَرْحَامِ كَيْفَ يَشَاءُ ۚ لَا إِلٰهَ إِلَّا هُوَ الْعَزِيْزُ الْحَكِيْمُ ۝ هُوَ الَّذِيْ اَنْزَلَ عَلَيْكَ الْكِتٰبَ مِنْهُ اٰيٰتٌ مُّحْكَمٰتٌ هُنَّ أُمُّ

of the Book: others are not entirely clear. But those in whose hearts is perversity follow the part thereof that is not entirely clear. Seeking discord, and searching for its interpretation, but no one knows its true meanings except Allah. And those who are firmly grounded in knowledge say: "We believe in it, the whole of it is from our Lord:" and none will grasp the Message except men of understanding.

8. "O Lord !" (they say), "Let not our hearts deviate now after Thou hast guided us, but grant us mercy from Thee: for Thou art the Grantor of bounties without measure.

9. "Our Lord ! Thou art He that will gather mankind together against a Day about which there is no doubt; for Allah never fails in His promise."

10. Those who reject Faith,—neither their possessions nor their (numerous) progeny will avail them aught against Allah: they are themselves but fuel for the Fire.

11. (Their plight will be) no better than that of the people of Pharaoh, and their predecessors: they denied our Signs, and Allah called them to account for their sins. For Allah is strict in punishment.

12. Say to those who reject Faith: "Soon will ye be vanquished and gathered together to Hell,—an evil bed indeed (to lie on) !

13. "There has already been for you a Sign in the two armies that met (in combat): one was fighting in the Cause of Allah, the other resisting Allah; these saw with their own eyes twice their number. But Allah

doth support with His aid whom He pleaseth. In this is a lesson for such as have eyes to see."

14. Fair in the eyes of men is the love of things they covet: women and sons; heaped-up hoards of gold and silver; horses branded (for blood and excellence); and (wealth of) cattle and well-tilled land. Such are the possessions of this world's life; but with Allah is the best of the goals (to return to).

15. Say: Shall I give you glad tidings of things far better than those ? For the righteous are Gardens in nearness to their Lord with rivers flowing beneath; therein is their eternal home; with spouses purified and the good pleasure of Allah. For in Allah's sight are (all) His servants,—

16. (Namely), those who say: "Our Lord ! we have indeed believed: forgive us, then, our sins, and save us from the agony of the Fire;"—

17. Those who show patience, (firmness and self-control;) who are true (in word and deed); who worship devoutly; who spend (in the way of Allah); and who pray for forgiveness in the early hours of the morning.

18. There is no god but He: that is the witness of Allah, His angels, and those endued with knowledge, standing firm on justice. There is no god but He, the Exalted in Power, the Wise.

19. The Religion before Allah is Islam (submission to His Will): nor did the People of the Book dissent therefrom except through envy of each other, after knowledge had come to them. But if any deny the

Signs of Allah, Allah is swift in calling to account.

20. So if they dispute with thee, say: "I have submitted my whole self to Allah and so have those who follow me." And say to the People of the Book and to those who are unlearned: "Do ye (also) submit yourselves ?" If they do, they are in right guidance, but if they turn back, thy duty is to convey the Message; and in Allah's sight are (all) His servants.

21. As to those who deny the Signs of Allah, and in defiance of right, slay the prophets, and slay those who teach just dealing with mankind, announce to them a grievous chastisement.

22. They are those whose works will bear no fruit in this world and in the Hereafter, nor will they have anyone to help.

23. Hast thou not turned thy thought to those who have been given a portion of the Book? They are invited to the Book of Allah, to settle their dispute, but a party of them turn back and decline (the arbitration).

24. This because they say: "The Fire shall not touch us but for a few numbered days"; for their forgeries deceive them as to their own religion.

25. But how (will they fare) when We gather them together against a Day about which there is no doubt, and each soul will be paid out just what it has earned, without (favour or) injustice?

26. Say: "O Allah! Lord of Power (and Rule), Thou givest Power to whom Thou

pleasest, and Thou strippest off Power from whom Thou pleasest: Thou enduest with honour whom Thou pleasest, and Thou bringest low whom Thou pleasest: in Thy hand is all Good. Verily, over all things thou hast power.

27. "Thou causest the Night to gain on the Day, and Thou causest the Day to gain on the Night; Thou bringest the Living out of the Dead, and Thou bringest the Dead out of the Living; and Thou givest sustenance to whom Thou pleasest without measure."
28. Let not the Believers take for friends or helpers Unbelievers rather than Believers: if any do that, shall have no relation left with Allah except by way of precaution, that ye may guard yourselves from them. But Allah cautions you (to fear) Himself; for the final goal is to Allah.

29. Say: "Whether ye hide what is in your hearts or reveal it, Allah knows it all: He knows what is in the heavens, and what is on earth. And Allah has power over all things.

30. "On the Day when every soul will be confronted with all the good it has done, and all the evil it has done, it will wish there were a great distance between it and its evil. But Allah cautions you (to fear) Him and Allah is full of kindness to those that serve Him."
31. Say: "If ye do love Allah, follow me: Allah will love you and forgive you your sins: for Allah is Oft-Forgiving, Most Merciful."
32. Say: "Obey Allah and His Messenger": but if they turn back, Allah loveth not those

who reject Faith.

33. Allah did choose Adam and Noah, the family of Abraham, and the family of 'Imrān above all people,–

34. Offspring, one of the other: and Allah heareth and knoweth all things.

35. Behold ! wife of 'Imrān said: "O my Lord ! I do dedicate into Thee what is in my womb for Thy special service: so accept this of me: for Thou hearest and knowest all things."

36. When she was delivered, she said: "O my Lord ! behold ! I am delivered of a female child !"—And Allah knew best what she brought forth—"And is not the male like the female. I have named her Mary, and I commend her and her offspring to Thy protection from Satan, the Rejected."

37. Right graciously did her Lord accept her: He made her grow in purity and beauty: to the care of Zakarīya was she assigned. Every time that he entered (her) chamber to see her, he found her supplied with sustenance. He said: "O Mary! Whence (comes) this to you ?" She said: "From Allah: for Allah provides sustenance to whom He pleases, without measure.

38. There did Zakariya pray to his Lord, saying: 'O my Lord ! Grant unto me from Thee a progeny that is pure: for Thou art He that heareth prayer !

39. While he was standing in prayer in the chamber, the angels called unto him: "Allah doth give thee glad tidings of Yahyā, confirming the truth of a Word

from Allah, and (be besides) noble, chaste, and a Prophet,—of the (goodly) company of the righteous."

40. He said: "O my Lord ! how shall I have a son, seeing I am very old, and my wife is barren?" "Thus," was the answer, "doth Allah accomplish what He willeth."

41. He said: "O my Lord ! give me a Sign !" "Thy Sign," was the answer, "shall be that thou shalt speak to no man for three days but with signals. Then celebrate the praises of thy Lord again and again, and glorify Him in the evening and in the morning."

42. Behold ! the angels said: "O Mary! Allah hath chosen thee and purified thee— chosen thee above the women of all nations.

43. "O Mary ! worship the Lord devoutly: prostrate thyself, and bow down (in prayer) with those who bow down."

44. This is part of the tidings of the things unseen, which We reveal unto thee (O Prophet !) by inspiration: thou wast not with them when they cast lots with pens, as to which of them should be charged with the care of Mary: nor wast thou with them when they disputed (the point).

45. Behold ! the angels said: "O Mary! Allah giveth thee glad tidings of a Word from Him: his name will be Christ Jesus, the son of Mary, held in honour in this world and the Hereafter and of (the company of) those nearest to Allah;

46. "He shall speak to the people in childhood and in maturity. And he shall be (of the company of) the righteous."

47. She said: "O my Lord ! how shall I

have a son when no man hath touched me? He said: "Even so; Allah createth what He willeth: when He hath decreed a matter, He but saith to it, 'Be,' and it is!

48. "And Allah will teach him the Book and Wisdom, the Torah and the Gospel,

49. "And (appoint him) a messenger to the Children of Israel, (with this message): "I have come to you, with a Sign from your Lord, in that I make for you out of clay, as it were, the figure of a bird, and breathe into it, and it becomes a bird by Allah's leave: and I heal those born blind, and the lepers, and I bring the dead into life, by Allah's leave; and I declare to you what ye eat, and what ye store in your houses. Surely therein is a Sign for you if ye did believe;

50. " '(I have come to you), to attest the Torah which was before me. And to make lawful to you part of what was (before) forbidden to you; I have come to you with a Sign from your Lord. So fear Allah, and obey me.

51. " 'It is Allah who is my Lord and your Lord; then worship Him. This is a Way that is straight.' "

52. When Jesus found unbelief on their part, he said: "Who will be my helpers to (the work of) Allah ? Said the Disciples:" We are Allah's helpers: we believe in Allah, and do thou bear witness that we are Muslims.

53. "Our Lord ! we believe in what Thou hast revealed, and we follow the Messenger: then write us down among those who bear witness."

54. And (the unbelievers) plotted and planned, and Allah too planned, and the best of planners is Allah.

55. Behold ! Allah said: "O Jesus! I will take thee and raise thee to Myself and clear thee (of the falsehoods) of those who blaspheme; I will make those who follow thee superior to those who reject Faith, to the Day of Resurrection: then shall ye all return unto Me, and I will judge between you of the matters wherein ye dispute.

56. "As to those who reject Faith, I will punish them with severe chastisement in this world and in the Hereafter nor will they have anyone to help.

57. "As to those who believe and work righteousness, Allah will pay them (in full) their reward; but Allah loveth not those who do wrong.

58. "This is what We rehearse unto thee of the Signs and the Message of Wisdom."

59. The similitude of Jesus before Allah is as that of Adam; He created him from dust, then said to him: "Be": and he was.

60. The Truth (comes) from thy Lord alone; so be not of those who doubt.

61. If anyone disputes in this matter with thee, now after (full) knowledge hath come to thee, say: "Come ! let us gather together,—our sons and your sons, our women and your women, ourselves and yourselves: then let us earnestly pray, and

invoke the curse of Allah on those who lie!"

62. This is the true account: there is no god except Allah; and Allah—He is indeed the Exalted in Power, the Wise.

63. But if they turn back, Allah hath full knowledge of those who do mischief.

64. Say: "O People of the Book ! come to common terms as between us and you: that we worship none but Allah; that we associate no partners with Him; that we erect not, from among ourselves, lords and patrons other than Allah." If then they turn back, say ye: "Bear witness that we (at least) are Muslims (bowing to Allah's Will)."

65. Ye People of the Book ! why dispute ye about Abraham, when the Torah and the Gospel were not revealed till after him ? Have ye no understanding ?

66. Ah ! Ye are those who fell to disputing (even) in matters of which ye had some Knowledge! But why dispute ye in matters of which ye have no knowledge? It is Allah Who knows, and ye who know not !

67 Abraham was not a Jew nor yet a Christian; but he was Upright, and bowed his will to Allah's, (which is Islam), and he joined not gods with Allah.

68. Without doubt, among men, the nearest of kin to Abraham, are those who follow him, as are also this Prophet and those who believe: and Allah is the Protector of those who have Faith.

69. It is the wish of a section of the People of the Book to lead you astray. But they shall lead astray (not you), but themselves, and they do not perceive !

لَعْنَتَ اللّٰهِ عَلَى الْكٰذِبِيْنَ ۞

اِنَّ هٰذَا لَهُوَ الْقَصَصُ الْحَقُّ ۚ وَمَا مِنْ اِلٰهٍ اِلَّا اللّٰهُ ۚ وَاِنَّ اللّٰهَ لَهُوَ الْعَزِيْزُ الْحَكِيْمُ ۞

فَاِنْ تَوَلَّوْا فَاِنَّ اللّٰهَ عَلِيْمٌ بِالْمُفْسِدِيْنَ ۞

قُلْ يٰٓاَهْلَ الْكِتٰبِ تَعَالَوْا اِلٰى كَلِمَةٍ سَوَآءٍۢ بَيْنَنَا وَبَيْنَكُمْ اَلَّا نَعْبُدَ اِلَّا اللّٰهَ وَلَا نُشْرِكَ بِهٖ شَيْئًا وَّلَا يَتَّخِذَ بَعْضُنَا بَعْضًا اَرْبَابًا مِّنْ دُوْنِ اللّٰهِ ۚ فَاِنْ تَوَلَّوْا فَقُوْلُوا اشْهَدُوْا بِاَنَّا مُسْلِمُوْنَ ۞

يٰٓاَهْلَ الْكِتٰبِ لِمَ تُحَآجُّوْنَ فِيْٓ اِبْرٰهِيْمَ وَمَآ اُنْزِلَتِ التَّوْرٰىةُ وَالْاِنْجِيْلُ اِلَّا مِنْۢ بَعْدِهٖ ۚ اَفَلَا تَعْقِلُوْنَ ۞

هٰٓاَنْتُمْ هٰٓؤُلَآءِ حَاجَجْتُمْ فِيْمَا لَكُمْ بِهٖ عِلْمٌ فَلِمَ تُحَآجُّوْنَ فِيْمَا لَيْسَ لَكُمْ بِهٖ عِلْمٌ ۚ وَاللّٰهُ يَعْلَمُ وَاَنْتُمْ لَا تَعْلَمُوْنَ ۞

مَا كَانَ اِبْرٰهِيْمُ يَهُوْدِيًّا وَّلَا نَصْرَانِيًّا وَّلٰكِنْ كَانَ حَنِيْفًا مُّسْلِمًا ۚ وَمَا كَانَ مِنَ الْمُشْرِكِيْنَ ۞

اِنَّ اَوْلَى النَّاسِ بِاِبْرٰهِيْمَ لَلَّذِيْنَ اتَّبَعُوْهُ وَهٰذَا النَّبِيُّ وَالَّذِيْنَ اٰمَنُوْا ۚ وَاللّٰهُ وَلِيُّ الْمُؤْمِنِيْنَ ۞

وَدَّتْ طَّآئِفَةٌ مِّنْ اَهْلِ الْكِتٰبِ لَوْ يُضِلُّوْنَكُمْ ۚ وَمَا يُضِلُّوْنَ اِلَّآ اَنْفُسَهُمْ وَمَا يَشْعُرُوْنَ ۞

70. Ye People of the Book ! why reject ye the Signs of Allah, of which ye are (yourselves) witnesses ?

71. Ye People of the Book! why do ye clothe truth with falsehood, and conceal the Truth, while ye have knowledge ?

72. A section of the People of the Book say: "Believe in the morning what is revealed to the Believers, but reject it at the end of the day: perchance they may (themselves) turn back;

73. "And believe no one unless he follows your religion." Say: "True guidance is the guidance of Allah: (fear ye) lest a revelation be sent to someone (else) like unto that which was sent unto you. Or that those (receiving such revelation) should engage you in argument before your Lord? Say: "All bounties are in the hand of Allah: He granteth them to whom He pleaseth: and Allah careth for all, and He knoweth all things."

74. For His Mercy He specially chooseth whom He pleaseth: for Allah is the Lord of bounties unbounded.

75. Among the People of the Book are some who, if entrusted with a hoard of gold, will (readily) pay it back; others, who, if entrusted with a single silver coin, will not repay it unless thou constantly stoodest demanding, because, they say: "There is no way over us as to the unlettered people," but they tell a lie against Allah, and (well) they know it.

76. Nay,—Those that keep their plighted faith and act aright,— verily Allah loves those who act aright.

77. As for those who sell the faith they

owe to Allah and their own solemn plighted word for a small price, they shall have no portion in the Hereafter: nor will Allah (deign to) speak to them or look at them on the Day of Judgment, nor will He cleanse them (of sin): they shall have a grievous Chastisement.

78. There is among them a section who distort the Book with their tongues; (as they read) so that you would think it is a part of the Book, but it is no part of the Book; and they say, "That is from Allah," but it is not from Allah: it is they who tell a lie against Allah, and (well) they know it !

79. It is not (possible) that a man, to whom is given the Book, and Wisdom, and the Prophetic Office, should say to people: "Be ye my worshippers rather than Allah's": on the contrary (he would say): "Be ye worshippers of Him (Who is truly the Cherisher of all): for ye have taught the Book and ye have studied it earnestly."

80. Nor would he instruct you to take angels and prophets for Lords and Patrons. What ! would he bid you to unbelief after ye have bowed your will (to Allah in Islam) ?

81. Behold ! Allah took the Covenant of the Prophets, saying: "I give you a Book and Wisdom: then comes to you a Messenger, confirming what is with you; do ye believe in him and render him help." Allah said: "Do ye agree, and take this My Covenant as binding on you ?" They said: "We agree." He said: "Then bear witness, and I am with you among the witnesses."

82. If any turn back after this, they are perverted transgressors.

83. Do they seek for other than the Religion of Allah?—while all creatures in the heavens and on earth have, willing or unwilling, bowed to His Will (accepted Islam), and to Him shall they all be brought back.

84. Say: "We believe in Allah, and in what has been revealed to us and what was revealed to Abraham, Isma'il: Isaac, Jacob, and the Tribes, and in (the Books) given to Moses, Jesus, and the Prophets, from their Lord: we make no distinction between one and another among them, and to Allah do we bow our will (in Islam)."

85. If anyone desires a religion other than Islam (submission to Allah), never will it be accepted of him; and in the Hereafter he will be in the ranks of those who have lost.

86. How shall Allah guide those who reject Faith after they accepted it and bore witness that the Messenger was true and that Clear Signs had come unto them ? But Allah guides not a people unjust.

87. Of such the reward is that on them (rests) the curse of Allah, of His angels, and of all mankind;—

88. In that will they dwell; nor will their punishment be lightened, nor respite be their (lot);—

89. Except for those that repent (even) after that, and make amends; for verily Allah is Oft-Forgiving, Most Merciful.

90. But those who reject Faith after they accepted it, and then go on adding to their defiance of Faith.— never will their

repentance be accepted: for they are those who have gone astray.

91. As to those who reject Faith, and die rejecting,—never would be accepted from any such as much gold as the earth contains, though they should offer it for ransom. For such is (in store) a chastisement grievous and they will find no helpers.

92. By no means shall ye attain righteousness unless ye give (freely) of that which ye love: and whatever ye give, Allah knoweth it well.

93. All food was lawful to the Children of Israel, except what Israel made unlawful for himself before the Torah was revealed. Say: "Bring ye the Torah and study it, if ye be men of truth."

94. If any, after this, invent a lie and attribute it to Allah, they are indeed unjust wrong-doers.

95. Say: "Allah speaketh the Truth: follow the religion of Abraham, the sane in faith: he was not of the Pagans."

96. The first House (of worship) appointed for men was that at Bakka: full of blessing and of guidance for all the worlds.

97. In it are Signs Manifest; the Station of Abraham; whoever enters it attains security; pilgrimage thereto is a duty men owe to Allah,—those who can afford the journey; but if any deny faith, Allah stands not in need of any of His creatures.

98. Say: "O People of the Book ! why reject ye the Signs of Allah, when Allah is

Himself witness to all ye do ?"

99. Say: "O ye People of the Book! why obstruct ye those who believe, from the Path of Allah, seeking to make it crooked, while ye were yourselves witnesses (to Allah's Covenant)? But Allah is not unmindful of all that ye do."

100. O ye who believe ! if ye listen to a faction among the People of the Book, they would (indeed) render you apostates after ye have believed!

101. And how would ye deny Faith while unto you are rehearsed the Signs of Allah, and among you lives the Messenger ? Whoever holds firmly to Allah will be shown a Way that is straight.

102. O ye who believe ! fear Allah as He should be feared, and die not except in a state of Islam.

103. And hold fast, all together, by the Rope which Allah (stretches out for you), and be not divided among yourselves; and remember with gratitude Allah's favour on you; for ye were enemies and He joined your hearts in love, so that by His Grace, ye became brethren; and ye were on the brink of the Pit of Fire, and He saved you from it. Thus doth Allah make His Signs clear to you: that ye may be guided.

104. Let there arise out of you a band of people inviting to all that is good, enjoining what is right, and forbidding what is wrong: they are the ones to attain felicity.

105. Be not like those who are divided amongst themselves and fall into disputations after receiving Clear Signs: for them is a dreadful Chastisement,—

106. On the Day when some faces will be (lit up with) white, and some faces will be (in the gloom of) black: to those whose faces will be black, (will be said): "Did ye reject Faith after accepting it ? Taste then the Chastisement for rejecting Faith."

107. But those whose faces will be (lit with) white,—they will be in (the light of) Allah's mercy: therein to dwell (for ever).

108. These are the Signs of Allah: We rehearse them to thee in Truth: and Allah means no injustice to any of His creatures.

109. To Allah belongs all that is in the heavens and earth: to Allah do all matters return.

110. Ye are the best of Peoples, evolved for mankind, enjoining what is right, forbidding what is wrong, and believing in Allah. If only the People of the Book had Faith, it were best for them: among them are some who have Faith, but most of them are perverted transgressors.

111. They will do you no harm, barring a trifling annoyance: if they come out to fight you, they will show you their backs, and no help shall they get.

112. Shame is pitched over them (like a tent) wherever they are found, except when under a covenant (of protection) from Allah and from men; they draw on themselves wrath from Allah, and pitched over them is (the tent of) destitution. This because they rejected the Signs of Allah. and slew the Prophets in defiance of right: this because they rebelled and transgressed beyond bounds.

113. Not all of them are alike: of the People of the Book are a portion that stand (for the

right); they rehearse the Signs of Allah all night long, and they prostrate themselves in adoration.

114. They believe in Allah and the Last Day; they enjoin what is right, and forbid what is wrong; and they hasten (in emulation) in (all) good works: they are in the ranks of the righteous.

115. Of the good that they do, nothing will be rejected of them; for Allah knoweth well those that do right.

116. Those who reject Faith,— neither their possessions nor their (numerous) progeny will avail them aught against Allah: they will be Companions of the Fire,— dwelling therein (for ever).

117. What they spend in the life of this (material) world may be likened to a Wind which brings a nipping frost: it strikes and destroys the harvest of men who have wronged their own souls: it is not Allah that hath wronged them, but they wrong themselves.

118. O ye who believe ! take not into your intimacy those outside your ranks: they will not fail to corrupt you. They only desire for you to suffer: rank hatred has already appeared from their mouths: what their hearts conceal is far worse. We have made plain to you the Signs, if ye have wisdom.

119. Ah ! ye are those who love them, but they love you not,—though ye believe in the whole of the Book, when they meet you, they say, "We believe": but when they are alone, they bite off the very tips of their fingers at you in their rage. Say: "Perish in

your rage; Allah knoweth well all the secrets of the heart."

120. If aught that is good befalls you, it grieves them; but if some misfortune overtakes you, they rejoice at it. But if ye are patient and do right, not the least harm will their cunning do to you; for Allah compasseth round about all that they do.

121. (Remember that morning) thou didst leave thy household (early) to post the Faithful at their stations for battle: and Allah heareth and knoweth all things:

122. Remember two of your parties meditated cowardice; but Allah was their protector, and in Allah should the Faithful (ever) put their trust.

123. Allah had helped you at Badr, when ye were helpless: then fear Allah; thus may ye show your gratitude.

124. Remember thou saidst to the Faithful: "Is it not enough for you that Allah should help you with three thousand angels (specially) sent down?

125. "Yea,—if ye remain firm, and act aright, even if the enemy should rush here on you in hot haste, your Lord would help you with five thousand angels clearly marked.

126. Allah made it but a message of hope for you, and an assurance to your hearts: (in any case) there is no victory except from Allah, the Exalted, the Wise:

127. That He might cut off a fringe of the Unbelievers or expose them to infamy, and

they should then be turned back, frustrated of their purpose.

128. Not for thee, (but for Allah), is the decision: whether He turn in mercy to them, or punish them; for they are indeed wrong-doers.

129. To Allah belongeth all that is in the heavens and on earth. He forgiveth whom He pleaseth and punisheth whom He pleaseth; but Allah is Oft-Forgiving, Most Merciful.

130. O ye who believe! devour not Usury, doubled and multiplied; but fear Allah; that ye may (really) prosper.

131. And fear the Fire, which is prepared for those who reject Faith:

132. And obey Allah and the Messenger; that ye may obtain mercy.

133. Be quick in the race for forgiveness from your Lord and for a Garden whose width is that (of the whole) of the heavens and of the earth, prepared for the righteous,—

134. Those who spend (freely), whether in prosperity, or in adversity; who restrain anger, and pardon (all) men;— for Allah loves those who do good:

135. And those who, having done an act of indecency or wronged their own souls. Remember Allah and ask for forgiveness for their sins,—and who can forgive sins except Allah?— and are never obstinate in persisting knowingly in (the wrong) they have done.

136. For such the reward is forgiveness from their Lord, and Gardens with rivers flowing underneath.— an eternal dwelling.

how excellent a recompense for those who work (and strive) !

137. There have been examples that have passed away before you: travel through the earth, and see what was the end of those who rejected Truth.

138. Here is a plain statement to men, a guidance and instruction to those who fear Allah !

139. So lose not heart, nor fall into despair: for ye must gain mastery if ye are true in Faith.

140. If a wound hath touched you, be sure a similar wound hath touched the others. Such days (of varying fortunes) We give to men and men by turns: that Allah may know those that believe, and that He may take to Himself from your ranks martyr-witnesses (to Truth). And Allah loveth not those that do wrong.

141. Allah's object also is to purge those that are true in Faith and to deprive of blessing those that resist Faith.

142. Did ye think that ye would enter Heaven without Allah testing those of you who fought hard (in His Cause) and remained steadfast ?

143. Ye did indeed wish for Death before ye encountered it: now ye have seen it with your own eyes, (and ye flinch !)

144. Muhammad is no more than a Messenger: many were the Messengers that passed away before Him. If he died or were slain, will ye then turn back on your heels? If any did turn back on his heels, not the least harm will he do to Allah; but Allah (on the other hand) will swiftly reward those who (serve him) with gratitude.

145. Nor can a soul die except by Allah's leave, the term being fixed as by writing. If any do desire a reward in this life, We shall give it to him; and if any do desire a reward in the Hereafter, We shall give it to him. And swiftly shall We reward those that (serve Us with) gratitude.

146. How many of the Prophets fought (in Allah's way), and with them (fought) large bands of godly men ? But they never lost heart if they met with disaster in Allah's way, nor did they weaken (in will) nor give in. And Allah loves those who are firm and steadfast.

147. All that they said was: "Our Lord ! forgive us our sins and anything we may have done that transgressed our duty: establish our feet firmly, and help us against those that resist Faith."

148. And Allah gave them a reward in this world, and the excellent reward of the Hereafter. For Allah loveth those who do good.

149. O ye who believe ! If ye obey the Unbelievers, they will drive you back on your heels, and ye will turn back (from Faith) to your own loss.

150. Nay, Allah is your Protector, and He is the best of helpers.

151. Soon shall We cast terror into the hearts of the Unbelievers, for that they joined partners with Allah, for which He had sent no authority: their abode will be the Fire: and evil is the home of the wrong-doers !

152. Allah did indeed fulfil His promise to you when ye with His permission were about to annihilate your enemy, until ye flinched

وَمَا كَانَ لِنَفْسٍ أَنْ تَمُوتَ إِلَّا بِإِذْنِ اللّٰهِ كِتَابًا مُّؤَجَّلًا ۚ وَمَن يُرِدْ ثَوَابَ الدُّنْيَا نُؤْتِهِ مِنْهَا ۚ وَمَن يُرِدْ ثَوَابَ الْآخِرَةِ نُؤْتِهِ مِنْهَا ۚ وَسَنَجْزِي الشَّاكِرِينَ ۝

وَكَأَيِّن مِّن نَّبِيٍّ قَاتَلَ مَعَهُ رِبِّيُّونَ كَثِيرٌ فَمَا وَهَنُوا لِمَا أَصَابَهُمْ فِي سَبِيلِ اللّٰهِ وَمَا ضَعُفُوا وَمَا اسْتَكَانُوا ۗ وَاللّٰهُ يُحِبُّ الصَّابِرِينَ

وَمَا كَانَ قَوْلَهُمْ إِلَّا أَن قَالُوا رَبَّنَا اغْفِرْ لَنَا ذُنُوبَنَا وَإِسْرَافَنَا فِي أَمْرِنَا وَثَبِّتْ أَقْدَامَنَا وَانصُرْنَا عَلَى الْقَوْمِ الْكَافِرِينَ ۝

فَآتَاهُمُ اللّٰهُ ثَوَابَ الدُّنْيَا وَحُسْنَ ثَوَابِ الْآخِرَةِ ۗ وَاللّٰهُ يُحِبُّ الْمُحْسِنِينَ ۝

يَا أَيُّهَا الَّذِينَ آمَنُوا إِن تُطِيعُوا الَّذِينَ كَفَرُوا يَرُدُّوكُمْ عَلَى أَعْقَابِكُمْ فَتَنقَلِبُوا خَاسِرِينَ ۝

بَلِ اللّٰهُ مَوْلَاكُمْ ۖ وَهُوَ خَيْرُ النَّاصِرِينَ ۝

سَنُلْقِي فِي قُلُوبِ الَّذِينَ كَفَرُوا الرُّعْبَ بِمَا أَشْرَكُوا بِاللّٰهِ مَا لَمْ يُنَزِّلْ بِهِ سُلْطَانًا ۖ وَمَأْوَاهُمُ النَّارُ ۚ وَبِئْسَ مَثْوَى الظَّالِمِينَ ۝

وَلَقَدْ صَدَقَكُمُ اللّٰهُ وَعْدَهُ إِذْ تَحُسُّونَهُم بِإِذْنِهِ ۖ حَتَّىٰ إِذَا فَشِلْتُمْ

and fell to disputing about the order, and disobeyed it after He brought you in sight (of the Victory) which ye covet. Among you are some that hanker after this world and some that desire the Hereafter. Then did He divert you from your foes in order to test you. But He forgave you: for Allah is full of grace to those who believe.

153. Behold ! ye were climbing up the high ground, without even casting a side glance at anyone, and the Messenger in your rear was calling you back. There did Allah give you one distress after another by way of requital, to teach you not to grieve for (the booty) that had escaped you and for (the ill) that had befallen you. For Allah is well aware of all that ye do.

154. After (the excitement) of the distress, He sent down calm on a band of you overcome with slumber, while another band was stirred to anxiety by their own feelings, moved by wrong suspicions of Allah— suspicions due to Ignorance. They said: "Have we any hand in the affair?" Say thou: "Indeed, this affair is wholly Allah's." They hide in their minds what they dare not reveal to thee. They say (to themselves); "If we had had anything to do with this affair, we should not have been in the slaughter here." Say: "Even if you had remained in your homes, those for whom death was decreed would certainly have gone forth to the place of their death": but (all this was) that Allah might test what is in your breasts and purge what is in your hearts. For Allah knoweth

well the secrets of your hearts.

155. Those of you who turned back on the day the two hosts met,—it was Satan who caused them to fail, because of some (evil) they had done. But Allah has blotted out (their fault): for Allah is Oft-Forgiving, Most Forbearing.

156. O ye who believe ! be not like the Unbelievers, who say of their brethren, when they are travelling through the earth or engaged in fighting: "If they had stayed with us, they would not have died, or been slain." This that Allah may make it a cause of sighs and regrets in their hearts. It is Allah that gives Life and Death, and Allah sees well all that ye do.

157. And if ye are slain, or die, in the way of Allah, forgiveness and mercy from Allah are far better than all they could amass:

158. And if ye die, or are slain, lo ! it is unto Allah that ye are brought together.

159. It is part of the Mercy of Allah that thou dost deal gently with them. Wert thou severe or harsh-hearted, they would have broken away from about thee: so pass over (their faults), and ask for (Allah's) forgiveness for them; and consult them in affairs (of moment). Then, when thou hast taken a decision, put thy trust in Allah. For Allah loves those who put their trust (in Him).

160. If Allah helps you, none can overcome you: if He forsakes you, who is there, after that, that can help you ? In Allah, then, let Believers put their trust.

161. No prophet could (ever) act dishonestly if any person acts dishonestly he shall, on

the Day of Judgment, restore what he misappropriated; then shall every soul receive its due whatever it earned,—and none shall be dealt with unjustly.

162. Is the man who follows the good pleasure of Allah like the man who draws on himself the wrath of Allah, and whose abode is in Hell?—a woeful refuge !

163. They are in varying grades in the sight of Allah, and Allah sees well all that they do.

164. Allah did confer a great favour on the Believers when He sent among them a Messenger from among themselves, rehearsing unto them the Signs of Allah, purifying them, and instructing them in Scripture and Wisdom, while, before that, they had been in manifest error.

165. What ! When a single disaster smites you, although ye smote (your enemies) with one twice as great, do ye say ?— "Whence is this?" Say (to them): "It is from yourselves: for Allah hath power over all things."

166. What ye suffered on the day the two armies met, was with the leave of Allah, in order that He might test the Believers,—

167. And the Hypocrites also. These were told: "Come, fight in the way of Allah, or (at least) drive (the foe from your city)." They said: "Had we known there would be a fight, we should certainly have followed you." They were that day nearer to Unbelief than to Faith, saying with their lips what was not in their hearts. But Allah hath full knowledge of all they conceal.

168. (They are) the ones that say, (of their brethren slain), while they themselves sit (at ease): "If only they had listened to us, they would not have been slain." Say: "Avert death from your own selves, if ye speak the truth."

الَّذِيْنَ قَالُوْا لِاِخْوَانِهِمْ وَقَعَدُوْا لَوْ اَطَاعُوْنَا مَا قُتِلُوْا ۖ قُلْ فَادْرَءُوْا عَنْ اَنْفُسِكُمُ الْمَوْتَ اِنْ كُنْتُمْ صٰدِقِيْنَ ۝

169. Think not of those who are slain in Allah's way as dead. Nay, they live, finding their sustenance from their Lord.

وَلَا تَحْسَبَنَّ الَّذِيْنَ قُتِلُوْا فِيْ سَبِيْلِ اللّٰهِ اَمْوَاتًا ۖ بَلْ اَحْيَاءٌ عِنْدَ رَبِّهِمْ يُرْزَقُوْنَ ۝

170. They rejoice in the Bounty provided by Allah: and with regard to those left behind, who have not yet joined them (in their bliss), the (martyrs) glory in the fact that on them is no fear, nor have they (cause to) grieve.

فَرِحِيْنَ بِمَا اٰتٰهُمُ اللّٰهُ مِنْ فَضْلِهٖ ۙ وَيَسْتَبْشِرُوْنَ بِالَّذِيْنَ لَمْ يَلْحَقُوْا بِهِمْ مِّنْ خَلْفِهِمْ ۙ اَلَّا خَوْفٌ عَلَيْهِمْ وَلَاهُمْ يَحْزَنُوْنَ ۝

171. They rejoice in the Grace and the Bounty from Allah, and in the fact that Allah suffereth not the reward of the Faithful to be lost (in the least).

يَسْتَبْشِرُوْنَ بِنِعْمَةٍ مِّنَ اللّٰهِ وَفَضْلٍ ۙ وَّاَنَّ اللّٰهَ لَا يُضِيْعُ اَجْرَ الْمُؤْمِنِيْنَ ۝

172. Of those who answered the call of Allah and the Messenger, even after being wounded, those who do right and refrain from wrong have a great reward;—

الَّذِيْنَ اسْتَجَابُوْا لِلّٰهِ وَالرَّسُوْلِ مِنْ بَعْدِ مَا اَصَابَهُمُ الْقَرْحُ ۛ لِلَّذِيْنَ اَحْسَنُوْا مِنْهُمْ وَاتَّقَوْا اَجْرٌ عَظِيْمٌ ۝

173. Those to whom men said: "A great army is gathering against you, so fear them": but it (only) increased their Faith: they said: "For us Allah sufficeth, and He is the best Guardian."

الَّذِيْنَ قَالَ لَهُمُ النَّاسُ اِنَّ النَّاسَ قَدْ جَمَعُوْا لَكُمْ فَاخْشَوْهُمْ فَزَادَهُمْ اِيْمَانًا ۖ وَّقَالُوْا حَسْبُنَا اللّٰهُ وَنِعْمَ الْوَكِيْلُ ۝

174. And they returned with Grace and Bounty from Allah: no harm ever touched them: for they followed the good pleasure of Allah: and Allah is the Lord of bounties unbounded.

فَانْقَلَبُوْا بِنِعْمَةٍ مِّنَ اللّٰهِ وَفَضْلٍ لَّمْ يَمْسَسْهُمْ سُوْءٌ ۙ وَّاتَّبَعُوْا رِضْوَانَ اللّٰهِ ۗ وَاللّٰهُ ذُوْ فَضْلٍ عَظِيْمٍ ۝

175. It is only the Satan that suggests to

اِنَّمَا ذٰلِكُمُ الشَّيْطٰنُ يُخَوِّفُ

you the fear of his votaries: be ye not afraid of them, but fear Me, if ye have Faith.

176. Let not those grieve thee who rush headlong into Unbelief: not the least harm will they do to Allah: Allah's Plan is that He will give them no portion in the Hereafter, but a severe punishment.

177. Those who purchase unbelief at the price of faith,— not the least harm will they do to Allah, but they will have a grievous punishment.

178. Let not the Unbelievers think that Our respite to them is good for themselves: We grant them respite that they may grow in their iniquity: but they will have a shameful punishment.

179. Allah will not leave the Believers in the state in which ye are now, until He separates what is evil from what is good nor will Allah disclose to you the secrets of the Unseen, but He chooses of His Messengers whom He pleases. So believe in Allah and His Messengers: and if ye believe and do right, ye have a great reward without measure.

180. And let not those who covetously withhold of the gifts which Allah hath given them of His Grace. think that it is good for them: nay, it will be the worse for them: soon it will be tied to their necks like a twisted collar, on the Day of Judgment. To Allah belongs the heritage of the heavens and the earth; and Allah is well-acquainted with all that ye do.

أَوْلِيَآءَ ۚ فَلَا تَخَافُوهُمْ وَخَافُونِ إِن كُنتُم مُّؤْمِنِينَ ۞

وَلَا يَحْزُنكَ الَّذِينَ يُسَارِعُونَ فِي الْكُفْرِ ۚ إِنَّهُمْ لَن يَضُرُّوا اللَّهَ شَيْئًا ۗ يُرِيدُ اللَّهُ أَلَّا يَجْعَلَ لَهُمْ حَظًّا فِي الْآخِرَةِ ۖ وَلَهُمْ عَذَابٌ عَظِيمٌ ۞

إِنَّ الَّذِينَ اشْتَرَوُا الْكُفْرَ بِالْإِيمَانِ لَن يَضُرُّوا اللَّهَ شَيْئًا ۖ وَلَهُمْ عَذَابٌ أَلِيمٌ ۞

وَلَا يَحْسَبَنَّ الَّذِينَ كَفَرُوا أَنَّمَا نُمْلِي لَهُمْ خَيْرٌ لِّأَنفُسِهِمْ ۚ إِنَّمَا نُمْلِي لَهُمْ لِيَزْدَادُوا إِثْمًا ۚ وَلَهُمْ عَذَابٌ مُّهِينٌ ۞

مَّا كَانَ اللَّهُ لِيَذَرَ الْمُؤْمِنِينَ عَلَىٰ مَا أَنتُمْ عَلَيْهِ حَتَّىٰ يَمِيزَ الْخَبِيثَ مِنَ الطَّيِّبِ ۗ وَمَا كَانَ اللَّهُ لِيُطْلِعَكُمْ عَلَى الْغَيْبِ وَلَٰكِنَّ اللَّهَ يَجْتَبِي مِن رُّسُلِهِ مَن يَشَاءُ ۖ فَآمِنُوا بِاللَّهِ وَرُسُلِهِ ۚ وَإِن تُؤْمِنُوا وَتَتَّقُوا فَلَكُمْ أَجْرٌ عَظِيمٌ ۞

وَلَا يَحْسَبَنَّ الَّذِينَ يَبْخَلُونَ بِمَا آتَاهُمُ اللَّهُ مِن فَضْلِهِ هُوَ خَيْرًا لَّهُم ۖ بَلْ هُوَ شَرٌّ لَّهُمْ ۖ سَيُطَوَّقُونَ مَا بَخِلُوا بِهِ يَوْمَ الْقِيَامَةِ ۗ وَلِلَّهِ مِيرَاثُ السَّمَاوَاتِ وَالْأَرْضِ ۗ وَاللَّهُ بِمَا تَعْمَلُونَ خَبِيرٌ ۞

181. Allah hath heard the taunt of those who say: "Truly, Allah is indigent and we are rich !"— We shall certainly record their word and (their act) of slaying the Prophets in defiance of right, and We shall say: "Taste ye the Chastisement of the scorching Fire !

182. "This is because of the (unrighteous deeds) which your hands sent on before ye: for Allah never do injustice to those who serve Him."

183. They (also) said: "Allah took our promise not to believe in a messenger unless he showed us a sacrifice consumed by fire (from heaven)." Say: "There came to you Messengers before me, with clear Signs and even with what ye ask for: why then did ye slay them, if ye speak the truth?"

184. Then if they reject thee, so were rejected messengers before thee, who came with clear Signs, and the Scriptures, and the Book of Enlightenment.

185. Every soul shall have a taste of death: and only on the Day of Judgment shall you be paid your full recompense. Only he who is saved far from the Fire and admitted to the Garden will have succeeded: for the life of this world is but goods and chattels of deception.

186. Ye shall certainly be tried and tested in your possessions and in yourselves; and ye shall certainly hear much that will grieve you, from those who received the Book before you and from those who worship partners besides Allah. But if ye persevere patiently, and guard against evil,—then that indeed is a matter of great resolution.

187. And remember Allah took a Covenant from the People of the Book, to make it known and clear to mankind, and not to

آل عمران ٣   لن تنالوا

hide it; but they threw it away behind their backs, and purchased with it some miserable gain ! And vile was the bargain they made !

188. Think not that those who exult in what they have brought about, and love to be praised for what they have not done,— think not that they can escape the Chastisement. For them is a Chastisement grievous indeed.

189. To Allah belongeth the dominion of the heavens and the earth; and Allah hath power over all things.

190. Behold ! In the creation of the heavens and the earth, and the alternation of Night and Day,— there are indeed Signs for men of understanding,—

191. Men who remember Allah standing, sitting, and lying down on their sides, and contemplate the (wonders of) creation in the heavens and the earth, (with the saying): "Our Lord not for naught hast Thou created (all) this ! Glory to Thee! Give us salvation from the Chastisement of the Fire.

192. "Our Lord ! any whom Thou dost admit to the Fire, truly Thou coverest with shame, and never will wrong-doers find any helpers!

193. "Our Lord ! we have heard the call of one calling (us) to Faith, 'Believe ye in the Lord,' and we have believed. Our Lord ! forgive us our sins, blot out from us our iniquities, and take to Thyself our souls in the company of the righteous.

194. "Our Lord ! Grant us what Thou didst promise unto us through Thy Messengers, and save us from shame on the Day of Judgment: for Thou never breakest Thy promise."

195. And their Lord hath accepted of them, and answered them: "Never will I suffer to be lost the work of any of you, be he male or female: ye are members, one of another: those who have left their homes, and were driven out therefrom, and suffered harm in My Cause, and fought and were slain,— verily, I will blot out from them their iniquites, and admit them into Gardens with rivers flowing beneath;—a reward from Allah and from Allah is the best of rewards."

196. Let not the strutting about of the Unbelievers through the land deceive thee:

197. Little is it for enjoyment: their Ultimate abode is Hell: what an evil bed (to lie on) !

198. On the other hand, for those who fear their Lord, are Gardens, with rivers flowing beneath; therein are they to dwell (for ever),— an entertainment from Allah; and that which is from Allah is the best (bliss) for the righteous.

199. And there are, certainly, among the People of the Book, those who believe in Allah, in the revelation to you, and in the revelation to them, bowing in humility to Allah: they will not sell the Signs of Allah for a miserable gain ! For them is a reward with their Lord, and Allah is swift in account.

200. O ye who believe ! persevere in patience and constancy; vie in such perseverance; strengthen each other; and fear Allah; that ye may prosper.

SÛRA–4
AN-NISÃA
(INTRODUCTION)

This Sûra is closely connected chronologically with Sûra 3. Its subject-matter deals with the social problems which the Muslim community had to face immediately after Uḥud. While the particular occasion made the necessity urgent, the principles laid down have permanently governed Muslim Law and social practice.

Broadly speaking, the Sûra consists of two parts: (1) that dealing with women, orphans, inheritance, marriage and family rights generally, and (2) that dealing with the recalcitrants in the larger family, the community at Madinah, viz. the Hypocrites and their accomplices.

An-Nisāa,
or The Women

In the name of Allah, Most Gracious Most Merciful.

1. O mankind ! fear your Guardian Lord, Who created you from a single Person, created, out of it, His mate, and from them twain scattered (like seeds) countless men and women;— fear Allah, through Whom ye demand your mutual (rights), and be heedful of the wombs (that bore you): for Allah ever watches over you.

2. To orphans restore their property (when they reach their age), nor substitute (your) worthless things for (their) good ones; and devour not their substance (by mixing it up) with your own. For this is indeed a great sin.

3. If ye fear that ye shall not be able to deal justly with the orphans, marry women of your choice, two, or three, or four; but if ye fear that ye shall not be able to deal justly (with them), then only one, or that which your right hands possess. That will be more suitable, to prevent you from doing injustice.

4. And give the women (on marriage) their dower as an obligation; but if they, of their own good pleasure, remit any part of it to you, take it and enjoy it with right good cheer.

5. To those weak of understanding give not your property which Allah has assigned to you to manage, but feed and clothe them therewith, and speak to them words of kindness and justice.

6. Make trial of orphans until they reach the age of marriage; if then ye find sound judgment in them, release their property to

فَادْفَعُوَاۤ اِلَيۡهِمۡ اَمۡوَالَهُمۡ وَلَا تَاۡكُلُوۡهَاۤ اِسۡرَافًا وَّبِدَارًا اَنۡ يَّكۡبَرُوۡا ؕ وَمَنۡ كَانَ غَنِيًّا فَلۡيَسۡتَعۡفِفۡ ۚ وَمَنۡ كَانَ فَقِيۡرًا فَلۡيَاۡكُلۡ بِالۡمَعۡرُوۡفِ ؕ فَاِذَا دَفَعۡتُمۡ اِلَيۡهِمۡ اَمۡوَالَهُمۡ فَاَشۡهِدُوۡا عَلَيۡهِمۡ ؕ وَكَفٰى بِاللّٰهِ حَسِيۡبًا ۝

7.   From what is left by parents and those nearest related there is a share for men and a share for women, whether the property be small or large,—a determinate share.

لِلرِّجَالِ نَصِيۡبٌ مِّمَّا تَرَكَ الۡوَالِدٰنِ وَالۡاَقۡرَبُوۡنَ ۪ وَلِلنِّسَاۤءِ نَصِيۡبٌ مِّمَّا تَرَكَ الۡوَالِدٰنِ وَالۡاَقۡرَبُوۡنَ مِمَّا قَلَّ مِنۡهُ اَوۡ كَثُرَ ؕ نَصِيۡبًا مَّفۡرُوۡضًا ۝

8.   But if at the time of division other relatives, or orphans, or poor, are present, give them out of the (property), and speak to them words of kindness and justice.

وَاِذَا حَضَرَ الۡقِسۡمَةَ اُولُوا الۡقُرۡبٰى وَالۡيَتٰمٰى وَالۡمَسٰكِيۡنُ فَارۡزُقُوۡهُمۡ مِّنۡهُ وَقُوۡلُوۡا لَهُمۡ قَوۡلًا مَّعۡرُوۡفًا ۝

9.   Let those (disposing of an estate) have the same fear in their minds as they would have for their own if they had left a helpless family behind: let them fear Allah, and speak appropriate words.

وَلۡيَخۡشَ الَّذِيۡنَ لَوۡ تَرَكُوۡا مِنۡ خَلۡفِهِمۡ ذُرِّيَّةً ضِعٰفًا خَافُوۡا عَلَيۡهِمۡ ۖ فَلۡيَتَّقُوا اللّٰهَ وَلۡيَقُوۡلُوۡا قَوۡلًا سَدِيۡدًا ۝

10.   Those who unjustly eat up the property of orphans, eat up a Fire into their own bodies: they will soon be enduring a blazing Fire !

اِنَّ الَّذِيۡنَ يَاۡكُلُوۡنَ اَمۡوَالَ الۡيَتٰمٰى ظُلۡمًا اِنَّمَا يَاۡكُلُوۡنَ فِىۡ بُطُوۡنِهِمۡ نَارًا ؕ وَسَيَصۡلَوۡنَ سَعِيۡرًا ۝

11.   Allah (thus) directs you as regards your children's (inheri-tance): to the male, a portion equal to that of two females: if only daughters, two or more, their share is two-thirds of the inheritance; if only one, her

يُوۡصِيۡكُمُ اللّٰهُ فِىۡۤ اَوۡلَادِكُمۡ ۖ لِلذَّكَرِ مِثۡلُ حَظِّ الۡاُنۡثَيَيۡنِ ۚ فَاِنۡ كُنَّ نِسَاۤءً فَوۡقَ اثۡنَتَيۡنِ فَلَهُنَّ ثُلُثَا مَا تَرَكَ ۚ وَاِنۡ كَانَتۡ وَاحِدَةً فَلَهَا النِّصۡفُ ؕ وَلِاَبَوَيۡهِ

share is a half.

For parents, a sixth share of the inheritance to each, if the deceased left children; if no children, and the parents are the (only) heirs, the mother has a third: if the deceased left brothers (or sisters), the mother has a sixth. (The distribution in all cases is) after the payment of legacies and debts. Ye know not whether your parents or your children are nearest to you in benefit. These are settled portions ordained by Allah: and Allah is All-knowing, All-wise.

12. In what your wives leave, your share is a half, if they leave no child, but if they leave a child, ye get a fourth; after payment of legacies and debts. In what ye leave, their share is a fourth, if ye leave no child; but if ye leave a child, they get an eighth; after payment of legacies and debts.

If the man or woman whose inheritance is in question, has left neither ascendants nor descendants, but has left a brother or a sister, each one of the two gets a sixth; but if more than two, they share in a third: after payment of legacies and debts;.so that no loss is caused (to anyone). Thus is it ordained by Allah; and Allah is All-knowing, Most Forbearing.

13. Those are limits set by Allah: those who obey Allah and His Messenger will be

admitted to Gardens with rivers flowing beneath, to abide therein (for ever) and that will be the Supreme achievement.

14. But those who disobey Allah and His Messenger and transgress His limits will be admitted to a Fire, to abide therein: and they shall have a humiliating punishment.

15. If any of your women are guilty of lewdness, take the evidence of four (reliable) witnesses from amongst you against them; and if they testify, confine them to houses until death do claim them, or Allah ordain for them some (other) way.

16. If two persons among you are guilty of lewdness, punish them both. If they repent and amend, leave them alone; for Allah is Oft-Returning, Most Merciful.

17. Allah accepts the repentance of those who do evil in ignorance and repent soon afterwards; to them will Allah turn in mercy: for Allah is full of knowledge and wisdom.

18. Of no effect is the repentance of those who continue to do evil, until death faces one of them, and he says, "Now have I repented indeed;" nor of those who die rejecting Faith: for them have We prepared a chastisement most grievous.

19. O ye who believe! ye are forbidden to inherit women against their will. Nor should ye treat them with harshness, that ye may take away part of the dower ye have given them,—except where they have been guilty

of open lewdness; on the contrary live with them on a footing of kindness and equity. If ye take a dislike to them it may be that ye dislike a thing, and Allah brings about through it a great deal of good.

مَا اتَيْتُمُوهُنَّ اِلَّا اَنْ يَّاتِيْنَ بِفَاحِشَةٍ مُّبَيِّنَةٍ ۚ وَعَاشِرُوْهُنَّ بِالْمَعْرُوْفِ ۚ فَاِنْ كَرِهْتُمُوْهُنَّ فَعَسٰۤى اَنْ تَكْرَهُوْا شَيْـًٔا وَّيَجْعَلَ اللهُ فِيْهِ خَيْرًا كَثِيْرًا ۞

20. But if ye decide to take one wife in place of another, even if ye had given the latter a whole treasure for dower, take not the least bit of it back: would ye take it by slander and a manifest sin?

وَاِنْ اَرَدْتُّمُ اسْتِبْدَالَ زَوْجٍ مَّكَانَ زَوْجٍ ۙ وَّاٰتَيْتُمْ اِحْدٰىهُنَّ قِنْطَارًا فَلَا تَاْخُذُوْا مِنْهُ شَيْـًٔا ۚ اَتَاْخُذُوْنَهٗ بُهْتَانًا وَّاِثْمًا مُّبِيْنًا ۞

21. And how could ye take it when ye have gone in unto each other, and they have taken from you a solemn covenant?

وَكَيْفَ تَاْخُذُوْنَهٗ وَقَدْ اَفْضٰى بَعْضُكُمْ اِلٰى بَعْضٍ وَّاَخَذْنَ مِنْكُمْ مِّيْثَاقًا غَلِيْظًا

22. And marry not women whom your fathers married,—except what is past: it was shameful and odious,—an abominable custom indeed.

وَلَا تَنْكِحُوْا مَا نَكَحَ اٰبَاۤؤُكُمْ مِّنَ النِّسَاۤءِ اِلَّا مَا قَدْ سَلَفَ ۚ اِنَّهٗ كَانَ فَاحِشَةً وَّمَقْتًا ۗ وَسَاۤءَ سَبِيْلًا ۞

23. Prohibited to you (for marriage) are:— your mothers, daughters, sisters; father's sisters, mother's sisters; brother's daughters, sister's daughters; foster-mothers (who gave you suck), foster-sisters; your wives' mothers; your step-daughters under your guardian-ship, born of your wives to whom ye have gone in,—no prohibition if ye have not gone in,— (those who have been) wives of your sons proceeding from your loins; and two sisters in wedlock at one and the same time, except for what is past; for Allah is Oft-Forgiving. Most Merciful;—

حُرِّمَتْ عَلَيْكُمْ اُمَّهٰتُكُمْ وَبَنٰتُكُمْ وَاَخَوٰتُكُمْ وَعَمّٰتُكُمْ وَخٰلٰتُكُمْ وَبَنٰتُ الْاَخِ وَبَنٰتُ الْاُخْتِ وَاُمَّهٰتُكُمُ الّٰتِيْۤ اَرْضَعْنَكُمْ وَاَخَوٰتُكُمْ مِّنَ الرَّضَاعَةِ وَاُمَّهٰتُ نِسَاۤئِكُمْ وَرَبَاۤئِبُكُمُ الّٰتِيْ فِيْ حُجُوْرِكُمْ مِّنْ نِّسَاۤئِكُمُ الّٰتِيْ دَخَلْتُمْ بِهِنَّ ۖ فَاِنْ لَّمْ تَكُوْنُوْا دَخَلْتُمْ بِهِنَّ فَلَا جُنَاحَ عَلَيْكُمْ ۖ وَحَلَاۤئِلُ اَبْنَاۤئِكُمُ الَّذِيْنَ مِنْ اَصْلَابِكُمْ ۙ وَاَنْ تَجْمَعُوْا بَيْنَ الْاُخْتَيْنِ اِلَّا مَا قَدْ سَلَفَ ۗ اِنَّ اللهَ كَانَ غَفُوْرًا رَّحِيْمًا ۞

24. Also (prohibited are) women already married, except those whom your right hands possess: thus hath Allah ordained (prohibitions) against you: except for these, all others are lawful, provided ye seek (them in marriage) with gifts from your property,— desiring chastity, not fornication. Give them their dowery for the enjoyment you have of them as a duty; but if, after a dower is prescribed, ye agree mutually (to vary it), there is no blame on you, and Allah is All-Knowing All-Wise.

25. If any of you have not the means wherewith to wed free believing women, they may wed believing girls from among those whom your right hands possess: and Allah hath full knowledge about your Faith. Ye are one from another: wed them with the leave of their owners, and give them their dowers, according to what is reasonable: they should be chaste, not fornicators, nor taking adulterous: when they are taken in wedlock, if they commit indecency their punishment is half that for free women. This (permission) is for those among you who fear sin; but it is better for you that ye practise self-restraint. And Allah is Oft-Forgiving, Most Merciful.

26. Allah doth wish to make clear to you and to guide you into the ways of those before you; and (He doth wish to) turn to you (in Mercy): and Allah is All-Knowing, All-Wise.

27. Allah doth wish to turn to you, but the wish of those who follow their lusts is that ye should turn away (from Him),— far, far away.

28. Allah doth wish to lighten your (burdens): for man was created weak (in resolution).

29. O ye who believe ! eat not up your property among yourselves in vanities: but let there be amongst you traffic and trade by mutual good-will: nor kill (or destroy) yourselves: for verily Allah hath been to you Most Merciful !

30. If any do that in rancour and injustice,— soon shall We cast him into the Fire: and easy it is for Allah.

31. If ye (but) eschew the most heinous of the things which ye are forbidden to do, We shall remit your evil deeds, and admit you to a Gate of great honour.

32. And in no wise covet those things in which Allah hath bestowed His gifts more freely on some of you than on others: to men is allotted what they earn, and to women what they earn: but ask Allah of His bounty. For Allah hath full knowledge of all things.

33. To (benefit) everyone, We have appointed sharers and heirs to property left by parents and relatives. To those, also, to whom your right hand was pledged, give their due portion. For truly Allah is witness to all things.

34. Men are the protectors and maintainers of women, because Allah has given the one more (strength) than the other, and because they support them from their means. Therefore the righteous women are devoutly obedient, and guard in (the husband's) absence what Allah would have

them guard. As to those women on whose part ye fear disloyalty and ill-conduct, admonish them (first), (next), refuse to share their beds, (and last) beat them (lightly); but if they return to obedience, seek not against them means (of annoyance): for Allah is Most High, Great (above you all).

35. If ye fear a breach between them twain, appoint (two) arbiters, one from his family, and the other from hers; if they seek to set things aright, Allah will cause their reconciliation: for Allah hath full knowledge, and is acquainted with all things.

36. Serve Allah, and join not any partners with Him; and do good— to parents, kinsfolk, orphans, those in need, neighbours who are of kin neighbours who are strangers, the Companion by your side, the way-farer (ye meet), and what your right hands possess: for Allah loveth not the arrogant, the vainglorious;—

37. (Nor) those who are niggardly, enjoin niggardliness on others, hide the bounties which Allah hath bestowed on them; for We have prepared, for those who resist Faith, a Punishment that steeps them in contempt;—

38. Nor those who spend of their substance, to be seen of men, and have no faith in Allah and the Last Day: if any take the Satan for their intimate, what a dreadful intimate he is !

39. And what burden were it on them if they had faith in Allah and in the Last Day, and they spent out of what Allah hath given

them for sustenance ? For Allah hath full knowledge of them.

40. Allah is never unjust in the least degree: if there is any good (done), He doubleth it, and giveth from His Own self a great reward.

41. How then if We brought from each People a witness, and We brought thee as a witness against these People !

42. On that day those who reject Faith and disobey the Messenger will wish that the earth were made one with them: but never will they hide a single fact from Allah!

43. O ye who believe ! approach not prayers in a state of intoxication, until ye can understand all that ye say,— nor in a state of ceremonial impurity except when you are passing by (through the mosque). Until after washing your whole body. If ye are ill, or on a journey, or one of you cometh from the privy, or ye have been in contact with women, and ye find no water. then take for yourselves clean sand (or earth), and rub therewith your faces and hands. For Allah doth blot out sins and forgive again and again.

44. Hast thou not turned thy thought to those who were given a portion of the Book? They traffic in error, and wish that ye should lose the right path.

45. But Allah hath full knowledge of your enemies: Allah is enough for a Protector, and Allah is enough for a Helper.

46. Of the Jews there are those who displace words from their (right) places, and say: "We near and we disobey": and "Here, may you not hear:" and *"Rā'ina"* with a twist of their tongues and a slander to Faith. If only they had said: "We hear

and we obey"; and "Do hear"; and "Do look at us": it would have been better for them, and more proper; but Allah hath cursed them for their Unbelief; and but few of them will believe.

47. O ye People of the Book ! believe in what We have (now) revealed, confirming what was (already) with you, before We change the face and fame of some (of you) beyond all recognition, and turn them hindwards, or curse them as We cursed the Sabbath-breakers, for the decision of Allah must be carried out.

48. Allah forgiveth not that partners should be set up with Him; but He forgiveth anything else, to whom he pleaseth: to set up partners with Allah is to devise a sin most heinous indeed.

49. Hast thou not turned thy thought to those who claim purity for themselves? Nay—but Allah doth purify whom He pleaseth. And they will not be wronged a whit.

50. Behold ! how they invent a lie against Allah! But that by itself is a manifest sin !

51. Hast thou not turned thy thought to those who were given a portion of the Book? They believe in Sorcery and Tagut and say to the Unbelievers that they are better guided in the (right) way than the Believers!

52. They are (men) whom Allah hath cursed: and those whom Allah hath cursed, thou wilt find, have no one to help.

53. Have they a share in dominion or power ? Behold, they give not a farthing to their fellow-men ?

54. Or do they envy mankind for what Allah hath given them of His bounty ? But We had already given the people of Abraham

the Book and Wisdom, and conferred upon them a great kingdom.

55. Some of them believed, and some of them averted their faces from him: and enough is Hell for a burning fire.

56. Those who reject our Signs, We shall soon cast into the Fire: as often as their skins are roasted through, We shall change them for fresh skins, that they may taste the Chastisement: for Allah is Exalted in Power, Wise.

57. But those who believe and do deeds of righteousness, We shall soon admit to Gardens, with rivers flowing beneath,— their eternal home: therein shall they have spouses purified We shall admit them to shades, cool and ever deepening.

58. Allah doth command you to render back your Trusts to those to whom they are due; and when ye judge between people that ye judge with justice: verily how excellent is the teaching which He giveth you ! For Allah is He Who heareth and seeth all things.

59. O ye who believe ! obey Allah, and obey the Messenger, and those charged with authority among you. If ye differ in anything among yourselves, refer it to Allah and His Messenger, if ye do believe in Allah and the Last Day: that is best, and most suitable for final determination.

60. Hast thou not turned thy thought to those who declare that they believe in the revelations that have come to thee and to those before thee? Their (real) wish is to resort together for judgment (in their disputes) to the Evil (Tagut) though they were ordered to reject him. But Satan's

wish is to lead them astray far away (from the Right).

61. When it is said to them: "Come to what Allah hath revealed, and to the Messenger": thou seest the Hypocrites avert their faces from thee in disgust.

62. How then, when they are seized by misfortune, because of the deeds which their hands have sent forth? Then they come to thee, swearing by Allah: "We meant no more than good-will and conciliation!"

63. Those men,—Allah knows what is in their heart; so keep clear of them but admonish them, and speak to them a word to reach their very souls.

64. We sent not a Messenger, but to be obeyed, in accordance with the leave of Allah. If they had only, when they were unjust to themselves, come unto thee and asked Allah's forgiveness. And the Messenger had asked forgiveness for them, they would have found Allah indeed Oft-Returning, Most Merciful.

65. But no, by thy Lord, they can have no (real) Faith, until they make thee judge in all disputes between them, and find in their souls no resistance against thy decisions, but accept them with the fullest conviction.

66. If We had ordered them to sacrifice their lives or to leave their homes, very few of them would have done it: but if they had done what they were (actually) told, it would have been best for them, and would have gone farthest to strengthen their (faith);

67. And We should then have given them from Ourselves a great reward;

68. And We should have shown them the Straight Way.

69. All who obey Allah and the Messenger are in the Company of those on whom is the Grace of Allah,—of the Prophets (who teach), the Sincere (lovers of Truth), the martyres, and the Righteous (who do good): Ah ! How beautiful is their Company.

70. Such is the Bounty from Allah: and sufficient is it that Allah knoweth all.

71. O ye who believe ! take your precautions, and either go forth in parties or go forth all together.

72. There are certainly among you men who would tarry behind: if a misfortune befalls you, they say: "Allah did favour us in that we were not present among them."

73. But if good fortune comes to you from Allah, they would be sure to say—as if there had never been ties of affection between you and them—"Oh! I wish I had been with them: a fine thing should I then have made of it !"

74. Let those fight In the cause of Allah who sell the life of this world for the Hereafter. To him who fighteth in the cause of Allah,— whether he is slain or gets victory— soon shall We give him a reward of great (value).

75. And why should ye not fight in the cause of Allah and of those who, being weak, are ill-treated (and oppressed)?— men, women, and children, whose cry is: "Our Lord ! rescue us from this town, whose people are oppressors; and raise for us from Thee one who will protect; and raise for us from Thee one who will help !"

76. Those who believe fight in the cause of Allah, and those who reject Faith fight in the cause of Evil (Tagut): so fight ye against the friends, of Satan: feeble indeed is the cunning of Satan.

77. Hast thou not turned thy thought to

those who were told to hold back their Hands (from fight) but establish regular prayers and spend in regular Zakat ? When (at length) the order for fighting was issued to them, behold ! a section of them feared men as—or even more than—they should have feared Allah: they said: "Our Lord! why hast Thou ordered us to fight? Wouldst Thou not grant us respite to our (natural) term, near (enough)? Say: "Short is the enjoyment of this world: the Hereafter is the best for those who do right: never will ye be dealt with unjustly in the very least!

78. "Wherever ye are, death will find you out, even if ye are in towers built up strong and high!"

If some good befalls them they say, "This is from Allah"; but if evil, they say, "This is from thee" (O Prophet). Say: "All things are from Allah." But what hath come to these people, that they fail to understand a single fact?

79. Whatever good, (O man !) happens to thee, is from Allah; but whatever evil happens to thee, is from thyself and We have sent thee as a Messenger to (instruct) mankind. And enough is Allah for a witness.

80. He who obeys the Messenger, obeys Allah: but if any turn away, We have not sent thee to watch over them.

81. They have "Obedience" on their lips; but when they leave thee, a section of them meditate all night on things very different from what thou tellest them. But Allah records their nightly (plots): so keep clear of them, and put thy trust in Allah, and enough is Allah as a disposer of affairs.

82. Do they not ponder on the Qur'an? Had it been from other than Allah, they would surely have found therein much discrepancy.

83. When there comes to them some matter touching (public) safety or fear, they divulge it. If they had only referred it to the Messenger or to those charged with authority among them, the proper investigators would have known it from them (direct). Were it not for the Grace and Mercy of Allah unto you, all but a few of you would have followed Satan.

84. Then fight in Allah's cause— thou art held responsible only for thyself—and rouse the Believers. It may be that Allah will restrain the fury of the Unbelievers; for Allah is the strongest in might and in punishment.

85. Whoever intercedes in a good cause becomes a partner therein: and whoever recommends and helps an evil cause, shares in its burden: and Allah hath power over all things.

86. When a (courteous) greeting is offered you, meet it with a greeting still more courteous, or (at least) of equal courtesy. Allah takes careful account of all things.

87. Allah ! There is no god but He: of a surety he will gather you together on the Day of Judgment, about which there is no doubt. And whose word can be truer than Allah's?

88. Why should ye be divided into two parties about the Hypocrites ? Allah hath cast them off for their (evil) deeds. Would ye guide those whom Allah hath thrown out of the Way ? For those whom Allah hath thrown out of the Way, never shalt thou find the Way.

89. They but wish that ye should reject Faith, as they do, and thus be on the same footing (as they): so take not friends from

their ranks until they flee in the way of Allah (from what is forbidden). But if they turn renegades, seize them and slay them wherever ye find them; and (in any case) take no friends or helpers from their ranks:—

90.   Except those who join a group between whom and you there is a treaty (of peace), or those who approach you with hearts restraining them from fighting you or fighting their own People. If Allah had pleased, He could have given them power over you, and they would have fought you: therefore if they withdraw from you but fight you not, and (instead) send you (guarantees of) peace, then Allah hath opened no way for you (to war against them).

91.   Others you will find that wish to be secure from you as well as that of their people: every time they are sent back to temptation, they succumb thereto: if they withdraw not from you nor give you (guarantees of peace besides restraining their hands, seize them and slay them wherever ye get them: in their case We have provided you with a clear argument against them.

92.   Never should a Believer kill a Believer; except by mistake, and whoever kills a Believer by mistake it is ordained that he should free a believing slave. And pay blood-money to the deceased's family, unless they remit it freely. If the deceased belonged to a people at war with you, and he was a Believer, the freeing of a believing slave (is enough). If he belonged to a people with whom ye have a treaty of mutual alliance, blood-money should be paid to his family, and a believing slave be freed. For those who find this beyond their means, (is prescribed) a fast for two months running: by way of repentance to Allah: for Allah

hath all knowledge and all wisdom.

93. If a man kills a Believer intentionally, his recompense is Hell, to abide therein (for ever): and the wrath and the curse of Allah are upon him, and a dreadful chastisement is prepared for him.

94. O ye who believe ! when ye go out in the cause of Allah, investigate carefully, and say not to anyone who offers you a salutation: "Thou art none of a Believer !" Coveting the perishable goods of this life: with Allah are profits and spoils abundant. Even thus were ye yourselves before, till Allah conferred on you His favours: therefore carefully investigate. For Allah is well aware of all that ye do.

95. Not equal are those Believers who sit (at home), except those who are disabled. And those who strive and fight in the cause of Allah with their goods and their persons. Allah hath granted a grade higher to those who strive and fight with their goods and persons than to those who sit (at home). Unto all (in Faith) hath Allah promised good: but those who strive and fight hath He distinguished above those who sit (at home) by a great reward.,—

96. Ranks specially bestowed by Him and Forgiveness and Mercy. For Allah is Oft-Forgiving, Most Merciful.

97. When angels take the souls of those who die in sin against their souls, they say: "In what (plight) were ye ?" They reply: "Weak and oppressed were we in the earth". They say: "Was not the earth of Allah spacious enough for you to move yourselves away (from evil)?" Such men will find their abode in Hell.—What an evil

Refuge!—

مَّصِيرًا ۞

98. Except those who are (really) weak and oppressed—men, women, and children who have no means in their power, nor can they find a way (to escape)

اِلَّا الْمُسْتَضْعَفِيْنَ مِنَ الرِّجَالِ وَالنِّسَآءِ وَالْوِلْدَانِ لَا يَسْتَطِيْعُوْنَ حِيْلَةً وَّلَا يَهْتَدُوْنَ سَبِيْلًا ۞

99. For these, there is hope that Allah will forgive: for Allah doth blot out (sins) and forgive again and again.

فَاُولٰٓئِكَ عَسَى اللّٰهُ اَنْ يَّعْفُوَ عَنْهُمْ وَكَانَ اللّٰهُ عَفُوًّا غَفُوْرًا ۞

100. He who forsakes his home in the cause of Allah, finds in the earth many a refuge. And abundance should he die as a refugee from home for Allah and His Messenger, His reward becomes due and sure with Allah: and Allah is Oft-Forgiving Most Merciful.

وَمَنْ يُّهَاجِرْ فِيْ سَبِيْلِ اللّٰهِ يَجِدْ فِي الْاَرْضِ مُرَاغَمًا كَثِيْرًا وَّسَعَةً وَمَنْ يَّخْرُجْ مِنْ بَيْتِهٖ مُهَاجِرًا اِلَى اللّٰهِ وَرَسُوْلِهٖ ثُمَّ يُدْرِكْهُ الْمَوْتُ فَقَدْ وَقَعَ اَجْرُهٗ عَلَى اللّٰهِ وَكَانَ اللّٰهُ غَفُوْرًا رَّحِيْمًا ۞

101. When ye travel through the earth, there is no blame on you if ye shorten your prayers, for fear the Unbelievers may attack you: for the Unbelievers are unto you open enemies.

وَاِذَا ضَرَبْتُمْ فِي الْاَرْضِ فَلَيْسَ عَلَيْكُمْ جُنَاحٌ اَنْ تَقْصُرُوْا مِنَ الصَّلٰوةِ اِنْ خِفْتُمْ اَنْ يَّفْتِنَكُمُ الَّذِيْنَ كَفَرُوْا اِنَّ الْكٰفِرِيْنَ كَانُوْا لَكُمْ عَدُوًّا مُّبِيْنًا

102. When thou (O Messenger) art with them, and standest to lead them in prayer, let one party of them stand up (in prayer) with thee. Taking their arms with them: when they finish their prostrations, let them take their position in the rear, and let the other party come up which hath not yet prayed—and let them pray with thee, taking all precautions, and bearing arms: the Unbelievers wish, if ye were negligent of your arms and your baggage, to assault you in a single rush. But there is no blame on you if ye put away your arms because of the inconvenience of rain or because ye are ill; but take (every) precaution for yourselves. For the Unbelievers Allah hath prepared a humiliating punishment.

وَاِذَا كُنْتَ فِيْهِمْ فَاَقَمْتَ لَهُمُ الصَّلٰوةَ فَلْتَقُمْ طَآئِفَةٌ مِّنْهُمْ مَّعَكَ وَلْيَأْخُذُوْا اَسْلِحَتَهُمْ فَاِذَا سَجَدُوْا فَلْيَكُوْنُوْا مِنْ وَّرَآئِكُمْ وَلْتَأْتِ طَآئِفَةٌ اُخْرٰى لَمْ يُصَلُّوْا فَلْيُصَلُّوْا مَعَكَ وَلْيَأْخُذُوْا حِذْرَهُمْ وَاَسْلِحَتَهُمْ وَدَّ الَّذِيْنَ كَفَرُوْا لَوْ تَغْفُلُوْنَ عَنْ اَسْلِحَتِكُمْ وَاَمْتِعَتِكُمْ فَيَمِيْلُوْنَ عَلَيْكُمْ مَّيْلَةً وَّاحِدَةً وَلَا جُنَاحَ عَلَيْكُمْ اِنْ كَانَ بِكُمْ اَذًى مِّنْ مَّطَرٍ اَوْ كُنْتُمْ مَّرْضٰٓى اَنْ تَضَعُوْا اَسْلِحَتَكُمْ وَخُذُوْا حِذْرَكُمْ اِنَّ اللّٰهَ اَعَدَّ لِلْكٰفِرِيْنَ عَذَابًا مُّهِيْنًا

103. When ye have performed the prayers, remember Allah, standing, sitting down, or lying down on your sides; but when ye are free from danger, set up regular Prayers: for such prayers are enjoined on Believers at stated times.

104. And slacken not in following up the enemy: if ye are suffering hardships, they are suffering similar hardships: but you hope from Allah, what they have not. And Allah is full of knowledge and wisdom.

105. We have sent down to thee the Book in truth, that thou mightest judge between people by that which Allah has shown thee; so be not an advocate for those who betray their trust;

106. But seek the forgiveness of Allah; for Allah is Oft-Forgiving, Most Merciful.

107. Contend not on behalf of such as betray their own souls; for Allah loveth not one given to perfidy and sin:—

108. They seek to hide themselves from the people but they cannot hide from Allah, while he is with them when they plot by night. In words that He cannot approve: and Allah doth ompass round all that they do.

109. Ah ! these are the sort of men on whose behalf ye may contend in this world; but who will contend with Allah on their behalf on the Day of Judgment, or who will carry their affairs through?

110. If anyone does evil or wrongs his own soul but afterwards seeks Allah's Forgiveness, he will find Allah Oft-Forgiving, Most Merciful.

111. And if anyone earns sin, he earns it against his own soul: for Allah is full of knowledge and wisdom.

112. But if anyone earns a fault or a sin and throws it on to one that is innocent. He carries (on himself) (both) a false charge and a flagrant sin.

113. But for the Grace of Allah to thee and His Mercy. a party of them would certainly have plotted to lead thee astray. But (in fact) they will only lead their own souls astray, and to thee they can do no harm in the least. For Allah hath sent down to thee the Book and Wisdom and taught thee what thou knewest not (before): and great is the Grace of Allah unto thee.

114. In most of their secret talks there is no good: but if one exhorts to a deed of charity or goodness or conciliation between people (secrecy is permis-sible): to him who does this, seeking the good pleasure of Allah, We shall soon give a reward of the highest (value).

115. If anyone contends with the Messenger even after guidance has been plainly conveyed to him, and follows a path other than that becoming to men to Faith, We shall leave him in the path he has chosen. and land him in Hell, what an evil refuge !

116. Allah forgiveth not (the sin of) joining other gods with Him; but He forgiveth whom He pleaseth other sins than this: one who joins other gods with Allah, hath strayed far. far away (from the Right).

117. (The Pagans), leaving Him. call but upon female deities: they call but upon Satan the persistent rebel !

118. Allah did curse him, but he said: "I will take of Thy servants a portion marked off:

119. "I will mislead them, and I will create in them false desires; I will order them to slit the ears of cattle, and to deface the (fair) nature created by Allah," Whoever. forsaking Allah, takes Satan for a friend, hath of a surety suffered a loss that is

النساء،   والمحصنته

خِيَرَ خُسْرَانًا مُّبِينًا ۝

manifest.

120. Satan makes them promises, and creates in them false hopes, but Satan's promises are nothing but deception.

يَعِدُهُمْ وَيُمَنِّيهِمْ ۖ وَمَا يَعِدُهُمُ الشَّيْطَنُ اِلَّا غُرُورًا ۝

121. They (his dupes) will have their dwelling in Hell, and from it they will find no way of escape.

اُولَٓئِكَ مَأْوَىٰهُمْ جَهَنَّمُ وَلَا يَجِدُونَ عَنْهَا مَحِيصًا ۝

122. But those who believe and do deeds of righteousness,—We shall soon admit them to Gardens, with rivers flowing beneath,—to dwell therein for ever. Allah's promise is the truth, and whose word can be truer than Allah's ?

وَالَّذِينَ اٰمَنُوا وَعَمِلُوا الصّٰلِحٰتِ سَنُدْخِلُهُمْ جَنّٰتٍ تَجْرِى مِنْ تَحْتِهَا الْاَنْهٰرُ خٰلِدِينَ فِيهَآ اَبَدًا ۖ وَعْدَ اللّٰهِ حَقًّا ۚ وَمَنْ اَصْدَقُ مِنَ اللّٰهِ قِيلًا ۝

123. Not your desires, nor those of the People of the Book (can prevail): whoever works evil, will be requited accordingly. Nor will he find, besides Allah, any protector or helper.

لَيْسَ بِاَمَانِيِّكُمْ وَلَا اَمَانِيِّ اَهْلِ الْكِتٰبِ ۗ مَنْ يَّعْمَلْ سُوٓءًا يُّجْزَ بِهٖ وَلَا يَجِدْ لَهٗ مِنْ دُونِ اللّٰهِ وَلِيًّا وَّلَا نَصِيرًا ۝

124. If any do deeds of righteousness,—be they male or female—and have faith, they will enter Heaven, and not the least injustice will be done to them.

وَمَنْ يَّعْمَلْ مِنَ الصّٰلِحٰتِ مِنْ ذَكَرٍ اَوْ اُنْثٰى وَهُوَ مُؤْمِنٌ فَاُولَٓئِكَ يَدْخُلُونَ الْجَنَّةَ وَلَا يُظْلَمُونَ نَقِيرًا ۝

125. Who can be better in religion than one who submits his whole self to Allah, does good, and follows the way of Abraham the true in faith? For Allah did take Abraham for a friend.

وَمَنْ اَحْسَنُ دِينًا مِّمَّنْ اَسْلَمَ وَجْهَهٗ لِلّٰهِ وَهُوَ مُحْسِنٌ وَّاتَّبَعَ مِلَّةَ اِبْرٰهِيمَ حَنِيفًا ۗ وَاتَّخَذَ اللّٰهُ اِبْرٰهِيمَ خَلِيلًا ۝

126. But to Allah belong all things in the heavens and on earth: and He it is that encompasseth all things.

وَلِلّٰهِ مَا فِى السَّمٰوٰتِ وَمَا فِى الْاَرْضِ ۚ وَكَانَ اللّٰهُ بِكُلِّ شَيْءٍ مُّحِيطًا ۝

127. They ask thy instruction concerning the Women. Say: Allah doth instruct you about them: and (remember) what hath been rehearsed unto you in the Book, concerning the orphaned women to whom ye give not the portions prescribed, and yet whom ye desire to marry, as also

وَيَسْتَفْتُونَكَ فِى النِّسَاءِ ۖ قُلِ اللّٰهُ يُفْتِيكُمْ فِيهِنَّ ۙ وَمَا يُتْلٰى عَلَيْكُمْ فِى الْكِتٰبِ فِى يَتٰمَى النِّسَاءِ الّٰتِى لَا تُؤْتُونَهُنَّ مَا كُتِبَ لَهُنَّ وَتَرْغَبُونَ اَنْ تَنْكِحُوهُنَّ وَالْمُسْتَضْعَفِينَ

concerning the children who are weak and oppressed: that ye stand firm for justice to orphans. There is not a good deed which ye do, but Allah is well-acquainted therewith.

128. If a wife fears cruelty or desertion on her husband's part, there is no blame on them if they arrange an amicable settlement between themselves; and such settlement is best; even though men's souls are swayed by greed. But if ye do good and practise self-restraint, Allah is well-acquainted with all that ye do.

129. Ye are never able to do justice between wives even if it is your ardent desire: but turn not away (from a woman) altogether, so as to leave her (as it were) hanging (in the air). If ye come to a friendly understanding, and practise self-restraint, Allah is Oft-Forgiving, Most Merciful.

130. But if they separate Allah will provide abundance for each of them from His all-reaching bounty: for Allah is He that careth for all and is Wise.

131. To Allah belong all things in the heavens and on earth. Verily We have directed the People of the Book before you, and you (O Muslims) to fear Allah. But if ye deny Him, lo! unto Allah belong all things in the heavens and on earth, and Allah is free of all wants, worthy of all praise.

132. Yea, unto Allah belong all things in the heavens and on earth, and enough is Allah to carry through all affairs.

133. If it were His Will, He could destroy you, O mankind, and create another race; for He hath power this to do.

134. If any one desires a reward in this life.

in Allah's (gift) is the reward (both) of this life and of the Hereafter: for Allah is He that heareth and seeth (all things).

135. O ye who believe ! stand out firmly for justice, as witnesses to Allah, even as against yourselves, or your parents, or your kin, and whether it be (against) rich or poor: for Allah can best protect both. Follow not the lusts (of your hearts), lest ye swerve, and if ye distort (justice) or decline to do justice, verily Allah is well-acquainted with all that ye do.

136. O ye who believe ! believe in Allah and His Messenger, and the scripture which He hath sent to His Messenger and the scripture which He sent to those before (him). Any who denieth Allah, His angels, His Books, His Messengers, and the Day of Judgment, hath gone far, far astray.

137. Those who believe, then reject Faith, then believe (again) and (again) reject Faith, and go on increasing in Unbelief,—Allah will not forgive them, nor guide them on the Way.

138. To the Hypocrites give the good tidings that there is for them a grievous Chastisement;—

139. Those who take for friends Unbelievers rather than Believers: is it honour they seek among them? Nay,— all honour is with Allah.

140. Already has He sent you in the Book, that when ye hear the Message of Allah held in defiance and ridicule, ye are not to sit with them unless they turn to a different theme: if ye did, ye would be like them. For Allah will collect the Hypocrites and those

فَعِنْدَ اللّٰهِ ثَوَابُ الدُّنْيَا وَالْاٰخِرَةِ ۗ وَكَانَ اللّٰهُ سَمِيْعًۢا بَصِيْرًا ۝

يٰۤاَيُّهَا الَّذِيْنَ اٰمَنُوْا كُوْنُوْا قَوّٰمِيْنَ بِالْقِسْطِ شُهَدَآءَ لِلّٰهِ وَلَوْ عَلٰۤى اَنْفُسِكُمْ اَوِ الْوَالِدَيْنِ وَالْاَقْرَبِيْنَ ۚ اِنْ يَّكُنْ غَنِيًّا اَوْ فَقِيْرًا فَاللّٰهُ اَوْلٰى بِهِمَا ۫ فَلَا تَتَّبِعُوا الْهَوٰۤى اَنْ تَعْدِلُوْا ۚ وَاِنْ تَلْوٗۤا اَوْ تُعْرِضُوْا فَاِنَّ اللّٰهَ كَانَ بِمَا تَعْمَلُوْنَ خَبِيْرًا ۝ يٰۤاَيُّهَا الَّذِيْنَ اٰمَنُوْۤا اٰمِنُوْا بِاللّٰهِ وَرَسُوْلِهٖ وَالْكِتٰبِ الَّذِيْ نَزَّلَ عَلٰى رَسُوْلِهٖ وَالْكِتٰبِ الَّذِيْۤ اَنْزَلَ مِنْ قَبْلُ ۗ وَمَنْ يَّكْفُرْ بِاللّٰهِ وَمَلٰٓئِكَتِهٖ وَكُتُبِهٖ وَرُسُلِهٖ وَالْيَوْمِ الْاٰخِرِ فَقَدْ ضَلَّ ضَلٰلًۢا بَعِيْدًا ۝

اِنَّ الَّذِيْنَ اٰمَنُوْا ثُمَّ كَفَرُوْا ثُمَّ اٰمَنُوْا ثُمَّ كَفَرُوْا ثُمَّ ازْدَادُوْا كُفْرًا لَّمْ يَكُنِ اللّٰهُ لِيَغْفِرَ لَهُمْ وَلَا لِيَهْدِيَهُمْ سَبِيْلًا ۝ بَشِّرِ الْمُنٰفِقِيْنَ بِاَنَّ لَهُمْ عَذَابًا اَلِيْمًا ۝

الَّذِيْنَ يَتَّخِذُوْنَ الْكٰفِرِيْنَ اَوْلِيَآءَ مِنْ دُوْنِ الْمُؤْمِنِيْنَ ۚ اَيَبْتَغُوْنَ عِنْدَهُمُ الْعِزَّةَ فَاِنَّ الْعِزَّةَ لِلّٰهِ جَمِيْعًا ۝ وَقَدْ نَزَّلَ عَلَيْكُمْ فِى الْكِتٰبِ اَنْ اِذَا سَمِعْتُمْ اٰيٰتِ اللّٰهِ يُكْفَرُ بِهَا وَيُسْتَهْزَاُ بِهَا فَلَا تَقْعُدُوْا مَعَهُمْ حَتّٰى يَخُوْضُوْا فِيْ حَدِيْثٍ غَيْرِهٖۤ ۖ اِنَّكُمْ اِذًا مِّثْلُهُمْ ۗ اِنَّ اللّٰهَ جَامِعُ

المُنۡفِقِیۡنَ وَالۡکٰفِرِیۡنَ فِیۡ جَهَنَّمَ جَمِیۡعًا ۟

who defy Faith—all in Hell;—

141. (These are) the ones who wait and watch about you: if ye do gain a victory from Allah, they say: "Were we not with you?"— but if the Unbelievers gain a success, they say (to them): "Did we not gain an advantage over you, and did we not guard you from the Believers?" But Allah will judge Betwixt you on the Day of Judgment. And never will Allah grant to the Unbelievers a way (to triumph) over the Believers.

142. The Hypocrites— they seek to deceive Allah but it is Allah Who deceive them. When they stand up to prayer, they stand without earnestness, to be seen of men, but little do they hold Allah in remembrance;

143. (They are) wavering between this and that belonging neither to these nor those whom Allah leaves straying,— never wilt thou find for him the Way.

144. O ye who believe ! take not for friends Unbelievers rather than Believers: do ye wish to offer Allah an open proof against yourselves?

145. The Hypocrites will be in the lowest depths of the Fire: no helper wilt thou find for them;—

146. Except for those who repent, mend (their life), hold fast to Allah, and make their religious devotion sincere to Allah: if so they will be (numbered) with the Believers. And soon will Allah grant to the Believers a reward of immense value.

147. What can Allah gain by your punishment, if ye are grateful and ye believe? Nay, it is Allah That recogniseth (all good), and knoweth all things.

148. Allah loveth not the shouting of evil words in public speech, except by one who has been wronged, for Allah is He Who heareth and knoweth all things.

149. Whether you do openly a good deed or conceal it or cover evil with pardon, surely Allah is ever pardoning Powerful.

150. Those who deny Allah and His Messengers, and wish to separate between Allah and His Messengers, saying: "We believe in some but reject others": and wish to take a course midway,—

151. They are in truth Unbelievers; and We have prepared for Unbelievers a humiliating punishement.

152. To those who believe in Allah and His messengers and make no distinction between any of the messengers, We shall soon give their (due) rewards: for Allah is Oft-Forgiving, Most Merciful.

153. The People of the Book ask thee to cause a book to descend to them from heaven: indeed they asked Moses for an even greater (miracle), for they said: "Show us Allah in public," but they were seized for their presumption, by thunder and lightning. Yet they worshipped the calf even after clear Signs had come to them; even so We forgave them; and gave Moses manifest proofs of authority.

154. And for their Covenant We raised over them the Mount (Sinai); and (on another occasion) We said: "Enter the gate with humility"; and (once again) We commanded them: "Transgress not in the matter of the Sabbath." And We took from them a solemn Covenant.

155. (They have incurred divine displeasure): in that they broke their Covenant; that they rejected the Signs of Allah; that they slew the Messengers in defiance of right; that they said, "Our hearts are the Wrappings";—nay, Allah hath set the seal on their hearts for their blasphemy, and little is it they believe;—

فَبِمَا نَقْضِهِم مِّيثَاقَهُمْ وَكُفْرِهِم بِآيَاتِ اللَّهِ وَقَتْلِهِمُ الْأَنْبِيَاءَ بِغَيْرِ حَقٍّ وَّقَوْلِهِمْ قُلُوبُنَا غُلْفٌ ۚ بَلْ طَبَعَ اللَّهُ عَلَيْهَا بِكُفْرِهِمْ فَلَا يُؤْمِنُونَ إِلَّا قَلِيلًا ۞

156. That they rejected Faith; that they uttered against Mary a grave false charge;

وَّبِكُفْرِهِمْ وَقَوْلِهِمْ عَلَىٰ مَرْيَمَ بُهْتَانًا عَظِيمًا ۞

157. That they said (in boast), "We killed Christ Jesus the son of Mary, the Messenger of Allah";— but they killed him not, nor crucified him. Only a likeness of that was shown to them. And those who differ therein are full of doubts, with no (certain) knowledge. But only conjecture to follow, for of a surety they killed him not:—

وَّقَوْلِهِمْ إِنَّا قَتَلْنَا الْمَسِيحَ عِيسَى ابْنَ مَرْيَمَ رَسُولَ اللَّهِ ۚ وَمَا قَتَلُوهُ وَمَا صَلَبُوهُ وَلَٰكِن شُبِّهَ لَهُمْ ۚ وَإِنَّ الَّذِينَ اخْتَلَفُوا فِيهِ لَفِي شَكٍّ مِّنْهُ ۚ مَا لَهُم بِهِ مِنْ عِلْمٍ إِلَّا اتِّبَاعَ الظَّنِّ ۚ وَمَا قَتَلُوهُ يَقِينًا ۞

158. Nay, Allah raised him up unto Himself; and Allah is Exalted in Power, Wise;—

بَل رَّفَعَهُ اللَّهُ إِلَيْهِ ۚ وَكَانَ اللَّهُ عَزِيزًا حَكِيمًا ۞

159. And there is none of the People of the Book but must believe in him before his death; and on the Day of Judgment He will be a witness against them;—

وَإِن مِّنْ أَهْلِ الْكِتَابِ إِلَّا لَيُؤْمِنَنَّ بِهِ قَبْلَ مَوْتِهِ ۖ وَيَوْمَ الْقِيَامَةِ يَكُونُ عَلَيْهِمْ شَهِيدًا ۞

160. For the iniquity of the Jews We made unlawful for them certain (foods) good and wholesome which had been lawful for them;—and that they hindered many from Allah's Way;—

فَبِظُلْمٍ مِّنَ الَّذِينَ هَادُوا حَرَّمْنَا عَلَيْهِمْ طَيِّبَاتٍ أُحِلَّتْ لَهُمْ وَبِصَدِّهِمْ عَن سَبِيلِ اللَّهِ كَثِيرًا ۞

161. That they took usury, though they were forbidden; and that they devoured men's wealth wrong-fully;— We have prepared for those among them who reject Faith a grievous chastisement.

وَّأَخْذِهِمُ الرِّبَا وَقَدْ نُهُوا عَنْهُ وَأَكْلِهِمْ أَمْوَالَ النَّاسِ بِالْبَاطِلِ ۚ وَأَعْتَدْنَا لِلْكَافِرِينَ مِنْهُمْ عَذَابًا أَلِيمًا ۞

162. But those among them who are well-grounded in knowledge, and the Believers, believe in what hath been revealed to thee and what was revealed before thee: and

لَٰكِنِ الرَّاسِخُونَ فِي الْعِلْمِ مِنْهُمْ وَالْمُؤْمِنُونَ يُؤْمِنُونَ بِمَا أُنزِلَ إِلَيْكَ وَمَا أُنزِلَ مِن قَبْلِكَ ۚ

(especially) those who establish regular prayer and pay Zakat and believe in Allah and in the Last Day: to them shall We soon give a great reward.

163. We have sent thee inspiration, as We sent it to Noah and the Messengers after him: We sent inspiration to Abraham. Ismā'îl, Isaac, Jacob and the Tribes, to Jesus, Job, Jonah, Aaron, and Solomon, and to David We gave the Psalms.

164. Of some messengers We have already told thee the story; of others We have not;— and to Moses Allah spoke direct;—

165. Messengers who gave good news as well as warning, that mankind, after (the coming) of the messengers, should have no plea against Allah: for Allah is Exalted in Power, Wise.

166. But Allah beareth witness that what He hath sent unto thee He hath sent with His (own) knowledge, and the angels bear witness: but enough is Allah for a witness.

167. Those who reject Faith and keep off (men) from the Way of Allah, have verily strayed far, far away from the Path.

168. Those who reject Faith and do wrong,— Allah will not forgive them, nor guide them to any way—

169. Except the way of Hell, to dwell therein for ever. And this to Allah is easy.

170. O mankind! the Messenger hath come to you in truth from Allah: believe in him: it is best for you. But if ye reject Faith, to Allah belong all things in the heavens and on

earth: and Allah is All-Knowing, All-Wise.

171 O People of the Book ! commit no excesses in your religion: nor say of Allah aught but the truth. Christ Jesus the son of Mary was (no more than) a Messenger of Allah, and His Word, which He bestowed on Mary, and a Spirit proceeding from Him: so believe in Allah and His Messengers. Say not "Three": desist: it will be better for you: for Allah is One God: glory be to Him: (far Exalted is He) above having a son. To Him belong all things in the heavens and on earth. And enough is Allah as a Disposer of affairs.

172. Christ disdaineth not to serve and worship Allah, nor do the angels, those nearest (to Allah): those who disdain His worship and are arrogant, He will gather them all together unto Himself to (answer).

173. But to those who believe and do deeds of righteousness, He will give their (due) rewards,—and more, out of His bounty: but those who are disdainful and arrogant, He will punish with a grievous chastisement: nor will they find, besides Allah, any to protect or help them.

174. O mankind ! Verily there hath come to you a convincing proof from your Lord for We have sent unto you a light (that is) manifest.

175. Then those who believe in Allah, and hold fast to Him,—soon will He admit them to Mercy and Grace from Himself, and guide them to Himself by a straight Way.

176. They ask thee for a legal decision. say: Allah directs (thus) about those

SÛRA–5
AL-MĀÎDAH
(INTRODUCTION)

This Sûra deals, by way of recapitulation, with the backsliding of the Jews and Christians from their pure religions, to which the coping stone was placed by Islam. It refers particularly to the Christians, and to their solemn Sacrament of the Last Supper, to whose mystic meaning they are declared to have been false.

As a logical corollary to the corruption of the earlier religions of Allah, the practical precepts of Islam, about food, cleanliness, justice, and fidelity are recapitulated.

The third verse contains the memorable declaration : "This day have I perfected your religion for you"; which was promulgated in 10 H., during the Apostle's last Pilgrimage to Makkah. Chronologically it was the last verse to be revealed.

who leave no descendants or ascendants as heirs. If it is a man, that dies, leaving a sister but no child, she shall have half the inheritance: if (such a deceased was) a woman, who left no child, her brother takes her inheritance: if there are two sisters, they shall have two-thirds of the inheritance (between them): if there are brothers and sisters, (they share), the male having twice the share of the female. Thus doth Allah make clear to you (His law), lest ye err. And Allah Hath knowledge of all things.

Al-Māîdah or
The Table Spread

In the name of Allah, Most Gracious, Most Merciful.

1.   O ye who believe ! fulfil (all) obligations. Lawful unto you (for food) are all beasts of cattle with the exceptions named: but animals of the chase are forbidden while ye are in the Sacred Precincts or in the state of pilgrimage: for Allah doth command according to His Will and Plan.

2.   O ye who believe ! violate not the sanctity of the rites of Allah, nor of the Sacred Month, nor of the animals brought for sacrifice, nor the garlands that mark out such animals, nor the people resorting to the Sacred House, seeking of the bounty and good pleasure of their Lord. But when ye are clear of the Sacred Precincts and of the state of pilgrimage, ye may hunt and let not the hatred of some people in (once) shutting you out of the Sacred Mosque lead you to transgression (and hostility on your part). Help ye one another in righteousness and piety, but help ye not one another in sin and rancour: fear Allah: for Allah is strict in punishment.

3.   Forbidden to you (for food) are: dead meat, blood, the flesh of swine, and that on which hath been invoked the name of other than Allah; that which hath been killed by strangling, or by a violent blow, or by a headlong fall, or by being gored to death; that which hath been (partly) eaten by a wild animal; unless ye are able to slaughter it (in due form); that which is sacrificed on stone (altars); (forbidden) also is the division (of meat) by raffling with arrows: that is impiety.

This day have those who reject Faith given up all hope of your religion: yet fear them not but fear Me. This day have I perfected your religion for you, completed My favour upon you, and have chosen for you Islam as your religion.

But if any is forced by hunger, with no inclination to transgression, Allah is indeed Oft-Forgiving, Most Merciful.

4.   They ask thee what is lawful to them (as food). Say: Lawful unto you are (all) things good and pure: and what ye have taught the beasts and birds of prey, training them to hunt in the manner directed to you by Allah: eat what they catch for you, but pronounce the name of Allah over it: and fear Allah; for Allah is swift in taking account.

5.   This day are (all) things good and pure made lawful unto you. The food of the People of the Book is lawful unto you and yours is lawful unto them. (Lawful unto you in marriage) are (not only) chaste women who are believers, but chaste women among the People of the Book, revealed before your time,— when ye give them their due dowers, and desire chastity. not lewdness. taking them as lovers. If any one

rejects faith, fruitless is his work, and in the Hereafter he will be in the ranks of those who have lost (all spiritual good).

6.   O ye who believe ! when ye prepare for prayer, wash your faces, and your hands (and arms) to the elbows; rub your heads (with water); and (wash) your feet to the ankles. If ye are in a state of ceremonial impurity, bathe your whole body. But if ye are ill, or on a journey, or one of you cometh from the privy, or ye have been in contact with women, and ye find no water, then take for yourselves clean sand or earth, and rub therewith your faces and hands. Allah doth not wish to place you in a difficulty, but to make you clean, and to complete His favour to you, that ye may be grateful.

7.   And call in remembrance the favour of Allah unto you, and His Covenant, which He ratified with you, when ye said: "We hear and we obey": and fear Allah, for Allah knoweth well the secrets of your hearts.

8.   O ye who believe ! stand out firmly for Allah, as witnesses to fair dealing, and let not the hatred of others to you make you swerve to wrong and depart from justice. Be just: that is next to Piety: and fear Allah. For Allah is well-acquainted with all that ye do.

9.   To those who believe and do deeds of righteousness hath Allah promised forgiveness and a great reward.

10.   Those who reject Faith and deny Our Signs will be Companions of Hell-fire.

11.   O ye who believe ! call in remembrance the favour of Allah unto you when certain

men formed the design to stretch out their hands against you, but (Allah) held back their hands from you: so fear Allah. And on Allah let Believers put (all) their trust.

12. Allah did aforetime take a Covenant from the Children of Israel, and We appointed twelve chieftains among them. And Allah said: "I am with you: if ye (but) establish regular Prayers, pay Zakat believe in My Messengers, honour and assist them, and loan to Allah a beautiful loan, verily I will wipe out from you your evils, and admit you to Gardens with rivers flowing beneath; but if any of you, after this, resisteth faith, he hath truly wandered from the path of rectitude."

13. But because of their breach of their Covenant, We cursed them, and made their hearts grow hard: they change the words from their (right) places and forget a good part of the Message that was sent them, nor wilt thou cease to find them— barring a few—ever bent on (new) deceits: but forgive them, and overlook (their misdeeds): for Allah loveth those who are kind.

14. From those, too, who call themselves Christians, We did take a Covenant, but they forgot a good part of the Message that was sent them: so We stirred up enmity and hatred between the one and the other, to the Day of Judgment. And soon will Allah show them what it is they have done.

15. O people of the Book ! there hath come to you Our Messenger, revealing to you much that ye used to hide in the Book, and passing over much (that is now unnecessary): there hath come to you from Allah a

جَاءَكُمْ مِّنَ اللهِ نُورٌ وَّكِتَبٌ مُّبِيْنٌ ۞

(new) light and a perspicuous Book,—

16. Wherewith Allah guideth all who seek His good pleasure to ways of peace and safety, and leadeth them out of darkness, by His Will, unto the light,—guideth them to a Path that is Straight.

يَّهْدِيْ بِهِ اللهُ مَنِ اتَّبَعَ رِضْوَانَهٗ سُبُلَ السَّلٰمِ وَيُخْرِجُهُمْ مِّنَ الظُّلُمٰتِ اِلَى النُّوْرِ بِاِذْنِهٖ وَيَهْدِيْهِمْ اِلٰى صِرَاطٍ مُّسْتَقِيْمٍ ۞

17. They disbelieved indeed those that say that Allah is Christ the son of Mary say: "Who then hath the least power against Allah, if His Will were to destroy Christ the son of Mary, his mother, and all—everyone that is on the earth? For to Allah belongeth the dominion of the heavens and the earth, and all that is between. He createth what He pleaseth. For Allah hath power over all things."

لَقَدْ كَفَرَ الَّذِيْنَ قَالُوٓا اِنَّ اللهَ هُوَ الْمَسِيْحُ ابْنُ مَرْيَمَ ۗ قُلْ فَمَنْ يَّمْلِكُ مِنَ اللهِ شَيْـًٔا اِنْ اَرَادَ اَنْ يُّهْلِكَ الْمَسِيْحَ ابْنَ مَرْيَمَ وَاُمَّهٗ وَمَنْ فِى الْاَرْضِ جَمِيْعًا ۗ وَلِلّٰهِ مُلْكُ السَّمٰوٰتِ وَالْاَرْضِ وَمَا بَيْنَهُمَا ۗ يَخْلُقُ مَا يَشَاءُ ۗ وَاللهُ عَلٰى كُلِّ شَيْءٍ قَدِيْرٌ ۞

18. (Both) the Jews and the Christians say: "We are sons of Allah, and His beloved." Say: "Why then doth He punish you for your sins? Nay, ye are but men,— of the men He hath created: He forgiveth whom He pleaseth. And He punisheth whom He pleaseth: and to Allah belongeth the dominion of the heavens and the earth, and all that is between: and unto Him is the final goal (of all)."

وَقَالَتِ الْيَهُوْدُ وَالنَّصٰرٰى نَحْنُ اَبْنٰٓؤُا اللهِ وَاَحِبَّاؤُهٗ ۗ قُلْ فَلِمَ يُعَذِّبُكُمْ بِذُنُوْبِكُمْ ۗ بَلْ اَنْتُمْ بَشَرٌ مِّمَّنْ خَلَقَ ۗ يَغْفِرُ لِمَنْ يَّشَاءُ وَيُعَذِّبُ مَنْ يَّشَاءُ ۗ وَلِلّٰهِ مُلْكُ السَّمٰوٰتِ وَالْاَرْضِ وَمَا بَيْنَهُمَا ۖ وَاِلَيْهِ الْمَصِيْرُ ۞

19. O People of the Book! now hath come unto you, making (things) clear unto you. Our Messenger, after the break in (the series of) our messengers, lest ye should say: "There came unto us no bringer of glad tidings and no warner": but now hath come unto you a bringer of glad tidings and a warner. And Allah hath power over all things.

يٰٓاَهْلَ الْكِتٰبِ قَدْ جَاءَكُمْ رَسُوْلُنَا يُبَيِّنُ لَكُمْ عَلٰى فَتْرَةٍ مِّنَ الرُّسُلِ اَنْ تَقُوْلُوْا مَا جَاءَنَا مِنْ بَشِيْرٍ وَّلَا نَذِيْرٍ ۖ فَقَدْ جَاءَكُمْ بَشِيْرٌ وَّنَذِيْرٌ ۗ وَاللهُ عَلٰى كُلِّ شَيْءٍ قَدِيْرٌ ۞

20. Remember Moses said to his pe-ople: "O my People! call in reme-mbrance the favour of Allah unto you, when He produced prophets among you, made you kings, and gave you what He had not given to any other among the peoples.

وَاِذْ قَالَ مُوْسٰى لِقَوْمِهٖ يٰقَوْمِ اذْكُرُوْا نِعْمَةَ اللهِ عَلَيْكُمْ اِذْ جَعَلَ فِيْكُمْ اَنْبِيَاءَ وَجَعَلَكُمْ مُّلُوْكًا ۖ وَّاٰتٰىكُمْ مَّا لَمْ يُؤْتِ اَحَدًا مِّنَ الْعٰلَمِيْنَ ۞

21. "O my people! enter the holy land

يٰقَوْمِ ادْخُلُوا الْاَرْضَ الْمُقَدَّسَةَ

which Allah hath assigned unto you, and turn not back ignominiously, for then will ye be overthrown, to your own ruin."

22. They said: "O Moses ! in this land are a people of exceeding strength: never shall we enter it until they leave it: If (once) they leave, then shall we enter."

23. (But) among (their) God-fearing men were two on whom Allah had bestowed His grace: they said: "Assault them at the (proper) Gate: when once ye are in, victory will be yours; but on Allah put your trust if ye have faith."

24. They said: "O Moses ! We shall never enter it as long as they are in it. Go thou, and thy Lord, and fight ye two, while we sit here."

25. He said: "O my Lord ! I have power only over myself and my brother: so separate us from this rebellious people!"

26. Allah said: "Therefore will the land be out of their reach for forty years: in distraction will they wander through the land: but sorrow thou not over these rebellious people."

27. Recite to them the truth of the story of the two sons of Adam. Behold ! they each presented a sacrifice (to Allah): it was accepted from one, but not from the other. Said the latter: "Be sure I will slay thee." "Surely," said the former, "Allah doth accept of the sacrifice of those who are righteous.

28. "If thou dost stretch thy hand against me, to slay me, it is not for me to stretch my hand against thee to slay thee: for I do fear Allah, the Cherisher of the Worlds.

29. "For me, I intend to let thee draw on thyself my sin as well as thine, for thou wilt be among the Companions of the Fire, and that is the reward of those who do wrong."

30. The (selfish) soul of the other led him to the murder of his brother: he murdered him, and became (himself) one of the lost ones.

31. Then Allah sent a raven, who scratched the ground, to show him how to hide the naked body of his brother. "Woe is me!" said he; "Was I not even able to be as this raven, and to hide the naked body of my brother?" Then he became full of regrets—

32. On that account: We ordained for the Children of Israel that if any one slew a person—unless it be for murder or for speading mischief in the land— it would be as if he slew the whole people: and if any one saved a life, It would be as if he saved the life of the whole people. Then although there came to them Our Messengers with Clear Signs, yet, even after that, many of them continued to commit excesses in the land.

33. The punishment of those who wage war against Allah and His Messenger, and strive with might and main for mischief through the land is: execution, or crucifixion, or the cutting off of hands and feet from opposite sides, or exile from the land: that is their disgrace in this world, and a heavy punishment is theirs in the Hereafter:

34. Except for those who repent before they fall into your Power: in that case, know that Allah is Oft-Forgiving, Most Merciful.

35. O ye who believe! do your duty to Allah, seek the means of approach unto

Him, and strive (with might and main) in His cause: that ye may prosper.

36. As to those who reject Faith,—if they had everything on earth, and twice repeated, to give as ransom for the Chastisement of the Day of Judgment, it would never be accepted of them. Theirs would be a grievous Chastisement.

37. Their wish will be to get out of the Fire. But never will they get out therefrom: their Chastisement will be one that endures.

38. As to the thief, Male or female, cut off his or her hands: a retribution for their deed and exemplary punishment from Allah, and Allah is Exalted in Power, full of Wisdom.

39. But if the thief repent after his crime, and amend his conduct, Allah turneth to him in forgiveness; for Allah is Oft-Forgiving, Most Merciful.

40. Knowest thou not that to Allah (alone) belongeth the dominion of the heavens and the earth ? He punisheth whom He pleaseth, and He forgiveth whom He pleaseth: and Allah hath power over all things.

41. O Messenger ! let not those grieve thee, who race each other into Unbelief: (whether it be) among those who say "We believe" with their lips but whose hearts have no faith; or it be among the Jews— men who will listen to any lie,—will listen even to others who have never so much as come to thee. They change the words from their (right) places they say, "If ye are given this, take it, but if not, beware!" If any one's trial is intended by Allah, thou hast no authority in the least for him against Allah. For such—it is not Allah's will to purify their

hearts. For them there is disgrace in this world, and in the Hereafter a heavy punishment.

42. (They are fond of) listening to falsehood, of devouring anything forbidden. If they do come to thee, either judge between them, or decline to interfere. If thou decline, they cannot hurt thee in the least. If thou judge, judge in equity between them. For Allah loveth those who judge in equity.

43. But why do they come to thee for decision, when they have (their own) Torah before them?—Therein is the (plain) Command of Allah; yet even after that, they would turn away. For they are not (really) People of Faith.

44. It was We who revealed the Torah (to Moses): therein was guidance and light. By its standard have been judged the Jews, by the Prophets who bowed (as in Islam) to Allah's Will, by the Rabbis and the Doctors of Law: for to them was entrusted the protection of Allah's Book, and they were witnesses thereto: therefore fear not men, but fear Me, and sell not My Signs for a miserable price. If any do fail to judge by what Allah hath revealed, they are Unbelievers.

45. We ordained therein for them: "Life for life, eye for eye, nose for nose, ear for ear, tooth for tooth, and wounds equal for equal." But if anyone remits the retaliation by way of charity, it is an act of atonement for himself. And if any fail to judge by what Allah hath revealed, they are wrong-doers.

فِتْنَتَهُ فَلَنْ تَمْلِكَ لَهُ مِنَ اللّٰهِ شَيْئًا ۚ اُولٰٓئِكَ الَّذِيْنَ لَمْ يُرِدِ اللّٰهُ اَنْ يُّطَهِّرَ قُلُوْبَهُمْ ۚ لَهُمْ فِى الدُّنْيَا خِزْيٌ ۖ وَّ لَهُمْ فِى الْاٰخِرَةِ عَذَابٌ عَظِيْمٌ ۝

سَمّٰعُوْنَ لِلْكَذِبِ اَكّٰلُوْنَ لِلسُّحْتِ ۚ فَاِنْ جَآءُوْكَ فَاحْكُمْ بَيْنَهُمْ اَوْ اَعْرِضْ عَنْهُمْ ۚ وَاِنْ تُعْرِضْ عَنْهُمْ فَلَنْ يَّضُرُّوْكَ شَيْئًا ۖ وَاِنْ حَكَمْتَ فَاحْكُمْ بَيْنَهُمْ بِالْقِسْطِ ۚ اِنَّ اللّٰهَ يُحِبُّ الْمُقْسِطِيْنَ ۝

وَكَيْفَ يُحَكِّمُوْنَكَ وَعِنْدَهُمُ التَّوْرٰىةُ فِيْهَا حُكْمُ اللّٰهِ ثُمَّ يَتَوَلَّوْنَ مِنْ بَعْدِ ذٰلِكَ ۚ وَمَآ اُولٰٓئِكَ بِالْمُؤْمِنِيْنَ ۝ اِنَّآ اَنْزَلْنَا التَّوْرٰىةَ فِيْهَا هُدًى وَّنُوْرٌ ۚ يَحْكُمُ بِهَا النَّبِيُّوْنَ الَّذِيْنَ اَسْلَمُوْا لِلَّذِيْنَ هَادُوْا وَالرَّبّٰنِيُّوْنَ وَالْاَحْبَارُ بِمَا اسْتُحْفِظُوْا مِنْ كِتٰبِ اللّٰهِ وَكَانُوْا عَلَيْهِ شُهَدَآءَ ۚ فَلَا تَخْشَوُا النَّاسَ وَاخْشَوْنِ وَلَا تَشْتَرُوْا بِاٰيٰتِيْ ثَمَنًا قَلِيْلًا ۚ وَمَنْ لَّمْ يَحْكُمْ بِمَآ اَنْزَلَ اللّٰهُ فَاُولٰٓئِكَ هُمُ الْكٰفِرُوْنَ ۝

وَكَتَبْنَا عَلَيْهِمْ فِيْهَآ اَنَّ النَّفْسَ بِالنَّفْسِ ۙ وَالْعَيْنَ بِالْعَيْنِ وَالْاَنْفَ بِالْاَنْفِ وَالْاُذُنَ بِالْاُذُنِ وَالسِّنَّ بِالسِّنِّ ۙ وَالْجُرُوْحَ قِصَاصٌ ۚ فَمَنْ تَصَدَّقَ بِهٖ فَهُوَ كَفَّارَةٌ لَّهُ ۚ وَمَنْ لَّمْ يَحْكُمْ بِمَآ اَنْزَلَ اللّٰهُ فَاُولٰٓئِكَ هُمُ الظّٰلِمُوْنَ ۝

46. And in their footsteps We sent Jesus the son of Mary, confirming the Torah that had come before him: We sent him the Gospel: therein was guidance and light. And confirmation of the Torah that had come before him: a guidance and an admonition to those who fear Allah.

47. Let the People of the Gospel judge by what Allah hath revealed therein. If any do fail to judge by what Allah hath revealed, they are those who rebel.

48. To thee We sent the Scripture in truth, confirming the scripture that came before it, and guarding it in safety: so judge between them by what Allah hath revealed, and follow not their vain desires, diverging from the Truth that hath come to thee. To each among you have We prescribed a Law and an Open Way. If Allah had so willed, He would have made you a single People, but (His Plan is) to test you in what He hath given you: so strive as in a race in all virtues. The goal of you all is to Allah; it is He that will show you the truth of the matters in which ye dispute;

49. And this (He commands): Judge thou between them by what Allah hath revealed, and follow not their vain desires, but beware of them lest they beguile thee from any of that (teaching) which Allah hath sent down to thee. And if they turn away, be assured that for some of their crimes it is Allah's purpose to punish them. And truly most men are rebellious.

50. Do they then seek after a judgment of (the Days of) Ignorance? But who, for a people whose faith is assured, can give better judgment than Allah?

51. O ye who believe ! take not the Jews and the Christians for your friends and protectors: they are but friends and protectors to each other. And he amongst you that turns to them (for friendship) is of them. Verily Allah guideth not a people unjust.

52. Those in whose hearts is a disease—thou seest how eagerly they run about amongst them, saying: "We do fear lest a change of fortune bring us disaster." Ah ! perhaps Allah will give (thee) victory, or a decision from Him then will they regret of the thoughts which they secretly harboured in their hearts.

53. And those who believe will say: "Are these the men who swore their strongest oaths by Allah, that they were with you ? All that they do will be in vain, and they will fall into (nothing but) ruin.

54. O ye who believe ! if any from among you turn back from his Faith, soon will Allah produce a people whom He will love as they will love Him,—lowly with the Believers, mighty against the Rejecters, fighting in the Way of Allah, and never afraid of the reproaches of such as find fault. That is the Grace of Allah, which He will bestow on whom He pleaseth. And Allah encompasseth all, and He knoweth all things.

55. Your (real) friends are (no less than) Allah, His Messenger, and the Believers,—those who establish regular prayers and pay Zakat and they bow down humbly (in worship).

56. As to those who turn (for friendship) to Allah, His Messenger, and the Believers,—it is the party of Allah that must certainly triumph.

57. O ye who believe ! take not for friends and protectors those who take your religion for a mockery or sport,—whether among

those who received the Scripture before you, or among those who reject Faith: but fear ye Allah, if ye have Faith (indeed).

58. When ye proclaim your call to prayer, they take it (but) as mockery and sport; that is because they are a people without understanding.

59. Say: "O people of the Book ! Do ye disapprove of us for no other reason than that we believe in Allah, and the revelation that hath come to us and that which came before (us), and (perhaps) that most of you are rebellious and disobedient?"

60. Say: "Shall I point out to you some-thing much worse than this, (as judged) by the treatment it received from Allah ? Those who incurred the curse of Allah and His wrath, those of whom some He transformed into apes and swine, those who worshipped Evil (Tagut)— these are (many times) worse in rank, and far more astray from the even Path!"

61. When they come to thee, they say: "We believe": but in fact they enter with a disbelief, and they go out with the same. But Allah knoweth fully all that they hide.

62. Many of them dost thou see, racing each other in sin and transgression and their eating of things forbidden. Evil indeed are the things that they do.

63. Why do not the Rabbis and the doctors of law forbid them from their (habit of) uttering sinful words and eating things forbidden ? Evil indeed are their works.

64. The Jews say: "Allah's hand is tied up," Be *their* hands tied up and be they accursed for the (blasphemy) they utter. Nay, both His hands are widely outstretched: He giveth and spendeth (of His bounty) as He pleaseth. But the revelation that cometh to thee from Allah increaseth in most of them their obstinate rebellion and blasphemy. Amongst them

We have placed enmity and hatred till the Day of Judgment. Every time they kindle the fire of war, Allah doth extinguish it; but they (ever) strive to do mischief on earth. And Allah loveth not those who do mischief.

65. If only the People of the Book had believed and been righteous. We should indeed have blotted out their iniquities and admitted them to Gardens of Bliss.

66. If only they had stood fast by the Torah, the Gospel, and all the revelation that was sent to them from their Lord, they would have eaten both from above them and from below their feet. There is from among them a party of the right course: but many of them follow a course that is evil.

67. O Messenger ! proclaim the (Message) which hath been sent to thee from thy Lord. If thou didst not, thou wouldst not have fulfilled and proclaimed His Mission. And Allah will defend thee from men (who mean mischief). For Allah guideth not those who reject Faith.

68. Say: "O People of the Book ! ye have no ground to stand upon unless ye stand fast by the Torah. The Gospel, and all the revelation that has come to you from your Lord." It is the revelation that cometh to thee from thy Lord, that increaseth in most of them their obstinate rebellion and blasphemy. But sorrow thou not over (these) people without Faith.

69. Those who believe (in the Qur'an). Those who follow the Jewish (scriptures), and the Sabians and the Christians,— any who believe in Allah and the Last Day, and work righteousness,— on them shall be no fear, nor shall they grieve.

70. We took the Covenant of the Children

of Israel and sent them Messengers. Every
time there came to them a Messenger with
what they them-selves desired not—some
(of these) they called impostors, and some
they slay.

71. They thought there would be no trial
(or punishment); so they became blind and
deaf; yet Allah (in mercy) turned to them;
yet again many of them became blind and
deaf. But Allah sees well all that they do.

72. Certainly they disbelieve who say:
"Allah is Christ the son of Mary." But said
Christ: "O Children of Israel! worship Allah,
my Lord and your Lord." Whoever joins
other gods with Allah,—Allah will forbid him
the Garden, and the Fire will be his abode.
There will for the wrong-doers be no one to
help.

73. They disbelieve who say: Allah is one
of three (in a Trinity:) for there is no god
except one God. If they desist not from their
word (of blasphemy), verily a grievous
chastisement will befall the disbelievers
among them.

74. Why turn they not to Allah and seek
His forgiveness? For Allah is Oft-Forgiving,
Most Merciful.

75. Christ the son of Mary was no more than
a Messenger; many were the Messengers
that passed away before him. His mother was
a woman of truth. They had both to eat their
(daily) food. See how Allah doth make His
Signs clear to them; yet see in what ways
they are deluded away from the truth!

76. Say: "Will ye worship, besides Allah,
something which hath no power either to
harm or benefit you? But Allah,—He it is
that heareth and knoweth all things."

77. Say: "O People of the Book ! Exceed not in your religion the bounds (of what is proper), trespassing beyond the truth, nor follow the vain desires of people who went wrong in times gone by,—who misled many, and strayed (themselves) from the even Way.

78 Curses were pronounced on those among the Children of Israel who rejected Faith, by the tongue of David and of Jesus the son of Mary: because they disobeyed and persisted in Excesses.

79. Nor did they forbid one another the iniquities which they committed: evil indeed were the deeds which they did.

80. Thou seest many of them turning in friendship to the Unbelievers. Evil indeed are (the works) which their souls have sent forward before them (with the result), that Allah's wrath is on them, and in torment will they abide.

81. If only they had believed in Allah, in the Prophet, and in what hath been revealed to him, never would they have taken them for friends and protectors, but most of them are rebellious wrong-doers.

82. Strongest among men in enmity to the Believers wilt thou find the Jews and Pagans; and nearest among them in love to the Believers wilt thou find those who say, "We are Christians": because amongst these are men devoted to learning. And men who have renounced the world, and they are not arrogant.

83. And when they listen to the revelation received by the Messenger, thou wilt see their eyes overflowing with tears, for they recognise the truth: they pray: "Our Lord ! we believe, write us down among the witnesses.

84. "What cause can we have not to believe in Allah and the truth which has come to us, seeing that we long for our

Lord to admit us to the company of the righteous ?"

85. And for this their prayer hath Allah rewarded them with Gardens, with rivers flowing underneath,—their eternal Home. Such is the recompense of those who do good.

86. But those who reject Faith and belie Our Signs,—they shall be Companions of Hell-fire.

87. O ye who believe ! make not unlawful the good things which Allah hath made lawful for you, but commit no excess: for Allah loveth not those given to excess.

88. Eat to the things which Allah hath provided for you, lawful and good: but fear Allah, in Whom ye believe.

89. Allah will not call you to account for what is void in your oaths. but He will call you to account for your deliberate oaths: for expiation, feed ten indigent persons, on a scale of the average for the food of your families; or clothe them; or give a slave his freedom. If that is beyond your means. fast for three days. That is the expiation for the oaths ye have sworn. But keep to your oaths. Thus doth Allah make clear to you His Signs, that ye May be grateful.

90. O ye who believe ! intoxicants and gambling, sacrificing to stones, and (divination by) arrows, are an abomination,— of Satan's handi-work: eschew such (abomination), that ye may prosper.

91. Satan's plan is (but) to excite enmity and hatred between you, with intoxicants and gambling, and hinder you from the remembrance of Allah, and from prayer.

will ye not then abstain?

92. Obey Allah, and obey the Messenger. And beware (of evil): if ye do turn back, know ye that it is Our Messenger's duty to proclaim (the Message) in the clearest manner.

93. On those who believe and do deeds of righteousness there is no blame for what they ate (in the past), when they guard themselves from evil, and believe, and do deeds of righteousness,— then again, guard themselves from evil and believe,— then again, guard themselves from evil and do good. For Allah loveth those who do good.

94. O ye who believe ! Allah doth but make a trial of you in a little matter of game well within reach of your hands and your lances, that He may test who feareth Him unseen: any who transgress thereafter, will have a grievous chastisement.

95. O ye who believe ! kill not game while in the Sacred precincts or in the state of pilgrimage if any of you doth so intentionally, the compensation is an offering, brought to the Ka'ba, of a domestic animal equivalent to the one he killed. As adjudged by two just men among you; or by way of atonement, the feeding of the indigent; or its equivalent in fasts: that he may taste of the penalty of his deed. Allah Forgives what is past: for repetition Allah will punish him for Allah is Exalted, and Lord of Retribution.

96. Lawful to you is the pursuit of water-game and its use for food,—for the benefit of yourselves and those who travel; but forbidden is the pursuit of land-game:—as long as ye are in the Sacred Precincts or in the state of pilgrimage and fear Allah, to Whom ye shall be gathered back.

97. Allah made the Ka'ba, the Sacred House, a means of support for men, as also

the Sacred Months, the animals for offerings, and the garlands that mark them: that ye may know that Allah hath knowledge of what is in the heavens and on earth and that Allah is well acquainted with all things.

98. Know ye that Allah is strict in punishment and that Allah is Oft-Forgiving, Most Merciful.

99. The Messenger's duty is but to proclaim (the Message). But Allah knoweth all that ye reveal and ye conceal.

100. Say: "Not equal are things that are bad and things that are good, even though the abundance of the bad may dazzle thee; so fear Allah, O ye that understand; that (so) ye may prosper."

101. O ye who believe ! ask not questions about things which, if made plain to you, may cause you trouble. But if ye ask about things when the Qur'an is being Revealed, they will be made plain to you, Allah will forgive those: for Allah is Oft-Forgiving, Most Forbearing.

102. Some people before you did ask such questions, and on that account lost their faith.

103. It was not Allah Who instituted (superstitions like those of) a slit-ear she-camel, or a she-camel let loose for free pasture, or idol sacrifices for twin-births in animals, or stallion-camels freed from work: it is the disbelievers who invent a lie against Allah; but most of them lack wisdom.

104. When it is said to them: "Come to what Allah hath revealed; come to the Messenger": they say: "Enough for us are the ways we found our fathers following." What! even though their fathers were void of knowledge and guidance ?

105. O ye who believe ! guard your own souls: if ye follow (right) guidance. No hurt can come to you from those who stray. The

return of you all is to Allah: it is He That will inform you of all that ye do.

106. O ye who believe ! when death approaches any of you, (take) witnesses among yourselves when making bequest,— two just men of your own (brotherhood) or others from outside if ye are journeying through the earth, and the chance of death befalls you (thus). If ye doubt (their truth), detain them both after prayer, and let them both swear by Allah: "We will not take for it a price even though the (beneficiary) be our near relation: we shall hide not the evidence we owe to Allah if we do, then behold ! we shall be sinners.

107. But if it gets known that these two were guilty of the sin (of perjury), let two others stand forth in their places,—nearest in kin from among those who claim a lawful right: let them swear by Allah: "We affirm that our witness is truer than that of those two, and that we have not trespassed (beyond the truth): if we did, behold ! we will be wrong-doers."

108. That is most suitable: that they may give the evidence in its true nature and shape, or else they would fear that other oaths would be taken after their oaths. But fear Allah, and listen (to His counsel): for Allah guideth not a rebellious people.

109. On the day when Allah will gather the Messengers together, and ask: "What was the response ye received (from men to your teaching)?" They will say: "We have no knowledge: it is Thou Who knowest in full all that is hidden."

110. Then will Allah say: "O Jesus the son of Mary ! recount My favour to thee and to thy mother. Behold ! I strengthened thee with the Holy Spirit. So that thou didst speak to the people in childhood and in old age. Behold ! I taught thee the Book and Wisdom,

the Torah and the Gospel. And behold!
thou makest out of clay, as it were, the
figure of a bird, by My leave. And thou
breathest into it, and it becometh a bird by
My leave, and thou healest those born blind,
and the lepers, by My leave. And behold !
thou bringest forth the dead by My leave.
And behold ! I did restrain the Children of
Israel from (violence to) thee when thou
didst show them the Clear Signs, and the
unbelievers among them said: 'This is
nothing but evident magic.'

111. "And behold ! I inspired the Disciples
to have faith in Me and Mine Messenger:
they said. 'We have faith, and do thou bear
witness that we bow to Allah as Muslims'."

112. Behold ! the Disciples said: "O Jesus
the son of Mary ! can thy Lord send down
to us a Table set (with viands) from
heaven?" Said Jesus: "Fear Allah, if ye
have faith".

113. They said: "We only wish to eat thereof
and satisfy our hearts, and to know that
thou has indeed told us the truth; and that
we ourselves may be witnesses to the
miracle."

114. Said Jesus the son of Mary: "O Allah
our Lord ! send us from heaven a Table set
(with viands), that there may be for us—for
the first and the last of us—a solemn festival
and a Sign from Thee; and provide for our
sustenance, for Thou art the best sustainer
(of our needs)."

115. Allah said: "I will send it down unto
you: but if any of you after that resisteth
faith, I will punish him with a chastisement
such as I have not inflicted on any one
among all the peoples."

116. And behold ! Allah will say:
'O Jesus the son of Mary ! didst thou say
unto men. 'Take me and my mother for

ṢŪRA–6
AL-AN'ĀM
(INTRODUCTION)

This is a Sûra of the late Makkan period. The greater part of it was revealed entire. Its place in the traditional order of arrangement is justified by logical considerations. We have alreay had the spiritual history of mankind, a discussion of the earlier revelations and how they were lost or corrupted, the regulations for the outer life of the new Community and the points in which the Jews and Christians failed to maintain the central doctrine of Islam—the unity of Allah. The next step now taken is to expound this doctrine in relation to Pagan Arabia.

two gods beside Allah'?" He will say: "Glory to Thee! never could I say what I had no right (to say). Had I said such a thing, Thou wouldst indeed have known it. Thou knowest what is in my heart, though I know not what is in Thine. For Thou knowest in full all that is hidden.

117. "Never said I to them aught except what Thou didst command me to say, to wit, 'Worship Allah, my Lord and your Lord': and I was a witness over them whilst I dwelt amongst them; when thou didst take me up Thou wast the Watcher over them, and Thou art a witness to all things.

118. "If Thou dost punish them, they are Thy servants: if Thou dost forgive them, Thou art the Exalted in power, the Wise."

119. Allah will say; "This is a day on which the truthful will profit from their truth: theirs are Gardens, with rivers flowing beneath,— their eternal home: Allah well-pleased with them, and they with Allah: that is the mighty Triumph (the fulfillment of all desires).

120. To Allah doth belong the dominion of the heavens and the earth, and all that is therein, and it is He who hath power over all things.

Al-An'ām, or Cattle.

In the name of Allah, Most Gracious, Most Merciful.

1. Praise be to Allah, Who created the heavens and the earth, and made the Darkness and the Light. Yet those who reject Faith hold (others) as equal with their Guardian Lord.

2. He it is Who created you from clay, and then decreed a stated term (for you).

And there is with Him another determined term; yet Ye doubt within yourselves !

3.　　And He is Allah in the heavens and in earth. He knoweth what ye hide, and what ye reveal, and He knoweth the (recompense) which ye earn (by your deeds).

4.　　But never did a single one of the Signs of their Lord reach them, but they turned away therefrom.

5.　　And now they reject the truth when it reaches them; but soon shall come to them the news of what they used to mock at.

6.　　See they not how many of those before them We did destroy?— Generations We had established on the earth, in strength such as We have not given to you—for whom We poured out rain from the skies in abundance, and gave streams flowing beneath their (feet): yet for their sins We destroyed them, and raised in their wake fresh generations (to succeed them).

7.　　If We had sent unto thee a written (Message) on parchment, so that they could touch it with their hands, the Unbelievers would have been sure to say: "This is nothing but obvious magic!"

8.　　They say: "Why is not an angel sent down to him ?" If We did send down an angel, the matter would be settled at once, and no respite would be granted them.

9.　　If We had made it an angel, We should have sent him as a man. And We should certainly have caused them confusion in a matter which they have already covered with confusion.

10.　Mocked were (many) Messengers before thee; but their scoffers were hemmed in by the thing that they mocked.

11.　Say: "Travel through the earth and see what was the end of those who rejected Truth."

12. Say: "To whom belongeth all that is in the heavens and on earth?" Say: "To Allah. He hath inscribed for Himself (the rule of) Mercy. That He will gather you together for the Day of Judgment, there is no doubt whatever, it is they who have lost their own souls, that will not believe.

13. To him belongeth all that dwelleth (or lurketh) in the Night and the Day, for He is the one Who heareth and knoweth all things.

14. Say: "Shall I take for my protector any other than Allah, the Maker of the heavens and the earth? And He it is that feedeth but is not fed." Say: "Nay! but I am commanded to be the first of those who bow to Allah (in Islam), and be not thou of the company of those who join gods with Allah."

15. Say: "I would, if I disobeyed my Lord, indeed have fear of the Chastisement of a Mighty Day.

16. "On that day, if the Penalty is aver-ted from any, it is due to Allah's Mercy; and that would be a Mighty Triumph.

17. "If Allah touch thee with affliction, none can remove it but He: if He touch thee with happiness, He hath power over all things.

18. "He is irresistibly Supreme over His servants. And He is the Wise, acquainted with all things."

19. Say: "What thing is most weighty in evidence ?" Say: "Allah is witness between me and you; this Qur'an hath been revealed to me by inspiration. That I may warn you and all whom it reaches. Can ye possibly bear witness that besides Allah there are other gods?" Say: "Nay! I cannot bear witness!" Say: "But in truth He is the One God. And I truly am innocent of (your blasphemy of) joining others with Him."

20. Those to whom We have given the Book know this as they know their own

قُل لِّمَن مَّا فِي السَّمَٰوَٰتِ وَالْأَرْضِ قُل لِّلَّهِ ۚ كَتَبَ عَلَىٰ نَفْسِهِ الرَّحْمَةَ ۚ لَيَجْمَعَنَّكُمْ إِلَىٰ يَوْمِ الْقِيَٰمَةِ لَا رَيْبَ فِيهِ ۚ الَّذِينَ خَسِرُوٓا۟ أَنفُسَهُمْ فَهُمْ لَا يُؤْمِنُونَ ۝

وَلَهُۥ مَا سَكَنَ فِي الَّيْلِ وَالنَّهَارِ ۚ وَهُوَ السَّمِيعُ الْعَلِيمُ ۝

قُلْ أَغَيْرَ اللَّهِ أَتَّخِذُ وَلِيًّا فَاطِرِ السَّمَٰوَٰتِ وَالْأَرْضِ وَهُوَ يُطْعِمُ وَلَا يُطْعَمُ ۗ قُلْ إِنِّيٓ أُمِرْتُ أَنْ أَكُونَ أَوَّلَ مَنْ أَسْلَمَ ۖ وَلَا تَكُونَنَّ مِنَ الْمُشْرِكِينَ ۝

قُلْ إِنِّيٓ أَخَافُ إِنْ عَصَيْتُ رَبِّي عَذَابَ يَوْمٍ عَظِيمٍ ۝

مَّن يُصْرَفْ عَنْهُ يَوْمَئِذٍ فَقَدْ رَحِمَهُۥ ۚ وَذَٰلِكَ الْفَوْزُ الْمُبِينُ ۝

وَإِن يَمْسَسْكَ اللَّهُ بِضُرٍّ فَلَا كَاشِفَ لَهُۥٓ إِلَّا هُوَ ۖ وَإِن يَمْسَسْكَ بِخَيْرٍ فَهُوَ عَلَىٰ كُلِّ شَيْءٍ قَدِيرٌ ۝

وَهُوَ الْقَاهِرُ فَوْقَ عِبَادِهِۦ ۚ وَهُوَ الْحَكِيمُ الْخَبِيرُ ۝

قُلْ أَيُّ شَيْءٍ أَكْبَرُ شَهَٰدَةً ۖ قُلِ اللَّهُ ۖ شَهِيدٌۢ بَيْنِي وَبَيْنَكُمْ ۚ وَأُوحِيَ إِلَيَّ هَٰذَا الْقُرْءَانُ لِأُنذِرَكُم بِهِۦ وَمَنۢ بَلَغَ ۚ أَئِنَّكُمْ لَتَشْهَدُونَ أَنَّ مَعَ اللَّهِ ءَالِهَةً أُخْرَىٰ ۚ قُل لَّآ أَشْهَدُ ۚ قُلْ إِنَّمَا هُوَ إِلَٰهٌ وَٰحِدٌ وَإِنَّنِي بَرِيٓءٌ مِّمَّا تُشْرِكُونَ ۝

الَّذِينَ ءَاتَيْنَٰهُمُ الْكِتَٰبَ يَعْرِفُونَهُۥ

sons. Those who have lost their own souls refuse therefore to believe.

21. Who doth more wrong than he who inventeth a lie against Allah or rejecteth His Signs ? But verily the wrong-doers never shall prosper.

22. On the day shall We gather them all together: We shall say to those who ascribed partners (to Us): "Where are the partners whom ye (invented and) talked about !

23. There will then be (left) no excuse for them but to say: "By Allah our Lord we were not those who joined gods with Allah."

24. Behold ! how they lie against themselves but the (lie) which they invented will leave them in the lurch.

25. Of them there are some who (pretend to) listen to thee; but We have thrown veils on their hearts, so they understand it not, and deafness in their ears; if they saw everyone of the Signs, they will not believe in them; in so much that when they come to thee, they (but) dispute with thee; the Unbelievers say: "These are nothing but tales of the ancients."

26. Others they forbid it and themselves they keep away; but they only destroy themselves and they perceive it not.

27. If thou couldst but see when they shall be made to stand by the Fire they will say: "Would that we were but sent back ! Then would we not reject the Signs of our Lord, but would be amongst those who believe!"

28. Yea, in their own (eyes) will become manifest what before they concealed. But if they were returned, they would certainly

relapse to the things they were forbidden, for they are indeed liars.

29. And they (sometimes) say: "There is nothing except our life on this earth, and never shall we be raised up again."

30. If thou couldst but see when they shall be made to stand before their Lord he will say: "Is not this the truth ?" They will say: "Yea, by our Lord" he will say: "Taste ye then the Chastisement because ye rejected Faith."

31. Lost indeed are they who treat it as a falsehood that they must meet Allah,—until on a sudden the hour is on them, and they say: "Ah! woe unto us that we neglected; for they bear their burdens on their backs, and evil indeed are the burdens that they bear?

32. Nothing is the life of this world but play and amusement. But best is the Home in the Hereafter, for those who are righteous. Will ye not then understand ?

33. We know indeed the grief which their words do cause thee: it is not thee they reject: it is the Signs of Allah, which the wicked deny.

34. Rejected were the Messengers before thee: with patience and constancy they bore their rejection and their persecution until Our aid did reach them: there is none that can alter the Words (and Decrees) of Allah already hast thou received some account of those Messengers.

35. If their spurning is hard on thee, yet if thou wert able to seek a tunnel in the ground or a ladder to the skies and bring them a Sign,— (what good ?). If it were Allah's Will, He could gather them together unto true guidance: so be not thou amongst those who are swayed byignorance (and

impatience)!

36. Those who listen (in truth), be sure, will accept: as to the dead, Allah will raise them up; then will they be returned unto Him.

37. They say: "Why is not a Sign sent down to him from his Lord !" Say: "Allah hath certainly power to send down a Sign: But most of them understand not."

38. There is not an animal (that lives) on the earth, nor a being that flies on its wings, but (forms part of) communities like you. Nothing have We omitted from the Book, and they (all) shall be gathered to their Lord in the end.

39. Those who reject our Signs are deaf and dumb,— in the midst of darkness profound: whom Allah willeth. He leaveth to wander: whom He willeth. He placeth on the Way that is Straight.

40. Say: "Think ye to yourselves, if there come upon you the Punishment of Allah, or the Hour (that ye dread). Would ye then call upon other than Allah ?— (reply) if ye are truthful !

41. "Nay,—on Him would ye call, and if it be his Will, He would remove (the distress) which occasioned your call upon Him, and ye would forget (the false gods) which ye join with Him !"

42. Before thee We sent (messengers) to many nations, and We afflicted the nations with suffering and adversity, that they call (Allah) in humility.

43. When the suffering reached them from Us, why then did they not call (Allah) in humility? On the contrary their hearts became hardened, and Satan made their (sinful) acts seem alluring to them.

44. But when they forgot the warning they had received, We opened to them the gates of all (good) things, until, in the midst of

their enjoyment of Our gifts, on a sudden, We called them to account, when lo! they were plunged in despair !

45. Of the wrong-doers the last remnant was cut off Praise be to Allah, the Cherisher of the Worlds.

46. Say: "Think ye, if Allah took away your hearing and your sight, and sealed up your hearts, who—a god other than Allah—could restore them to you ?" See how We explain the Signs by various (symbols); yet they turn aside.

47. Say: "Think ye, if the Punishment of Allah comes to you, whether suddenly or openly, will any be destroyed except those who do wrong?

48. We send the Messengers only to give good news and to warn: so those who believe and mend (their lives),—upon them shall be no fear, nor shall they grieve.

49. But those who reject our Signs,—them shall punishment touch, for that they ceased not from transgressing.

50. Say: "I tell you not that with me are the Treasures of Allah, nor do I know what is hidden. Nor do I tell you I am an angel. I but follow what is revealed to me." Say: "Can the blind be held equal to the seeing?" Will ye then consider not?

51. Give this warning to those in whose (hearts) is the fear that they will be brought (to Judgment) before their Lord: except for Him they will have no protector nor intercessor: that they may guard (against evil).

52. Send not away those who call on their Lord morning and evening, seeking His Face. In naught art thou accountable for them, and in naught are they accountable for thee, that thou shouldst turn them away,

and thus be (one) of the unjust.

فَتَنْظُرُ دَهُمْ فَتَكُوْنُوْا مِنَ الظّٰلِمِيْنَ ۞

53. Thus did We test some of them by others, that they should say: "Is it these then that Allah hath favoured from amongst us?" Doth not Allah know best those who are grateful?

وَكَذٰلِكَ فَتَنَّا بَعْضَهُمْ بِبَعْضٍ لِّيَقُوْلُوْٓا اَهٰٓؤُلَآءِ مَنَّ اللّٰهُ عَلَيْهِمْ مِّنْ بَيْنِنَا ۗ اَلَيْسَ اللّٰهُ بِاَعْلَمَ بِالشّٰكِرِيْنَ ۞

54. When those come to thee who believe in Our Signs, say: "Peace be on you: your Lord hath inscribed for Himself (the rule of) Mercy: verily, if any of you did evil in ingnorance, and thereafter repented, and amended (his conduct), lo! He is Oft-Forgiving, Most Merciful.

وَاِذَا جَآءَكَ الَّذِيْنَ يُؤْمِنُوْنَ بِاٰيٰتِنَا فَقُلْ سَلٰمٌ عَلَيْكُمْ كَتَبَ رَبُّكُمْ عَلٰى نَفْسِهِ الرَّحْمَةَ ۙ اَنَّهُ مَنْ عَمِلَ مِنْكُمْ سُوْٓءًا بِجَهَالَةٍ ثُمَّ تَابَ مِنْۢ بَعْدِهٖ وَ اَصْلَحَ فَاَنَّهُ غَفُوْرٌ رَّحِيْمٌ ۞

55. Thus do We explain the Signs in detail: that the way of the sinners may be shown up.

وَكَذٰلِكَ نُفَصِّلُ الْاٰيٰتِ وَلِتَسْتَبِيْنَ سَبِيْلُ الْمُجْرِمِيْنَ ۞

56. Say: "I am forbidden" to worship those—others than Allah—whom ye call upon," say: "I will not follow your vain desires: if I did, I would stray from the path, and be not of the company of those who receive guidance."

قُلْ اِنِّيْ نُهِيْتُ اَنْ اَعْبُدَ الَّذِيْنَ تَدْعُوْنَ مِنْ دُوْنِ اللّٰهِ ۗ قُلْ لَّآ اَتَّبِعُ اَهْوَآءَكُمْ ۙ قَدْ ضَلَلْتُ اِذًا وَّمَآ اَنَا مِنَ الْمُهْتَدِيْنَ ۞

57. Say: "For me, I am on a clear Sign from my Lord, but ye reject Him. What ye would see hastened, is not in my power. The Command rests with none but Allah: He declares the Truth, and He is the best of judges."

قُلْ اِنِّيْ عَلٰى بَيِّنَةٍ مِّنْ رَّبِّيْ وَكَذَّبْتُمْ بِهٖ ۗ مَا عِنْدِيْ مَا تَسْتَعْجِلُوْنَ بِهٖ ۗ اِنِ الْحُكْمُ اِلَّا لِلّٰهِ ۗ يَقُصُّ الْحَقَّ وَ هُوَ خَيْرُ الْفٰصِلِيْنَ ۞

58. Say: "If what ye would see hastened were in my power, the matter would be settled at once between you and me. But Allah knoweth best those who do wrong."

قُلْ لَّوْ اَنَّ عِنْدِيْ مَا تَسْتَعْجِلُوْنَ بِهٖ لَقُضِيَ الْاَمْرُ بَيْنِيْ وَبَيْنَكُمْ ۗ وَاللّٰهُ اَعْلَمُ بِالظّٰلِمِيْنَ ۞

59. With Him are the keys of the Unseen, the treasures that none knoweth but He. He knoweth whatever there is on the earth and in the sea. Not a leaf doth fall but with His knowledge: there is not a grain in the darkness (or depths) of the earth, nor anything fresh or dry (green or withered), but is (inscribed) in a Record clear (to those who can read).

وَعِنْدَهٗ مَفَاتِحُ الْغَيْبِ لَا يَعْلَمُهَآ اِلَّا هُوَ ۗ وَيَعْلَمُ مَا فِي الْبَرِّ وَالْبَحْرِ ۗ وَمَا تَسْقُطُ مِنْ وَّرَقَةٍ اِلَّا يَعْلَمُهَا وَلَا حَبَّةٍ فِيْ ظُلُمٰتِ الْاَرْضِ وَلَا رَطْبٍ وَّلَا يَابِسٍ اِلَّا فِيْ كِتٰبٍ مُّبِيْنٍ ۞

60. It is He Who doth take your souls by night, and hath knowledge of all that ye have done by day: by day doth He raise you up again; that a term appointed be fulfilled; in the end unto Him will be your return; then will He show you the truth of all that ye did.

61. He is Irresistibly, supreme over His servants and He sets guardians over you. At length, when death approaches one of you, Our angels take his soul, and they never fail in their duty.

62. Then are they returned unto Allah, their True Protector, surely His is the Command, and He is the Swiftest in taking account.

63. Say: "Who is it that delivereth you from the dark recesses of land and sea, when ye call upon Him in humility and in secret: 'If He only delivers us from these (dangers), (we vow) we shall truly show our gratitude'.?"

64. Say: "It is Allah That delivereth you from these and all (other) distres-ses: and yet ye worship false gods!"

65. Say: "He hath power to send calamities on you, from above and below, or to cover you with confusion in party strife, giving you a taste of mutual vengeance—each from the other". See how We explain the Signs in diverse ways; that they may understand.

66. But thy people reject this, though it is the Truth. Say: "Not mine is the responsibility for arranging your affairs;

67. For every Prophecy is a limit of time, and soon shall ye know it."

68. When thou seest men engaged in vain discourse about Our Signs, turn away from them unless they turn to a different theme. If Satan ever makes thee forget, then after

recollection, sit not thou in the company of those who do wrong.

69.   On their account no responsibility falls on the righteous, but (their duty) is to remind them, that they may (learn to) fear Allah.

70.   Leave alone those who take their religion to be mere play and amusement, and are deceived by the life of this world. But continue to admonish them with it (Al-Qur-ān) lest a soul is caught in its own ruin by its own action: it will find for itself no protector or intercessor except Allah: if it offered every ransom, (or reparation), none will be accepted: such is (the end of) those who deliver themselves to ruin by their own acts: they will have for drink (only) boiling water, and for punishment one most grievous: for they persisted in rejecting Allah.

71.   Say: "Shall we call on others besides Allah,—things that can do us neither good nor harm,—and turn on our heels after receiving guidance from Allah?—like one whom the Satans have made into a fool, wandering bewildered through the earth, his friends calling 'Come to us', (vainly) guiding him to the Path." Say: "Allah's guidance is the (only) guidance, and we have been directed to submit ourselves to the Lord of the worlds;—

72.   "To establish regular prayers and to fear Allah: for it is to Him that we shall be gathered together."

73.   It is He Who created the heavens and the earth with truth: the day He saith, "Be," behold! it is. His Word is the Truth. His will be the dominion the day the trumpet will be blown. He knoweth the Unseen as well as that which is Open. For He is the Wise, well acquainted (with all things).

74.   Lo! Abraham said to his father Āzar: "Takest thou idols for gods? For I see thee and thy people in manifest error."

75. So also did We show Abraham the kingdom of the heavens and the earth, that he might have certitude.

76. When the night covered him over, he saw a star: he said: "This is my Lord." But when it set, he said. "I love not those that set."

77. When he saw the moon rising in splendour, He said: "This is my Lord." But when the moon set, he said: "Unless my Lord guide me, I shall surely be among those who go astray."

78. When he saw the sun rising (in splendour,) he said: "This is my Lord; this is the greatest (of all)." But when the sun set, he said: "O my people! I am indeed free from your (guilt) of giving partners to Allah."

79. "For me, I have set my face, firmly and truly, towards Him Who created the heavens and the earth, and never shall I give partners to Allah."

80. His people disputed with him. He said: "(Come) ye to dispute with me, about Allah, when He (Himself) hath guided me? I fear not (the beings) ye associate with Allah: unless my Lord willeth, (nothing can happen), my Lord comprehendeth in His knowledge all things. Will ye not (yourselves) be admonished?

81. "How should I fear (the beings) ye associate with Allah, when ye fear not to give partners to Allah without any warrant having been given to you? Which of (us) two parties hath more right to security? (tell me) if ye know.

82. "It is those who believe and mix not their beliefs with wrong—that are (truly) in security, for they are on (right) guidance."

83. That was Our argument which We gave to Abraham (to use) against his people: We raise whom We will, degree after degree: for thy Lord is full of wisdom and knowledge.

84. We gave him Isaac and Jacob: all

(three) We guided: and before him, We guided Noah, and among his progeny, David, Solomon, Job, Joseph, Moses, and Aaron: thus do We reward those who do good:

85. And Zakariya and John, and Jesus and Elias: all in the ranks of the Righteous:

86. And Isma'il and Elisha, and Jonas, and Lot: and to all We gave favour above the nations:

87. (To them) and to their fathers, and progeny and brethren: We chose them, and We guided them to a straight Way.

88. This is the Guidance of Allah: He giveth that guidance to whom He pleaseth, of His servants if they were to join other gods with Him, all that they did would be vain for them.

89. These were the men to whom We gave the Book, and Judgement, and Prophethood: if these (their descendants) reject them, behold! We shall entrust their charge to a new People who reject them not.

90. Those were the (prophets) who received Allah's guidance. Follow the guidance they received; say: "No reward for this do I ask of you: this is but a Reminder to the nations.

91. No just estimate of Allah do they make when they say: "Nothing doth Allah send down to man (by way of revelation)": say: "Who then sent down the Book which Moses brought?—a light and guidance to man: but ye make it into (separate) sheets for show, while ye conceal much (of its contents): therein were ye taught that which ye knew not—neither ye nor your fathers." Say: "Allah (sent it down)": then leave them to plunge in vain discourse and trifling.

92. And this is a Book which We have sent down, bringing blessings, and confirming (the revelations) which came before it: that

thou mayest warn the Mother of Cities and all around her. Those who believe in the Hereafter believe in this (Book), and they are constant in guarding their Prayers.

93. Who can be more wicked than one who inventeth a lie against Allah, or saith, "I have received inspiration," when he hath received none, or (again) who saith, "I can reveal the like of what Allah hath revealed"? If thou couldst but see how the wicked (do fare) in the agonies of death!—the angels stretch forth their hands, (saying), "Yield up your souls: this day shall ye receive your reward,—a chastisement of disgrace, for that ye used to tell lies against Allah, and scornfully to reject of His Signs!"

94. "And behold! ye come to Us bare and alone as We created you for the first time: ye have left behind you all (the favours) which We bestowed on you: We see not with you your intercessors whom ye thought to be partners in your affairs: so now all relations between you have been cut off, and your (pet) fancies have left you in the lurch!

95. It is Allah Who causeth the seed-grain and the date-stone to split and sprout. He causeth the living to issue from the dead. And He is the One to cause the dead to issue from the living. That is Allah: then how are ye deluded away from the truth?

96. He it is that cleaveth the day-break (from the dark): He makes the night for rest and tranquillity, and the sun and moon for the reckoning (of time): such is the judgment and ordering of (Him), the Exalted in Power, the Omniscient.

97. It is He Who maketh the stars (as beacons) for you, that ye may guide yourselves, with their help, through the dark spaces of land and sea: We detail Our Signs for people who know.

98. It is He Who hath produced you from a single soul: then there is a resting place and a repository: We detail Our signs for people who understand.

99. It is He Who sendeth down rain from the skies: with it We produce vegetation of all kinds: from some We produce green (crops), out of which we produce, close-compounded grain out of the date-palm and its sheaths (or spathes) (come) clusters of dates hanging low and near: and (then there are) gardens of grapes, and olives, and pomegranates, each similar (in kind) yet different (in variety): when they begin to bear fruit, feast your eyes with the fruit and the ripeness thereof. Behold! in these things there are Signs for people who believe.

100. Yet they make the Jinns equals with Allah, though Allah did create the Jinns; and they falsely, having no knowledge, attribute to Him sons and daughters, praise and glory be to Him! (for He is) above what they attribute to Him!

101. Wonderful Originator of the heavens and the earth: how can He have a son when He hath no consort? He created all things, and He hath full knowledge of all things.

102. That is Allah, your Lord! there is no god but He, the Creator of all things: then worship ye Him: and He hath power to dispose of all affairs.

103. No vision can grasp Him, but His grasp is over all vision; He is subtle well-aware.

104. "Now have come to you, from your Lord proofs (to open your eyes): if any will see, it will be for (the good of) his own soul: if any will be blind, it will be to his own (Harm): I am not (here) to watch over your doings."

105. Thus do We explain the Signs by various (ways) that they may say, "Thou hast learnt this (from somebody), and that We may make the matter clear to those who know.

106. Follow what thou art taught by inspiration from thy Lord: there is no

وَهُوَ الَّذِى أَنْزَلَ مِنَ السَّمَاءِ مَاءً ۖ
فَأَخْرَجْنَا بِهِ نَبَاتَ كُلِّ شَيْءٍ فَأَخْرَجْنَا
مِنْهُ خَضِرًا نُخْرِجُ مِنْهُ حَبًّا مُّتَرَاكِبًا ۚ
وَمِنَ النَّخْلِ مِنْ طَلْعِهَا قِنْوَانٌ دَانِيَةٌ
وَّجَنّٰتٍ مِّنْ أَعْنَابٍ وَّالزَّيْتُونَ وَ
الرُّمَّانَ مُشْتَبِهًا وَّغَيْرَ مُتَشَابِهٍ ۗ
اُنْظُرُوا إِلٰى ثَمَرِهِ إِذَا أَثْمَرَ وَيَنْعِهِ ۚ
إِنَّ فِى ذٰلِكُمْ لَآيٰتٍ لِّقَوْمٍ
يُؤْمِنُونَ ۝

وَجَعَلُوا لِلّٰهِ شُرَكَاءَ الْجِنَّ وَخَلَقَهُمْ
وَخَرَقُوا لَهُ بَنِينَ وَبَنٰتٍ بِغَيْرِ عِلْمٍ ۚ
سُبْحٰنَهُ وَتَعٰلٰى عَمَّا يَصِفُونَ ۝

بَدِيعُ السَّمٰوٰتِ وَالْأَرْضِ ۖ أَنّٰى يَكُونُ
لَهُ وَلَدٌ وَّلَمْ تَكُنْ لَّهُ صَاحِبَةٌ ۗ وَخَلَقَ
كُلَّ شَيْءٍ ۖ وَهُوَ بِكُلِّ شَيْءٍ عَلِيمٌ ۝

ذٰلِكُمُ اللّٰهُ رَبُّكُمْ ۖ لَآ إِلٰهَ إِلَّا هُوَ ۖ
خَالِقُ كُلِّ شَيْءٍ فَاعْبُدُوهُ ۚ وَهُوَ
عَلٰى كُلِّ شَيْءٍ وَّكِيلٌ ۝

لَا تُدْرِكُهُ الْأَبْصَارُ ۖ وَهُوَ يُدْرِكُ
الْأَبْصَارَ ۖ وَهُوَ اللَّطِيفُ الْخَبِيرُ ۝

قَدْ جَاءَكُمْ بَصَائِرُ مِنْ رَّبِّكُمْ ۖ فَمَنْ
أَبْصَرَ فَلِنَفْسِهِ ۖ وَمَنْ عَمِيَ فَعَلَيْهَا ۚ وَ
مَا أَنَا عَلَيْكُمْ بِحَفِيظٍ ۝

وَكَذٰلِكَ نُصَرِّفُ الْآيٰتِ وَ
لِيَقُولُوا دَرَسْتَ وَلِنُبَيِّنَهُ لِقَوْمٍ
يَّعْلَمُونَ ۝

اِتَّبِعْ مَا أُوحِىَ إِلَيْكَ مِنْ رَّبِّكَ ۖ لَآ

god but He: and turn aside from those Who join gods with Allah.

107. If it had been Allah's Will, they would not have taken false gods: but We made thee not one to watch over their doings, nor art thou set over them to dispose of their affairs.

108. Revile not ye those whom they call upon besides Allah, lest they out of spite revile Allah in their ignorance. Thus have We made alluring to each people its own doings. In the end will they return to their Lord and He shall then tell them the truth of all that they did.

109. They swear their strongest oaths by Allah, that if a (special) Sign came to them, by it they would believe. Say: "Certainly (all) Signs are in the power of Allah: but what will make you (Muslims) realise that (even) if (special) Signs came, they will not believe."?

110. We (too) shall turn to (confusion) their hearts and their eyes, even as they refused to believe in this in the first instance: We shall leave them in their trespasses, to (stumble blindly)

111. Even if We did send unto them angels, and the dead did speak unto them, and We gathered together all things before their very eyes, they are not the ones to believe, unless it is in Allah's Plan. But most of them ignore (the truth).

112. Likewise did We make for every Messenger an enemy,— satans among men and Jinns, inspiring each other with flowery discourses by way of deception. If thy Lord had so willed, they would not have done it: so leave them and what they forge.

113. To such (deceit) let the hearts of those incline, who have no faith in the Hereafter:

and let them delight in it, and let them earn from it what they may.

114. Say: "Shall I seek for judge other than Allah?— When He it is Who hath sent unto you the Book, explained in detail." They know full well, to whom We have given the Book, that it hath been sent down from thy Lord in truth. Never be then of those who doubt.

115. The Word of thy Lord doth find its fulfilment in truth and in justice: none can change His Words: for He is the one Who heareth and knoweth all.

116. Wert thou to follow the common run of those on earth, they will lead thee away from the Way of Allah. They follow nothing but conjecture: they do nothing but lie.

117. Thy Lord knoweth best who strayeth from His Way: He knoweth best those who are rightly guided.

118. So eat of (meats) on which Allah's name hath been prono-unced, if ye have faith in His Signs.

119. Why should ye not eat of (meats) on which Allah's name hath been pronounced, when He hath explained to you in detail what is forbidden to you—except under compulsion of necessity? But many do mislead (men) by low desires without knowledge. Thy Lord knoweth best those who transgress.

120. Eschew all sin, open or secret: those who earn sin will get due recompense for their "earnings."

121. Eat not of (meats) on which Allah's name hath not been pronounced: that would be impiety. But the satans ever inspire their

friends to contend with you if ye were to obey them, ye would indeed be Pagans.

122. Can he who was dead, to whom We gave life, and a Light whereby he can walk amongst men, be like him who is in the depths of darkness, from which he can never come out? Thus to those without Faith their own deeds seem pleasing.

123. Thus have We placed leaders in every town, its wicked men, to plot (and burrow) therein: but they only plot against their own souls, and they perceive it not.

124. When there comes to them a Sign (from Allah), they say: "We shall not believe until we receive one (exactly) like those received by Allah's messengers." Allah knoweth best where to Place His mission. Soon will the wicked be overtaken by humiliation before Allah, and a severe chastisement, for all their plots.

125. Those whom Allah willeth to guide,— He openeth their breast to Islam; those whom He willeth to leave straying,— He maketh their breast close and constricted, as if they had to climb up to the skies: thus doth Allah lay abomination on those who refuse to believe.

126. This is the Way of thy Lord, leading straight: We have detailed the Signs for those who receive admonition.

127. For them will be a Home of Peace with their Lord: He will be their Friend, because they practised (righteousness).

128. On the day when He will gather them all together, (and say): "O ye assembly of Jinns much (toll) did ye take of men." Their

friends amongst men will say: "Our Lord! we made profit from each other: but (alas!) we reached our term—which Thou didst appoint for us." He will say: "The Fire be your dwelling-place: you will dwell therein for ever, except as Allah willeth. For thy Lord is full of wisdom and knowledge.

129. Thus do We make the wrong-doers turn to each other, because of what they earn.

130. "O ye assembly of Jinns and men! came there not unto you messengers from amongst you, setting forth unto you My Signs, and warning you of the meeting of this Day of yours?" They will say: "We bear witness against ourselves." It was the life of this world that deceived them. So against themselves will they bear witness that they rejected Faith.

131. (The messengers were sent) thus, for thy Lord would not destroy the towns unjustly whilst their occupants were unwarned.

132. To all are degrees (or ranks) according to their deeds: for thy Lord is not unmindful of anything that they do.

133. Thy Lord is Self-sufficient, full of Mercy: if it were His Will, He could destroy you, and in your place appoint whom He will as your successors, even as He raised you up from the posterity of other people.

134. All that hath been promised unto you will come to pass: nor can ye frustrate it (in the least bit).

135. Say: "O my people! do whatever ye can: I will do (my part): soon will ye know who it is whose end will be (best) in the Hereafter: certain it is that the wrong-doers will not prosper."

136. Out of what Allah hath produced in abundance in tilth and in cattle, they assigned Him a share: they say, according

to their fancies: "This is for Allah, and this"—for Our "partners"! But the share of their "partners" reacheth not Allah, whilst the share of Allah reacheth their "partners"! Evil (and unjust) is their judgment.

137. Even so, in the eyes of most of the Pagans, their "partners" made alluring the slaughter of their children, in order to lead them to their own destruction, and cause confusion in their religion if Allah had willed. they would not have done so: but leave alone them and what they forged.

138. And they say that such and such cattle and crops are forbidden, and none should eat of them except those whom—so they say—We wish; further, there are cattle forbidden to yoke or burden, and cattle on which, (at slaughter) the name of Allah is not pronounced:—forging a lie against Allah's name: soon will He requite them for what they forged.

139. They say: "What is in the wombs of such and such cattle is specially reserved (for food) for our men, and forbidden to our women; but if it is still-born, then all have shares therein. For their (false) attribution (of superstitions to Allah), He will soon punish them: for He is full of wisdom and knowledge.

140. Lost are those who slay their children, from folly, without knowledge, and forbid food which Allah hath provided for them, forging (lies) against Allah, they have indeed gone astray and heeded no guidance.

141. It is He who produceth gardens, with trellises and without. and dates, and tilth with produce of all kinds, and olives and pomegranates, similar (in kind) and different (in variety): eat of their fruit in their season, but render the dues that are proper on the day that the harvest is gathered. But waste not by excess: for Allah loveth not the

wasters.

142. Of the cattle are some for burden and some for meat: eat what Allah hath provided for you, and follow not the footsteps of Satan: for he is to you an avowed enemy.

143. (Take) eight (head of cattle) in (four) pairs: of sheep a pair; and of goats a pair, say, hath He forbidden the two males, or the two females, or (the young) which the wombs of the two females enclose? Tell me with knowledge if ye are truthful:

144. Of camels a pair, and of oxen a pair; say, hath He forbidden the two males, or the two females, or (the young) which the wombs of the two females enclose?—Were ye present when Allah ordered you such a thing? But who doth more wrong than one who invents a lie against Allah, to lead astray men without knowledge? For Allah guideth not people who do wrong.

145. Say: "I find not in the Message received by me by inspiration any (meat) forbidden to be eaten by one who wishes to eat it, unless it be dead meat, or blood poured forth, or the flesh of swine,—for it is an abomination—or what is impious, (meat) on which a name has been invoked, other than Allah's." But (even so), if a person is forced by necessity, without wilful disobedience, nor transgressing due limits,—thy Lord is Oft-Forgiving, Most Merciful.

146. For those who followed the Jewish Law, We forbade every (animal) with undivided hoof, and We forbade them the fat of the ox and the sheep, except what adheres to their backs or their entrails, or is mixed up with a bone: this in recompense for their wilful disobedience: for We are True (in Our ordinances).

147. If they accuse thee of falsehood, say: "Your Lord is full of mercy all-embracing; but from people in guilt never will His wrath be turned back.

148. Those who give partners (to Allah) will say: "If Allah had wished, we should not have given partners to Him, nor would our fathers; nor should we have had any forbidden thing." So did their ancestors argue falsely, until they tasted of Our wrath. Say: "Have ye any (certain) knowledge? If so, produce it before us. Ye follow nothing but conjecture: ye do nothing but lie."

149. Say: "With Allah is the argument that reaches home: if it had been His Will. He could indeed have guided you all."

150. Say: "Bring forward your witnesses to prove that Allah did forbid so and so." If they bring such witnesses, be not thou amongst them: nor follow thou the vain desires of such as treat Our Signs as falsehoods, and such as believe not in the Hereafter: for they hold others as equal with their Guardian Lord.

151. Say: "Come, I will rehearse what Allah hath (really) prohibited you from": join not anything with Him: Be good to your parents; kill not your children on a plea of want;— We provide sustenance for you and for them;—come not nigh to indecent deeds, whether open or secret; take not life, which Allah hath made sacred, except by way of justice and law: thus doth He command you, that ye may learn wisdom.

152. And come not nigh to the orphan's property, except to improve it, until he attain the age of full strength; give measure and weight with (full) justice;—no burden do

We place on any soul, but that which it can bear;— whenever ye speak, speak justly, even if a near relative is concerned; and fulfil the Covenant of Allah: thus doth He command you, that ye may remember.

153. Verily, this is My Way leading straight: follow it: follow not (other) paths: they will scatter you about from His Path: thus doth He command you, that ye may be righteous.

154. Moreover, We gave Moses the Book, completing (our favour) to those who would do right, and explaining all things in detail,— and a guide and a mercy, that they might believe in the meeting with their Lord.

155. And this is a Book which We have revealed as a blessing: so follow it and be righteous, that ye may receive mercy:

156. Lest ye should say: "The Book was sent down to two Peoples before us, and for our part, we remained unacquainted with all that they learned by assiduous study;"

157. Or lest ye should say: "If the Book had only been sent down to us, we should have followed its guidance better than they." Now then hath come unto you a Clear (Sign) from your Lord,—and a guide and a mercy: then who could do more wrong than one who rejecteth Allah's Signs, and turneth away therefrom? In good time shall We requite those who turn away from Our Signs, with a dreadful chastisement for their turning away.

158. Are they waiting to see if the angels come to them, or thy Lord (Himself), or certain of the Signs of thy Lord! the day that certain of the Signs of the Lord do come, no good will it do to a soul to believe then, if it believed not before nor earned righteousness through its Faith.

SÛRA-7
AL-A'RĀF
(INTRODUCTION)

This Sûra is closely connected, both chronologically and in respect of the argument, with the previous Sûra. But it expounds the doctrine of revelation and man's spiritual history by illustrations from Adam onwards, through various Prophets, and the details of Moses's struggles, to the time of the Apostle Muḥammad, in whom Allah's revelation is completed.

Say: "Wait ye: we too are waiting"

159. As for those who divide their religion and break up into sects, thou hast no part in them in the least: their affair is with Allah: He will in the end tell them the truth of all that they did.

160. He that doeth good shall have ten times as much to his credit: he that doeth evil shall only be recompensed according to his evil: no wrong shall be done unto them.

161. Say: "Verily, my Lord hath guided me to a Way that is straight,—a religion of right,—the Path (trod) by Abraham the true in faith, and he (certainly) joined not gods with Allah."

162. Say: "Truly, my prayer and my service of sacrifice, my life and my death, are (all) for Allah, the Cherisher of the Worlds:

163. No partner hath He: this am I commanded, and I am the first of those who submit to His Will.

164. Say: "Shall I seek for (my) Lord other than Allah. When He is the Cherisher of all things (that exist)? Every soul draws the meed of its acts on none but itself: no bearer of burdens can bear the burden of another. Your return in the end is towards Allah: He will tell you the truth of the things wherein ye disputed."

165. It is He Who hath made you the inheritors of the earth: He hath raised you in ranks, some above others: that He may try you in the gifts He hath given you: for thy Lord is quick in punishment: yet He is indeed Oft-Forgiving Most Merciful.

Al-A'ráf. or The Heights.

In the name of Allah, Most Gracious, Most Merciful.

1. Alif, Lam, Mim, Sad.

2. A Book revealed unto thee,—so let thy heart be oppressed no more by any difficulty on that account,—that with it thou

mightest warn (the erring) and a reminder
to the Believers.

3.　Follow (O men!) the revelation given
unto you from your Lord, and follow not, as
friends or protectors, other than Him. Little
it is ye remember of admonition.

4.　How many towns have We destroyed
(for their sins)? Our punishment took them
on a sudden by night or while they slept for
their afternoon rest.

5.　When (thus) Our punishment took
them, no cry did they utter but this: "Indeed
we did wrong."

6.　Then shall we question those to whom
Our Message was sent and those by whom
we sent it.

7.　And verily, We shall recount their whole
story with knowledge, for We were never
absent (at any time or place).

8.　The balance that day will be true (to a
nicety): those whose scale (of good) will be
heavy, will prosper:

9.　Those whose scale will be light, will
find their souls in perdition, for that they
wrongfully treated Our Signs.

10.　It is We Who have placed you with
authority on earth, and provided you therein
with means for the fulfilment of your life:
small are the thanks that ye give!

11.　It is We Who created you and gave you
shape: then We bade the angels prostrate to
Adam, and they prostrated, not so Iblis; he
refused to be of those who prostrate.

12.　(Allah) said: "What prevented thee from
prostrating when I commanded thee?" He
said: "I am better than he: Thou didst create
me from fire, and him from clay".

13.　(Allah) said: "Get thee down from it: it
is not for thee to be arrogant here: get out,
for thou art of the meanest (of creatures)."

14. He said: "Give me respite till the day they are raised up."

قَالَ أَنْظِرْنِيْ إِلَىٰ يَوْمِ يُبْعَثُوْنَ ۝

15. (Allah) said: "Be thou among those who have respite."

قَالَ إِنَّكَ مِنَ الْمُنْظَرِيْنَ ۝

16. He said: "Because thou hast thrown me out (of the Way), lo! I will lie in wait for them on Thy Straight Way:

قَالَ فَبِمَآ أَغْوَيْتَنِيْ لَأَقْعُدَنَّ لَهُمْ صِرَاطَكَ الْمُسْتَقِيْمَ ۝

17. "Then will I assault them from before them and behind them, from their right and their left: nor wilt Thou find, in most of them, gratitude (for Thy mercies)."

ثُمَّ لَآتِيَنَّهُمْ مِّنْ بَيْنِ أَيْدِيْهِمْ وَمِنْ خَلْفِهِمْ وَعَنْ أَيْمَانِهِمْ وَعَنْ شَمَآئِلِهِمْ وَلَا تَجِدُ أَكْثَرَهُمْ شَاكِرِيْنَ ۝

18. (Allah) said: "Get out from this, despised and expelled. If any of them follow thee,—hell will I fill with you all.

قَالَ اخْرُجْ مِنْهَا مَذْءُوْمًا مَّدْحُوْرًا لَمَنْ تَبِعَكَ مِنْهُمْ لَأَمْلَأَنَّ جَهَنَّمَ مِنْكُمْ أَجْمَعِيْنَ ۝

19. "O Adam! dwell thou and thy wife in the Garden, and enjoy (its good things) as ye wish: but approach not this tree, lest you become of the unjust."

وَيَا آدَمُ اسْكُنْ أَنْتَ وَزَوْجُكَ الْجَنَّةَ فَكُلَا مِنْ حَيْثُ شِئْتُمَا وَلَا تَقْرَبَا هٰذِهِ الشَّجَرَةَ فَتَكُوْنَا مِنَ الظّٰلِمِيْنَ ۝

20. Then began Satan to whisper suggestions to them, in order to reveal to them their shame that was hidden from them (before): he said: "Your Lord only forbade you this tree, lest ye should become angels or such beings as live for ever."

فَوَسْوَسَ لَهُمَا الشَّيْطٰنُ لِيُبْدِيَ لَهُمَا مَا وُوْرِيَ عَنْهُمَا مِنْ سَوْآتِهِمَا وَقَالَ مَا نَهٰكُمَا رَبُّكُمَا عَنْ هٰذِهِ الشَّجَرَةِ إِلَّآ أَنْ تَكُوْنَا مَلَكَيْنِ أَوْ تَكُوْنَا مِنَ الْخٰلِدِيْنَ ۝

21. And he swore to them both, that he was their sincere adviser.

وَقَاسَمَهُمَآ إِنِّيْ لَكُمَا لَمِنَ النّٰصِحِيْنَ ۝

22. So by deceit he brought about their fall: when they tasted of the tree, their shameful parts became manifest to them, and they began to sew together the leaves of the Garden over their bodies. And their Lord called unto them: "Did I not forbid you that tree, and tell you that Satan was an avowed enemy unto you?"

فَدَلّٰهُمَا بِغُرُوْرٍ فَلَمَّا ذَاقَا الشَّجَرَةَ بَدَتْ لَهُمَا سَوْآتُهُمَا وَطَفِقَا يَخْصِفٰنِ عَلَيْهِمَا مِنْ وَرَقِ الْجَنَّةِ وَنَادٰهُمَا رَبُّهُمَآ أَلَمْ أَنْهَكُمَا عَنْ تِلْكُمَا الشَّجَرَةِ وَأَقُلْ لَّكُمَآ إِنَّ الشَّيْطٰنَ لَكُمَا عَدُوٌّ مُّبِيْنٌ ۝

23. They said: "Our Lord we have wronged our own souls: if Thou for-give us not and bestow not upon us Thy Mercy, we shall certainly be lost.

قَالَا رَبَّنَا ظَلَمْنَآ أَنْفُسَنَا وَإِنْ لَّمْ تَغْفِرْ لَنَا وَتَرْحَمْنَا لَنَكُوْنَنَّ مِنَ الْخٰسِرِيْنَ ۝

24. (Allah) said: "Get ye down, with enmity between yourselves. On earth will be your dwelling-place and your means of livelihood,—for a time."

قَالَ اهْبِطُوْا بَعْضُكُمْ لِبَعْضٍ عَدُوٌّ وَلَكُمْ فِي الْأَرْضِ مُسْتَقَرٌّ وَّمَتَاعٌ إِلَىٰ حِيْنٍ ۝

25. He said: "Therein shall ye live, and therein shall ye die: but from it shall ye be taken out (at last)."

26. O ye Children of Adam! We have bestowed raiment upon you to cover your shame, as well as to be an adornment to you, but the raiment of righteousness— that is the best. Such are among the Signs of Allah, that they may receive admonition!

27. O ye Children of Adam! let not Satan seduce you, in the same manner as he got your parents out of the Garden, stripping them of their raiment, to expose their shame: for he and his tribe see you from a position where ye cannot see them: We made the Satans friends (only) to those without Faith.

28. When they commit an indecency, they say: "We found our fathers doing so"; and "Allah commanded us thus": Say: "Nay, Allah never command what is Indecent: do ye say of Allah what ye know not?

29. Say: "My Lord hath comman-ded justice; and that ye set your whole selves (to Him) at every time and place of prayer, and call upon Him, making your devotion sincere such as He created you in the beginning, so shall ye return."

30. Some He hath guided: others have deserved the loss of their way; in that they took the Satans in preference to Allah, for their friends and protectors, and think that they receive guidance.

31. O Children of Adam! wear your beautiful apparel at every time and place of prayer: eat and drink: but waste not by excess, for Allah loveth not the wasters.

32. Say: Who hath forbidden the beautiful (gifts) of Allah, which He hath produced for His servants, and the things, clean and pure, (which He hath provided) for sustenance? say: They are, in the life of

this world, for those who believe, (and)
purely for them on the Day of Judgment.
Thus do We explain the Signs in detail for
those who know.

33. Say: The things that my Lord hath
indeed forbidden are: indecent deeds,
whether open or secret; sins and trespasses
against truth or reason; assigning of
partners to Allah, for which He hath given
no authority; and saying things about Allah
of which ye have no knowledge.

34. To every People is a term appointed:
when their term is reached, not an hour can
they cause delay, nor (an hour) can they
advance (it in anticipation).

35. O ye Children of Adam! whenever
there come to you Messengers from
amongst you, rehearsing My Signs unto
you,—those who are righteous and mend
(their lives),— on them shall be no fear nor
shall they grieve.

36. But those who reject Our Signs and
treat them with arrogance,—they are Companions of the Fire, to dwell therein (for ever).

37. Who is more unjust than one who forges
a lie against Allah or rejects His Signs? For
such, their portion appointed must reach
them from the Book (of Decrees): until, when
Our messengers (of death) arrive and take
their souls, they say: "Where are the things
that ye used to invoke besides Allah?" They
will reply, "They have left us in the lurch,"
and they will bear witness against
themselves, that they had rejected Allah.

38. He will say: "Enter ye in the company
of the Peoples who passed away before
you—men and Jinns,—into the Fire. Every
time a new People enters, it curses its sister-
People (that went before), until they follow
each other, all into the Fire. Saith the last
about the first: "Our Lord! it is these that
misled us: so give them a double punishment
in the Fire." He will say: "Doubled for all":

but this ye do not know.

39. Then the first will say to the last: "See then! no advantage have ye over us; so taste ye of the Chastisement for all that ye did!"

40. To those who reject Our Signs and treat them with arrogance, no opening will there be of the gates of heaven, nor will they enter the Garden, until the camel can pass through the eye of the needle: such is Our reward for those in sin.

41. For them there is hell, as a couch (below) and folds and folds of covering above: such is Our requital of those who do wrong.

42. But those who believe and work righteousness,—no burden do We place on any soul, but that which it can bear,—they will be Companions of the Garden, therein to dwell (for ever).

43. And We shall remove from their hearts any rancour; beneath them will be rivers flowing;—and they shall say: "Praise be to Allah, Who hath guided us to this (felicity): never could we have found guidance, had it not been for the guidance of Allah: indeed it was the truth that the Messengers of our Lord brought unto us." And they shall hear the cry: "Behold! the Garden before you! Ye have been made its inheritors, for your deeds (of righteousness)."

44. The Companions of the Garden will call out to the Companions of the Fire: "We have indeed found the promises of our Lord to us true have you also found your Lord's promises true?" They shall say, "Yes": but a Crier shall proclaim between them: "The curse of Allah is on the wrong-doers;—

45. "Those who would hinder (men) from the path of Allah desiring to make something crooked: they were those who denied the Hereafter."

46. Between them shall be a veil, and on the Heights will be men who would know everyone by his marks: they will call out to

the Companions of the Garden, "Peace be upon you" they have not entered it, but they still hoped to (enter it).

47. When their eyes shall be turned towards the Companions of the Fire, they will say: "Our Lord! send us not to the company of the wrong-doers".

48. The men on the Heights will call to certain men whom they will know from their marks, saying "Of what profit to you were your hoards and your arrogant ways?

49. "Behold! are these not the men whom you swore that Allah with His Mercy would never bless? Enter ye the Garden: no fear shall be on you, nor shall ye grieve."

50. The Companions of the Fire will call to the Companions of the Garden: "Pour down to us water or anything that Allah doth provide for your sustenance." They will say: "Both these things hath Allah for-bidden to those who rejected Him;—

51. "Such as took their religion to be mere amusement and play, and were deceived by the life of the world." That day shall We forget them as they forgot the meeting of this day of theirs, and as they were wont to reject Our Signs.

52. For We had certainly sent unto them a Book, based on knowledge, which We explained in detail,—a guide and a mercy to all who believe.

53. Are they waiting for its fulfilment? On the day when it is fulfilled those who have forgotten it before will say: "The Messengers of our Lord did indeed bring true (tidings). Have we no intercessors now to intercede on our behalf? Or could we be sent back? Then should we behave differently from our behaviour in the past." In fact they will have lost their souls, and the things they

forged will leave them in the lurch.

54. Your Guardian Lord is Allah, Who created the heavens and the earth in six Days, then He settled Himself on the Throne: He draweth the night as a veil o'er the day, each seeking the other in rapid succession: and the sun, the moon, and the stars, (all) are subservient by His Command. Verily, His are the creation and the Command blessed be Allah, the Cherisher and Sustainer of the Worlds!

55. Call on your Lord with humility and in private: for Allah loveth not those who trespass beyond bounds.

56. Do not mischief on the earth, after it hath been set in order, but call on Him with fear and longing (in your hearts): for the Mercy of Allah is (always) near to those who do good.

57. It is He Who sendeth the Winds like heralds of glad tidings, going before His Mercy: when they have carried the heavy-laden clouds. We drive them to a land that is dead, make rain to descend thereon, and produce every kind of harvest therewith: thus shall We raise up the dead: perchance ye may remember.

58. From the land that is clean and good, by the Will of its Cherisher, springs up produce, (rich) after its kind: but from the land that is bad, springs up nothing but that which is scanty thus do we explain the Signs by various (symbols) to those who are grateful.

59. We sent Noah to his people. He said: "O my people ! worship Allah! ye have no other god but Him. I fear for you the Punishment of a dreadful Day!"

60. The leaders of his people Said: "Ah! we see thee in evident error."

61. He said: "O my people! there is no error in me: on the contrary I am a messenger from the Lord and Cherisher of the Worlds!"

62. "I but convey to you" the Message of my Lord. Sincere is my advice to you, and I know from Allah something that ye know not.

63. "Do ye wonder that there hath come to you a reminder from your Lord, through a man of your own people, to warn you,—so that ye may fear Allah and haply receive His Mercy?"

64. But they rejected him, and We delivered him, and those with him, in the Ark: but We overwhelmed in the Flood those who rejected Our Signs, they were indeed a blind people!

65. To the 'Ād people, (We sent) Hūd, one of their (own) brethren: he said: "O my people! worship Allah! ye have no other god but Him. Will ye not fear (Allah)?"

66. The leaders of the unbelievers among his people said: "Ah! we see thou art in folly!" and "We think thou art a liar!"

67. He said: "O my people! there is no folly in me" but (I am) a messenger from the Lord and Cherisher of the Worlds!

68. "I but convey to you the messages of my Lord: I am to you a sincere and trustworthy adviser".

69. "Do ye wonder that there hath come to you a message from your Lord through a man of your own people, to warn you? Call in remembrance that He made you inheritors after the people of Noah, and gave you a stature tall among the nations. Call in remembrance the benefits (ye have received) from Allah: that so ye may prosper."

70. They said: "Comest thou to us, that we may worship Allah alone, and give up that which our fathers used to worship bring us what thou threatenest us with, if so it be that thou tellest the truth!"

71. He said: "Punishment and wrath have already come upon you from your Lord: dispute ye with me over names which ye have devised—ye and your fathers,—without authority from Allah? Then wait: I am amongst you, also waiting."

قَالَ قَدۡ وَقَعَ عَلَيۡكُمۡ مِّنۡ رَّبِّكُمۡ رِجۡسٌ وَّغَضَبٌ ۖ أَتُجَادِلُونَنِي فِىٓ أَسۡمَآءٍ سَمَّيۡتُمُوهَآ أَنۡتُمۡ وَءَابَآؤُكُمۡ مَّا نَزَّلَ اللَّهُ بِهَا مِنۡ سُلۡطَٰنٍ ۚ فَانتَظِرُوٓاۡ إِنِّى مَعَكُم مِّنَ الۡمُنتَظِرِينَ ۝

72. We saved him and those who adhered to him, by Our Mercy and We cut off the roots of those who rejected Our Signs and did not believe.

فَأَنجَيۡنَٰهُ وَالَّذِينَ مَعَهُۥ بِرَحۡمَةٍ مِّنَّا وَقَطَعۡنَا دَابِرَ الَّذِينَ كَذَّبُواۡ بِـَٔايَٰتِنَا ۖ وَمَا كَانُواۡ مُؤۡمِنِينَ ۝

73. To the Thamūd people (We sent) Sālih, one of their own brethren: he said: "O my people! worship Allah; ye have no other god but Him. Now hath come unto you a clear (Sign) from your Lord! This she-camel of Allah is a Sign unto you: so leave her to graze in Allah's earth, and let her come to no harm, or ye shall be seized with a grievous punishment."

وَإِلَىٰ ثَمُودَ أَخَاهُمۡ صَٰلِحًا ۗ قَالَ يَٰقَوۡمِ اعۡبُدُواۡ اللَّهَ مَا لَكُم مِّنۡ إِلَٰهٍ غَيۡرُهُۥ ۖ قَدۡ جَآءَتۡكُم بَيِّنَةٌ مِّن رَّبِّكُمۡ ۖ هَٰذِهِۦ نَاقَةُ اللَّهِ لَكُمۡ ءَايَةً ۖ فَذَرُوهَا تَأۡكُلۡ فِىٓ أَرۡضِ اللَّهِ ۖ وَلَا تَمَسُّوهَا بِسُوٓءٍ فَيَأۡخُذَكُمۡ عَذَابٌ أَلِيمٌ ۝

74. "And remember how He made you inheritors After the 'Ād people and gave you habitations in the land: ye build for yourselves palaces and castles in (open) plains, and carve out homes in the mountains; so bring to remembrance the benefits (ye have received) from Allah, and refrain from evil and mischief on the earth."

وَاذۡكُرُوٓاۡ إِذۡ جَعَلَكُمۡ خُلَفَآءَ مِنۢ بَعۡدِ عَادٍ وَبَوَّأَكُمۡ فِى الۡأَرۡضِ تَتَّخِذُونَ مِن سُهُولِهَا قُصُورًا وَتَنۡحِتُونَ الۡجِبَالَ بُيُوتًا ۖ فَاذۡكُرُوٓاۡ ءَالَآءَ اللَّهِ وَلَا تَعۡثَوۡاۡ فِى الۡأَرۡضِ مُفۡسِدِينَ ۝

75. The leaders of the arrogant party among his people said to those who were reckoned powerless—those among them who believed: "Know ye indeed that Sālih is a messenger from his Lord?" They said: "We do indeed believe in the revelation which hath been sent through him."

قَالَ الۡمَلَأُ الَّذِينَ اسۡتَكۡبَرُواۡ مِن قَوۡمِهِۦ لِلَّذِينَ اسۡتُضۡعِفُواۡ لِمَنۡ ءَامَنَ مِنۡهُمۡ أَتَعۡلَمُونَ أَنَّ صَٰلِحًا مُّرۡسَلٌ مِّن رَّبِّهِۦ ۚ قَالُوٓاۡ إِنَّا بِمَآ أُرۡسِلَ بِهِۦ مُؤۡمِنُونَ ۝

76. The arrogant party said: "For our part, we reject what ye believe in."

قَالَ الَّذِينَ اسۡتَكۡبَرُوٓاۡ إِنَّا بِالَّذِىٓ ءَامَنتُم بِهِۦ كَٰفِرُونَ ۝

77. Then they ham-strung the she-camel, and insolently defied the order of their Lord, saying: "O Sālih! bring about thy threats, if

فَعَقَرُواۡ النَّاقَةَ وَعَتَوۡاۡ عَنۡ أَمۡرِ رَبِّهِمۡ وَقَالُواۡ يَٰصَٰلِحُ ائۡتِنَا بِمَا تَعِدُنَآ إِن كُنتَ

thou art a messenger (of Allah)!"

78. So the earthquake took them unawares, and they lay prostrate in their homes in the morning!

79. So Sālih left them, saying: "O my people! I did indeed convey to you the message for which I was sent by my Lord: I gave you good counsel, but ye love not good counsellors!"

80. We also (sent) Lût: he said to his people: "Do ye practise lewdness such as no people in creation (ever) committed before you?

81. "For ye practise your lusts on men in preference to women: ye are indeed a people transgressing beyond bounds".

82. And his people gave no answer but this: they said, "Drive them out of your city: these are indeed men who want to be clean and pure!"

83. But We saved him and his family, except his wife: she was of those who lagged behind

84. And we rained down on them a shower (of brimstone): then see what was the end of those who indulged in sin and crime!

85. To the Madyan people we sent Shu'aib, one of their own brethren: he said: "O my people! worship Allah; ye have no other god but Him. Now hath come unto you a clear (Sign) from your Lord! Give just measure and weight, nor withhold from the people the things that are their due; and do no mischief on the earth after it has been set in order: that will be best for you, if ye have Faith."

86. "And squat not on every road, breathing threats, hindering from the path of Allah those who believe in Him, and seek to make it crooked; but remember how ye were little,

were little, and He gave you increase. And see what was the end of those who did mischief.

87. "And if there is a party among you who believes in the Message with which I have been sent, and a party which does not believe, hold yourselves in patience until Allah doth decide between us: for He is the best to decide."

88. The leaders, the arrogant party among his people, said: "O Shu'aib! we shall certainly drive thee out of our city—(thee) and those who believe with thee; or else ye (thou and they) shall have to return to our religion." He said: "What! even though we do detest (them)?

89. "We should indeed forge a lie against Allah, if we returned to your religion after Allah hath rescued us therefrom; nor could we by any manner of means return thereto unless it be as in the will of Allah, our Lord. Our Lord comprehends all things in His knowledge in Allah is our trust. Our Lord ! Decide thou between us and our people in truth. for thou art the best to decide."

90. The leaders, the Unbelievers among his people, said: "If ye follow Shu'aib, be sure then ye are ruined!"

91. But the earthquake took them unawares, and they lay prostrate in their homes before the morning!

92. The men who rejected Shu'aib became as if they had never been in the homes where they had flourished: the men who rejected Shu'aib—it was they who were ruined!

93. So Shu'aib left them, saying: "O my people! i did indeed convey to you the Messages for which I was sent by my Lord: i gave you good counsel, but how shall I lament over a people who refuse to believe!"

94. Whenever We sent a prophet to a town, We took up its people in suffering and adversity, in order that they might call in humility.

وَمَآ أَرْسَلْنَا فِى قَرْيَةٍ مِّن نَّبِىٍّ إِلَّآ أَخَذْنَآ أَهْلَهَا بِٱلْبَأْسَآءِ وَٱلضَّرَّآءِ لَعَلَّهُمْ يَضَّرَّعُونَ ۝

95. Then We changed their suffering into prosperity, until they grew and multiplied, and began to say: "Our fathers (too) were touched by suffering and affluence". Behold! We took them to account of a sudden, while they realised not (their peril).

ثُمَّ بَدَّلْنَا مَكَانَ ٱلسَّيِّئَةِ ٱلْحَسَنَةَ حَتَّىٰ عَفَوا۟ وَّقَالُوا۟ قَدْ مَسَّ ءَابَآءَنَا ٱلضَّرَّآءُ وَٱلسَّرَّآءُ فَأَخَذْنَٰهُم بَغْتَةً وَّهُمْ لَا يَشْعُرُونَ ۝

96. If the people of the towns had but believed and feared Allah, We should indeed have opened out to them (all kinds of) blessings from heaven and earth; but they rejected (the truth), and We brought them to book for their misdeeds.

وَلَوْ أَنَّ أَهْلَ ٱلْقُرَىٰٓ ءَامَنُوا۟ وَٱتَّقَوْا۟ لَفَتَحْنَا عَلَيْهِم بَرَكَٰتٍ مِّنَ ٱلسَّمَآءِ وَٱلْأَرْضِ وَلَٰكِن كَذَّبُوا۟ فَأَخَذْنَٰهُم بِمَا كَانُوا۟ يَكْسِبُونَ ۝

97. Did the people of the towns feel secure against the coming of Our wrath by night while they were asleep?

أَفَأَمِنَ أَهْلُ ٱلْقُرَىٰٓ أَن يَأْتِيَهُم بَأْسُنَا بَيَٰتًا وَهُمْ نَآئِمُونَ ۝

98. Or else did they feel secure against its coming in broad daylight while they played about (care-free)?

أَوَأَمِنَ أَهْلُ ٱلْقُرَىٰٓ أَن يَأْتِيَهُم بَأْسُنَا ضُحًى وَهُمْ يَلْعَبُونَ ۝

99. Did they then feel secure against Allah's devising but no one can feel secure from the Plan of Allah. except those (doomed) to ruin!

أَفَأَمِنُوا۟ مَكْرَ ٱللَّهِ فَلَا يَأْمَنُ مَكْرَ ٱللَّهِ إِلَّا ٱلْقَوْمُ ٱلْخَٰسِرُونَ ۝

100. To those who inherit the earth in succession to its (previous) possessors, is it not a guiding (lesson) that, if We so willed, we could punish them (too) for their sins, and seal up their hearts so that they could not hear?

أَوَلَمْ يَهْدِ لِلَّذِينَ يَرِثُونَ ٱلْأَرْضَ مِنۢ بَعْدِ أَهْلِهَآ أَن لَّوْ نَشَآءُ أَصَبْنَٰهُم بِذُنُوبِهِمْ وَنَطْبَعُ عَلَىٰ قُلُوبِهِمْ فَهُمْ لَا يَسْمَعُونَ ۝

101. Such were the towns whose story We (thus) relate unto thee: there came indeed to them their Messengers with clear (Signs); but they would not believe what they had rejected before. Thus doth Allah seal up the hearts of those who reject Faith.

تِلْكَ ٱلْقُرَىٰ نَقُصُّ عَلَيْكَ مِنْ أَنۢبَآئِهَا وَلَقَدْ جَآءَتْهُمْ رُسُلُهُم بِٱلْبَيِّنَٰتِ فَمَا كَانُوا۟ لِيُؤْمِنُوا۟ بِمَا كَذَّبُوا۟ مِن قَبْلُ كَذَٰلِكَ يَطْبَعُ ٱللَّهُ عَلَىٰ قُلُوبِ ٱلْكَٰفِرِينَ ۝

102. Most of them We found not men (true) to their covenant: but most of them We

وَمَا وَجَدْنَا لِأَكْثَرِهِم مِّنْ عَهْدٍ ٥

found rebellious and disobedient.

103. Then after them We sent Moses with Our Signs to Pharaoh and his chiefs. But they wrongfully rejected them: so see what was the end of those who made mischief.

104. Moses said: "O Pharaoh!" I am a messenger from the Lord of the Worlds,–

105. One for whom it is right to say nothing but truth about Allah. Now have I come unto you (people), from your Lord with a clear (Sign): so let the Children of Israel depart along with me."

106. (Pharaoh) said: "If indeed thou hast come with a Sign, show it forth,—if thou tellest the truth."

107. Then (Moses) threw his rod, and behold! it was a serpent, plain (for all to see)!

108. And he drew out his hand, and behold! it was white to all beholders!

109. Said the Chiefs of the people of Pharaoh: "This is indeed a sorcerer well-versed.

110. "His plan is to get you out of your land: then what is it ye counsel?"

111. They said: "Keep him and his brother in suspense (for a while); and send to the cities men to collect—

112. And bring up to thee all (our) sorcerers well-versed."

113. So there came the sorcerers to Pharaoh: they said, "Of course we shall have a (suitable) reward if we win!"

114. He said: "Yea, (and more),—for ye shall in that case be (raised to posts) nearest (to my person)."

115. They said: "O Moses! wilt thou throw (first), or shall we have the (first) throw?"

116. Said Moses: "Throw ye (first)." So when they threw, they bewitched the eyes of the people, and struck terror into them:

وَإِن وَّجَدْنَآ أَكْثَرَهُمْ لَفٰسِقِيْنَ ۝

ثُمَّ بَعَثْنَا مِنْۢ بَعْدِهِمْ مُّوْسٰى بِاٰيٰتِنَآ إِلٰى فِرْعَوْنَ وَمَلَإِيْهٖ فَظَلَمُوْا بِهَا ۚ فَانْظُرْ كَيْفَ كَانَ عَاقِبَةُ الْمُفْسِدِيْنَ ۝

وَقَالَ مُوْسٰى يٰفِرْعَوْنُ إِنِّيْ رَسُوْلٌ مِّنْ رَّبِّ الْعٰلَمِيْنَ ۝

حَقِيْقٌ عَلٰى أَنْ لَّآ أَقُوْلَ عَلَى اللّٰهِ إِلَّا الْحَقَّ ۚ قَدْ جِئْتُكُمْ بِبَيِّنَةٍ مِّنْ رَّبِّكُمْ فَأَرْسِلْ مَعِيَ بَنِيْ إِسْرَآءِيْلَ ۝

قَالَ إِنْ كُنْتَ جِئْتَ بِاٰيَةٍ فَأْتِ بِهَآ إِنْ كُنْتَ مِنَ الصّٰدِقِيْنَ ۝

فَأَلْقٰى عَصَاهُ فَإِذَا هِيَ ثُعْبَانٌ مُّبِيْنٌ ۝

وَّنَزَعَ يَدَهُ فَإِذَا هِيَ بَيْضَآءُ لِلنّٰظِرِيْنَ ۝

قَالَ الْمَلَأُ مِنْ قَوْمِ فِرْعَوْنَ إِنَّ هٰذَا لَسٰحِرٌ عَلِيْمٌ ۝

يُّرِيْدُ أَنْ يُّخْرِجَكُمْ مِّنْ أَرْضِكُمْ ۚ فَمَاذَا تَأْمُرُوْنَ ۝

قَالُوْا أَرْجِهْ وَأَخَاهُ وَأَرْسِلْ فِي الْمَدَآئِنِ حٰشِرِيْنَ ۝

يَأْتُوْكَ بِكُلِّ سٰحِرٍ عَلِيْمٍ ۝

وَجَآءَ السَّحَرَةُ فِرْعَوْنَ قَالُوْٓا إِنَّ لَنَا لَأَجْرًا إِنْ كُنَّا نَحْنُ الْغٰلِبِيْنَ ۝

قَالَ نَعَمْ وَإِنَّكُمْ لَمِنَ الْمُقَرَّبِيْنَ ۝

قَالُوْا يٰمُوْسٰٓى إِمَّآ أَنْ تُلْقِيَ وَإِمَّآ أَنْ نَّكُوْنَ نَحْنُ الْمُلْقِيْنَ ۝

قَالَ أَلْقُوْا ۚ فَلَمَّآ أَلْقَوْا سَحَرُوْٓا أَعْيُنَ النَّاسِ وَاسْتَرْهَبُوْهُمْ وَجَآءُوْ

and they showed a great (feat of) magic.

بِسِحۡرٍ عَظِيۡمٍ ۟

117. We revealed to Moses "Throw thy rod": and behold! it swallows up all the falsehoods which they fake!

وَاَوۡحَيۡنَاۤ اِلٰى مُوۡسٰۤى اَنۡ اَلۡقِ عَصَاكَ ۚ فَاِذَا هِىَ تَلۡقَفُ مَا يَاۡفِكُوۡنَ ۚ

118. Thus truth was confirmed. And all that they did was made of no effect.

فَوَقَعَ الۡحَقُّ وَبَطَلَ مَا كَانُوۡا يَعۡمَلُوۡنَ ۚ

119. So they were vanquished there and then, and turned about humble.

فَغُلِبُوۡا هُنَالِكَ وَانۡقَلَبُوۡا صٰغِرِيۡنَ ۚ

120. But the sorcerers fell down prostrate in adoration.

وَاُلۡقِىَ السَّحَرَةُ سٰجِدِيۡنَ ۚ

121. Saying: "We believe in the Lord of the Worlds."

قَالُوۡۤا اٰمَنَّا بِرَبِّ الۡعٰلَمِيۡنَ ۙ

122. "The Lord of Moses and Aaron."

رَبِّ مُوۡسٰى وَهٰرُوۡنَ ۚ

123. Said Pharaoh: "Believe ye in Him before I give you permission? Surely this is a trick which ye have planned in the City to drive out its people: but soon shall ye know (the consequences)."

قَالَ فِرۡعَوۡنُ اٰمَنۡتُمۡ بِهٖ قَبۡلَ اَنۡ اٰذَنَ لَكُمۡ ۚ اِنَّ هٰذَا لَمَكۡرٌ مَّكَرۡتُمُوۡهُ فِى الۡمَدِيۡنَةِ لِتُخۡرِجُوۡا مِنۡهَاۤ اَهۡلَهَا ۚ فَسَوۡفَ تَعۡلَمُوۡنَ ۚ

124. "Be sure I will cut off your hands and your feet on opposite sides, and I will crucify you all."

لَاُقَطِّعَنَّ اَيۡدِيَكُمۡ وَاَرۡجُلَكُمۡ مِّنۡ خِلَافٍ ثُمَّ لَاُصَلِّبَنَّكُمۡ اَجۡمَعِيۡنَ ۚ

125. They said: "For us, we are but sent back unto our Lord."

قَالُوۡۤا اِنَّاۤ اِلٰى رَبِّنَا مُنۡقَلِبُوۡنَ ۚ

126. "But thou dost wreak thy vengeance on us simply because we believed in the Signs of our Lord when they reached us! Our Lord! pour out on us patience and cons-tancy, and take our souls unto Thee as Muslims (who bow to Thy Will)!"

وَمَا تَنۡقِمُ مِنَّاۤ اِلَّاۤ اَنۡ اٰمَنَّا بِاٰيٰتِ رَبِّنَا لَمَّا جَآءَتۡنَا ۚ رَبَّنَاۤ اَفۡرِغۡ عَلَيۡنَا صَبۡرًا وَّتَوَفَّنَا مُسۡلِمِيۡنَ ۚ

127. Said the chiefs of Pharaoh's people: "Wilt thou leave Moses and his people, to spread mischief in the land, and to abandon thee and thy gods?" He said "Their male children will we slay; (only) their females will we save alive; and we have over them (power) irresistible."

وَقَالَ الۡمَلَاُ مِنۡ قَوۡمِ فِرۡعَوۡنَ اَتَذَرُ مُوۡسٰى وَقَوۡمَهٗ لِيُفۡسِدُوۡا فِى الۡاَرۡضِ وَيَذَرَكَ وَاٰلِهَتَكَ ۚ قَالَ سَنُقَتِّلُ اَبۡنَآءَهُمۡ وَنَسۡتَحۡىٖ نِسَآءَهُمۡ ۚ وَاِنَّا فَوۡقَهُمۡ قَاهِرُوۡنَ ۚ

128. Said Moses to his people: "Pray for help from Allah," and (wait) in patience and constancy: for the earth is Allah's, to give as a heritage to such of His servants as He pleaseth; and the end is (best) for the righteous.

قَالَ مُوۡسٰى لِقَوۡمِهِ اسۡتَعِيۡنُوۡا بِاللّٰهِ وَاصۡبِرُوۡا ۚ اِنَّ الۡاَرۡضَ لِلّٰهِ يُوۡرِثُهَا مَنۡ يَّشَآءُ مِنۡ عِبَادِهٖ ۚ وَالۡعَاقِبَةُ لِلۡمُتَّقِيۡنَ ۚ

129. They said: "We have had (nothing but) trouble, both before and after thou camest to us." He said: "It may be that your Lord will destroy your enemy and make you inheritors in the earth; that so He may see how ye act."

130. We punished the people of Pharaoh with years (of drought) and shortness of crops; that they might receive admonition.

131. But when good (times) came, they said, "This is due to us;" when gripped by calamity, they ascribed it to evil omens connected with Moses and those with him! Behold! in truth the omens of evil are theirs in Allah's sight, but most of them do not understand!

132. They said (to Moses): "What-ever be the Signs Thou bringest, to work therewith thy sorcery on us, we shall never believe in thee."

133. So We sent on them: wholesale Death, Locusts, Lice, frogs, and Blood: Signs openly Self-explained: but they were steeped in arrogance, a people given to sin.

134. And when the Plague fell on them, they said: "O Moses! on our behalf call on thy Lord in virtue of his promise to thee: if thou wilt remove the Plague from us, we shall truly believe in thee, and we shall send away the Children of Israel with thee."

135. But when We removed the Plague from them according to a fixed term which they had to fulfil,—behold! they broke their word!

136. So We exacted retribution from them: We drowned them in the sea, because they rejected Our Signs, and failed to take warning from them.

137. And We made a people, considered weak (and of no account), inheritors of lands in both East and West,—lands whereon We sent down Our blessings. The fair promise of thy Lord was fulfilled for the Children of Israel, because they had

patience and constancy, and We levelled to the ground the great Works and fine Buildings which Pharaoh and his people erected (with such pride).

138. We took the Children of Israel (with safety) across the sea. They came upon a people devoted entirely to some idols they had. They said: "O Moses! fashion for us a god like unto the gods they have." He said: "Surely ye are a people without knowledge".

139. "As to these folk,—the cult they are in is bound to destruction, and vain is the (worship) which they practise."

140. He said: "Shall I seek for you a god other than Allah, when it is He who hath endowed you with gifts above the nations?"

141. And remember We rescued you from Pharaoh's people, who afflicted you with the worst of punishment who slew your male children and saved alive your females: in that was a momentous trial from your Lord.

142. We appointed for Moses thirty nights, and completed (the period) with ten (more): thus was completed the term with his Lord, forty nights. And Moses had charged his brother Aaron (before he went up): "Act for me amongst my people: do right, and follow not the way of those who do mischief."

143. When Moses came to the place appointed by Us, and his Lord addressed him, he said: "O my Lord! show (Thyself) to me, that I may look upon Thee." Allah said: "By no means canst thou see Me (direct); but look upon the mount; if it abide in its place, then shalt thou see Me." When his Lord manifested Himself to the Mount, He made it as dust, and Moses fell down in a swoon. When he recovered his senses he said: "Glory be to Thee! To Thee I turn in repentance, and I am the first to believe."

مَا كَانَ يَصْنَعُ فِرْعَوْنُ وَقَوْمُهُ وَمَا كَانُوا يَعْرِشُونَ ۞

وَجَاوَزْنَا بِبَنِيٓ إِسْرَآءِيلَ الْبَحْرَ فَأَتَوْا عَلَىٰ قَوْمٍ يَعْكُفُونَ عَلَىٰٓ أَصْنَامٍ لَّهُمْ ۚ قَالُوا يَٰمُوسَى اجْعَل لَّنَآ إِلَٰهًا كَمَا لَهُمْ ءَالِهَةٌ ۚ قَالَ إِنَّكُمْ قَوْمٌ تَجْهَلُونَ ۞

إِنَّ هَٰٓؤُلَآءِ مُتَبَّرٌ مَّا هُمْ فِيهِ وَبَٰطِلٌ مَّا كَانُوا يَعْمَلُونَ ۞

قَالَ أَغَيْرَ اللَّهِ أَبْغِيكُمْ إِلَٰهًا وَهُوَ فَضَّلَكُمْ عَلَى الْعَالَمِينَ ۞

وَإِذْ أَنجَيْنَاكُم مِّنْ ءَالِ فِرْعَوْنَ يَسُومُونَكُمْ سُوٓءَ الْعَذَابِ ۖ يُقَتِّلُونَ أَبْنَآءَكُمْ وَيَسْتَحْيُونَ نِسَآءَكُمْ ۚ وَفِي ذَٰلِكُم بَلَآءٌ مِّن رَّبِّكُمْ عَظِيمٌ ۞

وَوَٰعَدْنَا مُوسَىٰ ثَلَٰثِينَ لَيْلَةً وَأَتْمَمْنَاهَا بِعَشْرٍ فَتَمَّ مِيقَاتُ رَبِّهِ أَرْبَعِينَ لَيْلَةً ۚ وَقَالَ مُوسَىٰ لِأَخِيهِ هَٰرُونَ اخْلُفْنِي فِي قَوْمِي وَأَصْلِحْ وَلَا تَتَّبِعْ سَبِيلَ الْمُفْسِدِينَ ۞

وَلَمَّا جَآءَ مُوسَىٰ لِمِيقَاتِنَا وَكَلَّمَهُ رَبُّهُ قَالَ رَبِّ أَرِنِيٓ أَنظُرْ إِلَيْكَ ۚ قَالَ لَن تَرَانِي وَلَٰكِنِ انظُرْ إِلَى الْجَبَلِ فَإِنِ اسْتَقَرَّ مَكَانَهُ فَسَوْفَ تَرَانِي ۚ فَلَمَّا تَجَلَّىٰ رَبُّهُ لِلْجَبَلِ جَعَلَهُ دَكًّا وَخَرَّ مُوسَىٰ صَعِقًا ۚ فَلَمَّآ أَفَاقَ قَالَ سُبْحَانَكَ تُبْتُ إِلَيْكَ وَأَنَا أَوَّلُ الْمُؤْمِنِينَ ۞

144. (Allah) said: "O Moses! I have chosen thee above (other) men, by the messages I (have given thee) and the words I (have spoken to thee); take then the (revelation) which I give thee, and be of those who give thanks."

145. And We ordained for him in the Tablets in all matters, Admonition and explanation of all things, (and said): "Take and hold these with firmness, and enjoin thy people to hold fast by the best in the precepts: soon shall I show you the homes of the wicked,— (how they lie desolate)."

146. Those who behave arrogantly on the earth in defiance of right—them will I turn away from My Signs: even if they see all the Signs, they will not believe in them; and if they see the way of right conduct, they will not adopt it as the Way; but if they see the way of error, that is the Way they will adopt. For they have rejected our Signs, and failed to take warning from them.

147. Those who reject Our Signs and the Meeting in the Hereafter,— vain are their deeds: can they expect to be rewarded except as they have wrought?

148. The people of Moses made, in his absence, out of their ornaments, the body of a calf, (for worship): having lowing sound did they not see that it could neither speak to them, nor show them the Way? They took it for worship and they did wrong.

149. When they repented, and saw that they had erred, they said: "If our Lord have not mercy upon us and forgive us, we shall indeed be among the Losers.

150. When Moses came back to his people, angry and grieved, he said: "Evil it is that ye Have done in my place in my absence: did ye make haste to bring on the judgment of your Lord?" He put down the Tablets, seized his brother by (the hair of) his head, and dragged

him. To him Aaron said: "Son of my mother! The people did indeed reckon me as naught, and went near to slaying me! Make not the enemies rejoice over my misfortune, nor count thou me amongst the people of sin."

151. Moses prayed: "O my Lord! forgive me and my brother! Admit us to thy mercy! for Thou art the Most Merciful of those who show mercy!"

152. Those who took the calf (for worship) will indeed be overwhelmed with wrath from their Lord and with shame in this life: thus do We recompense those who invent (falsehoods).

153. But those who do wrong but repent thereafter and (truly) believe,—verily Thy Lord is thereafter Oft-Forgiving, Most Merciful.

154. When the anger of Moses was appeased, he took up the Tablets: in the writing thereon was Guidance and Mercy for such as fear their Lord.

155. And Moses chose seventy of his people for Our place of meeting: when they were seized with violent quaking, he prayed: "O my Lord! if it had been Thy Will thou couldst have destroyed, long before, both them and me: wouldst Thou destroy us for the deeds of the foolish ones among us? This is no more than thy trial: by it Thou causest whom Thou wilt stray, and Thou leadest whom Thou wilt into the right path. Thou art our Protector: so forgive us and give us Thy mercy; for Thou art the Best of those who forgive.

156. "And ordain for us that which is good, in this life and in the Hereafter: for we have turned unto Thee." He said: "I afflict My Punishment on whom I will; but My Mercy extendeth to all things. That (Mercy) I shall ordain for those who do right, and pay Zakat

and those who believe in Our Signs;—

157. "Those who follow the Messenger, the
unlettered Prophet, whom they find
mentioned in their own (Scriptures),— in
the Taurat and the Gospel;—for he
commands them what is just and forbids
them what is evil; he allows them as lawful
what is good (and pure) and prohibits them
from what is bad (and impure): He releases
them from their heavy burdens and from
the yokes that are upon them. So it is those
who believe in him, honour him, help him,
and follow the Light which is sent down
with him,—it is they who will prosper."

158. Say: "O men! I am sent unto you all,
as the Messenger of Allah, to Whom
belongeth the dominion of the heavens and
the earth: there is no god but He: it is He
that giveth both life and death. So believe
in Allah and His Messenger. The unlettered
Prophet, who believeth in Allah and His
Words: follow him that (so) ye may be
guided."

159. Of the people of Moses there is a
section who guide and do justice in the
light of truth.

160. We divided them into twelve Tribes or
nations. We directed Moses by inspiration,
when his (thirsty) people asked him for
Water: "Strike the rock with thy staff": out of
it there gushed forth twelve springs. each
group knew its own place for water. We
gave them the shade of clouds, and sent
down to them manna and quails, (saying):
"Eat of the good things We have provided
for you": (but they rebelled); to Us they did
no harm, but they harmed their own souls.

161. And remember it was said to them:
"Dwell in this town and eat therein as ye

wish, but say forgive (us) and enter the gate in a posture of humility: We shall forgive you your faults; We shall increase (the portion of) those who do good."

162. But the transgressors among them changed the word from that which had been given them so we sent on them a plague from heaven. For that they repeatedly transgressed.

163. Ask them concerning the town standing close by the sea. Behold! they transgressed in the matter of the Sabbath, for on the day of their Sabbath their fish did come to them, openly (holding up their heads,) but on the day they had no Sabbath, they came not: thus did We make a trial of them, for they were given to transgression.

164. When some of them said: "Why do ye preach to a people whom Allah will destroy or visit with a terrible punishment?" — said the preachers: "To discharge our duty to your Lord and perchance they may fear Him."

165. When they disregarded the warnings that had been given them, we rescued those who forbade evil; but We visited the wrong-doers with a grievous punishment, because they were given to transgression.

166. When in their insolence they transgressed (all) prohibitions, We said to them: "Be ye apes, despised and rejected."

167. Behold! thy Lord did declare that He would send against them, to the Day of Judgment, those who would afflict them with grievous Chastisement. Thy Lord is quick in retribution, but He is also Oft-Forgiving, Most Merciful.

168. We broke them up into sections on this earth. There are among them some that are the righteous, and some that are

the opposite. We have tried them with both prosperity and adversity: in order that they might turn (to Us).

169. After them succeeded an (evil) generation: they inherited the Book, but they chose (for themselves) the vanities of this world, saying (for excuse): "(Everything) will be forgiven us." (Even so), if similar vanities came their way, they would (again) seize them. Was not the Covenant of the Book taken from them, that they would not ascribe to Allah anything but the truth? And they study what is in the Book. But best for the righteous is the Home in the Hereafter. Will ye not understand?

170. As to those who hold fast by the Book and establish regular Prayer,—never shall we suffer the reward of the righteous to perish.

171. When We raised the Mount over them, as if it had been a canopy, and they thought it was going to fall on them (We said): "Hold firmly to what We have given you, and bring (ever) to remembrance what is therein; perchance ye may fear Allah".

172. When thy Lord drew forth from the Children of Adam—from their loins—their descendants, and made them testify concerning themselves, (saying): "Am I not your Lord (Who cherishes and sustains you)?"—They said. "Yea! we do testify!" (This), lest ye should say on the Day of Judgment: "Of this we were never mindful":

173. Or lest ye should say: "Our fathers before us took false gods, but we are (their) descendants after them: wilt Thou then destroy us because of the deeds of men who followed falsehood?"

174. Thus do We explain the Signs in detail; and perchance they may turn (unto Us).

175. Relate to them the story of the man to whom We sent Our Signs, but he passed them by: so Satan followed him up, and he went astray.

وَبَلَوْنَٰهُم بِٱلْحَسَنَٰتِ وَٱلسَّيِّئَاتِ لَعَلَّهُمْ يَرْجِعُونَ ۝

فَخَلَفَ مِنۢ بَعْدِهِمْ خَلْفٌ وَرِثُوا۟ ٱلْكِتَٰبَ يَأْخُذُونَ عَرَضَ هَٰذَا ٱلْأَدْنَىٰ وَيَقُولُونَ سَيُغْفَرُ لَنَا وَإِن يَأْتِهِمْ عَرَضٌ مِّثْلُهُۥ يَأْخُذُوهُ أَلَمْ يُؤْخَذْ عَلَيْهِم مِّيثَٰقُ ٱلْكِتَٰبِ أَن لَّا يَقُولُوا۟ عَلَى ٱللَّهِ إِلَّا ٱلْحَقَّ وَدَرَسُوا۟ مَا فِيهِ وَٱلدَّارُ ٱلْأَخِرَةُ خَيْرٌ لِّلَّذِينَ يَتَّقُونَ أَفَلَا تَعْقِلُونَ ۝

وَٱلَّذِينَ يُمَسِّكُونَ بِٱلْكِتَٰبِ وَأَقَامُوا۟ ٱلصَّلَوٰةَ إِنَّا لَا نُضِيعُ أَجْرَ ٱلْمُصْلِحِينَ ۝

وَإِذ نَتَقْنَا ٱلْجَبَلَ فَوْقَهُمْ كَأَنَّهُۥ ظُلَّةٌ وَظَنُّوٓا۟ أَنَّهُۥ وَاقِعٌۢ بِهِمْ خُذُوا۟ مَآ ءَاتَيْنَٰكُم بِقُوَّةٍ وَٱذْكُرُوا۟ مَا فِيهِ لَعَلَّكُمْ تَتَّقُونَ ۝

وَإِذْ أَخَذَ رَبُّكَ مِنۢ بَنِىٓ ءَادَمَ مِن ظُهُورِهِمْ ذُرِّيَّتَهُمْ وَأَشْهَدَهُمْ عَلَىٰٓ أَنفُسِهِمْ أَلَسْتُ بِرَبِّكُمْ قَالُوا۟ بَلَىٰ شَهِدْنَآ أَن تَقُولُوا۟ يَوْمَ ٱلْقِيَٰمَةِ إِنَّا كُنَّا عَنْ هَٰذَا غَٰفِلِينَ ۝

أَوْ تَقُولُوٓا۟ إِنَّمَآ أَشْرَكَ ءَابَآؤُنَا مِن قَبْلُ وَكُنَّا ذُرِّيَّةً مِّنۢ بَعْدِهِمْ أَفَتُهْلِكُنَا بِمَا فَعَلَ ٱلْمُبْطِلُونَ ۝

وَكَذَٰلِكَ نُفَصِّلُ ٱلْءَايَٰتِ وَلَعَلَّهُمْ يَرْجِعُونَ ۝
وَٱتْلُ عَلَيْهِمْ نَبَأَ ٱلَّذِىٓ ءَاتَيْنَٰهُ ءَايَٰتِنَا فَٱنسَلَخَ مِنْهَا فَأَتْبَعَهُ ٱلشَّيْطَٰنُ فَكَانَ مِنَ ٱلْغَاوِينَ ۝

176. If it had been Our Will. We should have elevated him with Our Signs: but he inclined to the earth, and followed his own vain desires. His similitude is that of a dog: if you attack him, he lolls out his tongue, or if you leave him alone, he (still) lolls out his tongue. That is the similitude of those who reject Our Signs; so relate the story; perchance they may reflect.

177. Evil as the example are people who reject Our Signs and wrong their own souls.

178. Whom Allah doth guide.—he is on the right path: whom He rejects from His guidance,—such are the persons who lose.

179. Many are the Jinns and men We have made for Hell: they have hearts wherewith they understand not, eyes wherewith they see not, and ears wherewith they hear not. They are like cattle,—nay more misguided: for they are heedless (of warning).

180. The most beautiful names belong to Allah: so call on Him by them; but shun such men as distort His names: for what they do, they will soon be requited.

181. Of those We have created are people who direct (others) with truth, and dispense justice therewith.

182. Those who reject Our Signs, We will lead them step by step to ruin while they know not:

183. Respite will I grant unto them: for My scheme is strong (and unfailing).

184. Do they not reflect? Their Companion is not seized with madness: he is but a perspicuous warner.

185. Do they see nothing in the kingdom of the heavens and the earth and all that Allah hath created? (Do they not see) that it may well be that their term is nigh drawing to an

end? In what Message after this will they then believe?

186. To such as Allah rejects from His guidance, there can be no guide: He will Leave them in their trespasses, wandering in distraction.

187. They ask thee about the (final) Hour—when will be its appointed time? Say: "The knowledge thereof is with my Lord (alone): none but He can reveal as to when it will occur. Heavy were its burden through the heavens and the earth. Only, all of a sudden will it come to you." They ask thee as if thou wert eager in search thereof: say: "The knowledge thereof is with Allah (alone), but most men know not."

188. Say: "I have no power over any good or harm to myself except as Allah willeth. If I had knowledge of the unseen, I should have multiplied all good, and no evil should have touched me: I am but a warner, and a bringer of glad tidings to those who have faith."

189. It is He Who created you from a single person, and made his mate of like nature, in order that he might dwell with her (in love). When they are united, she bears a light burden and carries it about (unnoticed). When she grows heavy, they both pray to Allah their Lord (saying): "if Thou givest us a goodly child, we vow we shall (ever) be grateful."

190. But when He giveth them a goodly child, they ascribe to others a share in the gift they have received: but Allah is exalted high above the partners they ascribe to Him.

191. Do they indeed ascribe to Him as partners things that can create nothing, but are themselves created?

192. No aid can they give them, nor can they aid themselves!

193. If ye call them to guidance, they will not obey: for you it is the same whether ye call them or ye keep silent.

أَجَلُهُمْ فَبِأَيِّ حَدِيثٍ بَعْدَهُ يُؤْمِنُونَ ۝

مَنْ يُضْلِلِ اللهُ فَلَا هَادِيَ لَهُ وَيَذَرُهُمْ فِي طُغْيَانِهِمْ يَعْمَهُونَ ۝

يَسْـَٔلُونَكَ عَنِ السَّاعَةِ أَيَّانَ مُرْسَاهَا قُلْ إِنَّمَا عِلْمُهَا عِنْدَ رَبِّي لَا يُجَلِّيهَا لِوَقْتِهَا إِلَّا هُوَ ثَقُلَتْ فِي السَّمَاوَاتِ وَالْأَرْضِ لَا تَأْتِيكُمْ إِلَّا بَغْتَةً يَسْـَٔلُونَكَ كَأَنَّكَ حَفِيٌّ عَنْهَا قُلْ إِنَّمَا عِلْمُهَا عِنْدَ اللهِ وَلَكِنَّ أَكْثَرَ النَّاسِ لَا يَعْلَمُونَ ۝

قُلْ لَا أَمْلِكُ لِنَفْسِي نَفْعًا وَلَا ضَرًّا إِلَّا مَا شَاءَ اللهُ وَلَوْ كُنْتُ أَعْلَمُ الْغَيْبَ لَاسْتَكْثَرْتُ مِنَ الْخَيْرِ وَمَا مَسَّنِيَ السُّوءُ إِنْ أَنَا إِلَّا نَذِيرٌ وَبَشِيرٌ لِقَوْمٍ يُؤْمِنُونَ ۝

هُوَ الَّذِي خَلَقَكُمْ مِنْ نَفْسٍ وَاحِدَةٍ وَجَعَلَ مِنْهَا زَوْجَهَا لِيَسْكُنَ إِلَيْهَا فَلَمَّا تَغَشَّاهَا حَمَلَتْ حَمْلًا خَفِيفًا فَمَرَّتْ بِهِ فَلَمَّا أَثْقَلَتْ دَعَوَا اللهَ رَبَّهُمَا لَئِنْ آتَيْتَنَا صَالِحًا لَنَكُونَنَّ مِنَ الشَّاكِرِينَ ۝

فَلَمَّا آتَاهُمَا صَالِحًا جَعَلَا لَهُ شُرَكَاءَ فِيمَا آتَاهُمَا فَتَعَالَى اللهُ عَمَّا يُشْرِكُونَ ۝ أَيُشْرِكُونَ مَا لَا يَخْلُقُ شَيْئًا وَهُمْ يُخْلَقُونَ ۝ وَلَا يَسْتَطِيعُونَ لَهُمْ نَصْرًا وَلَا أَنْفُسَهُمْ يَنْصُرُونَ ۝

وَإِنْ تَدْعُوهُمْ إِلَى الْهُدَى لَا يَتَّبِعُوكُمْ سَوَاءٌ عَلَيْكُمْ أَدَعَوْتُمُوهُمْ أَمْ أَنْتُمْ صَامِتُونَ ۝

194. Verily those whom ye call upon besides Allah are servants like unto you: call upon them, and let them listen to your prayer, if ye are (indeed) truthful!

195. Have they feet to walk with? Or hands to lay hold with? Or eyes to see with? Or ears to hear with? Say: "Call your 'god-partners', scheme (your worst) against me, and give me no respite!

196. "For my Protector is Allah. Who revealed the Book, (from time to time), and He will befriend the righteous.

197. "But those ye call upon besides Him, are unable to help you, and indeed to help themselves."

198. If thou callest them to guidance, they hear not. Thou wilt see them looking at thee, but they see not.

199. Hold to forgiveness; command what is right; but turn away from the ignorant.

200. If a suggestion from Satan assail thy (mind), seek refuge with Allah: for He heareth and knoweth (all things).

201. Those who fear Allah, when a thought of evil from Satan assaults them, bring Allah to remembrance, when lo! they see (aright)!

202. But their brethren (the evil ones) plunge them deeper into error, and never relax (their efforts).

203. If thou bring them not a reve-lation, they say: "Why hast thou not got it together?" Say: "I but follow what is revealed to me from my Lord: this is (nothing but) Lights

SÛRA–8
AL-ANFĀL
(INTRODUCTION)

In the previous Introductions to the Sûras we have shown how each Sûra is a step or gradation in the teaching of the Qur-ān. The first seven Sûras, comprising a little less than one-third of the Qur-ān, form a gradation, sketching the early spiritual history of man and leading up to the formation of the new Ummat or Community of the Holy Apostle. Now we begin another gradation, consolidating that Ummat and directing us as to various phases in our new collective life.

In this chapter we have the lessons of the Battle of Badr enforced in their larger aspects: (1) the question of war booty; (2) the true virtues necessary for fighting the good fight; (3) victory against odds; (4) clemency and consideration for one's own and for others in the hour of victory.

As regards booty taken in battle, the first point to note is that that should never be our aim in war. It is only an advertitious circumstance, a sort of windfall. Secondly, no soldier or troop has any inherent right to it. A righteous war is a community affair, and any accessions resulting from it belong to Allah, or the community or Cause. Thirdly, certain equitable principles of division should be laid down to check human greed and selfishness. A fifth share goes to the Commander, and he can use it at his discretion; for his own expenses, and for the relief of the poor and suffering, and the orphans and widows (8: 41). The remainder was divided, according to the Prophet's practice, not only among those who were actually in the fight physically, but all who were in the enterprise, young and old, provided they loyally did some duty assigned to them. Fourthly, there should be no disputes, as they interfere with internal discipline and harmony.

These principles are followed in the best modern practice of civilised nations. All acquisition of war belong absolutely to the Sovereign as representing the commonwealth. In the distribution of booty not only the actual captors but also the "joint captors" and the "constructive captors" share. See Sir R. Phillimore's *International Law* (1885), vol. 3, pp. 209-10, 221-4.

As regards the military virtues, which are the types of virtues throughtout life, we are shown by an analysis of the incidents of Badr how, against the greatest odds, Allah's help will give the victory if men are fighting not for themselves but for the sacred Cause of Allah. And directions are given for the treatment of prisoners and for maintaining the solidarity of the Muslim community.

The date of this Sûra is shortly after the battle of Badr, which was fought on Friday, the 17th of Ramadhān in the second year of the Hijra.

from your Lord, and Guidance, and Mercy,
for any who have Faith."

204. When the Qur'an is read, listen to it
with attention, and hold your peace: that ye
may receive Mercy.

205. And do thou (O reader!) bring thy Lord
to remembrance in thy (very) soul, with
humility and remember without loudness in
words, in the mornings and evenings; and
be not thou of those who are unheedful.

206. Those who are near to thy Lord, disdain
not to worship Him: they glorify Him and
prostrate before Him.

Al-Anfāl, or the Spoils of War

In the name of Allah, Most Gracious, Most
Merciful.

1. They ask thee concerning (things taken
as) spoils, of war. Say: "(Such) spoils are at
the disposal of Allah and the Messenger:
so fear Allah, and keep straight the relations
between yourselves: obey Allah and His
Messenger, if ye do believe."

2. For, believers are those who, when
Allah is mentioned, fell a tremor in their
hearts, and when they hear His revelations
rehearsed, find their faith strengthened, and
put (all) their trust in their Lord;

3. Who establish regular prayers and
spend (freely) out of the gifts We have
given them for sustenance:

4. Such in truth are the Believers: they
have grades of dignity with their Lord, and
forgiveness, and generous sustenance:

5. Just as thy Lord ordered thee out of
thy house in truth, even though a party
among the Believers disliked it.

6. Disputing with thee concerning the truth
after it was made manifest, as if they were
being driven to death while they see it.

7. Behold! Allah promised you one of the
two parties, that it should be yours: ye
wished that the one unarmed should be

yours, but Allah willed to establish the Truth according to His words, and to cut off the roots of the Unbelievers;–

الشَّوْكَةِ تَكُوْنُ لَكُمْ وَيُرِيْدُ اللّٰهُ اَنْ يُّحِقَّ الْحَقَّ بِكَلِمٰتِهٖ وَيَقْطَعَ دَابِرَ الْكٰفِرِيْنَ ۞

8. That He might establish Truth and prove Falsehood false, distasteful though it be to those in guilt.

لِيُحِقَّ الْحَقَّ وَيُبْطِلَ الْبَاطِلَ وَلَوْ كَرِهَ الْمُجْرِمُوْنَ ۞

9. Remember ye implored the assistance of your Lord. And He answered you: "I will assist you with a thousand of the angels, ranks on ranks."

اِذْ تَسْتَغِيْثُوْنَ رَبَّكُمْ فَاسْتَجَابَ لَكُمْ اَنِّيْ مُمِدُّكُمْ بِاَلْفٍ مِّنَ الْمَلٰٓئِكَةِ مُرْدِفِيْنَ ۞

10. Allah made it but a message of hope, and an assurance to your hearts: (in any case) there is no help except from Allah: and Allah is Exalted in Power, Wise.

وَمَا جَعَلَهُ اللّٰهُ اِلَّا بُشْرٰى وَلِتَطْمَئِنَّ بِهٖ قُلُوْبُكُمْ وَمَا النَّصْرُ اِلَّا مِنْ عِنْدِ اللّٰهِ اِنَّ اللّٰهَ عَزِيْزٌ حَكِيْمٌ ۞

11. Remember He covered you with drowsiness, to give you calm as from himself, and he caused rain to descend on you from heaven, to clean you therewith, to remove from you the stain of Satan, to strengthen your hearts, and to plant your feet firmly therewith.

اِذْ يُغَشِّيْكُمُ النُّعَاسَ اَمَنَةً مِّنْهُ وَ يُنَزِّلُ عَلَيْكُمْ مِّنَ السَّمَآءِ مَآءً لِّيُطَهِّرَكُمْ بِهٖ وَيُذْهِبَ عَنْكُمْ رِجْزَ الشَّيْطٰنِ وَ لِيَرْبِطَ عَلٰى قُلُوْبِكُمْ وَيُثَبِّتَ بِهِ الْاَقْدَامَ ۞

12. Remember thy Lord inspired the angels (with the message): "I am with you: give firmness to the Believers: I will instil terror into the hearts of the Unbelievers: smite ye above their necks and smite all their finger-tips off them."

اِذْ يُوْحِيْ رَبُّكَ اِلَى الْمَلٰٓئِكَةِ اَنِّيْ مَعَكُمْ فَثَبِّتُوا الَّذِيْنَ اٰمَنُوْا سَاُلْقِيْ فِيْ قُلُوْبِ الَّذِيْنَ كَفَرُوا الرُّعْبَ فَاضْرِبُوْا فَوْقَ الْاَعْنَاقِ وَاضْرِبُوْا مِنْهُمْ كُلَّ بَنَانٍ ۞

13. This because they contended against Allah and His Messenger: if any contend against Allah and His Messenger. Allah is strict in punishment.

ذٰلِكَ بِاَنَّهُمْ شَآقُّوا اللّٰهَ وَرَسُوْلَهٗ وَ مَنْ يُّشَاقِقِ اللّٰهَ وَرَسُوْلَهٗ فَاِنَّ اللّٰهَ شَدِيْدُ الْعِقَابِ ۞

14. Thus (will it be said): "Taste ye then of the (punishment): for those who reject is the chastisement of the Fire."

ذٰلِكُمْ فَذُوْقُوْهُ وَاَنَّ لِلْكٰفِرِيْنَ عَذَابَ النَّارِ ۞

15. O ye who believe! when ye meet the Unbelievers in hostile array, never turn your backs to them.

يٰٓاَيُّهَا الَّذِيْنَ اٰمَنُوْا اِذَا لَقِيْتُمُ الَّذِيْنَ كَفَرُوْا زَحْفًا فَلَا تُوَلُّوْهُمُ الْاَدْبَارَ ۞

16. If any do turn his back to them on such a day— unless it be in a stratagem of war, or to retreat to a troop (of his own)— he draws on himself the wrath of Allah, and his abode is Hell,— an evil refuge (indeed)!

وَمَن يُوَلِّهِمْ يَوْمَئِذٍ دُبُرَهُ إِلَّا مُتَحَرِّفًا لِّقِتَالٍ أَوْ مُتَحَيِّزًا إِلَىٰ فِئَةٍ فَقَدْ بَآءَ بِغَضَبٍ مِّنَ اللَّهِ وَمَأْوَاهُ جَهَنَّمُ وَبِئْسَ الْمَصِيرُ ۝

17. It is not ye who slew them; it was Allah: when thou threwest (a handful of dust), it was not thy act, but Allah's: in order that He might confer on the Believers a gracious benefit from Himself: for Allah is He Who heareth and knoweth (all things).

فَلَمْ تَقْتُلُوهُمْ وَلَٰكِنَّ اللَّهَ قَتَلَهُمْ وَمَا رَمَيْتَ إِذْ رَمَيْتَ وَلَٰكِنَّ اللَّهَ رَمَىٰ وَلِيُبْلِيَ الْمُؤْمِنِينَ مِنْهُ بَلَآءً حَسَنًا إِنَّ اللَّهَ سَمِيعٌ عَلِيمٌ ۝

18. That, and also because Allah is He Who makes feeble the Plans and strategems of the Unbelievers.

ذَٰلِكُمْ وَأَنَّ اللَّهَ مُوهِنُ كَيْدِ الْكَافِرِينَ ۝

19. (O Unbelievers!) if ye prayed for victory and judgment, now hath the judgment come to you: if ye desist (from wrong), it will be best for you: if ye return (to the attack), so shall We. Not the least good will your forces be to you even if they were multiplied: for verily Allah is with those who believe!

إِن تَسْتَفْتِحُوا فَقَدْ جَآءَكُمُ الْفَتْحُ وَإِن تَنتَهُوا فَهُوَ خَيْرٌ لَّكُمْ وَإِن تَعُودُوا نَعُدْ وَلَن تُغْنِيَ عَنكُمْ فِئَتُكُمْ شَيْئًا وَلَوْ كَثُرَتْ وَأَنَّ اللَّهَ مَعَ الْمُؤْمِنِينَ ۝

20. O ye who believe! obey Allah and His Messenger, and turn not away from him when ye hear (him speak).

يَٰٓأَيُّهَا الَّذِينَ آمَنُوا أَطِيعُوا اللَّهَ وَرَسُولَهُ وَلَا تَوَلَّوْا عَنْهُ وَأَنتُمْ تَسْمَعُونَ ۝

21. Nor be like those who say, "We hear," but listen not:

وَلَا تَكُونُوا كَالَّذِينَ قَالُوا سَمِعْنَا وَهُمْ لَا يَسْمَعُونَ ۝

22. For the worst of beasts in the sight of Allah are the deaf and the dumb,—those who understand not.

إِنَّ شَرَّ الدَّوَابِّ عِندَ اللَّهِ الصُّمُّ الْبُكْمُ الَّذِينَ لَا يَعْقِلُونَ ۝

23. If Allah had found in them any good, He would indeed have made them listen: (as it is), if He had made them listen, they would but have turned back and declined (faith).

وَلَوْ عَلِمَ اللَّهُ فِيهِمْ خَيْرًا لَّأَسْمَعَهُمْ وَلَوْ أَسْمَعَهُمْ لَتَوَلَّوا وَّهُم مُّعْرِضُونَ ۝

24. O ye who believe! give your response to Allah and His Messenger, when He calleth you to that which will give you life; and know that Allah cometh in between a man and his heart, and that it is He to Whom ye shall (all) be gathered.

يَٰٓأَيُّهَا الَّذِينَ آمَنُوا اسْتَجِيبُوا لِلَّهِ وَلِلرَّسُولِ إِذَا دَعَاكُمْ لِمَا يُحْيِيكُمْ وَاعْلَمُوا أَنَّ اللَّهَ يَحُولُ بَيْنَ الْمَرْءِ وَقَلْبِهِ وَأَنَّهُ إِلَيْهِ تُحْشَرُونَ ۝

25. And fear the trial which affecteth not in particular (only) those of you who do wrong:

وَاتَّقُوا فِتْنَةً لَّا تُصِيبَنَّ الَّذِينَ ظَلَمُوا مِنكُمْ خَآصَّةً وَاعْلَمُوا أَنَّ اللَّهَ شَدِيدُ

and know that Allah is strict in punishment.

26. Call to mind when ye were a small (band), deemed weak through the land, and afraid that men might despoil and kidnap you; but He pro-vided a safe asylum for you, strengthened you with His aid, and gave you good things for suste-nance: that ye might be grateful.

27. O ye that believe! betray not the trust of Allah and the Messenger, nor misappropriate knowingly things entrusted to you.

28. And know ye that your possessions and your progeny are but a trial: and that it is Allah with whom lies your highest reward.

29. O ye who believe! if ye fear Allah, He will grant you a Criterion (to judge between right and wrong), remove from you (all) evil deeds and forgive you: for Allah is the Lord of grace unbounded.

30. Remember how the Unbelievers plotted against thee, to keep thee in bonds, or slay thee, or get thee out (of thy home). They plot and plan, and Allah too plans, but the best of planners is Allah.

31. When Our Signs are rehearsed to them, they say: "We have heard this (before): if we wished, we could say (words) like these: these are nothing but tales of the ancients."

32. Remember how they said: "O Allah! if this is indeed the Truth from Thee, rain down on us a shower of stones from the sky, or send us a grievous chastisement."

33. But Allah was not going to send them a Chastisement: whilst thou wast amongst them; nor was He going to send it whilst they could ask for pardon.

34. But what plea have they that Allah should not punish them, when they keep out (men) from the Sacred Mosque—and they are not its guardians? No men can be its guardians except the righteous; but most of them do not understand.

35. Their prayer at the House (of Allah) is nothing but whistling and clapping of hands: (its only answer can be), "Taste ye the Chastise-ment because ye blasphemed."

36. The Unbelievers spend their wealth to hinder (men) from the path of Allah, and so will they continue to spend; but in the end they will have (only) regrets and sighs; at length they will be overcome: and the Unbelievers will be gathered together to Hell;—

37. In order that Allah may separate the impure from the pure. Put the impure, one on another, heap them together, and cast them into Hell. They will be the ones to have lost.

38. Say to the Unbelievers, if (now) they desist (from Unbelief), their past would be forgiven them; but if they persist, the punishment of those before them is already (a matter of warning for them).

39. And fight them on until there is no more persecution, and religion becomes Allah's in its entirety but if they cease, verily Allah doth see all that they do.

40. If they refuse, be sure that Allah is your Protector—the Best to protect and the Best to help.

41. And know that out of all the booty that ye may acquire (in war), a fifth share is assigned to Allah,—and to the Messenger, and to near relatives, orphans, the needy, and the wayfarer,— if ye do believe in Allah and in the revelation We sent down to Our Servant on the Day of Discrimination—the Day of the meeting of the two forces. For Allah hath power over all things.

42. Remember ye were on the hither side of the valley, and they on the farther side, and the caravan on lower ground than ye. Even if ye had made a mutual appointment to meet, ye would certainly have failed in the appointment: But (thus ye met), that Allah might accomplish a matter already

decided; that those who died might die after a clear Sign (had been given), and those who lived might live after a clear Sign (had been given). And verily Allah is He Who heareth and knoweth (all things).

43. Remember in thy dream Allah showed them to thee as few: if He had shown them to thee as many, ye would surely have been discouraged, and ye would surely have disputed in (your) decision: but Allah saved (you): for He knoweth well the (secrets) of (all) hearts.

44. And remember when ye met, He showed them to you as few in your eyes, and He made you appear as contemptible in their eyes: that Allah might accomplish a matter already decided and unto Allah are all matters returned.

45. O ye who believe! when ye meet a force, be firm, and call Allah in remembrance much (and often); that ye may prosper:

46. And obey Allah and His Messenger; and fall into no disputes, lest ye lose heart and your power depart; and be patient and persevering: for Allah is with those who patiently persevere:

47. And be not like those who started from their homes insolently and to be seen of men, and to hinder (men) from the path of Allah: for Allah compasseth all that they do.

48. Remember Satan made their (sinful) acts seem alluring to them, and said: "No one among men can overcome you this day, while I am near to you": but when the two forces came in sight of each other, he turned on his heels, and said: "Lo! I am clear of you; lo! I see what ye see not; lo! I fear Allah; for Allah is strict in punishment"

49. Lo! the Hypocrites and those in whose hearts is a disease: say: "these people,— their religion has misled them." But if any trust in Allah, behold! Allah is Exalted in might, Wise.

50. If thou couldst see, when the angels take the souls of the Unbelievers (at death), (how) they smite their faces and their backs, (saying): "Taste the chastisement of the blazing Fire—

وَلَوْ تَرَىٰٓ إِذْ يَتَوَفَّى الَّذِينَ كَفَرُوا الْمَلَٰٓئِكَةُ يَضْرِبُونَ وُجُوهَهُمْ وَأَدْبَٰرَهُمْ وَذُوقُوا عَذَابَ الْحَرِيقِ ٥٠

51. This is "because of (the deeds) which your (own) hands sent forth. For Allah is never unjust to His servants."

ذَٰلِكَ بِمَا قَدَّمَتْ أَيْدِيكُمْ وَأَنَّ اللَّهَ لَيْسَ بِظَلَّٰمٍ لِّلْعَبِيدِ ٥١

52. "(Deeds) after the manner of the People of Pharaoh and of those before them: they rejected the Signs of Allah, and Allah punished them for their crimes: for Allah is Strong, and Strict in punishment:

كَدَأْبِ آلِ فِرْعَوْنَ وَالَّذِينَ مِن قَبْلِهِمْ كَفَرُوا بِـَٔايَٰتِ اللَّهِ فَأَخَذَهُمُ اللَّهُ بِذُنُوبِهِمْ إِنَّ اللَّهَ قَوِيٌّ شَدِيدُ الْعِقَابِ ٥٢

53. "Because Allah will never change the Grace which He hath bestowed on a people until they change what is in their (own) souls: and verily Allah is He who heareth and knoweth (all things)."

ذَٰلِكَ بِأَنَّ اللَّهَ لَمْ يَكُ مُغَيِّرًا نِّعْمَةً أَنْعَمَهَا عَلَىٰ قَوْمٍ حَتَّىٰ يُغَيِّرُوا مَا بِأَنفُسِهِمْ وَأَنَّ اللَّهَ سَمِيعٌ عَلِيمٌ ٥٣

54. "(Deeds) after the manner of the People of Pharaoh and those before them": they treated as false the Signs of their Lord so We destroyed them for their crimes, and We drowned the People of Pharaoh: for they were all oppressors and wrong-doers.

كَدَأْبِ آلِ فِرْعَوْنَ وَالَّذِينَ مِن قَبْلِهِمْ كَذَّبُوا بِـَٔايَٰتِ رَبِّهِمْ فَأَهْلَكْنَٰهُم بِذُنُوبِهِمْ وَأَغْرَقْنَا آلَ فِرْعَوْنَ وَكُلٌّ كَانُوا ظَٰلِمِينَ ٥٤

55. For the worst of beasts in the sight of Allah are those who reject Him: they will not believe.

إِنَّ شَرَّ الدَّوَابِّ عِندَ اللَّهِ الَّذِينَ كَفَرُوا فَهُمْ لَا يُؤْمِنُونَ ٥٥

56. They are those with whom thou didst make a covenant, but they break their covenant every time, and they have not the fear (of Allah).

الَّذِينَ عَٰهَدتَّ مِنْهُمْ ثُمَّ يَنقُضُونَ عَهْدَهُمْ فِى كُلِّ مَرَّةٍ وَهُمْ لَا يَتَّقُونَ ٥٦

57. If ye gain the mastery over them in war, disperse, with them, those who follow them, that they may remember.

فَإِمَّا تَثْقَفَنَّهُمْ فِى الْحَرْبِ فَشَرِّدْ بِهِم مَّنْ خَلْفَهُمْ لَعَلَّهُمْ يَذَّكَّرُونَ ٥٧

58. If thou fearest treachery from any group, throw back (their Covenant) to them, (so as to be) on equal terms: for Allah loveth not the treacherous.

وَإِمَّا تَخَافَنَّ مِن قَوْمٍ خِيَانَةً فَانبِذْ إِلَيْهِمْ عَلَىٰ سَوَآءٍ إِنَّ اللَّهَ لَا يُحِبُّ الْخَآئِنِينَ ٥٨

59. Let not the Unbelievers think that they have escaped, they will never frustrate (them).

وَلَا يَحْسَبَنَّ الَّذِينَ كَفَرُوا سَبَقُوٓا إِنَّهُمْ لَا يُعْجِزُونَ ٥٩

60. Against them make ready your strength to the utmost of your power, including steeds of war, to strike terror into (the hearts of) the

وَأَعِدُّوا لَهُم مَّا اسْتَطَعْتُم مِّن قُوَّةٍ وَمِن رِّبَاطِ الْخَيْلِ تُرْهِبُونَ بِهِ عَدُوَّ

enemies, of Allah and your enemies, and others besides, whom ye may not know, but whom Allah doth know. Whatever ye shall spend in the Cause of Allah, shall be repaid unto you, and ye shall not be treated unjustly.

61. But if the enemy incline towards peace, do thou (also) incline towards peace, and trust in Allah: for He is the One that heareth and knoweth (all things).

62. Should they intend to deceive thee,— verily Allah sufficeth thee: He it is that hath strengthened thee with His aid and with (the company of) the Believers.

63. And (moreover) He hath put affection between their hearts: not if thou hadst spent all that is in the earth, couldst thou have produced that affection, but Allah Hath done it: for He is Exalted in might, Wise.

64. O Prophet ! Sufficient unto thee is Allah,—and unto those Who follow thee among the Believers.

65. O Prophet! rouse the Believers to the fight. If there are twenty amongst you, patient and persevering, they will vanquish two hundred: if a hundred. They will vanquish a thousand of the Unbelievers: for these are a people without understanding.

66. For tne present, Allah nath lightened your (burden), for He knoweth that there is a weak spot in you: but (even so), if there are a hundred of you, patient and persevering, they will vanquish two hundred, and if a thousand, they will vanquish two thousand, with the leave of Allah: for Allah is with those who patiently persevere.

67. It is not fitting for a Prophet that he should have prisoners of war until He hath thoroughly subdued the land. Ye look for the temporal goods of this world; but Allah looketh to the Hereafter: and Allah is Exalted

in might, Wise.

عَزِيزٌ حَكِيمٌ ۝

68. Had it not been for a previous ordainment from Allah, a severe punishment would have reached you for the (ransom) that ye took.

لَوْلَا كِتَابٌ مِّنَ اللَّهِ سَبَقَ لَمَسَّكُمْ فِيمَا أَخَذْتُمْ عَذَابٌ عَظِيمٌ ۝

69. But (now) enjoy what ye took in war, lawful and good: but fear Allah: for Allah is Oft-Forgiving, Most Merciful.

فَكُلُوا مِمَّا غَنِمْتُمْ حَلَالًا طَيِّبًا ۚ وَاتَّقُوا اللَّهَ ۚ إِنَّ اللَّهَ غَفُورٌ رَّحِيمٌ ۝

70. O Prophet! say to those who are captives in your hands: "If Allah findeth any good in your hearts, He will give you something better than what has been taken from you, and He will forgive you: for Allah is Oft-Forgiving, Most Merciful."

يَا أَيُّهَا النَّبِيُّ قُل لِّمَن فِي أَيْدِيكُم مِّنَ الْأَسْرَى إِن يَعْلَمِ اللَّهُ فِي قُلُوبِكُمْ خَيْرًا يُؤْتِكُمْ خَيْرًا مِّمَّا أُخِذَ مِنكُمْ وَيَغْفِرْ لَكُمْ ۗ وَاللَّهُ غَفُورٌ رَّحِيمٌ ۝

71. But if they have treacherous designs against thee, (O Messenger!), they have already been in treason against Allah, and so hath He given (thee) power over them. And Allah is He Who hath (full) knowledge and wisdom.

وَإِن يُرِيدُوا خِيَانَتَكَ فَقَدْ خَانُوا اللَّهَ مِن قَبْلُ فَأَمْكَنَ مِنْهُمْ ۗ وَاللَّهُ عَلِيمٌ حَكِيمٌ ۝

72. Those who believed, and emigrated and fought for the Faith, with their property and their persons, in the Cause of Allah, as well as those who gave (them) asylum and aid,—these are (all) Friends and protectors, one of another. As to those who believed but did not emigrate ye owe no duty of protection to them until they emigrate; but if they seek your aid in religion, it is your duty to help them, except against a people with whom ye have a treaty of mutual alliance. And (remember) Allah seeth all that ye do.

إِنَّ الَّذِينَ آمَنُوا وَهَاجَرُوا وَجَاهَدُوا بِأَمْوَالِهِمْ وَأَنفُسِهِمْ فِي سَبِيلِ اللَّهِ وَالَّذِينَ آوَوا وَّنَصَرُوا أُولَٰئِكَ بَعْضُهُمْ أَوْلِيَاءُ بَعْضٍ ۚ وَالَّذِينَ آمَنُوا وَلَمْ يُهَاجِرُوا مَا لَكُم مِّن وَلَايَتِهِم مِّن شَيْءٍ حَتَّىٰ يُهَاجِرُوا ۚ وَإِنِ اسْتَنصَرُوكُمْ فِي الدِّينِ فَعَلَيْكُمُ النَّصْرُ إِلَّا عَلَىٰ قَوْمٍ بَيْنَكُمْ وَبَيْنَهُم مِّيثَاقٌ ۗ وَاللَّهُ بِمَا تَعْمَلُونَ بَصِيرٌ ۝

73. The Unbelievers are protec-tors, one of another: unless ye do this, (Protect each other), there would be tumult and oppression on earth, and great mischief.

وَالَّذِينَ كَفَرُوا بَعْضُهُمْ أَوْلِيَاءُ بَعْضٍ ۚ إِلَّا تَفْعَلُوهُ تَكُن فِتْنَةٌ فِي الْأَرْضِ وَفَسَادٌ كَبِيرٌ ۝

74. Those who believe, and emigrate, and fight for the Faith, in the Cause of Allah, as well as those who give (them) asylum and aid,—these are (all) in very truth the Believers: for them is the forgiveness of sins and a provision most generous.

وَالَّذِينَ آمَنُوا وَهَاجَرُوا وَجَاهَدُوا فِي سَبِيلِ اللَّهِ وَالَّذِينَ آوَوا وَّنَصَرُوا أُولَٰئِكَ هُمُ الْمُؤْمِنُونَ حَقًّا ۚ لَّهُم مَّغْفِرَةٌ وَرِزْقٌ كَرِيمٌ ۝

75. And those who accept Faith subsequently, and emigrate, and fight

وَالَّذِينَ آمَنُوا مِن بَعْدُ وَهَاجَرُوا

SÛRA–9
AT-TAUBA
(INTRODUCTION)

Logically this Sûra follows up the argument of the last Sûra (8), and indeed may be considered a part of it, although chronologically the two are separated by an interval of seven years.

We saw that Sûra 8 dealt with the large questions arising at the outset of the life of a new Ummat or organised nation: questions of defence under attack, distribution of war acquisitions after victory, the virtues needed for concerted action, and clemency and consideration for one's own and for enemies in the hour of victory. We pass on in this Sûra to deal with the question : What is to be done if the enemy breaks faith and is guilty of treachery? No nation can go on with a treaty if the other party violates it at will; but it is laid down that a period of four months should be allowed by way of notice after denunciation of the treaty; that due protection should be accorded in the intervening period; that there should always be open the door to repentance and reunion with the people of Allah; and that if all these fail, and war must be undertaken, it must be pushed with utmost vigour.

These are the general principles deducible from the Sura. The immediate occasion for their promulgation may be considered in connection with the chronological place of the Sûra.

Chronologically, verses 1-29 were a notable declaration of State policy promulgated about the month of Shwwāi. A.H. 9, and read out by Hadhrat 'Ali at the Pilgrimage two months later in order to give the policy the widest publicity possible. The remainder of the Súra, verses 30-129, was revealed a little earlier, say, about the month of Ramadhān, A.H. 9, and sums up the lessons of the Apostle's Tabûk expedition in the summer of A.H. 9 (say October 630).

Tabûk is a place near the frontier of Arabia, quite close to what was then Byzantine territory in the Province of Syria (which includes Palestine). It is about 350 miles northwest of Madinah, and 150 miles south of Ma'ān. It had a fort and a spring of sweet water. In consequence of strong and persistent rumours that the Byzantines (Romans) were preparing to invade Arabia and that the Byzantine Emperor himself had arrived near the frontier for the purpose, the Apostle collected as large a force as he could, and marched to Tubûk. The Byzantine invasion did not come off. But the Apostle took the opportunity of consolidating the Muslim position in that direction and making treaties of alliance with certain Christain and Jewish tribes near the Gulf of 'Aqaba. On his return to Madinah he considered the situation. During his absence the Hypocrites had played, as always, a double game, and the policy hitherto followed, of free access to the sacred centre of Islam, to Muslims and Pagans alike, was now altered, as it had been abused by the enemies of Islam.

This is the only Sūra to which the usual formula of *Bismillāh* is not prefixed. It was among the last of the Sūras revealed, and though the Apostle had directed that it should follow Sūra 8, it was not clear whether it was to form a separate Sūra or only a part of Sūra 8. It is now treated as a separate Sūra, but the *Bismillāh* is not prefixed to it, as there is no warrant for supposing that the Apostle used the *Bismillāh* before it in his recittion of the Qur-ān. The Sūra is known under many names. the two most commonly used are (1) *Tauba* (Repentance), with reference to 9: 104 and (2) *Barāat* (Immunity), the opening word of the Sūra.

for the Faith in your company,—they are of you. But kindred by blood have prior rights against each other in the Book of Allah. Verily Allah is well—acquainted with all things.

At-Tauba (Repentance) or Barãat (Immunity)

1. A (declaration) of immunity from Allah and His Messenger, to those of the Pagans with whom ye have contracted mutual alliances:—

2. Go ye, then for four months, (as ye will), throughout the land, but know yet that ye cannot frustrate Allah (by your falsehood but that Allah will cover with shame those who reject Him.

3. And an announcement from Allah and His Messenger, to the people (assembled) on the day of the Great Pilgrimage,—that Allah and His Messenger dissolve (treaty) obligations with the Pagans. If, then, ye repent, it were best for you; but if ye turn away, know ye that ye cannot frustrate Allah, and proclaim a grievous chastisement to those who reject Faith.

4. (But the treaties are) not dissolved with those Pagans with whom ye have entered into alliance and who have not subsequently failed you in aught, nor aided anyone against you. So fulfil your engagements with them to the end of their term: for Allah loveth the righteous.

5. But when the forbidden months are past, then fight and slay the Pagans wherever ye find them, and seize them, beleaguer them, and lie in wait for them in every stratagem (of war); but if they repent, and establish regular prayers and pay Zakat then open the way for them: for Allah is Oft-Forgiving, Most Merciful.

6. If one amongst the Pagans ask thee for asylum, grant it to him, so that he may

وَجَاهَدُوا مَعَكُمْ نَأُولَئِكَ مِنْكُمْ ۚ وَأُولُوا الْأَرْحَامِ بَعْضُهُمْ أَوْلَى بِبَعْضٍ فِى كِتَابِ اللّٰهِ ۗ إِنَّ اللّٰهَ بِكُلِّ شَىْءٍ عَلِيمٌ ۞

بَرَآءَةٌ مِّنَ اللّٰهِ وَرَسُولِهِ إِلَى الَّذِينَ عَاهَدْتُّمْ مِّنَ الْمُشْرِكِينَ ۞

فَسِيحُوا فِى الْأَرْضِ أَرْبَعَةَ أَشْهُرٍ وَّاعْلَمُوا أَنَّكُمْ غَيْرُ مُعْجِزِى اللّٰهِ ۙ وَأَنَّ اللّٰهَ مُخْزِى الْكَافِرِينَ ۞

وَأَذَانٌ مِّنَ اللّٰهِ وَرَسُولِهِ إِلَى النَّاسِ يَوْمَ الْحَجِّ الْأَكْبَرِ أَنَّ اللّٰهَ بَرِىءٌ مِّنَ الْمُشْرِكِينَ ۙ وَرَسُولُهُ ۚ فَإِنْ تُبْتُمْ فَهُوَ خَيْرٌ لَّكُمْ ۚ وَإِنْ تَوَلَّيْتُمْ فَاعْلَمُوا أَنَّكُمْ غَيْرُ مُعْجِزِى اللّٰهِ ۗ وَبَشِّرِ الَّذِينَ كَفَرُوا بِعَذَابٍ أَلِيمٍ ۞

إِلَّا الَّذِينَ عَاهَدْتُّمْ مِّنَ الْمُشْرِكِينَ ثُمَّ لَمْ يَنْقُصُوكُمْ شَيْئًا وَّلَمْ يُظَاهِرُوا عَلَيْكُمْ أَحَدًا فَأَتِمُّوا إِلَيْهِمْ عَهْدَهُمْ إِلَى مُدَّتِهِمْ ۚ إِنَّ اللّٰهَ يُحِبُّ الْمُتَّقِينَ ۞

فَإِذَا انْسَلَخَ الْأَشْهُرُ الْحُرُمُ فَاقْتُلُوا الْمُشْرِكِينَ حَيْثُ وَجَدْتُّمُوهُمْ وَخُذُوهُمْ وَاحْصُرُوهُمْ وَاقْعُدُوا لَهُمْ كُلَّ مَرْصَدٍ ۚ فَإِنْ تَابُوا وَأَقَامُوا الصَّلَوٰةَ وَآتَوُا الزَّكَوٰةَ فَخَلُّوا سَبِيلَهُمْ ۚ إِنَّ اللّٰهَ غَفُورٌ رَّحِيمٌ ۞

وَإِنْ أَحَدٌ مِّنَ الْمُشْرِكِينَ اسْتَجَارَكَ

hear the Word of Allah; and then escort him to where he can be secure, that is because they are men without knowledge.

7.   How can there be a covenant before Allah and His Messenger, with the Pagans, except those with whom ye made a treaty near the Sacred Mosque? As long as these stand true to you, stand ye true to them: for Allah doth love the righteous.

8.   How (can there be such a covenant) seeing that if they get an advantage over you, they respect not in you the ties either of kinship or of covenant? With (fair words from) their mouths they please you, but their hearts are averse from you; and most of them are rebellious and wicked.

9.   The Words of Allah have they sold for a miserable price, and (many) have they hindered from His Way: evil indeed are the deeds thy have done.

10.   In a Believer they respect not the ties either of kinship or of covenant! It is they who have transgressed all bounds.

11.   But (even so), if they repent, establish regular prayers, and pay Zakat they are your brethren in Faith: (thus) do We explain the Signs in detail, for those who understand.

12.   But if they violate their oaths after their covenant, and attack your Faith,—fight ye the chiefs of Unfaith: for their oaths are nothing to them: that thus they may be restrained.

13.   Will ye not fight people who violated their oaths, plotted to expel the Messenger, and attacked you first? Do ye fear them? Nay, it is Allah Whom ye should more justly fear, if ye believe!

14. Fight them, and Allah will punish them by your hands, and disgrace them help you (to victory) over them, heal the breasts of Believers.

قَاتِلُوهُمْ يُعَذِّبْهُمُ اللّهُ بِأَيْدِيكُمْ وَيُخْزِهِمْ وَيَنْصُرْكُمْ عَلَيْهِمْ وَيَشْفِ صُدُورَ قَوْمٍ مُّؤْمِنِينَ ۞

15. And still the indignation of their hearts. For Allah will turn (in mercy) to whom He will: and Allah is All-Knowing, All-Wise.

وَيُذْهِبْ غَيْظَ قُلُوبِهِمْ وَيَتُوبُ اللّهُ عَلَى مَن يَشَاءُ وَاللّهُ عَلِيمٌ حَكِيمٌ ۞

16. Do you think that you would be left alone while Allah has not yet known those among you who strive with might and main, and take none for friends and protectors except Allah, His Messenger, and the (community of) Believers? And Allah is well-acquainted with (all) that ye do.

أَمْ حَسِبْتُمْ أَن تُتْرَكُوا وَلَمَّا يَعْلَمِ اللّهُ الَّذِينَ جَاهَدُوا مِنكُمْ وَلَمْ يَتَّخِذُوا مِن دُونِ اللّهِ وَلَا رَسُولِهِ وَلَا الْمُؤْمِنِينَ وَلِيجَةً وَاللّهُ خَبِيرٌ بِمَا تَعْمَلُونَ ۞

17. It is not for such as join gods with Allah, to maintain the mosques of Allah while they witness against their own souls to infidelity. The works of such bear no fruit: in Fire shall they dwell.

مَا كَانَ لِلْمُشْرِكِينَ أَن يَعْمُرُوا مَسَاجِدَ اللّهِ شَاهِدِينَ عَلَى أَنفُسِهِم بِالْكُفْرِ أُولَئِكَ حَبِطَتْ أَعْمَالُهُمْ وَفِي النَّارِ هُمْ خَالِدُونَ ۞

18. The mosques of Allah shall be visited and maintained by such as believe in Allah and the Last Day, establish regular prayers, and pay Zakat, and fear none (at all) except Allah it is they who are expected to be on true guidance.

إِنَّمَا يَعْمُرُ مَسَاجِدَ اللّهِ مَنْ آمَنَ بِاللّهِ وَالْيَوْمِ الْآخِرِ وَأَقَامَ الصَّلَوةَ وَآتَى الزَّكَوةَ وَلَمْ يَخْشَ إِلَّا اللّهَ فَعَسَى أُولَئِكَ أَن يَكُونُوا مِنَ الْمُهْتَدِينَ ۞

19. Do ye consider the giving of drink to pilgrims, or the maintenance of the Sacred Mosque, equal to (the pious service of) those who believe in Allah and the Last Day, and strive with might and main in the cause of Allah? They are not equal in the sight of Allah: and Allah guides not those who do wrong.

أَجَعَلْتُمْ سِقَايَةَ الْحَاجِّ وَعِمَارَةَ الْمَسْجِدِ الْحَرَامِ كَمَنْ آمَنَ بِاللّهِ وَالْيَوْمِ الْآخِرِ وَجَاهَدَ فِي سَبِيلِ اللّهِ لَا يَسْتَوُونَ عِندَ اللّهِ وَاللّهُ لَا يَهْدِي الْقَوْمَ الظَّالِمِينَ ۞

20. Those who believe, and emigrate and strive with might and main, in Allah's cause, with their goods and their persons have the highest rank in the sight of Allah: they are the people who will achieve (salvation).

الَّذِينَ آمَنُوا وَهَاجَرُوا وَجَاهَدُوا فِي سَبِيلِ اللّهِ بِأَمْوَالِهِمْ وَأَنفُسِهِمْ أَعْظَمُ دَرَجَةً عِندَ اللّهِ وَأُولَئِكَ هُمُ الْفَائِزُونَ ۞

21. Their Lord doth give them glad tidings of a Mercy from Himself, of His good pleasure. And of Gardens for them, wherein are delights that endure:

يُبَشِّرُهُمْ رَبُّهُم بِرَحْمَةٍ مِّنْهُ وَرِضْوَانٍ وَجَنَّاتٍ لَّهُمْ فِيهَا نَعِيمٌ مُّقِيمٌ ۞

22. They will dwell therein for ever. Verily

خَالِدِينَ فِيهَا أَبَدًا إِنَّ اللّهَ عِندَهُ

with Allah is a reward, the greatest (of all).

23. O ye who believe! Take not for protectors your fathers and your brothers if they love infidelity above Faith: if any of you do so, they do wrong.

24. Say: If it be that your fathers, your sons, your brothers, your mates, or your kindred; the wealth that ye have gained; the commerce in which ye fear a decline; or the dwellings in which ye delight— are dearer to you than Allah or His Messenger, or the striving in His cause;—then wait until Allah brings about His Decision: and Allah guides not the rebellious.

25. Assuredly Allah did help you in many battle-fields and on the day of Hunain: behold! your great numbers elated you, but they availed you naught; the land. For all that it is wide, did constrain you, and ye turned back in retreat.

26. But Allah did pour His calm on the Messenger and on the Believers and sent down forces which ye saw not: He punished the Unbelievers: thus doth He reward those without Faith.

27. Again will Allah, after this, turn (in mercy) to whom He will: for Allah is Oft-Forgiving, Most Merciful.

28. O ye who believe! Truly the Pagans are unclean; so let them not, after this year of theirs, approach the Sacred Mosque. And if ye fear poverty, soon will Allah enrich you, if He wills, out of His bounty, for Allah is All-Knowing, All-Wise.

29. Fight those who believe not in Allah nor the Last Day, nor hold that forbidden which hath been forbidden by Allah and

His Messenger. nor acknowledge the
Religion of Truth, from among the People of
the Book. until they pay the *Jizya* with willing
submission, and feel themselves subdued.

30. The Jews call 'Uzair a son of Allah,
and the Christians call Christ the Son of
Allah. That is a saying from their mouth: (in
this) they but imitate what the Unbelievers
of old used to say. Allah's curse be on
them: how they are deluded away from the
Truth!

31. They take their priests and their
anchorites to be their lords beside Allah.
And (they take as their Lord) Christ the son
of Mary: yet they were commanded to
worship but One God: there is no god but
He. Praise and glory to Him: (far is He)
from having the partners they associate
(with Him).

32. Fain would they extinguish Allah's
Light with their mouths. but Allah will not
allow but that His Light should be perfected,
even though the Unbelievers May detest
(it).

33. It is He Who hath sent His Messenger
with Guidance and the Religion of Truth, to
cause it to prevail over all religion. even
though the Pagans may detest (it).

34. O ye who believe! There are Indeed
many among the priests and anchorites,
who in falsehood devour the wealth of men
and hinder (them) from the Way of Allah.
And there are those who hoard gold and
silver and spend it not in the Way of Allah:
announce unto them a most grievous
chastisement—

35. On the Day when it will be heated in
the fire of Hell, and with it will be branded
their foreheads, their flanks, and their
backs,—"This is the (treasure) which ye
Hoarded for yourselves: taste ye, then, the
(treasures) ye hoarded"

36. The number of months in the sight of
Allah is twelve (in a year)— so ordained by
Him the day He created the heavens and
the earth; of them four are sacred: that is
the right religion so wrong not yourselves
therein, and fight the Pagans all together
as they fight you all together. But know that
Allah is with those who restrain themselves.

37. Verily the transposing (of a prohibited
month) is an addition to Unbelief: the
Unbelievers are led to wrong thereby: for
they make it lawful one year, and forbidden
another year, in order to agree with the
number of months forbidden by Allah and
make such forbidden ones Lawful. The evil
of their course seems pleasing to them.
But Allah guideth not those who reject Faith.

38. O ye who believe! what is the matter
with you, that, when ye are asked to go
forth in the Cause of Allah, ye cling heavily
to the earth? Do ye prefer the life of this
world to the Hereafter? But little is the
comfort of this life, as compared with the
Hereafter.

39. Unless ye go forth, He will punish you
with a grievous penalty, and put others in
your place; but Him ye would not harm in the
least, for Allah Hath power over all things.

40. If ye help not (the Prophet). (it is no
matter): for Allah did indeed help him, when
the Unbelievers drove him out: being the
second of the two they two were in the
Cave, and he said to his companion. "Have
no fear, for Allah is with us": then Allah sent
down His peace upon him, and
strengthened him with forces which ye saw
not. and humbled to the depths the word of
the Unbelievers. But the word of Allah is
exalted to the heights: for Allah is Exalted
in might. Wise.

41. Go ye forth, (whether equipped) lightly or heavily, and strive and struggle, with your goods and your persons, in the Cause of Allah. That is best for you, if ye (but knew).

42. If there had been immediate gain (in sight), and the journey easy, they would (all) without doubt have followed thee, but the distance was long, (and weighed) on them. They would indeed swear by Allah, "If we only could, We should certainly have come out with you:" They would destroy their own souls; for Allah doth know that they are certainly lying.

43. God give thee grace! Why didst thou grant them exemption until those who told the truth were seen by thee in a clear light, and thou hadst proved the liars?

44. Those who believe in Allah and the Last Day ask thee for no exemption from fighting with their goods and persons. And Allah knoweth well those who do their duty.

45. Only those ask thee for exemption who believe not in Allah and the Last Day, and whose hearts are in doubt, so that they are tossed in their doubts to and fro.

46. If they had intended to come out, they would certainly have made some preparation therefor: but Allah was averse to their being sent forth; so He made them lag behind, and they were told, "Sit ye among those who sit (inactive)."

47. If they had come out with you, they would not have added to your (strength) but only (made for) disorder, hurrying to and fro in your midst and sowing sedition among you, and there would have been some among you who would have listened to them. But Allah knoweth well those who do wrong.

48. Indeed they had plotted sedition before, and upset matters for thee,—until the Truth arrived, and the Decree of Allah became manifest, much to their disgust.

49. Among them is (many) a man who says: "Grant me exemption and draw me not into trial." Have they not fallen into trial already? And indeed Hell surrounds the Unbelievers (on all sides).

50. If good befalls thee, it grieves them; but if a misfortune befalls thee, they say, "We took indeed our precautions beforehand," and they turn away rejoicing.

51. Say: "Nothing will happen to us except what Allah has decreed for us: He is our Protector": and on Allah let the Believers put their trust.

52. Say: "Can you expect for us (any fate) other than one of two glorious things—(martyrdom or victory)? But we can expect for you either that Allah will send His punishment from Him or by our hands. So wait (Expectant); we too will wait with you."

53. Say: "Spend (for the Cause) willingly or unwillingly: not from you will it be accepted: for ye are indeed a people rebellious and wicked."

54. The only reasons why their contributions are not accepted are: that they reject Allah and His Messenger; that they come not to prayer save lazily and that they offer contributions unwillingly.

55. Let not their wealth nor their children dazzle thee: in reality Allah's Wish is to punish them with these things in this life, and that their souls may perish in their (very) denial of Allah.

56. They swear by Allah that they are indeed of you: but they are not of you: yet they are afraid (of you).

57. If they could find a place to flee to, or caves, or a place of concealment, they would Turn straight-way thereto with an obstinate rush.

58. And among them are men who slander

thee in the matter of (the distribution of) the alms. If they are given part thereof, they are pleased, but if not, behold! they are indignant!

59. If only they had been content with what Allah and His Messenger gave them, and had said, "Sufficient unto us is Allah! Allah and His mesenger will soon give us of His bounty: to Allah do we turn our hopes!" (That would have been the right Course).

60. Alms are for the poor and the needy, and those employed to administer the (funds): for those whose hearts have been (recently) reconciled (to Truth); for those in bondage and in debt; in the cause of Allah: and for the wayfarer: (thus is it) ordained by Allah. And Allah is full of knowledge and wisdom.

61. Among them are men who molest the Prophet and say, "He is (all) ear." Say, "He listens to what is best for you: he believes in Allah, has faith in the Believers, and is a Mercy to those of you who believe." But those who molest the Prophet will have a grievous chastisement

62. To you they swear by Allah. In order to please you: but it is more fitting that they should please Allah and His Messenger, if they are Believers.

63. Know they not that for those who oppose Allah and His Messenger, is the Fire of Hell?—wherein they shall dwell. That is the supreme disgrace.

64. The Hypocrites are afraid lest a Sūra should be sent down about them, showing them what is (really passing) in their hearts. Say: "Mock ye! But verily Allah will bring to light all that ye fear (should be revealed).

65. If thou dost question them, they declare (with emphasis): "We were only talking idly and in play.": Say: "Was it at Allah, and His Signs, and His Messenger, that ye were mocking?"

66. Make ye no excuses: ye have rejected Faith after ye had accepted it. If We pardon

some of you, We will punish others amongst you, for that they are sinners.

67. The Hypocrites, men and women, are alike: they enjoin evil, and forbid what is just, and tighten their purse's strings. They have forgotten Allah: so He Hath forgotten them. Verily the Hypocrites are rebellious and perverse.

68. Allah hath promised the Hypocrites men and women, and the rejecters, of Faith, the fire of Hell: therein shall they dwell: sufficient is it for them: for them is the curse of Allah. And an enduring punishment,—

69. As in the case of those before you: they were mightier than you in power, and more flourishing in wealth and children. They had their enjoyment of their portion: and ye have of yours, as did those before you; and ye indulge in idle talk as they did. They!—their works are fruitless in this world and in the Hereafter, and they are the Losers.

70. Hath not the story reached them of those before them?—The people of Noah, and 'Ād, and Thamud; the people of Abraham, the men of Midian, and the Cities overthrown. To them came their messengers with Clear Signs. It is not Allah Who wrongs them, but they wrong their own souls.

71. The Believers, men and women, are protectors, one of another: they enjoin what is just, and forbid what is evil: they observe regular prayers, pay Zakat and obey Allah and His Messenger. On them will Allah pour His mercy: for Allah is Exalted in power, Wise.

72. Allah hath promised to Believers, men and women, Gardens under which rivers flow, to dwell therein, and beautiful mansions in Gardens of everlasting stay

but the greatest bliss is the Good Pleasure of Allah: that is the supreme triumph.

73. O Prophet! strive hard against the Unbelievers and the Hypocrites, and be firm against them. Their abode is Hell,—an evil refuge indeed.

74. They swear by Allah that they said nothing (evil), but indeed they uttered blasphemy, and they uttered it after accepting Islam: and they meditated a plot which they were unable to carry out: this revenge of theirs was (their) only return for the bounty with which Allah and His Messenger had enriched them! If they repent, it will be best for them: but if they turn back (to their evil ways), Allah will punish them with a grievous chastisement in this life and in the Hereafter: they shall have none on earth to protect or help them.

75. Amongst them are men who made a Covenant with Allah, that if He bestowed on them of His bounty, they would give (largely) in charity, and be truly amongst those who are righteous.

76. But when He did bestow of His bounty, they became misers, and turned back (from their Covenant), averse (from its fulfilment).

77. So He hath put as a consequence hypocrisy into their hearts, (to last) till the Day whereon they shall meet Him: because they broke their Covenant with Allah, and because they lied (again and again).

78. Know they not that Allah doth know their secret (thoughts) and their secret counsels, and that Allah knoweth well all things unseen?

79. Those who slander such of the Believers as give themselve freely to (deeds of) charity, as well as those who give according to their means,—and throw ridicule on them,—Allah will throw back their ridicule on them: and they shall have a grievous chastisement.

80. Whether thou ask for their forgiveness, or not, (their) sin is unforgivable: if thou ask seventy times for their forgiveness, Allah will not forgive them: because they have

rejected Allah and His Messenger: and Allah guideth not those who are perversely rebellious.

81. Those who were left behind (in the Tabûk expedition) rejoiced in their sitting back behind the Messenger of Allah: they hated to strive and fight, with their goods and their persons, in the Cause of Allah: they said, "Go not forth in the heat ." Say, "The fire of Hell is fiercer in heat," if only they could understand!

82. Let them laugh a little: much will they weep: a recompense for the (evil) that they do.

83. If, then, Allah bring thee back to any of them, and they ask Thy permission to come out (with thee), say: "Never shall ye come out with me, nor fight an enemy with me: for ye preferred to sit inactive on the first occasion: then sit ye (now) with those who stay behind."

84. Nor do thou ever pray for any of them that dies, nor stand at his grave; for they rejected Allah and His Messenger, and died in a state of perverse rebellion.

85. Nor let their wealth nor their children dazzle thee: Allah's Wish is to punish them with these things in this world, and that their souls may depart while they are unbelievers.

86. When a Sûra comes down, enjoining them to believe in Allah and to strive and fight along with His Messenger, those with wealth and influence among them ask thee for exemption, and say: "Leave us (behind): we would be with those who sit (at home)."

87. They prefer to be with (the women), who remain behind (at home): their hearts are sealed and so they understand not.

88. But the Messenger, and those who believe with him. strive and fight with their wealth and their persons: for them

are (all) good things: and it is they who will prosper.

89. Allah hath prepared for them Gardens under which rivers flow, to dwell therein: that is the supreme triumph.

90. And there were, among the desert Arabs (also), men who made excuses and came to claim exemption: and those who were false to Allah and His Messenger (merely) sat behind: soon will a grievous chastisement seize the Unbelievers among them.

91. There is no blame on those who are infirm, or ill, or who find no resources to spend (on the Cause), if they are sincere (in duty) to Allah and His Messenger: no ground (of complaint) can there be against such as do right: and Allah is Oft-Forgiving, Most Merciful.

92. Nor (is there blame) on those who came to thee to be provided with mounts. And when thou saidst, "I can find no mounts for you," they turned back, their eyes streaming with tears of grief that they had no resources wherewith to provide the expenses.

93. The ground (of complaint) is only against such as claim exemption while they are rich. They prefer to stay with the (women) who remain behind: Allah hath sealed their hearts: so they know not.

94. They will present their excuses to you when ye return to them. Say thou: "Present no excuses, we shall not believe you: Allah hath already informed us of the true state of matters concerning you: it is your actions that Allah and His Messenger will observe: in the end will ye be brought back to Him who knoweth what is hidden and what is open: then will He show you the truth of all that ye did."

95. They will swear to you by Allah, when ye return to them, that ye may leave them alone. So leave them alone: for they are an abomination, and Hell is their dwelling-place,—a fitting recom-pense for the (evil) that they did.

96. They will swear unto you, that ye may be pleased with them. But if ye are pleased with them. Allah is not pleased with those who disobey.

97. The Bedouin Arabs are the worst in unbelief and hypocrisy, and most fitted to be in ignorance of the command which Allah hath sent down to His Messenger: but Allah is All-Knowing, All-Wise.

98. Some of the Bedouin Arabs look upon their payments as a fine, and watch for disasters for you: on them be the disaster of Evil: for Allah is He that heareth and knoweth (all things).

99. But some of the Bedouin Arabs believe in Allah and the Last Day, and look on their payments as pious gifts bringing them nearer to Allah and obtaining the prayers of the Messenger. Aye, indeed they bring them nearer (to Him): soon will Allah Admit them to His Mercy: for Allah is Oft-Forgiving, Most Merciful.

100. The vanguard (of Islam)—the first of those who forsook (their homes) and of those who gave them aid, and (also) those who follow them in (all) good deeds,—Well-pleased is Allah with them, as are they with Him: for them hath He prepared Gardens under which rivers flow, to dwell therein for ever: that is the supreme Triumph.

101. Certain of the desert Arabs round about you are Hypocrites, as well as among the Madinah folk: they are obstinate in nypocrisy: thou knowest them not: We know

them: twice shall We punish them: and in addition shall they be sent to a grievous Chastisement.

102. Others (there are who) have acknowledged their wrong-doings: they have mixed an act that was good with another that was evil. Perhaps Allah will turn unto them (in mercy): for Allah is Oft-Forgiving, Most Merciful.

103. Of their wealth take alms, that so thou mightest purify and sanctify them; and pray on their behalf. Verily thy prayers are a source of security for them: And Allah is One Who heareth and knoweth.

104. Know they not that Allah doth accept repentance from His votaries and receives their gifts of charity, and that Allah is verily He, the Oft-Returning, Most Merciful?

105. And say: "Work (righteous-ness): soon will Allah observe your work, and His Messenger, and the Believers: soon will ye be brought back to the Knower of what is hidden and what is open: then will He show you the truth of all that ye did."

106. There are (yet) others, held in suspense for the command of Allah, whether He will punish them, or turn in mercy to them: and Allah is All-Knowing, Wise.

107. And there are those who put up a mosque by way of mischief and infidelity—to disunite the Believers—and in preparation for one who warred against Allah and His Messenger aforetime. They will indeed swear that their intention is nothing but good; but Allah doth declare that they are certainly liars.

108. Never stand thou forth therein. There is a mosque whose foundation was laid from the first day on piety; it is more worthy of thy standing forth (for prayer) therein. In it are men who love to be purified; and Allah loveth those who make themselves pure.

109. Which then is best?—he that layeth his foundation on piety to Allah and His

Good Pleasure?—or he that layeth his
foundation on an undermined sand-cliff
ready to crumble to pieces? And it doth
crumble to pieces with him, into the fire of
Hell. And Allah guideth not People that do
wrong.

110. The foundation of those who so build
is never free from suspicion and shakiness
in their hearts, until their hearts are cut to
pieces. And Allah is All-Knowing, Wise.

111. Allah hath purchased of the Believers
their persons and their goods; for theirs (in
return) is the Garden (of Paradise): they
fight in His Cause, and slay and are slain: a
promise binding on Him in Truth, through
the Torah, the Gospel, and the Qur'an: and
who is more faithful to his Covenant than
Allah? Then rejoice in the bargain which ye
have concluded: that is the achievement
supreme.

112. Those that turn (to Allah) in repentance:
that serve Him, and praise Him: that wander
in devotion to Cause of Allah: that bow down
and prostrate themselves in　prayer; that
enjoin good and forbid evil; and observe the
limits set by Allah,—(these do rejoice). So
proclaim the glad tidings to the Believers.

113. It is not fitting, for the Prophet and
those who believe, that they should pray
for forgiveness for Pagans, even though
they be of kin, after it is clear to them that
they are companions of the Fire.

114. And Abraham prayed for his father's
forgiveness only because of a promise he
had made to him. But when it became clear
to him that he was an enemy to Allah, he
dissociated himself from him: for Abraham
was most tender hearted, forbearing.

115. And Allah will not mislead a people
after He hath guided them until he makes
clear to them as to what they should avoid,
for Allah hath knowledge of all things.

116. Unto Allah belongeth the dominion of the heavens and the earth. He giveth life and He taketh it. Except for Him ye have no protector nor helper.

117. Allah turned with favour to the Prophet, the Muhajirs. And the Ansār,—who followed Him in a time of distress, after that the hearts of a part of them had nearly swerved (from duty); but He turned to them (also): for He is unto them Most Kind, Most Merciful.

118. (He turned in mercy also) to the three who were left behind; (they felt guilty) to such a degree that the earth seemed constrained to them, for all its speciousness, and their (very) souls seemed straitened to them,—and they perceived that there is no fleeing from Allah (and no refuge) but to Himself. Then He turned to them, that they might repent: for Allah is Oft-Returning, Most Merciful.

119. O ye who believe! Fear Allah and be with those who are truthful.

120. It was not fitting for the people of Madinah and the Bedouin Arabs of the neighbourhood, to stay behind Allah's Messenger, nor to prefer their own lives to his: because nothing could they suffer or do, but was reckoned to their credit as a deed of righteousness,—whether they suffered thirst, or fatigue, or hunger, in the Cause of Allah, or trod paths to raise the ire of the Unbelievers, or gain any gain from an enemy: for Allah suffereth not the reward to be lost of those who do good;—

121. Nor could they spend anything (for the Cause)—small or great—nor cut across a valley, but the deed is inscribed to their credit; that Allah may requite them with the best (possible reward).

122. It is not for the Believers to go forth together: if a contingent from every

expedition go forth to devote themselves to studies in religion, and admonish the people when they return to them,--that thus they (may learn) to guard themselves (against evil).

فَلَوْلَا نَفَرَ مِنْ كُلِّ فِرْقَةٍ مِّنْهُمْ طَآئِفَةٌ لِّيَتَفَقَّهُوا فِى الدِّينِ وَلِيُنْذِرُوا قَوْمَهُمْ إِذَا رَجَعُوٓا إِلَيْهِمْ لَعَلَّهُمْ يَحْذَرُونَ ۝

123. O ye who believe! Fight the Unbelievers who are near to you and let them find harshness in you: and know that Allah is with those who fear Him.

يَآأَيُّهَا الَّذِينَ ءَامَنُوا قَاتِلُوا الَّذِينَ يَلُونَكُمْ مِّنَ الْكُفَّارِ وَلْيَجِدُوا فِيكُمْ غِلْظَةً وَاعْلَمُوٓا أَنَّ اللَّهَ مَعَ الْمُتَّقِينَ ۝

124. Whenever there cometh down a Sûra, some of them say: "Which of you has had His faith increased by it?" Yea, those who believe,—their faith is increased, and they do rejoice.

وَإِذَا مَآ أُنْزِلَتْ سُورَةٌ فَمِنْهُمْ مَّنْ يَقُولُ أَيُّكُمْ زَادَتْهُ هَذِهِ إِيمَانًا فَأَمَّا الَّذِينَ ءَامَنُوا فَزَادَتْهُمْ إِيمَانًا وَهُمْ يَسْتَبْشِرُونَ ۝

125. But those in whose hearts is a disease,—it will add doubt to their doubt, and they will die in a state of Unbelief.

وَأَمَّا الَّذِينَ فِى قُلُوبِهِمْ مَّرَضٌ فَزَادَتْهُمْ رِجْسًا إِلَى رِجْسِهِمْ وَمَاتُوا وَهُمْ كَافِرُونَ ۝

126. See they not that they are tried every year once or twice? Yet they turn not in repentance, and they take no heed.

أَوَلَا يَرَوْنَ أَنَّهُمْ يُفْتَنُونَ فِى كُلِّ عَامٍ مَّرَّةً أَوْ مَرَّتَيْنِ ثُمَّ لَا يَتُوبُونَ وَلَا هُمْ يَذَّكَّرُونَ ۝

127. Whenever there cometh down a Sûra, they look at each other, (saying), "Doth anyone see you?" Then they turn away: Allah hath turned their hearts (from the light); for they are a people that understand not.

وَإِذَا مَآ أُنْزِلَتْ سُورَةٌ نَّظَرَ بَعْضُهُمْ إِلَى بَعْضٍ هَلْ يَرَاكُمْ مِّنْ أَحَدٍ ثُمَّ انْصَرَفُوا صَرَفَ اللَّهُ قُلُوبَهُمْ بِأَنَّهُمْ قَوْمٌ لَّا يَفْقَهُونَ ۝

128. Now hath come unto you a Messenger from amongst yourselves: it grieves him that ye should suffer, ardently anxious is he over you: to the Believers is he most kind and merciful.

لَقَدْ جَآءَكُمْ رَسُولٌ مِّنْ أَنْفُسِكُمْ عَزِيزٌ عَلَيْهِ مَا عَنِتُّمْ حَرِيصٌ عَلَيْكُمْ بِالْمُؤْمِنِينَ رَءُوفٌ رَّحِيمٌ ۝

129. But if they turn away, say: "Allah sufficeth me: there is no god but He on Him is my trust,— He the Lord of the Throne Supreme!"

فَإِنْ تَوَلَّوْا فَقُلْ حَسْبِيَ اللَّهُ لَآ إِلَهَ إِلَّا هُوَ عَلَيْهِ تَوَكَّلْتُ وَهُوَ رَبُّ الْعَرْشِ الْعَظِيمِ ۝

SÛRA–10
YÛNUS
(INTRODUCTION)

Chronologically this Sûra and the five that follow (Sûras 9, 12, 13, 14, and 15) are closely connected, and were revealed in the late Makkan period, as the great event of the Hijrat was gradually approaching down the stream of Time. But their chronology has no particular significance.

On the other hand their arrangement in the gradation of Quranic teaching fits in with the subject-matter. S. 8 and S. 9 were mainly concerned with the first questions that arose on the formation of the new and organised Community of Islam in its conflict with those who wished to suppress or destroy it or use force to prevent its growth and the consolidation of its ideals. See Introductions to those Sûras. The present group leads us to the questions that face us when external hostility has been met, and our relations to Allah have to be considered from a higher standpoint than that of sale-preservation. How does revelation work? What is the meaning of divine grace and its withdrawal? How do the Messengers of Allah deliver their Message? How should we receive it?

All these question revolve round the revelation of the Qur-ān and each Sûra of this group except the 13 has the Abbreviated Letters A.L.R. attached to it. S. 13 has the letters A.L.M.R., and we shall discuss this variation when we come to S. 13.

The Abbreviated Letters are mystic symbols, about whose meaning there is no authoritative explanation. If the present group A.L.R. is cognate to the group A.L.M., we have to consider and form some idea in our minds as to the probable meaning of the variation. We think A.L.M. to be a symbol of those Sûras that deal with the beginning, the middle, and the end of man's spiritual history,—the origin, the present position, and the things to come in the Last Days (eschatology, to use a theological term). A.L. stand as symbols of the first two, and M. of the last. In the present group of Sûras we find hardly any eschatological matter, and therefore we can understand the absence of M., the symbol standing for such matter. In its place comes R., which is phonetically allied to L. L. is produced by the impact of the tongue to the front of the palate, and R. to the middle of the palate. In many languages the letters L. and R. are interchangeable; e.g. in Arabic, al-Raḥmān becomes ar-Raḥmān, and R. in imperfect enunciation becomes L., as in Chinese lallations. If L. is a symbol of present-day things looking to the future, we may take R. as a symbol of present-day things looking within, i.e. into the interior of the organisation of the Ummat. And this symbolism fits in with the subject-matter of the Sûras in question. But no one should be dogmatic in speculation about mystic Symbols.

Let us now consider Sûra 10 alone. The central theme is that Allah's wonderful Creation must not be viewed by us as a creation of material things only, once made and finished with. Most wonderful of all is how He reveals Himself to men through Apostles and Scriptures; how apostles are rejected by men, and the Message disbelieved until it is too late for repentance; and how, as in the case of Yûnus (Jonah) and his people, even the rejection (when repentance supervenes) does not prevent Allah's grace and mercy from working, and how far that working is beyond man's comprehension.

Yûnus, or Jonah

In the name of Allah, Most Gracious, Most Merciful!

1. **A. L. R.** These are the Ayats of the Book of Wisdom.

2. Is it a matter of wonderment to men that We have sent our inspiration to a man from among themselves?—that he should warn mankind (of their danger), and give the good news to the Believers that they have before their Lord the good actions they have advanced (but) say the Unbelievers: "This is indeed an evident sorcerer!"

3. Verily your Lord is Allah, who created the heavens and the earth in six Days, then He established Himself on the Throne, regulating and governing all things. No intercessor (can plead with Him) except after His leave (hath been obtained). This is Allah your Lord; Him therefore serve ye; will ye not receive admonition?

4. To Him will be your return—of all of you. The promise of Allah is true and sure. It is He who beginneth the process of creation, and repeateth it, that He may reward with justice those who believe and work righteousness; but those who reject Him will have draughts of boiling fluids, and a Chastisement grievous, because they did reject Him.

5. It is He Who made the sun to be a shining glory and the moon to be a light (of beauty), and measured out stages for it, that ye might know the number of years and the count (of time). Nowise did Allah create this but in truth and righteousness. (Thus) doth He explain His Signs in detail, for those who know!

6. Verily, in the alternation of the Night and the Day, and in all that Allah hath created, in the heavens and the earth, are Signs for those who fear Him!

7. Those who rest not their hope on their meeting with Us, but are pleased and satisfied with the life of the Present, and

.hose who heed not Our Signs,—

8. Their abode is the Fire. because of the (evil) they earned.

9. Those who believe, and work righteously,— their Lord will guide them because of their Faith: beneath them will flow rivers in Gardens of Bliss.

10. (This will be) their prayer therein: "Glory to Thee, O Allah!" and "Peace" will be their greeting therein and the end of their prayer will be: "Praise be to Allah, the Cheri-sher and Sustainer of the Worlds!"

11. If Allah were to hasten for men the ill (they have earned) as they would fain hasten on the good.—then would their respite be settled at once. But We leave those who rest not their hope on their meeting with Us, in their trespasses, wandering in distraction blindly.

12. When trouble toucheth a man, he crieth unto Us (in all postures)—lying down on his side, or sitting, or standing. But when We have removed his affliction, he passeth on his way as if he had never cried to Us for the affliction that touched him! Thus do the deeds of transgressors seem fair in their eyes!

13. Generations before you We destroyed when they did wrong: their Messengers came to them with clear Signs, but they would not believe! Thus do We requite those who sin!

14. Then We made you heirs in the land after them, to see how ye would behave!

15. But when Our clear Signs are rehearsed unto them, those who rest not their hope on their meeting with Us, say: "Bring us a Qur'an other than this, or change this," Say: "It is not for me, of my own accord, to change it: I follow naught but

what is revealed unto me: if I were to disobey my Lord, I should myself fear the Chastisement of a Great Day (to come)."

16. Say: "If Allah had so willed, I should not have rehearsed it to you, nor should He have made it known to you. A whole lifetime before this have I tarried amongst you: will ye not then understand?"

17. Who doth more wrong than such as forge a lie against Allah, or deny His Signs? But never will prosper those who sin.

18. They serve, besides Allah, what can hurt them not nor profit them, and they say: "These are our intercessors with Allah." Say: "Do ye indeed inform Allah of something He knows not, in the heavens or on earth?—Glory to Him! And far is He above the partners they ascribe (to Him)!"

19. Mankind was but one nation, but differed (later). Had it not been for a Word that went forth before from thy Lord, their differences would have been settled between them.

20. They say: "Why is not a Sign sent down to him from his Lord?" Say: "The Unseen is only for Allah (to know). Then wait ye: I too will wait with you".

21. When We make mankind taste of some mercy after adversity hath touched them, behold! they take to plotting against Our Signs! Say: "Swifter to plan is Allah!" Verily, Our messengers record all the plots that ye make!

22. He it is who enableth you to traverse through land and sea; till when ye even board ships;—they sail with them with a favourable wind, and they rejoice thereat: then comes a stormy wind and the waves come to them from all sides, and they think

they are being overwhelmed: they pray unto Allah, sincerely offering (their) duty unto Him, saying, "If Thou dost deliver us from this, we shall truly show our gratitude!"

23. But when he delivereth them, behold! they transgress insolently through the earth in defiance of right! O mankind! your insolence is against your own souls,—an enjoyment of the life of the Present: in the end, to Us is your return, and We shall show you the truth of all that ye did.

24. The likeness of the life of the Present is as the rain which We send down from the skies: by its mingling arises the produce of the earth—which provides food for men and animals: (it grows) till the earth is clad with its golden ornaments and is decked out (in beauty): the people to whom it belongs think they have all powers of disposal over it: there reaches it Our command by night or by day, and We make it like a harvest clean-mown, as if it had not flourished only the day before! Thus do We explain the Signs in detail for those who reflect.

25. But Allah doth call to the Home of Peace: He doth guide whom He pleaseth to a Way that is straight.

26. To those who do right is a goodly (reward)—Yea, more (than in measure)! No darkness nor abasement shall cover their faces! They will Companions of the Garden; they will abide therein (for aye)!

27. But those who have earned evil will have a reward of like evil: ignominy will cover their (faces): no defender will they have from (the wrath of) Allah: their faces will be covered, as it were, with pieces from the depth of the darkness of Night: they are Inhabitants of the Fire: they will abide therein (for aye)!

28. One Day shall We gather them all together. Then shall We say to those who joined gods (with Us): "To your place! ye and those ye joined as 'partners'." We shall separate them, and their "partners" shall

say: "It was not us that ye worshipped!

29. "Enough is Allah for a witness between us and you: we certainly knew nothing of your worship of us!"

30. There will every soul see (the fruits of) the deeds it sent before: they will be brought back to Allah their rightful Lord, and their invented falsehoods will leave them in the lurch.

31. Say: "Who is it that sustains you (in life) from the sky and from the earth? Or who is it that has power over hearing and sight? And who is it that brings out the living from the dead and the dead from the living? And who is it that rules and regulates all affairs?" They will soon say, "Allah". Say, "Will ye not then show piety (to Him)?"

32. Such is Allah, your true Lord: apart from the Truth, what (remains) but error? How then are ye turned away?

33. Thus is the Word of thy Lord proved true against those who rebel: verily they will not believe.

34. Say: "Of your 'partners', can any originate creation and repeat it?" Say: "It is Allah Who originates creation and repeats it: then how are ye deluded away (from the truth)?"

35. Say: "Of your 'partners' is there any that can give any guidance towards Truth?" Say: "It is Allah Who gives guidance towards Truth. Is then He Who gives guidance to Truth more worthy to be followed, or he who finds not guidance (Himself) unless he is guided? What then is the matter with you? How judge ye?

36. But most of them follow nothing but conjecture: truly conjecture can be of no avail against Truth. Verily Allah is well aware of all that they do.

37. This Qur'an is not such as can be produced by other than Allah; on the contrary it is a confirmation of (revelations)

that went before it, and a fuller explanation of the Book—wherein there is no doubt—from the Lord of the Worlds.

38. Or do they say, "He forged it"? Say: "Bring then a Sûra like unto it, and call (to your aid) anyone you can, besides Allah, if it be ye speak the truth!"

39. Nay, they charge with falsehood that whose knowledge they cannot compass, even before the interpretation thereof hath reached them: thus did those before them make charges of falsehood: but see what was the end of those who did wrong!

40. Of them there are some who believe therein, and some who do not: and thy Lord knoweth best those who are out for mischief.

41. If they charge thee with falsehood, say: "My work to me, and yours to you! Ye are free from responsibility for what I do, and I for what ye do!"

42. Among them are some who (pretend to) listen to thee: but canst thou make the deaf to hear,—even though they are without understanding?

43. And among them are some who look at thee: but canst thou guide the blind,—even though they will not see?

44. Verily Allah will not deal unjustly with man in aught: it is man that wrongs his own soul.

45. And on the day when He will gather them together: (it will be) as if they had tarried but an hour of a day: they will recognise each other: assuredly those will be lost who denied the meeting with Allah and refused to receive true guidance.

46. Whether We show thee (realised in thy life-time) some part of what We promise

them,—or We take thy soul (before that),—
in any case, to Us is their return: ultimately
Allah is witness to all that they do.

47. To every people (was sent) a Messenger:
when their Messenger comes (before them),
the matter will be judged between them with
justice, and they will not be wronged.

48. They say: "When will this promise
come to pass,—if ye speak the truth?"

49. Say: "I have no power over any harm
or profit to myself except as Allah willeth.
To every People is a term appointed: when
their term is reached, not an hour can they
cause delay, not (an hour) can they advance
(it in anticipation)."

50. Say: Do ye see,—if His punishment
should come to you by night or by day,—
what portion of it would the Sinners wish to
hasten?

51. "Would ye then believe in it at last,
when it actually cometh to pass? (It will
then be said:) 'Ah! now? and ye wanted
(aforetime) to hasten it on!'

52. "At length will be said to the wrong-
doers: 'Taste ye the enduring punishment!
Ye get but the recompense of what ye
earned!'"

53. They seek to be informed by thee: "Is
that true?" Say: "Aye! by my Lord! It is the
very truth! And ye cannot frustrate it!"

54. Every soul that hath sinned, if it
possessed all that is on earth, would fain
give it in ransom: they would declare (their)
repentance when they see the
Chastisement: but the judgment between
them will be with justice, and no wrong will
be done unto them.

55. Is it not (the case) that to Allah
belongeth whatever is in the heavens and
on earth? Is it not (the case) that Allah's
promise is assuredly true? Yet most of them
do not know.

56. It is He who giveth life and who taketh
it, and to Him shall ye all be brought back.

أَوْ نَتَوَفَّيَنَّكَ فَإِلَيْنَا مَرْجِعُهُمْ ثُمَّ اللَّهُ
شَهِيدٌ عَلَى مَا يَفْعَلُونَ ۝

وَلِكُلِّ أُمَّةٍ رَّسُولٌ فَإِذَا جَاءَ رَسُولُهُمْ
قُضِيَ بَيْنَهُمْ بِالْقِسْطِ وَهُمْ لَا يُظْلَمُونَ ۝

وَيَقُولُونَ مَتَى هَذَا الْوَعْدُ إِنْ كُنْتُمْ
صَادِقِينَ ۝

قُلْ لَا أَمْلِكُ لِنَفْسِى ضَرًّا وَلَا نَفْعًا
إِلَّا مَا شَاءَ اللَّهُ ۗ لِكُلِّ أُمَّةٍ أَجَلٌ ۚ
إِذَا جَاءَ أَجَلُهُمْ فَلَا يَسْتَأْخِرُونَ
سَاعَةً وَلَا يَسْتَقْدِمُونَ ۝

قُلْ أَرَأَيْتُمْ إِنْ أَتَاكُمْ عَذَابُهُ بَيَاتًا
أَوْ نَهَارًا مَّاذَا يَسْتَعْجِلُ مِنْهُ الْمُجْرِمُونَ ۝

أَثُمَّ إِذَا مَا وَقَعَ آمَنْتُمْ بِهِ ۚ آلْآنَ
وَقَدْ كُنْتُمْ بِهِ تَسْتَعْجِلُونَ ۝

ثُمَّ قِيلَ لِلَّذِينَ ظَلَمُوا ذُوقُوا عَذَابَ
الْخُلْدِ ۚ هَلْ تُجْزَوْنَ إِلَّا بِمَا كُنْتُمْ
تَكْسِبُونَ ۝

وَيَسْتَنْبِئُونَكَ أَحَقٌّ هُوَ ۖ قُلْ إِي وَرَبِّي
إِنَّهُ لَحَقٌّ ۖ وَمَا أَنْتُمْ بِمُعْجِزِينَ ۝

وَلَوْ أَنَّ لِكُلِّ نَفْسٍ ظَلَمَتْ مَا فِي الْأَرْضِ
لَافْتَدَتْ بِهِ ۗ وَأَسَرُّوا النَّدَامَةَ لَمَّا
رَأَوُا الْعَذَابَ ۖ وَقُضِيَ بَيْنَهُمْ بِالْقِسْطِ
وَهُمْ لَا يُظْلَمُونَ ۝

أَلَا إِنَّ لِلَّهِ مَا فِي السَّمَوَاتِ وَالْأَرْضِ ۗ
أَلَا إِنَّ وَعْدَ اللَّهِ حَقٌّ وَلَكِنَّ أَكْثَرَهُمْ
لَا يَعْلَمُونَ ۝

هُوَ يُحْيِي وَيُمِيتُ وَإِلَيْهِ تُرْجَعُونَ ۝

57. O mankind! there hath come to you an admonition from your Lord and a healing for the (diseases) in your hearts,—and for those who believe, a Guidance and a Mercy.

58. Say: "In the Bounty of Allah. And in His Mercy,—in that let them rejoice": that is better than the (wealth) they hoard.

59. Say: "See ye what things Allah hath sent down to you for sustenance? Yet ye hold forbidden some things thereof and (some things) lawful." Say: "Hath Allah indeed permitted you, or do ye forge (things) to attribute to Allah?"

60. And what think those who forge lies against Allah, on the Day of Judgment? Verily Allah is full of Bounty to mankind, but most of them are ungrateful.

61. In whatever business thou mayest be, and whatever portion thou mayest be reciting from the Qur'an,—and whatever deed ye (mankind) may be doing,—We are Witnesses thereof when ye are deeply engrossed therein. Nor is hidden from the Lord (so much as) the weight of an atom on the earth or in heaven. And not the smallest and not the greatest of these things but are recorded in a clear Record.

62. Behold! verily on the friends of Allah there is no fear, nor shall they grieve;

63. Those who believe and (constantly) guard against evil;—

64. For them are Glad Tidings, in the life of the Present and in the Hereafter: no change can there be in the Words of Allah. This is indeed the supreme Triumph.

65. Let not their speech grieve thee: for all power and honour belong to Allah: It is He Who heareth and knoweth (all things).

66. Behold! verily to Allah belong all

creatures, in the heavens and on earth.
What do they follow who worship as His
"partners" other than Allah? They follow
nothing but conjecture, and they do nothing
but lie.

67. He it is that hath made you the Night
that ye may rest therein, and the Day to
make things visible (to you). Verily in this
are Signs for those who listen (to His
Message).

68. They say, "Allah hath begotten a
son!"—Glory be to Him! He is Self-Sufficient!
His are all things in the heavens and on
earth! No warrant have ye for this! Say ye
about Allah what ye know not?

69. Say: "Those who forge a lie against
Allah will never prosper."

70. A little enjoyment in this world!—and
then, to Us will be their return. Then shall
We make them taste the severest
Chastisement for their disbelief.

71. Relate to them the story of Noah.
Behold! he said to his People: "O my People,
if it be hard on your (mind) that I should stay
(with you) and remind (you) the Signs of
Allah,—yet I put my trust in Allah get ye then
an agreement about your plan and among
your Partners, so your plan be not to you
dark and dubious. Then pass your sentence
on me, and give me no respite.

72. But if ye turn back, (consider): no reward
have I asked of you: my reward is only due
from Allah, and I have been commanded to
be of those who submit to Allah's Will (in
Islām)."

73. They rejected him, but We delivered
him, and those with him, in the Ark, and We
made them inherit (the earth), while We
drowned in the Flood those who rejected
Our Signs. Then see what was the end of
those who were warned (but heeded not)!

الْأَرْضِ وَمَا يَتَّبِعُ الَّذِينَ يَدْعُونَ
مِنْ دُونِ اللَّهِ شُرَكَاءَ إِنْ يَتَّبِعُونَ
إِلَّا الظَّنَّ وَإِنْ هُمْ إِلَّا يَخْرُصُونَ ۝

هُوَ الَّذِي جَعَلَ لَكُمُ اللَّيْلَ لِتَسْكُنُوا
فِيهِ وَالنَّهَارَ مُبْصِرًا إِنَّ فِي ذَلِكَ لَآيَاتٍ
لِقَوْمٍ يَسْمَعُونَ ۝

قَالُوا اتَّخَذَ اللَّهُ وَلَدًا سُبْحَانَهُ هُوَ الْغَنِيُّ
لَهُ مَا فِي السَّمَوَاتِ وَمَا فِي الْأَرْضِ إِنْ
عِنْدَكُمْ مِنْ سُلْطَانٍ بِهَذَا أَتَقُولُونَ
عَلَى اللَّهِ مَا لَا تَعْلَمُونَ ۝

قُلْ إِنَّ الَّذِينَ يَفْتَرُونَ عَلَى اللَّهِ الْكَذِبَ
لَا يُفْلِحُونَ ۝

مَتَاعٌ فِي الدُّنْيَا ثُمَّ إِلَيْنَا مَرْجِعُهُمْ ثُمَّ
نُذِيقُهُمُ الْعَذَابَ الشَّدِيدَ بِمَا كَانُوا
يَكْفُرُونَ ۝

وَاتْلُ عَلَيْهِمْ نَبَأَ نُوحٍ إِذْ قَالَ لِقَوْمِهِ يَا قَوْمِ
إِنْ كَانَ كَبُرَ عَلَيْكُمْ مَقَامِي وَتَذْكِيرِي
بِآيَاتِ اللَّهِ فَعَلَى اللَّهِ تَوَكَّلْتُ فَأَجْمِعُوا
أَمْرَكُمْ وَشُرَكَاءَكُمْ ثُمَّ لَا يَكُنْ أَمْرُكُمْ عَلَيْكُمْ
غُمَّةً ثُمَّ اقْضُوا إِلَيَّ وَلَا تُنْظِرُونِ ۝

فَإِنْ تَوَلَّيْتُمْ فَمَا سَأَلْتُكُمْ مِنْ أَجْرٍ
إِنْ أَجْرِيَ إِلَّا عَلَى اللَّهِ وَأُمِرْتُ أَنْ
أَكُونَ مِنَ الْمُسْلِمِينَ ۝

فَكَذَّبُوهُ فَنَجَّيْنَاهُ وَمَنْ مَعَهُ فِي الْفُلْكِ
وَجَعَلْنَاهُمْ خَلَائِفَ وَأَغْرَقْنَا الَّذِينَ
كَذَّبُوا بِآيَاتِنَا فَانْظُرْ كَيْفَ كَانَ عَاقِبَةُ
الْمُنْذَرِينَ ۝

74. Then after him We sent (many) messengers to their Peoples: they brought them Clear Signs, but they would not believe what they had already rejected beforehand. Thus do We seal the hearts of the transgressors.

75. Then after them sent We Moses and Aaron to Pharaoh and his chiefs with Our Signs. But they were arrogant: they were a wicked people.

76. When the Truth did come to them from Us, they said: "This is indeed evident sorcery!"

77. Said Moses: "Say ye (this) about the Truth when it hath (actually) reached you? Is it sorcery (like) this? But sorcerers will not prosper."

78. They said: "Hast thou come to us to turn us away from the ways we found our fathers following,—in order that thou and thy brother may have greatness in the land? But not we shall believe in you!"

79. Said Pharaoh: "Bring me every sorcerer well versed."

80. When the sorcerers came, Moses said to them: "Throw ye what ye (wish) to throw!"

81. When they had had their throw, Moses said: "What ye have brought is sorcery: Allah will surely make it of no effect: for Allah Prospereth not the work of those who make mischief.

82. "And Allah by His Words doth prove and establish the Truth, however much the Sinners may hate it!"

83. But none believed in Moses except some children of his People, because of the fear of Pharaoh and his chiefs, lest they should persecute them; and certainly Pharaoh was mighty on the earth and one who transgressed all bounds.

84. Moses said: "O my People! If ye do (really) believe in Allah, then in Him put

your trust if ye submit (your will to His)."

85. They said: "In Allah do we put our trust. Our Lord make us not a trial for those who practise oppression;

86. "And deliver us by Thy Mercy from those who reject (Thee)."

87. We inspired Moses and his brother with this Message: "Provide dwellings for your People in Egypt, make your dwellings into places of worship, and establish regular prayers: and give Glad Tidings to those who believe!"

88. Moses prayed: "Our Lord! Thou hast indeed bestowed on Pharaoh and his Chiefs splendour and wealth in the life of the Present, and so, our Lord they mislead (men) from Thy Path. Deface our Lord the features of their wealth, and send hardness to their hearts, so they will not believe until they see the grievous Chastisement."

89. Allah said: "Accepted is your prayer (O Moses and Aaron)! So stand ye straight, and follow not the path of those who know not."

90. We took the Children of Israel across the sea: Pharaoh and his hosts followed them in insolence and spite. At length, when overwhelmed with the flood, he said: "I believe that there is no god except Him Whom the Children of Israel believe in: I am of those who submit (to Allah in Islām)."

91. (It was said to him:) "Ah now!—but a little while before, wast thou in rebellion!—and thou didst mischief (and violence)!

92. "This day shall We save thee in thy body, that thou mayest be a Sign to those who come after thee! But verily, many among mankind are heedless of Our Signs!"

93. We settled the Children of Israel in an honourable dwelling-place, and provided for them sustenance of the best: it was after knowledge had been granted to them, that they fell into schisms. Verily Allah will

judge between them as to the schisms amongst them, on the Day of Judgment.

94. If thou wert in doubt as to what We have revealed unto thee, then ask those who have been reading the Book from before thee: the Truth hath indeed come to thee from thy Lord: so be in no wise of those in doubt.

95. Nor be of those who reject the Signs of Allah, or thou shalt be of those who perish

96. Those against whom the Word of thy Lord hath been verified would not believe—

97. Even if every Sign was brought unto them,—until they see (for them-selves) the Chastisement Grievous.

98. If only there had been a single township (among those We warned), which believed,— so its Faith should have profited it,—except the People of Jonah? When they believed, We removed from them the Chastisement of Ignominy in the life of the Present, and permitted them to enjoy (their life) for a while.

99. If it had been thy Lord's Will, they would all have believed,— all who are on earth! Wilt thou then compel mankind, against their will, to believe!

100. No soul can believe, except by the Will of Allah, and He will place abomination on those who will not understand.

101. Say: "Behold all that is in the heavens and on earth"; but neither Signs nor Warners profit those who believe not.

102. Do they then expect (any thing) but the like of (what happened in) the days of the men who passed away before them? Say: "Wait ye then: for I, too, will wait with you."

103. In the end We deliver Our messengers and those who believe: thus is it fitting on Our part that We should deliver those who believe!

بَيْنَهُمْ يَوْمَ الْقِيٰمَةِ فِيْمَا كَانُوْا فِيْهِ يَخْتَلِفُوْنَ ۝

فَاِنْ كُنْتَ فِىْ شَكٍّ مِّمَّآ اَنْزَلْنَآ اِلَيْكَ فَسْـَٔلِ الَّذِيْنَ يَقْرَءُوْنَ الْكِتٰبَ مِنْ قَبْلِكَ ۚ لَقَدْ جَآءَكَ الْحَقُّ مِنْ رَّبِّكَ فَلَا تَكُوْنَنَّ مِنَ الْمُمْتَرِيْنَ ۝

وَلَا تَكُوْنَنَّ مِنَ الَّذِيْنَ كَذَّبُوْا بِاٰيٰتِ اللّٰهِ فَتَكُوْنَ مِنَ الْخٰسِرِيْنَ ۝

اِنَّ الَّذِيْنَ حَقَّتْ عَلَيْهِمْ كَلِمَتُ رَبِّكَ لَا يُؤْمِنُوْنَ ۝

وَلَوْ جَآءَتْهُمْ كُلُّ اٰيَةٍ حَتّٰى يَرَوُا الْعَذَابَ الْاَلِيْمَ ۝

فَلَوْلَا كَانَتْ قَرْيَةٌ اٰمَنَتْ فَنَفَعَهَآ اِيْمَانُهَآ اِلَّا قَوْمَ يُوْنُسَ ۗ لَمَّآ اٰمَنُوْا كَشَفْنَا عَنْهُمْ عَذَابَ الْخِزْيِ فِى الْحَيٰوةِ الدُّنْيَا وَمَتَّعْنٰهُمْ اِلٰى حِيْنٍ ۝

وَلَوْ شَآءَ رَبُّكَ لَاٰمَنَ مَنْ فِى الْاَرْضِ كُلُّهُمْ جَمِيْعًا ۗ اَفَاَنْتَ تُكْرِهُ النَّاسَ حَتّٰى يَكُوْنُوْا مُؤْمِنِيْنَ ۝

وَمَا كَانَ لِنَفْسٍ اَنْ تُؤْمِنَ اِلَّا بِاِذْنِ اللّٰهِ ۗ وَيَجْعَلُ الرِّجْسَ عَلَى الَّذِيْنَ لَا يَعْقِلُوْنَ ۝ قُلِ انْظُرُوْا مَاذَا فِى السَّمٰوٰتِ وَالْاَرْضِ ۗ وَمَا تُغْنِى الْاٰيٰتُ وَالنُّذُرُ عَنْ قَوْمٍ لَّا يُؤْمِنُوْنَ ۝

فَهَلْ يَنْتَظِرُوْنَ اِلَّا مِثْلَ اَيَّامِ الَّذِيْنَ خَلَوْا مِنْ قَبْلِهِمْ ۗ قُلْ فَانْتَظِرُوْا اِنِّىْ مَعَكُمْ مِّنَ الْمُنْتَظِرِيْنَ ۝

ثُمَّ نُنَجِّىْ رُسُلَنَا وَالَّذِيْنَ اٰمَنُوْا كَذٰلِكَ ۚ حَقًّا عَلَيْنَا نُنْجِ الْمُؤْمِنِيْنَ ۝

SÛRA–11

HÛD

(INTRODUCTION)

For the chronological place of this Sûra and the general arguments of Sûras 10 to 15, see Introduction to S.10.

In subject-matter this Sûra supplements the preceding one. In the last Sûra stress was laid on that side of Allah's dealings with man which leads to Mercy: here stress is laid on the side which deals with justice and the punishment of Sin when all Grace is resisted.

104. Say: "O ye men! If ye are in doubt as to my religion, (behold!) I worship not what ye worship other than Allah! But I worship Allah— Who will take your souls (at death): I am commanded to be (in the ranks) of the Believers,

105. "And further (thus): set thy face towards Religion with true piety, and never in any wise be of the Unbelievers;

106. "Nor call on any, other than Allah;— such can neither profit thee nor hurt thee: if thou dost, behold! thou shalt certainly be of those who do wrong."

107. If Allah do touch thee with hurt, there is none can remove it but He: if He do design some benefit for thee, there is none can keep back His favour: He causeth it to reach whomsoever of His servants He pleaseth. And He is the Oft-Forgiving, Most Merciful.

108. Say: "O ye men! Now Truth hath reached you from your Lord! Those, who receive guidance, do so for the good of their own souls; those who stray, do so to their own loss: and I am not (set) over you to arrange your affairs."

109. Follow thou the inspiration sent unto thee, and be patient and constant, till Allah, do decide: for He is the Best to decide.

Hûd (The Prophet Hûd)

In the name of Allah, Most Gracious, Most Merciful.

1. **A. L. R.** (This is) a Book, with verses fundamental (of established meaning), further explained in detail,— from One Who is Wise and Well-Acquainted (with all things):

2. (It teacheth) that ye should worship none but Allah. (Say:) "Verily I am (sent) unto you from Him to warn and to bring Glad tidings:

3. "(And to preach thus), 'Seek ye the forgiveness of your Lord, and turn

to Him in repentance; that He may grant you enjoyment, good (and true), for a term appointed, and bestow His abounding grace on all who abound in merit! But if ye turn away, then I fear for you the Chastisement of a Great Day:

4. "To Allah is your return, and He hath power over all things."

5. Behold! they fold up their hearts, that they may lie hid from Him! Ah! even when they cover themselves with their garments, He knoweth what they conceal, and what they reveal: for He knoweth well the (inmost secrets) of the hearts.

6. There is no moving creature on earth but its sustenance dependeth on Allah: He knoweth its resting place and its temporary deposit: all is in a clear Record.

7. He it is Who created the heavens and the earth in six Days—and His Throne was over the Waters—that He might try you, which of you is best in conduct. But if thou wert to say to them, "Ye shall indeed be raised up after death", the Unbelievers would be sure to say, "This is nothing but obvious sorcery!"

8. If We delay the chastisement for them for a definite term, they are sure to say, "What keeps it back?" Ah! On the day it (actually) reaches them, nothing will turn it away from them, and they will be completely encircled by that which they used to mock at!

9. If We give man a taste of mercy from Ourselves, and then withdraw it from him, behold! he is in despair and (falls into) ingratitude.

10. But if We give him a taste of (Our) favours after adversity hath touched him, he is sure to say, "All evil has departed from me:" behold! he falls into exultation and pride.

11. Not so do those who show patience and constancy, and work righteousness; for them is forgive-ness (of sins) and a great reward.

12. Perchance thou mayest (feel the inclination) to give up a part of what is revealed unto thee, and thy heart feeleth straitened because they say, "Why is not a treasure sent down unto him, or why does not an angel come down with him?" But thou art there only to warn! It is Allah that arrangeth all affairs!

13. Or they may say, "He forged it." Say. "Bring ye then ten Suras forged, like unto it, and call (to your aid) whomsoever ye can, other than Allah!—If ye speak the truth!

14. "If then they (your false gods) answer not your (call), know ye that this Revelation is sent down (replete) with the knowledge of Allah, and that there is no god but He! Will ye even then submit (to Islam)?"

15. Those who desire the life of the Present and its glitter,—to them We shall pay (the price of) their deeds therein,—without diminution.

16. They are those for whom there is nothing in the Hereafter but the Fire: vain are the designs they frame therein, and of no effect are the deeds that they do!

17. Can they be (like) those who accept a Clear (Sign) from their Lord and followed by a witness from Him and before him is the Book of Moses—a guide and a mercy? They believe therein; but those of the Sects that reject it,—the Fire will be their promised meeting-place. Be not then in doubt thereon: for it is the Truth from thy Lord: yet many among men do not believe!

18. Who doth more wrong than those who forge a lie against Allah? They will be

brought before their Lord, and the witnesses will say, "These are the ones who lied against their Lord! Behold! the Curse of Allah is on those who do wrong!—

19. "Those who hinder (men) from the path of Allah and wish it, to be crooked: these were they who denied the Hereafter!"

20. They will not escape in earth, nor have they protectors besides Allah! Their chastisement will be doubled! They could not hear, nor they could see!

21. They are the ones who have lost their own souls: and the (fancies) they forged have left them in the lurch!

22. Without a doubt, these are the very ones who will lose most in the Hereafter!

23. But those who believe and work righteousness, and humble themselves before their Lord—they will be Companions of the Garden, to dwell therein for aye!

24. These two kinds (of men) may be compared to the blind and deaf, and those who can see and hear well. Are they equal when com-pared? Will ye not then take heed?

25. We sent Noah to his People (with a mission); "I have come to you as a clear warner.

26. "That ye serve none but Allah: verily I do fear for you the punishment of a Grievous Day.

27. But the Chiefs of the Unbelievers among his People said: "We see (in) thee nothing but a man like ourselves: nor do we see that any follow thee but the meanest among us, apparently nor do we see in you (all) any merit above us: in fact we think ye are liars!"

28. He said: "O my People! see ye if (it be that) I have a Clear Sign from my Lord and that He hath sent Mercy unto me from Him, but that the Mercy hath been obscured from your sight? Shall we compel you to accept it when ye are averse to it?

29. "And O my People! I ask you for no wealth I return: my reward is from none but Allah: but I will not drive away (in contempt) those who believe: for verily they are to meet their Lord, and ye I see are the ignorant ones!

30. "And O my People! who would help me against Allah if I drove them away? Will ye not then take heed?

31. "I tell you not that with me are the Treasures of Allah, nor do I know what is hidden, nor claim I to be an angel. Nor yet do I say, of those whom your eyes do despise that Allah will not grant them (all) that is good: Allah knoweth best what is in their souls: I should, if I did, indeed be a wrong-doer."

32. They said: "O Noah! thou hast disputed with us, and (much) hast thou prolonged the dispute with us: now bring upon us what thou threatenest us with, if thou speakest the truth!?"

33. He said: "Truly, Allah will bring it on you if He wills,—and then, ye will not be able to frustrate it!

34. "Of no profit will be my counsel to you, much as I desire to give you (good) counsel, if it be that Allah willeth to leave you astray: He is your Lord! and to Him will ye return!"

35. Or do they say, "He has forged it"? Say: "If I had forged it, on me were my sin! And I am free of the sins of which ye are guilty!

36. It was revealed to Noah: "None of thy People will believe except those who have believed already! So grieve no longer over

their (evil) deeds.

37. "But construct an Ark under Our eyes and Our inspiration, and add-ress Me no (further) on behalf of tho-se who are in sin: for they are about to be overwhelmed (in the Flood)."

38. Forthwith he (starts) construc-ting the Ark: every time that the Chiefs of his People passed by him, they threw ridicule on him. He said: "If ye ridicule us now. we (in our turn) can look down on you with ridicule likewise!

39. "But soon will ye know who it is on whom will descend a Chastisement that will cover them with shame,—on whom will be unloosed a Chastisement lasting.:"

40. At length, behold! there came Our Com-mand, and the fountains of the earth gushed forth! We said: "Embark therein, of each kind two. male and female, and your fami-ly—except those against whom the Word has already gone forth,— and the believ-ers." But only a few believed with him.

41. So he said: "Embark ye on the Ark in the name of Allah, whether it move or be at rest! For my Lord is, be sure, Oft-Forgiving, Most Merciful!"

42. So the Ark sailed with them on the waves (towering) like mountains, and Noah called out to his son, who had separated himself (from the rest): "O my son! embark with us, and be not with the Unbelievers!"

43. The son replied: "I will betake myself to some mountain: it will save me from the water." Noah said: "This day nothing can save, from the Command of Allah, any but those on whom He hath mercy!"— and the waves came between them, and the son was among those who were drowned.

44. Then the word went forth: "O earth! swallow up thy water. and O sky! withhold (thy rain)!" And the water abated, and the matter was ended. The Ark rested on Mount Jûdî, and the word went forth: "Away with those who do wrong!"

45. And Noah called upon His Lord and said: "O my Lord! surely my son is of my

family and Thy promise is true, and Thou art the Justest of Judges!"

46. He said: "O Noah! he is not of thy family: for his conduct is unrighteous. So ask not of Me that of which thou hast no knowledge! I give thee counsel, lest thou become one of the ignorants!"

47. Noah said: "O my Lord! I do seek refuge with Thee, from asking Thee for that of which I have no knowledge and unless Thou forgive me and have Mercy on me, I should indeed be among the losers!

48. The word came: "O Noah! come down (from the Ark) with Peace from Us, and Blessing on thee and on some of the Peoples (who will spring) from those with thee: but (there will be other) Peoples to whom We shall grant their pleasures (for a time), but in the end will a grievous Chastisement reach them from Us."

49. Such are some of the stories of the Unseen, which We have revealed unto thee: before this, neither thou nor thy People knew them. So persevere patiently: for the End is for those who are righteous.

50. To the 'Ad People (We sent) Hûd, one of their own brethren. He said: "O my people! worship Allah! ye have no other god but Him. You are only forgers.

51. "O my people! I ask of you no reward for this (Message). My reward is from none but Him who created me: will ye not then understand?

52. "And O my people! Ask forgiveness of your Lord, and turn to Him (in repentance): He will send you the skies pouring abundant rain, and add strength to your strength: so turn ye not back in sin!"

53. They said: "O Hûd! no Clear (Sign) hast thou brought us, and we are not the

ones to desert our gods on thy word! Nor shall we believe in thee!

54. "We say nothing but that (perhaps) some of our gods may have seized thee with evil." He said: "I call Allah to witness, and do ye bear witness, that I am free from the sin of ascribing, to Him,

55. "Other gods as partners! so scheme (your worst) against me, all of you, and give me no respite.

56. "I put my trust in Allah, my Lord and your Lord! There is not a moving creature, but He hath grasp of its fore-lock. Verily, it is my Lord that is on a straight Path.

57. "If ye turn away,—I (at least) have conveyed the Message with which I was sent to you. My Lord will make another People to succeed you, and you will not harm Him in the least. For my Lord hath care and watch over all things."

58. So when Our decree issued, We saved Hūd and those who believed with him, by (special) Grace from Us: We saved them from a severe Chastisement.

59. Such were the 'Ād People: they rejected the Signs of their Lord and Cherisher; disobeyed His Messengers; and followed the command of every powerful, obstinate Transgressor.

60. And they were pursued by a Curse in this Life,—and on the Day of Judgment. Ah! Behold! For the 'Ād rejected their Lord and Cherisher! Away with 'Ād the People of Hūd!

61. To the Thamud People (We sent) Sālih, one of their own brethren he said: "O my People! worship Allah: ye have no other God but Him. It is He Who hath produced you from the earth and settled you therein: then ask forgiveness of Him, and turn to Him (in repentance): for my Lord is (always) near, ready to answer."

ومآ من دآبة

62. They Said: "O Sālih! Thou hast been of us!—A centre of our hopes hitherto! Dost thou (now) forbid us the worship of what our fathers worshipped? But we are really in suspicious (disquieting) doubt as to that to which thou invitest us."

63. He said: "O my people! Do ye see?—If I have a Clear (Sign) from my Lord and He hath sent Mercy unto me from Himself,—who then can help me against Allah if I were to disobey Him? What then would ye add to my (portion) but perdition?

64. "And O my people! This she-camel of Allah is a sign to you: leave her to feed on Allah's (free) earth, and inflict no harm on her, or a swift Punishment will seize you!"

65. But they did ham-string her. So he said: "Enjoy yourselves in your homes for three days: (then will be your ruin): (behold) there a promise not to be belied!"

66. When Our Decree issued, We saved Sālih and those who believed with him, by (special) Grace from Us—and from the Ignominy of that Day. For thy Lord—He is the Strong One, and the Mighty.

67. The (mighty) Blast overtook the wrong-doers, and they lay prostrate in their homes before the morning,—

68. As if they had never dwelt and flourished there. Ah! Behold! For the Thamûd rejected their Lord and Cherisher! So away with the Thamûd

69. There came Our Messengers to Abraham with glad tidings. They said, "Peace!" He answered, "Peace!" and hastened to entertain them with a roasted calf.

70. But when he saw their hands not reaching towards the (meal), he felt some mistrust of them, and conceived a fear of them. They said: "Fear not: we have been sent against the people of Lût."

71. And his wife was standing (there), and she laughed: but We gave her glad tidings of Isaac, and after him, of Jacob.

72. She said: "Alas for me! Shall I bear a child, seeing I am an old woman, and my husband here is an old man? That would indeed be a wonderful thing!"

73. They said: "Dost thou wonder at Allah's decree? The grace of Allah and His blessings on you, O ye people of the house! for He is indeed worthy of all praise, full of all glory!"

74. When fear had passed from (the mind of) Abraham and the glad tidings had reached him, he began to plead with Us for Lût's people.

75. For Abraham was, without doubt, forbearing (of faults), compa-ssionate, and given to penitence.

76. O Abraham! seek not this. The decree of thy Lord hath gone forth: for them there cometh a Chastisement that cannot be turned back!

77. When Our Messengers came to Lût, he was grieved on their account and felt himself powerless (to protect) them. He said: "This is a distressful day."

78. And his people came rushing towards him, and they had been long in the habit of practising abominations. He said: "O my people! here are my daughters: they are purer for you (if ye marry)! Now fear Allah, and cover me not with disgrace about my guests! Is there not among you a single right-minded man?"

79. They said: "Well dost thou know we have no need of thy daughters: indeed thou knowest quite well what we want!"

80. He said: "Would that I had power to suppress you or that I could betake myself to some powerful support".

81. (The Messengers) said: "O Lût! we are Messengers from thy Lord! By no means shall they reach thee! Now travel with thy family while yet a part of the night remains, and let not any of you look back: but thy wife (will remain behind): to her will happen

what happens to the people. Morning is their time appointed: is not the morning nigh?"

82. When Our decree issued. We turned (the cities) upside down, and rained down on them brimstones hard as baked clay, spread, layer on layer,—

83. Marked from thy Lord; nor are they ever far from those who do wrong!

84. To the Madyan people (We sent) Shu'aib, one of their own brethren: he said: "O my people! worship Allah: ye have no other god but Him. And give not short measure or weight: I see you in prosperity, but I fear for you the Chastisement of a Day that will compass (you) all round.

85. "And O my people! give just measure and weight, nor withhold from the people the things that are their due: commit not evil in the land with intent to do mischief.

86. That which is left you by Allah is best for you, if ye (but) believed! But I am not set over you to keep watch!"

87. They said: "O Shu'aib! does thy prayer command thee that we leave off the worship which our fathers practised, or that we leave off doing what we like with our property? Truly, thou art the one that forbeareth with faults and is right-minded!"

88. He said: "O my people! see ye whether I have a Clear (Sign) from my Lord, and He hath given me sustenance (pure and) good as from Himself? I wish not, in opposition to you, to do that which I forbid you to do. I only desire (your) betterment to the best of my power; and my success (in my task) can only come from Allah. In Him I trust, and unto Him I turn.

89. "And O my people! let not my dissent (from you) cause you to sin, lest ye suffer a fate similar to that of the people of Noah or of Hûd or of Sālih, nor are the people of Lût far off from you!

90. "But ask forgiveness of your Lord, and turn unto Him (in repentance): for my Lord is indeed full of mercy and loving-kindness."

91. They said: "O Shu'aib! much of what thou sayest we do not understand! In fact among us we see that thou hast no strength! Were it not for thy family, we should certainly have stoned thee! For thou hast among us no great position!"

92. He said: "O my people! is then my family of more consideration with you than Allah? For ye cast Him away behind your backs (with contempt). But verily my Lord encompasseth all that ye do!

93. "And O my people! do whatever ye can: I will do (my part): soon will ye know who it is on whom des-cends the Chastisement of ignominy, and who is a liar! And watch ye! For I too am watching with you!"

94. When Our decree issued, We saved Shu'aib and those who believed with him, by (special) Mercy from Us: but the (mighty) Blast did seize the wrong-doers, and they lay prostrate in their homes by the morning,—

95. As if they had never dwelt and flourished there! So away with Madyan as were Thamûd gone away.

96. And We sent Moses, with Our Clear (Signs) and an authority manifest,

97. Unto Pharaoh and his Chiefs: but they followed the command of Pharaoh, and the command of Pharaoh was not rightly guided.

98. He will go before his people on the Day of Judgment, and lead them into the Fire but woeful indeed will be the place to which they are led!

99. And they are followed by a curse in this (life) and on the Day of Judgment: and woeful is the gift which shall be given (unto them)!

100. These are some of the stories of communities which We relate unto thee: of them some are standing, and some have been mown down (by the sickle of time).

101. It was not We that wronged them: they wronged their own souls: the deities, other than Allah, whom they invoked, profited them no whit when there issued the decree of thy Lord: nor did they add aught (to their lot) but perdition!

102. Such is the chastisement of thy Lord when He chastises communities in the midst of their wrong: grievous, indeed, and severe is His chastisement.

103. In that is a Sign for those who fear the Chastisement of the Hereafter: that is a Day for which mankind will be gathered together: that will be a Day of Testimony.

104. Nor shall We delay it but for a term appointed.

105. The day it arrives, no soul shall speak except by His leave: of those (gathered) some will be wretched and some will be blessed.

106. Those who are wretched shall be in the Fire: there will be for them therein (nothing but) the heaving of sighs and sobs:

107. They will dwell therein so long as the heavens and the earth endure, except as thy Lord willeth: for thy Lord is the (sure) Accomplisher of what He planneth.

108. And those who are blessed shall be in the Garden: they will dwell therein so long as the heavens and the earth endure, except as thy Lord willeth: a gift without break.

109. Be not then in doubt as to what these men worship. They worship nothing but what their fathers worshipped before (them): but verily We shall pay them back (in full) their portion without (the least) abatement.

110. We certainly gave the Book to Moses, but differences arose therein: had it not

been that a Word had gone forth before from thy Lord the matter would have been deci-ded between them: but they are in suspicious doubt concerning it.

111. And, of a surety, to all will your Lord pay back (in full the recompense) of their deeds: for He knoweth well all that they do.

112. Therefore stand firm (in the straight Path) as thou art commanded,— thou and those who with thee turn (unto Allah); and transgress not (from the Path): for He seeth well all that ye do.

113. And incline not to those who do wrong, or the Fire will touch you; and ye have no protectors other than Allah, nor shall ye be helped.

114. And establish regular prayers at the two ends of the day and at the approaches of the night: for those things that are good remove those that are evil: that is a reminder for the mindful.

115. And be steadfast in patience; for verily Allah will not suffer the reward of the righteous to perish.

116. If only there had been of the generations before you, men of righteousness who prohibited men from mischief in the earth (but there were none) except a few among them whom We saved (from harm)? But the wrong-doers pursued the enjoyment of the good things of life which were given them, and persisted in sin.

117. Nor would thy Lord be the One to destroy the towns unjustly while their people are Righteous.

118. If thy Lord had so willed, He could have made mankind one People: but they will not cease to differ,

119. Except those on whom thy Lord hath bestowed His Mercy: and for this did He create them: and the Word of thy Lord shall be fulfilled: "I will fill Hell with jinns and men all together."

120. All that we relate to thee of the stories of the messengers.—with it

For the chronological place of this Sûra and the general argument of Sûras 10 to 15 see Introduction to Sura 10.

In subject-matter this Sûra is entirely taken up with the story (recapitulated rather than told) of Joseph, the youngest (but one) of the twelve sons of the patriarch Jacob.The story is called the most beautiful of stories (12:3) for many reasons: (1) it is the most detailed of any in the Qur-ān; (2) it is full of human vicissitudes, and has therefore deservedly appealed to men and women of all classes; (3) it paints in vivid colours, with their spiritual implications, the most varied aspects of life—the patriarch's old age and the confidence between him and his litle best-beloved son, the elder brother's jealousy of this little son, their plot and their father's grief, the sale of the father's darling into slavery for a miserable little price, carnal love contrasted with purity and chastity, false charges, prison, the interpretation of dreams, low life and high life, Innocence raised to honour; the sweet "revenge" of Forgiveness and Benevolence, high matters of State and administration, humility in exaltation, filial love, and the beauty of Piety and Truth.

The story is similar to but not identical with the Biblical story; but the atmosphere is wholly diferent. The Biblical story is like a folk-tale in which morality has no place. Its tendency is to exalt the clever and financially-minded Jew against the Egyptian, and to explain certain ethnic and tribal peculiarities in later Jewish history. Joseph is shown as buying up all the cattle and the land of the poor Egyptians for the State under the stress of famine conditions, and making the Israelites "rulers" over Pharaoh's cattle. The Quranic story, on the other hand, is less a narrative than a highly spiritual sermon of allegory explaining the seeming contradictions in life, the enduring nature of virtue in a world full of flux and change, and the marvellous working of Allah's eternal purpose in His Plan as unfolded to us on the wide canvas of history. This aspect of the matter has been a favourite with Muslim poets and Ṣufi exegetists.

We make firm thy heart: in them there cometh to thee the Truth, as well as an exhortation and a message of remembrance to those who believe.

121. Say to those who do not believe: "Do whatever ye can: we shall do our part;

122. "And wait ye! We too shall wait."

123. To Allah do belong the unseen (secrets) of the heavens and the earth, and to Him goeth back every affair (for decision): so worship Him, and put thy trust in Him: and thy Lord is not Unmindful of aught that ye do.

Yûsuf, or Joseph

In the name of Allah, Most Gracious, Most Merciful.

1. **A. L. R.** These are the Verses of the Perspicuous Book.

2. We have sent it down as an Arabic Qur'an, in order that ye may learn wisdom.

3. We do relate unto thee the most beautiful of stories, in that We reveal to thee this (portion of the) Qur'an: before this, thou too was among those who knew it not.

4. Behold, Joseph said to his father: "O my father! I did see eleven stars and the sun and the moon: I saw them prostrate themselves to me!"

5. Said (the father): "My (dear) little son! relate not thy vision to thy brothers, lest they concoct a plot against thee: for Satan is to man an avowed enemy!

6. "Thus will thy Lord choose thee and teach thee the interpretation of stories (and events) an perfect His favour to thee and to the posterity of Jacob—even as He perfected it to thy fathers Abraham and Isaac aforetime! For thy Lord is full of

knowledge and wisdom.

عٰلِيْمٌ حَكِيْمٌ ۞

7.   Verily in Joseph and his brethren are Signs for Seekers (after Truth)

لَقَدْ كَانَ فِيْ يُوْسُفَ وَاِخْوَتِهٖ اٰيٰتٌ لِّلسَّآئِلِيْنَ ۞

8.   They said: "Truly Joseph and his brother are loved more by our father than we: but we are a goodly body! Really our father is obviously in error!

اِذْ قَالُوا لَيُوْسُفُ وَاَخُوْهُ اَحَبُّ اِلٰى اَبِيْنَا مِنَّا وَنَحْنُ عُصْبَةٌ ؕ اِنَّ اَبَانَا لَفِيْ ضَلٰلٍ مُّبِيْنِ ۞

9.   "Slay ye Joseph or cast him out to some (unknown) land, that so the favour of your father may be given to you alone: (there will be time enough) for you to be righteous after that!

اۨقْتُلُوْا يُوْسُفَ اَوِ اطْرَحُوْهُ اَرْضًا يَّخْلُ لَكُمْ وَجْهُ اَبِيْكُمْ وَتَكُوْنُوْا مِنْۢ بَعْدِهٖ قَوْمًا صٰلِحِيْنَ ۞

10.   Said one of them: "Slay not Joseph, but if ye must do something, throw him down to the bottom of the well: he will be picked up by some caravan of travellers."

قَالَ قَآئِلٌ مِّنْهُمْ لَا تَقْتُلُوْا يُوْسُفَ وَ اَلْقُوْهُ فِيْ غَيٰبَتِ الْجُبِّ يَلْتَقِطْهُ بَعْضُ السَّيَّارَةِ اِنْ كُنْتُمْ فٰعِلِيْنَ ۞

11.   They said: "O our father! why dost thou not Trust us with Joseph,—seeing we are indeed his sincere well-wishers?

قَالُوْا يٰٓاَبَانَا مَا لَكَ لَا تَاْمَنَّا عَلٰى يُوْسُفَ وَاِنَّا لَهٗ لَنٰصِحُوْنَ ۞

12.   "Send him with us tomorrow to enjoy himself and play, and we shall take every care of him."

اَرْسِلْهُ مَعَنَا غَدًا يَّرْتَعْ وَيَلْعَبْ وَاِنَّا لَهٗ لَحٰفِظُوْنَ ۞

13.   (Jacob) said: "Really it saddens me that ye should take him away: I fear lest the wolf should devour him while ye attend not to him."

قَالَ اِنِّيْ لَيَحْزُنُنِيْٓ اَنْ تَذْهَبُوْا بِهٖ وَ اَخَافُ اَنْ يَّاْكُلَهُ الذِّئْبُ وَاَنْتُمْ عَنْهُ غٰفِلُوْنَ ۞

14.   They said: "If the wolf were to devour him while we are (so large) a party, then should we be the losers!"

قَالُوْا لَئِنْ اَكَلَهُ الذِّئْبُ وَنَحْنُ عُصْبَةٌ اِنَّآ اِذًا لَّخٰسِرُوْنَ ۞

15.   So they did take him away, and they all agreed to throw him down to the bottom of the well: and We put into his heart (this Message): 'Of a surety thou shall (one day) tell them the truth of this their affair while they perceive not.'

فَلَمَّا ذَهَبُوْا بِهٖ وَاَجْمَعُوْٓا اَنْ يَّجْعَلُوْهُ فِيْ غَيٰبَتِ الْجُبِّ ۚ وَاَوْحَيْنَآ اِلَيْهِ لَتُنَبِّئَنَّهُمْ بِاَمْرِهِمْ هٰذَا وَهُمْ لَا يَشْعُرُوْنَ ۞

16.   Then they came to their father in the early part of the night, weeping.

وَجَآءُوْٓ اَبَاهُمْ عِشَآءً يَّبْكُوْنَ ۞

17.   They said: "O our father! we went racing with one another, and left Joseph with our things; and the wolf devoured him.

قَالُوْا يٰٓاَبَانَآ اِنَّا ذَهَبْنَا نَسْتَبِقُ وَتَرَكْنَا يُوْسُفَ عِنْدَ مَتَاعِنَا فَاَكَلَهُ الذِّئْبُ

But thou wilt never believe us even though we tell the truth."

18. They stained his shirt with false blood. He said: "Nay, but your minds have made up a tale (that may pass) with you, (for me) patience is most fitting: against that which ye assert, it is Allah (alone) Whose help can be sought"...

19. Then there came a caravan of travellers: they sent their water-carrier (for water), and he let down his bucket (into the well)... He said: "Ah there! Good news! Here is a (fine) young man!" So they concealed him as a treasure! But Allah knoweth well all that they do!

20. The (Brethren) sold him for a miserable price,— for a few dirhams counted out: in such low estimation did they hold him!

21. The man in Egypt who bought him, said to his wife: "Make his stay (among us) honourable: may be he will bring us much good, or we shall adopt him as a son." Thus did We establish Joseph in the land, that We might teach him the interpretation of stories (and events). And Allah Hath full power and control over His affairs; but most among mankind know it not.

22. When Joseph attained His full manhood, We gave him power and knowledge: thus do We reward those who do right.

23. But she in whose house he was, sought to seduce him and she fastened the doors, and said: "Now come," He said: "Allah forbid! truly (thy husband) is my lord! he made my sojourn agreeable! truly to no good come those who do wrong"

24. And (with passion) did she desire him, and he would have desired her, but that he saw the evidence of his Lord: thus (did We order) that We might turn away from him (all) evil and indecent deeds: for he was one of Our servants chosen.

25. So they both raced each other to the door, and she tore his shirt from the back:

وَمَآ أَنتَ بِمُؤۡمِنٍ لَّنَا وَلَوۡ كُنَّا صَٰدِقِينَ ۝

وَجَآءُو عَلَىٰ قَمِيصِهِۦ بِدَمٍ كَذِبٍ ۚ قَالَ بَلۡ سَوَّلَتۡ لَكُمۡ أَنفُسُكُمۡ أَمۡرًا ۖ فَصَبۡرٌ جَمِيلٌ ۖ وَٱللَّهُ ٱلۡمُسۡتَعَانُ عَلَىٰ مَا تَصِفُونَ ۝

وَجَآءَتۡ سَيَّارَةٌ فَأَرۡسَلُوا۟ وَارِدَهُمۡ فَأَدۡلَىٰ دَلۡوَهُۥ ۖ قَالَ يَٰبُشۡرَىٰ هَٰذَا غُلَٰمٌ ۚ وَأَسَرُّوهُ بِضَٰعَةً ۚ وَٱللَّهُ عَلِيمٌۢ بِمَا يَعۡمَلُونَ ۝

وَشَرَوۡهُ بِثَمَنٍۭ بَخۡسٍ دَرَٰهِمَ مَعۡدُودَةٍ وَكَانُوا۟ فِيهِ مِنَ ٱلزَّٰهِدِينَ ۝

وَقَالَ ٱلَّذِي ٱشۡتَرَىٰهُ مِن مِّصۡرَ لِٱمۡرَأَتِهِۦٓ أَكۡرِمِي مَثۡوَىٰهُ عَسَىٰٓ أَن يَنفَعَنَآ أَوۡ نَتَّخِذَهُۥ وَلَدًا ۚ وَكَذَٰلِكَ مَكَّنَّا لِيُوسُفَ فِي ٱلۡأَرۡضِ وَلِنُعَلِّمَهُۥ مِن تَأۡوِيلِ ٱلۡأَحَادِيثِ ۚ وَٱللَّهُ غَالِبٌ عَلَىٰٓ أَمۡرِهِۦ وَلَٰكِنَّ أَكۡثَرَ ٱلنَّاسِ لَا يَعۡلَمُونَ ۝

وَلَمَّا بَلَغَ أَشُدَّهُۥٓ ءَاتَيۡنَٰهُ حُكۡمًا وَعِلۡمًا ۚ وَكَذَٰلِكَ نَجۡزِي ٱلۡمُحۡسِنِينَ ۝

وَرَٰوَدَتۡهُ ٱلَّتِي هُوَ فِي بَيۡتِهَا عَن نَّفۡسِهِۦ وَغَلَّقَتِ ٱلۡأَبۡوَٰبَ وَقَالَتۡ هَيۡتَ لَكَ ۚ قَالَ مَعَاذَ ٱللَّهِ ۖ إِنَّهُۥ رَبِّيٓ أَحۡسَنَ مَثۡوَايَ ۖ إِنَّهُۥ لَا يُفۡلِحُ ٱلظَّٰلِمُونَ ۝

وَلَقَدۡ هَمَّتۡ بِهِۦ ۖ وَهَمَّ بِهَا لَوۡلَآ أَن رَّءَا بُرۡهَٰنَ رَبِّهِۦ ۚ كَذَٰلِكَ لِنَصۡرِفَ عَنۡهُ ٱلسُّوٓءَ وَٱلۡفَحۡشَآءَ ۚ إِنَّهُۥ مِنۡ عِبَادِنَا ٱلۡمُخۡلَصِينَ ۝

وَٱسۡتَبَقَا ٱلۡبَابَ وَقَدَّتۡ قَمِيصَهُۥ مِن

they both found her lord near the door. She said: "What is the (fitting) punishment for one who formed an evil design against thy wife, but prison or a grievous chastisement?"

26. He said: "It was she that sought to seduce me — from my (true) self." And one of her household saw (this) and bore witness, (thus):— "If it be that his shirt is rent from the front, then is her tale true, and he is a liar!

27. "But if it be that his shirt is torn from the back, then is she the liar, and he is telling the truth!"

28. So when he saw his shirt,—that it was torn at the back,—(her husband) said: "Behold! it is a snare of you women! Truly, mighty is your snare!

29. "O Joseph, pass this over! (O wife), ask forgiveness for thy sin, for truly thou hast been at fault!"

30. Ladies said in the City: "The wife of the (great) 'Aziz is seeking to seduce her slave truly hath he inspired her with violent love: we see she is evidently going astray."

31. When she heard of their malicious talk, she sent for them and prepared a banquet for them: she gave each of them a knife: and she said (to Joseph), "Come out before them." When they saw him, they did extol him, and (in their amazement) cut their hands: they said, "Allah preserve us! no mortal is this! This is none other than a noble angel!"

32. She said: "There before you is the man about whom ye did blame me! I did seek to seduce him from his (true) self but he did firmly save himself guiltless!... And now, if he doth not my bidding, he shall

certainly be cast into prison, and (what is more) be of the company of the vilest!"

33. He said: "O my Lord! The prison is dearer to my liking than that to which they invite me: unless Thou turn away their snare from me, I should feel inclined towards them and join the ranks of the ignorant."

34. So his Lord hearkened to him (in his prayer) and turned away from him their snare: verily He heareth and knoweth (all things).

35. Then it occurred to them after they had seen the Signs, (that it was best) to imprison him for a time.

36. Now with him there came into the prison two young men. Said one of them; "I see myself (in a dream) pressing wine." Said the other: "I see myself (in a dream) carrying bread on my head, and birds are eating thereof." "Tell us" (they said) "the truth and meaning thereof: for we see thou art one that doth good (to all).

37. He said: "Before any food comes (in due course) to feed either of you I will surely reveal to you the truth and meaning of this ere it befall you. That is part of the (Duty) which my Lord hath taught me! have (I assure you) abandoned the ways of a people that believe not in Allah and that (even) deny the Hereafter.

38. "And I follow the ways of my fathers,— Abraham, Isaac and Jacob; and never could we attribute any partners whatever to Allah: that (comes) of the grace of Allah to us and to mankind; yet Most men are not grateful.

39. "O my two companions. Of the prison! (I ask you): are many lords differing among themselves better, or Allah the One, Supreme and Irresistible?

40. Whatever ye worship apart from Him is nothing but names which ye have named, ye and your fathers,— for which Allah hath

sent down no authority: the Command is
for none but Allah: He hath commanded
that ye worship none but Him: that is the
right religion, but most men understand
not...

41. "O my two companions of the prison!
As to one of you, he will pour out the wine
for his lord to drink; as for the other, he will
hang from the cross, and the birds will eat
from off his head. (So) hath been decreed
that matter whereof ye twain do enquire"...

42. And of the two, to that one whom he
considered about to be saved, he said:
"Mention me to thy lord," but Satan made
him forget to mention him to his lord: and
(Joseph) lingered in prison a few (more)
years.

43. The king (of Egypt) said: "I do see (in a
vision) seven fat kine, whom seven lean
ones devour,—and seven green ears of
corn, and seven (others) withered. O ye
chiefs! expound to me my vision if it be that
ye can interpret visions."

44. They said: "A confused medley of
dreams: and we are not skilled in the
interpretation of dreams."

45. But the man who had been released,
one of the two (who had been in prison) and
who now remem-bered him after (so long) a
space of time, said: "I will tell you the truth of
its interpretation: send ye me (therefore)."

46. "O Joseph!" (he said) "O man of truth!
expound to us (the dream) of seven fat kine
whom seven lean ones devour, and of
seven green ears of corn and (seven) others
withered: that I may return to the people,
and that they may know "

47. (Joseph) said: "For seven years
shall ye diligently sow as is your wont, and
the harvests that ye reap, ye shall

leave them in the ear,—except a little, of which ye shall eat.

48. "Then will come after that (period) seven dreadful (years), which will devour what ye shall have laid by in advance for them,—(all) except a little which ye shall have (specially) guarded.

49. "Then will come after that (period) a year in which the people will have abundant water, and in which they will press (wine and oil.)"

50. So the king said: "Bring ye him unto me." But when the messenger came to him, (Joseph) said: "Go thou back to thy lord, and ask him, 'What was the matter with the ladies who cut their hands'? For my Lord is certainly well aware of their snare."

51. (The king) said (to the ladies): "What was your affair when ye did seek to seduce Joseph?" The ladies said: "Allah preserve us! no evil know we against him!" Said the 'Aziz's wife: "Now is the truth manifest (to all): it was I who sought to seduce him he is indeed of those who are (ever) true (and virtuous).

52. 'This (say I), in order that he may know that I have never been false to him in his absence, and that Allah will never guide the snare of the false ones

53. "Yet I do not absolve myself (of blame): the (human) soul certainly incites evil. unless my Lord do bestow His Mercy: but surely my Lord is Oft-Forgiving, Most Merciful."

54. So the king said: "Bring him unto me; I will take him specially to serve about my own person." Therefore when he had spoken to him, he said: "Be assured this day, thou art of high standing with us, invested with all trust."

55. (Joseph) said: "Set me over the store-houses of the land: I am a good keeper, knowledgeable."

56. Thus did we give established power to Joseph in the land, to take possession therein as, when, or where he pleased. We bestow of Our mercy on whom We please, and We suffer not, to be lost, the reward of those who do good.

57. But verily the reward of the Hereafter is the best, for those who believe, and are constant in righteousness.

58. Then came Joseph's brethren: They entered his presence, and he knew them, but they knew him not.

59. And when he had furnished them forth with provisions (suitable) for them, he said: "Bring unto me a brother ye have, of the same father as yourselves, (but a different mother): see ye not that I pay out full measure, and that I do provide the best hospitality?

60. "Now if ye bring him not to me, ye shall have no measure (of corn) from me, nor shall ye (even) come near me."

61. They said: "We shall try to win him from his father: indeed we shall do it."

62. And (Joseph) told his servants to put their stock-in-trade (with which they had bartered) into their saddle-bags, so they should know it only when they returned to their people, in order that they might come back

63. Now when they returned to their father, they said: "O our father! No more measure of grain shall we get (unless we take our brother): so send our brother with us, that we may get our measure; and we will indeed take every care of him."

64. He said: "Shall I trust you with him with any result other than when I trusted you with his brother afore-time? But Allah is the best to take care (of him), and He is the Most Merciful of those who show mercy!"

65. Then when they opened their baggage, they found their stock-in-trade had been returned to them. They said: "O our father! What (more) can we desire? This our Stock-in-trade has been returned to us: so we

shall get (more) food for our family; we shall take care of our brother; and add (at the same time) a full camel's load (of grain to our provisions). This is but a small quantity.

66. (Jacob) said: "Never will I send him with you until ye swear a solemn oath to me, in Allah's name, that ye will be sure to bring him back to me unless ye are yourselves Hemmed in (and made powerless)." And when they had sworn their solemn oath, He said: "Over all that we say, be Allah the Witness and Guardian!"

67. Further he said: "O my sons! enter not all by one gate: enter ye by different gates. Not that I can profit you aught against Allah (with my advice): none can command except Allah: on Him do I put my trust: and let all that trust put their trust on Him."

68. And when they entered in the manner their father had enjoined, it did not profit them in the least against (the Plan of) Allah: it served only to satisfy Jacob's heartfelt desire. For he was, by Our instruction, full of knowledge (and experience): but most men know not.

69. Now when they came into Joseph's presence, he received his (full) brother to stay with him. He said (to him): "Behold! I am thy (own) brother; so grieve not at aught of their doings."

70. At length when he had furnished them forth with provisions (suitable) for them, he put the drinking cup into his brother's saddle-bag. Then shouted out a Crier: "O ye (in) the Caravan! behold! ye are thieves, without doubt!"

71. They said, turning towards them: "What is it that ye miss?"

72. They said: "We miss the great beaker of the king; for him who produces it. Is (the reward of) a camel load; I will be bound by it."

73. (The brothers) said: "By Allah! well ye know that we came not to make mischief in the land, and we are no thieves!"

74. (The Egyptians) said: "What then shall be the penalty of this, if ye are (proved) to have lied?"

75. They said: "The penalty should be that he in whose saddle-bag it is found, should be held (as bondman) to atone for the (crime). Thus it is we punish the wrong-doers!"

76. So he began (the search) with their baggage, before (he came to) the baggage of his brother: at length he brought it out of his brother's baggage. Thus did We plan for Joseph. He could not take his brother by the law of the king except that Allah willed it (so). We raise to degrees (of wisdom) whom We please: but over all endued with knowledge is One, the All-Knowing.

77. They said: "If he steals, there was a brother of his who did steal before (him)." But these things did Joseph keep locked in his heart, revealing not the secrets to them he (simply) said (to himself): "Ye are the worse situated; and Allah know-eth best the truth of what ye assert!"

78. They said: "O exalted one! Behold! he has a father, aged and venerable, (who will grieve for him); so take one of us in his place; for we see that thou art (gracious) in doing good."

79. He said: "Allah forbid that we take other than him with whom we found our property: indeed (if we did so), we should be acting wrongfully.

80. Now when they saw no hope of his (yielding), they held a conference in private. The leader among them said: "Know ye not that your father did take an oath from you in Allah's name, and how before this, ye did fail in your duty with Joseph? Therefore will I not leave this land until my father permits me, or Allah judges for me; and He is the best to judge.

81. "Turn ye back to your father, and say, 'O our father! behold! thy son committed theft! We bear witness only to what we know, and we could not well guard against the unseen!

82. "Ask at the town where we have been and the caravan in which we returned, and (you will find) we are indeed telling the truth."

قَالُوْا جَزَآؤُهٗ مَنْ وُّجِدَ فِىْ رَحْلِهٖ فَهُوَ جَزَآؤُهٗ ؕ كَذٰلِكَ نَجْزِى الظّٰلِمِيْنَ ۞

فَبَدَاَ بِاَوْعِيَتِهِمْ قَبْلَ وِعَآءِ اَخِيْهِ ثُمَّ اسْتَخْرَجَهَا مِنْ وِّعَآءِ اَخِيْهِ ؕ كَذٰلِكَ كِدْنَا لِيُوْسُفَ ؕ مَا كَانَ لِيَاْخُذَ اَخَاهُ فِىْ دِيْنِ الْمَلِكِ اِلَّاۤ اَنْ يَّشَآءَ اللّٰهُ ؕ نَرْفَعُ دَرَجٰتٍ مَّنْ نَّشَآءُ ؕ وَفَوْقَ كُلِّ ذِىْ عِلْمٍ عَلِيْمٌ ۞

قَالُوْۤا اِنْ يَّسْرِقْ فَقَدْ سَرَقَ اَخٌ لَّهٗ مِنْ قَبْلُ ۚ فَاَسَرَّهَا يُوْسُفُ فِىْ نَفْسِهٖ وَلَمْ يُبْدِهَا لَهُمْ ۚ قَالَ اَنْتُمْ شَرٌّ مَّكَانًا ؕ وَاللّٰهُ اَعْلَمُ بِمَا تَصِفُوْنَ ۞

قَالُوْا يٰۤاَيُّهَا الْعَزِيْزُ اِنَّ لَهٗۤ اَبًا شَيْخًا كَبِيْرًا فَخُذْ اَحَدَنَا مَكَانَهٗ ۚ اِنَّا نَرٰىكَ مِنَ الْمُحْسِنِيْنَ ۞

قَالَ مَعَاذَ اللّٰهِ اَنْ نَّاْخُذَ اِلَّا مَنْ وَّجَدْنَا مَتَاعَنَا عِنْدَهٗۤ ۙ اِنَّاۤ اِذًا لَّظٰلِمُوْنَ ۞

فَلَمَّا اسْتَيْـَٔسُوْا مِنْهُ خَلَصُوْا نَجِيًّا ؕ قَالَ كَبِيْرُهُمْ اَلَمْ تَعْلَمُوْۤا اَنَّ اَبَاكُمْ قَدْ اَخَذَ عَلَيْكُمْ مَّوْثِقًا مِّنَ اللّٰهِ وَمِنْ قَبْلُ مَا فَرَّطْتُّمْ فِىْ يُوْسُفَ ۚ فَلَنْ اَبْرَحَ الْاَرْضَ حَتّٰى يَاْذَنَ لِىْۤ اَبِىْۤ اَوْ يَحْكُمَ اللّٰهُ لِىْ ۚ وَهُوَ خَيْرُ الْحٰكِمِيْنَ ۞

اِرْجِعُوْۤا اِلٰۤى اَبِيْكُمْ فَقُوْلُوْا يٰۤاَبَانَاۤ اِنَّ ابْنَكَ سَرَقَ ۚ وَمَا شَهِدْنَاۤ اِلَّا بِمَا عَلِمْنَا وَمَا كُنَّا لِلْغَيْبِ حٰفِظِيْنَ ۞

وَسْـَٔلِ الْقَرْيَةَ الَّتِىْ كُنَّا فِيْهَا وَالْعِيْرَ الَّتِىْۤ اَقْبَلْنَا فِيْهَا ؕ وَاِنَّا لَصٰدِقُوْنَ ۞

83. Jacob said: "Nay, but ye have yourselves contrived a story (good enough) for you. So patience is most fitting (for me). May be Allah will bring them (back) all to me (in the end). For He is indeed full of knowledge and wisdom."

84. And he turned away from them, and said: "How great is my grief for Joseph! And his eyes became white with sorrow, and he was suppressed with silent sorrow.

85. They said: "By Allah! (never) wilt thou cease to remember Joseph until thou reach the last ex-tremity of illness, or until thou die!"

86. He said: "I only complain of my distraction and anguish to Allah, and I know from Allah that which ye know not...

87. "O my sons! go ye and enquire about Joseph and his brother, and never give up hope of Allah's soothing Mercy: truly no one despairs of Allah's soothing Mercy, except those who have no faith."

88. Then, when they came (back) into (Joseph's) presence they said: "O exalted one! distress has seized us and our family: we have (now) brought but scanty capital: so pay us full measure, (we pray thee), and treat it as charity to us; for Allah doth reward the charitable."

89. He said: "Know ye how ye dealt with Joseph and his brother, not knowing (what ye were doing)?"

90. They said: "Art thou indeed Joseph?" He said, "I am Joseph, and this is my brother: Allah has indeed been gracious to us (all): behold, he that is righteous and patient,—never will Allah suffer the reward to be lost, of those who do right."

91. They said: "By Allah! Indeed has Allah preferred thee above us, and we certainly have been guilty of sin!"

92. He said: "This day let no reproach be (cast) on you: Allah will forgive you, and He

is the Most Merciful of those who show mercy!

93. "Go with this my shirt, and cast it over the face of my father: he will come to see (clearly). Then come ye (here) to me together with all your family."

94. When the Caravan left (Egypt), their father said: "I do indeed scent the presence of Joseph: nay, think me not a dotard."

95. They said: "By Allah! truly thou art in thine old wandering illusion."

96. Then when the bearer of the good news came, he cast (the shirt) over his face, and he forthwith regained clear sight. He said: "Did I not say to you, 'I know from Allah that which ye know not?'"

97. They said: "O our father! ask for us forgiveness for our sins, for we were truly at fault.

98. He said: "Soon will I ask my Lord for forgiveness for you: for He is indeed Oft-Forgiving, Most Merciful."

99. Then when they entered the presence of Joseph, he provided a home for his parents with himself, and said: "Enter ye Egypt (all) in safety if it please Allah.

100. And he raised his parents high on the throne and they fell down in prostration, (all) before him. He said: "O my father! this is the fulfilment of my vision of old! Allah hath made it come true! He was indeed good to me when he took me out of prison and brought you (all here) out of the desert, (even) after Satan had sown enmity between me and my brothers. Verily my Lord is Gracious to whom He wills for verily He is full of knowledge and wisdom.

101. "O my Lord! Thou hast indeed bestowed on me some power, and taught me

something of the interpretation of dreams,—
O thou Creator of the heavens and the
earth! Thou art my Protector in this world
and in the Hereafter. Take Thou my soul
(at death) as one submitting to Thy Will (as
a Muslim), and unite me with the righteous."

102. Such is one of the stories of what
happened unseen, which We reveal by
inspiration unto thee: nor wast thou (present)
with them when they concerted their plans
together in the process of weaving their plots.

103. Yet no faith will the greater part of
mankind have, however ardently thou dost
desire it.

104. And no reward dost thou ask of them
for this: it is no less than a Message for all
creatures.

105. And how many Signs in the heavens
and the earth do they pass by? Yet they
turn (their faces) away from them!

106. And most of them believe not in Allah
without associating (others as partners) with
Him!

107. Do they then feel secure from the
coming against them of the covering veil of
the wrath of Allah.— Or of the coming
against them of the (final) Hour all of a
sudden while they perceive not?

108. Say thou. "This is my Way; I do invite
unto Allah,—with a certain knowledge I and
whoever follows me. Glory to Allah! and
never will I join gods with Allah!"

109. Nor did We send before thee (as
Messengers) any but men, whom We did
inspire, —(men) from the peoples of the
towns. Do they not travel through the earth,
and see what was the end of those before
them? But the home of the Hereafter is
best, for those who do right. Will ye not
then understand?

110. (Respite will be granted) until, when
the messengers give up hope (of their
people) and (come to) think that they
were treated as liars, there reaches

SÛRA–13
AR-RA'D
(INTRODUCTION)

The chronological place of this Sûra and the general argument of Sûras 10 to 15 has been described in the Introduction to S. 10.

The special argument of this Sûra deals with that aspect of Allah's revelation of Himself to man and His dealings with him, which is concerned with certain contrasts which are here pointd out. There is the revelation to the Prophets, which comes in spoken words adapted to the language of the various men and groups of men to whom it comes; and there is the parallel revelation or Signs in the constant laws of external nature, on this earth and in the visible heavens. There is the contrast between recurring life and death already in the external world: why should men disbelieve in the life after death? They mock at the idea of punishment because it is deferred: but can they not see Allah's power and glory in thunder and the forces of nature? All creation praises Him: it is the good that endures and the evil that is swept away like froth or scum. Not only in miracles but in the normal working of the world, are shown Allah's power and mercy. What is Punishment in this world, compared to that in the life to come? Even here there are Signs of the working of His law: plot or plan as men will, it is Allah's Will that must prevail. This is illustrated in Joseph's story in the preceding Sûra.

them Our help, and those whom We will are delivered into safety. But never will be warded off Our punishment from those who are in sin.

111. There is, in their stories, instruction for men endued with understanding. It is not a tale invented, but a confirmation of what went before it,— a detailed exposition of all things, and a Guide and a Mercy to any such as believe.

فَنُنَجِّى مَنْ نَّشَاءُ ۖ وَلَا يُرَدُّ بَأْسُنَا عَنِ الْقَوْمِ الْمُجْرِمِينَ ۝

لَقَدْ كَانَ فِى قَصَصِهِمْ عِبْرَةٌ لِّأُولِى الْأَلْبَابِ ۗ مَا كَانَ حَدِيثًا يُّفْتَرَىٰ وَ لَـٰكِن تَصْدِيقَ الَّذِى بَيْنَ يَدَيْهِ وَ تَفْصِيلَ كُلِّ شَىْءٍ وَّهُدًى وَّرَحْمَةً لِّقَوْمٍ يُّؤْمِنُونَ ۝

Ar-Ra'd, or Thunder

In the name of Allah, Most Gracious, Most Merciful.

بِسْمِ اللَّهِ الرَّحْمَٰنِ الرَّحِيمِ ۝

1. **A.L.M.R.** These are the verses of the Book: that which hath been revealed unto thee from thy Lord is the Truth; but most men believe not.

الٓمٓر ۚ تِلْكَ آيَاتُ الْكِتَابِ ۗ وَالَّذِى أُنزِلَ إِلَيْكَ مِن رَّبِّكَ الْحَقُّ وَلَـٰكِنَّ أَكْثَرَ النَّاسِ لَا يُؤْمِنُونَ ۝

2. Allah is He Who raised the heavens without any pillars that ye can see; then He established Himself on the Throne. He has subjected the sun and the moon! Each one runs (its course) for a term appointed. He doth regulate all affairs, explaining the Signs in detail, that ye may believe with certainty in the meeting with your Lord.

اللَّهُ الَّذِى رَفَعَ السَّمَاوَاتِ بِغَيْرِ عَمَدٍ تَرَوْنَهَا ۖ ثُمَّ اسْتَوَىٰ عَلَى الْعَرْشِ ۖ وَ سَخَّرَ الشَّمْسَ وَالْقَمَرَ ۖ كُلٌّ يَّجْرِى لِأَجَلٍ مُّسَمًّى ۚ يُدَبِّرُ الْأَمْرَ يُفَصِّلُ الْآيَاتِ لَعَلَّكُم بِلِقَاءِ رَبِّكُمْ تُوقِنُونَ ۝

3. And it is He Who spread out the earth, and set thereon Mountains standing firm, and (flowing) rivers: and fruit of every kind He made in pairs, two and two: He draweth the Night as a veil O'er the Day. Behold, verily in these things there are Signs for those who consider!

وَهُوَ الَّذِى مَدَّ الْأَرْضَ وَجَعَلَ فِيهَا رَوَاسِىَ وَأَنْهَارًا ۖ وَمِن كُلِّ الثَّمَرَاتِ جَعَلَ فِيهَا زَوْجَيْنِ اثْنَيْنِ ۖ يُغْشِى الَّيْلَ النَّهَارَ ۚ إِنَّ فِى ذَٰلِكَ لَآيَاتٍ لِّقَوْمٍ يَّتَفَكَّرُونَ ۝

4. And in the earth are tracts (diverse though) neighbouring, and gardens of vines and fields sown with corn, and palm trees— growing out of single roots or otherwise: watered with the same water, yet some of them We make more excellent than others

وَفِى الْأَرْضِ قِطَعٌ مُّتَجَاوِرَاتٌ وَّجَنَّاتٌ مِّنْ أَعْنَابٍ وَّزَرْعٌ وَّنَخِيلٌ صِنْوَانٌ وَّغَيْرُ صِنْوَانٍ يُّسْقَىٰ بِمَاءٍ وَّاحِدٍ وَ نُفَضِّلُ بَعْضَهَا عَلَىٰ بَعْضٍ فِى الْأُكُلِ ۚ

to eat. Behold, verily in these things there are Signs for those who understand!

5. If thou dost marvel (at their want of faith), strange is their saying: "When we are (actually) dust, shall we indeed then be in a creation renewed?" They are those who deny their Lord! They are those round whose necks will be yokes (of servitude): they will be Companions of the Fire, to dwell therein (for aye)!

6. They ask thee to hasten on the evil in preference to the good yet have come to pass, before them, (many) exemplary punishments! But verily thy Lord is full of forgiveness for mankind for their wrong-doing. And verily thy Lord is (also) strict in punishment.

7. And the Unbelievers say: "Why is not a Sign sent down to him from his Lord?" But thou art truly a warner, and to every people a guide.

8. Allah doth know what every female (womb) doth bear, by how much the wombs fall short (of their time or number) or do exceed. Every single thing is with Him in (due) proportion.

9. He knoweth the Unseen and that which is open: He is the Great, the most High.

10. It is the same (to Him) whether any of you conceal his speech or declare it openly; whether he lie hid by night or walk forth freely by day.

11. For each (such person) there are (angels) in succession, before and behind him; they guard him by command of Allah. Verily never will Allah change the condition of a people until they change what is in themselves but when (once) Allah willeth a people's punishment, there can be no turning it back, nor will they find, besides Him, any to protect

12. It is He Who doth show you the lightning, by way both of fear and of hope: it

is He Who doth raise up the clouds, heavy with (fertilising) rain!

13. Nay, thunder repeateth His praises, and so do the angels, with awe: He flingeth the loud-voiced Thunder-bolts, and therewith He striketh whomsoever He will... yet these (are the men) the while they are disputing about Allah He is Mighty in Power.

14. To Him is due the true prayer any others that they call upon besides Him·hear them no more than if they were to stretch forth their hands for water to reach their mouths but it reaches them not: for the prayer of those without Faith is nothing but vain prayer.

15. Whatever beings there are in the heavens and the earth do prostrate themselves to Allah —with good-will or in spite of themselves: so do their shadows in the mornings and evenings.

16. Say: "Who is the Lord and Sustainer of the heavens and the earth?" Say:"(It is) Allah." Say: "Do ye then take (for worship) protectors other than Him, such as have no power either for good or for harm to themselves?" Say: "Are the blind equal with those who see? Or the depths of darkness equal with Light?" Or do they assign to Allah partners who have created (anything) as He has created, so that the creation seemed to them similar? Say: "Allah is the Creator of all things: He is the One, the Supreme and Irresistible."

17. He sends down water from the skies, and the channels flow, each according to its measure: But the torrent bears away the foam that mounts up to the surface. Even so, from that (ore) which they heat in the fire, to make ornaments or utensils therewith, there is a scum likewise. Thus doth Allah (by parables) show forth Truth and falsehood. For the scum disappears like froth cast out; while that which is for the good of mankind remains on the earth. Thus doth Allah set forth parables.

18. For those who respond to their Lord, are (all) good things. But those who respond not to Him,—even if they had all that is in the heavens and on earth, and as much more, (in vain) would they offer it for ransom. For them will the reckoning be terrible: their abode will be Hell,—what a bed of misery!

19. Is then one who doth know that that which hath been revealed unto thee from thy Lord is the Truth, like one who is blind? It is those who are endued with understanding that receive admonition;—

20. Those who fulfil the Covenant of Allah and fail not in their plighted word;

21. Those who join together those things which Allah hath commanded to be joined, hold their Lord in awe, and fear the terrible reckoning;

22. Those who patiently persevere, seeking the countenance of their Lord; establish regular prayers; spend, out of (the gifts) We have bestowed for their sustenance, secretly and openly; and turn off Evil with good: for such there is the final attainment of the (Eternal) Home,—

23. Gardens of perpetual bliss: they shall enter there, as well as the righteous among their fathers, their spouses and their offspring and angels shall enter unto them from every gate (with the salutation)

24. "Peace unto you for that ye persevered in patience! Now how excellent is the final Home!"

25. But those who break the Covenant of Allah, after having plighted their word thereto, and cut asunder those things which Allah has commanded to be joined, and work mischief in the land; — on them is the Curse; for them is the terrible Home!

26. Allah doth enlarge, or grant by (strict) measure, the Sustenance (which He giveth)

to whomso He pleaseth. (The worldly) rejoice in the life of this world: but the life of this world is but little comfort compared to the Hereafter.

27. The Unbelievers say: "Why is not a Sign sent down to him from his Lord?" Say: "Truly Allah leaveth, to stray, whom He will; but He guideth to Himself those who turn to Him in penitence,—

28. "Those who believe, and whose hearts find satisfaction in the remembrance of Allah: for without doubt in the remembrance of Allah do hearts find satisfaction.

29. "For those who believe and work righteousness, is (every) blessedness, and a beautiful place of (final) return."

30. Thus have We sent thee amongst a People before whom (long since) have (other) Peoples (gone and) passed away; in order that thou mightest rehearse unto them what We send down unto thee by ins-piration; yet do they reject (Him), the Most Gracious! Say: "He is my Lord! There is no god but He! On Him is my trust, and to Him do I turn!"

31. If there were a Qur'an with which mountains were moved, or the earth were cloven asunder, or the dead were made to speak, (this would be the one!) but, truly, the Command is with Allah in all things! Do not the Believers know, that, had Allah (so) willed, He could have guided all mankind (to the Right)? But the Unbelievers,—never will disaster cease to seize them for their (ill) deeds, or to settle close to their homes, until the promise of Allah come to pass, for, verily, Allah will not fail in His promise.

32. Mocked were (many) messengers before thee: but I granted respite to the Unbelievers, and finally I punished them: then how (terrible) was My requital!

33. Is then He Who standeth over every soul (and knoweth) all that it doth, (like any others)? And yet they ascribe partners to Allah. Say: "But name them! Is it that ye will inform Him of something He Knoweth not on earth, or is it (just) a show of words?" Nay! to those who believe not, their devising seems pleasing, but they are kept back (thereby) from the Path. And those whom Allah leads astray, no one can guide

34. For them is a Penalty in the life of this world, but harder, truly, is the Chastisement of the Hereafter: and defender have they none against Allah.

35. The parable of the Garden which the righteous are promised!—beneath it flow rivers: perpetual is the fruits thereof and the shade therein: such is the End of the Righteous: and the End of Unbelievers is the Fire.

36. Those to whom We have given the Book rejoice at what hath been revealed unto thee: but there are among the clans those who reject a part thereof. Say: "I am commanded to worship Allah, and not to join partners with Him. Unto Him do I call, and unto Him is my return."

37. Thus have We revealed it to be a judgment of authority in Arabic. Wert thou to follow their (vain) desires after the knowledge which hath reached thee, then wouldst thou find neither protector nor defender against Allah.

38. We did send messengers before thee, and appointed for them wives and children: and it was never the part of a messenger to bring a Sign except as Allah permitted (or commanded). For each period is an appointment).

39. Allah doth blot out or confirm what He pleaseth: with Him is the Mother of the Book.

SÛRA–14
IBRÂHÎM
(INTRODUCTION)

For the chronology and the general argument of this Sûra in the series Sûras 10 to 15, see Introduction to S. 10.

The special subject-matter of this Sûra is a continuation of the conculding portion of the last Sûra, which explained how Allah's revelation gains ground in spite of selfish men's opposition. Here illustrations are given from the story of Moses and Abraham, and Abraham's Prayer for Makkah forms the core of the Sûra.

40. Whether We shall show thee (within thy life-time) part of what We promised them or take to Us thy soul (before it is all accomplished). Thy duty is to make (the Message) reach them: It is Our part to call them to account.

41. See they not that We gradually reduce the land from its outlying borders? (Where) Allah commands, there is none to put back His command: and He is Swift in calling to account.

42. Those before them did (also) devise plots; but in all things Allah is the devising altogether. He knoweth the doings of every soul: and soon will the Unbelievers know who gets home in the End.

43. The Unbelievers say: "No messenger art thou." Say: "Enough for a witness between me and you is Allah, and such as have knowledge of the Book."

Ibrāhīm, or Abraham

In the name of Allah, Most Gracious, Most Merciful.

1. **A. L. R.** A Book which We have revealed unto thee, in order that thou mightest lead mankind out of the depths of darkness into light—by the leave of their Lord—to the Way of (Him) the Exalted in Power, Worthy of all Praise!—

2. Of Allah, to Whom do belong all things in the heavens and on earth! But alas for the Unbelievers for a terrible Chastisement (their Unfaith will bring them)!—

3. Those who prefer the life of this world to the Hereafter, who hinder (men) from the Path of Allah and seek to make it crooked: they are astray by a long distance.

4. We sent not a messenger except (to teach) in the language of his (own) people, in order to make (things) clear to them. So Allah leads astray those whom He pleases

and guides whom He pleases and He is Exalted in power, Full of Wisdom.

5.   We sent Moses with Our Signs (and the command). "Bring out thy people from the depths of darkness into light, and remind them of the Days of Allah." Verily in this there are Signs for such as are firmly patient and constant,—grateful and appreciative.

6.   Remember! Moses said to his people: "Call to mind the favour of Allah to you when He delivered you from the people of Pharaoh: they set you hard tasks and punishments, slaughtered your sons, and let your women-folk live: therein was a tremendous trial from your Lord."

7.   And remember! your Lord caused to be declared (publicly): "If ye are grateful, I will add more (favours) unto you; but if ye show ingratitude, truly My punishment is terrible indeed."

8.   And Moses said: "If ye show ingratitude, ye and all on earth together,— yet is Allah free of all wants, Worthy of all praise.

9.   Has not the story reached you, (O people!), of those who (went) before you?— of the People of Noah, and 'Ād, and Thamūd?— And of those who (came) after them? None knows them but Allah. To them came Messengers with Clear (Signs); but they put their hands up to their mouths, and said: "We do deny (the mission) on which ye have been sent, and we are really in suspicious (disquieting) doubt as to that to which ye invite us."

10.   Their messengers said: "Is there a doubt about Allah, the Creator of the heavens and the earth? It is He Who invites you, in order that He may forgive you your sins and give you respite for a term appointed!" They said: "Ah! ye are no more

than human, like ourselves! Ye wish to turn us away from what our fathers used to worship; then bring us some clear authority.

11. Their messengers said to them: "True, we are human like yourselves, but Allah doth grant His grace to such of His servants as He pleases. It is not for us to bring you an authority except as Allah permits. And on Allah let all men of faith put their trust.

12. Why we should not put our trust on Allah. Indeed He has guided us to the Ways we (follow). We shall certainly bear with patience all the hurt you caused us. For those who put their trust should put their trust on Allah."

13. And the Unbelievers said to their messengers: "Be sure we shall drive you out of our land, or ye shall return to our religion." But their Lord inspired (this Message) to them: "Verily We shall cause the wrong-doers to perish!

14. "And verily, We shall cause you to abide in the land, and succeed them. This for such as fear the time when they shall stand before My tribunal,—such as fear My Punishment."

15. But they sought victory and decision (there and then), and frustration was the lot of every powerful obstinate transgressor.

16. In front of such a one is Hell, and he is given, for drink, boiling fetid water.

17. In gulps will he sip it, but never will he be near swallowing it down his throat; death will come to him from every quarter, yet will he not die; and in front of him will be a chastisement unrelenting.

18. The parable of those who raject their Lord is that their works are as ashes, on which the wind blows furiously on a tempestuous day: no power have they over aught that they have earned: that is the straying far, far (from the goal).

19. Seest thou not that Allah created the heavens and the earth in Truth? If He so will, He can remove you and put (in your place) a new Creation?

20. Nor is that for Allah any great matter.

21. They will all be marshalled before Allah together: then will the weak say to those who were arrogant, "For us, we but followed you; can ye then avail us at all against the Wrath of Allah?" They will reply, "If we had received the guidance of Allah, we should have given it to you; to us it makes no difference (now) whether we rage, or bear (these torments) with patience: for ourselves there is no way of escape."

22. And Satan will say when the matter is decided: "It was Allah Who gave you a promise of Truth: I too promised, but I failed in my promise to you. I had no authority over you except to call you, but ye listened to me; then reproach not me, but reproach your own souls. I cannot listen to your cries, nor can ye listen to mine. I reject your former act in associating me with Allah. For wrong-doers there must be a grievous Chastisement."

23. But those who believe and work righteousness will be admitted to Gardens beneath which rivers flow,—to dwell therein for aye with the leave of their Lord. Their greeting therein will be: "Peace!"

24. Seest thou not how Allah sets forth a parable?—A goodly Word like a goodly tree, whose root is firmly fixed, and its branches (reach) to the heavens,—

25. It brings forth its fruit at all times, by the leave of its Lord so Allah sets forth parables for men, in order that they may receive admonition.

26. And the parable of an evil Word is that of an evil tree: it is torn up by the root from the surface of the earth: it has no stability.

وَمَثَلُ كَلِمَةٍ خَبِيثَةٍ كَشَجَرَةٍ خَبِيثَةٍ
اجْتُثَّتْ مِنْ فَوْقِ الْأَرْضِ مَا لَهَا
مِنْ قَرَارٍ ۝

27. Allah will establish in strength those who believe, with the Word that stands firm, in this world and in the Hereafter; but Allah will leave, to stray, those who do wrong: Allah doeth what He willeth.

يُثَبِّتُ اللهُ الَّذِيْنَ اٰمَنُوْا بِالْقَوْلِ الثَّابِتِ
فِي الْحَيٰوةِ الدُّنْيَا وَفِي الْاٰخِرَةِ ۚ وَيُضِلُّ
اللهُ الظّٰلِمِيْنَ ۚ وَيَفْعَلُ اللهُ مَا يَشَاءُ ۞

28. Hast thou not turned thy thought to those who exchanged the favour of Allah with ingratitude and caused their people to descend to the House of Perdition?—

اَلَمْ تَرَ اِلَى الَّذِيْنَ بَدَّلُوْا نِعْمَتَ
اللهِ كُفْرًا وَّاَحَلُّوْا قَوْمَهُمْ
دَارَ الْبَوَارِ ۞

29. Into Hell? They will burn therein,—an evil place to stay in!

جَهَنَّمَ ۚ يَصْلَوْنَهَا ۚ وَبِئْسَ الْقَرَارُ ۞

30. And they set up (idols) as equal to Allah, to mislead (men) from His Path! Say: "Enjoy (your brief power)! But verily ye are making straightway for Hell!"

وَجَعَلُوْا لِلّٰهِ اَنْدَادًا لِّيُضِلُّوْا عَنْ
سَبِيْلِهٖ ۚ قُلْ تَمَتَّعُوْا فَاِنَّ مَصِيْرَكُمْ
اِلَى النَّارِ ۞

31. Speak to my servants who have believed, that they may establish regular prayers, and spend (in charity) out of the Sustenance We have given them, secretly and openly, before the coming of a Day in which there will be neither mutual bargaining nor befriending.

قُلْ لِّعِبَادِيَ الَّذِيْنَ اٰمَنُوْا يُقِيْمُوا
الصَّلٰوةَ وَيُنْفِقُوْا مِمَّا رَزَقْنٰهُمْ سِرًّا
وَّعَلَانِيَةً مِّنْ قَبْلِ اَنْ يَّأْتِيَ يَوْمٌ
لَّا بَيْعٌ فِيْهِ وَلَا خِلٰلٌ ۞

32. It is Allah Who hath created the heavens and the earth and sendeth down rain from the skies, and with it bringeth our fruits wherewith to feed you; it is He Who hath made the ships subject to you, that they may sail through the sea by His Command; and the rivers (also) hath He made subject to you.

اَللهُ الَّذِيْ خَلَقَ السَّمٰوٰتِ وَالْاَرْضَ
وَاَنْزَلَ مِنَ السَّمَاءِ مَاءً فَاَخْرَجَ بِهٖ
مِنَ الثَّمَرٰتِ رِزْقًا لَّكُمْ ۚ وَسَخَّرَ لَكُمُ
الْفُلْكَ لِتَجْرِيَ فِي الْبَحْرِ بِاَمْرِهٖ ۚ وَسَخَّرَ
لَكُمُ الْاَنْهٰرَ ۞

33. And He hath made subject to you the sun and the moon, both diligently pursuing their courses; and the Night and the Day hath He (also) made subject to you.

وَسَخَّرَ لَكُمُ الشَّمْسَ وَالْقَمَرَ دَائِبَيْنِ ۚ
وَسَخَّرَ لَكُمُ الَّيْلَ وَالنَّهَارَ ۞

34. And He giveth you of all that ye ask for but if ye count the favours of Allah, never will ye be able to number them. Verily, man is given up to injustice and ingratitude.

وَاٰتٰىكُمْ مِّنْ كُلِّ مَا سَاَلْتُمُوْهُ ۚ وَاِنْ
تَعُدُّوْا نِعْمَتَ اللهِ لَا تُحْصُوْهَا ۚ اِنَّ
الْاِنْسَانَ لَظَلُوْمٌ كَفَّارٌ ۞

35. Remember Abraham said: "O my Lord! make this city one of peace and security; and preserve me and my sons from worshipping idols.

36. "O my Lord! they have indeed led astray many among mankind; he then who follows my (ways) is of me, and he that disobeys me,—but Thou art indeed Oft-Forgiving, Most Merciful.

37. "O our Lord! I have made some of my offspring to dwell in a valley without cultivation, by Thy Sacred House; in order, O our Lord! that they may establish regular Prayer: so fill the hearts of some among men with love towards them, and feed them with Fruits: so that they may give thanks.

38. "O our Lord! truly Thou dost know what we conceal and what we reveal: for nothing whatever is hidden from Allah, whether on earth or in heaven.

39. "Praise be to Allah, Who hath granted unto me in old age Ismā'īl and Isaac: for truly my Lord is He, the Hearer of Prayer!

40. "O my Lord! make me one who establishes regular Prayer, and also (raise such) among my offspring O our Lord! and accept Thou my Prayer.

41. "O our Lord! cover (us) with Thy Forgiveness— me, my parents, and (all) Believers, on the Day that the Reckoning will be established!

42. Think not that Allah doth not heed the deeds of those who do wrong. He but giveth them respite against a Day when the eyes will fixedly stare in horror,—

43. They running forward with necks outstretched, their heads uplifted, their gaze returning not towards them, and their hearts

a (gaping) void!

هَوَآءٌ ۞

44. So warn mankind of the Day when the Wrath will reach them: then will the wrong-doers say: "Our Lord respite us (if only) for a short Term we will answer Thy Call. and follow the messengers!" "What! were ye not wont to swear aforetime that ye should suffer no decline?

وَاَنْذِرِ النَّاسَ يَوْمَ يَأْتِيهِمُ الْعَذَابُ فَيَقُوْلُ الَّذِيْنَ ظَلَمُوْا رَبَّنَآ اَخِّرْنَآ اِلٰٓى اَجَلٍ قَرِيْبٍ نُّجِبْ دَعْوَتَكَ وَ نَتَّبِعِ الرُّسُلَ ؕ اَوَلَمْ تَكُوْنُوْٓا اَقْسَمْتُمْ مِّنْ قَبْلُ مَالَكُمْ مِّنْ زَوَالٍ ۙ۞

45. "And ye dwelt in the dwellings of men who wronged themselves ye were clearly shown how We dealt with them; and We put forth (many) Parables in your behoof!"

وَّسَكَنْتُمْ فِيْ مَسٰكِنِ الَّذِيْنَ ظَلَمُوْٓا اَنْفُسَهُمْ وَتَبَيَّنَ لَكُمْ كَيْفَ فَعَلْنَا بِهِمْ وَضَرَبْنَا لَكُمُ الْاَمْثَالَ ۞

46. Mighty indeed were the plots which they made, but their plots were (well) within the sight of Allah, even though they were such as to shake the hills!

وَقَدْ مَكَرُوْا مَكْرَهُمْ وَعِنْدَ اللّٰهِ مَكْرُهُمْ ؕ وَاِنْ كَانَ مَكْرُهُمْ لِتَزُوْلَ مِنْهُ الْجِبَالُ ۞

47. Never think that Allah would fail His messengers in His promise: for Allah is Exalted in Power,—the Lord of Retribution.

فَلَا تَحْسَبَنَّ اللّٰهَ مُخْلِفَ وَعْدِهٖ رُسُلَهٗ ؕ اِنَّ اللّٰهَ عَزِيْزٌ ذُوانْتِقَامٍ ؕ۞

48. One day the Earth will be changed to a different Earth, and so will be the Heavens, and (men) will be marshalled forth, before Allah, the One, the Irresistible,

يَوْمَ تُبَدَّلُ الْاَرْضُ غَيْرَ الْاَرْضِ وَ السَّمٰوٰتُ وَبَرَزُوْا لِلّٰهِ الْوَاحِدِ الْقَهَّارِ ۞

49. And thou wilt see the Sinners that day bound together in fetters:—

وَتَرَى الْمُجْرِمِيْنَ يَوْمَئِذٍ مُّقَرَّنِيْنَ فِى الْاَصْفَادِ ۙ۞

50 Their garments of liquid pitch, and their faces covered with Fire;

سَرَابِيْلُهُمْ مِّنْ قَطِرَانٍ وَّتَغْشٰى وُجُوْهَهُمُ النَّارُ ۙ۞

51. That Allah may requite each soul according to its deserts; and verily Allah is Swift in calling to account.

لِيَجْزِيَ اللّٰهُ كُلَّ نَفْسٍ مَّا كَسَبَتْ ؕ اِنَّ اللّٰهَ سَرِيْعُ الْحِسَابِ ۞

52. Here is a Message for mankind: that they may take warning therefrom, and may know that He is One Allah: let men of understanding take heed.

هٰذَا بَلٰغٌ لِّلنَّاسِ وَلِيُنْذَرُوْا بِهٖ وَلِيَعْلَمُوْٓا اَنَّمَا هُوَ اِلٰهٌ وَّاحِدٌ وَّلِيَذَّكَّرَ اُولُوا الْاَلْبَابِ ۞

SÛRA–15
AL-ḤIJR
(INTRODUCTION)

This is the last of the six Sûras of the A.L.M. series (10 to 15). Its place in chronology is the late Makkan period, probably somewhere near the middle of that period. See Introduction to S. 10 where will be found also an indication of the general subject-matter of the whole series in the gradation of Quranic teaching.

The special subject-matter of this, Sûra is the protection of Allah's Revelation and Allah's Truth. Evil arose from Pride and the warping of man's will, but Allah's Mercy is the antidote, as was proved in the case of Abraham and Lot, and might have been proved by the people of the Aika and the Ḥijr if they had only attended to Allah's "Signs". The Qur-ān, beginning with the Seven Oft-repeated Verses, is the precious vehicle for the praises of Allah.

Al-Hijr, or The Rocky Tract

In the name of Allah, Most Gracious, Most Merciful.

1. **A.L.R.** These are the Ayats of Revelation,— of a Qur'an that makes things clear.

2. Often will those who disbelieve, wish that they had been Muslims.

3. Leave them alone, to eat and enjoy and (false) hope distract them: soon for they will soon know.

4. Never did We destroy a population that had not a term decreed and assigned beforehand.

5. Neither can a people anticipate its Term, nor delay it.

6. They say: "O thou to whom the Message is being revealed! Truly thou art mad (or possessed)!

7. "Why bringest thou not angels to us if it be that thou hast the Truth?"

8. We send not the angels down except for just cause: if they came (to the ungodly), behold! no respite would they have!

9. We have, without doubt, sent down the Message; and We will assuredly guard it (from corruption).

10. We did send messengers before thee amongst the sects of old:

11. But never came a messenger to them but they mocked him.

12. Even so do We let it creep into the hearts of the sinners—

13. They do not believe in the Message, such has been the way of those who went before them.

14. Even if We opened out to them a gate from heaven, and they were to continue (all

day) ascending therein,

15. They would only say: "Our eyes have been intoxicated: nay, we have been bewitched by sorcery."

16. It is We Who have set out constellations in the heavens and made them fair-seeming to (all) beholders;

17. And (moreover) We have guar-ded them from every accursed Satan.

18. But any that gains a hearing by stealth, is pursued by a fiery comet, bright (to see).

19. And the earth We have spread out (like a carpet); set thereon mountains firm and immovable; and produced therein all kinds of things in due balance.

20. And We have provided therein means of subsistence,—for you and for those for whose sustenance ye are not responsible.

21. And there is not a thing but its (sources and) treasures (inexhaustible) are with Us; but We only send down thereof in due and ascertainable measures.

22. And We send the fecundating winds, then cause the rain to descend from the sky, therewith providing you with water (in abundance), though ye are not the guardians of its stores.

23. And verily, it is We Who give life, and Who give death: it is We Who remain inheritors (after all else passes away).

24. To Us are known those of you who hasten forward, and those who lag behind.

25. Assuredly it is thy Lord who will gather them together: for He is Perfect in Wisdom and Knowledge.

26. We created man from sounding clay, from mud moulded into shape;

27. And the Jinn race, We had created before, from the fire of a scorching wind.

28. Behold! thy Lord said to the angels: "I am about to creat man, from sounding clay from mud moulded into shape;

29. "When I have fashioned him (in due proportion) and breathed into him of My spirit, fall ye down in obeisance unto him."

30. So the angels prostrated themselves, all of them together:

31. Not so Iblîs: he refused to be among those who prostrated themselves.

32. (Allah) said: "O Iblîs! What is your reason for not being among those who prostrated themselves?"

33. (Iblîs) said: "I am not one to prostrate myself to man, whom Thou didst create from sounding clay, from mud moulded into shape."

34. (Allah) said: "Then get thee out fr-om here; for thou art rejected, accursed.

35. "And the Curse shall be on thee till the Day of Judgment."

36. (Iblîs) said: "O my Lord! give me then respite till the Day the (dead) are raised."

37. (Allah) said: "Respite is granted thee—

38. "Till the Day of the Time Appointed."

39. (Iblîs) said: "O my Lord! because Thou hast put me in the wrong, I will make (wrong) fair-seeming to them on the earth, and I will put them all in the wrong.—

40. "Except Thy chosen servants among them,

41. (Allah) said: "This is for me a straight path.

42. "For over My servants no authority shalt thou have. except such as put themselves in the wrong and follow thee."

43. And verily, Hell is the promised abode for them all!

44. To it are seven Gates: for each of those Gates is a (special) class (of sinners) assigned.

45. The righteous (will be) amid Garde-ns and fountains (of clear-flowing water)

46. (Their greeting will be); "Enter ye here in Peace and Security."

47. And We shall remove from their hearts any lurking sense of injury; (they will be) brothers (Joyfully) facing each other on raised couches.

48. There no sense of fatigue shall touch them, nor shall they (ever) be asked to leave.

49. Tell My servants that I am indeed the Oft-Forgiving, Most Merciful;

50. And that My Chastisement will be indeed the most grievous Chastisement

51. Tell them about the guests of Abraham.

52. When they entered his presence and said, "Peace!" He said, "We feel afraid of you!"

53. They said: "Fear not! We give thee glad tidings of a son endowed with knowledge"

54. He said: "Do ye give me such glad tidings even though old age has seized me? Of what, then, is your good news?"

55. They said: "We give thee glad tidings in truth; be not then in despair!"

56. He said: "And who despairs of the mercy of his Lord, but such as go astray?"

57. Abraham said: "What then is the business on which ye (have come), O ye Messengers (of Allah)?"

58. They said: "We have been sent to a people (deep) in sin,

59. "Excepting the adherents of Lût: them we are certainly (charged) to save (from harm),—all—

60. "Except his wife, who, We bave ascertained, will be among those who will lag behind."

61. At length when the messengers arrived among the adherents of Lût.

62. He said; "Ye appear to be uncommon folk."

63. They said: "Yea, We have come to thee to accomplish that of which they doubt.

64. "We have come to thee with the Truth and assuredly We tell the truth.

65. "Then travel by night with thy

household, when a portion of the night (yet remains), and do thou go behind them: let no one amongst you look back, but pass on whither ye are ordered."

66. And We made known this decree to him, that the last remnants of those (sinners) should be cut off by the morning.

67. The inhabitants of the City came in (mad) joy (at news of the young men).

68. Lūt said: "These are my guests: disgrace me not:

69. "But fear Allah, and shame me not."

70. They said: "Did we not forbid thee (to speak) for all and sundry?"

71. He said: "There are my daugh-ters (to marry), if ye must act (so)."

72. Verily, by thy life (O Prophet), in their wild intoxication, they wander in distraction, to and fro.

73. But the (mighty) Blast overtook them at sunrise,

74. And We turned (the cities) upside down, and rained down on them brimstones hard as baked clay.

75. Behold! in this are Signs for those who by tokens do understand.

76. And the (Cities were) right on the high-road.

77. Behold! in this is a Sign for those who believe!

78. And the Companions of the Wood were also wrong-doers.

79. So We exacted retribution from them. They were both on an open highway, plain to see.

80. The Companions of the Rocky Tract also rejected the messengers:

81. We sent them Our Signs, but they persisted in turning away from them.

82. Out of the mountains did they hew (their) edifices, (feeling themselves) secure.

83. But the (mighty) Blast seized them of a morning,

84. And of no avail to them was all that they did (with such art and care)!

85. We created not the heavens, the earth, and all between them, but for just ends. And the Hour is surely coming (when this will be manifest). So overlook (any human faults) with gracious forgiveness.

86. For verily it is thy Lord Who is the All-Creator, Knowing all things.

أَدْبَارَهُمْ وَلَا يَلْتَفِتْ مِنكُمْ أَحَدٌ وَّامْضُوا حَيْثُ تُؤْمَرُونَ ۞

وَقَضَيْنَا إِلَيْهِ ذٰلِكَ الْأَمْرَ أَنَّ دَابِرَ هٰؤُلَاءِ مَقْطُوعٌ مُّصْبِحِينَ ۞

وَجَاءَ أَهْلُ الْمَدِينَةِ يَسْتَبْشِرُونَ ۞

قَالَ إِنَّ هٰؤُلَاءِ ضَيْفِي فَلَا تَفْضَحُونِ ۞

وَاتَّقُوا اللَّهَ وَلَا تُخْزُونِ ۞

قَالُوا أَوَلَمْ نَنْهَكَ عَنِ الْعَالَمِينَ ۞

قَالَ هٰؤُلَاءِ بَنَاتِي إِنْ كُنْتُمْ فَاعِلِينَ ۞

لَعَمْرُكَ إِنَّهُمْ لَفِي سَكْرَتِهِمْ يَعْمَهُونَ ۞

فَأَخَذَتْهُمُ الصَّيْحَةُ مُشْرِقِينَ ۞

فَجَعَلْنَا عَالِيَهَا سَافِلَهَا وَأَمْطَرْنَا عَلَيْهِمْ حِجَارَةً مِّنْ سِجِّيلٍ ۞

إِنَّ فِي ذٰلِكَ لَآيَاتٍ لِّلْمُتَوَسِّمِينَ ۞

وَإِنَّهَا لَبِسَبِيلٍ مُّقِيمٍ ۞

إِنَّ فِي ذٰلِكَ لَآيَةً لِّلْمُؤْمِنِينَ ۞

وَإِنْ كَانَ أَصْحَابُ الْأَيْكَةِ لَظَالِمِينَ ۞

فَانْتَقَمْنَا مِنْهُمْ وَإِنَّهُمَا لَبِإِمَامٍ مُّبِينٍ ۞

وَلَقَدْ كَذَّبَ أَصْحَابُ الْحِجْرِ الْمُرْسَلِينَ ۞

وَآتَيْنَاهُمْ آيَاتِنَا فَكَانُوا عَنْهَا مُعْرِضِينَ ۞

وَكَانُوا يَنْحِتُونَ مِنَ الْجِبَالِ بُيُوتًا آمِنِينَ ۞

فَأَخَذَتْهُمُ الصَّيْحَةُ مُصْبِحِينَ ۞

فَمَا أَغْنَى عَنْهُمْ مَّا كَانُوا يَكْسِبُونَ ۞

وَمَا خَلَقْنَا السَّمَاوَاتِ وَالْأَرْضَ وَمَا بَيْنَهُمَا إِلَّا بِالْحَقِّ وَإِنَّ السَّاعَةَ لَآتِيَةٌ فَاصْفَحِ الصَّفْحَ الْجَمِيلَ ۞

إِنَّ رَبَّكَ هُوَ الْخَلَّاقُ الْعَلِيمُ ۞

SÛRA–16
AN-NAḤL
(INTRODUCTION)

Chronologically this Sûra, like the six which preceded it, belongs to the late Makkan period, except perhaps verse 110 and some of the verses that follow, but the chronology has no significance. In subject-matter it sums up, from a new point of view, the arguments on the great questions of Allah's dealings with man, His Self-revelation to man and how the Messengers and the Message are writ large in every phase of Allah's Creation and the life of Man. The new point of view is that Nature points to Nature's Allah.

87. And We have bestowed upon thee the Seven Oft-repeated (Verses) and the Grand Qur-ān.

وَلَقَدْ أَتَيْنَاكَ سَبْعًا مِّنَ الْمَثَانِى وَ الْقُرْآنَ الْعَظِيمَ ۝

88. Strain not thine eyes (wistfully) at what We have bestowed on certain classes of them, nor grieve over them. but lower thy wing (in gentleness) to the Believers.

لَا تَمُدَّنَّ عَيْنَيْكَ إِلَى مَا مَتَّعْنَا بِهٖ أَزْوَاجًا مِّنْهُمْ وَلَا تَحْزَنْ عَلَيْهِمْ وَ اخْفِضْ جَنَاحَكَ لِلْمُؤْمِنِينَ ۝

89. And say: "I am indeed he that warneth openly and without ambiguity."—

وَقُلْ إِنِّى أَنَا النَّذِيرُ الْمُبِينُ ۝

90. (Of just such wrath) as We sent down on those who divided (Scripture into arbitrary parts).—

كَمَا أَنْزَلْنَا عَلَى الْمُقْتَسِمِينَ ۝

91. (So also on such) who have made Qur-an into shreds (as they please).

الَّذِينَ جَعَلُوا الْقُرْآنَ عِضِينَ ۝

92. Therefore, by thy Lord, we will, of a surety, call them to account.

فَوَرَبِّكَ لَنَسْأَلَنَّهُمْ أَجْمَعِينَ ۝

93. For all their deeds.

عَمَّا كَانُوا يَعْمَلُونَ ۝

94. Therefore expound openly what thou art commanded, and turn away from those who join false gods with Allah.

فَاصْدَعْ بِمَا تُؤْمَرُ وَأَعْرِضْ عَنِ الْمُشْرِكِينَ ۝

95. For sufficient are We unto thee against those who scoff.—

إِنَّا كَفَيْنَاكَ الْمُسْتَهْزِئِينَ ۝

96. Those who adopt, with Allah, another god: but soon will they come to know.

الَّذِينَ يَجْعَلُونَ مَعَ اللّٰهِ إِلٰهًا آخَرَ فَسَوْفَ يَعْلَمُونَ ۝

97. We do indeed know how thy heart is distressed at what they say.

وَلَقَدْ نَعْلَمُ أَنَّكَ يَضِيقُ صَدْرُكَ بِمَا يَقُولُونَ ۝

98. But celebrate the praises of thy Lord and be of those who prostrate themselves in adoration.

فَسَبِّحْ بِحَمْدِ رَبِّكَ وَكُنْ مِّنَ السَّاجِدِينَ ۝

99. And serve thy Lord until there come unto thee the Hour that is Certain.

وَاعْبُدْ رَبَّكَ حَتّٰى يَأْتِيَكَ الْيَقِينُ ۝

An-Nahl, or The Bee

In the name of Allah, Most Gracious, Most Merciful.

بِسْمِ اللّٰهِ الرَّحْمٰنِ الرَّحِيمِ

1. (Inevitable) cometh (to pass) the Command of Allah: seek ye not then to hasten it: glory to Him, and far is He above having the partners they ascribe unto Him!

أَتَى أَمْرُ اللّٰهِ فَلَا تَسْتَعْجِلُوهُ سُبْحَانَهُ وَتَعَالَى عَمَّا يُشْرِكُونَ ۝

2. He doth send down His angels with inspiration of His Command, to such of His servants as He pleaseth, (saying): "Warn (Man) that there is no god but I: so do your duty unto Me."

يُنَزِّلُ الْمَلٰئِكَةَ بِالرُّوحِ مِنْ أَمْرِهٖ عَلَى مَنْ يَشَاءُ مِنْ عِبَادِهٖ أَنْ أَنْذِرُوا أَنَّهُ لَا إِلٰهَ إِلَّا أَنَا فَاتَّقُونِ ۝

3.   He has created the heavens and the earth with truth far is He above having the partners they ascribe to Him!

4.   He has created man from a sperm-drop and behold this same (man) becomes an open disputer!

5.   And cattle He has created for you (men): from them ye derive warmth. and numerous benefits, and of their (meat) ye eat.

6.   And ye have a sense of pride and beauty in them as ye drive them home in the evening, and as ye lead them forth to pasture in the morning.

7.   And they carry your heavy loads to lands that ye could not (otherwise) reach except with souls distressed: for your Lord is indeed Most Kind, Most Merciful.

8.   And (He has created) horses, mules, and donkeys, for you to ride and as an adornment; and He has created (other) things of which ye have no knowledge.

9.   Allah alone can show the right path but there are ways that turn aside: if Allah had willed, He could have guided all of you.

10.   It is He Who sends down rain from the sky from it ye drink, and out of it (grows) the vegetation on which ye feed your cattle.

11.   With it He produces for you corn. olives, date-palms, grapes, and every kind of fruit: verily in this is a Sign for those who give thought.

12.   He has made subject to you the Night and the Day; the Sun and the Moon: and the Stars are in subjection by His Command: verily in this are Signs for men who are wise.

13.   And the things on this earth which He has multiplied in varying colours (and qualities): verily in this is a Sign for men who are mindful.

14.   It is He Who has made the sea subject, that ye may eat thereof flesh that is fresh and tender, and that ye may extract

therefrom ornaments to wear; and thou seest the ships therein that plough the waves, that ye may seek (thus) of the bounty of Allah and that ye may be grateful.

15. And He has set up on the earth mountains standing firm, lest it should shake with you; and rivers and ways: that ye may guide yourselves;

16. And marks and sign-posts; and by the stars (men) guide themselves.

17. Is then He Who creates like one that creates not? Will ye not receive admonition?

18. If ye would count up the favours of Allah, never would ye be able to number them: for Allah is Oft-Forgiving, Most Merciful.

19. And Allah doth know what ye conceal, and what ye reveal.

20. Those whom they invoke besides Allah create nothing and are themselves created.

21. (They are things) dead, lifeless: nor do they know when they will be raised up.

22. Your God is One God: as to those who believe not in the Hereafter, their hearts refuse to know, and they are arrogant.

23. Undoubtedly Allah doth know What they conceal, and what they reveal: verily He loveth not the arrogant.

24. When it is said to them, "What is it that your Lord has revealed?" they say, "Tales of the ancients!"

25. That they may bear, on the Day of Judgment, their own burdens in full, and also (something) of the burdens of those without knowledge, whom they misled. Alas, how grievous the burdens they will bear!

26. Those before them did also plot (against Allah's Way): but Allah took their structures from their foundations, and the roof fell down on them from above; and the

Wrath seized them from directions they did not perceive.

27. Then, on the Day of Judgment, He will cover them with shame, and say: "Where are My 'partners' concerning whom ye used to dispute (with the godly)?" Those endued with knowledge will say: "This Day, indeed, are the Unbelievers covered with Shame and Misery,—

28. "(Namely) those whose lives the angels take in a state of wrong-doing to their own souls." Then would they offer submission (with the pre-tence), We did no evil (knowingly)." (The angels will reply). "Nay, but verily Allah knoweth all that ye did;

29. "So enter the gates of Hell, to dwell therein. Thus evil indeed is the abode of the arrogant."

30. To the righteous (when) it is said, "What is it that your Lord has revealed?" they say, "All that is good." To those who do good, there is good in this world, and the Home of the Hereafter is even better and excellent indeed is the Home of the righteous,—

31. Gardens of Eternity which they will enter: beneath them flow (pleasant) rivers: they will have therein all that they wish: thus doth Allah reward the righteous,—

32. (Namely) those whose lives the angels take in a state of purity, saying (to them). "Peace be on you; enter ye the Garden, because of (the good) which ye did (in the world)."

33. Do the (ungodly) wait but for the angels to come to them, or there comes the Command of thy Lord (for their doom)? So did those who went before them. But Allah wronged them not: nay, they wronged their own souls.

34. But the evil results of their deeds overtook them, and that every (Wrath) at which they had scoffed hemmed them in.

35. The worshippers of false gods say: "If Allah had so willed, we should not have worshipped aught but Him—neither we nor our fathers,—nor should we have prescribed prohibitions other than His." So did those who went before them. But what is the mission of messengers but to preach the Clear Message?

36. For We assuredly sent amongst every People a Messenger, (with the Command), "Serve Allah, and eschew Evil": of the people were some whom Allah guided, and some on whom Error became inevitably (established). So travel through the earth, and see what was the end of those who denied (the Truth).

37. If thou art anxious for their guidance, yet Allah guideth not such as he leaves to stray, and there is none to help them.

38. They swear their strongest oath by Allah, that Allah will not raise up those who die: nay, but it is a promise (binding) on Him in truth: but most among mankind know it not.

39. (They must be raised up), in order that He may manifest to them the truth of that wherein they differ, and that the rejecters of Truth may realise that they were liars.

40. For to anything which We have willed, We but say "Be," and it is.

41. To those who leave their homes in the cause of Allah, after suffering oppression,—We will assuredly give a goodly home in this world; but truly the reward of the Hereafter will be greater. If they only realised (this)!

42. (They are) those who persevere in patience, and put their trust on their Lord.

43. And before thee We sent none but men, to whom We granted inspiration: if ye realise this not, ask of those who possess the Message.

44. (We sent them) with Clear Signs and Scriptures and We have sent down unto

thee (also) the Message; that thou mayest explain clearly to men what is sent for them, and that they may give thought.

45. Do then those who devise evil (plots) feel secure that Allah will not cause the earth to swallow them up, or that the Wrath will not seize them from directions they little perceive?—

46. Or that He may not call them to account in the midst of their goings to and fro, without a chance of their frustrating Him?—

47. Or that He may not call them to account by a process of slow wastage—for thy Lord is indeed full of kindness and mercy.

48. Do they not look at Allah's creation. Among things,—how their shadows turn round, from the right and the left, prostrating themselves to Allah, and that in the humblest manner?

49. And to Allah doth prostrate all that is in the heavens and on earth, whether moving creatures or the angels: for none are arrogant (before their Lord).

50. They all fear their Lord, high above them, and they do all that they are commanded.

51. Allah has said: "Take not (for worship two gods: for He is just One God: then fear Me (and Me alone)."

52. To Him belongs whatever is in the heavens and on earth and to Him is the religion always: then will ye fear other—than Allah?

53. And ye have no good thing but is from Allah: and moreover, when ye are touched by distress, unto Him ye cry with groans,

54. Yet, when He removes the distress from you, behold! Some of you turn to other gods to join with their Lord—

55. To show their ingratitude for the favours We have bestowed on them! Then enjoy (your brief day); but soon will ye know (your folly)!

56. And they (even) assign, to things they do not know, a portion out of that which We have bestowed for their sustenance! By Allah, ye shall certainly be called to account for your false inventions.

57. And they assign daughters for Allah!— Glory be to Him!— and for themselves what they desire!

58. When news is brought to one of them, of (the birth of) a female (child), his face darkens, and he is filled with inward grief!

59. With shame does he hide himself from his people, because of the bad news he has had! Shall he retain it on (sufferance and) Contempt, or bury it in the dust? Ah! what an evil (choice) they decide on?

60. To those who believe not in the Hereafter, applies the similitude of evil: to Allah applies the highest similitude: for He is the Exalted in Power, full of Wisdom.

61. If Allah were to punish men for their wrong-doing, he would not leave, on the (earth), a single living creature: but He gives them respite for a stated Term: when their Term expires, they would not be able to delay (the punishment) for a single hour, just as they would not be able to anticipate it (for a single hour).

62. They attribute to Allah what they hate (for themselves), and their tongues assert the falsehood that the reward most fair is for themselves: without doubt for them is the Fire, and they will be the first to be hastened on into it!

63. By Allah, We (also) sent (our prophets) to Peoples before thee; but Satan Madm, (to the wicked), their own acts seem alluring: he is their patron today, so but they shall have a most grievous chastisement.

64. And We sent down the Book to thee so that that thou shouldst make clear to

وَيَجْعَلُونَ لِمَا لَا يَعْلَمُونَ نَصِيبًا مِّمَّا رَزَقْنَاهُمْ تَاللّٰهِ لَتُسْأَلُنَّ عَمَّا كُنتُمْ تَفْتَرُونَ ۝

وَيَجْعَلُونَ لِلّٰهِ الْبَنَاتِ سُبْحَانَهُ وَلَهُم مَّا يَشْتَهُونَ ۝

وَإِذَا بُشِّرَ أَحَدُهُم بِالْأُنثَى ظَلَّ وَجْهُهُ مُسْوَدًّا وَّهُوَ كَظِيمٌ ۝

يَتَوَارَى مِنَ الْقَوْمِ مِن سُوءِ مَا بُشِّرَ بِهِ أَيُمْسِكُهُ عَلَى هُونٍ أَمْ يَدُسُّهُ فِي التُّرَابِ أَلَا سَاءَ مَا يَحْكُمُونَ ۝

لِلَّذِينَ لَا يُؤْمِنُونَ بِالْآخِرَةِ مَثَلُ السَّوْءِ وَلِلّٰهِ الْمَثَلُ الْأَعْلَى وَهُوَ الْعَزِيزُ الْحَكِيمُ ۝

وَلَوْ يُؤَاخِذُ اللّٰهُ النَّاسَ بِظُلْمِهِم مَّا تَرَكَ عَلَيْهَا مِن دَابَّةٍ وَّلٰكِن يُؤَخِّرُهُمْ إِلَى أَجَلٍ مُّسَمًّى فَإِذَا جَاءَ أَجَلُهُمْ لَا يَسْتَأْخِرُونَ سَاعَةً وَّلَا يَسْتَقْدِمُونَ ۝

وَيَجْعَلُونَ لِلّٰهِ مَا يَكْرَهُونَ وَتَصِفُ أَلْسِنَتُهُمُ الْكَذِبَ أَنَّ لَهُمُ الْحُسْنَى لَا جَرَمَ أَنَّ لَهُمُ النَّارَ وَأَنَّهُم مُّفْرَطُونَ ۝

تَاللّٰهِ لَقَدْ أَرْسَلْنَا إِلَى أُمَمٍ مِّن قَبْلِكَ فَزَيَّنَ لَهُمُ الشَّيْطَانُ أَعْمَالَهُمْ فَهُوَ وَلِيُّهُمُ الْيَوْمَ وَلَهُمْ عَذَابٌ أَلِيمٌ ۝

وَمَا أَنزَلْنَا عَلَيْكَ الْكِتَابَ إِلَّا لِتُبَيِّنَ

them those things in which they differ, and that it should be a guide and a mercy to those who believe.

65. And Allah sends down rain from the skies, and gives therewith life to the earth after its death: verily in this is a sign for those who listen.

66. And verily in cattle (too) will ye find an instructive Sign. From what is within their bodies, between excretions and blood, we produce, for your drink, milk, pure and agreeable to those who drink it.

67. And from the fruit of the date-palm and the vine, ye get out strong drink, and wholesome food: behold, in this also is a sign for those who are wise.

68. And thy Lord taught the Bee to build its cells in hills, on trees, and in (men's) habitations;

69. Then to eat of all the produce (of the earth), and follow the ways of Thy Lord made smooth: there issues from within their bodies a drink of varying colours, wherein is healing for men: verily in this is a Sign for those who give thought.

70. It is Allah Who creates you and takes your souls at death; and of you there are some who are sent back to a feeble age, so that they know nothing after having known (much): for Allah is All-Knowing, All-Powerful.

71. Allah has bestowed His gifts of sustenance more freely on some of you than on others: those more favoured are not going to throw back their gifts to those whom their right hands possess, so as to be equal in that respect. Will they then deny the favours of Allah?

72. And Allah has made for you mates of your own nature, and made for you, out of them, sons and daughters and grandchildren, and provided for you sustenance of the best: will they then believe in vain things, and be ungrateful for Allah's favours?—

وَاللّٰهُ جَعَلَ لَكُمۡ مِّنۡ أَنۡفُسِكُمۡ أَزۡوَاجًا وَّجَعَلَ لَكُمۡ مِّنۡ أَزۡوَاجِكُمۡ بَنِيۡنَ وَحَفَدَةً وَّرَزَقَكُمۡ مِّنَ الطَّيِّبٰتِ ۚ أَفَبِالۡبَاطِلِ يُؤۡمِنُوۡنَ وَبِنِعۡمَتِ اللّٰهِ هُمۡ يَكۡفُرُوۡنَ ۟

73. And worship others than Allah,— such as have no power of providing them, for sustenance, with anything in heavens or earth, and cannot possibly have such power?

وَيَعۡبُدُوۡنَ مِنۡ دُوۡنِ اللّٰهِ مَا لَا يَمۡلِكُ لَهُمۡ رِزۡقًا مِّنَ السَّمٰوٰتِ وَالۡأَرۡضِ شَيۡئًا وَّلَا يَسۡتَطِيۡعُوۡنَ ۟

74. Invent not similitudes for Allah: for Allah knoweth, and ye know not.

فَلَا تَضۡرِبُوۡا لِلّٰهِ الۡأَمۡثَالَ ۚ إِنَّ اللّٰهَ يَعۡلَمُ وَأَنۡتُمۡ لَا تَعۡلَمُوۡنَ ۟

75. Allah sets forth the Parable (of two men: one) a slave under the dominion of another; he has no power of any sort; and (the other) a man on whom We have bestowed goodly favours from Ourselves, and he spends thereof (freely), privately and publicly: are the two equal? (By no means;) praise be to Allah. But most of them know not.

ضَرَبَ اللّٰهُ مَثَلًا عَبۡدًا مَّمۡلُوۡكًا لَّا يَقۡدِرُ عَلٰى شَيۡءٍ وَّمَنۡ رَّزَقۡنٰهُ مِنَّا رِزۡقًا حَسَنًا فَهُوَ يُنۡفِقُ مِنۡهُ سِرًّا وَّجَهۡرًا ۗ هَلۡ يَسۡتَوُنَ ؕ الۡحَمۡدُ لِلّٰهِ ؕ بَلۡ أَكۡثَرُهُمۡ لَا يَعۡلَمُوۡنَ ۟

76. Allah sets forth (another) parable of two men: one of them dumb, with no power of any sort; a wearisome burden is he to his master; whichever way he directs him, he brings no good: is such a man equal with one who commands justice, and is on a Straight Way?

وَضَرَبَ اللّٰهُ مَثَلًا رَّجُلَيۡنِ أَحَدُهُمَا أَبۡكَمُ لَا يَقۡدِرُ عَلٰى شَيۡءٍ وَّهُوَ كَلٌّ عَلٰى مَوۡلٰىهُ ۙ أَيۡنَمَا يُوَجِّهۡهُّ لَا يَأۡتِ بِخَيۡرٍ ؕ هَلۡ يَسۡتَوِىۡ هُوَ وَمَنۡ يَّأۡمُرُ بِالۡعَدۡلِ ۙ وَهُوَ عَلٰى صِرَاطٍ مُّسۡتَقِيۡمٍ ۟

77. To Allah belongeth the Unseen of the heavens and the earth. And the matter of the Hour (of Judgement) is as the twinkling of an eye, or even quicker: for Allah hath power over all things.

وَلِلّٰهِ غَيۡبُ السَّمٰوٰتِ وَالۡأَرۡضِ ؕ وَمَا أَمۡرُ السَّاعَةِ إِلَّا كَلَمۡحِ الۡبَصَرِ أَوۡ هُوَ أَقۡرَبُ ؕ إِنَّ اللّٰهَ عَلٰى كُلِّ شَيۡءٍ قَدِيۡرٌ ۟

78. It is He Who brought you forth from the wombs of your mothers when ye knew nothing; and He gave you hearing and sight and intelligence and affections: that ye may

وَاللّٰهُ أَخۡرَجَكُمۡ مِّنۡ بُطُوۡنِ أُمَّهٰتِكُمۡ لَا تَعۡلَمُوۡنَ شَيۡئًا ۙ وَّجَعَلَ لَكُمُ السَّمۡعَ وَالۡأَبۡصَارَ وَالۡأَفۡـِٔدَةَ ۙ لَعَلَّكُمۡ

give thanks (to Allah).

79. Do they not look at the birds, held poised in the midst of (the air and) the sky? Nothing holds them up but (the power of) Allah. Verily in this are Signs for those who believe.

80. It is Allah Who made your habitations homes of rest and quiet for you; and made for you, out of the skins of animals, (tents for) dwellings, which ye find so light (and handy) when ye travel and when ye stop (in your travels), and out of their wool, and their soft fibres (between wool and hair), and their rich stuff and articles of convenience (to serve you) for a time.

81. It is Allah Who made out of the things He created, some things to give you shade; of the hills He made some for your shelter; He made you garments to protect you from heat, and coats of mail to protect you from your (mutual) violence. Thus does He complete his favours on you, that ye may surrender to His Will (in Islām).

82. But if they turn away, thy duty is only to preach the Clear Message.

83. They recognise the favours of Allah; then they deny them; and most of them are (creatures) ungrateful.

84. On the Day We shall raise from all Peoples a Witness; then will no excuse be accepted from Unbelievers, nor will they be allowed to make amends.

85. When the wrong-doers (actually) see the Chastisement then will it in no way be mitigated, nor will they then receive respite.

86. When those who gave part-ners to Allah will see their "partners", they will say: "Our Lord! These are our 'partners', those whom we used to invoke besides Thee," But they will throw their word at them (and say): "Indeed ye are liars!"

87. That day shall they (openly) show (their) submission to Allah; and all their

inventions shall leave them in the lurch.

88. Those who reject Allah and hinder (men) from the Path of Allah—for them will We add Chastisement to Chastisement; for that they used to spread mischief.

عَنْهُمْ مَّا كَانُوْا يَفْتَرُوْنَ ۞
اَلَّذِيْنَ كَفَرُوْا وَصَدُّوْا عَنْ سَبِيْلِ
اللّٰهِ زِدْنٰهُمْ عَذَابًا فَوْقَ الْعَذَابِ
بِمَا كَانُوْا يُفْسِدُوْنَ ۞

89. On the day We shall raise from all Peoples a witness against them, from amongst themselves: and We shall bring thee as a witness against these (thy people): and We have sent down to thee the Book explaining all things, a Guide, a Mercy and Glad Tidings to Muslims.

وَيَوْمَ نَبْعَثُ فِيْ كُلِّ اُمَّةٍ شَهِيْدًا عَلَيْهِمْ
مِّنْ اَنْفُسِهِمْ وَجِئْنَا بِكَ شَهِيْدًا عَلٰى
هٰٓؤُلَاءِ ۚ وَنَزَّلْنَا عَلَيْكَ الْكِتٰبَ تِبْيَانًا
لِّكُلِّ شَيْءٍ وَّهُدًى وَّرَحْمَةً وَّبُشْرٰى
لِلْمُسْلِمِيْنَ ۞

90. Allah commands justice, the doing of good, and giving to kith and kin, and He forbids all indecent deeds, and evil and rebellion: He instructs you, that ye may receive admonition.

اِنَّ اللّٰهَ يَأْمُرُ بِالْعَدْلِ وَالْاِحْسَانِ
وَاِيْتَاۤئِ ذِى الْقُرْبٰى وَيَنْهٰى عَنِ
الْفَحْشَاۤءِ وَالْمُنْكَرِ وَالْبَغْيِ ۚ يَعِظُكُمْ
لَعَلَّكُمْ تَذَكَّرُوْنَ ۞

91. Fulfil the Covenant of Allah when ye have entered into it, and break not your oaths after ye have confirmed them; indeed ye have made Allah your surety; for Allah knoweth all that ye do.

وَاَوْفُوْا بِعَهْدِ اللّٰهِ اِذَا عَاهَدْتُّمْ
وَلَا تَنْقُضُوا الْاَيْمَانَ بَعْدَ تَوْكِيْدِهَا
وَقَدْ جَعَلْتُمُ اللّٰهَ عَلَيْكُمْ كَفِيْلًا ۚ
اِنَّ اللّٰهَ يَعْلَمُ مَا تَفْعَلُوْنَ ۞

92. And be not like a woman who breaks into untwisted strands the yarn which she has spun, after it has become strong. Using your oaths to deceive one another, lest one party should be more numerous than another: for Allah will test you by this; and on the Day of Judgment He will certainly make clear to you (the truth of) that wherein ye disagree.

وَلَا تَكُوْنُوْا كَالَّتِيْ نَقَضَتْ غَزْلَهَا
مِنْ بَعْدِ قُوَّةٍ اَنْكَاثًا ۚ تَتَّخِذُوْنَ
اَيْمَانَكُمْ دَخَلًا بَيْنَكُمْ اَنْ تَكُوْنَ
اُمَّةٌ هِيَ اَرْبٰى مِنْ اُمَّةٍ ۚ اِنَّمَا يَبْلُوْكُمُ
اللّٰهُ بِهٖ ۚ وَلَيُبَيِّنَنَّ لَكُمْ يَوْمَ الْقِيٰمَةِ
مَا كُنْتُمْ فِيْهِ تَخْتَلِفُوْنَ ۞

93. If Allah so willed, He could make you all one People: but He leaves straying whom He pleases, and He guides whom He pleases: but ye shall certainly be called to account for all your actions.

وَلَوْ شَاۤءَ اللّٰهُ لَجَعَلَكُمْ اُمَّةً وَّاحِدَةً
وَّلٰكِنْ يُّضِلُّ مَنْ يَّشَاۤءُ وَيَهْدِيْ مَنْ
يَّشَاۤءُ ۚ وَلَتُسْئَلُنَّ عَمَّا كُنْتُمْ تَعْمَلُوْنَ ۞

94. And take not your oaths, to practise deception between yourselves. With the

وَلَا تَتَّخِذُوْا اَيْمَانَكُمْ دَخَلًا بَيْنَكُمْ

result that someone's foot may slip after it was firmly planted, and ye may have to taste the evil (consequences) of having hindered (men) from the Path of Allah and a mighty Wrath descend on you.

95. Nor sell the Covenant of Allah for a miserable price: for with Allah is (a prize) far better for you, if ye only knew.

96. What is with you must vanish: what is with Allah will endure. And We will certainly bestow, on those who patiently persevere, their reward according to the best of their actions.

97. Whoever works righteousness, man or woman, and has Faith, verily, to him will We give a life that is good and pure, and We will bestow on such their reward according to the best of their actions.

98. When thou dost read the Qur'an, seek Allah's protection from Satan the Rejected One.

99. No authority has he over those who believe and put their trust in their Lord.

100. His authority is over those only, who take him as patron and who join partners with Allah.

101. When We substitute one revelation for another,—and, Allah knows best what He reveals (in stages),— they say, "Thou art but a forger" but most of them know not.

102. Say, the Holy Spirit has brought the revelation from the Lord in truth, in other to strengthen those who believe, and as a Guide and Glad Tidings to Muslims.

103. We know indeed that they say, "It is a man that teaches him." The tongue of him they wickedly point to is notably foreign, while this is Arabic, pure and clear.

104. Those who believe not in the Signs of Allah,— Allah will not guide them, and their will be a grievous Chastisement.

105. It is those who believe not in the Signs of Allah, that forge falsehood: it is they who lie!

106. Anyone who, after accepting faith in Allah, utters Unbelief,—except under compulsion, his heart remaining firm in Faith—but such as open their breast to Unbelief,—on them is Wrath from Allah, and theirs will be a dreadful Chastisement.

107. This because they love the life of this world better than the Hereafter: and Allah will not guide those who reject Faith.

108. Those are they whose hearts, ears, and eyes Allah has sealed up and they take no heed.

109. Without doubt, in the Hereafter they will be the losers.

110. But verily thy Lord,—to those who leave their homes after trials and persecutions,— and who thereafter strive and fight for the Faith and patiently persevere,—thy Lord after all this is Oft-Forgiving, Most Merciful.

111. On the Day every soul will come up pleading for itself, and every soul will be recompensed (fully) for all its actions, and none will be unjustly dealt with.

112. Allah sets forth a Parable: a city enjoying security and quiet, abundantly supplied with sustenance from every place: yet was it ungrateful for the favours of Allah: so Allah made it taste of hunger and terror

إِنَّ الَّذِينَ لَا يُؤْمِنُونَ بِآيَاتِ اللهِ لَا يَهْدِيهِمُ اللهُ وَلَهُمْ عَذَابٌ أَلِيمٌ ۞

إِنَّمَا يَفْتَرِى الْكَذِبَ الَّذِينَ لَا يُؤْمِنُونَ بِآيَاتِ اللهِ وَأُولَٰئِكَ هُمُ الْكَاذِبُونَ ۞

مَنْ كَفَرَ بِاللهِ مِنْ بَعْدِ إِيمَانِهِ إِلَّا مَنْ أُكْرِهَ وَقَلْبُهُ مُطْمَئِنٌّ بِالْإِيمَانِ وَلَٰكِنْ مَنْ شَرَحَ بِالْكُفْرِ صَدْرًا فَعَلَيْهِمْ غَضَبٌ مِنَ اللهِ وَلَهُمْ عَذَابٌ عَظِيمٌ ۞

ذَٰلِكَ بِأَنَّهُمُ اسْتَحَبُّوا الْحَيَوٰةَ الدُّنْيَا عَلَى الْآخِرَةِ وَأَنَّ اللهَ لَا يَهْدِى الْقَوْمَ الْكَافِرِينَ ۞

أُولَٰئِكَ الَّذِينَ طَبَعَ اللهُ عَلَىٰ قُلُوبِهِمْ وَسَمْعِهِمْ وَأَبْصَارِهِمْ وَأُولَٰئِكَ هُمُ الْغَافِلُونَ ۞

لَا جَرَمَ أَنَّهُمْ فِى الْآخِرَةِ هُمُ الْخَاسِرُونَ ۞

ثُمَّ إِنَّ رَبَّكَ لِلَّذِينَ هَاجَرُوا مِنْ بَعْدِ مَا فُتِنُوا ثُمَّ جَاهَدُوا وَصَبَرُوا إِنَّ رَبَّكَ مِنْ بَعْدِهَا لَغَفُورٌ رَحِيمٌ ۞ يَوْمَ تَأْتِى كُلُّ نَفْسٍ تُجَادِلُ عَنْ نَفْسِهَا وَتُوَفَّىٰ كُلُّ نَفْسٍ مَّا عَمِلَتْ وَهُمْ لَا يُظْلَمُونَ ۞

وَضَرَبَ اللهُ مَثَلًا قَرْيَةً كَانَتْ آمِنَةً مُطْمَئِنَّةً يَأْتِيهَا رِزْقُهَا رَغَدًا مِنْ كُلِّ مَكَانٍ فَكَفَرَتْ بِأَنْعُمِ اللهِ

(in extremes) (closing in on it) like a garment (from every side), because of the (evil) which (its people) wrought.

فَاَذَاقَهَا اللّٰهُ لِبَاسَ الْجُوْعِ وَالْخَوْفِ بِمَا كَانُوْا يَصْنَعُوْنَ ۝

113. And there came to them a Messenger from among themselves, but they falsely rejected him; so the Wrath seized them even in the midst of their iniquities.

وَلَقَدْ جَآءَهُمْ رَسُوْلٌ مِّنْهُمْ فَكَذَّبُوْهُ فَاَخَذَهُمُ الْعَذَابُ وَهُمْ ظٰلِمُوْنَ ۝

114. So eat of the sustenance which Allah has provided for you, lawful and good; and be grateful for the favours of Allah, if it is He Whom ye serve.

فَكُلُوْا مِمَّا رَزَقَكُمُ اللّٰهُ حَلٰلًا طَيِّبًا ۖ وَّاشْكُرُوْا نِعْمَتَ اللّٰهِ اِنْ كُنْتُمْ اِيَّاهُ تَعْبُدُوْنَ ۝

115. He has only forbidden you dead meat, and blood, and the flesh or swine, and any (food) over which the name of other than Allah has been invoked. But if one is forced by necessity, without wilful disobedience, nor transgressing due limits,— then Allah is Oft-Forgiving, Most Merciful.

اِنَّمَا حَرَّمَ عَلَيْكُمُ الْمَيْتَةَ وَالدَّمَ وَلَحْمَ الْخِنْزِيْرِ وَمَآ اُهِلَّ لِغَيْرِ اللّٰهِ بِهٖ ۚ فَمَنِ اضْطُرَّ غَيْرَ بَاغٍ وَّلَا عَادٍ فَاِنَّ اللّٰهَ غَفُوْرٌ رَّحِيْمٌ ۝

116. But say not—for any false thing that your tongues may put forth,— "This is lawful, and this is forbidden," so as to ascribe false things to Allah. For those who ascribe false things to Allah, will never prosper.

وَلَا تَقُوْلُوْا لِمَا تَصِفُ اَلْسِنَتُكُمُ الْكَذِبَ هٰذَا حَلٰلٌ وَّهٰذَا حَرَامٌ لِّتَفْتَرُوْا عَلَى اللّٰهِ الْكَذِبَ ۚ اِنَّ الَّذِيْنَ يَفْتَرُوْنَ عَلَى اللّٰهِ الْكَذِبَ لَا يُفْلِحُوْنَ ۝

117. In such falsehood is but a paltry profit; but they will have a most grievous Chastisement.

مَتَاعٌ قَلِيْلٌ ۖ وَّلَهُمْ عَذَابٌ اَلِيْمٌ ۝

118. To the Jews We prohibited such things as We have mentioned to thee before: We did them no wrong, but they were used to doing wrong to themselves.

وَعَلَى الَّذِيْنَ هَادُوْا حَرَّمْنَا مَا قَصَصْنَا عَلَيْكَ مِنْ قَبْلُ ۚ وَمَا ظَلَمْنٰهُمْ وَلٰكِنْ كَانُوْا اَنْفُسَهُمْ يَظْلِمُوْنَ ۝

119. But verily the Lord, to those who do wrong in ignorance, but who thereafter repent and make amends, thy Lord after all this, is Oft-Forgiving, Most Merciful.

ثُمَّ اِنَّ رَبَّكَ لِلَّذِيْنَ عَمِلُوا السُّوْٓءَ بِجَهَالَةٍ ثُمَّ تَابُوْا مِنْ بَعْدِ ذٰلِكَ وَ اَصْلَحُوْٓا ۙ اِنَّ رَبَّكَ مِنْ بَعْدِهَا لَغَفُوْرٌ رَّحِيْمٌ ۝

120. Abraham was indeed a model, devoutly obedient to Allah, (and) true in faith, and he joined not gods with Allah.

اِنَّ اِبْرٰهِيْمَ كَانَ اُمَّةً قَانِتًا لِّلّٰهِ حَنِيْفًا ۚ وَلَمْ يَكُ مِنَ الْمُشْرِكِيْنَ ۝

121. He showed his gratitude for the favours of Allah, who chose him, and

شَاكِرًا لِّاَنْعُمِهٖ ۚ اِجْتَبٰهُ وَهَدٰىهُ اِلٰى

SÛRA–17
AL-ISRÃA
(INTRODUCTION)

In the gradation of spiritual teaching (see Introduction to Sûra 7), we saw that the first seven Sûras sketched the early spiritual history of man, and led up to the formation of the new Ummat of Islam. Sûras 8 to 16 formed another series dealing with the formation of the new Ummat and its consolidation, and Allah's dealing with man taken as an Ummat and considered in his social relation in organised communities (see Introduction to Sûras 8, 10, and 16). We now come to a fresh series, (Sûras 17-29), which may be considered in three parts. Sûras 17-21 begin with an allusion to the *Mi'rãj* (of which more later), and proceed to spiritual history as touching individuals rather than nations. The old prophets and stories of the past are now referred to from this point of view. Sûras 22-25 refer to Ḥajj (pilgrimage), worship and prayer, chastity, privacy, etc., as related to a man's individual spiritual growth. Sûras 26-29 go back to the old prophets and stories of the past, as illustrating the growth of the individual soul in the reactions against the lives of the communities, and the reactions of the communities to the lives of its great individual souls.

Let us now consider S. 17 itself. It opens with the mystic Vision of the Ascension of the Holy Prophet: he was transported from the Sacred Mosque (of Makkah) to the Farthest Mosque (of Jerusalem) in a night and shown some of the Signs of Allah. The majority of Commentators take this Night Journey literally, but allow that there were other occasions on which a spiritual Journey or Vision occurred. Even on the supposition of a miraculous bodily Journey, it is conceded that the body was almost transformed into a spiritual fineness. The Ḥadîth literature gives details of this Journey and its study helps to elucidate its mystic meaning. The Holy Prophet was first transported to the seat of the earlier revelations in Jerusalem, and then taken throutgh the seven heavens, even to the Sublime Throne, and initiated into the spiritual mysteries of the human soul struggling in Space and Time. The Spaniard, Miguel Asin, Arabic Professor in the University of Madrid, has shown that this *Mi'rāj* literature had a great influence on the Mediaeval literature of Europe, and especially on the great Italian poem, the *Divine Comedy* (or Drama) of Dante, which towers like a landmark in mediaeval European literature.

The reference to this great mystic story of the *Mi'rāj* is a fitting prelude to the journey of the human soul in its spiritual growth in life. The first steps in such growth must be through moral conduct—the reciprocal rights of parents and childern, kindness to our fellow-men, courage and firmness in the hour of danger, a sense of personal responsibility, and a sense of Allah's Presence through prayer and praise.

The *Mi'rāj* is usually dated to the 27th night of the month of Rajab (though other dates, e.g. 17th of Rabi' I, are also given) in the year before the Hijra. This fixes the date of the opening verse of the Sûra, though portions of the Sûra may have been a little earlier.

guided him to a Straight Way.

122. And We gave him Good in this world, and he will be, in the Hereafter, in the ranks of the Righteous.

123. Then We revealed to thee "Follow the ways of Abraham the True in Faith, and he joined not gods with Allah."

صِرَاطٍ مُّسْتَقِيْمٍ ۞

وَاٰتَيْنٰهُ فِي الدُّنْيَا حَسَنَةً ۖ وَإِنَّهٗ فِي الْاٰخِرَةِ لَمِنَ الصّٰلِحِيْنَ ۞

ثُمَّ اَوْحَيْنَاۤ اِلَيْكَ اَنِ اتَّبِعْ مِلَّةَ اِبْرٰهِيْمَ حَنِيْفًا ۖ وَمَا كَانَ مِنَ الْمُشْرِكِيْنَ ۞

124. The Sabbath was only made (strict) for those who disagreed (as to its observance); but Allah will judge between them on the Day of Judgement, as to their differences.

125. Invite (all) to the Way of the Lord with wisdom and beautiful preaching; and argue with them in ways that are best and most gracious: for thy Lord knoweth best, who have strayed from His path, and who receive guidance.

126. And if ye punish, let your punishment be proportionate to the wro-ng that has been done to you: but if ye show patience, that is indeed the best (course) for those who are patient.

127. And do thou be patient, for thy patience is but with the help from Allah; nor grieve over them: and distress not thyself because of their plots.

128. For Allah is with those who restrain themselves, and those who do good.

اِنَّمَا جُعِلَ السَّبْتُ عَلَى الَّذِيْنَ اخْتَلَفُوْا فِيْهِ ۖ وَإِنَّ رَبَّكَ لَيَحْكُمُ بَيْنَهُمْ يَوْمَ الْقِيٰمَةِ فِيْمَا كَانُوْا فِيْهِ يَخْتَلِفُوْنَ ۞

اُدْعُ اِلٰى سَبِيْلِ رَبِّكَ بِالْحِكْمَةِ وَ الْمَوْعِظَةِ الْحَسَنَةِ وَجَادِلْهُمْ بِالَّتِيْ هِيَ اَحْسَنُ ۚ اِنَّ رَبَّكَ هُوَ اَعْلَمُ بِمَنْ ضَلَّ عَنْ سَبِيْلِهٖ وَهُوَ اَعْلَمُ بِالْمُهْتَدِيْنَ ۞

وَإِنْ عَاقَبْتُمْ فَعَاقِبُوْا بِمِثْلِ مَا عُوْقِبْتُمْ بِهٖ ۖ وَلَئِنْ صَبَرْتُمْ لَهُوَ خَيْرٌ لِّلصّٰبِرِيْنَ ۞

وَاصْبِرْ وَمَا صَبْرُكَ اِلَّا بِاللّٰهِ وَلَا تَحْزَنْ عَلَيْهِمْ وَلَا تَكُ فِيْ ضَيْقٍ مِّمَّا يَمْكُرُوْنَ ۞

اِنَّ اللّٰهَ مَعَ الَّذِيْنَ اتَّقَوْا وَّالَّذِيْنَ هُمْ مُّحْسِنُوْنَ ۞

Bani Isrā'īi, or the Children of Israel or Al-Isrāa

In the name of Allah, Most Gracious Most Merciful.

1. Glory to (Allah) Who did take His Servant for a Journey by night from the Sacred Mosque to the Farthest Mosque whose precincts We did bless,—in order that We might show him some of Our Signs: for He is the One Who heareth and seeth (all things).

2. We gave Moses the Book, and made it a Guide to the Children of Israel,

بِسْمِ اللّٰهِ الرَّحْمٰنِ الرَّحِيْمِ

سُبْحٰنَ الَّذِيْ اَسْرٰى بِعَبْدِهٖ لَيْلًا مِّنَ الْمَسْجِدِ الْحَرَامِ اِلَى الْمَسْجِدِ الْاَقْصَا الَّذِيْ بٰرَكْنَا حَوْلَهُ لِنُرِيَهٗ مِنْ اٰيٰتِنَا ۚ اِنَّهٗ هُوَ السَّمِيْعُ الْبَصِيْرُ ۞

وَاٰتَيْنَا مُوْسَى الْكِتٰبَ وَجَعَلْنٰهُ هُدًى لِّبَنِيْ اِسْرَآءِيْلَ اَلَّا تَتَّخِذُوْا مِنْ

(commanding): "Take not other than Me as Disposer of (your) affairs."

3. O ye that are sprung from those whom We carried (in the Ark) with Noah! verily he was a devotee most grateful.

4. And we decreed for the Children of Israel in the Book, that twice would they do mischief on the earth and be elated with mighty arrogance (and twice would they be punished)!

5. When the first of the warnings came to pass, We sent against you Our servants given to terrible warfare: they entered the very inmost parts of your homes; and it was a warning (completely) fulfilled.

6. Then did We grant you victory over them: We gave you increase in resources and sons, and made you the more numerous in man-power.

7. If ye did well, ye did well for yourselves; if ye did evil, (ye did it) against yourselves. So when the second of the warnings came to pass, (We permitted your enemies) to disfigure your faces, and to enter your Temple as they had entered it before, and to visit with destruction all that fell into their power.

8. It may be that your Lord may (yet) show mercy unto you; but if ye revert (to your sins), We shall revert (to Our punishments): and We have made Hell a prison for those who reject (all Faith).

9. Verily this Qur'an doth guide to that which is most right (or stable), and giveth the glad tidings to the Believers who work deeds of righteousness, that they shall have a magnificent reward;

10. And to those who believe not in the Hereafter, (it announceth) that We have prepared for them a Chastisement grievous (indeed).

11. Man prays for evil as fervently as he prays for good for man is given to haste.

12. We have made the Night and the Day as two (of Our) Signs: the Sign of the Night have We made dark while the Sign of the Day We have made bright that ye may seek bounty from your Lord and that ye may know the number and count of the years: all things have We explained in detail.

وَجَعَلْنَا الَّيْلَ وَالنَّهَارَ اٰيَتَيْنِ فَمَحَوْنَا اٰيَةَ الَّيْلِ وَجَعَلْنَا اٰيَةَ النَّهَارِ مُبْصِرَةً لِّتَبْتَغُوْا فَضْلًا مِّنْ رَّبِّكُمْ وَلِتَعْلَمُوْا عَدَدَ السِّنِيْنَ وَالْحِسَابَ ۗ وَكُلَّ شَيْءٍ فَصَّلْنٰهُ تَفْصِيْلًا ۝

13. Every man's fate We have fastened on his own neck: on the Day of Judgment We shall bring out for him a scroll, which he will see spread open.

وَكُلَّ إِنْسَانٍ أَلْزَمْنٰهُ طٰٓئِرَهٗ فِيْ عُنُقِهٖ ۗ وَنُخْرِجُ لَهٗ يَوْمَ الْقِيٰمَةِ كِتٰبًا يَّلْقٰىهُ مَنْشُوْرًا ۝

14. (It will be said to him:) "Read thine (own) record: sufficient is thy soul this day to make out an account against thee."

إِقْرَأْ كِتٰبَكَ ۗ كَفٰى بِنَفْسِكَ الْيَوْمَ عَلَيْكَ حَسِيْبًا ۝

15. Who receiveth guidance, receiveth it for his own benefit: who goeth astray doth so to his own loss: no bearer of burdens can bear the burden of another: nor would We punish until We had sent a messenger (to give warning).

مَنِ اهْتَدٰى فَإِنَّمَا يَهْتَدِيْ لِنَفْسِهٖ ۚ وَمَنْ ضَلَّ فَإِنَّمَا يَضِلُّ عَلَيْهَا ۚ وَلَا تَزِرُ وَازِرَةٌ وِّزْرَ أُخْرٰى ۗ وَمَا كُنَّا مُعَذِّبِيْنَ حَتّٰى نَبْعَثَ رَسُوْلًا ۝

16. When We decide to destroy a town, We command those among them who are given the good things of this life (to be obedient) but they continued to transgress; so that the word is proved true against them: then We destroy them utterly.

وَإِذَآ أَرَدْنَآ أَنْ نُّهْلِكَ قَرْيَةً أَمَرْنَا مُتْرَفِيْهَا فَفَسَقُوْا فِيْهَا فَحَقَّ عَلَيْهَا الْقَوْلُ فَدَمَّرْنٰهَا تَدْمِيْرًا ۝

17. How many generations have We destroyed after Noah? And enough is thy Lord to note and see the sins of His servants.

وَكَمْ أَهْلَكْنَا مِنَ الْقُرُوْنِ مِنْ بَعْدِ نُوْحٍ ۗ وَكَفٰى بِرَبِّكَ بِذُنُوْبِ عِبَادِهٖ خَبِيْرًۢا بَصِيْرًا ۝

18. If any do wish for the transitory things (of this life), We readily grant them—such things as We will, to such persons as We will: in the end have We provided Hell for them: they will burn therein, disgraced and rejected.

مَنْ كَانَ يُرِيْدُ الْعَاجِلَةَ عَجَّلْنَا لَهٗ فِيْهَا مَا نَشَآءُ لِمَنْ نُّرِيْدُ ثُمَّ جَعَلْنَا لَهٗ جَهَنَّمَ ۚ يَصْلٰىهَا مَذْمُوْمًا مَّدْحُوْرًا ۝

19. Those who do wish for the (things of) the Hereafter, and strive therefor with all due striving, and have Faith,—they are the ones whose striving will be thanked (by Allah).

وَمَنْ أَرَادَ الْاٰخِرَةَ وَسَعٰى لَهَا سَعْيَهَا وَهُوَ مُؤْمِنٌ فَأُولٰٓئِكَ كَانَ سَعْيُهُمْ مَّشْكُوْرًا ۝

20. Of the bounties of thy Lord We bestow freely on all—these as well as those: the

كُلًّا نُّمِدُّ هٰٓؤُلَآءِ وَهٰٓؤُلَآءِ مِنْ عَطَآءِ

bounties of thy Lord are not closed (to anyone).

21. See how We have bestowed more on some than on others; but verily the Hereafter is more in rank and gradation and more in excellence.

22. Take not with Allah another god; or thou (O man!) wilt sit in disgrace and destitution.

23. Thy Lord hath decreed that ye worship none but Him, and that ye be kind to parents. Whether one or both of them attain old age in thy life, say not to them a word of contempt, nor repel them but address them, in terms of honour.

24. And, out of kindness, lower to them the wing of humility, and say: "My Lord! bestow on them Thy Mercy even as they cherished me in childhood."

25. Your Lord knoweth best what is in your hearts: if ye do deeds of righteousness, verily He is Most Forgiving to those who turn to Him again and again (in true penitence).

26. And render to the kindred their due rights, as (also) to those in want and to the wayfarer: but squander not (your wealth) in the manner of a spendthrift.

27. Verily spendthrifts are brothers of the Satans; and the Satan is to his Lord (Himself) ungrateful.

28. And even if thou hast to turn away from them in pursuit of the Mercy from thy Lord which thou dost expect, yet speak to them a word of easy kindness.

29. Make not thy hand tied (Like a niggard's) to thy neck, nor stretch it forth to its utmost reach, so that thou become blameworthy and destitute.

30. Verily thy Lord doth provide sustenance in abundance for whom He

pleaseth, and He straiten it for He doth know and regard all His servants.

وَيَقْدِرُ إِنَّهُ كَانَ بِعِبَادِهٖ خَبِيرًۢا بَصِيرًا ۞

31. Kill not your children for fear of want: We shall provide, sustenance for them as well as for you. Verily the killing of them is a great sin.

وَلَا تَقْتُلُوٓا أَوْلَادَكُمْ خَشْيَةَ إِمْلَاقٍ نَحْنُ نَرْزُقُهُمْ وَإِيَّاكُمْ إِنَّ قَتْلَهُمْ كَانَ خِطْأً كَبِيرًا ۞

32. Nor come nigh to adultery: for it is an indecent (deed) and an evil way

وَلَا تَقْرَبُوا الزِّنَىٰٓ إِنَّهُ كَانَ فَاحِشَةً وَسَآءَ سَبِيلًا ۞

33. Nor take life—which Allah has made sacred—except for just cause. And if anyone is slain wrongfully, We have given his heir authority (to demand Qisās or to forgive): but let him not exceed bounds in the matter of taking life; for he is helped (by the Law).

وَلَا تَقْتُلُوا النَّفْسَ الَّتِي حَرَّمَ اللّٰهُ إِلَّا بِالْحَقِّ وَمَنْ قُتِلَ مَظْلُومًا فَقَدْ جَعَلْنَا لِوَلِيِّهٖ سُلْطَانًا فَلَا يُسْرِفْ فِّى الْقَتْلِ إِنَّهُ كَانَ مَنْصُورًا ۞

34. Come not nigh to the orphan's property except to improve it, until he attains the age of full strength; and fulfil (every) engagement, for (every) engagement will be enquired into (on the Day of Reckoning).

وَلَا تَقْرَبُوا مَالَ الْيَتِيمِ إِلَّا بِالَّتِي هِيَ أَحْسَنُ حَتّٰى يَبْلُغَ أَشُدَّهٗ وَ أَوْفُوا بِالْعَهْدِ إِنَّ الْعَهْدَ كَانَ مَسْئُولًا ۞

35. Give full measure when ye measure, and weigh with a balance that is straight: that is better and fairer in the final determination.

وَأَوْفُوا الْكَيْلَ إِذَا كِلْتُمْ وَزِنُوا بِالْقِسْطَاسِ الْمُسْتَقِيمِ ذٰلِكَ خَيْرٌ وَّأَحْسَنُ تَأْوِيلًا ۞

36. And pursue not that of which thou hast no knowledge; for surely the hearing, the sight, the heart all of those shall be questioned of.

وَلَا تَقْفُ مَا لَيْسَ لَكَ بِهٖ عِلْمٌ إِنَّ السَّمْعَ وَالْبَصَرَ وَالْفُؤَادَ كُلُّ أُولٰٓئِكَ كَانَ عَنْهُ مَسْئُولًا ۞

37. Nor walk on the earth with insolence: for thou canst not rend the earth asunder, nor reach the mountains in height.

وَلَا تَمْشِ فِى الْأَرْضِ مَرَحًا إِنَّكَ لَنْ تَخْرِقَ الْأَرْضَ وَلَنْ تَبْلُغَ الْجِبَالَ طُولًا ۞

38. Of all such things the evil is hateful in the sight of thy Lord.

كُلُّ ذٰلِكَ كَانَ سَيِّئُهٗ عِنْدَ رَبِّكَ مَكْرُوهًا ۞

39. These are among the (precepts of) wisdom, which thy Lord has revealed to

ذٰلِكَ مِمَّآ أَوْحٰىٓ إِلَيْكَ رَبُّكَ مِنَ

thee. Take not, with Allah, another object of worship, lest thou shouldst be thrown into Hell, blameworthy and rejected.

40. Has then your Lord, (O Pagans!) preferred for you sons, and taken for Himself daughters among the angels? Truly ye utter a most dreadful saying!

41. We have explained (things) in various (ways) in this Qur'an, in order that they may receive admonition, but it only increases their flight (from the Truth)!

42. Say: if there had been (other) gods with Him,—as they say,—behold, they would certainly have sought out a way in submitting to the Lord of the Throne!

43. Glory to Him! He is high above all that they say! Exalted and Great (beyond measure)!

44. The seven heavens and the earth, and all beings therein, declare His glory: there is not a thing but celebrates His praise; and yet ye understand not how they declare His glory! Verily He is Oft-Forbearing, Most Forgiving!

45. When thou dost recite the Qur-ān, We put, between thee and those who believe not in the Hereafter, a veil invisible:

46. And We put coverings over their hearts (and minds) lest they should understand the Qur'an, and deafness into their ears: when thou dost mention thy Lord—and Him alone—in the Qur'an, they turn on their backs, fleeing (from the Truth).

47. We know best what it is they listen, when they listen to thee; and when they meet in private behold, the wicked say, "Ye follow none other than a man bewitched!"

48. See what similes they strike for thee: but they have gone astray, and never can

they find a way.

49. They say: "What! when we are reduced to bones and dust, should we really be raised up (to be) a new creation?

50. Say: (Nay!) be ye stones or iron,

51. "Or any created matter which, in your minds, is hardest (to be raised up,)— (yet shall ye be raised up)!" Then will they say: "Who will cause us to return?" Say: "He Who created you first!" Then will they wag their heads towards thee, and say, "When will that be?" Say, "May be it will be quite soon!

52. "It will be on the Day when He will call you, and ye will answer (His call) with (words of) His praise, and ye will think that ye tarried but a little while!"

53. Say to My servants that they should (only) say those things that are best: for Satan doth sow dissensions among them: for Satan is to man an avowed enemy.

54. It is your Lord That knoweth you best: if He please, He granteth you mercy, or if He please, punishment: We have not sent thee to be a disposer of their affairs for them.

55. And it is your Lord That knoweth best all beings that are in the heavens and on earth: and We made some of the Prophets to excel others and We gave to David the Psalms.

56. Say: "Call on those—besides Him— whom ye fancy: they have neither the power to remove your troubles from you nor to change them."

57. Those whom they call upon do seek (for themselves) means of access to their Lord,—as to who are nearest: they hope for His Mercy and fear His Wrath: for the

Wrath of thy Lord is something to take heed of.

58. There is not a population but We shall destroy it before the Day of Judgment or punish it with a dreadful Chastisement. That is written in the (eternal) Record.

59. And We refrain from sending the Signs, only because the men of former generations treated them as false: We sent the She-camel to the <u>Thamūd</u>—a visible Sign— but they treated her wrongfully: We only sent the Signs by way of frightening (and warning from evil).

60. Behold! We told thee that thy Lord doth encompass mankind round about: We granted the vision which We showed thee, but as a trial for men,— as also the Cursed Tree (mentioned) in the Qur'an: We put fear (and warning) into them, but it only increases their inordinate transgression!

61. Behold! We said to the angels: "Prostrate unto Adam": they prostrated except Iblīs: he said, "Shall I prostrate to one whom Thou didst create from clay?"

62. He said, "Seest Thou? This is the one whom Thou hast honoured above me! If Thou wilt but respite me to the Day of Judgment, I will surely bring his descendants under my sway—all but a few!"

63. (Allah) said: "Go thy way; if any of them follow thee, verily Hell will be the recompense of you (all)— an ample recompense.

64. And Arouse those whom thou canst among them, with thy (seductive) voice; make assaults on them with thy cavalry and thy infantry; mutually share with them wealth and children; and make promises to them." But Satan promises them nothing but deceit.

65. "As for My servants, no authority shalt thou have over them:" Enough is thy Lord for a Disposer of affairs.

66. Your Lord is He That maketh the Ship go smoothly for you through the sea, in

order that ye may seek of His Bounty. For He is unto you Most Merciful.

67. When distress seizes you at sea, those that ye call upon—besides Himself—leave you in the lurch! but when He brings you back safe to land, ye turn away (from Him). Most ungrateful is man!

68. Do ye then feel secure that He will not cause you to be swallowed up beneath the earth when ye are on land, or that He will not send against you a violent tornado (with showers of stones) so that ye shall find no protector

69. Or do ye feel secure that He will not send you back a second time to sea and send against you a heavy gale to drown you because of your ingratitude, so that ye find no helper therein against Us?

70. We have honoured the sons of Adam; provided them with transport on land and sea; given them for sustenance things good and pure; and conferred on them special favours, above a great part of Our Creation.

71. On the day We shall call together all human beings with their (respective) Imāms: those who are given their record in their right hand will read it (with pleasure), and they will not be dealt with unjustly in the least.

72. But those who were blind in this world, will be blind in the Hereafter, and most astray from the Path.

73. And their purpose was to tempt thee away from that which We had revealed unto thee, to substitute in Our name something quite different: (in that case), behold! they would certainly have made thee (their) friend!

74. And had We not given thee strength, thou wouldst nearly have inclined to them a little.

75. In that case We should have made thee taste double portion (of punishment) in this life, and an equal portion in death: and moreover thou wouldst have found none to help thee against Us!

76. Their purpose was to scare thee off the land, in order to expel thee; but in that case they would not have stayed (therein) after thee, except for a little while.

77. (This was Our) way with the messengers We sent before thee: thou wilt find no change in Our ways.

78. Establish regular prayers—at the sun's decline till the darkness of the night, and the recital of the Qur'an in morning prayer for the recital of dawn is witnessed.

79. And as for the night keep awake a part of it as an additional prayer for thee: soon will thy Lord raise thee to a Station of Praise and Glory!

80. Say: "O my Lord! let my entry be by the Gate of Truth and Honour, and likewise my exit by the Gate of Truth and Honour; and grant me from Thee an authority to aid (me)

81. And say: "Truth has (now) arrived, and Falsehood perished: for Falsehood is (by its nature) bound to perish."

82. We send down (stage by stage) of the Qur'an that which is a healing and a mercy to those who believe: to the unjust it causes nothing but loss after loss.

83. Yet when We bestow Our favours on man, he turns away and becomes remote on his side (instead of coming to Us), and when evil seizes him he gives himself up to despair!

84. Say: "Everyone acts according to his own disposition: but your Lord knows best who it is that is best guided on the Way."

85. They ask thee concerning the Spirit say: "The Spirit is of the command of my Lord of knowledge it is only a little that is comm-unicated to you, (O men!)"

86. If it were Our Will, We could take away that which We have sent thee by inspiration: then wouldst thou find none to plead thy affair in that matter as against Us,—

87. Except for Mercy from thy Lord; for His Bounty is to thee (indeed) great.

88. Say: "If the whole of mankind and Jinns were to gather together to produce the like of this Qur'an, they could not produce the like thereof, even if they backed up each other with help and support.

89. And We have explained to man, in this Qur'an, every kind of similitude: yet the greater part of men refuse (to receive it) except with ingratitude!

90. They say: "We shall not believe in thee, until thou cause a spring to gush forth for us from the earth,

91. "Or (until) thou have a garden of date trees and vines, and cause rivers to gush forth in their midst, carrying abundant water;

92. "Or thou cause the sky to fall in pieces, as thou sayest (will happen), against us; or thou bring Allah and the angels before (us) face to face;

93. "Or thou have a house adorned with gold, or thou mount a ladder right into the skies. No, we shall not even believe in thy mounting until thou send down to us a book that we could read." Say: "Glory to my Lord! Am I aught but a man,— a messenger?"

94. What kept men back from Belief when Guidance came to them, was nothing but this: they said, "Has Allah sent a man (like us) to be (His) Messenger?"

95. Say, "If there were settled, on earth, angels walking about in peace and quiet. We should certainly have sent them down from the heavens an angel for a messenger."

96. Say: "Enough is Allah for a witness between me and you: for He is well acquainted with His servants, and He sees (all things).

97. It is he whom Allah guides, that is on true guidance; but he whom He leaves astray—for such wilt thou find no protector besides Him. On the Day of Judgment We shall gather them together, prone on their faces, blind, dumb, and deaf: their abode will be Hell: every time it shows abatement, We shall increase for them the fierceness of the Fire.

98. That is their recompense, because they rejected Our Signs, and said, "When we are reduced to bones and broken dust, should we really be raised up (to be) a new Creation?"

99. See they not that Allah, Who created the heavens and the earth, has power to create the like of them (anew)? Only He has decreed a term appointed, of which there is no doubt. But the unjust refuse (to receive it) except with ingratitude.

100. Say: "If ye had Control of the Treasures of the Mercy of my Lord, behold, ye would keep them back, for fear of spending them: for man is (ever) niggardly!"

101. To Moses We did give nine Clear Signs: ask the Children of Israel: when he came to them, Pharaoh said to him: "O Moses! i consider thee, indeed, to have been worked upon by sorcery!

102. Moses said, "Thou knowest well that these things have been sent down by none but the Lord of the heavens and the earth as eye-opening evidence: and I consider thee indeed, O Pharaoh, to be one doomed to destruction!"

103. So he resolved to remove them from the face of the earth: but We did drown him and all who were with him.

104. And We said thereafter to the Children of Israel, "Dwell securely in

It has been explained in the Introduction to S. 17 how the five Sûras 17 to 21 develop the theme of the individual soul's spiritual history, and how they fit into the general scheme of exposition.

This particular Makkan Sûra may be called a lesson on the brevity and mystery of Life. First there is the story of the Companions of the Cave who slept therein for a long period, and yet thought they had been there only a day or less. Then there is the story of the mysterious Teacher who shows Moses how Life itself is a parable. And further there is the story of Zul-qarnain, the two horned one, the powerful ruler of west and east, who made an iron wall to protect the weak against the strong. The parables refer to the brevity, uncertainty, and vanity of this life; to the many paradoxes in it, which can only be understood by patience and the fulness of knowledge; and to the need of guarding our spiritual gains against the incursions of evil.

the land (of promise)": but when the second of the warnings came to pass, We gathered you together in a mingled crowd.

105. We sent down the (Qur'an) in Truth, and in Truth has it descended: and We sent thee but to give Glad Tidings and to warn (sinners).

106. (It is) a Qur-ān which We have divided (into parts from time to time), in order that thou mightest recite it to men at intervals: We have revealed it by stages.

107. Say "Whether ye believe in it or not, it is true that those who were given knowledge beforehand, when it is recited to them, fall down on their faces in humble prostration,

108. "And they say: 'Glory to our Lord! Truly has the promise of our Lord been fulfilled!'

109. They fall down on their faces in tears, and it increases their (earnest) humility.

110. Say: "Call upon Allah, or call upon Rahmān: by whatever name ye call upon Him, (it is well): for to Him belong the Most Beautiful Names. Neither speak thy Prayer aloud, nor speak it in a low tone, but seek a middle course between."

111. Say: "Praise be to Allah, Who begets no son, and has no partner in (His) dominion: nor (needs) He any to protect Him from humiliation: yea, magnify Him for His greatness and glory!"

Al-Kahf, or the Cave

In the name of Allah, Most Gracious, Most Merciful.

1. Praise be to Allah, Who hath sent to His Servant the Book, and hath allowed therein no Crookedness:

2. (He hath made it) Straight (and Clear) in order that He may warn (the godless) of a terrible Punishment from Him, and that He may give Glad Tidings to the Believers

who work Righteous deeds, that they shall have a goodly Reward,

3.   Wherein they shall remain for ever:

4.   Further, that He may warn those (also) who say, "Allah hath begotten a son":

5.   No knowledge have they of such a thing, nor had their fathers. It is a grievous thing that issues from their mouths as a saying. What they say is nothing but falsehood!

6.   Thou wouldst only, perchance, Fret thyself to death, following after them, in grief, if they believe not in this Message.

7.   That which is on earth We have made but as a glittering show for it, in order that We may test them—as to which of them are best in conduct.

8.   Verily what is on earth We shall make but as dust and dry soil (without growth or herbage).

9.   Or dost thou think that the Companions of the Cave and of the Inscription were wonders among Our Signs?

10.   Behold, the youths betook themselves to the Cave: they said, "Our Lord! bestow on us mercy from Thyself, and dispose of our affair for us in the right way!"

11.   Then We drew (a veil) over their ears, for a number of years, in the Cave, (so that they heard not):

12.   Then We roused them, in order to test which of the two parties was best at calculating the term of years they had tarried!

13.   We relate to thee their story in truth: they were youths who believed in their Lord, and We increased them in guidance:

14.   We gave strength to their hearts: behold, they stood up and said: "Our Lord is the Lord of the heavens and of the earth: never shall we call upon any god other than Him: if we did, we should indeed have

uttered an enormity!

كُلْنَآ إِذًا شَطَطًا ۝

15. "These our people have taken for worship gods other than Him: why do they not bring forward an authority clear (and convincing) for what they do? Who doth more wrong than such as invent a falsehood against Allah?

هٰٓؤُلَآءِ قَوْمُنَا اتَّخَذُوْا مِنْ دُوْنِهٖۤ اٰلِهَةً ۖ لَوْلَا يَأْتُوْنَ عَلَيْهِمْ بِسُلْطٰنٍۭ بَيِّنٍ ۖ فَمَنْ أَظْلَمُ مِمَّنِ افْتَرٰى عَلَى اللّٰهِ كَذِبًا ۝

16. "When ye turn away from them and the things they worship other than Allah, betake yourselves to the Cave: your Lord will shower His mercies on you and dispose of your affair towards comfort and ease."

وَإِذِ اعْتَزَلْتُمُوْهُمْ وَمَا يَعْبُدُوْنَ إِلَّا اللّٰهَ فَأْوٗۤا إِلَى الْكَهْفِ يَنْشُرْ لَكُمْ رَبُّكُمْ مِّنْ رَّحْمَتِهٖ وَيُهَيِّئْ لَكُمْ مِّنْ أَمْرِكُمْ مِّرْفَقًا ۝

17. Thou wouldst have seen the sun, when it rose, declining to the right from their Cave, and when it set, turning away from them to the left, while they lay in the open space in the midst of the Cave. Such are among the Signs of Allah: he whom Allah guides is rightly guided; but he whom Allah leaves to stray,—for him wilt thou find no protector to lead him to the Right Way.

وَتَرَى الشَّمْسَ إِذَا طَلَعَتْ تَّزٰوَرُ عَنْ كَهْفِهِمْ ذَاتَ الْيَمِيْنِ وَإِذَا غَرَبَتْ تَّقْرِضُهُمْ ذَاتَ الشِّمَالِ وَهُمْ فِيْ فَجْوَةٍ مِّنْهُ ۖ ذٰلِكَ مِنْ اٰيٰتِ اللّٰهِ ۗ مَنْ يَّهْدِ اللّٰهُ فَهُوَ الْمُهْتَدِ ۖ وَمَنْ يُّضْلِلْ فَلَنْ تَجِدَ لَهٗ وَلِيًّا مُّرْشِدًا ۝

18. Thou wouldst have thought them awake, whilst they were asleep, and We turned them on their right and on their left sides: their dog stretching forth his two fore-legs on the threshold: if thou hadst looked at them, thou wouldst have certainly turned back from them in flight, and wouldst certainly have been filled with terror of them.

وَتَحْسَبُهُمْ أَيْقَاظًا وَّهُمْ رُقُوْدٌ ۖ وَّنُقَلِّبُهُمْ ذَاتَ الْيَمِيْنِ وَذَاتَ الشِّمَالِ ۖ وَكَلْبُهُمْ بَاسِطٌ ذِرَاعَيْهِ بِالْوَصِيْدِ ۚ لَوِ اطَّلَعْتَ عَلَيْهِمْ لَوَلَّيْتَ مِنْهُمْ فِرَارًا وَّلَمُلِئْتَ مِنْهُمْ رُعْبًا ۝

19. Such (being their state), We raised them up (from sleep), that they might question each other. Said one of them, "How long have ye stayed (here)?" They said, "We have stayed (perhaps) a day, or part of a day." (At length) they (all) said, "Allah (alone) knows best how long ye have stayed here... Now send ye then one of you with this money of yours to the town: let him find out which is the best food (to be had) and bring some to you, (that ye may satisfy your hunger therewith) and let him behave with care and courtesy, and let him not inform anyone about you.

وَكَذٰلِكَ بَعَثْنٰهُمْ لِيَتَسَآءَلُوْا بَيْنَهُمْ ۚ قَالَ قَآئِلٌ مِّنْهُمْ كَمْ لَبِثْتُمْ ۖ قَالُوْا لَبِثْنَا يَوْمًا أَوْ بَعْضَ يَوْمٍ ۚ قَالُوْا رَبُّكُمْ أَعْلَمُ بِمَا لَبِثْتُمْ ۖ فَابْعَثُوْۤا أَحَدَكُمْ بِوَرِقِكُمْ هٰذِهٖۤ إِلَى الْمَدِيْنَةِ فَلْيَنْظُرْ أَيُّهَآ أَزْكٰى طَعَامًا فَلْيَأْتِكُمْ بِرِزْقٍ مِّنْهُ وَلْيَتَلَطَّفْ وَلَا يُشْعِرَنَّ بِكُمْ أَحَدًا ۝

20. "For if they should come upon you, they would stone you or force you to return to their religion, and in that case ye would never attain prosperity."

21. Thus did We make their case know to the people, that they might know that the promise of Allah is true, and that there can be no doubt about the Hour of Judgment. Behold, they dispute among themselves as to their affair. (Some) said, "Construct a building over them": their Lord knows best about them: those who prevailed over their affair said, "Let us surely build a place of worship over them."

22. (Some) say they were three, the dog being the fourth among them; (others) say they were five, the dog being the sixth,—doubtfully guessing at the unknown; (yet others) say they were seven, the dog being the eighth. Say thou: "My Lord knoweth best their number; it is but few that know their (real case)." Enter not, therefore, into controversies concerning them, except on a matter that is clear, nor consult any of them about (the affair of) the Sleepers.

23. Nor say of anything, "I shall be sure to do so and so tomorrow"—

24. Except "If Allah so wills" and remember thy Lord when thou forgettest, and say, "I hope that my Lord will guide me ever closer (even) than this to the right course."

25. So they stayed in their Cave three hundred years, and nine (more).

26. Say: "Allah knows best how long they stayed: with Him is (the knowledge of) the secrets of the heavens and the earth: how clearly He sees, how finely He hears (everything)! They have no protector other than Him; nor does He share His Command with any person whatsoever.

27. And recite (and teach) what has been revealed to thee of the Book of thy Lord: none can change His Words, and none wilt thou find as a refuge other than Him.

28. And keep yourself content with those who call on their Lord morning and evening,

seeking His Face; and let not thine eyes pass beyond them, seeking the pomp and glitter of this Life; nor obey any whose heart We have permitted to neglect the remembrance of Us, one who follows his own desires, and his affair has become all excess.

29. Say, "The Truth is from your Lord" let him who will, believe, and let him who will, reject (it): for the wrong-doers We have prepared a Fire whose (smoke and flames), like the walls and roof of a tent, will hem them in: if they implore relief they will be granted water like melted·brass, that will scald their faces, how dreadful the drink! How uncomfor-table a couch to recline on!

30. As to those who believe and work righteousness, verily We shall not suffer to perish the reward of any who do a (single) righteous deed.

31. For them will be Gardens of Eternity; beneath them rivers will flow: they will be adorned therein with bracelets of gold, and they will wear green garments of fine silk and heavy brocade; they will recline therein on raised thrones. How good the recompense! How beautiful a couch to recline on!

32. Set forth to them the parable of two men: For one of them We provided two gardens of grape-vines and surrounded them with date palms; in between the two We placed tillage.

33. Each of those gardens brought forth its produce, and failed not in the least therein: in the midst of them We caused a river to flow.

34. (Abundant) was the produce this man had: he said to his companion, in the course of a mutual argument: "More wealth have I than you, and more honour and power in (my following of) men."

35. He went into his garden while he wronged himself: he said, "I deem not that this will ever perish."

36. "Nor do I deem that the Hour (of Judgment) will (ever) come: even if I am brought back to my Lord. I shall surely find (there) something better in exchange."

37. His companion said to him, in the course of the argument with him: "Dost thou deny Him Who created thee out of dust, then out of a sperm-drop, then fashioned thee into a man?

38. "But as for my part Allah is my Lord, and none shall I associate with my Lord.

39. "Why didst thou not, as thou wentest into Thy garden, say: 'Allah's Will (be done)! There is no power but from Allah!' If thou dost see me less than thee in wealth and sons,

40. "It may be that my Lord will give me something better than thy garden, and that He will send on thy garden thunderbolts (by way of reckoning) from heaven, making it (but) slippery sand!—

41. "Or the water of the garden will run off underground so that thou wilt never be able to find it."

42. So his fruits were encompassed (with ruin), and he remained twisting and turning his hands over what he had spent on his property, which had (now) tumbled to pieces to its very foundations, and he could only say, "Woe is me! Would I had never ascribed partners to my Lord and Cherisher!"

43. Nor had he numbers to help him against Allah, nor was he able to deliver himself.

44. There, the (only) protection comes from Allah, the True One. He is the Best to reward, and the Best to give success.

45. Set forth to them the similitude of the life of this world: it is like the rain which We send down from the skies: the earth's vegetation absorbs it, but soon it becomes dry stubble, which the winds do scatter: it is

(only) Allah Who prevails over all things.

تَذَرُوهُ الرِّيحُ وَكَانَ اللهُ عَلَى كُلِّ
شَىْءٍ مُقْتَدِرًا ۝

46. Wealth and sons are allurements of the life of this world: but the things that endure, Good Deeds, are best in the sight of thy Lord, as rewards, and best as (the foundation for) hopes.

اَلْمَالُ وَالْبَنُوْنَ زِيْنَةُ الْحَيٰوةِ الدُّنْيَا
وَالْبٰقِيٰتُ الصّٰلِحٰتُ خَيْرٌ عِنْدَ رَبِّكَ
ثَوَابًا وَّخَيْرٌ اَمَلًا ۝

47. On the Day We shall remove the mountains, and thou wilt see the earth as a level stretch, and We shall gather them, all together, nor shall We leave out anyone of them.

وَيَوْمَ نُسَيِّرُ الْجِبَالَ وَتَرَى الْاَرْضَ
بَارِزَةً وَّحَشَرْنٰهُمْ فَلَمْ نُغَادِرْ مِنْهُمْ
اَحَدًا ۝

48. And they will be marshalled before thy Lord in ranks (with the announcement) , "Now have ye come to Us (bare) as We created you first: aye, ye thought We shall not fulfil the appointment made to you to meet (Us)!":

وَعُرِضُوا عَلٰى رَبِّكَ صَفًّا لَقَدْ
جِئْتُمُوْنَا كَمَا خَلَقْنٰكُمْ اَوَّلَ مَرَّةٍ
بَلْ زَعَمْتُمْ اَلَّنْ نَّجْعَلَ لَكُمْ
مَّوْعِدًا ۝

49. And the Book (of Deeds) will be placed (before you); and thou wilt see the sinful in great terror because of what is (recorded) therein; they will say, "Ah! woe to us! What a book is this! It leaves out nothing small or great, but takes account thereof!" They will find all that they did, placed before them: and not one will thy Lord treat with injustice.

وَوُضِعَ الْكِتٰبُ فَتَرَى الْمُجْرِمِيْنَ
مُشْفِقِيْنَ مِمَّا فِيْهِ وَيَقُوْلُوْنَ يٰوَيْلَتَنَا
مَالِ هٰذَا الْكِتٰبِ لَا يُغَادِرُ صَغِيْرَةً
وَّلَا كَبِيْرَةً اِلَّا اَحْصٰهَا وَوَجَدُوْا مَا
عَمِلُوْا حَاضِرًا وَلَا يَظْلِمُ رَبُّكَ اَحَدًا ۝

50. Behold! We said to the angels, "Prostrate to Adam": they prostrated except Iblîs. He was one of the Jinns, and he broke the Command of his Lord will ye then take him and his progeny as protectors rather than Me? And they are enemies to you! Evil would be the exchange for the wrong-doers!

وَاِذْ قُلْنَا لِلْمَلٰئِكَةِ اسْجُدُوْا لِاٰدَمَ
فَسَجَدُوْا اِلَّا اِبْلِيْسَ كَانَ مِنَ الْجِنِّ
فَفَسَقَ عَنْ اَمْرِ رَبِّهِ اَفَتَتَّخِذُوْنَهُ
وَذُرِّيَّتَهُ اَوْلِيَاءَ مِنْ دُوْنِيْ وَهُمْ
لَكُمْ عَدُوٌّ بِئْسَ لِلظّٰلِمِيْنَ
بَدَلًا ۝

51. I called them not to witness the creation of the heavens and the earth, not (even) their own creation: nor is it for Me to take as helpers such as Lead (men) astray!

مَا اَشْهَدْتُّهُمْ خَلْقَ السَّمٰوٰتِ وَ
الْاَرْضِ وَلَا خَلْقَ اَنْفُسِهِمْ وَمَا كُنْتُ
مُتَّخِذَ الْمُضِلِّيْنَ عَضُدًا ۝

52. On the Day He will say, "Call on those whom ye thought to be My partners." And

وَيَوْمَ يَقُوْلُ نَادُوْا شُرَكَآءِيَ الَّذِيْنَ

they will call on them, but they will not listen to them; and We shall make for them a place of common perdition.

53. And the Sinful shall see the Fire and apprehend that they have to fall therein: no means will they find to turn away therefrom.

54. We have explained in detail in this Qur'an, for the benefit of mankind, every kind of similitude: but man is, in most things, contentious.

55. And what is there to keep back men from believing, now that guidance has come to them, nor from praying for forgiveness from their Lord but that (they wait for) the ways of the ancients to overtake them, or the Wrath be brought to them face to face?

56. We only send the Messengers to give glad tidings and to give warnings: but the Unbelievers dispute with vain argument, in order therewith to weaken the truth, and they treat My Signs and warnings as a jest.

57. And who doth more wrong than one who is reminded of the Signs of his Lord but turns away from them, forgetting the (deeds) which his hands have sent forth? Verily We have set veils over their hearts so that they understand this not, and over their ears, deafness. If thou callest them to guidance, even then will they never accept guidance.

58. But your Lord is Most Forgiving, full of Mercy. If He were yo call them (at once) to account for what they have earned, then surely He would have hastened their Punishment: but they have their appointed time, beyond which they will find no refuge.

59. Such were the towns We destroyed when they committed iniquities; but We fixed an appointed time tor their destruction.

60. Behold. Moses said to his attendant, "I will not give up until I reach the junction of

the two seas or (until) I spend years and years in travel."

61. But when they reached the Junction, they forgot (about) their Fish, which took its course through the sea (straight) as in a tunnel.

62. When they had passed on (some distance), Moses said to his attendant: "Bring us our early meal; truly we have suffered much fatigue at this (stage of) our journey."

63. He replied: "Sawest thou (what happened) when we betook ourselves to the rock? I did indeed forget (about) the Fish: none but Satan made me forget to tell (you) about It: it took its course through the sea in a marvellous way!"

64. Moses said: "That was what we were seeking after: so they went back on their footsteps, following (the path they had come).

65. So they found one of Our servants. On whom We had bestowed Mercy from Ourselves and whom We had taught knowledge from Our own presence.

66. Moses said to him: "May I follow thee, on the footing that Thou teach me something of the (Higher) Truth which thou hast been taught?"

67. (The other) said: "Verily Thou wilt not be able to have patience with me!

68. "For how canst thou have patience about things which are beyond your knowledge?"

69. Moses said: "Thou wilt find me, if Allah so will, (truly) patient: nor shall I disobey thee in aught."

70. The other said: "If then thou wouldst follow me, ask me no questions about anything until I Myself speak to thee concerning it."

71. So they both proceeded: until, when they were in the boat, he scutt-led it. Said Moses: "Hast thou scuttled it in order to drown those in it? Truly a strange thing hast thou done!"

72. He answered: "Did I not tell thee that thou canst have no patience with me?"

73. Moses said: Rebuke me not for forgetting, nor grieve me by raising

أَبْلُغَ مَجْمَعَ الْبَحْرَيْنِ أَوْ أَمْضِىَ حُقُبًا ۝

فَلَمَّا بَلَغَا مَجْمَعَ بَيْنِهِمَا نَسِيَا حُوتَهُمَا فَاتَّخَذَ سَبِيلَهُ فِى الْبَحْرِ سَرَبًا ۝

فَلَمَّا جَاوَزَا قَالَ لِفَتَاهُ ءَاتِنَا غَدَآءَنَا لَقَدْ لَقِينَا مِنْ سَفَرِنَا هَذَا نَصَبًا ۝

قَالَ أَرَءَيْتَ إِذْ أَوَيْنَآ إِلَى الصَّخْرَةِ فَإِنِّى نَسِيتُ الْحُوتَ وَمَآ أَنْسَانِيهُ إِلَّا الشَّيْطَنُ أَنْ أَذْكُرَهُ وَاتَّخَذَ سَبِيلَهُ فِى الْبَحْرِ عَجَبًا ۝

قَالَ ذَلِكَ مَا كُنَّا نَبْغِ فَارْتَدَّا عَلَى ءَاثَارِهِمَا قَصَصًا ۝

فَوَجَدَا عَبْدًا مِّنْ عِبَادِنَآ ءَاتَيْنَهُ رَحْمَةً مِّنْ عِنْدِنَا وَعَلَّمْنَهُ مِنْ لَّدُنَّا عِلْمًا ۝

قَالَ لَهُ مُوسَى هَلْ أَتَّبِعُكَ عَلَى أَنْ تُعَلِّمَنِ مِمَّا عُلِّمْتَ رُشْدًا ۝

قَالَ إِنَّكَ لَنْ تَسْتَطِيعَ مَعِيَ صَبْرًا ۝

وَكَيْفَ تَصْبِرُ عَلَى مَا لَمْ تُحِطْ بِهِ خُبْرًا ۝

قَالَ سَتَجِدُنِى إِنْ شَآءَ اللَّهُ صَابِرًا وَّلَآ أَعْصِى لَكَ أَمْرًا ۝

قَالَ فَإِنِ اتَّبَعْتَنِى فَلَا تَسْئَلْنِى عَنْ شَىْءٍ حَتَّى أُحْدِثَ لَكَ مِنْهُ ذِكْرًا ۝

فَانْطَلَقَا حَتَّى إِذَا رَكِبَا فِى السَّفِينَةِ خَرَقَهَا قَالَ أَخَرَقْتَهَا لِتُغْرِقَ أَهْلَهَا لَقَدْ جِئْتَ شَيْئًا إِمْرًا ۝

قَالَ أَلَمْ أَقُلْ إِنَّكَ لَنْ تَسْتَطِيعَ مَعِيَ صَبْرًا ۝

قَالَ لَا تُؤَاخِذْنِى بِمَا نَسِيتُ وَلَا

difficulties in my case."

74. Then they proceeded: until, when they met a young boy, he slew him. Moses said: "Hast thou slain an innocent person who had slain none? Truly a foul (unheard-of) thing hast thou done!"

75. He answered: "Did I not tell thee that thou canst have no patience with me?"

76. (Moses) said: "If ever I ask thee about anything after this, keep me not in thy company: then wouldst thou have received (full) excuse from my side.

77. Then they proceeded: until, when they came to the inhabitants of a town, they asked them for food, but they refused them hospitality. They found there a wall on the point of falling down, but he set it up straight. (Moses) said: "If thou hadst wished, surely thou couldst have exacted some recompense for it!

78. He answered: "This is the parting between me and thee: now will I tell thee the interpretation of (those things) over which thou wast unable to hold patience.

79. "As for the boat, it belonged to certain men in dire want: they plied on the water: I but wished to render it unserviceable, for there was after them a certain king who seized on every boat by force.

80. "As for the youth, his parents were people of Faith, and we feared that he would grieve them by obstinate rebellion and ingratitude (to Allah).

81. "So we desired that their Lord would give them in exchange (a son) better in purity (of conduct) and closer in affection.

82. "As for the wall, it belonged to two youths, orphans, in the Town; there was, beneath it, a buried treasure, to which they were entitled; their father had been a righteous man: so thy Lord desired that

they should attain their age of full strength and get out their treasure—a mercy (and favour) from thy Lord. I did it not of my own accord. Such is the interpretation of (those things) over which thou wast unable to hold patience."

83. They ask thee concerning *Zul-qarnain.* Say, "I will rehearse to you something of his story."

84. Verily We established his power on earth, and We gave him the ways and the means to all ends.

85. One (such) way he followed,

86. Until, when he reached the setting of the sun, he found it set in a spring of murky water: near it he found a People: We said: "O *Zul-qarnain!* (thou hast authority,) either to punish them, or to treat them with kindness."

87. He said: "Whoever doth wrong, him shall we punish; then shall he be sent back to his Lord; and He will punish him with a punishment unheard-of (before).

88. "But whoever believes, and works righteousness,—he shall have a goodly reward, and easy will be his task as we order it by our command."

89. Then followed he (another) way,

90. Until, when he came to the rising of the sun, he found it rising on a people for whom We had provided no covering protection against the sun.

91. (He left them) as they were: We completely understood what was before him.

92. Then followed he (another) way,

93. Until, when he reached (a tract) between two mountains, he found, beneath them, a people who scarcely understood a word.

94. They said: "O *Zul-qarnain!* the Gog and Magog (people) do great mischief on earth: shall we then render thee tribute in order that thou mightest erect a barrier

between us and them?

95. He said: "(The power) in which my Lord has established me is better (than tribute): help me therefore with strength (and labour): I will erect a strong barrier between you and them:

96. "Bring me blocks of iron." At length, when he had filled up the space between the two steep mountain-sides, he said, "Blow (with your bellows)" then, when he had made it (red) as fire, he said: "Bring me, that I may pour over it, molten lead."

97. Thus were they made powerless to scale it or to dig through it.

98. He said: "This is a mercy from my Lord: but when the promise of my Lord comes to pass, He will make it into dust; and the promise of my Lord is true."

99. On that day We shall leave them to surge like waves on one another: the trumpet will be blown, and We shall collect them all together.

100. And We shall present Hell that day for Unbelievers to see, all spread out,—

101. (Unbelievers) whose eyes had been under a veil from Remembrance of Me, and who had been unable even to hear.

102. Do the Unbelievers think that they can take My servants as protectors besides Me? Verily We have prepared Hell for the Unbelievers for (their) entertainment.

103. Say: "Shall we tell you of those who lose most in respect of their deeds?—

104. "Those whose efforts have been wasted in this life, while they thought that they were acquiring

SÛRA-19
MARYAM
(INTRODUCTION)

The spiritual growth of man as an individual soul having been explained in S. 17 as beginning with the first principles of moral conduct and in S. 18 as being dependent upon our realisation of the brevity and mystery of this life and the true use of power as in the story of Ẓul-qarnain, we now pass on to the story of individual Messengers of Allah in their personal relations with their environment,—Yaḥyā with his father Zakarîya, Jesus with his mother Mary, Abraham with his unbelieving father, Moses with his brother Aaron, Ismā'îl with his family, and Idrîs in the high station to which he was called. Seeing how these great ones fited into the scheme of life, man is condemned for his want of faith, or for degrading his faith to superstition, and warned of the Hereafter.

In chronology, it was revealed before the first resort of the batch of Muslims to Abyssinia, say seven years before the Hijrat.

good by their works?".

105. They are those who deny the Signs of their Lord and the fact of their having to meet Him (in the Hereafter): vain will be their works, nor shall We, on the Day of Judgment, give them any Weight.

106. That is their reward, Hell; because they rejected Faith, and took My Signs and My Messengers by way of jest.

107. As to those who believe and work righteous deeds, they have, for their entertainment, the Gardens of Paradise,

108. Wherein they shall dwell (for aye): no change will they wish for from them.

109. Say: "If the ocean were ink (wherewith to write out) the words of my Lord, sooner would the ocean be exhausted than would the words of my Lord, even if we added another ocean like it, for its aid."

110. Say: "I am but a man like yourselves, (but) the inspiration has come to me, that your God is One God: whoever expects to meet his Lord, let him work righteousness, and, in the worship of his Lord, admit no one as partner.

Maryam, or Mary

In the name of Allah, Most Gracious, Most Merciful.

1. Kāf. Hā. Yā. 'Ain. Sād.

2. (This is) a mention of the Mercy of thy Lord to His servant Zakarīya.

3. Behold! he cried to his Lord in secret.

4. Praying: "O my Lord! infirm indeed are my bones, and the hair of my head doth glisten with grey: but never am I unblest, O my Lord, in my prayer to Thee!

5. "Now I fear (what) my relatives (and colleagues) (will do) after me: but my wife is barren: so give me an heir as from Thyself,—

6. "(One that) will (truly) inherit me. and inherit the posterity of Jacob; and make him, O my Lord! One with whom Thou art well-pleased!"

7. (His prayer was answered). "O Zakariya! We give thee good news of a son: his name shall be Yahya: on none by that name have We conferred distinction before."

8. He said: "O my Lord! how shall i have a son, when my wife is barren and I have grown quite decrepit from old age?"

9. He said: "So (it will be): thy Lord saith, 'That is easy for Me: I did indeed create thee before, when thou hadst been nothing!'"

10. (Zakariya) said: "O my Lord! give me a Sign." "Thy Sign," was the answer, "Shall be that thou shalt speak to no man for three nights, although thou art not dumb."

11. So Zakariya came out to his people from his chamber: he told them by signs to celebrate Allah's praises in the morning and in the evening.

12. (To his son came the command): "O Yahya! take hold of the Book with might": and We gave him Wisdom even as a youth,

13. And pity (for all creatures) as from Us, and purity: he was devout,

14. And kind to his parents, and he was not overbearing or rebellious.

15. So Peace on him the day he was born, the day that he dies, and the day that he will be raised up to life (again)!

16. Relate in the Book (the story of) Mary, when she withdrew from her family to a place in the East.

17. She placed a screen (to screen herself) from them: then We sent to her Our angel, and he appeared before her as a man in all respects.

18. She said: "I seek refuge from thee to (Allah) Most Gracious: (come not near) if thou dost fear Allah."

19. He said: "Nay, I am only a messenger from thy Lord (to announce) to thee the gift of a pure son."

20. She said: "How shall I have a son, seeing that no man has touched me, and I am not unchaste?"

21. He said: "So (it will be): thy Lord saith, 'That is easy for Me: and (We wish) to appoint him as a Sign unto men and a Mercy from Us': it is a matter (so) decreed."

22. So she conceived him, and she retired with him to a remote place.

23. And the pains of childbirth drove her to the trunk of a palm-tree: she cried (in her anguish): "Ah! would that I had died before this! would that I had been a thing forgotten."

24. But (a voice) cried to her from beneath the (palm-tree): "Grieve not! for thy Lord hath provided a rivulet beneath thee;

25. "And shake towards thyself the trunk of the palm-tree: it will let fall fresh ripe dates upon thee.

26. "So eat and drink and cool (thine) eye. And if thou dost see any man, say, 'I have vowed a fast to (Allah) Most Gracious, and this day will I enter into no talk with any human being".'

27. At length she brought the (babe) to her people, carrying him (in her arms), they said: "O Mary! truly a strange thing has thou brought!

28. "O sister of Aaron! thy father was not a man of evil, nor thy mother a woman unchaste!"

29. But she pointed to the babe. They said: "How can we talk to one who is a child in the cradle?"

30. He said: "I am indeed a servant of Allah: He hath given me revelation and made me a prophet:

قَالَ اِنَّمَآ اَنَا رَسُوْلُ رَبِّكِ لِاَهَبَ لَكِ غُلٰمًا زَكِيًّا ۞

قَالَتْ اَنّٰى يَكُوْنُ لِيْ غُلٰمٌ وَّ لَمْ يَمْسَسْنِيْ بَشَرٌ وَّ لَمْ اَكُ بَغِيًّا ۞

قَالَ كَذٰلِكِ ۚ قَالَ رَبُّكِ هُوَ عَلَيَّ هَيِّنٌ ۚ وَ لِنَجْعَلَهٗٓ اٰيَةً لِّلنَّاسِ وَ رَحْمَةً مِّنَّا ۚ وَ كَانَ اَمْرًا مَّقْضِيًّا ۞

فَحَمَلَتْهُ فَانْتَبَذَتْ بِهٖ مَكَانًا قَصِيًّا ۞

فَاَجَآءَهَا الْمَخَاضُ اِلٰى جِذْعِ النَّخْلَةِ ۚ قَالَتْ يٰلَيْتَنِيْ مِتُّ قَبْلَ هٰذَا وَ كُنْتُ نَسْيًا مَّنْسِيًّا ۞

فَنَادٰىهَا مِنْ تَحْتِهَآ اَلَّا تَحْزَنِيْ قَدْ جَعَلَ رَبُّكِ تَحْتَكِ سَرِيًّا ۞

وَ هُزِّيْٓ اِلَيْكِ بِجِذْعِ النَّخْلَةِ تُسٰقِطْ عَلَيْكِ رُطَبًا جَنِيًّا ۞

فَكُلِيْ وَ اشْرَبِيْ وَ قَرِّيْ عَيْنًا ۚ فَاِمَّا تَرَيِنَّ مِنَ الْبَشَرِ اَحَدًا ۙ فَقُوْلِيْٓ اِنِّيْ نَذَرْتُ لِلرَّحْمٰنِ صَوْمًا فَلَنْ اُكَلِّمَ الْيَوْمَ اِنْسِيًّا ۞

فَاَتَتْ بِهٖ قَوْمَهَا تَحْمِلُهٗ ۚ قَالُوْا يٰمَرْيَمُ لَقَدْ جِئْتِ شَيْئًا فَرِيًّا ۞

يٰٓاُخْتَ هٰرُوْنَ مَا كَانَ اَبُوْكِ امْرَاَ سَوْءٍ وَّ مَا كَانَتْ اُمُّكِ بَغِيًّا ۞

فَاَشَارَتْ اِلَيْهِ ۚ قَالُوْا كَيْفَ نُكَلِّمُ مَنْ كَانَ فِى الْمَهْدِ صَبِيًّا ۞

قَالَ اِنِّيْ عَبْدُ اللّٰهِ ۚ اٰتٰىنِيَ الْكِتٰبَ وَ جَعَلَنِيْ نَبِيًّا ۞

31. "And He hath made me blessed wheresoever I be, and hath enjoined on me prayer and zakat as long as I live;

وَجَعَلَنِىْ مُبٰرَكًا اَيْنَ مَا كُنْتُ وَاَوْصٰنِىْ بِالصَّلٰوةِ وَالزَّكٰوةِ مَا دُمْتُ حَيًّا ۙ۞

32. "(He hath made me) kind to my mother, and not overbearing or unblest;

وَبَرًّۢا بِوَالِدَتِىْ ۖ وَلَمْ يَجْعَلْنِىْ جَبَّارًا شَقِيًّا ۞

33. "So Peace is on me the day I was born, the day that I die, and the day that I shall be raised up to life (again)"!

وَالسَّلٰمُ عَلَىَّ يَوْمَ وُلِدْتُّ وَيَوْمَ اَمُوْتُ وَيَوْمَ اُبْعَثُ حَيًّا ۞

34. Such (was) Jesus the son of Mary: (it is) a statement of truth, about which they (vainly) dispute.

ذٰلِكَ عِيْسَى ابْنُ مَرْيَمَ ۚ قَوْلَ الْحَقِّ الَّذِىْ فِيْهِ يَمْتَرُوْنَ ۞

35. It is not befitting to (the majesty of) Allah that He should beget a son. Glory be to Him! when He determines a matter, He only says to it, "Be", and it is.

مَا كَانَ لِلّٰهِ اَنْ يَّتَّخِذَ مِنْ وَّلَدٍ ۙ سُبْحٰنَهٗ ۚ اِذَا قَضٰۤى اَمْرًا فَاِنَّمَا يَقُوْلُ لَهٗ كُنْ فَيَكُوْنُ ۞

36. Verily Allah is my Lord and your Lord: Him therefore serve ye: this is a Way that is straight.

وَاِنَّ اللّٰهَ رَبِّىْ وَرَبُّكُمْ فَاعْبُدُوْهُ ۚ هٰذَا صِرَاطٌ مُّسْتَقِيْمٌ ۞

37. But the sects differ among themselves: and woe to the Unbe-lievers because of the (coming) Judgment of an awful Day!

فَاخْتَلَفَ الْاَحْزَابُ مِنْۢ بَيْنِهِمْ ۚ فَوَيْلٌ لِّلَّذِيْنَ كَفَرُوْا مِنْ مَّشْهَدِ يَوْمٍ عَظِيْمٍ ۞

38. How plainly will they see and hear, the Day that they will appear before Us! but the unjust today are in error manifest!

اَسْمِعْ بِهِمْ وَاَبْصِرْ ۙ يَوْمَ يَأْتُوْنَنَا لٰكِنِ الظّٰلِمُوْنَ الْيَوْمَ فِىْ ضَلٰلٍ مُّبِيْنٍ ۞

39. But warn them of the Day of Distress, when the matter will be determined: for (behold,) they are negligent and they do not believe!

وَاَنْذِرْهُمْ يَوْمَ الْحَسْرَةِ اِذْ قُضِىَ الْاَمْرُ ۘ وَهُمْ فِىْ غَفْلَةٍ وَّهُمْ لَا يُؤْمِنُوْنَ ۞

40. It is We Who will inherit the earth, and all beings thereon: to Us will they all be returned.

اِنَّا نَحْنُ نَرِثُ الْاَرْضَ وَمَنْ عَلَيْهَا وَاِلَيْنَا يُرْجَعُوْنَ ۞

41. (Also) mention in the Book (the story of) Abraham: he was a man of Truth, a prophet.

وَاذْكُرْ فِى الْكِتٰبِ اِبْرٰهِيْمَ ۬ ۚ اِنَّهٗ كَانَ صِدِّيْقًا نَّبِيًّا ۞

42. Behold, he said to his father: "O my father! why worship that which heareth not and seeth not, and can profit thee nothing?

اِذْ قَالَ لِاَبِيْهِ يٰۤاَبَتِ لِمَ تَعْبُدُ مَا لَا يَسْمَعُ وَلَا يُبْصِرُ وَلَا يُغْنِىْ عَنْكَ شَيْـًٔا ۞

43. "O my father! to me hath come knowledge which hath not reached thee: so follow me: I will guide thee to a Way that is even and straight.

يٰۤاَبَتِ اِنِّىْ قَدْ جَاۤءَنِىْ مِنَ الْعِلْمِ مَا لَمْ يَأْتِكَ فَاتَّبِعْنِىْ اَهْدِكَ صِرَاطًا سَوِيًّا ۞

44. "O my father! serve not Satan: for Satan is a rebel against (Allah) Most Gracious.

45. "O my father! I fear lest a Chastisement afflict thee from (Allah) Most Gracious, so that thou become to Satan a friend."

46. (The father) replied: art thou shrinking from my gods, O Abraham? If thou forbear not, I will indeed stone thee: now get away from me for a good long while!"

47. Abraham said: "Peace be on thee: I will pray to my Lord for thy forgiveness: for He is to me Most Gracious.

48. "And I will turn away from you (all) and from those whom ye invoke besides Allah: I will call on my Lord perhaps, by my prayer to my Lord, I shall be not unblest."!

49. When he had turned away from them and from those whom they worshipped besides Allah, We bestowed on him Isaac and Jacob, and each one of them We made a prophet.

50. And We bestowed of Our Mercy on them, and We granted them lofty honour on the tongue of truth.

51. Also mention in the Book (the story of) Moses: for he was specially chosen. And he was a messenger and a prophet.

52. And We called him from the right side of Mount (Sinai), and made him draw near to Us, for converse in secret

53. And, out of Our Mercy, We gave him his brother Aaron, (also) a prophet.

54. Also mention in the Book (the story of) Ismā'īl: he was (strictly) true to what he promised, and he was a messenger (and) a prophet.

55. He used to enjoin on his people Prayer and zakat and he was most acceptable in the sight of his Lord.

56. Also mention in the Book Idrîs: he was a man of truth (and sincerity), (and) a prophet:

وَاذْكُرْ فِى الْكِتَٰبِ إِدْرِيسَ ۚ إِنَّهُ كَانَ صِدِّيقًا نَّبِيًّا ۞

57. And We raised him to a lofty station.

وَرَفَعْنَٰهُ مَكَانًا عَلِيًّا ۞

58. Those were some of the prophets on whom Allah did bestow His Grace,—of the posterity of Adam, and of those whom We carried (in the Ark) with Noah, and of the posterity of Abraham and Israel—of those whom We guided and chose. Whenever the Signs of (Allah) Most Gracious were rehearsed to them, they would fall down in prostrate adoration and in tears.

أُو۟لَٰٓئِكَ الَّذِينَ أَنْعَمَ اللَّهُ عَلَيْهِم مِّنَ النَّبِيِّـۧنَ مِن ذُرِّيَّةِ ءَادَمَ وَمِمَّنْ حَمَلْنَا مَعَ نُوحٍ وَمِن ذُرِّيَّةِ إِبْرَٰهِيمَ وَإِسْرَٰٓءِيلَ وَمِمَّنْ هَدَيْنَا وَاجْتَبَيْنَا ۚ إِذَا تُتْلَىٰ عَلَيْهِمْ ءَايَٰتُ الرَّحْمَٰنِ خَرُّوا۟ سُجَّدًا وَبُكِيًّا ۩

59. But after them there followed a posterity who missed prayers and followed after lusts soon, then, will they face Destruction,—

فَخَلَفَ مِنۢ بَعْدِهِمْ خَلْفٌ أَضَاعُوا۟ الصَّلَوٰةَ وَاتَّبَعُوا۟ الشَّهَوَٰتِ ۖ فَسَوْفَ يَلْقَوْنَ غَيًّا ۞

60. Except those who repent and believe, and work Righteousness: for these will enter the Garden and will not be wronged in the least,—

إِلَّا مَن تَابَ وَءَامَنَ وَعَمِلَ صَٰلِحًا فَأُو۟لَٰٓئِكَ يَدْخُلُونَ الْجَنَّةَ وَلَا يُظْلَمُونَ شَيْـًٔا ۞

61. Gardens of Eternity, those which (Allah) Most Gracious has promised to His servants in the Unseen: for His promise must (necessarily) come to pass.

جَنَّٰتِ عَدْنٍ الَّتِى وَعَدَ الرَّحْمَٰنُ عِبَادَهُ بِالْغَيْبِ ۚ إِنَّهُ كَانَ وَعْدُهُ مَأْتِيًّا ۞

62. They will not there hear any vain discourse, but only salutations of Peace: and they will have therein their sustenance, morning and evening.

لَّا يَسْمَعُونَ فِيهَا لَغْوًا إِلَّا سَلَٰمًا ۖ وَلَهُمْ رِزْقُهُمْ فِيهَا بُكْرَةً وَعَشِيًّا ۞

63. Such is the Garden which We give as an inheritance to those of Our Servants who guard against evil.

تِلْكَ الْجَنَّةُ الَّتِى نُورِثُ مِنْ عِبَادِنَا مَن كَانَ تَقِيًّا ۞

64. (The angels say:) "We descend not but by command of thy Lord: to Him belongeth what is before us and what is behind us, and what is between: and thy Lord never doth forget,—

وَمَا نَتَنَزَّلُ إِلَّا بِأَمْرِ رَبِّكَ ۖ لَهُ مَا بَيْنَ أَيْدِينَا وَمَا خَلْفَنَا وَمَا بَيْنَ ذَٰلِكَ ۚ وَمَا كَانَ رَبُّكَ نَسِيًّا ۞

65. Lord of the heavens and of the earth, and of all that is between them: so worship Him, and be constant and patient in His worship: knowest thou of any who is worthy of the same Name as He?

رَّبُّ السَّمَٰوَٰتِ وَالْأَرْضِ وَمَا بَيْنَهُمَا فَاعْبُدْهُ وَاصْطَبِرْ لِعِبَادَتِهِ ۚ هَلْ تَعْلَمُ لَهُ سَمِيًّا ۞

66. Man says: "What! when I am dead,

وَيَقُولُ الْإِنسَٰنُ أَءِذَا مَا مِتُّ لَسَوْفَ

shall I then be raised up alive?"

67. But does not man call to mind that We created him before out of nothing?

68. So, by thy Lord, without doubt, We shall gather them together, and (also) Satans (with them); then shall We bring them forth on their knees round about Hell;

69. Then shall We certainly drag out from every sect all those who were worst in obstinate rebellion against (Allah) Most Gracious.

70. And certainly We know best those who are most worthy of being burned therein.

71. Not one of you but will pass over it: this is, with thy Lord, a Decree which must be accomplished.

72. But We shall save those who guarded against evil, and We shall leave the wrong-doers therein, (humbled) to their knees.

73. When Our Clear Signs are rehearsed to them, the Unbelievers say to those who believe, "Which of the two sides is best in point of position and fairer in assembly,"

74. But how many (countless) generations before them have We destroyed, who were even better in equipment and in glitter to the eye?

75. Say: "Whoever goes astray, (Allah) Most Gracious extends (the rope) to them, until, when they see the warning of Allah (being fulfilled)—either in punishment or in (the approach of) the Hour,—they will at length realise who is worst in position, and (who) weakest in forces!

76. "And Allah doth increase in guidance those who seek guidance: and the things that endure, Good Deeds, are best in the sight of thy Lord, as rewards, and best in respect of (their) eventual returns."

77. Has thou then seen the (sort of) man who rejects Our Signs, yet says: "I shall certainly be given wealth and children?"

78. Has he penetrated to the Unseen, or has he taken a promise with the Most Gracious?

اَطَّلَعَ الْغَيْبَ اَمِ اتَّخَذَ عِنْدَ الرَّحْمٰنِ عَهْدًا ۞

79. Nay! We shall record what he says, and We shall add and add to his punishment.

كَلَّا ۚ سَنَكْتُبُ مَا يَقُوْلُ وَنَمُدُّ لَهٗ مِنَ الْعَذَابِ مَدًّا ۞

80. To Us shall return all that he talks of, and he shall appear before Us bare and alone.

وَّنَرِثُهٗ مَا يَقُوْلُ وَيَأْتِيْنَا فَرْدًا ۞

81. And they have taken (for worship) gods other than Allah, to give them power and glory!

وَاتَّخَذُوْا مِنْ دُوْنِ اللّٰهِ اٰلِهَةً لِّيَكُوْنُوْا لَهُمْ عِزًّا ۞

82. Instead, they shall reject their worship, and become adversaries against them.

كَلَّا ۚ سَيَكْفُرُوْنَ بِعِبَادَتِهِمْ وَيَكُوْنُوْنَ عَلَيْهِمْ ضِدًّا ۞

83. Seest thou not that We have set Satans on against the Unbelievers, to incite them with fury?

اَلَمْ تَرَ اَنَّا اَرْسَلْنَا الشَّيٰطِيْنَ عَلَى الْكٰفِرِيْنَ تَؤُزُّهُمْ اَزًّا ۞

84. So make no haste against them, for We but count out to them a (limited) number (of days).

فَلَا تَعْجَلْ عَلَيْهِمْ ۚ اِنَّمَا نَعُدُّ لَهُمْ عَدًّا ۞

85. The day We shall gather the righteous to (Allah) Most Gracious, like a band (presented before a king for honours.)

يَوْمَ نَحْشُرُ الْمُتَّقِيْنَ اِلَى الرَّحْمٰنِ وَفْدًا ۞

86. And We shall drive the sinners to hell, (like thirsty cattle driven down to water,—)

وَّنَسُوْقُ الْمُجْرِمِيْنَ اِلٰى جَهَنَّمَ وِرْدًا ۞

87. None shall have the power of intercession, but such a one as has received permission (or promise) from (Allah) Most Gracious.

لَا يَمْلِكُوْنَ الشَّفَاعَةَ اِلَّا مَنِ اتَّخَذَ عِنْدَ الرَّحْمٰنِ عَهْدًا ۞

88. They say: "The Most Gracious has betaken a son!"

وَقَالُوا اتَّخَذَ الرَّحْمٰنُ وَلَدًا ۞

89. Indeed ye have put forth a thing most monstrous!

لَقَدْ جِئْتُمْ شَيْئًا اِدًّا ۞

90. At it the skies are about to burst, the earth to split asunder, and the mountains to fall down in utter ruin,

تَكَادُ السَّمٰوٰتُ يَتَفَطَّرْنَ مِنْهُ وَتَنْشَقُّ الْاَرْضُ وَتَخِرُّ الْجِبَالُ هَدًّا ۞

91. That they attributed a son to the Most Gracious.

اَنْ دَعَوْا لِلرَّحْمٰنِ وَلَدًا ۞

92. For it is not consonant with the majesty of the Most Gracious that He should beget a son.

وَمَا يَنْۢبَغِيْ لِلرَّحْمٰنِ اَنْ يَّتَّخِذَ وَلَدًا ۞

93. Not one of the beings in the heavens and the earth but must come to the Most Gracious as a servant.

اِنْ كُلُّ مَنْ فِى السَّمٰوٰتِ وَالْاَرْضِ اِلَّا اٰتِى الرَّحْمٰنِ عَبْدًا ۞

94. He does take an account of them (all), and hath numbered them (all) exactly.

لَقَدْ اَحْصٰهُمْ وَعَدَّهُمْ عَدًّا ۞

95. And everyone of them will come to Him singly on the Day of Judgment.

وَكُلُّهُمْ اٰتِيْهِ يَوْمَ الْقِيٰمَةِ فَرْدًا ۞

96. On those who believe and work

اِنَّ الَّذِيْنَ اٰمَنُوْا وَعَمِلُوا الصّٰلِحٰتِ

SÛRA–20
ṬĀ-HĀ
(INTRODUCTION)

The chronology of this Sûra has some significance: it has some relation to the spiritual lessons which it teaches.

It was used with great effect in that remarkable scene which resulted in Ḥaḍhrat 'Umar's conversion, and which took place about the seventh year before the Hijrat.

The scene is described with dramatic details by Ibn Hishãm. 'Umar had previously been one of the greatest enemies and persecutors of Islam. Like his blood-thirsty kinsmen the Quraish, he meditated slaying the Prophet, when it was suggested to him that there were near relations of his that had embraced Islam. His sister Fāṭima and her husband Sa'îd were Muslims, but in those days of persecution they had kept their faith secret. When 'Umar went to their house, he heard them reciting this Sûra from a written copy they had. For a while they concealed the copy. 'Umar attacked his sister and her husband, but they bore the attack with exemplary patience, and declared their faith. 'Umar was so struck with their sincerity and fortitude that he asked to see the leaf from which they had been reading. It was given to him: his soul was touched, and he not only came into the Faith but became one of its strongest supporters and champions.

The leaf contained some portion of this Sûra, perhaps the introductory portion. The mystic leters ṬĀ-HĀ are prefixed to this Sûra. What do they mean? The earliest tradition is that they denote a dialectical interjection meaning "O man!" If so, the title is particularly appropriate in two ways: (1) It was a direct and personal address to a man in a high state of excitement tempted by his temper to do grievous wrong, but called by Allah's Grace, as by a personal appeal, to face the realities, for Allah knew his inmost secret thoughts (20: 7) : the revelation was sent by Allah Most Gracious, out of His Grace and Mercy (20: 5). (2) It takes up the story from the last Sûra, of man as a spiritual being and illustrates it in further details. It tells the story of Moses in the crisis of his life when he received Allah's Commission and in his personal relations with his mother, and how he came to be brought up in the Pharaoh's house, to learn all the wisdom of the Egyptians, for use in Allah's service, and in his personal relations with Pharaoh, whom we take to be his adoptive father (28: 9). If further tells the story of a fallen soul who misled the Israelites into idolatry, and recalls how man's Arch-enemy Satan caused his fall. Prayer and praise are necessary to man to cure his spiritual blindness and enable him to appreciate Allah's revelation.

deeds of righteousness, will the Most Gracious bestow Love.

97. So have We made the (Qur-ān) easy in thine own tongue, that with it thou mayest give glad tidings to the righteous, and warnings to people given to contention.

98. But how many (countless) generations before them have We destroyed? Canst thou find a single one of them (now) or hear (so much as) a whisper of them?

Ṭā-Hā

In the name of Allah, Most Gracious, Most Merciful.

1. Ṭā-Hā.

2. We have not sent down the Qur'an to thee to be (an occasion) for thy distress,

3. But only as an admonition to those who fear (Allah),—

4. A revelation from Him Who created the earth and the heavens on high.

5. The Most Gracious is firmly established on the throne.

6. To Him belongs what is in the heavens and on earth, and all between them, and all beneath the soil.

7. If thou pronounce the word aloud, (it is no matter): for verily He knoweth what is secret and what is yet more hidden.

8. Allah! there is no god but He! To Him belong the Most Beautiful Names.

9. Was the story of Moses reached thee?

10. Behold, he saw a fire: so he said to his family, "Tarry ye; I perceive a fire; perhaps I can bring you some burning brand therefrom, or find some guidance at the fire."

11. But when he came to the fire, He was called "O Moses!

12. "Verily I am thy Lord! Therefore put off thy shoes: thou art in the sacred valley Tuwā.

13. "I have chosen thee: listen, then to the inspiration (given to thee).

14. "Verily, I am Allah: there is no god but

I: so serve thou Me (only), and establish regular prayer for My remembrance.

15. "Verily the Hour is coming— I have almost kept it hidden—for every soul to receive its reward by the measure of its Endeavour.

16. "Therefore let not such as believe not therein but follow their own lusts, divert thee therefrom, lest thou perish!"...

17. "And what is that in thy right hand, O Moses?"

18. He said, "It is my rod: on it I lean; with it I beat down fodder for my flocks; and in it I find other uses."

19. (Allah) said, "Throw it, O Moses!"

20. He threw it, and behold! it was a snake, active in motion.

21. (Allah) said, "Seize it, and fear not: We shall return it at once to its former condition"...

22. "Now draw thy hand close to thy side: it shall come forth white (and shining), without harm (or stain),—as another Sign,—

23. "In order that We may show thee of our Greater Signs.

24. "Go thou to Pharaoh, for he has indeed transgressed all bounds."

25. (Moses) said: "O my Lord! expand me my breast;

26. "Ease my task for me;

27. "And remove the impediment from my speech,

28. "So they may understand what I say:

29. "And give me a Minister from my family,

30. "Aaron, my brother;

31. "Add to my strength through him.

32. "And make him share My task:

33. "That we may celebrate Thy praise without stint,

34. "And remember Thee without stint:

35. "For Thou art ever seeing

36. (Allah) said: "Granted is thy prayer, O Moses!"

37. "And indeed We conferred a favour on thee another time (before).

38. "Behold! We sent to thy mother, by inspiration, the message:

39. " 'Throw (the child) into the chest, and throw (the chest) into the river: the river will cast him up on the bank, and he will be taken up by one who is an enemy to Me and an enemy to him': but I endued thee with love from Me: and (this) in order that thou mayest be reared under Mine eye.

40. "Behold! thy sister goeth forth and saith, 'Shall I show you one who will nurse and rear the (child)?' So We brought thee back to thy mother, that her eye might be cooled and she should not grieve. Then thou didst slay a man, but We saved thee from trouble, and We tried thee in various ways. Then didst thou tarry a number of years with the people of Midian. Then didst thou come hither as ordained, O Moses!

41. "And I have prepared thee for Myself (for service)"...

42. Go, thou and thy brother, with My signs, and slacken not, either of you, in keeping Me in remembrance.

43. "Go, both of you, to Pharaoh, for he has indeed transgressed all bounds;

44. "But speak to him mildly; perchance he may take warning or fear (Allah)."

45. They (Moses and Aaron) said: "Our Lord! we fear lest he hasten with insolence against us, or lest he transgress all bounds."

46. He said: "Fear not: for I am with you: I hear and see (everything).

47. "So go ye both to him, and say, 'Verily we are messengers sent by thy Lord: send forth, therefore, the Children of Israel with

اِنَّكَ كُنْتَ بِنَا بَصِيْرًا ۞

قَالَ قَدْ اُوْتِيْتَ سُؤْلَكَ يٰمُوْسٰى ۞

وَلَقَدْ مَنَنَّا عَلَيْكَ مَرَّةً اُخْرٰى ۞

اِذْ اَوْحَيْنَا اِلٰٓى اُمِّكَ مَا يُوْحٰى ۞

اَنِ اقْذِفِيْهِ فِى التَّابُوْتِ فَاقْذِفِيْهِ فِى الْيَمِّ فَلْيُلْقِهِ الْيَمُّ بِالسَّاحِلِ يَأْخُذْهُ عَدُوٌّ لِّيْ وَعَدُوٌّ لَّهٗ ۚ وَاَلْقَيْتُ عَلَيْكَ مَحَبَّةً مِّنِّيْ ۚ وَلِتُصْنَعَ عَلٰى عَيْنِيْ ۞

اِذْ تَمْشِيْٓ اُخْتُكَ فَتَقُوْلُ هَلْ اَدُلُّكُمْ عَلٰى مَنْ يَّكْفُلُهٗ ۚ فَرَجَعْنٰكَ اِلٰٓى اُمِّكَ كَيْ تَقَرَّ عَيْنُهَا وَلَا تَحْزَنَ ۚ وَقَتَلْتَ نَفْسًا فَنَجَّيْنٰكَ مِنَ الْغَمِّ وَفَتَنّٰكَ فُتُوْنًا ۚ فَلَبِثْتَ سِنِيْنَ فِيْٓ اَهْلِ مَدْيَنَ ۚ ثُمَّ جِئْتَ عَلٰى قَدَرٍ يّٰمُوْسٰى ۞

وَاصْطَنَعْتُكَ لِنَفْسِيْ ۚ ۞

اِذْهَبْ اَنْتَ وَاَخُوْكَ بِاٰيٰتِيْ وَلَا تَنِيَا فِيْ ذِكْرِيْ ۚ ۞

اِذْهَبَآ اِلٰى فِرْعَوْنَ اِنَّهٗ طَغٰى ۚ ۞

فَقُوْلَا لَهٗ قَوْلًا لَّيِّنًا لَّعَلَّهٗ يَتَذَكَّرُ اَوْ يَخْشٰى ۞

قَالَا رَبَّنَآ اِنَّنَا نَخَافُ اَنْ يَّفْرُطَ عَلَيْنَآ اَوْ اَنْ يَّطْغٰى ۞

قَالَ لَا تَخَافَآ اِنَّنِيْ مَعَكُمَآ اَسْمَعُ وَاَرٰى ۞

فَأْتِيٰهُ فَقُوْلَآ اِنَّا رَسُوْلَا رَبِّكَ فَاَرْسِلْ مَعَنَا بَنِيْٓ اِسْرَآءِيْلَ ۚ وَلَا تُعَذِّبْهُمْ ۚ

us, and afflict them not: with a Sign, indeed,
have we come from thy Lord! And Peace to
all who follow guidance!

48. " 'Verily it has been revealed to us that
the Chastisement (awaits) those who reject
and turn away.' "

49. (When this message was delivered),
(Pharaoh) said: "Who then, O Moses, is the
Lord of you two?"

50. He said: "Our Lord He Who gave to
each (created) thing its form then, gave (it)
guidance."

51. (Pharaoh) said: "What then is the
condition of previous generations?"

52. He replied: "The knowledge of that is
with my Lord, duly recorded: my Lord never
errs, nor forgets,—

53. "He Who has made for you the earth
like a carpet spread out; has enabled you
to go about therein by roads (and channels);
and has sent down water from the sky."
With it have We produced diverse pairs of
plants each separate from the others.

54. Eat (for yourselves) and pasture your
cattle: verily, in this are Signs for men
endued with understanding.

55. From the (earth) did We create you,
and into it shall We return you, and from it
shall We bring you out once again.

56. And We showed Pharaoh all Our
Signs, but he did reject and refuse.

57. He said: "Hast thou come to drive us
out of our land with thy magic, O Moses?

58. "But we can surely produce magic to
match thine! So make a tryst between us
and thee, which we shall not fail to keep—
neither we nor thou— in a place where
both shall have even chances."

59. Moses said: "Your tryst is the Day of
the Festival, and let the people be
assembled when the sun is well up,"

60. So Pharaoh withdrew: He concerted
his plan, and then came (back).

61. Moses said to them "Woe to you! Forge
not ye a lie against Allah, lest He destroy

you (at once) utterly by chastisement: the forger must suffer failure."

62. So they disputed, one with another, over their affair, but they kept their talk secret.

63. They said: "These two are certainly (expert) magicians: their object is to drive you out from your land with their magic, and to do away with your most cherished way.

64. "Therefore concert your plan, and then assemble in (serried) ranks: he wins (all along) today who gains the upper hand."

65. They said: "O Moses! whether wilt thou that thou throw (first) or that we be the first to throw?"

66. He said, "Nay, throw ye first!" Then behold their ropes and their rods—so it seemed to him on account of their magic—began to be in lively motion!

67. So Moses conceived in his mind a (sort of) fear.

68. We said: "Fear not! for thou hast indeed the upper hand:

69. "Throw that which is in thy right hand: quickly will it swallow up that which they have faked: what they have faked is but a magician's trick: and the magician succeeds not."

70. So the magicians were thrown down to prostration: they said, "We believe in the Lord of Aaron and Moses".

71. (Pharaoh) said: "Believe ye in Him before I give you permission? Surely this must be your leader, who has taught you magic! Be sure I will cut off your hands and feet on opposite sides, and I will have you crucified on trunks of palm-trees: so shall ye know for certain, which of us can give the more severe and the more lasting Punishment!"

72. They said: "Never shall we prefer thee to what has come to us of the Clear Signs Him Who created us! So decree whatever

thou desirest to decree: for thou canst only decree (touching) the life of this world.

73. "For us, we have believed in our Lord: may He forgive us our faults, and the magic to which thou didst compel us: for Allah is Best and Most Abiding."

74. Verily he who comes to his Lord as a sinner (at Judgment),—for him is Hell: therein shall he neither die nor live.

75. But such as come to Him as Believers who have worked righteous deeds,—for them are ranks exalted,—

76. Gardens of Eternity, beneath which flow rivers: they will dwell therein for aye: such is the reward of those who purify themselves (from evil).

77. We sent an inspiration to Moses: "Travel by night with My servants, and strike a dry path for them through the sea, without fear of being overtaken (by Pharaoh) and without (any other) fear."

78. Then Pharaoh pursued them with his forces, but the waters completely over-whelmed them and covered them up.

79. Pharaoh led his people astray instead of leading them aright.

80. O ye Children of Israel! We delivered you from your enemy, and We made a Convenant with you on the right side of Mount (Sinai), and We sent down to you Manna and quails:

81. "Eat of the good things We have provided for your sustenance, but commit no excess therein, lest My Wrath should descend on you: and those on whom descends My Wrath do perish indeed!

82. "But, without doubt, I am (also) He that forgives again and again, to those who repent, believe, and do right, —who, in fine, are on true guidance."

83. (When Moses was up on the Mount, Allah said:) "What made thee hasten in advance of thy people, O Moses?"

84. He replied: "Behold, they are close on

my footsteps: I hastened to Thee, O my Lord, to please Thee."

85. (Allah) said: "We have tested thy people in thy absence: the Sāmiri has led them Astray."

86. So Moses returned to his people in a state of anger and sorrow. He said: "O my people! did not your Lord make a handsome promise to you? Did then the promise seem to you long (in coming)? Or did ye desire that Wrath should descend from your Lord on you. and so ye broke your promise to me?"

87. They said: "We broke not the promise to thee, as far as lay in our power: but we were made to carry the weight of the ornaments of the (whole) people, and we threw them (into the fire), and that was what the Sāmiri suggested.

88. "Then he brought out (of the fire) before the (people) the image of a calf: it seemed to low: so they said: 'This is your god, and the god of Moses, but (Moses) has forgotten!"

89. Could they not see that it could not return them a word (for answer), and that it had no power either to harm them or to do them good?

90. Aaron had already, before this said to them: "O my people! ye are being tested in this: for verily your Lord is (Allah) Most Gracious: so follow me and obey my command."

91. They had said: "We will not cease to worship it, will devote ourselves to it until Moses returns to us."

92. (Moses) said: "O Aaron! what kept thee back, when thou sawest them going wrong.

93. "From following me? Didst thou then disobey my order?"

94. (Aaron) replied: "O son of my mother! Seize (me) not by my beard nor by (the hair of) my head! Truly I feared lest thou shouldst say, 'Thou hast caused a division among the Children of Israel, and thou didst not

observe my word!' "

95. (Moses) said: "What then is thy case, O Sāmirī?"

96. He replied: "I saw what they saw not: so I took a handful (of dust) from the footprint of the Messenger, and threw it (into the calf): thus did my soul suggest to me."

97. (Moses) said: "Get thee gone! But thy (punishment) in this life will be that thou wilt say, 'Touch me not'; and moreover (for a future penalty) thou hast a promise that will not fail: now look at thy god, of whom thou hast become a devoted worshipper: we will certainly burn it in a blazing fire and scatter it broadcast in the sea!"

98. But the God of you all is Allah: there is no god but He: all things He comprehends in His knowledge.

99. Thus do We relate to thee some stories of what happened before: for We have sent thee a reminder from Us.

100. If any do turn away therefrom, verily they will bear a burden on the Day of Judgment;

101. They will abide in this (state): and grievous will the burden be to them on that Day.—

102. The Day when the Trumpet will be sounded: that Day, We shall gather the sinful, blear-eyed (with terror).

103. In whispers will they consult each other: "Ye tarried not longer than ten (Days)";

104. We know best what they will say, when the best of them in judgment will say: "Ye tarried not longer than a day!"

105. They ask thee concerning the Mountains: say, "My Lord will uproot them and scatter them as dust;

106. "He will leave them as plains smooth and level;

107. "Nothing crooked or curved wilt thou see in their place."

108. On that Day will they follow the caller (straight): no crookedness in him: and the voices will be hushed to The Most Gracious: so that thou hearest not but murmuring.

109. On that Day shall no intercession avail except for those for whom permission has been granted by The Most Gracious and whose word is acceptable to Him.

110. He knows what is before or after or behind them: but they shall comprehend Him not.

111. (All) faces shall be humbled before—the Living, the Self-Subsisting, The Sustainer: hopeless indeed will be the man that carries iniquity (on his back).

112. But he who works deeds of righteousness, and has faith, will have no fear of harm nor of any curtailment (of what is his due).

113. Thus have We sent this down—an Arabic Qur'an—and explained therein in detail some of the warnings, in order that they may fear Allah, or that it may cause their remembrance (of Him).

114. High above all is Allah, the King, the Truth! Be not in haste with the Qur'an before its revelation to thee is completed, but say, "O my Lord! increase me in knowledge."

115. We had already, beforehand, taken the covenant of Adam, but he forgot: and We found on his part no firm resolve.

116. When We said to the angels, "Prostrate yourselves to Adam", they prostrated themselves, but not Iblīs: he refused.

117. Then We said: "O Adam! verily, this is an enemy to thee and thy wife: so let him not get you both out of the Garden, so that thou art landed in misery.

118. "There is therein (enough provision) for thee not to go hungry nor to go naked,

119. "Nor to suffer from thirst, nor from the sun's heat."

120. But Satan whispered evil to him: he

said, "O Adam! shall I lead thee to the Tree of Eternity and to a kingdom that never decays?"

هَلْ أَدُلُّكَ عَلَى شَجَرَةِ الْخُلْدِ وَمُلْكٍ لَّا يَبْلَى ۝

121. In the result, they both ate of the tree, and so their nakedness appeared to them: they began to sew together, for their covering, leaves from the Garden: thus did Adam disobey his Lord, and fell into error.

فَأَكَلَا مِنْهَا فَبَدَتْ لَهُمَا سَوْآتُهُمَا وَطَفِقَا يَخْصِفَانِ عَلَيْهِمَا مِنْ وَّرَقِ الْجَنَّةِ وَعَصَى اٰدَمُ رَبَّهُ فَغَوَى ۝

122. But his Lord chose him (for His Grace): He turned to him, and gave him guidance.

ثُمَّ اجْتَبٰهُ رَبُّهُ فَتَابَ عَلَيْهِ وَهَدَى ۝

123. He said: "Get ye down, both of you,— all together, from the Garden, with enmity one to another: but if, as is sure, there comes to you guidance from Me, whosoever follows My guidance, will not Lose his way, nor fall into misery.
124. "But whosoever turns away from My Message, verily for him is a life narrowed down, and We shall raise him up blind on the Day of Judgment."

قَالَ اهْبِطَا مِنْهَا جَمِيعًا بَعْضُكُمْ لِبَعْضٍ عَدُوٌّ فَإِمَّا يَأْتِيَنَّكُمْ مِّنِّي هُدًى فَمَنِ اتَّبَعَ هُدَايَ فَلَا يَضِلُّ وَلَا يَشْقَى ۝ وَمَنْ أَعْرَضَ عَنْ ذِكْرِي فَإِنَّ لَهُ مَعِيشَةً ضَنْكًا وَّنَحْشُرُهُ يَوْمَ الْقِيَامَةِ أَعْمَى ۝

125. He will say: "O my Lord! why hast thou raised me up blind, while I had sight (before)?"

قَالَ رَبِّ لِمَ حَشَرْتَنِي أَعْمَى وَقَدْ كُنْتُ بَصِيرًا ۝

126. (Allah) will say: "Thus didst thou, when Our Signs came unto thee, forgot them: so wilt thou, this day, be forgotten."

قَالَ كَذٰلِكَ أَتَتْكَ اٰيَاتُنَا فَنَسِيتَهَا وَكَذٰلِكَ الْيَوْمَ تُنْسَى ۝

127. And thus do We recompense him who transgresses beyond bounds and believes not in the Signs of his Lord: and the Chastisement of the Hereafter is far more grievous and more enduring.

وَكَذٰلِكَ نَجْزِي مَنْ أَسْرَفَ وَلَمْ يُؤْمِنْ بِاٰيَاتِ رَبِّهِ وَلَعَذَابُ الْاٰخِرَةِ أَشَدُّ وَأَبْقَى ۝

128. Is it not a guidance to such men (to call to mind) how many generations before them We destroyed, in whose haunts they (now) move? Verily, in this are Signs for men endued with understanding.

أَفَلَمْ يَهْدِ لَهُمْ كَمْ أَهْلَكْنَا قَبْلَهُمْ مِّنَ الْقُرُونِ يَمْشُونَ فِي مَسَاكِنِهِمْ إِنَّ فِي ذٰلِكَ لَاٰيَاتٍ لِّأُولِي النُّهَى ۝

129. Had it not been for a Word that went forth before from thy Lord, (their punishment) must necessarily have come; but there is a term appointed (for respite)..

وَلَوْلَا كَلِمَةٌ سَبَقَتْ مِنْ رَّبِّكَ لَكَانَ لِزَامًا وَّأَجَلٌ مُّسَمًّى ۝

130. Therefore be patient with what they say, and celebrate (constantly) the praises of thy Lord, before the rising of

فَاصْبِرْ عَلَى مَا يَقُولُونَ وَسَبِّحْ بِحَمْدِ رَبِّكَ قَبْلَ طُلُوعِ الشَّمْسِ وَقَبْلَ

SÛRA–21
AL-ANBIYÃA
(INTRODUCTION)

The last Sûra dealt with the individual story (spiritual) of Moses and Aaron, and contrasted it with the growth of evil in individuals like Pharaoh and the Samirî, and ended with a warning against Evil, and an exhortation to the purification of the soul with prayer and praise. This Sûra begins with the external obstacles placed by Evil against such purification, and gives the assurance of Allah's power to defend men, illustrating this with reference to Abraham's fight against idolatry, Lot's fight against unnatural wickedness, Noah's against unbelief, that of David and Solomon against injustice and failure to proclaim Allah's glory by making full use of man's Allah-given faculties and powers, that of Job against impatience and want of self-confidence, that of Isma'îl Idrîs and Zul-kifl against want of steady perseverance, that of Zun-nun against hasty anger, that of Zakariyã against spiritual isolation, and that of Mary against the lusts of this world. In each illusion there is a special point about the soul's purification. The common point is that the Prophets were not, as the vulgar suppose, just irresistible men. They had to win their ground inch by inch against all kinds of resistance from evil.

The chronology of this Sûra has no significance. It probably dates from the middle of the Makkan period of inspiration.

the sun, and before its sett-ing; yea, celebrate them for part of the hours of the night, and at the sides of the day: that thou may be pleased.

131. Nor strain thine eyes in longing for the things We have given for enjoyment to par-ties of them, the splendour of the life of this world, through which We test them: but the provision of thy Lord is better and more enduring.

132. Enjoin prayer on thy people, And be constant therein. We ask thee not to provide sustenance: We provide it for thee. But the (fruit of) the Hereafter is for Righteousness.

133. They say: "Why does he not bring us a Sign from his Lord?" Has not a Clear Sign come to them of all that was in the former Books of revelation?

134. Had We destroyed them with a pun-ishment before this. They would have said: "Our Lord! If only thou Hadst sent us a messenger, we should certainly have fol-lowed Thy Signs before we were humbled and put to shame."

135. Say: "Each one (of us) is waiting: wait ye, therefore, and soon shall ye know who it is that is on the straight and even way, and who it is that has received guidance."

Al-Anbiyāa, or The Prophets

In the name of Allah, Most Gracious, Most Merciful.

1. Closer and closer to mankind comes their Reckoning: yet they heed not and they turn away.

2. Never comes (aught) to them of a renewed Message from their Lord, but they listen to it as in jest,—

3. Their hearts toying as with trifles. The wrong-doers conceal their private counsels, (saying, "Is this (one) more than a man like yourselves? Will ye go to witchcraft with your eyes open?"

4.　Say: "My Lord knoweth (every) word (spoken) in the heavens and on earth: He is the One that heareth and knoweth (all things)."

5.　"Nay," they say, "(these are) medleys of dreams!—Nay, he forged it!—Nay, he is (but) a poet! Let him then bring us a Sign like the ones that were sent to (Prophets) of old!"

6.　(As to those) before them, not one of the towns which We destroyed believed: will these believe?

7.　Before thee, also, the messengers We sent were but men, to whom We granted inspiration: if ye know this not, ask of those who possess the Message.

8.　Nor did We give them bodies that ate no food, nor were they immortals.

9.　Then We fulfilled to them Our promise, and We saved them and those whom We willed but We destroyed those who transgressed beyond bounds.

10.　We have revealed for you (O men!) a book which will give you eminence. Will ye not then understand?

11.　How many were the towns We utterly destroyed because of their iniquities, setting up in their places other peoples?

12.　Yet, when they felt Our Punishment (coming), behold, they (tried to) flee from it.

13.　Flee not, but return to the good things of this life which were given you, and to your homes, in order that ye may be called to account.

14.　They said: "Ah! woe to us! We were indeed wrong-doers!"

15.　And that cry of theirs ceased not, till We made them as a field that is mown, as ashes silent and quenched.

16.　Not for (idle) sport did We create the

heavens and the earth and all that is between!

17. If it had been Our wish to take (just) a pastime, We should surely have taken it from the things nearest to Us, if We would do (such a thing)!

18. Nay, We hurl the Truth against falsehood, and it knocks out its brain, and behold, falsehood doth perish! Ah! woe be to you for the (false) things ye ascribe (to Us).

19. To Him belong all (creatures) in the heavens and on earth: even those who are with Him are not too proud to serve Him, nor are they (ever) weary (of His service):

20. They celebrate His praises night and day, nor do they ever flag or intermit.

21. Or have they taken (for worship) gods from the earth who can raise (the dead)?

22. If there were, in the heavens and the earth, other gods besides Allah, there would have been ruin in both! But glory to Allah, the Lord of the Throne: (High is He) above what they attribute to Him!

23. He cannot be questioned for His acts, but they will be questioned (for theirs).

24. Or have they taken for worship (other) gods besides Him? Say, "Bring your convincing proof: this is the Message of those with me and the Message of those before me." But most of them know not the Truth, and so turn away.

25. Not a messenger did We send before thee without this inspiration sent by Us to him: that there is no god but I; therefore worship and serve Me.

26. And they say: "The Most Gracious has taken a son." Glory to Him! They are (but) servants raised to honour.

27. They speak not before He speaks, and they act (in all things) by His command.

28. He knows what is before them, and what is behind them, and they offer no intercession except for those with whom He is well-pleased and they stand in awe and reverence of His (glory).

29. If any of them should say, "I am a god besides Him", such a one We should reward with Hell: thus do We reward those who do wrong.

30. Do not the Unbelievers see that the heavens and the earth were joined together (as one unit of Creation), before We clove them asunder? We made from water every living thing. Will they not then believe?

31. And We have set on the earth mountains standing firm, lest it should shake with them. and We have made therein broad highways (between mountains) for them to pass through: that they may find their way.

32. And We have made the heavens as a canopy well guarded: yet do they turn away from the Signs which these things (point to)!

33. It is He Who created the Night and the Day, and the sun and the moon: all (the celestial bodies) swim along, each in its rounded course.

34. We granted not to any man before thee permanent life (here): if then thou shouldst die, would they live permanently?

35. Every soul shall have a taste of death: and We test you by evil and by good by way of trial. To Us must ye return.

36. When the Unbelievers see thee, they treat thee not except with ridicule. "Is this," (they say), "The one who talks of your gods?" And they blaspheme at the mention of The Most Gracious!

37. Man is a creature of haste: soon (enough) will I show you My Signs; so ask Me not to hasten them!

38. They say: "When will this promise

come to pass, if ye are telling the truth?"

39. If only the Unbelievers knew (the time) when they will not be able to ward off the Fire from their faces, nor yet from their backs, and (when) no help can reach them!

40. Nay, it may come to them all of a sudden and confound them: no power will they have then to avert it, nor will they (then) get respite.

41. Mocked were (many) messengers before thee; but their scoffers were hemmed in by the thing that they mocked.

42. Say, "Who can keep you safe by night and by day from (the Wrath of) The Most Gracious?" Yet they turn away from the remembrance of their Lord.

43. Or have they gods that can guard them from Us? They have no power to aid themselves, nor can they be defended from Us.

44. Nay, We gave the good things of this life to these men and their fathers until the period grew long for them; see they not that We gradually reduce the land (in their control) from its outlying borders? Is it then they who will win?

45. Say, "I do but warn you according to revelation": but the deaf will not hear the call, (even) when they are warned!

46. If but a breath of the Wrath of thy Lord do touch them they will then say, "Woe to us! we did wrong indeed!"

47. We shall set up scales of justice for the day of Judgment, so that not a soul will be dealt with unjustly in the least. And if there be (no more than) the weight of a mustard seed, We will bring it (to account): and enough are We to take account.

48. In the past We granted to Moses and Aaron the Criterion (for judgment). And a Light and a Mess-age for those who would do right,—

وَلَقَدْ اٰتَيْنَا مُوْسٰى وَهٰرُوْنَ الْفُرْقَانَ وَضِيَاءً وَذِكْرًا لِلْمُتَّقِيْنَ ۞

49. Those who fear their Lord in their most secret thoughts, and who hold the Hour (of Judgment) in awe.

الَّذِيْنَ يَخْشَوْنَ رَبَّهُمْ بِالْغَيْبِ وَهُمْ مِّنَ السَّاعَةِ مُشْفِقُوْنَ ۞

50. And this is a blessed Message which We have sent down: will ye then reject it?

وَهٰذَا ذِكْرٌ مُّبٰرَكٌ اَنْزَلْنٰهُ اَفَاَنْتُمْ لَهٗ مُنْكِرُوْنَ ۞

51. We bestowed aforetime on Abraham his rectitude of conduct, and well were We acquainted with him.

وَلَقَدْ اٰتَيْنَا اِبْرٰهِيْمَ رُشْدَهٗ مِنْ قَبْلُ وَكُنَّا بِهٖ عٰلِمِيْنَ ۞

52. Behold! he said to his father and his people, "What are these images, to which ye are (so assiduously) devoted?"

اِذْ قَالَ لِاَبِيْهِ وَقَوْمِهٖ مَا هٰذِهِ التَّمَاثِيْلُ الَّتِيْ اَنْتُمْ لَهَا عٰكِفُوْنَ ۞

53. They said, "We found our fathers worshipping them."

قَالُوْا وَجَدْنَا اٰبَاءَنَا لَهَا عٰبِدِيْنَ ۞

54. He said, "Indeed ye have been in manifest error—ye and your fathers."

قَالَ لَقَدْ كُنْتُمْ اَنْتُمْ وَاٰبَاؤُكُمْ فِيْ ضَلٰلٍ مُّبِيْنٍ ۞

55. They said, "Have you brought us the Truth, or are you one of those who jest?"

قَالُوْا اَجِئْتَنَا بِالْحَقِّ اَمْ اَنْتَ مِنَ اللّٰعِبِيْنَ ۞

56. He said, "Nay, your Lord is the Lord of the heavens and the earth, He Who created them (from nothing): and I am a witness to this (truth).

قَالَ بَلْ رَّبُّكُمْ رَبُّ السَّمٰوٰتِ وَالْاَرْضِ الَّذِيْ فَطَرَهُنَّ وَاَنَا عَلٰى ذٰلِكُمْ مِّنَ الشّٰهِدِيْنَ ۞

57. "And by Allah, I will certainly plan against your idols—after ye go away and turn your backs"...

وَتَاللّٰهِ لَاَكِيْدَنَّ اَصْنَامَكُمْ بَعْدَ اَنْ تُوَلُّوْا مُدْبِرِيْنَ ۞

58. So he broke them to pieces, (all) but the biggest of them, that they might turn (and address themselves) to it.

فَجَعَلَهُمْ جُذَاذًا اِلَّا كَبِيْرًا لَّهُمْ لَعَلَّهُمْ اِلَيْهِ يَرْجِعُوْنَ ۞

59. They said, "Who has done this to our gods? He must indeed be one of the unjust one.

قَالُوْا مَنْ فَعَلَ هٰذَا بِاٰلِهَتِنَا اِنَّهٗ لَمِنَ الظّٰلِمِيْنَ ۞

60. They said, "We heard a youth talk of them: he is called Abraham."

قَالُوْا سَمِعْنَا فَتًى يَّذْكُرُهُمْ يُقَالُ لَهٗ اِبْرٰهِيْمُ ۞

61. They said, "Then bring him before the eyes of the people, that they may bear witness:"

قَالُوْا فَأْتُوْا بِهٖ عَلٰى اَعْيُنِ النَّاسِ لَعَلَّهُمْ يَشْهَدُوْنَ ۞

62. They said, "Art thou the one that did this with our gods, O Abraham?"

قَالُوٓاءَاَنْتَ فَعَلْتَ هٰذَا بِاٰلِهَتِنَا يَاۤبْرٰهِيْمُ ۞

63. He said: "Nay, this was done by this the biggest one! Ask them, if they can talk."

قَالَ بَلْ فَعَلَهٗ كَبِيْرُهُمْ هٰذَا فَسْـَٔلُوْهُمْ اِنْ كَانُوْا يَنْطِقُوْنَ ۞

64. So they turned to themselves and said, "Surely ye are the ones in the wrong!"

فَرَجَعُوْٓا اِلٰٓى اَنْفُسِهِمْ فَقَالُوْٓا اِنَّكُمْ اَنْتُمُ الظّٰلِمُوْنَ ۞

65. Then were they confounded with shame: (they said), "Thou knowest full well that these (idols) do not speak!"

ثُمَّ نُكِسُوْا عَلٰى رُءُوْسِهِمْ لَقَدْ عَلِمْتَ مَا هٰٓؤُلَآءِ يَنْطِقُوْنَ ۞

66. (Abraham) said, "Do ye then worship, besides Allah, things that can neither be of any good to you nor do you harm?

قَالَ اَفَتَعْبُدُوْنَ مِنْ دُوْنِ اللهِ مَا لَا يَنْفَعُكُمْ شَيْـًٔا وَّلَا يَضُرُّكُمْ ۞

67. "Fie upon you, and upon the things that ye worship besides Allah! Have ye no sense?"...

اُفٍّ لَّكُمْ وَلِمَا تَعْبُدُوْنَ مِنْ دُوْنِ اللهِ اَفَلَا تَعْقِلُوْنَ ۞

68. They said, "Burn him and protect your gods, if ye do (anything at all)!"

قَالُوْا حَرِّقُوْهُ وَانْصُرُوْٓا اٰلِهَتَكُمْ اِنْ كُنْتُمْ فٰعِلِيْنَ ۞

69. We said, "O Fire! be thou cool, and (a means of) safety for Abraham!"

قُلْنَا يٰنَارُ كُوْنِيْ بَرْدًا وَّسَلٰمًا عَلٰٓى اِبْرٰهِيْمَ ۞

70. Then they planned against him: but We made them the Greater losers.

وَاَرَادُوْا بِهٖ كَيْدًا فَجَعَلْنٰهُمُ الْاَخْسَرِيْنَ ۞

71. But We delivered him and (his nephew) Lût (and directed them) to the land which We have blessed for the nations.

وَنَجَّيْنٰهُ وَلُوْطًا اِلَى الْاَرْضِ الَّتِيْ بٰرَكْنَا فِيْهَا لِلْعٰلَمِيْنَ ۞

72. And We bestowed on him Isaac and, as an additional gift, (a grandson), Jacob, and We made righteous men of every one (of them).

وَوَهَبْنَا لَهٗٓ اِسْحٰقَ وَيَعْقُوْبَ نَافِلَةً وَكُلًّا جَعَلْنَا صٰلِحِيْنَ ۞

73. And We made them leaders, guiding (men) by Our Command, and We inspired them to do good deeds, to establish regular prayers, and to Give zakat and they constantly served Us (and Us only).

وَجَعَلْنٰهُمْ اَئِمَّةً يَّهْدُوْنَ بِاَمْرِنَا وَاَوْحَيْنَآ اِلَيْهِمْ فِعْلَ الْخَيْرٰتِ وَاِقَامَ الصَّلٰوةِ وَاِيْتَآءَ الزَّكٰوةِ ۚ وَكَانُوْا لَنَا عٰبِدِيْنَ ۞

74. And to Lût, too, We gave Judgment and Knowledge, and We saved him from the town which practised abominations: truly they were

وَلُوْطًا اٰتَيْنٰهُ حُكْمًا وَّعِلْمًا وَّنَجَّيْنٰهُ مِنَ الْقَرْيَةِ الَّتِيْ كَانَتْ تَّعْمَلُ الْخَبٰٓئِثَ ۚ

a people given to Evil, a rebellious people.

75. And We admitted him to Our Mercy: for he was one of the Righteous.

اِنَّهُمْ كَانُوْا قَوْمَ سَوْءٍ فٰسِقِيْنَ ۝

وَاَدْخَلْنٰهُ فِيْ رَحْمَتِنَا ۗ اِنَّهٗ مِنَ الصّٰلِحِيْنَ ۝

76. (Remember) Noah, when he cried (to Us) aforetime: We listened to his (prayer) and delivered him and his family from great distress.

وَنُوْحًا اِذْ نَادٰى مِنْ قَبْلُ فَاسْتَجَبْنَا لَهٗ فَنَجَّيْنٰهُ وَاَهْلَهٗ مِنَ الْكَرْبِ الْعَظِيْمِ ۝

77. We helped him against people who rejected Our Signs: truly they were a people given to Evil: so We drowned them (in the Flood) all together.

وَنَصَرْنٰهُ مِنَ الْقَوْمِ الَّذِيْنَ كَذَّبُوْا بِاٰيٰتِنَا ۗ اِنَّهُمْ كَانُوْا قَوْمَ سَوْءٍ فَاَغْرَقْنٰهُمْ اَجْمَعِيْنَ ۝

78. And remember David and Solomon, when they gave judgment in the matter of the field into which the sheep of certain people had strayed by night: We did witness their judgment.

وَدَاوٗدَ وَسُلَيْمٰنَ اِذْ يَحْكُمٰنِ فِى الْحَرْثِ اِذْ نَفَشَتْ فِيْهِ غَنَمُ الْقَوْمِ ۚ وَكُنَّا لِحُكْمِهِمْ شٰهِدِيْنَ ۝

79. To Solomon We inspired the (right) understanding of the matter: to each (of them) We gave Judgment and Knowledge; it was Our power that made the hills and the birds celebrate Our praises, with David: it was We Who did (all these things).

فَفَهَّمْنٰهَا سُلَيْمٰنَ ۚ وَكُلًّا اٰتَيْنَا حُكْمًا وَّعِلْمًا ۗ وَّسَخَّرْنَا مَعَ دَاوٗدَ الْجِبَالَ يُسَبِّحْنَ وَالطَّيْرَ ۚ وَكُنَّا فٰعِلِيْنَ ۝

80. It was We Who taught him the making of coats of mail for your bene-fit, to guard you from each other's violence: will ye then be grateful?

وَعَلَّمْنٰهُ صَنْعَةَ لَبُوْسٍ لَّكُمْ لِتُحْصِنَكُمْ مِّنْ بَاْسِكُمْ ۚ فَهَلْ اَنْتُمْ شٰكِرُوْنَ ۝

81. (It was Our power that made) the violent (unruly) wind flow (tamely) for Solomon, to his order, to the land which We had blessed: for We do know all things.

وَلِسُلَيْمٰنَ الرِّيْحَ عَاصِفَةً تَجْرِيْ بِاَمْرِهٖ اِلَى الْاَرْضِ الَّتِيْ بٰرَكْنَا فِيْهَا ۚ وَكُنَّا بِكُلِّ شَيْءٍ عٰلِمِيْنَ ۝

82. And of Satans were some who dived for him, and did other work besides; and it was We Who guarded them.

وَمِنَ الشَّيٰطِيْنِ مَنْ يَّغُوْصُوْنَ لَهٗ وَيَعْمَلُوْنَ عَمَلًا دُوْنَ ذٰلِكَ ۚ وَكُنَّا لَهُمْ حٰفِظِيْنَ ۝

83. And (remember) Job, when he cried to his Lord "Truly distress has seized me, but Thou art the Most Merciful of those that are Merciful."

وَاَيُّوْبَ اِذْ نَادٰى رَبَّهٗ اَنِّيْ مَسَّنِيَ الضُّرُّ وَاَنْتَ اَرْحَمُ الرّٰحِمِيْنَ ۝

84. So We listened to him: We removed the distress that was on him, and We

فَاسْتَجَبْنَا لَهٗ فَكَشَفْنَا مَا بِهٖ مِنْ ضُرٍّ وَّاٰتَيْنٰهُ اَهْلَهٗ وَمِثْلَهُمْ مَّعَهُمْ

restored his people to him, and doubled their number,—as a Grace from Ourselves, and a thing for commemoration, for all who serve Us.

85. And (remember) Ismā'īl Idrîs, and Zul-kifl, all (men) of constancy and patience;

86. We admitted them to Our Mercy: for they were of the Righteous ones.

87. And remember Zun-nûn, when he departed in wrath: he imagined that We had no power over him! but he cried through the depths of darkness, "There is no god but Thou: glory to Thee: I was indeed wrong!"

88. So We listened to him: and delivered him from distress: and thus do We deliver those who have faith.

89. And (remember) Zakariyā, when he cried to his Lord: "O my Lord! leave me not without offspring, tho-ugh Thou art the best of inheritors."

90. So We listened to him: and We granted him Yahyā: We cured his wife's (barrenness) for him. These (three) were ever quick in doing in good works: they used to call on Us in yearning and awe and humble themselves before Us.

91. And (remember) her who guarded her chastity: We breathed into her from Our spirit, and We made her and her son a Sign for all peoples.

92. Verily, this Ummah of yours is a single Ummah and I am your Lord and Cherisher: therefore serve Me (and no other).

93. But (later generations) cut off their affair (of unity), one from another: (yet) will they all return to Us.

94. Whoever works any act of Righteous-ness and has Faith,— his endeavour will not be rejected: We shall record it in his favour.

95. But there is a ban on any population which We have destroyed: that they shall not return,

96. Until the Gog and Magog (people) are let through (their barrier), and they swiftly swarm from every hill.

97. Then will the True Promise draw nigh (of fulfilment): then behold! the eyes of the Unbelievers will fixedly stare in horror: "Ah! woe to us! we were indeed heedless of this; nay; we truly did wrong!"

98. Verily ye, (Unbelievers), and the (false) gods that ye worship besides Allah, are (but) fuel for Hell! To it will ye (surely) come!

99. If these had been gods, they would not have got there! But each one will abide therein.

100. There, sobbing will be their lot, nor will they there hear (aught else).

101. Those for whom the Good from Us has gone before, will be removed far therefrom.

102. Not the slightest sound will they hear of Hell: what their souls desired, in that will they dwell.

103. The Great Terror will bring them no grief: but the angels will meet them (with mutual greetings): "This is your Day,—(the Day) that ye were promised."

104. The Day that We roll up the heavens like a scroll rolled up for books (completed),— even as We produced the first Creation, so shall We produce a new one: a promise We have undertaken: truly shall We fulfil it.

105. Before this We wrote in the Psalms, after the Message (given to Moses): "My servants, the righteous, shall inherit the earth."

106. Verily in this (Qur'an) is a Message for people who would (truly) worship Allah.

وَحَرَامٌ عَلَىٰ قَرْيَةٍ أَهْلَكْنَاهَا أَنَّهُمْ لَا يَرْجِعُونَ ۝

حَتَّىٰ إِذَا فُتِحَتْ يَأْجُوجُ وَمَأْجُوجُ وَهُم مِّن كُلِّ حَدَبٍ يَنسِلُونَ ۝

وَاقْتَرَبَ الْوَعْدُ الْحَقُّ فَإِذَا هِيَ شَاخِصَةٌ أَبْصَارُ الَّذِينَ كَفَرُوا يَٰوَيْلَنَا قَدْ كُنَّا فِي غَفْلَةٍ مِّنْ هَٰذَا بَلْ كُنَّا ظَالِمِينَ ۝

إِنَّكُمْ وَمَا تَعْبُدُونَ مِن دُونِ اللَّهِ حَصَبُ جَهَنَّمَ أَنتُمْ لَهَا وَارِدُونَ ۝

لَوْ كَانَ هَٰؤُلَاءِ آلِهَةً مَّا وَرَدُوهَا وَكُلٌّ فِيهَا خَالِدُونَ ۝

لَهُمْ فِيهَا زَفِيرٌ وَهُمْ فِيهَا لَا يَسْمَعُونَ ۝

إِنَّ الَّذِينَ سَبَقَتْ لَهُم مِّنَّا الْحُسْنَىٰ أُولَٰئِكَ عَنْهَا مُبْعَدُونَ ۝

لَا يَسْمَعُونَ حَسِيسَهَا وَهُمْ فِي مَا اشْتَهَتْ أَنفُسُهُمْ خَالِدُونَ ۝

لَا يَحْزُنُهُمُ الْفَزَعُ الْأَكْبَرُ وَتَتَلَقَّاهُمُ الْمَلَائِكَةُ هَٰذَا يَوْمُكُمُ الَّذِي كُنتُمْ تُوعَدُونَ ۝

يَوْمَ نَطْوِي السَّمَاءَ كَطَيِّ السِّجِلِّ لِلْكُتُبِ كَمَا بَدَأْنَا أَوَّلَ خَلْقٍ نُّعِيدُهُ وَعْدًا عَلَيْنَا إِنَّا كُنَّا فَاعِلِينَ ۝

وَلَقَدْ كَتَبْنَا فِي الزَّبُورِ مِن بَعْدِ الذِّكْرِ أَنَّ الْأَرْضَ يَرِثُهَا عِبَادِيَ الصَّالِحُونَ ۝

إِنَّ فِي هَٰذَا لَبَلَاغًا لِّقَوْمٍ عَابِدِينَ ۝

SÛRA–22

AL-ḤAJJ

(INTRODUCTION)

We now come to a new series of four Sûras, dealing with the environments and methods contributing to our spiritual progress, as the last five Sûras dealt with the Messengers who came in various ways to proclaim the Truth and conquer evil. See Introduction to S. 17.

The subject-matter of this particular Sûra is concerned mainly with the spiritual implications of the Sacred House, the Pilgrimage, the Sacrifices, Striving and Fighting in defence of Truth when attacked, and other acts that make for Unselfishness and uproot Falsehood.

On the chronology of this Sûra, opinion is divided. Some parts were probably revealed in the later Makkan period, and some in Madinah. But the chronological question has no significance here.

107. We sent thee not, but as a Mercy for all creatures.

108. Say: "What has come to me by inspiration is that your God is One God: will ye therefore bow to His Will (in Islām)?"

109. But if they turn back, say: "I have proclaimed the Message to you all alike and in truth; but I know not whether that which ye are promised is near or far.

110. "It is He Who knows what is open in speech and what ye hide (in your hearts).

111. "I know not but that it may be a trial for you, and a grant of (worldly) livelihood (to you) for a time."

112. Say: "O my Lord! judge Thou in truth!" "Our Lord Most Gracious is the One Whose assistance should be sought against the blasphemies ye utter!"

Al-Ḥajj, or The Pilgrimage

In the name of Allah, Most Gracious, Most Merciful.

1.   O mankind! Fear your Lord! for the convulsion of the Hour (of Judgment) will be a thing terrible!

2.   The Day ye shall see it, every mother giving suck shall forget her suckling-babe, and every pregnant female shall drop her load (unformed): thou shalt see mankind as in a drunken riot, yet not drunk: but dreadful will be the Chastisement of Allah.

3.   And yet among men there are such as dispute about Allah, without knowledge, and follow every Satan obstinate in rebellion!

4.   About whom (Satan) it is decreed that whoever turns to him for friendship, him will he lead astray, and he will guide him to the Chastisement of the Fire.

5.   O mankind! if ye have a doubt about the Resurrection, (consider) that We created you out of dust, then out of sperm, then out of a leech-like clot, then out of a morsel of flesh, partly formed and partly unformed, in

order that We may manifest (Our power) to you; and We cause whom We will to rest in the wombs for an appointed term, then do We bring you out as babes, then (foster you) that ye may reach your age of full strength; and some of you are called to die, and some are sent back to the feeblest old age, so that they know nothing after having known (much). And (further), thou seest the earth barren and lifeless, but when We pour down rain on it, it is stirred (to life), it swells, and it puts forth every kind of beautiful growth (in pairs).

6. This is so, because Allah is the Reality: it is He Who gives life to the dead, and it is He Who has power over all things.

7. And verily the Hour will come: there can be no doubt about it, or about (the fact) that Allah will raise up all who are in the graves.

8. Yet there is among men such a one as disputes about Allah, without knowledge, without guidance, and without a Book of Enlightenment,—

9. (Disdainfully) bending his side, in order to lead (men) astray from the Path of Allah: for him there is disgrace in this life, and on the Day of Judgment We shall make him taste the chastisement of burning (Fire).

10. (It will be said): "This is because of the deeds which thy hands sent forth, for verily Allah is not unjust to His servants."

11. There are among men some who serve Allah, as it were, on the verge: if good befalls them, they are, therewith, well content; but if a trial comes to them, they turn on their faces: they lose both this world and the Hereafter: that is indeed the manifest loss.

12. They call on such deities, besides Allah, as can neither hurt nor profit them: that is straying far indeed (from the Way)!

13. (Perhaps) they call on one whose hurt is nearer than his profit: evil, indeed, is the

patron, and evil the companion (for help)!

14. Verily Allah will admit those who believe and work righteous deeds. to Gardens, beneath which rivers flow: for Allah carries out all that He desires.

15. If any think that Allah will not help him (His Messenger) in this world and the Hereafter, let him stretch out a rope to the ceiling and cut (himself) off: then let him see whether his plan will remove that which enrages (him)!

16. Thus have We sent down Clear Signs; and verily Allah doth guide whom He will!

17. Those who believe (in the Qur-ān), those who follow the Jewish (scriptures), and the Sabians, Christians, Magians, and Polytheists,— Allah will judge between them on the Day of Judgment: for Allah is witness of all things.

18. Seest thou not that to Allah prostrate all things that are in the heavens and on earth,— the sun, the moon, the stars; the hills, the trees, the animals; and a great number among mankind? But a great number are (also) such as unto whom the Chastisement is justly due. And such as Allah shall disgrace,— none can raise to honour: for Allah carries out all that He wills.

19. These two antagonists dispute with each other about their Lord: but those who deny (their Lord),—for them will be cut out a garment of Fire: over their heads will be poured out boiling water.

20. With it will be melted what is within their bodies, as well as (their) skins.

21. in addition there will be maces of iron (to punish) them.

22. Every time they wish to get away

therefrom, from anguish, they will be forced back therein, and (it will be said). "Taste ye the Chastisement of Burning!"

23. Allah will admit those who believe and work righteous deeds, to Gardens beneath which rivers flow: they shall be adorned therein with bracelets of gold and pearls; and their garments there will be of silk.

24. For they have been guided (in this life) to the purest of speeches; they have been guided to the Path of Him Who is Worthy of (all) Praise.

25. As to those who have rejected (Allah), and would keep back (men) from the Way of Allah, and from the Sacred Mosque, which We have made (open) to (all) men—equal is the dweller there and the visitor from the country— and any whose purpose therein is profanity wrongfully them will We cause to taste of a most grievous Chastisement.

26. Behold! We pointed the site, to Abraham, of the (Sacred) House, (saying): "Associate not anything (in worship) with Me; and sanctify My House for those who compass it round, or stand up, or bow, or prostrate themselves (therein in prayer).

27. "And proclaim the Pilgrimage among men: they will come to thee on foot and (mounted) on every camel, lean (on account of journeys) through deep and distant mountain highways;

28. "That they may witness the benefits (provided) for them, and celebrate the name of Allah, through the Days appointed, over the cattle which He has provided for them (for sacrifice): then eat ye thereof and feed the distressed ones in want.

29. "Then let them complete the rites prescribed for them, fulfil their vows, and (again) circumambulate the Ancient House."

30. Such (is the Pilgrimage): whoever honours the sacred rites of Allah, for him it is good in the sight of his Lord. Lawful to

you (for food in Pilgrimage) are cattle, except those mentioned to you (as exceptions): so shun the abomination of idols, and shun the word that is false,—

31. Being true in faith to Allah, and never assigning partners to Him: if anyone assigns partners to Allah, he is as if he had fallen from heaven and been snatched up by birds, or the wind had swooped (like a bird on its prey) and thrown him into a far-distant place.

32. Such (is his state): and whoever holds in honour the Rites of Allah, (in the sacrifice of animals), such (honour) should come truly from piety of heart.

33. In them ye have benefits for a term appointed: in the end their place of sacrifice is near the Ancient House.

34. To every people did We appoint rites (of sacrifice), that they might celebrate the name of Allah over the sustenance He gave them from animals (fit for food). But your God is One God: submit then your wills to Him (in Islam): and give thou the good news to those who humble themselves,—

35. To those whose hearts, when Allah is mentioned, are filled with fear, who show patient perseverance over their afflictions, keep up regular prayer, and spend (in charity) out of what We have bestowed upon them.

36. The sacrificial camels We have made for you as among the Signs from Allah: in them is (much) good for you: then pronounce the name of Allah over them as they line up (for sacrifice): when they are down on their sides (after slaughter), eat ye thereof, and feed such as (beg not but) live in contentment, and such as beg with due humility: thus have We made animals subject to you, that ye may be grateful.

37. It is not their meat nor their blood, that reaches Allah: it is your piety that reaches Him: He has thus made them subject to you, that ye may glorify Allah for His guidance to you: and proclaim the Good News to all who do good.

38. Verily Allah will defend (from ill) those who believe: verily, Allah loveth not any

that is unfaithful, ungrateful.

39. To those against whom war is made, permission is given to (fight), because they are wronged;— and verily, Allah is Most Powerful for their aid;—

40. (They are those who have been expelled from their homes in defiance of right,— (for no cause) except that they say, "Our Lord is Allah". Did not Allah check one set of people by means of another, there would surely have been pulled down monasteries, churches, synagogues, and mosques, in which the name of Allah is commemorated in abundant measure. Allah will certainly aid those who aid His (cause);— for verily Allah is Full of strength, Exalted in Might, (Able to enforce His Will).

41. (They are) those who, if We establish them in the land, establish regular prayer and give zakat, enjoin the right and forbid wrong: with Allah rests the end (and decision) of (all) affairs.

42. If they disbelieve you so did the Peoples before them (with their Prophets),— the People of Noah, and 'Ad and Thamûd;

43. And those of Abraham and Lût;

44. And the Companions of the Madyan people; and Moses was rejected (in the same way). But I granted respite to the Unbelievers, and (only) after that did I punish them: but how (terrible) was My punishment (of them)!

45. How many populations have We destroyed, which were given to wrong-doing? They tumbled down on their roofs. And how many wells are lying idle and neglected, and castles lofty and well-built?

46. Do they not travel through the land, so that their hearts (and minds) may thus learn wisdom and their ears may thus learn to hear? Truly it is not the eyes that are blind, but the hearts which are in their breasts.

47. Yet they ask thee to hasten on the Punishment! But Allah will not fail in His promise. Verily a Day in the sight of thy Lord is like a thousand years of your reckoning.

48. And to how many populations did I give respite, which were given to wrong-doing? In the end I punished them. To Me is the destination (of all).

49. Say: O men! I am (sent) to you only to give a clear warning:

50. "Those who believe and work righteousness, for them is forgiveness and a sustenance most generous.

51. "But those who strive against Our Signs, to frustrate them,—they will be companions of the Fire."

52. Never did We send a messenger or a prophet before thee, but, when he framed a desire, Satan threw some (vanity) into his desire: but Allah will cancel anything (vain) that Satan throws in, and Allah will confirm (and establish) His Signs: for Allah is full of knowledge and wisdom:

53. That He may make the suggestions thrown in by Satan, but a trial for those in whose hearts is a disease and who are hardened of heart: verily the wrong-doers are in a schism far (from the Truth):

54. And that those on whom knowledge has been bestowed may learn that the (Qur'an) is the Truth from thy Lord, and that they may believe therein, and their hearts may be made humbly (open) to it: for verily Allah is the Guide of those who believe, to the Straight Way.

55. Those who reject Faith will not cease to be in doubt concerning (Revelation) until the Hour (of Judgment) comes suddenly upon them. or there comes to them the Chastisement of a barren day.

56. On that Day the Dominion will be that of Allah: He will judge between them: so those who believe and work righteous deeds will be in Gardens of Delight.

57. And for those who reject Faith and deny Our Signs, there will be a humiliating punishment.

58. Those who leave their homes in the cause of Allah, and are then slain or die,— on them will Allah bestow verily a goodly Provision: truly Allah is He Who bestows the best Provision.

59. Verily He will admit them to a place with which they shall be well pleased: for Allah is All-Knowing, Most Forbearing.

60. That (is so). And if one has retaliated to no greater extent than the injury he received, and is again set upon inordinately, Allah will help Him: for Allah is One That blots out (sins) and forgives (again and again).

61. That is because Allah merges Night into Day, and He merges Day into Night, and verily it is Allah Who hears and sees (all things).

62. That is because Allah—He is the Reality; and those besides Him whom they invoke,— they are but vain Falsehood: verily Allah is He, Most High, Most Great.

63. Seest thou not that Allah sends down rain from the sky, and forthwith the earth becomes clothed with green? For Allah is All-subtle, All-Aware.

64. To Him belongs all that is in the heavens and on earth: for verily Allah,—He is free of all wants, worthy of all praise.

65. Seest thou not that Allah has made subject to you (men) all that is on the earth, and the ships that sail through the sea by His command? He withholds the sky from

falling on the earth except by His leave: for Allah is Most Kind and Most Merciful to man.

66. It is He Who gave you life, will cause you to die, and will again give you Life: truly man is a most ungrateful creature!

67. To every People have We appointed rites which they must follow: let them not then dispute with thee on the matter, but do thou invite (them) to thy Lord: for thou art assuredly on the Right Way.

68. If they do wrangle with thee, say, "Allah knows best what it is ye are doing."

69. "Allah will judge between you on the Day of Judgment concerning the matters in which ye differ."

70. Knowest thou not that Allah knows all that is in heaven and on earth? Indeed it is all in a record, and that is easy for Allah.

71. Yet they worship, besides Allah, things for which no authority has been sent down to them, and of which they have (really) no knowledge: for those that do wrong there is no helper.

72. When Our Clear Signs are rehearsed to them, thou wilt notice a denial on the faces of the Unbelievers! They nearly attack with violence those who rehearse Our Signs to them. Say, "Shall I tell you of something (far) worse than that? It is the Fire (of Hell)! Allah has promised it to the Unbelievers! And evil is that destination!"

73. O men! Here is a parable set forth! Listen to it! Those on whom, besides Allah, ye call, cannot create (even) a fly, if they all met together for the purpose! And if the fly should snatch away anything from them, they would have no power to release it from the fly.

SÛRA–23
AL-MÛMINÛN
(INTRODUCTION)

This Sûra deals with the virtues which are the seed-bed of Faith, especially in an environment in which Truth is denied and its votaries insulted and persecuted. But Truth is One and must prevail. Those who do wrong will be filled with vain regrets when it is too late for repentance.

It belongs to the late Makkan period.

Feeble are those who petition and those whom they petition!

74. They do not have right estimate of Allah, for Allah is Powerful and Mighty.

75. Allah chooses Messengers from angels and from men for Allah is He Who hears and sees (all things).

76. He knows what is before them and what is behind them: and to Allah go back all affairs (for decision).

77. O ye who believe! bow down, prostrate yourselves, and adore your Lord; and do good; that ye may prosper.

78. And strive in His cause as ye ought to strive, (with sincerity and under discipline). He has chosen you, and has imposed no difficulties on you in religion; it is the religion of your father Abraham. It is He Who has named you Muslims, both before and in this (Revelation); that the Messenger may be a witness for you, and ye be witnesses for mankind! So establish regular Prayer, give zakat and hold fast to Allah! He is your Protector—the Best to protect and the Best to help!

Al-Mûminûn, or The Believers

In the name of Allah, Most Gracious, Most Merciful.

1. Successful indeed are the Believers,—

2. Those who humble themselves in their prayers;

3. Who avoid vain talk;

4. Who are active in giving zakat;

5. Who guard their modesty,

6. Except with those joined to them in the marriage bond, or (the captives) whom their right hands possess,— for (in their case) they are free from blame,

7. But those whose desires exceed those

limits are transgressors;—

8.   Those who faithfully observe their trusts and their covenants;

9.   And who (strictly) guard their prayers;—

10.   These will be the heirs,

11.   Who will inherit Paradise: they will dwell therein (for ever).

12.   Man We did create from a quintessence (of clay);

13.   Then We placed him as (a drop of) sperm in a place of rest, firmly fixed;

14.   Then We made the sperm into a clot of congealed blood; then of that clot We made a (foetus) lump; then We made out of that lump bones and clothed the bones with flesh; then We developed out of it another creature. So blessed be Allah, the Best to create!

15.   After that, at length ye will die.

16.   Again, on the Day of Judgment, will ye be raised up.

17.   And We have made, above you, seven tracts; and We are never unmindful of (Our) Creation.

8.   And We send down water from the sky according to (due) measure, and We cause it to soak in the soil; and We certainly are able to drain it off (with ease).

19.   With it We grow for you gardens of date-palms and vines: in them have ye abundant fruits: and of them ye eat (and have enjoyment),—

20.   Also a tree springing out of Mount Sinai, which produces oil, and relish for those who use it for food.

21.   And in cattle (too) ye have an instructive example: from within their bodies

We produce (milk) for you to drink; there are, in them, (besides), numerous (other) benefits for you; and of their (meat) ye eat;

22. And on them, as well as in ships, ye ride.

23. And certainly we sent Noah to his people: he said, "O my people! worship Allah! Ye have no other god but Him. Will ye not fear (Him)?"

24. The chiefs of the Unbelievers among his people said: "he is no more than a man like yourselves: his wish is to assert his superiority over you: if Allah had wished (to send messengers), He could have sent down angels: never did we hear such a thing (as he says), among our ancestors of old."

25. (And some said): "He is only a man possessed: wait (and have patience) with him for a time."

26. (Noah) said: "O my Lord! help me: for that they accuse me of falsehood!"

27. So We inspired him (with this message); "Construct the Ark within Our sight and under Our guidance: then when comes Our command, and the oven gushes forth, take thou on board pairs of every species, male and female, and thy family—except those of them against whom the Word has already gone forth: and address Me not in favour of the wrong-doers: for they shall be drowned (in the Flood).

28. And when thou hast embarked On the Ark—thou and those with thee,—say: "Praise be to Allah, Who has saved us from the people who do wrong."

29. And say: "O my Lord! enable me to disembark with Thy blessing: for Thou Art the Best to enable (us) to disembark."

30. Verily in this there are Signs (for men to understand); lo! We put (men) to test.

31. Then We raised after them another generation.

32. And We sent to them a messenger from among themselves, (saying), "Worship

Allah! Ye have no other god but Him. Will ye not fear (Him)?"

اللهَ مَالَكُمْ مِّنْ اِلٰهٍ غَيْرُهٗ ۗ اَفَلَا تَتَّقُوْنَ ۞

33. And the chiefs of his people, who disbelieved and denied the Meeting in the Hereafter, and on whom We had bestowed the good things of this life, said: "He is no more than a man like yourselves: he eats and drinks of what ye drink.

وَقَالَ الْمَلَاُ مِنْ قَوْمِهِ الَّذِيْنَ كَفَرُوْا وَكَذَّبُوْا بِلِقَآءِ الْاٰخِرَةِ وَاَتْرَفْنٰهُمْ فِى الْحَيٰوةِ الدُّنْيَا ۙ مَا هٰذَا اِلَّا بَشَرٌ مِّثْلُكُمْ ۙ يَأْكُلُ مِمَّا تَأْكُلُوْنَ مِنْهُ وَيَشْرَبُ مِمَّا تَشْرَبُوْنَ ۞

34. "If ye obey a man like yourselves, behold, it is certain ye will be lost.

وَلَئِنْ اَطَعْتُمْ بَشَرًا مِّثْلَكُمْ ۙ اِنَّكُمْ اِذًا لَّخٰسِرُوْنَ ۞

35. "Does he promise that when ye die and become dust and bones, ye shall be brought forth (again)?

اَيَعِدُكُمْ اَنَّكُمْ اِذَا مِتُّمْ وَكُنْتُمْ تُرَابًا وَّعِظَامًا اَنَّكُمْ مُّخْرَجُوْنَ ۞

36. "Far, very far is that which ye are promised!

هَيْهَاتَ هَيْهَاتَ لِمَا تُوْعَدُوْنَ ۞

37. "There is nothing but our life in this world! We shall die and we live! But we shall never be raised up again!

اِنْ هِيَ اِلَّا حَيَاتُنَا الدُّنْيَا نَمُوْتُ وَنَحْيَا وَمَا نَحْنُ بِمَبْعُوْثِيْنَ ۞

38. "He is only a man who invents a lie against Allah, but we are not the ones to believe in him!

اِنْ هُوَ اِلَّا رَجُلُ ﹰ افْتَرٰى عَلَى اللهِ كَذِبًا وَّمَا نَحْنُ لَهٗ بِمُؤْمِنِيْنَ ۞

39. (The prophet) said: "O my Lord help me: for that they accuse me of falsehood."

قَالَ رَبِّ انْصُرْنِيْ بِمَا كَذَّبُوْنِ ۞

40. (Allah) said: "In but a little while, they are sure to be sorry!"

قَالَ عَمَّا قَلِيْلٍ لَّيُصْبِحُنَّ نٰدِمِيْنَ ۞

41. Then the Blast overtook them with justice, and We made them as rubbish of dead leaves so away with the people who do wrong!

فَاَخَذَتْهُمُ الصَّيْحَةُ بِالْحَقِّ فَجَعَلْنٰهُمْ غُثَآءً ۚ فَبُعْدًا لِّلْقَوْمِ الظّٰلِمِيْنَ ۞

42. Then We raised after them other generations.

ثُمَّ اَنْشَأْنَا مِنْ بَعْدِهِمْ قُرُوْنًا اٰخَرِيْنَ ۞

43. No people can hasten their term, nor can they delay (it).

مَا تَسْبِقُ مِنْ اُمَّةٍ اَجَلَهَا وَمَا يَسْتَأْخِرُوْنَ ۞

44. Then sent We Our messengers in succession: every time there came to a people their messenger, they accused him of falsehood: so We made them follow each other (in punishment): We made them as a tale (that is told): so away with a people that will not believe!

ثُمَّ اَرْسَلْنَا رُسُلَنَا تَتْرَا ۗ كُلَّ مَا جَآءَ اُمَّةً رَّسُوْلُهَا كَذَّبُوْهُ فَاَتْبَعْنَا بَعْضَهُمْ بَعْضًا وَّجَعَلْنٰهُمْ اَحَادِيْثَ ۚ فَبُعْدًا لِّقَوْمٍ لَّا يُؤْمِنُوْنَ ۞

45. Then We sent Moses and his brother

ثُمَّ اَرْسَلْنَا مُوْسٰى وَاَخَاهُ هٰرُوْنَ ۙ

Aaron, with Our Signs and authority manifest,

46. To Pharaoh and his Chiefs: but these behaved insolently: they were an arrogant people.

47. They said: "Shall we believe in two men like ourselves? And their people are subject to us!"

48. So they rejected them and they became of those who were destroyed.

49. And We gave Moses the Book, in order that they might receive guidance.

50. And We made the son of Mary and his mother as a Sign: We gave them both shelter on high ground, affording rest and security and furnished with springs.

51. O ye messengers! enjoy (all) things good and pure, and work righteousness: for I am well-acquainted with (all) that ye do.

52. And verily this Ummah of yours is a single Ummah and I am your Lord and Cherisher: therefore fear Me (and no other).

53. But people have cut off their affair (of unity), between them, into sects: each party rejoices in that which is with itself.

54. But leave them in their confused ignorance for a time.

55. Do they think that because We have granted them abundance of wealth and sons,

56. We would hasten them on in every good? Nay they do not perceive.

57. Verily those who live in awe for fear of their Lord;

58. Those who believe in the Signs of their Lord;

59. Those who join not (in worship) partners with their Lord;

60. And those who dispense their charity with their hearts full of fear, because they will return to their Lord;—

بِاٰيٰتِنَا وَسُلْطٰنٍ مُّبِيْنٍ ۝

اِلٰى فِرْعَوْنَ وَمَلَا۟ىِٕهٖ فَاسْتَكْبَرُوْا وَكَانُوْا قَوْمًا عَالِيْنَ ۝

فَقَالُوْٓا اَنُؤْمِنُ لِبَشَرَيْنِ مِثْلِنَا وَقَوْمُهُمَا لَنَا عٰبِدُوْنَ ۝

فَكَذَّبُوْهُمَا فَكَانُوْا مِنَ الْمُهْلَكِيْنَ ۝

وَلَقَدْ اٰتَيْنَا مُوْسَى الْكِتٰبَ لَعَلَّهُمْ يَهْتَدُوْنَ ۝

وَجَعَلْنَا ابْنَ مَرْيَمَ وَاُمَّهٗٓ اٰيَةً وَّ اٰوَيْنٰهُمَآ اِلٰى رَبْوَةٍ ذَاتِ قَرَارٍ وَّمَعِيْنٍ ۝

يٰٓاَيُّهَا الرُّسُلُ كُلُوْا مِنَ الطَّيِّبٰتِ وَ اعْمَلُوْا صَالِحًا ۖ اِنِّيْ بِمَا تَعْمَلُوْنَ عَلِيْمٌ ۝

وَاِنَّ هٰذِهٖٓ اُمَّتُكُمْ اُمَّةً وَّاحِدَةً وَّ اَنَا رَبُّكُمْ فَاتَّقُوْنِ ۝

فَتَقَطَّعُوْٓا اَمْرَهُمْ بَيْنَهُمْ زُبُرًا ۖ كُلُّ حِزْبٍۭ بِمَا لَدَيْهِمْ فَرِحُوْنَ ۝

فَذَرْهُمْ فِيْ غَمْرَتِهِمْ حَتّٰى حِيْنٍ ۝

اَيَحْسَبُوْنَ اَنَّمَا نُمِدُّهُمْ بِهٖ مِنْ مَّالٍ وَّبَنِيْنَ ۝

نُسَارِعُ لَهُمْ فِي الْخَيْرٰتِ ۖ بَلْ لَّا يَشْعُرُوْنَ ۝

اِنَّ الَّذِيْنَ هُمْ مِّنْ خَشْيَةِ رَبِّهِمْ مُّشْفِقُوْنَ ۝

وَالَّذِيْنَ هُمْ بِاٰيٰتِ رَبِّهِمْ يُؤْمِنُوْنَ ۝

وَالَّذِيْنَ هُمْ بِرَبِّهِمْ لَا يُشْرِكُوْنَ ۝

وَالَّذِيْنَ يُؤْتُوْنَ مَآ اٰتَوْا وَّ قُلُوْبُهُمْ وَجِلَةٌ اَنَّهُمْ اِلٰى رَبِّهِمْ رٰجِعُوْنَ ۝

61. It is these who hasten in every good work, and these who are foremost in them.

أُولَٰٓئِكَ يُسَارِعُونَ فِى الْخَيْرَٰتِ وَهُمْ لَهَا سَٰبِقُونَ ۝

62. On no soul do We place a burden greater than it can bear: before Us is a record which clearly speaks the truth. They will never be wronged.

وَلَا نُكَلِّفُ نَفْسًا إِلَّا وُسْعَهَا وَلَدَيْنَا كِتَٰبٌ يَنطِقُ بِالْحَقِّ وَهُمْ لَا يُظْلَمُونَ ۝

63. But their hearts are in confused ignorance of this; and there are, besides that, deeds of theirs, which they will (continue) to do,—

بَلْ قُلُوبُهُمْ فِى غَمْرَةٍ مِّنْ هَٰذَا وَلَهُمْ أَعْمَٰلٌ مِّن دُونِ ذَٰلِكَ هُمْ لَهَا عَٰمِلُونَ ۝

64. Until, when We seize in Punishment those of them who received the good things of this world, behold, they will groan in supplication!

حَتَّىٰٓ إِذَآ أَخَذْنَا مُتْرَفِيهِم بِالْعَذَابِ إِذَا هُمْ يَجْـَٔرُونَ ۝

65. (It will be said): "Groan not in supplication this day; for ye shall certainly not be helped by Us.

لَا تَجْـَٔرُوا الْيَوْمَ إِنَّكُم مِّنَّا لَا تُنصَرُونَ ۝

66. "My Signs used to be rehearsed to you, but ye used to turn back on your heels—

قَدْ كَانَتْ ءَايَٰتِى تُتْلَىٰ عَلَيْكُمْ فَكُنتُمْ عَلَىٰٓ أَعْقَٰبِكُمْ تَنكِصُونَ ۝

67. "In arrogance: talking nonsense about the (Qur'an), like one telling fables by night."

مُسْتَكْبِرِينَ بِهِۦ سَٰمِرًا تَهْجُرُونَ ۝

68. Do they not ponder over the Word (of Allah), or has anything (new) come to them that did not come to their fathers of old?

أَفَلَمْ يَدَّبَّرُوا الْقَوْلَ أَمْ جَآءَهُم مَّا لَمْ يَأْتِ ءَابَآءَهُمُ الْأَوَّلِينَ ۝

69. Or do they not recognise their Messenger, that they deny him?

أَمْ لَمْ يَعْرِفُوا رَسُولَهُمْ فَهُمْ لَهُۥ مُنكِرُونَ ۝

70. Or do they say, "He is Possessed"? Nay, he has brought them the Truth, but most of them hate the Truth.

أَمْ يَقُولُونَ بِهِۦ جِنَّةٌۢ بَلْ جَآءَهُم بِالْحَقِّ وَأَكْثَرُهُمْ لِلْحَقِّ كَٰرِهُونَ ۝

71. If the Truth had been in accord with their desires, truly the heavens and the earth, and all beings therein would have been in ruin nay, We have sent them their admonition, but they turn away from their admonition.

وَلَوِ اتَّبَعَ الْحَقُّ أَهْوَآءَهُمْ لَفَسَدَتِ السَّمَٰوَٰتُ وَالْأَرْضُ وَمَن فِيهِنَّ ۚ بَلْ أَتَيْنَٰهُم بِذِكْرِهِمْ فَهُمْ عَن ذِكْرِهِم مُّعْرِضُونَ ۝

72. Or is it that thou asked them for some recompense? But the recompense of thy Lord is best: He is the Best of those who give sustenance.

أَمْ تَسْـَٔلُهُمْ خَرْجًا فَخَرَاجُ رَبِّكَ خَيْرٌ وَهُوَ خَيْرُ الرَّٰزِقِينَ ۝

73. But verily thou callest them to the Straight Way;

وَإِنَّكَ لَتَدْعُوهُمْ إِلَىٰ صِرَٰطٍ مُّسْتَقِيمٍ ۝

74. And verily those who believe not in the Hereafter are deviating from that Way.

وَإِنَّ الَّذِينَ لَا يُؤْمِنُونَ بِالْءَاخِرَةِ عَنِ الصِّرَٰطِ لَنَٰكِبُونَ ۝

75. If We had mercy on them and removed the distress which is on them, they would obstinately persist in their transgression, wandering in distraction to and fro.

76. We inflicted Punishment on them, but they humbled not themselves to their Lord, nor do they submissively entreat (Him)!—

77. Until We open on them a gate leading to a severe Punishment: then lo! they will be plunged in despair therein!

78. It is He Who has created for you (the faculties of) hearing, sight, feeling and understanding: little thanks it is ye give!

79. And He Has multiplied you through the earth, and to Him shall ye be gathered back.

80. It is He Who gives life and death, and to Him (is due) the alternation of Night and Day: will ye not then understand?

81. On the contrary they say things similar to what the ancients said.

82. They say: "What! When we die and become dust and bones, could we really be raised up again?

83. "Such things have been promised to us and to our fathers before! They are nothing but tales of the ancients!"

84. Say: "To whom belong the earth and all beings therein? (Say) if ye know!"

85. They will say, "To Allah!" Say: "Yet will ye not receive admonition?"

86. Say: "Who is the Lord of the seven heavens, and the Lord of the Mighty Throne

87. They will say, "(They belong) to Allah." Say: "Will ye not then fear.

88. Say: "Who is it in whose hands is the sovereignty of all things,—Who protects (all), but is not protected (of any)? (Say) if ye know."

89. They will say, "(It belongs) to Allah." Say: "Then how are ye deluded?"

90. We have sent them the Truth: but they indeed are liars.

91. No son did Allah beget, nor is there any god along with Him: (if there were many gods), behold, each god would have taken away what he had created, and some would have lorded it over others! Glory to Allah! (He is free) from the (sort of) things they attribute to Him!

92. He knows what is hidden and what is open: too high is He for the partners they attribute to Him!

93. Say: "O my Lord! if Thou wilt show me (in my lifetime) that which they are warned against,—

94. "Then, O my Lord! put me not amongst the people who do wrong!"

95. And We are certainly able to show thee (in fulfilment) that against which they are warned.

96. Repel evil with that which is best: We are well acquainted with the things they say.

97. And say "O my Lord! I seek refuge with Thee from the suggestions of the Satans.

98. "And I seek refuge with Thee O my Lord! lest they should come near me."

99. Until, when death comes to one of them, he says: "O my Lord! send me back (to life),—

100. "In order that I may work righteousness in the things I neglected."— "By no means! it is but a word he says."—Before them is a Partition till the Day they are raised up.

101. Then when the Trumpet is blown, there will be no more relationships between them that day, nor will one ask after another!

102. Then those whose balance (of good deeds) is heavy,—they will be successful.

103. But those whose balance is light, will be those who have lost their souls; in Hell will they abide.

104. The Fire will burn their faces, and they will therein grin, with their lips displaced.

تَلْفَحُ وُجُوهَهُمُ النَّارُ وَهُمْ فِيهَا كَالِحُونَ ۝

105. "Were not My Signs rehearsed to you, and ye did but treat them as falsehoods?"

اَلَمْ تَكُنْ اٰيٰتِى تُتْلٰى عَلَيْكُمْ فَكُنْتُمْ بِهَا تُكَذِّبُوْنَ ۝

106. They will say: "Our Lord! our misfortune overwhelmed us, and we became a people astray!

قَالُوْا رَبَّنَا غَلَبَتْ عَلَيْنَا شِقْوَتُنَا وَكُنَّا قَوْمًا ضَآلِّيْنَ ۝

107. "Our Lord! bring us out of this: if ever we return (to evil), then shall we be wrong-doers indeed!"

رَبَّنَا اَخْرِجْنَا مِنْهَا فَاِنْ عُدْنَا فَاِنَّا ظٰلِمُوْنَ ۝

108. He will say: "Be ye driven into it (with ignominy)! and speak ye not to Me!

قَالَ اخْسَـُٔوْا فِيْهَا وَلَا تُكَلِّمُوْنِ ۝

109. "A part of My servants there was, who used to pray, 'Our Lord! we believe; then do Thou forgive us, and have mercy upon us: for Thou art the Best of those who show mercy!'

اِنَّهٗ كَانَ فَرِيْقٌ مِّنْ عِبَادِىْ يَقُوْلُوْنَ رَبَّنَاۤ اٰمَنَّا فَاغْفِرْ لَنَا وَارْحَمْنَا وَاَنْتَ خَيْرُ الرّٰحِمِيْنَ ۝

110. "But ye treated them with ridicule, so much so that (ridicule of) them made you forget My Message while ye were laughing at them!

فَاتَّخَذْتُمُوْهُمْ سِخْرِيًّا حَتّٰۤى اَنْسَوْكُمْ ذِكْرِىْ وَكُنْتُمْ مِّنْهُمْ تَضْحَكُوْنَ ۝

111. "I have rewarded them this day for their patience and constancy: they are indeed the ones that have achieved Bliss..."

اِنِّىْ جَزَيْتُهُمُ الْيَوْمَ بِمَا صَبَرُوْۤا اَنَّهُمْ هُمُ الْفَآئِزُوْنَ ۝

112. He will say: "What number of years did ye stay on earth?"

قٰلَ كَمْ لَبِثْتُمْ فِى الْاَرْضِ عَدَدَ سِنِيْنَ ۝

113. They will say: "We stayed a day or part of a day: but ask those who keep account."

قَالُوْا لَبِثْنَا يَوْمًا اَوْ بَعْضَ يَوْمٍ فَسْـَٔلِ الْعَآدِّيْنَ ۝

114. He will say: "Ye stayed not but a little,—if ye had only known!

قٰلَ اِنْ لَّبِثْتُمْ اِلَّا قَلِيْلًا لَّوْ اَنَّكُمْ كُنْتُمْ تَعْلَمُوْنَ ۝

115. "Did ye then think that We had created you in jest, and that ye would not be brought back to Us (for account)?"

اَفَحَسِبْتُمْ اَنَّمَا خَلَقْنٰكُمْ عَبَثًا وَّاَنَّكُمْ اِلَيْنَا لَا تُرْجَعُوْنَ ۝

116. Therefore exalted be Allah, the King, the Reality: there is no god but He, the Lord of the Throne of Honour!

فَتَعٰلَى اللّٰهُ الْمَلِكُ الْحَقُّ ۚ لَاۤ اِلٰهَ اِلَّا هُوَ ۚ رَبُّ الْعَرْشِ الْكَرِيْمِ ۝

117. If anyone invokes, besides Allah, any other god, he has no authority thereof; and his reckoning will be only

وَمَنْ يَّدْعُ مَعَ اللّٰهِ اِلٰهًا اٰخَرَ لَا بُرْهَانَ لَهٗ بِهٖ فَاِنَّمَا حِسَابُهٗ عِنْدَ رَبِّهٖ ۚ اِنَّهٗ

SÛRA–24
AN-NÛR
(INTRODUCTION)

The environmental and social influences which most frequently wreck our spiritual ideals have to do with sex, and especially with its misuse, whether in the form of unregulated behaviour, of false charges or scandals, or breach of the refined conventions of personal or domestic privacy. Our complete conquest of all pitfalls in such matters enables us to rise to the higher regions of Light and of Allah-created Nature, about which a mystic doctrine is suggested. This subject is continued in the next Sûra.

As the reprobation of false slanders about women (24: 11-20) is connected with an incident that happened to Hadhrat 'Āi-sha in A.H. 5-6, that fixes the chronological place of this Madinah Sûra.

with his Lord! and verily the Unbelievers shall not prosper.

118. So say; "O my lord! grant Thou forgiveness and mercy! for Thou art the Best of those who show mercy!"

An-Nūr, or Light

In the name of Allah, Most Gracious, Most Merciful.

1. A Sūra which We have sent down and which We have ordained: in it have We sent down Clear Signs, in order that ye may receive admonition.

2. The woman and the man guilty of fornication,— flog each of them with a hundred stripes: let not compassion move you in their case, in a matter prescribed by Allah, if ye believe in Allah and the Last Day: and let a party of the Believers witness their punishment.

3. The adulterer cannot have sexual relations with any but an adulteress or an idolatress, and the adulteress, none can have sexual relations with her but an adulterer or an idolater; to the believers such a thing is forbidden.

4. And those who launch a charge against chaste women, and produce not four witnesses (to support their allegations),— flog them with eighty stripes; and reject their evidence ever after: for such men are wicked transgressors;—

5. Except those who repent thereafter and mend (their conduct); for Allah is Oft-Forgiving, Most Merciful.

6. And for those who launch a charge against their wives, and have (in support) no evidence but their own,— let one of them testify four times by Allah that he is of those who speak the Truth.

7. And the fifth (oath) (should be) that he solemnly invokes the curse of Allah on

لَا يُفْلِحُ الْكَافِرُونَ ﴿١١٧﴾

وَقُلْ رَّبِّ اغْفِرْ وَارْحَمْ وَأَنْتَ خَيْرُ الرَّاحِمِيْنَ ﴿١١٨﴾

سُوْرَةُ النُّوْرِ مَدَنِيَّةٌ وَّهِيَ أَرْبَعٌ وَّسِتُّوْنَ اٰيَةً

بِسْمِ اللهِ الرَّحْمٰنِ الرَّحِيْمِ

سُوْرَةٌ أَنْزَلْنَاهَا وَفَرَضْنَاهَا وَأَنْزَلْنَا فِيْهَا اٰيٰتٍ بَيِّنٰتٍ لَّعَلَّكُمْ تَذَكَّرُوْنَ ﴿١﴾

اَلزَّانِيَةُ وَالزَّانِيْ فَاجْلِدُوْا كُلَّ وَاحِدٍ مِّنْهُمَا مِائَةَ جَلْدَةٍ ۖ وَّلَا تَأْخُذْكُمْ بِهِمَا رَأْفَةٌ فِيْ دِيْنِ اللهِ إِنْ كُنْتُمْ تُؤْمِنُوْنَ بِاللهِ وَالْيَوْمِ الْاٰخِرِ ۖ وَلْيَشْهَدْ عَذَابَهُمَا طَائِفَةٌ مِّنَ الْمُؤْمِنِيْنَ ﴿٢﴾

اَلزَّانِيْ لَا يَنْكِحُ إِلَّا زَانِيَةً أَوْ مُشْرِكَةً ۖ وَّالزَّانِيَةُ لَا يَنْكِحُهَا إِلَّا زَانٍ أَوْ مُشْرِكٌ ۖ وَحُرِّمَ ذٰلِكَ عَلَى الْمُؤْمِنِيْنَ ﴿٣﴾

وَالَّذِيْنَ يَرْمُوْنَ الْمُحْصَنٰتِ ثُمَّ لَمْ يَأْتُوْا بِأَرْبَعَةِ شُهَدَاءَ فَاجْلِدُوْهُمْ ثَمٰنِيْنَ جَلْدَةً وَّلَا تَقْبَلُوْا لَهُمْ شَهَادَةً أَبَدًا ۚ وَأُولٰئِكَ هُمُ الْفٰسِقُوْنَ ﴿٤﴾

إِلَّا الَّذِيْنَ تَابُوْا مِنْ بَعْدِ ذٰلِكَ وَأَصْلَحُوْا ۖ فَإِنَّ اللهَ غَفُوْرٌ رَّحِيْمٌ ﴿٥﴾

وَالَّذِيْنَ يَرْمُوْنَ أَزْوَاجَهُمْ وَلَمْ يَكُنْ لَّهُمْ شُهَدَاءُ إِلَّا أَنْفُسُهُمْ فَشَهَادَةُ أَحَدِهِمْ أَرْبَعُ شَهَادَاتٍ بِاللهِ إِنَّهُ لَمِنَ الصّٰدِقِيْنَ ﴿٦﴾

وَالْخَامِسَةُ أَنَّ لَعْنَتَ اللهِ عَلَيْهِ إِنْ

himself if he tells a lie.

8. But it would avert the punishment from the wife, if she bears witness four times (with an oath) by Allah, that (her husband) is telling a lie;

9. And the fifth (oath) should be that she solemnly invokes the wrath of Allah on herself if (her accuser) is telling the truth.

10. If it were not for Allah's grace and mercy on you, and that Allah is Oft-Returning, full of Wisdom,— (ye would be ruined indeed).

11. Those who brought forward the lie are a body among yourselves: think it not to be an evil to you; on the contrary it is good for you: to every man among them (will come the punishment) of the sin that he earned, and to him who took on himself the lead among them, will be a Chastisement grievous.

12. Why did not the Believers—men and women —when ye heard of the affair,— thought well of their people and say, "This (charge) is an obvious lie"?

13. Why did they not bring four witnesses to prove it? When they have not brought the witnesses, such men, in the sight of Allah, (stand forth) themselves as liars!

14. Were it not for the grace and mercy of Allah on you, in this world and the Hereafter, a grievous chastisement would have seized you in that ye rushed glibly into this affair.

15. Behold, ye received it on your tongues, and said out of your mouths things of which ye had no knowledge; and ye thought it to be a light matter, while it was most serious in the sight of Allah.

16. And why did ye not, when ye heard it, say?— "It is not right of us to speak of this: glory to Thee (our Lord) this is a most serious slander!"

17. Allah doth admonish you, that ye may never repeat such (conduct), if ye are (true) Believers.

18. And Allah makes the Signs plain to you: for Allah is full of knowledge and wisdom.

19. Those who love (to see) scandal circulate among the Believers, will have a grievous Chastisement in this life and in the Hereafter: Allah knows, and ye know not.

20. Were it not for the grace and mercy of Allah on you, and that Allah is full of kindness and mercy, (ye would be ruined indeed).

21. O ye who believe! follow not Satan's footsteps: if any will follow the footsteps of Satan, he will (but) command what is indecent and wrong: and were it not for the grace and mercy of Allah on you, not one of you would ever have been pure: but Allah doth purify whom He pleases: and Allah is One Who hears and knows (all things).

22. Let not those among you who are endued with grace and amplitude of means resolve by oath against helping their kinsmen, those in want, and those who have left their homes in Allah's cause: let them forgive and overlook, do you not wish that Allah should forgive you? For Allah is Oft-Forgiving, Most Merciful.

23. Those who slander chaste, indiscreet and believing women are cursed in this life and in the Hereafter: for them is a grievous Chastisement—

24. On the Day when their tongues, their hands, and their feet will bear witness against them as to their actions.

25. On that Day Allah will pay them back (all) their just dues, and they will realise that Allah is the (very) Truth, that makes all things manifest.

26. Women impure are for men impure,

and men impure for women impure, and
women of purity are for men of purity, and
men of purity are for women of purity: these
are innocent of all what people say: for
them there is forgiveness, and a provision
honourable.

27. O ye who believe! enter not houses
other than your own, until ye have asked
permission and saluted those in them: that
is best for you, in order that ye may heed
(what is seemly).

28. If ye find no one in the house, enter
not until permission is given to you: if ye
are asked to go back, go back: that makes
for greater purity for yourselves: and Allah
knows well all that ye do.

29. It is no fault on your part to enter
houses not used for living in, which serve
some (other) use for you: and Allah has
knowledge of what ye reveal and what ye
conceal.

30. Say to the believing men that they
should lower their gaze and guard their
modesty: that will make for greater purity
for them: and Allah is well acquainted with
all that they do.

31. And say to the believing women that
they should lower their gaze and guard
their modesty; that they should not display
their beauty and ornaments except what
(ordinarily) appear thereof; that they should
draw their veils over their bosoms and not
display their beauty except to their
husbands, their fathers, their husbands'
fathers, their sons, their husbands' sons,
their brothers or their brothers' sons, or
their sisters' sons, or their women, or the
slaves whom their right hands possess, or
male attendants free of sexual desires. Or

small children who have no carnal knowledge of women; and that they should not strike their feet in order to draw attention to their hidden ornaments. And O ye Believers! turn ye all together towards Allah in repentance that ye may be successful.

32. Marry those among you who are single, and the virtuous ones among your slaves, male or female: if they are in poverty, Allah will give them means out of His grace: for Allah is Ample-giving, and He knoweth all things.

33. Let those who find not the wherewithal for marriage keep themselves chaste, until Allah gives them means out of His grace. And if any of your slaves ask for a deed in writing (for emancipation) give them such a deed if ye know any good in them; yea, give them something yourselves out of the means which Allah has given to you. But force not your maids to prostitution when they desire chastity, in order that ye may make a gain in the goods of this life. But if anyone compels them, yet, after such compulsion, is Allah Oft-Forgiving, Most Merciful (to them).

34. We have already sent down to you verses making things clear, an illustration from (the story of) people who passed away before you, and an admonition for those who fear (Allah).

35. Allah is the Light of the heavens and the earth. The parable of His Light is as if there were a Niche and within it a Lamp: the Lamp enclosed in Glass: the glass as it were a brilliant star: lit from a blessed Tree, an Olive, neither of the East nor of the West, whose Oil is well-nigh luminous, though fire scarce touched it: Light upon Light! Allah doth guide whom He will to His Light: Allah doth set forth Parables for men: and Allah doth know all things.

36. (Lit is such a Light) in houses, which
Allah hath permitted to be raised to honour;
for the celebration, in them, of His name: in
them is He glorified in the mornings and in
the evenings, (again and again),—

37. By men whom neither trade nor sale
can divert from the Remembrance of Allah,
nor from regular Prayer, nor from paying
zakat their (only) fear is for the Day when
hearts and eyes will be turned about,—

38. That Allah may reward them according
to the best of their deeds, and add even
more for them out of His Grace: for Allah
doth provide for those whom He will, without
measure.

39. But the Unbelievers,— their deeds are
like a mirage in sandy deserts, which the
man parched with thirst mistakes for water;
until when he comes up to it, he finds it to
be nothing: but he finds Allah there, and
Allah will pay him his account: and Allah is
swift in taking account.

40. Or (the Unbelievers' state) is like the
depths of darkness in a vast deep ocean,
overwhelmed with billow topped by billow,
topped by (dark) clouds: depths of darkness,
one above another: if a man stretches out
his hand, he can hardly see it! For any to
whom Allah giveth not light, there is no light!

41. Seest thou not that it is Allah Whose
praises all being in the heavens and on
earth do celebrate, and the birds (of the air)
with wings outspread? Each one knows its
own (mode of) prayer and praise. And Allah
knows well all that they do.

42. Yea, to Allah belongs the dominion of
the heavens and the earth; and to Allah is
the return.

43. Seest thou not that Allah makes the
clouds move gently, then joins them together,
then makes them into a heap?—

then wilt thou see rain issue forth from their midst. And He sends down from the sky mountain masses (of clouds) wherein is hail: He strikes therewith whom He pleases and He turns it away from whom He pleases. The vivid flash of its lightning well-nigh blinds the sight.

44. It is Allah Who alternates the Night and the Day: verily in these things is an instructive example for those who have vision!

45. And Allah has created every animal from water: of them there are some that creep on their bellies; some that walk on two legs: and some that walk on four. Allah creates what He wills; for verily Allah has power over all things.

46. We have indeed sent down Signs that make things manifest: and Allah guides whom He wills to a Way that is straight.

47. They say, "We believe in Allah and in the Messenger, and we obey": but even after that, some of them turn away: they are not (really) Believers.

48. When they are summoned to Allah and His Messenger, in order that he may judge between them, behold, some of them decline (to come).

49. But if the right is on their side, they come to him with all submission.

50. Is it that there is a disease in their hearts? Or do they doubt, or are they in fear, that Allah and His Messenger will deal unjustly with them? Nay, it is they themselves who do wrong.

51. The answer of the Believers, when summoned to Allah and His Messenger, in order that he may judge between them, is no other than this: they say, "We hear and we obey": it is such as these that will prosper.

52. It is such as obey Allah and His Messenger, and fear Allah and do right, that will triumph.

53. They swear their strongest oaths by Allah that, if only thou wouldst command them, they would leave (their homes). Say: "Swear ye not; obedience is (more) reasonable; verily, Allah is well acquainted with all that ye do."

وَأَقْسَمُوا بِاللَّهِ جَهْدَ أَيْمَانِهِمْ لَئِنْ أَمَرْتَهُمْ لَيَخْرُجُنَّ ۖ قُلْ لَّا تُقْسِمُوا ۖ طَاعَةٌ مَّعْرُوفَةٌ ۚ إِنَّ اللَّهَ خَبِيرٌ بِمَا تَعْمَلُونَ ۝

54. Say: "Obey Allah, and obey the Messenger: but if ye turn away, he is only responsible for the duty placed on him and ye for that placed on you. If ye obey him, ye shall be on right guidance. The Messenger's duty is only to preach the clear (Message)".

قُلْ أَطِيعُوا اللَّهَ وَأَطِيعُوا الرَّسُولَ ۖ فَإِن تَوَلَّوْا فَإِنَّمَا عَلَيْهِ مَا حُمِّلَ وَعَلَيْكُمْ مَّا حُمِّلْتُمْ ۖ وَإِن تُطِيعُوهُ تَهْتَدُوا ۚ وَمَا عَلَى الرَّسُولِ إِلَّا الْبَلَاغُ الْمُبِينُ ۝

55. Allah has promised, to those among you who believe and work righteous deeds, that He will, of a surety, grant them in the land, inheritance (of power), as He granted it to those before them; that He will establish in authority their religion—the one which He has chosen for them; and that He will change (their state), after the fear in which they (lived), to one of security and peace: 'They will worship Me (alone) and not associate aught with Me. If any do reject Faith after this, they are rebellious and wicked.

وَعَدَ اللَّهُ الَّذِينَ آمَنُوا مِنكُمْ وَعَمِلُوا الصَّالِحَاتِ لَيَسْتَخْلِفَنَّهُمْ فِي الْأَرْضِ كَمَا اسْتَخْلَفَ الَّذِينَ مِن قَبْلِهِمْ وَلَيُمَكِّنَنَّ لَهُمْ دِينَهُمُ الَّذِي ارْتَضَىٰ لَهُمْ وَلَيُبَدِّلَنَّهُم مِّن بَعْدِ خَوْفِهِمْ أَمْنًا ۚ يَعْبُدُونَنِي لَا يُشْرِكُونَ بِي شَيْئًا ۚ وَمَن كَفَرَ بَعْدَ ذَٰلِكَ فَأُولَٰئِكَ هُمُ الْفَاسِقُونَ ۝

56. So establish regular Prayer and give zakat and obey the Messenger; that ye may receive mercy.

وَأَقِيمُوا الصَّلَاةَ وَآتُوا الزَّكَاةَ وَأَطِيعُوا الرَّسُولَ لَعَلَّكُمْ تُرْحَمُونَ ۝

57. Never think thou that the Unbelievers can escape in the earth their abode is the Fire,— and it is indeed an evil refuge!

لَا تَحْسَبَنَّ الَّذِينَ كَفَرُوا مُعْجِزِينَ فِي الْأَرْضِ ۚ وَمَأْوَاهُمُ النَّارُ ۖ وَلَبِئْسَ الْمَصِيرُ ۝

58. O ye who believe! let those whom your right hands possess, and the (children) among you who have not come of age ask your permission (before they come to your presence), on three occasions: before morning prayer; the while ye doff your clothes for the noonday heat; and after the late-night prayer: these are your three times of undress: outside those times it is not wrong for you or for them to move about attending to each other: thus does Allah make clear the Signs to you: for Allah is full of knowledge and wisdom.

يَا أَيُّهَا الَّذِينَ آمَنُوا لِيَسْتَأْذِنكُمُ الَّذِينَ مَلَكَتْ أَيْمَانُكُمْ وَالَّذِينَ لَمْ يَبْلُغُوا الْحُلُمَ مِنكُمْ ثَلَاثَ مَرَّاتٍ ۚ مِّن قَبْلِ صَلَاةِ الْفَجْرِ وَحِينَ تَضَعُونَ ثِيَابَكُم مِّنَ الظَّهِيرَةِ وَمِن بَعْدِ صَلَاةِ الْعِشَاءِ ۚ ثَلَاثُ عَوْرَاتٍ لَّكُمْ ۚ لَيْسَ عَلَيْكُمْ وَلَا عَلَيْهِمْ جُنَاحٌ بَعْدَهُنَّ ۚ طَوَّافُونَ عَلَيْكُم بَعْضُكُمْ عَلَىٰ بَعْضٍ ۚ كَذَٰلِكَ يُبَيِّنُ اللَّهُ لَكُمُ الْآيَاتِ ۗ وَاللَّهُ عَلِيمٌ حَكِيمٌ ۝

59. But when the children among you come of age, let them (also) ask for permission, as do those before them: thus does Allah make clear His Signs to you: for Allah is full of knowledge and wisdom.

وَاِذَا بَلَغَ الْاَطْفَالُ مِنْكُمُ الْحُلُمَ فَلْيَسْتَأْذِنُوْا كَمَا اسْتَأْذَنَ الَّذِيْنَ مِنْ قَبْلِهِمْ كَذٰلِكَ يُبَيِّنُ اللّٰهُ لَكُمْ اٰيٰتِهٖ وَاللّٰهُ عَلِيْمٌ حَكِيْمٌ ۝

60. Such elderly women as are past the prospect of marriage,— there is no blame on them if they lay aside their (outer) garments, provided they make not a wanton display of their beauty: but it is best for them to be modest: and Allah is One Who sees and knows all things.

وَالْقَوَاعِدُ مِنَ النِّسَاءِ الّٰتِيْ لَا يَرْجُوْنَ نِكَاحًا فَلَيْسَ عَلَيْهِنَّ جُنَاحٌ اَنْ يَّضَعْنَ ثِيَابَهُنَّ غَيْرَ مُتَبَرِّجٰتٍۭ بِزِيْنَةٍ ۗ وَاَنْ يَّسْتَعْفِفْنَ خَيْرٌ لَّهُنَّ ۗ وَاللّٰهُ سَمِيْعٌ عَلِيْمٌ ۝

61. It is no fault in the blind nor in one born lame, nor in one afflicted with illness, nor in yourselves, that ye should eat in your own houses, or those of your fathers, or your mothers, or your brothers, or your sisters, or your father's brothers or your father's sisters, or your mother's brothers, or your mother's sisters, or in houses of which the keys are in your possession, or in the house of a sincere friend of yours: there is no blame on you, whether ye eat in company or separately. But if ye enter houses, salute each other—a greeting of blessing and purity as from Allah. Thus does Allah make clear the Signs to you: that ye may understand.

لَيْسَ عَلَى الْاَعْمٰى حَرَجٌ وَّلَا عَلَى الْاَعْرَجِ حَرَجٌ وَّلَا عَلَى الْمَرِيْضِ حَرَجٌ وَّلَا عَلٰى اَنْفُسِكُمْ اَنْ تَأْكُلُوْا مِنْۢ بُيُوْتِكُمْ اَوْ بُيُوْتِ اٰبَآئِكُمْ اَوْ بُيُوْتِ اُمَّهٰتِكُمْ اَوْ بُيُوْتِ اِخْوَانِكُمْ اَوْ بُيُوْتِ اَخَوٰتِكُمْ اَوْ بُيُوْتِ اَعْمَامِكُمْ اَوْ بُيُوْتِ عَمّٰتِكُمْ اَوْ بُيُوْتِ اَخْوَالِكُمْ اَوْ بُيُوْتِ خٰلٰتِكُمْ اَوْ مَا مَلَكْتُمْ مَّفَاتِحَهٗ اَوْ صَدِيْقِكُمْ ۗ لَيْسَ عَلَيْكُمْ جُنَاحٌ اَنْ تَأْكُلُوْا جَمِيْعًا اَوْ اَشْتَاتًا ۗ فَاِذَا دَخَلْتُمْ بُيُوْتًا فَسَلِّمُوْا عَلٰى اَنْفُسِكُمْ تَحِيَّةً مِّنْ عِنْدِ اللّٰهِ مُبٰرَكَةً طَيِّبَةً ۗ كَذٰلِكَ يُبَيِّنُ اللّٰهُ لَكُمُ الْاٰيٰتِ لَعَلَّكُمْ تَعْقِلُوْنَ ۝

62. Only those are Believers, who believe in Allah and His Messenger: when they are with him on a matter requiring collective action, they do not depart until they have asked for his leave; those who ask for the leave are those who believe in Allah and His Messenger; so when they ask for thy leave, for some business of their, give leave to those of them whom thou wilt, and ask Allah for their forgiveness; for

اِنَّمَا الْمُؤْمِنُوْنَ الَّذِيْنَ اٰمَنُوْا بِاللّٰهِ وَرَسُوْلِهٖ وَاِذَا كَانُوْا مَعَهٗ عَلٰى اَمْرٍ جَامِعٍ لَّمْ يَذْهَبُوْا حَتّٰى يَسْتَأْذِنُوْهُ ۗ اِنَّ الَّذِيْنَ يَسْتَأْذِنُوْنَكَ اُولٰٓئِكَ الَّذِيْنَ يُؤْمِنُوْنَ بِاللّٰهِ وَرَسُوْلِهٖ ۚ فَاِذَا اسْتَأْذَنُوْكَ لِبَعْضِ شَأْنِهِمْ فَأْذَنْ لِّمَنْ شِئْتَ مِنْهُمْ وَاسْتَغْفِرْ لَهُمُ

SÛRA–25
AL-FURQĀN
(INTRODUCTION)

This Sûra further develops the contrast between Light and Darkness, as symbolical of knowledge and ignorance, righteousness and sin, spiritual progress and degradation. It closes with a definition of the deeds by which the righteous are known in the environement of this world.

It is mainly an early Makkan Sûra, but its date has no significance.

Allah is Oft-Forgiving, Most Merciful.

63. Deem not the summons of the Messenger among yourselves like the summons of one of you to another: Allah doth know those of you who slip away under shelter of some excuse: then let those beware who withstand the Messenger's order, lest some trial befall them, or a grievous Chastisement be inflicted on them.

64. Be quite sure that to Allah doth belong whatever is in the heavens and on earth. Well doth He know what ye are intent upon: and the day they will be brought back to Him, He will tell them the truth of what they did: for Allah doth know all things.

Al-Furqān, or The Criterion

In the name of Allah, Most Gracious Most Merciful.

1. Blessed is He Who sent down the Criterion to His servant, that it may be an admonition to all creatures;—

2. He to Whom belongs the dominion of the heavens and the earth: no son has He begotten, nor has He a partner in His dominion: it is He Who created all things, and ordered them in due proportions.

3. Yet have they taken, besides Him, gods that can create nothing but are themselves created; that have no control of hurt or good to themselves; nor can they control Death nor Life nor Resurrection.

4. But the Misbelievers say: "Naught is this but a lie which he has forged, and others have helped him at it." In truth it is they who have put forward an iniquity and a falsehood.

5. And they say: "Tales of the ancients, which he has caused to be written: and they are dictated before him morning and evening."

6. Say: "The (Qur'an) was sent down by Him Who knows the secret (that is) in the heavens and the earth: verily He is Oft-Forgiving, Most Merciful."

قُلْ أَنزَلَهُ الَّذِى يَعْلَمُ السِّرَّ فِى السَّمَوَاتِ وَالْأَرْضِ ۚ إِنَّهُ كَانَ غَفُورًا رَّحِيمًا ۞

7. And they say: "What sort of a messenger is this, who eats food, and walks through the streets? Why has not an angel been sent down to him to give admonition with him?

وَقَالُوا مَالِ هَذَا الرَّسُولِ يَأْكُلُ الطَّعَامَ وَيَمْشِى فِى الْأَسْوَاقِ ۖ لَوْلَا أُنزِلَ إِلَيْهِ مَلَكٌ فَيَكُونَ مَعَهُ نَذِيرًا ۞

8. "Or (why) has not a treasure been bestowed on him, or why has he (not) a garden for enjoyment?" The wicked say: "Ye follow none other than a man bewitched."

أَوْ يُلْقَىٰ إِلَيْهِ كَنزٌ أَوْ تَكُونُ لَهُ جَنَّةٌ يَأْكُلُ مِنْهَا ۚ وَقَالَ الظَّالِمُونَ إِن تَتَّبِعُونَ إِلَّا رَجُلًا مَّسْحُورًا ۞

9. See what kinds of comparisons they make for thee! But they have gone astray, and never a way will they be able to find!

أُنظُرْ كَيْفَ ضَرَبُوا لَكَ الْأَمْثَالَ فَضَلُّوا فَلَا يَسْتَطِيعُونَ سَبِيلًا ۞

10. Blessed is He Who, if that were His Will, could give thee better (things) than those,—Gardens beneath which rivers flow; and He could give thee Palaces (secure to dwell in).

تَبَارَكَ الَّذِى إِن شَاءَ جَعَلَ لَكَ خَيْرًا مِّن ذَلِكَ جَنَّاتٍ تَجْرِى مِن تَحْتِهَا الْأَنْهَارُ وَيَجْعَل لَّكَ قُصُورًا ۞

11. Nay, they deny the Hour (of the Judgment to come): but We have prepared a Blazing Fire for such as deny the Hour:

بَلْ كَذَّبُوا بِالسَّاعَةِ ۖ وَأَعْتَدْنَا لِمَن كَذَّبَ بِالسَّاعَةِ سَعِيرًا ۞

12. When it sees them from a place far off, they will hear its fury and its raging sigh.

إِذَا رَأَتْهُم مِّن مَّكَانٍ بَعِيدٍ سَمِعُوا لَهَا تَغَيُّظًا وَزَفِيرًا ۞

13. And when they are cast, bound together, into a constricted place therein, they will plead for destruction there and then!

وَإِذَا أُلْقُوا مِنْهَا مَكَانًا ضَيِّقًا مُّقَرَّنِينَ دَعَوْا هُنَالِكَ ثُبُورًا ۞

14. "This day plead not for a single destruction: plead for destruction oft-repeated!"

لَا تَدْعُوا الْيَوْمَ ثُبُورًا وَاحِدًا وَادْعُوا ثُبُورًا كَثِيرًا ۞

15. Say: "Is that best, or the eternal Garden, promised to the righteous? For them, that is a reward as well as a final abode.

قُلْ أَذَلِكَ خَيْرٌ أَمْ جَنَّةُ الْخُلْدِ الَّتِى وُعِدَ الْمُتَّقُونَ ۚ كَانَتْ لَهُمْ جَزَاءً وَّمَصِيرًا ۞

16. "For them there will be therein all that they wish for: they will dwell (there) for aye: a promise binding upon thy Lord."

لَّهُمْ فِيهَا مَا يَشَاءُونَ خَالِدِينَ ۚ كَانَ عَلَىٰ رَبِّكَ وَعْدًا مَّسْئُولًا ۞

17. The Day He will gather them together as well as those whom they

وَيَوْمَ يَحْشُرُهُمْ وَمَا يَعْبُدُونَ مِن

worship besides Allah, He will ask: "Was it ye who led these My servants astray, or did they stray from the Path themselves?"

18.   They will say: "Glory to Thee! not meet was it for us that we should take for protectors others besides Thee: but Thou didst bestow, on them and their fathers, good things (in life), until they forgot the Message: for they were a people destroyed".

19.   (Allah will say): "Now have they proved you liars in what ye say: so ye cannot avert (your penalty) nor (get) help." And whoever among you does wrong, him shall We cause to taste of a grievous Chastisement.

20.   And the messengers whom We sent before thee were all (men) who ate food and walked through the markets. We have made some of you as a trial for others: will ye have patience? For Allah is One Who sees (all things).

21.   Those who do not hope to meet Us (for Judgment) say: "Why are not the angels sent down to us, or (why) do we not see our Lord?" Indeed they have an arrogant conceit of themselves, and mighty is the insolence of their impiety!

22.   The Day they see the angels,—no joy will there be to the sinners that Day: the (angels) will say: "There is a barrier forbidden (to you) altogether!"

23.   And We shall turn to whatever deeds they did (in this life), and We shall make such deeds as floating dust scattered about.

24.   The Companions of the Garden will be well, that Day, in their abode, and have the fairest of places for repose.

25.   The Day the heaven shall be rent asunder with clouds, and angels shall be sent down, Descending (in ranks),—

26.   That Day, the dominion right by shall be (wholly) for The Most Gracious: it will be a Day of dire difficulty for the Misbelievers.

دُونِ اللّهِ فَيَقُولُ ءَاَنتُمۡ اَضۡلَلۡتُمۡ عِبَادِىۡ هٰٓؤُلَآءِ اَمۡ هُمۡ ضَلُّوا السَّبِيۡلَ ۞

قَالُوۡا سُبۡحٰنَكَ مَا كَانَ يَنۢبَغِىۡ لَنَآ اَن نَّتَّخِذَ مِنۡ دُوۡنِكَ مِنۡ اَوۡلِيَآءَ وَلٰكِنۡ مَّتَّعۡتَهُمۡ وَاٰبَآءَهُمۡ حَتّٰى نَسُوا الذِّكۡرَۚ وَكَانُوۡا قَوۡمًاۢ بُوۡرًا ۞

فَقَدۡ كَذَّبُوۡكُمۡ بِمَا تَقُوۡلُوۡنَ فَمَا تَسۡتَطِيۡعُوۡنَ صَرۡفًا وَّلَا نَصۡرًاۚ وَمَنۡ يَّظۡلِمۡ مِّنۡكُمۡ نُذِقۡهُ عَذَابًا كَبِيۡرًا ۞

وَمَآ اَرۡسَلۡنَا قَبۡلَكَ مِنَ الۡمُرۡسَلِيۡنَ اِلَّآ اِنَّهُمۡ لَيَاۡكُلُوۡنَ الطَّعَامَ وَيَمۡشُوۡنَ فِى الۡاَسۡوَاقِۚ وَجَعَلۡنَا بَعۡضَكُمۡ لِبَعۡضٍ فِتۡنَةً اَتَصۡبِرُوۡنَۚ وَكَانَ رَبُّكَ بَصِيۡرًا ۞

وَقَالَ الَّذِيۡنَ لَا يَرۡجُوۡنَ لِقَآءَنَا لَوۡلَآ اُنۡزِلَ عَلَيۡنَا الۡمَلٰٓئِكَةُ اَوۡ نَرٰى رَبَّنَاۗ لَقَدِ اسۡتَكۡبَرُوۡا فِىۡٓ اَنۡفُسِهِمۡ وَعَتَوۡ عُتُوًّا كَبِيۡرًا ۞

يَوۡمَ يَرَوۡنَ الۡمَلٰٓئِكَةَ لَا بُشۡرٰى يَوۡمَئِذٍ لِّلۡمُجۡرِمِيۡنَ وَيَقُوۡلُوۡنَ حِجۡرًا مَّحۡجُوۡرًا ۞

وَقَدِمۡنَآ اِلٰى مَا عَمِلُوۡا مِنۡ عَمَلٍ فَجَعَلۡنٰهُ هَبَآءً مَّنۡثُوۡرًا ۞

اَصۡحٰبُ الۡجَنَّةِ يَوۡمَئِذٍ خَيۡرٌ مُّسۡتَقَرًّا وَّاَحۡسَنُ مَقِيۡلًا ۞

وَيَوۡمَ تَشَقَّقُ السَّمَآءُ بِالۡغَمَامِ وَنُزِّلَ الۡمَلٰٓئِكَةُ تَنۡزِيۡلًا ۞

اَلۡمُلۡكُ يَوۡمَئِذِ ِۨالۡحَقُّ لِلرَّحۡمٰنِۚ وَكَانَ يَوۡمًا عَلَى الۡكٰفِرِيۡنَ عَسِيۡرًا ۞

27. The Day that the wrong-doer will bite at his hands, he will say, "Oh! would that I had taken a (straight) path with the Messenger!

28. "Ah! woe is me! would that I had never taken such a one for a friend!

وَيَوْمَ يَعَضُّ الظَّالِمُ عَلَى يَدَيْهِ يَقُوْلُ يٰلَيْتَنِى اتَّخَذْتُ مَعَ الرَّسُوْلِ سَبِيْلاً ۞ يٰوَيْلَتٰى لَيْتَنِىْ لَمْ اَتَّخِذْ فُلَانًا خَلِيْلاً ۞

29. "He did lead me astray from the Message (of Allah) after it had come to me! Ah! the Satan is but a traitor to man!

30. Then the Messenger will say: "O my Lord, Truly my people treated this Qur-ān with neglect."

لَقَدْ اَضَلَّنِىْ عَنِ الذِّكْرِ بَعْدَ اِذْ جَآءَنِىْ وَكَانَ الشَّيْطٰنُ لِلْاِنْسَانِ خَذُوْلاً ۞ وَقَالَ الرَّسُوْلُ يٰرَبِّ اِنَّ قَوْمِى اتَّخَذُوْا هٰذَا الْقُرْاٰنَ مَهْجُوْرًا ۞

31. Thus have We made for every prophet an enemy among the sinners: but enough is thy Lord to guide and to help.

32. Those who reject Faith say: "Why is not the Qur-ān revealed to him all at once? Thus (is it revealed), that We may strengthen thy heart thereby, and We have rehearsed it to thee in slow, well-arranged stages, gradually.

33. And no question do they bring to thee but We reveal to thee the truth and the best explanation (thereof).

34. Those who will be gathered to Hell (prone) on their faces,— they will be in an evil plight, and, as to Path, most astray.

وَكَذٰلِكَ جَعَلْنَا لِكُلِّ نَبِىٍّ عَدُوًّا مِّنَ الْمُجْرِمِيْنَ ۗ وَكَفٰى بِرَبِّكَ هَادِيًا وَّنَصِيْرًا ۞ وَقَالَ الَّذِيْنَ كَفَرُوْا لَوْلَا نُزِّلَ عَلَيْهِ الْقُرْاٰنُ جُمْلَةً وَّاحِدَةً ۚ كَذٰلِكَ ۚ لِنُثَبِّتَ بِهٖ فُؤَادَكَ وَرَتَّلْنٰهُ تَرْتِيْلاً ۞ وَلَا يَأْتُوْنَكَ بِمَثَلٍ اِلَّا جِئْنٰكَ بِالْحَقِّ وَاَحْسَنَ تَفْسِيْرًا ۞ اَلَّذِيْنَ يُحْشَرُوْنَ عَلٰى وُجُوْهِهِمْ اِلٰى جَهَنَّمَ ۙ اُولٰٓئِكَ شَرٌّ مَّكَانًا وَّاَضَلُّ سَبِيْلاً ۞

35. (Before this), We sent Moses the Book, and appointed his brother Aaron with him as Minister;

36. And We commanded: "Go ye both, to the people who have rejected our Signs:" and those (people) We destroyed with utter destruction.

37. And the people of Noah,—when they rejected the messengers, We drowned them, and We made them as a Sign for mankind; and We have prepared for (all) wrong-doers a grievous Chastisement:

38. As also 'Ād and Thamūd, and the Companions of the Rass, and many a generation between them.

39. To each one We set forth Parables and examples; and each one We broke to

وَلَقَدْ اٰتَيْنَا مُوْسَى الْكِتٰبَ وَجَعَلْنَا مَعَهٗ اَخَاهُ هٰرُوْنَ وَزِيْرًا ۞ فَقُلْنَا اذْهَبَا اِلَى الْقَوْمِ الَّذِيْنَ كَذَّبُوْا بِاٰيٰتِنَا ۚ فَدَمَّرْنٰهُمْ تَدْمِيْرًا ۞ وَقَوْمَ نُوْحٍ لَّمَّا كَذَّبُوا الرُّسُلَ اَغْرَقْنٰهُمْ وَجَعَلْنٰهُمْ لِلنَّاسِ اٰيَةً ۖ وَاَعْتَدْنَا لِلظّٰلِمِيْنَ عَذَابًا اَلِيْمًا ۞ وَّعَادًا وَّثَمُوْدَا۠ وَاَصْحٰبَ الرَّسِّ وَقُرُوْنًا بَيْنَ ذٰلِكَ كَثِيْرًا ۞ وَكُلًّا ضَرَبْنَا لَهُ الْاَمْثَالَ ۖ وَكُلًّا تَبَّرْنَا

utter annihilation (for their sins).

تَبْتِيْرًا ٣٩

وَلَقَدْ اَتَوْا عَلَى الْقَرْيَةِ الَّتِيْ اُمْطِرَتْ

40. And the (Unbelievers) must indeed have passed by the town on which was rained a shower of evil: did they not then see it (with their own eyes)? But they expect not to be raised again.

مَطَرَ السَّوْءِ ط اَفَلَمْ يَكُوْنُوْا يَرَوْنَهَا ط بَلْ

كَانُوْا لَا يَرْجُوْنَ نُشُوْرًا ٤٠

41. When they see thee, they treat thee no otherwise than in mockery: "Is this the one whom Allah has sent as a messenger?"

وَاِذَا رَاَوْكَ اِنْ يَّتَّخِذُوْنَكَ اِلَّا هُزُوًا ط اَهٰذَا

الَّذِيْ بَعَثَ اللّٰهُ رَسُوْلًا ٤١

42. "He indeed would well-nigh have misled us from our gods, had it not been that we were constant to them!"—Soon will they know, when they see the Chastisement, who it is that is most misled in Path!

اِنْ كَادَ لَيُضِلُّنَا عَنْ اٰلِهَتِنَا لَوْ لَا

اَنْ صَبَرْنَا عَلَيْهَا ط وَسَوْفَ يَعْلَمُوْنَ

حِيْنَ يَرَوْنَ الْعَذَابَ مَنْ اَضَلُّ

سَبِيْلًا ٤٢

43. Seest thou such a one as taketh for his god his own passion (or impulse)? Couldst thou be a disposer of affairs for him?

اَرَءَيْتَ مَنِ اتَّخَذَ اِلٰهَهٗ هَوٰىهُ ط اَفَاَنْتَ

تَكُوْنُ عَلَيْهِ وَكِيْلًا ٤٣

44. Or thinkest thou that most of them listen or understand? They are only like cattle,—nay, they are farther astray from the way.

اَمْ تَحْسَبُ اَنَّ اَكْثَرَهُمْ يَسْمَعُوْنَ اَوْ

يَعْقِلُوْنَ ط اِنْ هُمْ اِلَّا كَالْاَنْعَامِ بَلْ

هُمْ اَضَلُّ سَبِيْلًا ٤٤

45. Hast thou not seen how thy Lord?—Doth prolong the Shadow! If He willed, He could make it stationary! Then do We make the sun its guide;

اَلَمْ تَرَ اِلٰى رَبِّكَ كَيْفَ مَدَّ الظِّلَّ ط وَلَوْ شَآءَ

جَعَلَهٗ سَاكِنًا ج ثُمَّ جَعَلْنَا الشَّمْسَ

عَلَيْهِ دَلِيْلًا ٤٥

46. Then We draw it in towards Ourselves,— a contraction by easy stages.

ثُمَّ قَبَضْنٰهُ اِلَيْنَا قَبْضًا يَّسِيْرًا ٤٦

47. And He it is Who makes the Night as a Robe for you, and Sleep as Repose and makes the Day (as it were) a Resurrection.

وَهُوَ الَّذِيْ جَعَلَ لَكُمُ الَّيْلَ لِبَاسًا وَّ

النَّوْمَ سُبَاتًا وَّجَعَلَ النَّهَارَ نُشُوْرًا ٤٧

48. And He it is Who sends the Winds as heralds of glad tidings, going before His Mercy, and We send down pure water from the sky,—

وَهُوَ الَّذِيْ اَرْسَلَ الرِّيٰحَ بُشْرًا بَيْنَ يَدَيْ

رَحْمَتِهٖ ج وَاَنْزَلْنَا مِنَ السَّمَآءِ مَآءً طَهُوْرًا ٤٨

49. That with it We may give life to a dead land, and slake the thirst of things We have created,— cattle and men in great numbers.

لِّنُحْيِۦ بِهٖ بَلْدَةً مَّيْتًا وَّنُسْقِيَهٗ مِمَّا خَلَقْنَا

اَنْعَامًا وَّاَنَاسِيَّ كَثِيْرًا ٤٩

50. And We have distributed the (water) amongst them, in order that they may be mindful but most men are averse (to aught) but (rank) ingratitude.

وَلَقَدْ صَرَّفْنٰهُ بَيْنَهُمْ لِيَذَّكَّرُوْا ز فَاَبٰى

اَكْثَرُ النَّاسِ اِلَّا كُفُوْرًا ٥٠

51. Had it been Our Will, We could have sent a warner to every town.

52. Therefore listen not to the Unbelievers, but strive against them with the utmost strenuousness, with the (Qur'an).

53. It is He Who has let free the two bodies of flowing water: one palatable and sweet, and the other salt and bitter; yet has He made a barrier between them, a partition that is not to be passed.

54. It is He Who has created man from water: then has He established relationships of lineage and marriage: for thy Lord has power (over all things).

55. Yet do they worship, besides Allah, things that can neither profit them nor harm them: and the misbeliever is a helper (of Evil), against his own Lord!

56. But thee We only sent to give glad tidings and warnings.

57. Say: "No reward do I ask of you for it but this: that each one who will may take a (straight) Path to his Lord."

58. And put thy trust in Him Who lives and dies not; and celebrate His praise; and enough is He to be acquainted with the faults of His servants;—

59. He Who created the heavens and the earth and all that is between, in six days, then He established Himself on the Throne: Allah Most Gracious: ask thou, then, about Him of any acquainted (with such things).

60. When it is said to them, "Adore ye the Most Gracious!", They say, "And what is (Allah) Most Gracious? Shall we adore that which thou commandest us?" And it increases them in aversion.

61. Blessed is He Who made constellations in the skies, and placed therein a Lamp and a Moon giving light;

62. And it is He Who made the Night and the Day to follow each other for such as desire to be mindful or to show their

gratitude.

شُكُوْرًا ۝

63. And the servants of (Allah) Most Gracious are those who walk on the earth in humility, and when the ignorant address them, they say, "Peace!";

وَعِبَادُ الرَّحْمٰنِ الَّذِيْنَ يَمْشُوْنَ عَلَى الْأَرْضِ هَوْنًا وَّاِذَا خَاطَبَهُمُ الْجٰهِلُوْنَ قَالُوْا سَلٰمًا ۝

64. Those who spend the night in adoration of their Lord prostrate and standing;

وَالَّذِيْنَ يَبِيْتُوْنَ لِرَبِّهِمْ سُجَّدًا وَّ قِيَامًا ۝

65. Those who say, "Our Lord! avert from us the Wrath of Hell, for its Wrath is indeed an affliction grievous,—

وَالَّذِيْنَ يَقُوْلُوْنَ رَبَّنَا اصْرِفْ عَنَّا عَذَابَ جَهَنَّمَ اِنَّ عَذَابَهَا كَانَ غَرَامًا ۝

66. "Evil indeed is it as an abode, and as a place to rest in";

اِنَّهَا سَآءَتْ مُسْتَقَرًّا وَّمُقَامًا ۝

67. Those who, when they spend, are not extravagant and not niggardly, but hold a just (balance) between those (extremes);

وَالَّذِيْنَ اِذَا اَنْفَقُوْا لَمْ يُسْرِفُوْا وَلَمْ يَقْتُرُوْا وَكَانَ بَيْنَ ذٰلِكَ قَوَامًا ۝

68. Those who invoke not, with Allah, any other god, nor slay such life as Allah has made sacred, except for just cause, nor commit fornication;—and any that does this (not only) meets punishment,

وَالَّذِيْنَ لَا يَدْعُوْنَ مَعَ اللّٰهِ اِلٰهًا اٰخَرَ وَلَا يَقْتُلُوْنَ النَّفْسَ الَّتِيْ حَرَّمَ اللّٰهُ اِلَّا بِالْحَقِّ وَلَا يَزْنُوْنَ ۚ وَمَنْ يَّفْعَلْ ذٰلِكَ يَلْقَ اَثَامًا ۝

69. (But) the Chastisement on the Day of Judgment will be doubled to him, and he will dwell therein in ignominy,—

يُّضٰعَفْ لَهُ الْعَذَابُ يَوْمَ الْقِيٰمَةِ وَ يَخْلُدْ فِيْهِ مُهَانًا ۝

70. Unless he repents, believes, and works righteous deeds, for Allah will change the evil of such persons into good, and Allah is Oft-Forgiving, Most Merciful,

اِلَّا مَنْ تَابَ وَاٰمَنَ وَعَمِلَ عَمَلًا صَالِحًا فَاُولٰٓئِكَ يُبَدِّلُ اللّٰهُ سَيِّاٰتِهِمْ حَسَنٰتٍ ۚ وَكَانَ اللّٰهُ غَفُوْرًا رَّحِيْمًا ۝

71. And whoever repents and does good has truly turned to Allah in repentance:

وَمَنْ تَابَ وَعَمِلَ صَالِحًا فَاِنَّهٗ يَتُوْبُ اِلَى اللّٰهِ مَتَابًا ۝

72. Those who witness no falsehood and, if they pass by futility, they pass by it with honourable (avoidance);

وَالَّذِيْنَ لَا يَشْهَدُوْنَ الزُّوْرَ ۙ وَاِذَا مَرُّوْا بِاللَّغْوِ مَرُّوْا كِرَامًا ۝

73. Those who, when they are admonished with the Signs of their Lord, droop not down at them as if they were deaf or blind;

وَالَّذِيْنَ اِذَا ذُكِّرُوْا بِاٰيٰتِ رَبِّهِمْ لَمْ يَخِرُّوْا عَلَيْهَا صُمًّا وَّعُمْيَانًا ۝

74. And those who pray, "Our Lord! Grant unto us wives and offspring who

وَالَّذِيْنَ يَقُوْلُوْنَ رَبَّنَا هَبْ لَنَا مِنْ

SÛRA–26
ASH-SHU'ARÃA
(INTRODUCTION)

This Sûra begins a new series of four Sûras (26-29), which illustrate the contrast between the spirit of Prophecy and spiritual Light and the reaction to it in the communities among whom it appeared, by going back to old Prophets and the stories of the Past, as explained in the Introduction to S. 17.

In this particular Sûra we have the story of Moses in his fight with Pharaoh and of Pharaoh's discomfiture. Other Prophets mentioned are Abraham, Noah, Hûd, Ṣāliḥ, Lut and Shu'aib. The lesson is drawn that the Qur-ān is a continuation and fulfilment of previous Revelations, and is pure Truth, unlike the poerty of vain poets.

Chronologically, the Sûra belongs to the middle Makkan period, when the contact of the Light of Prophecy with the milieu of Pagan Makkah was testing the Makkans in their most arrogant mood.

will be the comfort of our eyes, and give us (the grace) to lead the righteous."

75. Those are the ones who will be rewarded with the highest place in heaven, because of their patient constancy: therein shall they be met with salutations and peace,

76. Dwelling therein;—how beautiful an abode and place of rest!

77. Say (to the Rejecters): "My Lord would not concern Himself with you but for your call on Him: but ye have indeed rejected (Him), and soon will come the inevitable (punishment)!"

Ash-Shu'araa, or The Poets

In the name of Allah, Most Gracious, Most Merciful.

1. Tā. Sīn. Mīm.

2. These are Verses of the Book that makes (things) clear.

3. It may be thou will kill thyself with grief, that they do not become Believers.

4. If (such) were Our Will, We could send down to them from the sky a Sign, to which they would bend their necks in humility.

5. But there comes not to them a newly-revealed Message from The Most Gracious, but they turn away therefrom.

6. They have indeed rejected (the Message): so they will know soon (en-ough) the truth of what they mocked at!

7. Do they not look at the earth, —how many noble things of all kinds We have produced therein?

8. Verily, in this is a Sign: but most of them do not believe.

9. And verily, thy Lord is He, the Exalted in Might, Most Merciful.

10. Behold, thy Lord called Moses: "Go to the people of iniquity,—

11. "The people of Pharaoh: will they not fear Allah?"

12. He said: "O my Lord! I do fear that they will charge me with falsehood:

13. "My breast will be straitened, and my tongue will not speak (plainly): so send unto Aaron.

14. "And (further), they have a charge of crime against me; and I fear they may slay me."

15. Allah said: "By no means! proceed then, both of you, with Our Signs; We are with you, and will listen (to your call).

16. "So go forth, both of you, to Pharaoh, and say: 'We have been sent by the Lord and Cherisher of the Worlds;

17. " 'Send thou with us the Children of Israel.' "

18. (Pharaoh) said: "Did we not cherish thee as a child among us, and didst thou not stay in our midst many years of thy life?

19. "And thou didst a deed of thine which (thou knowest) thou didst, and thou art an ungrateful!"

20. Moses said: "I did it then, when I was in error.

21. "So I fled from you (all) when I feared you; but my Lord has (since) invested me with judgment (and wisdom) and appointed me as one of the messengers.

22. "And this is the favour with which thou dost reproach me,—that you hast enslaved the Children of Israel!"

23. Pharaoh said: "And what is the Lord and Cherisher of the Worlds?"

24. (Moses) said: "The Lord and Cherisher of the heavens and the earth, and all between,—— if ye had but sure belief."

25. (Pharaoh) said to those around: "Do ye not listen (to what he says)?"

26. (Moses) said: "Your Lord and the Lord of your fathers from the beginning!"

27. (Pharaoh) said: "Truly your messenger who has been sent to you is a veritable madman!"

28. (Moses) said: "Lord of the East and the West, and all between! If ye only had sense!"

29. (Pharaoh) said: "If thou takest any god other than me, I will certainly put thee in

مِنَ الْمَسْجُونِينَ ۞

prison!"

30. (Moses) said: "Even if I showed you something clear (and) convincing?"

قَالَ أَوَلَوْجِئْتُكَ بِشَيْءٍ مُّبِينٍ ۞

31. (Pharaoh) said: "Show it then, if thou tellest the truth!"

قَالَ فَأْتِ بِهِ إِن كُنتَ مِنَ الصَّادِقِينَ ۞

32. So (Moses) threw his rod, and behold, it was a serpent, plain (for all to see)!

فَأَلْقَى عَصَاهُ فَإِذَا هِيَ ثُعْبَانٌ مُّبِينٌ ۞

33. And he drew out his hand. and behold, it was white to all beholders!

وَنَزَعَ يَدَهُ فَإِذَا هِيَ بَيْضَاءُ لِلنَّاظِرِينَ ۞

34. (Pharaoh) said to the Chiefs around him: "This is indeed a sorcerer well-versed:

قَالَ لِلْمَلَإِ حَوْلَهُ إِنَّ هَـٰذَا لَسَاحِرٌ عَلِيمٌ ۞

35. "His plan is to get you out of your land by his sorcery; then what is it ye counsel?"

يُرِيدُ أَن يُخْرِجَكُم مِّنْ أَرْضِكُم بِسِحْرِهِ فَمَاذَا تَأْمُرُونَ ۞

36. They said: "Keep him and his brother in suspense (for a while), and dispatch to the Cities heralds to collect—

قَالُوا أَرْجِهْ وَأَخَاهُ وَابْعَثْ فِي الْمَدَائِنِ حَاشِرِينَ ۞

37. "And bring up to thee all (our) sorcerers well-versed."

يَأْتُوكَ بِكُلِّ سَحَّارٍ عَلِيمٍ ۞

38. So the sorcerers were got together for the appointment of a day well-known.

فَجُمِعَ السَّحَرَةُ لِمِيقَاتِ يَوْمٍ مَّعْلُومٍ ۞

39. And the people were told: "Are ye (now) assembled?"—

وَقِيلَ لِلنَّاسِ هَلْ أَنتُم مُّجْتَمِعُونَ ۞

40. "That we may follow the sorcerers if they win?"

لَعَلَّنَا نَتَّبِعُ السَّحَرَةَ إِن كَانُوا هُمُ الْغَالِبِينَ ۞

41. So when the sorcerers arrived, they said to Pharaoh: "Of course—shall we have a (suitable) reward if we win?"

فَلَمَّا جَاءَ السَّحَرَةُ قَالُوا لِفِرْعَوْنَ أَئِنَّ لَنَا لَأَجْرًا إِن كُنَّا نَحْنُ الْغَالِبِينَ ۞

42. He said: "Yea, (and more),— for ye shall in that case be (raised to posts) nearest (to my person).

قَالَ نَعَمْ وَإِنَّكُمْ إِذًا لَّمِنَ الْمُقَرَّبِينَ ۞

43. Moses said to them: "Throw ye–that which ye are about to throw!"

قَالَ لَهُم مُّوسَى أَلْقُوا مَا أَنتُم مُّلْقُونَ ۞

44. So they threw their ropes and their rods, and said: "By the might of Pharaoh, it is we who will certainly win!"

فَأَلْقَوْا حِبَالَهُمْ وَعِصِيَّهُمْ وَقَالُوا بِعِزَّةِ فِرْعَوْنَ إِنَّا لَنَحْنُ الْغَالِبُونَ ۞

45. Then Moses threw his rod, when, behold, it straightway swallows up all the falsehoods which they fake!

فَأَلْقَى مُوسَى عَصَاهُ فَإِذَا هِيَ تَلْقَفُ مَا يَأْفِكُونَ ۞

46. Then did the sorcerers fall down, prostrate in adoration,

فَأُلْقِيَ السَّحَرَةُ سَاجِدِينَ ۞

47. Saying: "We believe in the Lord of the Worlds.

قَالُوا آمَنَّا بِرَبِّ الْعَالَمِينَ ۞

48. "The Lord of Moses and Aaron."

رَبِّ مُوسَى وَهَارُونَ ۞

49. Said (Pharaoh): "Believe ye in Him before I give you permission? Surely he is

قَالَ آمَنتُمْ لَهُ قَبْلَ أَنْ آذَنَ لَكُمْ إِنَّهُ لَكَبِيرُكُمُ الَّذِي عَلَّمَكُمُ السِّحْرَ

your leader, who has taught you sorcery!
But soon shall ye know! "Be sure I will cut
off your hands and your feet on opposite
sides, and I will crucify you all"

50. They said: "No matter! For us, we shall
but return to our Lord!

51. "Only, our desire is that our Lord will
forgive us our faults since we are the first to
believe."

52. By inspiration We told Moses: "Travel
by night with My servants; for surely ye
shall be pursued."

53. Then Pharaoh sent heralds to (all) the
Cities,

54. (Saying): "These (Israelites) are but a
small band,

55. "And they have surely enraged us:

56. "And we are a multitude amply fore-
warned."

57. So We expelled them from gardens,
springs,

58. Treasures, and every kind of
honourable position;

59. Thus it was, but We made the Children
of Israel inheritors of such things.

60. So they pursued them at sunrise.

61. And when the two bodies saw each
other, the people of Moses said: "We are
sure to be overtaken."

62. (Moses) said: "By no means! My Lord
is with me! Soon will He guide me!"

63. Then We told Moses by inspiration:
"Strike the sea with thy rod." So it divided,
and each separate part became like the
huge, firm mass of a mountain.

64. And We made the other party approach
thither.

65. We delivered Moses and all who were
with him;

66. But We drowned the others.

67. Verily in this is a Sign: but most of
them do not believe.

68. And verily thy Lord is He, the Exalted in Might, Most Merciful.

69. And rehearse to them (something of) Abraham's story.

70. Behold, he said to his father and his people: "What worship ye?"

71. They said: "We worship Idols, and we remain constantly in attendance on them."

72. He said: "Do they listen to you when ye call (on them),

73. Or do you good or harm?"

74. They said: "Nay, but we found our fathers doing thus (what we do)."

75. He said: "Do ye then see whom ye have been worshipping,—

76. "Ye and your fathers before you?—

77. "For they are enemies to me; not so the Lord and Cherisher of the Worlds;

78. "Who created me, and it is He Who guides me;

79. "Who gives me food and drink,

80. "And when I am ill, it is He who cures me;

81. "Who will cause me to die, and then to live (again);

82. "And who, I hope, will forgive me my faults on the Day of Judgment.

83. "O my Lord! bestow wisdom on me, and join me with the righteous;

84. "Grant me honourable mention on the tongue of truth among the latest (generations);

85. "Make me one of the inheritors of the Garden of Bliss;

86. "Forgive my father, for that He is among those astray;

87. "And let me not be in disgrace on the Day when (men) will be raised up;—

88. "The Day whereon neither wealth nor sons will avail,

89. "But only he (will prosper) that brings to Allah a sound heart;

90. "To the righteous, the Garden will be brought near,

91. "And to those straying in evil, the Fire will be placed in full view:

92. "And it shall be said to them: 'Where are the (gods) ye worshipped—93.

'Besides Allah? Can they help you or help themselves?' "

94. "Then they will be thrown headlong into the (Fire),--they and those straying in evil,

95. "And the whole hosts of Iblis together.

96. "They will say there in their mutual bickerings:

97. " 'By Allah, we were truly in an error manifest,

98. " 'When we held you as equals with the Lord of the Worlds;

99. " 'And our seducers were only those who were steeped in guilt.

100. " 'Now, then, we have none to intercede (for us),

101. " 'Nor a single intimate friend

102. " 'Now if we only had a chance of return, we shall truly be of those who believe!' "

103. Verily in this is a Sign but most of them do not believe.

104. And verily thy Lord is He, the Exalted in Might, Most Merciful.

105. The people of Noah rejected the messengers.

106. Behold, their brother Noah said to them: "Will ye not Fear (Allah)?

107. "I am to you a trustworthy messenger

108. "So fear Allah, and obey me.

109. "No reward do I ask of you for it: my reward is only from the Lord of the Worlds:

110. "So fear Allah, and obey me."

111. They said: "Shall we believe in thee when it is the meanest that follow thee?"

112. He said: "And what do I know as to what they do?

113. "Their account is only with my Lord, if ye could (but) understand.

114. "I am not one to drive away those who believe.

115. "I am sent only as a plain warner".

116. They said: "If thou desist not, O Noah! thou shalt be stoned (to death).

يَنتَصِرُونَ ۞

فَكُبْكِبُوا فِيهَا هُمْ وَالْغَاوُونَ ۞

وَجُنُودُ إِبْلِيسَ أَجْمَعُونَ ۞

قَالُوا وَهُمْ فِيهَا يَخْتَصِمُونَ ۞

تَاللَّهِ إِن كُنَّا لَفِي ضَلَالٍ مُّبِينٍ ۞

إِذْ نُسَوِّيكُم بِرَبِّ الْعَالَمِينَ ۞

وَمَا أَضَلَّنَا إِلَّا الْمُجْرِمُونَ ۞

فَمَا لَنَا مِن شَافِعِينَ ۞

وَلَا صَدِيقٍ حَمِيمٍ ۞

فَلَوْ أَنَّ لَنَا كَرَّةً فَنَكُونَ مِنَ الْمُؤْمِنِينَ ۞

إِنَّ فِي ذَلِكَ لَآيَةً وَمَا كَانَ أَكْثَرُهُم مُّؤْمِنِينَ ۞

وَإِنَّ رَبَّكَ لَهُوَ الْعَزِيزُ الرَّحِيمُ ۞

كَذَّبَتْ قَوْمُ نُوحٍ الْمُرْسَلِينَ ۞

إِذْ قَالَ لَهُمْ أَخُوهُمْ نُوحٌ أَلَا تَتَّقُونَ ۞

إِنِّي لَكُمْ رَسُولٌ أَمِينٌ ۞

فَاتَّقُوا اللَّهَ وَأَطِيعُونِ ۞

وَمَا أَسْأَلُكُمْ عَلَيْهِ مِنْ أَجْرٍ إِنْ أَجْرِيَ إِلَّا عَلَى رَبِّ الْعَالَمِينَ ۞

فَاتَّقُوا اللَّهَ وَأَطِيعُونِ ۞

قَالُوا أَنُؤْمِنُ لَكَ وَاتَّبَعَكَ الْأَرْذَلُونَ ۞

قَالَ وَمَا عِلْمِي بِمَا كَانُوا يَعْمَلُونَ ۞

إِنْ حِسَابُهُمْ إِلَّا عَلَى رَبِّي لَوْ تَشْعُرُونَ ۞

وَمَا أَنَا بِطَارِدِ الْمُؤْمِنِينَ ۞

إِنْ أَنَا إِلَّا نَذِيرٌ مُّبِينٌ ۞

قَالُوا لَئِن لَّمْ تَنتَهِ يَا نُوحُ لَتَكُونَنَّ مِنَ الْمَرْجُومِينَ ۞

117. He said: "O my Lord! truly my people have rejected me.

قَالَ رَبِّ إِنَّ قَوْمِي كَذَّبُونِ ۝

118. "Judge thou, then, between me and them openly, and deliver me and those of the Believers who are with me."

فَافْتَحْ بَيْنِي وَبَيْنَهُمْ فَتْحًا وَنَجِّنِي وَمَن مَّعِيَ مِنَ الْمُؤْمِنِينَ ۝

119. So We delivered him and those with him. In the Ark filled (with all creatures).

فَأَنجَيْنَاهُ وَمَن مَّعَهُ فِي الْفُلْكِ الْمَشْحُونِ ۝

120. Thereafter We drowned those who remained behind.

ثُمَّ أَغْرَقْنَا بَعْدُ الْبَاقِينَ ۝

121. Verily in this is a Sign: but most of them do not believe.

إِنَّ فِي ذَٰلِكَ لَآيَةً ۖ وَمَا كَانَ أَكْثَرُهُم مُّؤْمِنِينَ ۝

122. And verily thy Lord is He, the Exalted in Might, Most Merciful.

وَإِنَّ رَبَّكَ لَهُوَ الْعَزِيزُ الرَّحِيمُ ۝

123. The 'Ād (people) rejected the messengers.

كَذَّبَتْ عَادٌ الْمُرْسَلِينَ ۝

124. Behold, their brother Hūd said to them: "Will ye not fear (Allah)?

إِذْ قَالَ لَهُمْ أَخُوهُمْ هُودٌ أَلَا تَتَّقُونَ ۝

125. "I am to you a messenger worthy of all trust:

إِنِّي لَكُمْ رَسُولٌ أَمِينٌ ۝

126. "So fear Allah and obey me.

فَاتَّقُوا اللَّهَ وَأَطِيعُونِ ۝

127. "No reward do I ask of you for it: my reward is only from the Lord of the Worlds.

وَمَا أَسْأَلُكُمْ عَلَيْهِ مِنْ أَجْرٍ ۖ إِنْ أَجْرِيَ إِلَّا عَلَىٰ رَبِّ الْعَالَمِينَ ۝

128. "Do ye build a landmark on eve-ry high place to amuse yourselves?

أَتَبْنُونَ بِكُلِّ رِيعٍ آيَةً تَعْبَثُونَ ۝

129. "And do ye get for yourselves fine buildings in the hope of living therein (for ever)?

وَتَتَّخِذُونَ مَصَانِعَ لَعَلَّكُمْ تَخْلُدُونَ ۝

130. "And when ye strike you strike like tyrants.

وَإِذَا بَطَشْتُم بَطَشْتُمْ جَبَّارِينَ ۝

131. "Now fear Allah, and obey me.

فَاتَّقُوا اللَّهَ وَأَطِيعُونِ ۝

132. "Yea, fear Him Who has bestowed on you freely all that ye know.

وَاتَّقُوا الَّذِي أَمَدَّكُم بِمَا تَعْلَمُونَ ۝

133. "Freely has He bestowed on you cattle and sons,—

أَمَدَّكُم بِأَنْعَامٍ وَبَنِينَ ۝

134. "And Gardens and Springs.

وَجَنَّاتٍ وَعُيُونٍ ۝

135. "Truly I fear for you the Chastisement of a Great Day."

إِنِّي أَخَافُ عَلَيْكُمْ عَذَابَ يَوْمٍ عَظِيمٍ ۝

136. They said: "It is the same to us whether thou admonish us or be not among (our) admonishers!

قَالُوا سَوَاءٌ عَلَيْنَا أَوَعَظْتَ أَمْ لَمْ تَكُن مِّنَ الْوَاعِظِينَ ۝

137. "This is no other than a customary device of the ancients,

إِنْ هَٰذَا إِلَّا خُلُقُ الْأَوَّلِينَ ۝

138. "And we are not the ones to receive Pains and Chastisement!"

وَمَا نَحْنُ بِمُعَذَّبِينَ ۝

139. So they rejected him, and We destroyed them. Verily in this is a Sign: but

فَكَذَّبُوهُ فَأَهْلَكْنَاهُمْ ۗ إِنَّ فِي ذَٰلِكَ لَآيَةً

rnost of them do not believe.

140. And verily thy Lord is He, the Exalted in Might, Most Merciful.

141. The Thamūd (people) rejected the messengers.

142. Behold, their brother Sālih said to them: "Will you not fear (Allah)?

143. "I am to you a messenger worthy of all trust.

144. "So fear Allah, and obey me.

145. "No reward do I ask of you for it: my reward is only from the Lord of the Worlds.

146. "Will ye be left secure, in (the enjoyment of) all that ye have here?—

147. "Gardens and Springs,

148. "And corn-fields and date palms with spathes near breaking (with the weight of fruit)?

149. "And ye carve houses out of (rocky) mountains with great skill.

150. "But fear Allah and obey me;

151. "And follow not the bidding of those who are extravagant,—

152. "Who make mischief in the land, and mend not (their ways)."

153. They said: "Thou art only one of those bewitched!

154. "Thou art no more than a mortal like us: then bring us a Sign, if thou tellest the truth!"

155. He said: "Here is a she-camel: she has a right of watering, and ye have a right of watering, (severally) on a day appointed.

156. "Touch her not with harm, lest the Chastisement of a Great Day seize you."

157. But they hamstrung her: then did they become full of regrets.

158. But the Chastisement seized them. Verily in this is a Sign: but most of them do not believe.

159. And verily thy Lord is He, the Exalted in Might, Most Merciful.

160. The people of Lūt rejected the messengers.

161. Behold, their brother Lût said to them: "Will ye not fear (Allah)?

162. "I am to you a messenger worthy of all trust.

163. "So fear Allah and obey me.

164. "No reward do I ask of you for it: my reward is only from the Lord of the Worlds.

165. "Of all the creatures in the world, will ye approach males,

166. "And leave those whom Allah has created for you to be your mates? Nay, ye are a people transgressing (all limits)!"

167. They said: "If thou desist not, O Lût ! thou wilt assuredly be cast out!"

168. He said: "I do detest your doings."

169. "O my Lord! deliver me and my family from such things as they do!"

170. So We delivered him and his family,—all

171. Except an old woman who lingered behind.

172. Then the rest We destroyed utterly.

173. We rained down on them a shower (of brimstone): and evil was the shower on those who were admonished (But heeded not)!

174. Verily in this is a Sign: but most of them do not believe.

175. And verily thy Lord is He, the Exalted in Might Most Merciful.

176. The Companions of the Wood rejected the messengers.

177. Behold, Shu'aib said to them: "Will ye not fear (Allah)?

178. "I am to you a messenger worthy of all trust.

179. "So fear Allah and obey me.

180. "No reward do I ask of you for it: my reward is only from the Lord of the Worlds.

181. "Give just measure, and cause no loss (to others by fraud).

182. "And weigh with scales true and upright.

183. "And withhold not things justly due to men, nor do evil in the land, working mischief.

184. "And fear Him Who created you and (Who created) the generations before (you)."

185. They said: "Thou art only one of those bewitched!

186. "Thou art no more than a mortal like us, and indeed we think thou art a liar!

187. "Now cause a piece of the sky to fall on us, if thou art truthful!"

188. He said: "My Lord knows best what ye do."

189. But they rejected him. Then the punishment of a day of overshadowing gloom seized them, and that was the Chastisement of a Great Day.

190. Verily in that is a Sign: but most of them do not believe.

191. And verily thy Lord is He, the Exalted in Might Most Merciful.

192. Verily this is a Revelation from the Lord of the Worlds:

193. With it came down the Truthful spirit

194. To thy heart that thou mayest admonish

195. In the perspicuous Arabic tongue.

196. Without doubt it is (announced) in the revealed Books of former peoples.

197. Is it not a Sign to them that the Learned of the Children of Israel knew it (as true)?

198. Had We revealed it to any of the non-Arabs,

199. And had he recited it to them, they would not have believed in it.

200. Thus have We caused it to enter the hearts of the Sinners.

201. They will not believe in it until they see the grievous Chastisement

202. But it will come to them of a sudden, while they perceive it not;

203. Then they will say: "Shall we be respited?"

204. Do they then ask for Our Chastisement to be hastened on?

205. Seest thou? If We do let them enjoy (this life) for a few years,

206. Yet there comes to them at length the (Punishment) which they were promised!

207. It will profit them not the enjoyment they were given.

208. Never did We destroy a town but had its warners—

209. By way of reminder; and We never are unjust.

210. The Satans did not bring it down:

211. It is not meet for them, nor is it in their power

212. Indeed they are banished from hearing it.

213. So call not on any other god with Allah, or thou wilt be among those who will be punished.

214. And admonish thy nearest kinsmen,

215. And lower thy wing to the Believers who follow thee.

216. Then if they disobey thee, say: "I am free (of responsibility) from what ye do!"

217. And put thy trust on the Exalted in Might, the Merciful,

218. Who seeth thee standing forth (in prayer),

219. And thy movements among those who prostrate themselves.

220. For it is He Who heareth and knoweth all things.

221. Shall I inform you, (O people), on whom it is that the Satans descend?

222. They descend on every lying, wicked person,

223. They listen eagerly and most of them are liars.

224. And the Poets,— it is those straying in Evil, who follow them:

225. Seest thou not that they wan-der distracted in every valley?—

226. And that they say what they practise not?—

227. Except those who believe, work

SÛRA-27

AN-NAML

(INTRODUCTION)

This Sûra is cognate in subject to the one preceding it and the two following it. Its chronological place is also in the same group of four.

Here there is much mystic symbolism. Wonders in the physical world are types of greater wonders in the spiritual world. The Fire, the White Hand and the Rod, in the story of Moses; the speech of birds, the crowds of Jinns and men pitted against a humble ant, and the Hoopoe and the Queen of Sheba, in Solomon's story; the defeat of the plot of the nine wicked men in the story of Ṣāliḥ; and the crime of sin with open eyes in the story of Lot;— lead up to the lessons of true and false worship and the miracles of Allah's grace and revelation.

righteousness, engaged much in the remembrance of Allah, and defend themselves after they are unjustly attacked. And soon will the unjust know what vicissitudes their affairs will take!

An-Naml, or the Ants

In the name of Allah, Most Gracious, Most Merciful.

1. Tā. Sîn. These are verses of the Qur-ān,— A Book that makes (things) clear;

2. A Guide; and Glad Tidings for the Believers,—

3. Those who establish regular prayers and give zakat, and also have sure faith in the Hereafter.

4. As to those who believe not in the Hereafter, We have made their deeds pleasing in their eyes; and so they wander blindly.

5. Such are they for whom a grievous Chastisement is (waiting): and in the Hereafter theirs will be the greatest loss.

6. As for thee, thou receivest the Qur'an from One All-Wise, All-Knowing.

7. Behold! Moses said to his family: "I perceive a fire; soon will I bring you from there some information, or I will bring you a burning brand (to light our fuel,) that ye may warm yourselves.

8. But when he came to the (Fire), a voice was heard: "Blessed are those in the Fire and those around: and Glory to Allah, the Lord of the Worlds.

9. "O Moses! Verily, I am Allah, the Exalted in Might, the Wise!...

10. "Now do thou throw thy rod!" But when he saw it moving (of its own accord) as if it had been a snake, He turned back in retreat, and retraced not his steps: "O Moses!" (it was said), "Fear not: truly, in My presence, those called as messengers have no fear,—

11. "But if any have done wrong and have thereafter substituted good to take the place of evil, truly, I am Oft-Forgiving, Most Merciful.

12. "Now put thy hand into thy bosom, and it will come forth white without stain (or

harm): (these are) among the nine Signs (thou wilt take) to Pharaoh and his people: for they are a people rebellious in transgression."

13. But when Our Signs came to them, visibly they said: "This is sorcery manifest!"

14. And they denied them, though their souls acknowledged them wrongfully and out of pride: so see what was the end of those who acted corruptly!

15. We gave knowledge to David and Solomon: and they both said: "Praise be to Allah, Who has favoured us above many of His servants who believe!"

16. And Solomon was David's heir. He said: "O ye people! we have been taught the speech of Birds, and we have been given of everything this is indeed Grace manifest (from Allah.)"

17. And before Solomon were marshalled his hosts,—of Jinns and men and birds, and they were all kept in order and ranks.

18. At length, when they came to a valley of ants, one of the ants said: "O ye ants, get into your habitations, lest Solomon and his hosts crush you (under foot) without knowing it."

19. So he smiled, amused at her speech; and he said: "O my Lord! so order me that I may be grateful for Thy favours, which Thou has bestowed on me and on my parents, and that I may work the righteousness that will please Thee: and admit me, by Thy Grace, to the ranks of Thy righteous Servants."

20. And he took a muster of the Birds; and he said: "Why is it I see not the Hoopoe? Or is he among the absentees?

21. "I will certainly punish him with a severe punishment, or execute him, unless he bring me a clear reason (for absence)."

22. But the Hoopoe tarried not far: he (came up and) said: "I have compassed

which thou hast not compassed, and I have come to thee from Sabā with tidings true.

23. "I found (there) a woman ruling over them and provided with every requisite; and she has a magnificent throne.

24. "I found her and her people worshipping the sun besides Allah: Satan has made their deeds seem pleasing in their eyes, and has kept them away from the Path,—so they receive no guidance,—

25. "So that they worship not Allah who brings forth what is hidden in the heavens and the earth, and knows what ye hide and what ye reveal.

26. "Allah!—there is no god but He!—Lord of the Throne Supreme!"

27. (Solomon) said: "Soon shall we see whether thou hast told the truth or lied!

28. "Go thou, with this letter of mine, and deliver it to them: then draw back from them, and (wait to) see what answer they return"...

29. (The Queen) said: "Ye chiefs! here is—delivered to me—a letter worthy of respect.

30. "It is from Solomon, and is (as follows): 'In the name of Allah, Most Gracious, Most Merciful:

31. " 'Be ye not arrogant against me, but come to me in submission (to the true Religion).' "

32. She said: "Ye chiefs! advise me in (this) my affair: no affair have I decided except in your presence."

33. They said: "We are endued with strength, and given to vehement war: but the command is with thee; so consider what thou wilt command."

34. She said: "Kings, when they enter a country, despoil it, and make the noblest of its people its meanest thus do they behave.

35. "But I am going to send him a present, and (wait) to see with what (answer) return

(my) ambassadors."

يَرْجِعُ الْمُرْسَلُونَ ۝

36. Now when (the embassy) came to Solomon, he said: "Will ye give me abundance in wealth? But that which Allah has given me is better than that which He has given you! Nay it is ye who rejoice in your gift!

فَلَمَّا جَاءَ سُلَيْمٰنَ قَالَ اَتُمِدُّونَنِ بِمَالٍ فَمَا اٰتٰىنِۦَ اللّٰهُ خَيْرٌ مِّمَّا اٰتٰىكُمْ بَلْ اَنْتُمْ بِهَدِيَّتِكُمْ تَفْرَحُونَ ۝

37. "Go back to them, and be sure we shall come to them with such hosts as they will never be able to meet: we shall expel them from there in disgrace, and they will feel humbled (indeed)."

اِرْجِعْ اِلَيْهِمْ فَلَنَأْتِيَنَّهُمْ بِجُنُودٍ لَّا قِبَلَ لَهُمْ بِهَا وَلَنُخْرِجَنَّهُمْ مِّنْهَا اَذِلَّةً وَّهُمْ صٰغِرُونَ ۝

38. He said (to his own men): "Ye Chiefs! which of you can bring me her throne before they come to me in submission?"

قَالَ يٰٓاَيُّهَا الْمَلَؤُا اَيُّكُمْ يَأْتِيْنِيْ بِعَرْشِهَا قَبْلَ اَنْ يَّأْتُوْنِيْ مُسْلِمِيْنَ ۝

39. A stalwart of the Jinn said: "I will bring it to thee before thou rise from thy council: indeed I have full strength for the purpose, and may be trusted."

قَالَ عِفْرِيْتٌ مِّنَ الْجِنِّ اَنَا اٰتِيْكَ بِهٖ قَبْلَ اَنْ تَقُوْمَ مِنْ مَّقَامِكَ وَاِنِّيْ عَلَيْهِ لَقَوِيٌّ اَمِيْنٌ ۝

40. Said one who had knowledge of the Book: "I will bring it to thee before ever thy glance returns to thee. Then when (Solomon) saw it placed firmly before him, he said: "This is by the grace of my Lord!— to test me whether I am grateful or ungrateful! And if any is grateful, truly his gratitude is (a gain) for his own soul; but if any is ungrateful, truly my Lord is Free of all Needs, Supreme in Honour!"

قَالَ الَّذِيْ عِنْدَهٗ عِلْمٌ مِّنَ الْكِتٰبِ اَنَا اٰتِيْكَ بِهٖ قَبْلَ اَنْ يَّرْتَدَّ اِلَيْكَ طَرْفُكَ فَلَمَّا رَاٰهُ مُسْتَقِرًّا عِنْدَهٗ قَالَ هٰذَا مِنْ فَضْلِ رَبِّيْ لِيَبْلُوَنِيْٓ ءَاَشْكُرُ اَمْ اَكْفُرُ وَمَنْ شَكَرَ فَاِنَّمَا يَشْكُرُ لِنَفْسِهٖ وَمَنْ كَفَرَ فَاِنَّ رَبِّيْ غَنِيٌّ كَرِيْمٌ ۝

41. He said: "Disguise her throne. Let us see whether she is guided (to the truth) or is one of those who are not rightly guided."

قَالَ نَكِّرُوْا لَهَا عَرْشَهَا نَنْظُرْ اَتَهْتَدِيْٓ اَمْ تَكُوْنُ مِنَ الَّذِيْنَ لَا يَهْتَدُوْنَ ۝

42. So when she arrived, she was asked, "Is this thy throne?" She said, "It seems the same. And knowledge was bestowed on us in advance of this, and we have submitted to Allah (in Islām)."

فَلَمَّا جَاءَتْ قِيْلَ اَهٰكَذَا عَرْشُكِ قَالَتْ كَاَنَّهٗ هُوَ وَاُوْتِيْنَا الْعِلْمَ مِنْ قَبْلِهَا وَكُنَّا مُسْلِمِيْنَ ۝

43. And he diverted her from the worship of others besides Allah: for she was (sprung) of a people that had no faith.

وَصَدَّهَا مَا كَانَتْ تَّعْبُدُ مِنْ دُوْنِ اللّٰهِ اِنَّهَا كَانَتْ مِنْ قَوْمٍ كٰفِرِيْنَ ۝

44. She was asked to enter the lofty Palace: but when she saw it, she thought it was a lake of water, and she (tucked up her skirts), uncovering her legs. He said: "This is but a palace paved smooth with slabs of

قِيْلَ لَهَا ادْخُلِي الصَّرْحَ فَلَمَّا رَاَتْهُ حَسِبَتْهُ لُجَّةً وَّكَشَفَتْ عَنْ سَاقَيْهَا قَالَ اِنَّهٗ صَرْحٌ مُّمَرَّدٌ مِّنْ قَوَارِيْرَ

glass." She said: "O my Lord! I have indeed wronged my soul: I do (now) submit (in Islām), with Solomon, to the Lord of the Worlds."

45. We sent (aforetime), to the Thamūd, their brother Sālih, saying, "Serve Allah": but behold, they became two factions quarrelling with each other.

46. He said: "O my people! why ask ye to hasten on the evil before the good? If only ye ask Allah for forgiveness, ye may hope to receive mercy."

47. They said: "Ill omen do we augur from thee and those that are with thee". He said: "Your ill omen is with Allah; yea, ye are a people under trial."

48. There were in the City nine men, who made mischief in the land, and would not reform.

49. They said: "Swear a mutual oath by Allah that we shall make a secret night attack on him and his people, and that we shall then say to his heir (when he seeks vengeance): 'We were not present at the slaughter of his people, and we are positively telling the truth'."

50. They plotted and planned, but We too planned, even while they perceived it not.

51. Then see what was the end of their plot!—this, that We destroyed them and their people, all (of them).

52. Now such were their houses,—in utter ruin,—because they practised wrong-doing. Verily in this is a Sign for people of knowledge.

53. And We saved those who believed and practised righteousness.

54. (We also sent) Lūt (as a messenger): behold, he said to his people, "Do ye do what is indecent though ye see (its iniquity)?

55. Would ye really approach men in your lusts rather than women? Nay, ye are a people (grossly) ignorant!

56. But his people gave no other answer but this: They said, "Drive

out the followers of Lút from your city: these
are indeed men who want to be clean and
pure!"

57. But We saved him and his family,
except his wife: her We desti-ned to be of
those who lagged behind.

58. And We rained down on them a shower
(of brimstone): and evil was the shower on
those who were admonished (but heeded
not)!

59. Say: Praise be to Allah, and Peace on
His servants whom He has chosen (for His
Message). (Who) is better?—Allah or the
false gods they associate (with Him)?

60. On who has created the heavens and
the earth, and who sends you down rain
from the sky? Yea, with it We cause to grow
well-planted orchards full of beauty and
delight: it is not in your power to cause the
growth of the trees in them. (Can there be
another) god besides Allah? Nay, they are a
people who swerve from justice.

61. Or, who has made the earth firm to live
in; made rivers in its midst; set thereon
mountains immovable; and made a
separating bar between the two seas (can
there be another) god besides Allah? Nay,
most of them know not.

62. Or, who listens to the distressed when
he calls on Him, and Who relieves his
suffering, and makes you (mankind)
inheritors of the earth? (Can there be
another) god besides Allah? Little it is that
ye heed!

63. Or, who guides you through the depths
of darkness on land and sea, and who sends
the winds as heralds of glad tidings, going
before His Mercy? (Can there be another)
god besides Allah?—High is Allah above
what they associate with Him!

64. Or, who originates Creation, then
repeats it, and who gives you sustenance
from heaven and earth? (Can there be
another) god besides Allah? Say, "Bring
forth your argument, if ye are telling the
truth!"

65. Say: None in the heavens or on earth,
except Allah, knows what is hidden: nor can

they perceive when they shall be raised up (for Judgment).

الْغَيْبَ إِلَّا اللهُ وَمَا يَشْعُرُونَ أَيَّانَ يُبْعَثُونَ ۞

66. Nay, but their knowledge fails as to the Hereafter, they are in doubt and uncertainty thereanent; nay, they are blind thereunto!

بَلِ ادَّارَكَ عِلْمُهُمْ فِي الْأَخِرَةِ بَلْ هُمْ فِى شَكٍّ مِنْهَا بَلْ هُمْ مِنْهَا عَمُونَ ۞

67. The Unbelievers say "What! when we become dust,— we and our fathers,—shall we really be raised (from the dead)?

وَقَالَ الَّذِينَ كَفَرُوٓا أَءِذَا كُنَّا تُرَابًا وَّ اٰبَاؤُنَآ أَئِنَّا لَمُخْرَجُونَ ۞

68. "It is true we were promised this,—we and our fathers before (us): these are nothing but tales of the ancients."

لَقَدْ وُعِدْنَا هٰذَا نَحْنُ وَاٰبَاؤُنَا مِنْ قَبْلُ إِنْ هٰذَآ إِلَّآ أَسَاطِيرُ الْأَوَّلِينَ ۞

69. Say: "Go ye through the earth and see what has been the end of those guilty (of sin)."

قُلْ سِيرُوْا فِي الْأَرْضِ فَانْظُرُوْا كَيْفَ كَانَ عَاقِبَةُ الْمُجْرِمِينَ ۞

70. But grieve not over them, nor distress thyself because of their plots.

وَلَا تَحْزَنْ عَلَيْهِمْ وَلَا تَكُنْ فِي ضَيْقٍ مِمَّا يَمْكُرُونَ ۞

71. They also say: "When will this promise (come to pass)? If ye are truthful."

وَيَقُولُونَ مَتٰى هٰذَا الْوَعْدُ إِنْ كُنْتُمْ صٰدِقِينَ ۞

72. Say: "It may be that some of the events which ye wish to hasten on may be (close) in your pursuit!"

قُلْ عَسٰى أَنْ يَّكُونَ رَدِفَ لَكُمْ بَعْضُ الَّذِي تَسْتَعْجِلُونَ ۞

73. But verily thy Lord is full of grace to mankind: yet most of them are ungrateful.

وَإِنَّ رَبَّكَ لَذُوْ فَضْلٍ عَلَى النَّاسِ وَ لٰكِنَّ أَكْثَرَهُمْ لَا يَشْكُرُونَ ۞

74. And verily thy Lord knoweth all that their hearts do hide, as well as all that they reveal.

وَإِنَّ رَبَّكَ لَيَعْلَمُ مَا تُكِنُّ صُدُورُهُمْ وَمَا يُعْلِنُونَ ۞

75. And there is nothing hidden in heaven or earth, but is (recorded) in a clear record.

وَمَا مِنْ غَآئِبَةٍ فِي السَّمَآءِ وَالْأَرْضِ إِلَّا فِي كِتٰبٍ مُبِينٍ ۞

76. Verily this Qur-ān doth explain to the Children of Israel most of the matters in which they disagree.

إِنَّ هٰذَا الْقُرْاٰنَ يَقُصُّ عَلٰى بَنِيٓ إِسْرَآءِيلَ أَكْثَرَ الَّذِي هُمْ فِيهِ يَخْتَلِفُونَ ۞

77. And it certainly is a Guide and a Mercy to those who believe.

وَإِنَّهُ لَهُدًى وَّرَحْمَةٌ لِلْمُؤْمِنِينَ ۞

78. Verily thy Lord will decide between them by His Decree: and He is Exalted in Might, All-Knowing.

إِنَّ رَبَّكَ يَقْضِي بَيْنَهُمْ بِحُكْمِهِ وَهُوَ الْعَزِيزُ الْعَلِيمُ ۞

79. So put thy trust in Allah: for thou art on (the Path of) manifest Truth.

80. Truly thou canst not cause the Dead to listen, nor canst thou cause the Deaf to hear the call, (especially) when they turn back in retreat.

81. Nor canst thou be a guide to the Blind, (to prevent them) from straying: only those wilt thou get to listen who believe in Our Signs, so they submit.

82. And when the Word is fulfilled against them (the unjust), We shall bring forth from the earth a Beast to speak unto them because mankind had no faith in Our Signs.

83. The Day We shall gather together from every people a troop of those who reject Our Signs, and they shall be kept in ranks,—

84. Until, when they come (before the Judgment-seat), (Allah) will say: "Did ye reject My Signs, though ye comprehended them not in knowledge, or what was it ye did?"

85. And the Word will be fulfilled against them, because of their wrong-doing, and they will be unable to speak (in plea).

86. See they not that We have made the Night for them to rest in and the Day to give them light? Verily in this are Signs for any people that believe!

87. And the Day that the Trumpet will be sounded—then will be smitten with terror those who are in the heavens, and those who are on earth, except such as Allah will please (to exempt): and all shall come to Him in utter humility.

88. Thou seest the mountains and thinkest them firmly fixed: but they shall pass away as the clouds pass away: (such is) the artistry of Allah, who disposes of all things in perfect order: for He is well acquainted with all that ye do.

89. If any do good, he will have better than it. And they will be secure from terror that Day.

SÛRA-28
AL-QAṢAṢ
(INTRODUCTION)

This Sûra continues the subject of Revelation and its reception by those to whom it is sent. But it emphasises new points : how the recipient of inspiration is prepared for his high destiny, even in the growth of his ordinary life, and how the rejection of Allah's Message by groups of men or by individuals is caused by overweening arrogance or avarice. The plight of those who reject the Truth is contrasted with the reward of the righteous.

With the possible exception of a few verses, it belongs to the late Makkan period, just preceding the Hijrat.

90. And if any do evil, their faces will be thrown headlong into the Fire: "Do ye receive a reward other than that which ye have earned by your deeds?"

91. For me, I have been commanded to serve the Lord of this City, Him Who has sanctified it and to Whom (belong) all things: and I am commanded to be of those who bow in Islam to Allah's Will,—

92. And to rehearse the Qur'an: and if any accept guidance, they do it for the good of their own souls, and if any stray, say: "I am only a Warner".

93. And say: "Praise be to Allah, Who will soon show you His Signs, so that ye shall know them:" and thy Lord is not unmindful of all that ye do.

Al-Qaṣaṣ, or the Narration

In the name of Allah, Most Gracious, Most Merciful.

1. Tā. Sîn. Mîm.

2. These are Verses of the Book that makes (things) clear.

3. We rehearse to thee some of the story of Moses and Pharaoh in Truth, for people who believe.

4. Truly Pharaoh elated himself in the land and divided its people into sections, depressing a group among them: their sons he slew, but he kept alive their females: for he was indeed an evil-doer.

5. And We wished to be gracious to those who were being depressed in the land, to make them leaders (in faith) and make them heirs,

6. To establish a firm place for them in the land, and to show Pharaoh, Hāmān, and their hosts, what they were dreading from them.

7. So We sent this inspiration to the mother of Moses: "Suckle (thy child), but when thou hast fears about him, cast him into the river, but fear not nor grieve: for We shall restore him to thee, and We shall

make him one of Our messengers."

8.   Then the people of Pharaoh picked him up (from the river): (it was intended) that (Moses) should be to them an adversary and a cause of sorrow: for Pharaoh and Hāmān and (all) their hosts were men of sin.

9.   The wife of Pharaoh said: "(Here is) a joy of the eye for me and for thee: slay him not. It may be that he will be of use to us, or we may adopt him as a son." And they perceived not (what they were doing)!

10.   And the heart of the mother of Moses became void: she was going almost to disclose his (case), had We not strengthened her heart (with faith), so that she might remain a (firm) believer.

11.   And she said to the sister of (Moses), "Trace him". So she (the sister) watched him from a distance and they perceived not.

12.   And We ordained that he refused suck at first, until (his sister came up and) said: "Shall I point out to you the people of a house that will nourish and bring him up for you and take care of him."

13.   Thus did We restore him to his mother, that her eye might be comforted, that she might not grieve, and that she might know that the promise of Allah is true: but most of them do not know.

14.   When he reached full age, and was firmly established (in life), We bestowed on him wisdom and knowledge: for thus do We reward those who do good.

15.   And he entered the City at a time when its people were not watching: and he found there two men fighting,— one of his own people, and the other, of his foes. Now the man of his own people appealed to him against his foe, and Moses struck him with his fist and killed him. He said: "This is a work of Satan: for he is an enemy that manifestly misleads!"

16.   He prayed: "O my Lord! I have indeed wronged my soul! Do Thou then forgive

me!" So (Allah) forgave him: for He is the Oft-Forgiving, Most Merciful.

17. He said: "O my Lord! for that Thou hast bestowed Thy Grace on me, never shall I be a help to those who sin!"

18. In the morning, he was in the city, fearful and vigilant when behold, the man who had, the day before, sought his help called aloud for his help (again). Moses said to him: "Thou art truly, one erring manifestly."

19. Then, when he was about to lay his hands on their enemy the man said: "O Moses! is it thy intention to slay me as thou slewest a man yesterday? Thou only desire to become a tyrant in the land, and not to be one who sets things right!"

20. And there came a man, running, from the furthest end of the City. He said: "O Moses! the Chiefs are taking counsel together about thee, to slay thee: so get thee away, for I do give thee sincere advice."

21. He therefore got away therefrom, looking about, in a state of fear. He prayed: "O my Lord! save me from people given to wrong-doing."

22. Then, when he turned his face towards (the land of) Madyan, he said: "I do hope that my Lord will sh-ow me the smooth and straight Path."

23. And when he arrived at the watering (place) in Madyan, he found there a group of men watering (their flocks), and besides them he found two women who were keeping back (their flocks). He said: "What is the matter with you?" They said: "We cannot water (our flocks) until the shepherds take back (their flocks): and our father is a very old man."

24. So he watered (their flocks) for them; then he turned back to the shade, and said: "O my lord! truly am I in (desperate) need of any good that Thou dost send me!"...

25. Afterwards one of the (damsels) came (back) to him, walking bashfully. She said:

"My father invites thee that he may reward thee for having watered (our flocks) for us." So when he came to him and narrated the story, he said: "Fear thou not: (well) hast thou escaped from unjust people."

قَالَتْ اِنَّ اَبِيْ يَدْعُوْكَ لِيَجْزِيَكَ اَجْرَ مَا سَقَيْتَ لَنَا فَلَمَّا جَاءَهُ وَقَصَّ عَلَيْهِ الْقَصَصَ قَالَ لَا تَخَفْ نَجَوْتَ مِنَ الْقَوْمِ الظّٰلِمِيْنَ ۞

26. Said one of the (damsels): "O my (dear) father! engage him on wages: truly the best of men for thee to employ is the (man) who is strong and trusty"...

قَالَتْ اِحْدٰىهُمَا يَاَبَتِ اسْتَأْجِرْهُ اِنَّ خَيْرَ مَنِ اسْتَأْجَرْتَ الْقَوِيُّ الْاَمِيْنُ ۞

27. He said: "I intend to wed one of these my daughters to thee, on condition that thou serve me for eight years; but if thou complete ten years, it will be (grace) from thee. But I intend not to place thee under a difficulty: thou wilt find me, indeed, if Allah wills, one of the righteous."

قَالَ اِنِّيْ اُرِيْدُ اَنْ اُنْكِحَكَ اِحْدَى ابْنَتَيَّ هٰتَيْنِ عَلٰى اَنْ تَأْجُرَنِيْ ثَمٰنِيَ حِجَجٍ فَاِنْ اَتْمَمْتَ عَشْرًا فَمِنْ عِنْدِكَ وَمَا اُرِيْدُ اَنْ اَشُقَّ عَلَيْكَ سَتَجِدُنِيْ اِنْ شَاءَ اللّٰهُ مِنَ الصّٰلِحِيْنَ ۞

28. He said: "Be that (the agreement between me and thee: whichever of the two terms I fulfil, let there be no injustice to me. Be Allah a witness to what we say."

قَالَ ذٰلِكَ بَيْنِيْ وَبَيْنَكَ اَيَّمَا الْاَجَلَيْنِ قَضَيْتُ فَلَا عُدْوَانَ عَلَيَّ وَاللّٰهُ عَلٰى مَا نَقُوْلُ وَكِيْلٌ ۞

29. Now when Moses had fulfilled the term, and was travelling with his family, he perceived a fire in the direction of Mount Tûr. He said to his family: "Tarry ye; I perceive a fire; I hope to bring you from there some information, or a burning firebrand, that ye may warm yourselves."

فَلَمَّا قَضٰى مُوْسَى الْاَجَلَ وَسَارَ بِاَهْلِهٖ اٰنَسَ مِنْ جَانِبِ الطُّوْرِ نَارًا قَالَ لِاَهْلِهِ امْكُثُوْا اِنِّيْ اٰنَسْتُ نَارًا لَّعَلِّيْ اٰتِيْكُمْ مِّنْهَا بِخَبَرٍ اَوْ جَذْوَةٍ مِّنَ النَّارِ لَعَلَّكُمْ تَصْطَلُوْنَ ۞

30. But when he came to the (Fire), he was called from the right bank of the valley, from a tree in hallowed ground: "O Moses! Verily I am Allah, the Lord of the Worlds...
31. "Now do thou throw thy rod!" But when he saw it moving (of its own accord) as if it had been a snake, he turned back in retreat, and retraced not his steps: "O Moses!" (it was said), "Draw near, and fear not: for thou art of those who are secure.
32. "Thrust thy hand into thy bosom, and it will come forth white without stain (or harm).

فَلَمَّا اَتٰىهَا نُوْدِيَ مِنْ شَاطِئِ الْوَادِ الْاَيْمَنِ فِي الْبُقْعَةِ الْمُبٰرَكَةِ مِنَ الشَّجَرَةِ اَنْ يّٰمُوْسَى اِنِّيْ اَنَا اللّٰهُ رَبُّ الْعٰلَمِيْنَ ۞ وَاَنْ اَلْقِ عَصَاكَ فَلَمَّا رَاٰهَا تَهْتَزُّ كَاَنَّهَا جَانٌّ وَلّٰى مُدْبِرًا وَّلَمْ يُعَقِّبْ يٰمُوْسَى اَقْبِلْ وَلَا تَخَفْ اِنَّكَ مِنَ الْاٰمِنِيْنَ ۞ اُسْلُكْ يَدَكَ فِيْ جَيْبِكَ تَخْرُجْ بَيْضَاءَ

and draw thy hand close to thy side (to guard) against fear. Those are the two credentials From thy Lord to Pharaoh and his Chiefs: for truly they are a people rebellious and wicked."

33. He said: "O my Lord! I have slain a man among them, and I fear lest they slay me.

34. "And my brother Aaron—he is more eloquent in speech than I: so send him with me as a helper, to confirm (and strengthen) me: for I fear that they may accuse me of falsehood."

35. He said: "We will certainly strengthen thy arm through thy brother, and invest you both with authority, so they shall not be able to touch you: with Our Signs shall ye triumph,—you two as well as those who follow you."

36. When Moses came to them with Our Clear Signs, they said: "This is nothing but sorcery faked up: never did we hear the like among our fathers of old!"

37. Moses said: "My Lord knows best who it is that comes with guidance from Him and whose End will be best in the Hereafter: certain it is that the wrong-doers will not prosper."

38. Pharaoh said: "O Chiefs! no god do I know for you but myself: therefore, O Hāmān! light me a (kiln to bake bricks) out of clay, and build me a lofty palace, that I may mount up to the god of Moses: but as far as I am concerned, I think (Moses) is a liar!"

39. And he was arrogant and insolent in the land, beyond reason.— he and his hosts: they thought that they would not have to return to Us!"

40. So We seized him and his hosts, and We flung them into the sea: now behold what was the End of those who did wrong!

41. And We made them (but) leaders inviting to the Fire; and on the Day of Judgment no help shall they find.

42. In this world We made a Curse to follow them: and on the Day of Judgment they will be among the loathed (and despised).

43. We did reveal to Moses the Book after We had destroyed the earlier generations, (to give) Insight to men, and Guidance and Mercy, that they might receive admonition.

44. Thou wast not on the Western side when We decreed the Commission to Moses, nor wast thou a witness (of those events).

45. But We raised up (new) generations, and long were the ages that passed over them; but thou wast not a dweller among the people of Madyan, rehearsing Our Signs to them; but it is We Who send Messengers (with inspiration).

46. Nor wast thou at the side of (the Mountain of) Tûr when We called (to Moses). Yet (art thou sent) as a Mercy from thy Lord, to give warning to a people to whom no warner had come before thee: in order that they may receive admonition.

47. If (We had) not (sent thee to the Quraish),—in case a calamity should seize them for (the deeds) that their hands have sent forth, they might say: "Our Lord! why didst Thou not send us a messenger? We should then have followed the Signs and been amongst those who believe!"

48. But (now), when the Truth has come to them from Ourselves, they say, "Why are not (Signs) sent to him, like those which were sent to Moses?" Do they not then reject (the Signs) which were formerly sent to Moses? They say: "Two kinds of sorcery, each assisting the other!" And they say: "For us, we reject all! (such things)!"

49. Say: "Then bring ye a Book from Allah, which is a better Guide than either of them, that I may follow it! (Do), if ye are truthful!"

50. But if they hearken not to thee, know that they only follow their own lusts: and who is more astray than one who follows his own lusts, devoid of guidance from Allah? For Allah guides not people given to wrong-doing.

قُلْ فَأْتُوا بِكِتَٰبٍ مِّنْ عِنْدِ اللَّهِ هُوَ أَهْدَىٰ مِنْهُمَآ أَتَّبِعْهُ إِن كُنتُمْ صَٰدِقِينَ ۝ فَإِن لَّمْ يَسْتَجِيبُوا لَكَ فَاعْلَمْ أَنَّمَا يَتَّبِعُونَ أَهْوَآءَهُمْ ۚ وَمَنْ أَضَلُّ مِمَّنِ اتَّبَعَ هَوَٰهُ بِغَيْرِ هُدًى مِّنَ اللَّهِ ۚ إِنَّ اللَّهَ لَا يَهْدِى الْقَوْمَ الظَّٰلِمِينَ ۝

51. Now have We brought them the Word in order that they may receive admonition.

وَلَقَدْ وَصَّلْنَا لَهُمُ الْقَوْلَ لَعَلَّهُمْ يَتَذَكَّرُونَ ۝

52. Those to whom We sent the Book before this,—they do believe in this (Revelation);

الَّذِينَ ءَاتَيْنَٰهُمُ الْكِتَٰبَ مِن قَبْلِهِۦ هُم بِهِۦ يُؤْمِنُونَ ۝

53. And when it is recited to them, they say: "We believe therein, for it is the Truth from our Lord: indeed we have been Muslims (bowing to Allah's Will) from before this."

وَإِذَا يُتْلَىٰ عَلَيْهِمْ قَالُوٓا ءَامَنَّا بِهِۦ إِنَّهُ الْحَقُّ مِن رَّبِّنَآ إِنَّا كُنَّا مِن قَبْلِهِۦ مُسْلِمِينَ ۝

54. Twice will they be given their reward, for that they have persevered, that they avert Evil with Good, and that they spend (in charity) out of what We have given them.

أُو۟لَٰٓئِكَ يُؤْتَوْنَ أَجْرَهُم مَّرَّتَيْنِ بِمَا صَبَرُوا وَيَدْرَءُونَ بِالْحَسَنَةِ السَّيِّئَةَ وَمِمَّا رَزَقْنَٰهُمْ يُنفِقُونَ ۝

55. And when they hear vain talk, they turn away therefrom and say: "To us our deeds, and to you yours; peace be to you: we seek not the ignorant."

وَإِذَا سَمِعُوا اللَّغْوَ أَعْرَضُوا عَنْهُ وَقَالُوا لَنَآ أَعْمَٰلُنَا وَلَكُمْ أَعْمَٰلُكُمْ سَلَٰمٌ عَلَيْكُمْ لَا نَبْتَغِى الْجَٰهِلِينَ ۝

56. It is true thou wilt not be able to guide everyone whom thou lovest; but Allah guides those whom He will and He knows best those who receive guidance.

إِنَّكَ لَا تَهْدِى مَنْ أَحْبَبْتَ وَلَٰكِنَّ اللَّهَ يَهْدِى مَن يَشَآءُ ۚ وَهُوَ أَعْلَمُ بِالْمُهْتَدِينَ ۝

57. They say: "If we were to follow the guidance with thee, we should be snatched away from our land." Have We not established for them a secure sanctuary, to which are brought as tribute fruits of all kinds,—a provision from Ourselves? But

وَقَالُوٓا إِن نَّتَّبِعِ الْهُدَىٰ مَعَكَ نُتَخَطَّفْ مِنْ أَرْضِنَآ ۚ أَوَلَمْ نُمَكِّن لَّهُمْ حَرَمًا ءَامِنًا يُجْبَىٰ إِلَيْهِ ثَمَرَٰتُ كُلِّ شَىْءٍ رِّزْقًا مِّن لَّدُنَّا وَلَٰكِنَّ أَكْثَرَهُمْ

most of them understand not.

58. And how many towns We destroyed, which exulted in their life (of ease and plenty)! Now those habitations of theirs, after them, are deserted,— all but a (miserable) few! And We are their heirs!

59. Nor was thy Lord the one to destroy a town until He had sent to its Centre a messenger, rehearsing to them Our Signs; nor are We going to destroy a population except when its members practise iniquity.

60. The (material) things which ye are given are but the conveniences of this life and the glitter thereof; but that which is with Allah is better and more enduring: will ye not then be wise?

61. Are (these two) alike?—One to whom We have made a goodly promise, and who is going to reach its (fulfilment), and one to whom We have given the good things of this life, but who, on the Day of judgment, is to be among those brought up (for punishment)?

62. That Day (Allah) will call to them, and say: "Where are My 'partners'?— whom ye imagined (to be such)?"

63. Those against whom the charge will be proved, will say: "Our Lord! these are the ones whom we led astray: we led them astray, as we were astray ourselves: we free ourselves (from them) to you. It was not us they worshipped."

64. It will be said (to them): "Call upon your 'partners' (for help)": they will call upon them, but they will not listen to them; and they will see the Chastisement (before them); (how they will wish) 'If only they had been open to guidance!'

65. That Day (Allah) will call to them, and say: "What was the answer ye gave to the messengers?"

66. Then the arguments that day will be obscure to them and they will not be able (even) to question each other.

لَا يَعْلَمُونَ ۝

وَكَمْ أَهْلَكْنَا مِن قَرْيَةٍ بَطِرَتْ مَعِيشَتَهَا فَتِلْكَ مَسَاكِنُهُمْ لَمْ تُسْكَن مِّن بَعْدِهِمْ إِلَّا قَلِيلًا وَكُنَّا نَحْنُ الْوَارِثِينَ ۝

وَمَا كَانَ رَبُّكَ مُهْلِكَ الْقُرَىٰ حَتَّىٰ يَبْعَثَ فِي أُمِّهَا رَسُولًا يَتْلُو عَلَيْهِمْ آيَاتِنَا وَمَا كُنَّا مُهْلِكِي الْقُرَىٰ إِلَّا وَأَهْلُهَا ظَالِمُونَ ۝

وَمَا أُوتِيتُم مِّن شَيْءٍ فَمَتَاعُ الْحَيَوٰةِ الدُّنْيَا وَزِينَتُهَا وَمَا عِندَ اللَّهِ خَيْرٌ وَأَبْقَىٰ أَفَلَا تَعْقِلُونَ ۝

أَفَمَن وَعَدْنَاهُ وَعْدًا حَسَنًا فَهُوَ لَاقِيهِ كَمَن مَّتَّعْنَاهُ مَتَاعَ الْحَيَوٰةِ الدُّنْيَا ثُمَّ هُوَ يَوْمَ الْقِيَامَةِ مِنَ الْمُحْضَرِينَ ۝

وَيَوْمَ يُنَادِيهِمْ فَيَقُولُ أَيْنَ شُرَكَائِيَ الَّذِينَ كُنتُمْ تَزْعُمُونَ ۝

قَالَ الَّذِينَ حَقَّ عَلَيْهِمُ الْقَوْلُ رَبَّنَا هَٰؤُلَاءِ الَّذِينَ أَغْوَيْنَا أَغْوَيْنَاهُمْ كَمَا غَوَيْنَا تَبَرَّأْنَا إِلَيْكَ مَا كَانُوا إِيَّانَا يَعْبُدُونَ ۝

وَقِيلَ ادْعُوا شُرَكَاءَكُمْ فَدَعَوْهُمْ فَلَمْ يَسْتَجِيبُوا لَهُمْ وَرَأَوُا الْعَذَابَ لَوْ أَنَّهُمْ كَانُوا يَهْتَدُونَ ۝

وَيَوْمَ يُنَادِيهِمْ فَيَقُولُ مَاذَا أَجَبْتُمُ الْمُرْسَلِينَ ۝

فَعَمِيَتْ عَلَيْهِمُ الْأَنبَاءُ يَوْمَئِذٍ فَهُمْ لَا يَتَسَاءَلُونَ ۝

67. But any that (in this life) had repented, believed, and worked righteousness, haply he shall be one of the successful.

فَأَمَّا مَن تَابَ وَءَامَنَ وَعَمِلَ صَالِحًا فَعَسَى أَن يَكُونَ مِنَ الْمُفْلِحِينَ ٦٧

68. Thy Lord does create and choose as He pleases: no choice have they (in the matter): Glory to Allah! and far is He above the partners they ascribe (to Him)!

وَرَبُّكَ يَخْلُقُ مَا يَشَاءُ وَيَخْتَارُ مَا كَانَ لَهُمُ الْخِيَرَةُ سُبْحَنَ اللَّهِ وَتَعَلَى عَمَّا يُشْرِكُونَ ٦٨

69. And thy Lord knows all that their hearts conceal and all that they reveal.

وَرَبُّكَ يَعْلَمُ مَا تُكِنُّ صُدُورُهُمْ وَمَا يُعْلِنُونَ ٦٩

70. And He is Allah: there is no god but He. To Him be praise, at the first and at the last: for Him is the Command, and to Him shall ye (all) be brought back.

وَهُوَ اللَّهُ لَا إِلَهَ إِلَّا هُوَ لَهُ الْحَمْدُ فِي الْأُولَى وَالْءَاخِرَةِ وَلَهُ الْحُكْمُ وَإِلَيْهِ تُرْجَعُونَ ٧٠

71. Say: See ye? If Allah were to make the Night perpetual over you to the Day of Judgment, what god is there other than Allah, who can give you light? Will ye not then hearken?

قُلْ أَرَءَيْتُمْ إِن جَعَلَ اللَّهُ عَلَيْكُمُ الَّيْلَ سَرْمَدًا إِلَى يَوْمِ الْقِيَمَةِ مَنْ إِلَهٌ غَيْرُ اللَّهِ يَأْتِيكُم بِضِيَاءٍ أَفَلَا تَسْمَعُونَ ٧١

72. Say: See ye? If Allah were to make the Day perpetual over you to the Day of Judgment, what god is there other than Allah, who can give you a Night in which ye can rest? Will ye not then see?

قُلْ أَرَءَيْتُمْ إِن جَعَلَ اللَّهُ عَلَيْكُمُ النَّهَارَ سَرْمَدًا إِلَى يَوْمِ الْقِيَمَةِ مَنْ إِلَهٌ غَيْرُ اللَّهِ يَأْتِيكُم بِلَيْلٍ تَسْكُنُونَ فِيهِ أَفَلَا تُبْصِرُونَ ٧٢

73. It is out of His Mercy that He has made for you Night and Day,—that ye may rest therein, and that ye may seek of His Grace;— and in order that ye may be grateful.

وَمِن رَّحْمَتِهِ جَعَلَ لَكُمُ الَّيْلَ وَالنَّهَارَ لِتَسْكُنُوا فِيهِ وَلِتَبْتَغُوا مِن فَضْلِهِ وَلَعَلَّكُمْ تَشْكُرُونَ ٧٣

74. The Day that He will call on them, He will say: "Where are My 'partners'? Whom ye imagined (to be such)?"

وَيَوْمَ يُنَادِيهِمْ فَيَقُولُ أَيْنَ شُرَكَاءِيَ الَّذِينَ كُنتُمْ تَزْعُمُونَ ٧٤

75. And from each people shall We draw a witness, and We shall say: "Produce your Proof": then shall they know that the Truth is with Allah (alone), and the (lies) which they invented will leave them in the lurch.

وَنَزَعْنَا مِن كُلِّ أُمَّةٍ شَهِيدًا فَقُلْنَا هَاتُوا بُرْهَانَكُمْ فَعَلِمُوا أَنَّ الْحَقَّ لِلَّهِ وَضَلَّ عَنْهُم مَّا كَانُوا يَفْتَرُونَ ٧٥

76. Qārūn was doubtless, of the people of

إِنَّ قَارُونَ كَانَ مِن قَوْمِ مُوسَى فَبَغَى

Moses; but he acted insolently towards them: such were the treasures We had bestowed on him, that their very keys would have been a burden to a body of strong men. Behold, his people said to him: "Exult not, for Allah loveth not those who exult (in riches).

عَلَيْهِمْ وَءَاتَيْنَهُ مِنَ الْكُنُوزِ مَآ اِنَّ مَفَاتِحَهُ لَتَنُوٓاُ بِالْعُصْبَةِ أُولِى الْقُوَّةِ اِذْ قَالَ لَهُ قَوْمُهُ لَا تَفْرَحْ اِنَّ اللّٰهَ لَا يُحِبُّ الْفَرِحِيْنَ ۟

77. "But seek, with the (wealth) which Allah has bestowed on thee, the Home of the Hereafter, nor forget thy portion in this world: but do thou good, as Allah has been good to thee, and seek not (occasions for) mischief in the land: for Allah loves not those who do mischief."

وَابْتَغِ فِيْمَآ ءَاتَىٰكَ اللّٰهُ الدَّارَ الْاٰخِرَةَ وَلَا تَنْسَ نَصِيْبَكَ مِنَ الدُّنْيَا وَأَحْسِنْ كَمَآ أَحْسَنَ اللّٰهُ اِلَيْكَ وَلَا تَبْغِ الْفَسَادَ فِى الْاَرْضِ اِنَّ اللّٰهَ لَا يُحِبُّ الْمُفْسِدِيْنَ

78. He said: "This has been given to me because of a certain knowledge which I have." Did he not know that Allah had destroyed, before him, (whole) generations,—which were superior to him in strength and greater in the amount (of riches) they had collected? But the wicked are not called (immediately) to account for their sins.

قَالَ اِنَّمَآ أُوتِيْتُهُ عَلَىٰ عِلْمٍ عِنْدِىْ ۚ أَوَلَمْ يَعْلَمْ أَنَّ اللّٰهَ قَدْ أَهْلَكَ مِنْ قَبْلِهِ مِنَ الْقُرُوْنِ مَنْ هُوَ أَشَدُّ مِنْهُ قُوَّةً وَّأَكْثَرُ جَمْعًا ۚ وَلَا يُسْئَلُ عَنْ ذُنُوْبِهِمُ الْمُجْرِمُوْنَ ۟

79. So he went forth among his people in the (pride of his worldly) glitter. Said those whose aim is the life of this World: "Oh! that we had the like of what Qārūn has got! for he is truly a lord of mighty good fortune!"

فَخَرَجَ عَلَىٰ قَوْمِهِ فِىْ زِيْنَتِهِ ۖ قَالَ الَّذِيْنَ يُرِيْدُوْنَ الْحَيٰوةَ الدُّنْيَا يٰلَيْتَ لَنَا مِثْلَ مَآ أُوتِىَ قَارُوْنُ ۙ اِنَّهُ لَذُوْ حَظٍّ عَظِيْمٍ ۟

80. But those who had been granted (true) knowledge said: "Alas for you! The reward of Allah (in the Hereafter) is best for those who believe and work righteousness: but this none shall attain, save those who steadfastly persevere (in good)."

وَقَالَ الَّذِيْنَ أُوتُوا الْعِلْمَ وَيْلَكُمْ ثَوَابُ اللّٰهِ خَيْرٌ لِّمَنْ ءَامَنَ وَعَمِلَ صَالِحًا ۚ وَلَا يُلَقّٰىهَآ اِلَّا الصّٰبِرُوْنَ ۟

81. Then We caused the earth to swallow up him and his house; and he had not (the least little) party to help him against Allah, nor could he defend himself.

فَخَسَفْنَا بِهِ وَبِدَارِهِ الْاَرْضَ ۖ فَمَا كَانَ لَهُ مِنْ فِئَةٍ يَّنْصُرُوْنَهُ مِنْ دُوْنِ اللّٰهِ ۖ وَمَا كَانَ مِنَ الْمُنْتَصِرِيْنَ ۟

82. And those who had envied his position the day before began to say on the morrow: "Ah! it is indeed Allah Who enlarges the provision or restricts it, to any of His servants He pleases! Had it not been that Allah was gracious to us, He could have caused the earth

وَأَصْبَحَ الَّذِيْنَ تَمَنَّوْا مَكَانَهُ بِالْاَمْسِ يَقُوْلُوْنَ وَيْكَأَنَّ اللّٰهَ يَبْسُطُ الرِّزْقَ لِمَنْ يَّشَآءُ مِنْ عِبَادِهِ وَيَقْدِرُ ۖ لَوْلَا أَنْ مَّنَّ اللّٰهُ عَلَيْنَا لَخَسَفَ بِنَا ۖ وَيْكَأَنَّهُ

SÛRA-29
AL-'ANKABÛT
(INTRODUCTION)

This Sûra is the last of the series begun with S. 17 in which the growth of the spiritual man as an individual in considered, especially illustrated by the way in which the great apostles were prepared for their work and received their mission, and the nature of Revelation in relation to the environments in which it was promulgated. (See Introduction to S. 17). It also closes the sub-series beginning with S. 26 which is concerned with the spiritual Light, and the reactions to it at certain periods of spiritual history. (See Introduction to S. 26).

The last Sûra closed with a reference to the doctrine of the *Ma'ad*, or final Return of man to Allah. This theme is further developed here, and as it is continued in the subsequent three Sûras all bearing the Abbreviated Letters A.L.M., it forms a connecting link between the present series and those three Sûras.

In particular, emphasis is laid here on the necessity of linking actual conduct with the reception of Allah's revelation, and reference is again made to the stories of Noah, Abraham, and Lot among the apostles, and the stories of Midian, Ãd, Thamûd, and Pharaoh among the rejecters of Allah's Message. This world's life is contrasted with the real Life of the Hereafter.

Chronologically, the main Sûra belongs to the late Middle Makkan period, but the chronology has no significance except as showing how clearly the vision of the Future was revealed long before the Hijrat, to the struggling Brotherhood of Islam.

to swallow us up! Ah! those who reject Allah will assuredly never prosper."

83. That Home of the Hereafter We shall give to those who intend not high-handedness or mischief on earth: and the End is (best) for the righteous.

84. If any does good, the reward to him is better than his deed, but if any does evil, the doers of evil are only punished (to the extent) of their deeds.

85. Verily He Who ordained the Qur-ān for thee, will bring thee back to the Place of Return. Say: "My Lord knows best who it is that brings true guidance, and who is in manifest error."

86. And thou hadst not expected that the Book would be sent to thee except as a Mercy from thy Lord: therefore lend not thou support in any way to those who reject (Allah's Message).

87. Let no one turn you away from Allah's revelations after they have been revealed to thee: and invite (men) to thy Lord and be not of the company of those who join gods with Allah.

88. And call not, besides Allah, on another god. There is no god but He. Everything (that exists) will perish except His Face. To Him belongs the Command, and to Him will ye (all) be brought back.

Al-'Ankabût, or the Spider

In the name of Allah, Most Gracious, Most Merciful.

1. A. L. M.

2. Do men think that they will be left alone on saying, "We believe", and that they will not be tested?

3. We did test those before them, and Allah will certainly know those who are true from those who are false.

4. Do those who practise evil think that

they will outstrip Us? Evil is their judgment!

5.   For those whose hopes are in the meeting with Allah, the Term (appointed) by Allah is surely coming: and He hears and knows (all things).

6.   And if any strive (with might and main), they do so for their own souls: for Allah is free of all needs from all creation.

7.   Those who believe and work righteous deeds,—from them shall We blot out all misdeeds that they have committed, and We shall reward them according to the best of their deeds.

8.   We have enjoined on man kindness to parents: but if they (either of them) strive (to force) thee to join with Me (in worship) anything of which thou hast no knowledge, obey them not. Ye have (all) to return to Me, and I will tell you (the truth) of all that ye did.

9.   And those who believe and work righteous deeds,—them shall We admit to the company of the Righteous.

10.   Then there are among men such as say. "We believe in Allah"; but when they suffer affliction in (the cause of) Allah, they treat men's oppression as if it were the Wrath of Allah! And if help comes (to thee) from thy Lord, they are sure to say, "We have (always) been with you!" Does not Allah know best all that is in the hearts of all Creation!

11.   And Allah most certainly knows those who believe, and as certainly those who are Hypocrites.

12.   And the Unbelievers say to those who believe: "Follow our path, and we will bear (the consequences) of your faults." Never in the least will they bear their faults: in fact they are liars!

13.   They will bear their own burdens, and (other) burdens along with their own, and on the Day of Judgment they will be called to account for their falsehoods.

14. We did send Noah to his people, and he tarried among them a thousand years less fifty: but the Deluge overwhelmed them while they (persisted in) sin.

15. But We saved him and the Companions of the Ark, and We made the (Ark) a Sign for all Peoples!

16. And (We also saved) Abraham: behold, he said to his people, "Serve Allah and fear Him: that will be best for you— if ye understand!

17. "For ye do worship idols besides Allah, and ye invent falsehood. The things that ye worship besides Allah have no power to give you sustenance: then seek ye sustenance from Allah, serve Him, and be grateful to Him: to Him will be your return.

18. "And if ye reject (the Message), so did generations before you: and the duty of the messenger is only to preach publicly (and clearly)."

19. See they not how Allah originates creation, then repeats it: truly that is easy for Allah.

20. Say: "Travel through the earth and see how Allah did originate creation; so will Allah produce a later creation: for Allah has power over all things.

21. "He punishes whom He pleases, and He grants mercy to whom He pleases, and towards Him are ye turned.

22. "Not on earth nor in heaven will ye be able (fleeing) to frustrate (His Plan), nor have ye, besides Allah, any protector or helper."

23. Those who reject the Signs of Allah and the Meeting with Him (in the Hereafter),— it is they who shall despair of

My mercy: it is they who will (suffer) a most grievous Chastisement

24. So naught was the answer of (Abraham's) people except that they said: "Slay him or burn him." But Allah did save him from the Fire. Verily in this are Signs for people who believe.

25. And he said: "For you, ye have taken (for worship) idols besides Allah, out of mutual love and regard between yourselves in this life; but on the Day of Judgment ye shall disown each other and curse each other: and your abode will be the Fire. and ye shall have none to help."

26. But Lût believed him: he said: "I will leave home for the sake of my Lord: for He is Exalted in Might, and Wise."

27. And We gave (Abraham) Isaac and Jacob, and ordained among his progeny Prophethood and Revelation, and We Granted him his reward in this life; and he will be in the Hereafter of the Righteous.

28. And (remember) Lût: behold, he said to his people: "Ye do commit lewdness, such as no people in Creation (ever) committed before you.

29. "Do ye indeed approach men, and cut off the highway?— and practise wickedness (even) in your councils?" But his people gave no answer but this: they said: "Bring us the Wrath of Allah if thou tellest the truth."

30. He said: "O my Lord! help Thou me against people who do mischief!"

31. When Our Messengers came to Abraham with the good news, they said: "We are indeed going to destroy the people of this township: for truly they are wicked men."

32. He said: "But there is Lût there." They said: "We know well who is there: we will

certainly save him and his following,—
except his wife: she is of those who lag
behind!"

33. And when Our Messengers came to
Lût, he was grieved on their account, and
felt himself powerless (to protect) them: but
they said: "Fear thou not, nor grieve: We
are (here) to save thee and thy following,
except thy wife: she is of those who lag
behind.

34. "For we are going to bring down on the
people of this township a Punishment from
heaven, because they have been wickedly
rebellious."

35. And We have left thereof an evident
Sign, for any people who (care to)
understand.

36. To the Madyan (people) (We sent) their
brother Shu'aib. Then he said: "O my
people! serve Allah, and fear the Last Day:
nor commit evil on the earth, with intent to
do mischief."

37. But they rejected him: then the mighty
Blast seized them, and they lay prostrate in
their homes by the morning.

38. (Remember also) the 'Ād and the
Thamûd (people): clearly will appear to you
from (the traces) of their buildings (their
fate): Satan made their deeds alluring to
them, and kept them back from the Path,
though they were keen-sighted.

39. (Remember also) Qārûn, Pharaoh, and
Hāmān: there came to them Moses with
Clear Signs, but they behaved with
insolence on the earth; yet they could not
overreach (Us).

40. Each one of them We seized for his
crime: of them, against some We sent a
violent tornado (with showers of stones);
some were caught by a (mighty) Blast; some
We caused the earth to swallow up; and
some We drowned (in the waters): it was
not Allah Who wronged them: they wronged
themselves.

41. The parable of those who take protectors other than Allah is that of the Spider, who builds (to itself) a house; but truly the flimsiest of houses is the Spider's house;— if they but knew.

مَثَلُ الَّذِيْنَ اتَّخَذُوْا مِنْ دُوْنِ اللهِ
اَوْلِيَاءَ كَمَثَلِ الْعَنْكَبُوْتِ ۖ اتَّخَذَتْ بَيْتًا ۖ
وَاِنَّ اَوْهَنَ الْبُيُوْتِ لَبَيْتُ الْعَنْكَبُوْتِ ۘ
لَوْ كَانُوْا يَعْلَمُوْنَ ۝

42. Verily Allah doth know of (every thing) whatever that they call upon besides Him: and He is Exalted (in power), Wise.

اِنَّ اللهَ يَعْلَمُ مَا يَدْعُوْنَ مِنْ دُوْنِهٖ
مِنْ شَيْءٍ ۚ وَهُوَ الْعَزِيْزُ الْحَكِيْمُ ۝

43. And such are the Parables We set forth for mankind, but only those understand them who have Knowledge.

وَتِلْكَ الْاَمْثَالُ نَضْرِبُهَا لِلنَّاسِ ۚ وَمَا
يَعْقِلُهَا اِلَّا الْعَالِمُوْنَ ۝

44. Allah created the heavens and the earth in truth: verily in that is a Sign for those who believe.

خَلَقَ اللهُ السَّمٰوٰتِ وَالْاَرْضَ بِالْحَقِّ ۗ
اِنَّ فِيْ ذٰلِكَ لَاٰيَةً لِّلْمُؤْمِنِيْنَ ۝

45. Recite what is sent of the Book by inspiration to thee, and establish regular Prayer: for Prayer restrains from shameful and evil deeds; and remembrance of Allah is the greatest (thing in life) without doubt. And Allah knows the (deeds) that ye do.

اُتْلُ مَا اُوْحِيَ اِلَيْكَ مِنَ الْكِتٰبِ
وَاَقِمِ الصَّلٰوةَ ۖ اِنَّ الصَّلٰوةَ تَنْهٰى عَنِ
الْفَحْشَاءِ وَالْمُنْكَرِ ۗ وَلَذِكْرُ اللهِ اَكْبَرُ ۗ
وَاللهُ يَعْلَمُ مَا تَصْنَعُوْنَ ۝

46. And dispute ye not with the People of the Book, except in the best way, unless it be with those of them who do wrong but say, "We believe in the Revelation which has come down to us and in that which came down to you; our God and your God is One; and it is to Him we submit (in Islām)."

وَلَا تُجَادِلُوْٓا اَهْلَ الْكِتٰبِ اِلَّا بِالَّتِيْ هِيَ
اَحْسَنُ ۖ اِلَّا الَّذِيْنَ ظَلَمُوْا مِنْهُمْ وَقُوْلُوْٓا
اٰمَنَّا بِالَّذِيْٓ اُنْزِلَ اِلَيْنَا وَاُنْزِلَ اِلَيْكُمْ
وَاِلٰهُنَا وَاِلٰهُكُمْ وَاحِدٌ وَّنَحْنُ لَهٗ
مُسْلِمُوْنَ ۝

47. And thus (it is) that We have sent down the Book to thee. So the People of the Book believe therein, as also do some of these (Pagan Arabs): and none but Unbelievers reject Our Signs.

وَكَذٰلِكَ اَنْزَلْنَآ اِلَيْكَ الْكِتٰبَ ۗ فَالَّذِيْنَ
اٰتَيْنٰهُمُ الْكِتٰبَ يُؤْمِنُوْنَ بِهٖ ۚ وَمِنْ هٰٓؤُلَاءِ
مَنْ يُّؤْمِنُ بِهٖ ۚ وَمَا يَجْحَدُ بِاٰيٰتِنَآ اِلَّا
الْكٰفِرُوْنَ ۝

48. And thou wast not (able) to recite a Book before this (Book came), nor art thou (able) to transcribe it with thy right hand: in that case, indeed, would the talkers of vanities have doubted.

وَمَا كُنْتَ تَتْلُوْا مِنْ قَبْلِهٖ مِنْ كِتٰبٍ وَّلَا
تَخُطُّهٗ بِيَمِيْنِكَ اِذًا لَّارْتَابَ الْمُبْطِلُوْنَ ۝

49. Nay, here are Signs self-evident in the hearts of those endowed with knowledge:

بَلْ هُوَ اٰيٰتٌۢ بَيِّنٰتٌ فِيْ صُدُوْرِ الَّذِيْنَ
اُوْتُوا الْعِلْمَ ۗ وَمَا يَجْحَدُ بِاٰيٰتِنَآ اِلَّا

and none but the unjust reject Our Signs.

50. Yet they say: "Why are not Signs sent down to him from his Lord?" Say: "The Signs are indeed with Allah: and I am indeed a clear Warner."

51. And is it not enough for them that We have sent down to thee the Book which is rehearsed to them? Verily, in it is Mercy and a Reminder to those who believe.

52. Say: "Enough is Allah for a Witness between me and you: He knows what is in the heavens and on earth." And it is those who believe in vanities and reject Allah, that are the losers.

53. They ask thee to hasten on the Punishment (for them): had it not been for a term (of respite) appointed, the Punishment would certainly have come to them: and it will certainly reach them,— of a sudden, while they perceive not!

54. They ask thee to hasten on the Punishment: but, of a surety, Hell will encompass the rejecters of Faith!—

55. On the Day that the Punishment shall cover them from above them and from below them, and (a Voice) shall say: "Taste ye (the fruits) of your deeds"!

56. O My servants who believe! truly, spacious is My Earth: therefore serve ye Me— (and Me alone)!

57. Every soul shall have a taste of death: in the end to Us shall ye be brought back.

58. But those who believe and work deeds of righteousness— to them shall We give a Home in Heaven,— lofty mansions beneath which flow rivers,—to dwell therein for aye;—an excellent reward for those who do (good)!—

59. Those who persevere in patience, and put their trust in their Lord and Cherisher.

60. How many are the creatures that carry

not their own sustenance? It is Allah Who feeds (both) them and you: for He hears and knows (all things).

61. If indeed thou ask them who has created the heavens and the earth and subjected the sun and the moon (to His Law), they will certainly reply, "Allah". How are they then deluded away (from the truth)?

62. Allah enlarges the sustenance (which He gives) to whichever of His servants He pleases; and He (similarly) grants by (strict) measure, (as He pleases): for Allah has full knowledge of all things.

63. And if indeed thou ask them who it is that sends down rain from the sky, and gives life therewith to the earth after its death, they will certainly reply, "Allah!" Say, "Praise be to Allah!" But most of them understand not.

64. What is the life of this world but amusement and play? But verily the Home of the Hereafter,—that is life indeed, if they but knew.

65. Now, if they embark on a boat, they call on Allah, making their devotion sincerely (and exclusively) to Him; but when He has delivered them safely to (dry) land, behold! they give a share (of their worship to others)!—

66. Disdaining ungratefully Our gifts, and giving themselves up to (worldly) enjoyment! But soon will they know.

67. Do they not then see that We have made a Sanctuary secure, and that men are being snatched away from all around them? Then, do they believe in that which is vain, and reject the Grace of Allah?

68. And who does more wrong than he who invents a lie against Allah or rejects the Truth when it reaches him? Is there not a home in Hell for those who reject Faith?

69. And those who strive in Our (Cause),— We will certainly guide them to Our Paths: for verily Allah is with those who do right.

SÛRA–30
AR-RÛM
(INTRODUCTION)

This Sûra, as remarked in the Introduction to the last Sûra, deals with the question of Ma'âd or the Final End of Things, from various points of view. In the last Sûra, we saw that Revelation was linked up with Life and Conduct, and Time (looking backwards and forwards) figured forth the frailty of this Life. In this Sûra the Time theme and its mystery are brought into relation with human history in the foreground and the evolution of the world in all its aspects in the background. The corruption introduced by man is cleared away by Allah, Whose Universal Plan points to the Hereafter. We shall see that the next two Sûras (31 and 32) present the theme in other aspects. All four are introduced with the Abbreviated Letters A.L.M. which (without being dogmatic) I have suggested as symbolical of the Past, Present and Future.

The choronology of this Sûra is significant. It was revealed about the 7th or the 6th year *before* the Hijrat, corresponding to 615-16 of the Christian era, when the tide of Persian conquest over the Roman Empire was running strong. The Christian Empire of Rome had lost Jerusalem to the Persians, and Christianity had been humbled in the dust. At that time it seemed outside the bounds of human possibility, even to one intimately acquainted with the inner resources and conditions of the Persian and Roman armies and empires, that the tables would be turned and the position reversed within the space of eight or nine years. The pro-Persian Pagan Quraish rejoiced exceedingly, and redoubled their taunts and persecution against the Holy Prophet, whose Message was a renewal of the Message of Christ preached in Jerusalem. Then was this passage 30: 1-6 revealed, clearly foreshadowing the final defeat of Persia as a prelude to the destruction of the Persian Empire. There is no doubt about the probhecy and its fulfilment. For the exulting Pagans of Makka laid a heavy wager against the fulfilment of the prophecy with Ḥadhrat Abû Bakr, and they lost it on its fulfilment.

But the rise and fall even of such mighty empires as the Persian and Roman Empires were but small events on the chequer-board of Time, compared to a mightier movement that was taking birth in the promulgation of Islam. In the seventh or sixth year *before* the Hijrat, and for a year or two after the Hijrat, Islam was struggling in the world like the still small voice in the conscience of humanity. It was scarcely heeded, and when it sought to insist upon its divine claim, it was insulted, assaulted, persecuted, boycotted, and (as it seemed) suppressed. The agony of Ṭā-if (two years before the Hijrat) and the murder-plot on the eve of the Hijrat were yet to come. But the purpose of Allah is not to be thwarted. Badr (A.H. 2=A.D. 624), rightly called the critical Day of Decision, began to redress the balance of outward events in early Islam, in the same year in which Issus began to redress the balance of outward events in Perso-Roman relations. Mightier events were yet to come. A new inner World was being created through Islam. This spiritual Revolution was of infinitely greater moment in world-history. The toppling down of priestcraft and false worship, the restoration of simplicity in faith and life, the rehabilitation of this life as the first step to the understanding of the Hereafter, the displacement of superstition and hairsplitting theology by a spirit of rational inquiry and knowledge, and the recognition of the divine as covering not merely an isolated thing called "Religion" but the whole way of Life, Thought, and Feeling,—this was and is the true Message of Islam and its mission. Its struggle—its fight—continues, but it is not without effect, as may be seen in the march of centuries in world-history.

Ar-Rûm, or The Romans

In the name of Allah, Most Gracious. Most Merciful.

1. A. L. M.

2. The Romans have been defeated—

3. In a land close by: but they, (even) after (this) defeat of theirs, will soon be victorious—

4. Within a few years, with Allah is the Command in the Past and in the Future: on that Day shall the Believers rejoice—

5. With the help of Allah. He gives victory to whom He will, and He is Exalted in Might, Most Merciful.

6. (It is) the promise of Allah. Never does Allah fail from His promise: but most men know not.

7. They know but the outer (things) in the life of this world: but of the Hereafter they are heedless.

8. Do they not reflect in their own minds? Not but in truth and for a term appointed, did Allah create the heavens and the earth, and all between them: yet are there truly many among men who deny the meeting with their Lord (at the Resurrection)!

9. Do they not travel through the earth, and see what was the End of those before them? They were superior to them in strength: they tilled the soil and populated it in greater numbers than these have done: there came to them their messengers with Clear (Signs), (which they rejected, to their own destruction): it was not Allah who wronged them, but they wronged their own souls.

10. In the long run evil will be the End of those who do evil; for that they rejected the Signs of Allah, and held them up to ridicule.

11. It is Allah Who begins the creation; then repeats it; then shall ye be brought back to Him.

12. On the Day when the Hour will come the guilty will be struck dumb with despair.

13. No intercessor will they have among their "Partners", and they will (themselves) reject their "Partners".

14. On the Day when the Hour will come that Day shall (all men) be sorted out.

15. Then those who have believed and worked righteous deeds, shall be made happy in a Mead (of Delight).

16. And those who have rejected Faith and falsely denied Our Signs and the meeting of the Hereafter,—such shall be brought forth to Punishment.

17. So glory be to Allah, when ye reach eventide and when ye rise in the morning;

18. Yea, to Him be praise, in the heavens and on earth; and in the late afternoon and when the day begins to decline.

19. It is He Who brings out the living from the dead, and brings out the dead from the living, and Who gives life to the earth after it is dead: and thus shall ye be brought out (from the dead).

20. Among His Signs is this, that He created you from dust; and then,—behold, ye are men scattered (far and wide)!

21. And among His Signs is this, that He created for you mates from among yourselves, that ye may dwell in tranquillity with them, and He has put love and mercy between your (hearts): verily in that are Signs for those who reflect.

22. And among His Signs is the creation of the heavens and the earth, and the variations in your languages and your colours: verily in that are Signs for those who know.

23. And among His Signs is the sleep that ye take by night and by day, and the quest that ye (make for livelihood) out of His Bounty: verily in that are Signs for those who hearken.

24. And among His Signs, He shows you the lightning, by way both of fear and of hope, and He sends down rain from the sky and with it gives life to the earth after it is dead: verily in that are Signs for those who are wise.

25. And among His Signs is this, that heaven and earth stand by His Command: then when He calls you, by a single call, from the earth, behold, ye (straightway) come forth.

26. To Him belongs every being that is in the heavens and on earth: all are devoutly obedient to Him.

27. It is He Who begins the creation; then repeats it; and for Him it is most easy. To Him belongs the loftiest similitude (we can think of) in the heavens and the earth: for He is Exalted in Might, full of wisdom.

28. He does propound to you a similitude from yourselves: do ye have partners among those whom your right hands possess, to share as equals in the wealth We have bestowed on you? Do ye fear them as ye fear each other? Thus do We explain the Signs in detail to a people that understand.

29. Nay, the wrong-doers (merely) follow their own desires being devoid of knowledge. But who will guide those whom Allah leaves astray? To them there will be no helpers.

30. So set thou thy face truly to the religion being upright, the nature in which Allah has made mankind: no change (there is) in the work (wrought) by Allah: that is the true Religion: but most among mankind know not.

31. Turn ye in repentance to Him, and fear Him: establish regular prayers, and be not ye among those who join gods with Allah,—

32. Those who split up their Religion, and become (Mere) Sects,—each party rejoicing in that which is with itself!

33. When trouble touches men, they cry to their Lord turning back to Him in repentance: but when He gives them a taste of Mercy from Himself, behold, some of them pay part-worship to other gods besides their Lord,—

34. (As if) to show their ingratitude for the (favours) We have bestowed on them! Then enjoy (your brief day); but soon will ye know (your folly).

35. Or have We sent down authority to them, which speaks to them the things to which the pay part-worship?

36. When We give men a taste of Mercy, they exult thereat: and when some evil afflicts them because of what their (own) hands have sent forth, behold, they are in despair!

37. See they not that Allah enlarges the provision and restricts it, to whomsoever He pleases? Verily in that are Signs for those who believe.

38. So give what is due to kindred, the needy, and the wayfarer, that is best for those who seek the Countenance, of Allah, and it is they who will prosper.

39. That which you give in usury for increase through the property of (other) people, will have no increase with Allah: but that which you give for charity, seeking the Countenance of Allah, (will increase): it is these who will get a recompense multiplied.

40. It is Allah Who has created you: further, He has provided for your sustenance; then He will cause you to die; and again He will give you life. Are there any of your (false) "Partners" who can do any single one of these things? Glory to Him! and High is He

above the partners they attribute (to Him)!

41. Mischief has appeared on land and sea because of (the meed) that the hands of men have earned, that (Allah) may give them a taste of some of their deeds: in order that they may turn back (from evil).

42. Say: "Travel through the earth and see what was the End of those before (you): most of them were idolaters.

43. But set thou thy face to the right Religion, before there come from Allah the Day which there is no chance of averting: on that Day shall men be divided (in two).

44. Those who reject Faith will suffer from that rejection: and those who work righteousness will make provision for themselves (in heaven):

45. That He may reward those who believe and work righteous deeds, out of His Bounty. For He loves not those who reject Faith.

46. Among His Signs is this, that He sends the Winds, as heralds of Glad Tidings, giving you a taste of His Mercy,— that the ships may sail by His Command and that ye may seek of His Bounty: in order that ye may be grateful.

47. We did indeed send, before thee, messengers to their (respective) peoples, and they came to them with Clear Signs: then, to those who transgressed, We meted out Retribution: and it was a duty incumbent upon Us to aid those who believed.

48. It is Allah Who sends the Winds, and they raise the Clouds: then does He spread them in the sky as He wills, and break them into fragments, until thou seest rain-drops issue from the midst thereof: then when He has made them reach such of His servants as He wills, behold, they do rejoice!—

عَمَّا يُشْرِكُوْنَ ۞

ظَهَرَ الْفَسَادُ فِي الْبَرِّ وَالْبَحْرِ بِمَا كَسَبَتْ اَيْدِى النَّاسِ لِيُذِيقَهُمْ بَعْضَ الَّذِىْ عَمِلُوْا لَعَلَّهُمْ يَرْجِعُوْنَ ۞

قُلْ سِيْرُوْا فِي الْاَرْضِ فَانْظُرُوْا كَيْفَ كَانَ عَاقِبَةُ الَّذِيْنَ مِنْ قَبْلُ ۖ كَانَ اَكْثَرُهُمْ مُّشْرِكِيْنَ ۞

فَاَقِمْ وَجْهَكَ لِلدِّيْنِ الْقَيِّمِ مِنْ قَبْلِ اَنْ يَّاْتِىَ يَوْمٌ لَّا مَرَدَّ لَهُ مِنَ اللّٰهِ يَوْمَئِذٍ يَّصَّدَّعُوْنَ ۞

مَنْ كَفَرَ فَعَلَيْهِ كُفْرُهٗ ۚ وَمَنْ عَمِلَ صَالِحًا فَلِاَنْفُسِهِمْ يَمْهَدُوْنَ ۞

لِيَجْزِيَ الَّذِيْنَ اٰمَنُوْا وَعَمِلُوا الصّٰلِحٰتِ مِنْ فَضْلِهٖ ۚ اِنَّهٗ لَا يُحِبُّ الْكٰفِرِيْنَ ۞

وَمِنْ اٰيٰتِهٖٓ اَنْ يُّرْسِلَ الرِّيَاحَ مُبَشِّرٰتٍ وَّلِيُذِيْقَكُمْ مِّنْ رَّحْمَتِهٖ وَلِتَجْرِيَ الْفُلْكُ بِاَمْرِهٖ وَلِتَبْتَغُوْا مِنْ فَضْلِهٖ وَلَعَلَّكُمْ تَشْكُرُوْنَ ۞

وَلَقَدْ اَرْسَلْنَا مِنْ قَبْلِكَ رُسُلًا اِلٰى قَوْمِهِمْ فَجَآءُوْهُمْ بِالْبَيِّنٰتِ فَانْتَقَمْنَا مِنَ الَّذِيْنَ اَجْرَمُوْا ۚ وَكَانَ حَقًّا عَلَيْنَا نَصْرُ الْمُؤْمِنِيْنَ ۞

اَللّٰهُ الَّذِيْ يُرْسِلُ الرِّيَاحَ فَتُثِيْرُ سَحَابًا فَيَبْسُطُهٗ فِي السَّمَآءِ كَيْفَ يَشَآءُ وَيَجْعَلُهٗ كِسَفًا فَتَرَى الْوَدْقَ يَخْرُجُ مِنْ خِلٰلِهٖ فَاِذَآ اَصَابَ بِهٖ مَنْ يَّشَآءُ مِنْ عِبَادِهٖٓ اِذَا هُمْ يَسْتَبْشِرُوْنَ ۞

49. Even though, before they received (the rain)—just before this—they were dumb with despair!

50. Then behold (O man!) the tokens of Allah's Mercy!— how He gives life to the earth after its death: verily the Same will give life to the men who are dead: for He has power over all things.

51. And if We (but) send a Wind from which they see (their tilth) turn yellow,— behold, they become, thereafter, ungrateful (Unbelievers)!

52. So verily thou canst not make the dead to hear, nor canst thou make the deaf to hear the call, when they show their backs and turn away.

53. Nor canst thou lead back the blind from their straying: only those wilt thou make to hear, who believe in Our Signs and submit (their wills in Islām).

54. It is Allah Who created you in a state of (helpless) weakness, then gave (you) strength after weakness, then, after strength, gave (you) weakness and a hoary head: He creates whatever He wills, and it is He who has all knowledge and power.

55. On the Day that the Hour (of reckoning) will be established, the transgressors will swear that they tarried not but an hour: thus were they used to being deluded!

56. But those endued with knowledge and faith will say: "Indeed ye did tarry, within Allah's Decree, to the Day of Resurrection, and this is the Day of Resurrection: but ye—ye did not know!"

57. So on that Day no excuse of theirs will avail the Transgressors, nor will they be allowed to make amends.

58. Verily We have propounded for men, in this Qur-ān. Every kind of Parable: but if thou bring to them any Sign, the Unbelievers are sure to say, "Ye do nothing but talk vanities."

SÛRA-31
LUQMÃN
(INTRODUCTION)

The argument of the Final End of Things is here continued from another point of view. What is Wisdom? Where shall she be found? Will she solve the mysteries of Time and Nature, and that world higher than physical Nature, which brings us nearer to Allah? "Yes," is the answer: "if, as in the advice of Luqmãn the Wise, human wisdom looks to Allah in true worship, enables every act of life with true kindness, but avoids the false indulgence that infringes the divine law,—and in short follows the golden mean of virtue." And this is indicated by every Sign in Nature.

The chronology of the Sûra has no significance. In the main, it belongs to the late Makkan period.

59. Thus does Allah seal up the hearts of those who understand not.

كَذٰلِكَ يَطْبَعُ اللّٰهُ عَلٰى قُلُوبِ الَّذِيْنَ لَا يَعْلَمُوْنَ ۝

60. So patiently persevere: for verily the promise of Allah is true: nor let those excite thee, who have (themselves) no certainty of faith.

فَاصْبِرْ اِنَّ وَعْدَ اللّٰهِ حَقٌّ وَّلَا يَسْتَخِفَّنَّكَ الَّذِيْنَ لَا يُوْقِنُوْنَ ۝

Luqmān (the Wise)

In the name of Allah, Most Gracious, Most Merciful.

بِسْمِ اللّٰهِ الرَّحْمٰنِ الرَّحِيْمِ ۝

1. **A. L. M.**

2. These are Verses of the Wise Book,—

3. A Guide and a Mercy to the Doers of Good,—

الٓمّٓ ۝ تِلْكَ اٰيٰتُ الْكِتٰبِ الْحَكِيْمِ ۝ هُدًى وَّرَحْمَةً لِّلْمُحْسِنِيْنَ ۝

4. Those who establish regular Prayer, and give zakat and have sure faith in the Hereafter.

الَّذِيْنَ يُقِيْمُوْنَ الصَّلٰوةَ وَيُؤْتُوْنَ الزَّكٰوةَ وَهُمْ بِالْاٰخِرَةِ هُمْ يُوْقِنُوْنَ ۝

5. These are on (true) guidance from their Lord; and these are the ones who will prosper.

اُولٰٓئِكَ عَلٰى هُدًى مِّنْ رَّبِّهِمْ وَاُولٰٓئِكَ هُمُ الْمُفْلِحُوْنَ ۝

6. But there are, among men, those who purchase idle tales, without knowledge (or meaning), to mislead (men) from the Path of Allah and throw ridicule (on the Path): for such there will be a humiliating Chastisement.

وَمِنَ النَّاسِ مَنْ يَّشْتَرِيْ لَهْوَ الْحَدِيْثِ لِيُضِلَّ عَنْ سَبِيْلِ اللّٰهِ بِغَيْرِ عِلْمٍ وَّيَتَّخِذَهَا هُزُوًا اُولٰٓئِكَ لَهُمْ عَذَابٌ مُّهِيْنٌ ۝

7. When Our Signs are rehearsed to such a one, he turns away in arrogance, as if he heard them not, as if there were deafness in both his ears: announce to him a grievous Chastisement.

وَاِذَا تُتْلٰى عَلَيْهِ اٰيٰتُنَا وَلّٰى مُسْتَكْبِرًا كَاَنْ لَّمْ يَسْمَعْهَا كَاَنَّ فِيْ اُذُنَيْهِ وَقْرًا فَبَشِّرْهُ بِعَذَابٍ اَلِيْمٍ ۝

8. For those who believe and work righteous deeds, there will be Gardens of Bliss,—

اِنَّ الَّذِيْنَ اٰمَنُوْا وَعَمِلُوا الصّٰلِحٰتِ لَهُمْ جَنّٰتُ النَّعِيْمِ ۝

9. To dwell therein. The promise of Allah is true: and He is Exalted in power, Wise.

خٰلِدِيْنَ فِيْهَا وَعْدَ اللّٰهِ حَقًّا وَهُوَ الْعَزِيْزُ الْحَكِيْمُ ۝

10. He created the heavens without any pillars that ye can see; He set on the earth mountains standing firm, lest it should shake with you; and He scattered through it beasts of all kinds. We send down rain from the sky, and produce on the earth every kind of

خَلَقَ السَّمٰوٰتِ بِغَيْرِ عَمَدٍ تَرَوْنَهَا وَاَلْقٰى فِي الْاَرْضِ رَوَاسِيَ اَنْ تَمِيْدَ بِكُمْ وَبَثَّ فِيْهَا مِنْ كُلِّ دَابَّةٍ وَاَنْزَلْنَا مِنَ السَّمَاءِ مَاءً فَاَنْبَتْنَا فِيْهَا مِنْ كُلِّ

noble creature, in pairs.

زَوْجٍ كَرِيْمٍ ۝

11. Such is the Creation of Allah: now show Me what is there that others besides Him have created: nay, but the Transgressors are in manifest error.

هٰذَا خَلْقُ اللّٰهِ فَاَرُوْنِیْ مَاذَا خَلَقَ الَّذِیْنَ مِنْ دُوْنِهٖ ۚ بَلِ الظّٰلِمُوْنَ فِیْ ضَلٰلٍ مُّبِیْنٍ ۝

12. We bestowed (in the past) wisdom on Luqmān: "Show (thy) gratitude to Allah." Any who is (so) grateful does so to the profit of his own soul: but if any is ungrateful, verily Allah is free of all wants, worthy of all praise.

وَلَقَدْ اٰتَیْنَا لُقْمٰنَ الْحِکْمَةَ اَنِ اشْکُرْ لِلّٰهِ ؕ وَمَنْ یَّشْکُرْ فَاِنَّمَا یَشْکُرُ لِنَفْسِهٖ ۚ وَمَنْ کَفَرَ فَاِنَّ اللّٰهَ غَنِیٌّ حَمِیْدٌ ۝

13. Behold, Luqmān said to his son admonishing him "O my son! join not in worship (others) with Allah: for false worship is indeed the highest wrong-doing."

وَاِذْ قَالَ لُقْمٰنُ لِابْنِهٖ وَهُوَ یَعِظُهٗ یٰبُنَیَّ لَا تُشْرِکْ بِاللّٰهِ ؔ اِنَّ الشِّرْکَ لَظُلْمٌ عَظِیْمٌ ۝

14. And We have enjoined on man (to be good) to his parents: in travail upon travail did his mother bear him. And in years twain was his weaning (hear the command), "Show gratitude to Me and to thy parents to Me is (thy final) Goal.

وَوَصَّیْنَا الْاِنْسَانَ بِوَالِدَیْهِ ۚ حَمَلَتْهُ اُمُّهٗ وَهْنًا عَلٰی وَهْنٍ وَّفِصٰلُهٗ فِیْ عَامَیْنِ اَنِ اشْکُرْ لِیْ وَلِوَالِدَیْکَ ؕ اِلَیَّ الْمَصِیْرُ ۝

15. "But if they strive to make thee join in worship with Me things of which thou hast no knowledge, obey them not; yet bear them company in this life with justice (and consideration), and follow the way of those who turn to Me: in the End the return of you all is to Me, and I will tell you all that ye did.

وَاِنْ جَاهَدٰکَ عَلٰۤی اَنْ تُشْرِکَ بِیْ مَا لَیْسَ لَکَ بِهٖ عِلْمٌ فَلَا تُطِعْهُمَا وَ صَاحِبْهُمَا فِی الدُّنْیَا مَعْرُوْفًا ؗ وَّاتَّبِعْ سَبِیْلَ مَنْ اَنَابَ اِلَیَّ ۚ ثُمَّ اِلَیَّ مَرْجِعُکُمْ فَاُنَبِّئُکُمْ بِمَا کُنْتُمْ تَعْمَلُوْنَ ۝

16. "O my son! (said Luqmān), "If there be (but) the weight of a mustard-seed and it were (hidden) in a rock, or (anywhere) in the heavens or on earth, Allah will bring it forth: for Allah is subtle and Aware.

یٰبُنَیَّ اِنَّهَاۤ اِنْ تَکُ مِثْقَالَ حَبَّةٍ مِّنْ خَرْدَلٍ فَتَکُنْ فِیْ صَخْرَةٍ اَوْ فِی السَّمٰوٰتِ اَوْ فِی الْاَرْضِ یَاْتِ بِهَا اللّٰهُ ؕ اِنَّ اللّٰهَ لَطِیْفٌ خَبِیْرٌ ۝

17. "O my son! establish regular prayer, enjoin what is just, and forbid what is wrong: and bear with patient constancy whate'er betide thee; for this is firmness (of purpose) in (the conduct of) affairs.

یٰبُنَیَّ اَقِمِ الصَّلٰوةَ وَاْمُرْ بِالْمَعْرُوْفِ وَانْهَ عَنِ الْمُنْکَرِ وَاصْبِرْ عَلٰی مَاۤ اَصَابَکَ ؕ اِنَّ ذٰلِکَ مِنْ عَزْمِ الْاُمُوْرِ ۝

18. "And swell not thy cheek (for pride) at men. Nor walk in insolence through the earth: for Allah loveth not any arrogant

وَلَا تُصَعِّرْ خَدَّکَ لِلنَّاسِ وَلَا تَمْشِ فِی الْاَرْضِ مَرَحًا ؕ اِنَّ اللّٰهَ لَا یُحِبُّ کُلَّ

boaster.

19. "And be moderate in thy pace, and lower thy voice; for the harshest of sounds without doubt is the braying of the ass."

20. Do ye not see that Allah has subjected to your (use) all things in the heavens and on earth, and has made His bounties flow to you in exceeding measure, (both) seen and unseen? Yet there are among men those who dispute about Allah, without knowledge and without guidance, and without a Book to enlighten them!

21. When they are told to follow the (Revelation) that Allah Has sent down, they say: "Nay, we shall follow the ways that we found our fathers (following)." What! even if it is Satan beckoning them to the Chastisement of the (Blazing) Fire?

22. Whoever submits his whole self to Allah, and is a doer of good, has grasped indeed the firmest hand-hold: and to Allah shall all things return.

23. But if any reject Faith, let not his rejection grieve thee: to Us is their Return, and We shall tell them the truth of their deeds: for Allah knows well all that is in (men's) hearts.

24. We grant them their pleasure for a little while: in the end shall We drive them to a chastisement unrelenting.

25. If thou ask them, who it is that created the heavens and the earth. They will certainly say, "Allah", say: "Praise be to Allah!" But most of them know not.

26. To Allah belong all things in heaven and earth: verily Allah is He (that is) free of all wants, worthy of all praise.

27. And if all the trees on earth were pens and the Ocean (were ink), with seven

Oceans behind it to add to its (supply), yet would not the Words of Allah be exhausted (in the writing): for Allah is Exalted in power, full of Wisdom.

28. And your creation or your resurrection is in no wise but as an individual soul: for Allah is He Who hears and sees (all things).

29. Seest thou not that Allah merges Night into Day and He merges Day into Night; that He has subjected the sun and the moon (to His Law), each running its course for a term appointed; and that Allah is well acquainted with all that ye do?

30. That is because Allah is the Truth and because whatever else they invoke besides Him is Falsehood; and because Allah,— He is the Most High, Most Great.

31. Seest thou not that the ships sail through the Ocean by the grace of Allah?— that He may show you of His Signs? Verily, in this are Signs for all who constantly persevere and give thanks.

32. When a wave covers them like the canopy (of clouds), they call upon Allah, offering Him sincere devotion. But when He has delivered them safely to land, there are among them those that falter between (right and wrong). But none reject Our Signs except only a perfidious ungrateful (wretch)!

33. O mankind! do your duty to your Lord and fear (the coming of) a Day when no father can avail aught for his son. nor a son avail aught for his father. Verily, the promise of Allah is true: let not then this present life deceive you, nor let the Chief Deceiver deceive you about Allah.

34. Verily the knowledge of the Hour is with Allah (alone). It is He Who sends down rain, and He Who knows what is

SÛRA–32
AS-SAJDA
(INTRODUCTION)

This short Sûra closes the series of the four A.L.M. Sûras, which began with the 29th. Its theme is the mystery of Creation, the mystery of Time and the mystery of the *Ma'ād* (the Final End) as viewed through the light of Allah's revelation. The contemplation of these mysteries should lead to Faith and the adoration of Allah. In chronology it belongs to the middle Makkan period and is therefore a little earlier than the last, but its chronology has no significance.

in the wombs. Nor does anyone know what it is that he will earn on the morrow: nor does anyone know in what land he is to die. Verily with Allah is full knowledge and He is acquainted (with all things).

As-Sajda, or Adoration

In the name of Allah, Most Gracious, Most Merciful.

1. **A. L. M.**

2. (This is) the revelation of the Book in which there is no doubt,—from the Lord of the Worlds.

3. Or do they say, "He has forged it"? Nay, it is the Truth from thy Lord that thou mayest admonish a people to whom no warner has come before thee: in order that they may be rightly guided.

4. It is Allah Who has created the heavens and the earth, and all between them, in six Days, then He established Himself on the Throne: ye have none, besides Him, to protect or intercede (for you): will ye not then receive admonition?

5. He directs the affairs from the heavens to the earth: then it ascends unto Him, on a Day the measure of which is a thousand years of your reckoning.

6. Such is He, the Knower of all things, hidden and open, the Exalted (in power), the Merciful;—

7. He Who created all things in the Best way and He began the creation of man from clay.

8. And made his progeny from a quintessence of despised fluid.

9. But He fashioned him in due proportion, and breathed into him of His spirit. And He gave you (the faculties of) hearing and sight and understanding little thanks do ye give!

10. And they say: "What! when we lie, hidden and lost, in the earth, shall we indeed be in a Creation renewed? Nay, they deny

the Meeting with their Lord!"

11. Say: "The Angel of Death, put in charge of you, will (duly) take your souls: then shall ye be brought back to your Lord."

12. If only thou couldst see when the guilty ones will bend low their heads before their Lord, (saying:) "Our Lord! We have seen and we have heard: now then send us back (to the world): we will work righteousness: for we do indeed (now) believe.

13. If We had so willed, we could certainly have brought every soul its true guidance: but the Word from Me will come true, "I will fill Hell with Jinns and men all together."

14. "Taste ye then—for ye forgot the Meeting of this Day of yours, and We too will forget you—taste ye the chastisement of Eternity for your (evil) deeds!"

15. Only those believe in Our Signs, who, when they are recited to them fall down in adoration, and celebrate the praises of their Lord, nor are they (ever) puffed up with pride.

16. They forsake their beds of sleep, the while they call on their Lord, in Fear and Hope: and they spend (in charity) out of the sustenance which We have bestowed on them.

17. Now no person knows what delights of the eye are kept hidden (in reserve) for them—as a reward for their (good) Deeds.

18. Is then the man who believes no better than the man who is rebellious and wicked? Not equal are they.

19. For those who believe and do righteous deeds, are Gardens as hospitable homes, for their (good) deeds.

20. As to those who are rebellious and wicked, their abode will be the Fire: every time they wish to get away therefrom, they will be forced thereinto, and it will be said to them: "Taste ye the Chastisement of the

Fire, the which ye were wont to reject as false."

21. And indeed We will make them taste of the lighter Chastisement before the greater Chastisement in order that they may (repent and) return.

22. And who does more wrong than one to whom are recited the Signs of his Lord, and who then turns away therefrom? Verily from those who transgress We shall exact (due) Retribution.

23. We did indeed aforetime give the Book to Moses: be not then in doubt of its reaching (thee): and We made it a guide to the Children of Israel.

24. And We appointed, from among them, Leaders, giving guidance under Our command, so long as they persevered with patience and continued to have faith in Our Signs.

25. Verily thy Lord will judge between them on the Day of Judgment, in the matters wherein they differ (among themselves).

26. Does it not teach them a lesson, how many generations We destroyed before them, in whose dwellings they (now) go to and fro? Verily in that are Signs: do they not then listen?

27. And do they not see that We do drive Rain to parched soil (bare of herbage), and produce therewith crops, providing food for their cattle and themselves? Have they not the vision?

28. They say: "When will this Decision be, if ye are telling the truth?"

29. Say: "On the Day of Decision, no profit will it be to Unbelievers if they (then) believe! Nor will they be granted a respite."

30. So turn away from them, and wait: they too are waiting.

SÛRA–33
AL-AḤZĀB
(INTRODUCTION)

The series of mystic Sûras beginning with S. 26 having been closed with the last Sûra, we now come back to the hard facts of this life. Two questions are mainly considered there, viz. (1) the attempt by violence and brute force to crush the truth, and (2) the attempt, by slander or unseemly conduct, to poison the relations of women with men.

As regards the first, the story of the Aḥzāb or Confederates, who tried to surround and annihilate the Muslim community in Madinah, is full of underhand intrigues on the part of such diverse enemies as the Pagan Quraish, the Jews (Banû Nadhîr) who had been already expelled from Madinah for their treachery, the Gaṭafān tribe of Bedouin Arabs from the interior, and the Jewish tribe Banû Quraiẓa in Madinah. This was the unholy Confederacy against Islam. But though they caused a great deal of anxiety and suffering to the beleaguered Muslims, Islam came triumphantly out of the trial and got more firmly established than ever.

The Quraish in Makkah had tried all sorts of persecution, boycott, insult, and bodily injuries to the Muslims, leading to their partial *hijrat* to Abyssinia and their Hijrat as a body to Madinah. The first armed conflict between them and the Muslims took place at Badr in Ramadhān A.H. 2, when the Quraish were signally defeated. Next year (Shauwāl A.H. 3) they came to take revenge on Madinah. The battle was fought at Uḥud, and though the Muslims suffered severely. Madinah was saved and the Makkans had to return to Makkah with their object frustrated. Then they began to make a network of intrigues and alliances, and besieged Madinah with a force of 10,000 men in Shauwāl and Ẕul-qaʻd A.H. 5. This is the siege

siege of the Confederates referred to in 33: 9-27, which lasted over two weeks: some accounts give 27 days. It caused much suffering, from hunger, cold, an unceasing shower of arrows, and constant general or concentrated assaults. But it ended in the discomfiture of the Confederates, and established Islam firmer than ever. It was a well organised and formidable attack, but the Muslims had made preparations to meet it. One of the preparations, which took the enemy by surprise, was the Trench (*Khandaq*) dug round Madinah by the Prophet's order and under the supervision of Salmān the Persian. The siege and battle are therefore known as the Battle of the Trench or the Battle of the Confederates.

As regards the position and dignity of the ladies of the Prophet's Household and the Muslim women generally, salutary principles are laid down to safeguard their honour and protect them from slander and insult. The ladies of the Household interested themselves in social work and work of instruction for the Muslim women, and Muslim women were being trained more and more in community service. Two of them (the two Zainabs) devoted themselves to the poor. The nursing of the wounded on or by the battlefield was specially necessary in those days of warfare. The Prophet's daughter Fāṭima, then aged about 19 to 20, lovingly nursed her father's wounds at Uḥud (A.H. 3); Rufaida nursed Saʿd ibn Muāʿẓ's wounds at the Siege of Madinah by the Confederates (A.H. 5) and in the Khaibar expedition (A.H. 7) Muslim women went out from Madinah for nursing service.

A portion of this Sûra sums up the lessons of the Battle of the Trench and must have been revealed sometime after that Battle (Shauwāl A.H. 5). The marriage with Zainab referred to in verse 37 also took place in the same year. Some portions (e.g. verse 27) were probably revealed in A.H. 7 after the Khaibar settlement.

Al-Aḥzāb, or The Confederates

سُوْرَةُ الْأَحْزَابِ مَدَنِيَّةٌ وَهِيَ تِسْعٌ وَسَبْعُوْنَ اٰيَةً وَتِسْعُ رُكُوْعَاتٍ

In the name of Allah, Most Gracious, Most Merciful.

بِسْمِ اللهِ الرَّحْمٰنِ الرَّحِيْمِ

1.   O Prophet! Fear Allah, and hearken not to the Unbelievers and the Hypocrites: verily Allah is full of knowledge and wisdom.

يٰٓاَيُّهَا النَّبِيُّ اتَّقِ اللهَ وَلَا تُطِعِ الْكٰفِرِيْنَ وَالْمُنٰفِقِيْنَ ۚ اِنَّ اللهَ كَانَ عَلِيْمًا حَكِيْمًا ۙ

2.   But follow that which comes to thee by inspiration from thy Lord: for Allah is well acquainted with (all) that ye do.

وَّاتَّبِعْ مَا يُوْحٰٓى اِلَيْكَ مِنْ رَّبِّكَ ۗ اِنَّ اللهَ كَانَ بِمَا تَعْمَلُوْنَ خَبِيْرًا ۙ

3.   And put thy trust in Allah, and enough is Allah as a Disposer of affairs.

وَّتَوَكَّلْ عَلَى اللهِ ۚ وَكَفٰى بِاللهِ وَكِيْلًا ۞

4.   Allah has not made for any man two hearts in his breast: nor has He made your wives whom ye divorce by Ziḥār your mothers: nor has He made your adopted sons your sons. Such is (only) your (manner of) speech by your mouths. But Allah tells (you) the Truth, and He shows the (right) Way.

مَا جَعَلَ اللهُ لِرَجُلٍ مِّنْ قَلْبَيْنِ فِيْ جَوْفِهٖ ۚ وَمَا جَعَلَ اَزْوَاجَكُمُ الّٰٓـئِيْ تُظٰهِرُوْنَ مِنْهُنَّ اُمَّهٰتِكُمْ ۚ وَمَا جَعَلَ اَدْعِيَآءَكُمْ اَبْنَآءَكُمْ ۗ ذٰلِكُمْ قَوْلُكُمْ بِاَفْوَاهِكُمْ ۗ وَاللهُ يَقُوْلُ الْحَقَّ وَهُوَ يَهْدِى السَّبِيْلَ ۞

5.   Call them by after their fathers: that is juster in the sight of Allah. But if ye know not their father's names, (then they are) your Brothers in faith, or your friends but there is no blame on you if ye make a mistake therein: (what counts is) the intention of your hearts: and Allah is Oft-Forgiving, Most Merciful.

اُدْعُوْهُمْ لِاٰبَآئِهِمْ هُوَ اَقْسَطُ عِنْدَ اللهِ ۚ فَاِنْ لَّمْ تَعْلَمُوْٓا اٰبَآءَهُمْ فَاِخْوَانُكُمْ فِى الدِّيْنِ وَمَوَالِيْكُمْ ۚ وَلَيْسَ عَلَيْكُمْ جُنَاحٌ فِيْمَآ اَخْطَاْتُمْ بِهٖ وَلٰكِنْ مَّا تَعَمَّدَتْ قُلُوْبُكُمْ ۗ وَكَانَ اللهُ غَفُوْرًا رَّحِيْمًا ۞

6.   The Prophet is closer to the Believers than their own selves, and his wives are their mothers. Blood-relations among each other have closer personal ties, in the Book of Allah, than (the Brotherhood of) Believers and Muhājirs: nevertheless do ye what is just to your closest friends: such is the writing in the Book (of Allah).

اَلنَّبِيُّ اَوْلٰى بِالْمُؤْمِنِيْنَ مِنْ اَنْفُسِهِمْ وَاَزْوَاجُهٗٓ اُمَّهٰتُهُمْ ۗ وَاُولُوا الْاَرْحَامِ بَعْضُهُمْ اَوْلٰى بِبَعْضٍ فِيْ كِتٰبِ اللهِ مِنَ الْمُؤْمِنِيْنَ وَالْمُهٰجِرِيْنَ اِلَّآ اَنْ تَفْعَلُوْٓا اِلٰٓى اَوْلِيَآئِكُمْ مَّعْرُوْفًا ۗ كَانَ ذٰلِكَ فِى الْكِتٰبِ مَسْطُوْرًا ۞

7.   And remember We took from the Prophets their Covenant: and from thee: from Noah, Abraham, Moses, and Jesus the son of Mary: We took from them a solemn Covenant:

وَاِذْ اَخَذْنَا مِنَ النَّبِيّٖنَ مِيْثَاقَهُمْ وَمِنْكَ وَمِنْ نُّوْحٍ وَّاِبْرٰهِيْمَ وَمُوْسٰى وَعِيْسَى ابْنِ مَرْيَمَ ۖ وَاَخَذْنَا مِنْهُمْ مِّيْثَاقًا غَلِيْظًا ۙ

اتل ما أوحى ٢١

8. That (Allah) may question the Truthful about their truthfulness and He has prepared for the Unbelievers a grievous Chastisement.

9. O ye who believe! remember the Grace of Allah, (bestowed) on you, when there came down on you hosts (to overwhelm you): but We sent against them a hurricane and forces that ye saw not: but Allah sees (clearly) all that ye do.

10. Behold! they came on you from above you and from below you, and behold, the eyes swerved and the hearts gaped up to the throats, and ye imagined various (vain) thoughts about Allah!

11. In that situation were the Believers tried: they were shaken as by a tremendous shaking.

12. And behold! The Hypocrites and those in whose hearts is a disease say: "Allah and His Messenger promised us nothing but delusions!"

13. Behold! A party among them said: "Ye men of Yathrib! Ye cannot stand (the attack)! Therefore go back!" And a band of them ask for leave of the Prophet, saying, "Truly our houses are bare and exposed," though they were not exposed: they intended nothing but to run away.

14. And if an entry had been effected to them from the sides of the (City), and they had been incited to sedition. They would certainly have brought it to pass, with none but a brief delay!

15. And yet they had already Covenanted with Allah not to turn their backs, and a covenant with Allah must (surely) be answered for.

16. Say: "Running away will not profit you if ye are running away from death or slaughter; and even if (ye do escape), no more than a brief (respite) will ye be allowed to enjoy!"

17. Say: "Who is it that can screen you from Allah if it be His wish to give you

لِيَسْـَٔلَ الصّٰدِقِيْنَ عَنْ صِدْقِهِمْ ۚ وَاَعَدَّ لِلْكٰفِرِيْنَ عَذَابًا اَلِيْمًا ۞

يٰٓاَيُّهَا الَّذِيْنَ اٰمَنُوا اذْكُرُوْا نِعْمَةَ اللّٰهِ عَلَيْكُمْ اِذْ جَآءَتْكُمْ جُنُوْدٌ فَاَرْسَلْنَا عَلَيْهِمْ رِيْحًا وَّجُنُوْدًا لَّمْ تَرَوْهَا ۚ وَكَانَ اللّٰهُ بِمَا تَعْمَلُوْنَ بَصِيْرًا ۞

اِذْ جَآءُوْكُمْ مِّنْ فَوْقِكُمْ وَمِنْ اَسْفَلَ مِنْكُمْ وَاِذْ زَاغَتِ الْاَبْصَارُ وَبَلَغَتِ الْقُلُوْبُ الْحَنَاجِرَ وَتَظُنُّوْنَ بِاللّٰهِ الظُّنُوْنَا ۞

هُنَالِكَ ابْتُلِيَ الْمُؤْمِنُوْنَ وَزُلْزِلُوْا زِلْزَالًا شَدِيْدًا ۞

وَاِذْ يَقُوْلُ الْمُنٰفِقُوْنَ وَالَّذِيْنَ فِيْ قُلُوْبِهِمْ مَّرَضٌ مَّا وَعَدَنَا اللّٰهُ وَرَسُوْلُهٗٓ اِلَّا غُرُوْرًا ۞

وَاِذْ قَالَتْ طَّآئِفَةٌ مِّنْهُمْ يٰٓاَهْلَ يَثْرِبَ لَا مُقَامَ لَكُمْ فَارْجِعُوْا ۚ وَيَسْتَاْذِنُ فَرِيْقٌ مِّنْهُمُ النَّبِيَّ يَقُوْلُوْنَ اِنَّ بُيُوْتَنَا عَوْرَةٌ ۛ وَمَا هِيَ بِعَوْرَةٍ ۛ اِنْ يُّرِيْدُوْنَ اِلَّا فِرَارًا ۞

وَلَوْ دُخِلَتْ عَلَيْهِمْ مِّنْ اَقْطَارِهَا ثُمَّ سُئِلُوا الْفِتْنَةَ لَاٰتَوْهَا وَمَا تَلَبَّثُوْا بِهَآ اِلَّا يَسِيْرًا ۞

وَلَقَدْ كَانُوْا عَاهَدُوا اللّٰهَ مِنْ قَبْلُ لَا يُوَلُّوْنَ الْاَدْبَارَ ۚ وَكَانَ عَهْدُ اللّٰهِ مَسْـُٔوْلًا ۞

قُلْ لَّنْ يَّنْفَعَكُمُ الْفِرَارُ اِنْ فَرَرْتُمْ مِّنَ الْمَوْتِ اَوِ الْقَتْلِ وَاِذًا لَّا تُمَتَّعُوْنَ اِلَّا قَلِيْلًا ۞

قُلْ مَنْ ذَا الَّذِيْ يَعْصِمُكُمْ مِّنَ اللّٰهِ

Punishment or to give you Mercy?" Nor will they find for themselves, besides Allah, any protector or helper.

18. Verily Allah knows those among you who keep back (men) and those who say to their brethren, "Come along to us", but come not to the fight except for just a little while,'

19. Covetous over you. Then when fear comes, thou wilt see them looking to thee, their eyes revolving, like one who faints from death: but when the fear is past, they will smite you with sharp tongues, covetous of goods. Such men have no faith, and so Allah has made their deeds of none effect: and that is easy for Allah.

20. They think that the Confederates have not withdrawn; and if, the Confederates should come (again), they would wish they were in the deserts (wandering) among the Bedouins, and seeking news about you (from a safe distance); and if they were in your midst, they would fight but little.

21. Ye have indeed in the Messenger of Allah an excellent exemplar for him who hopes in Allah and the Final Day, and who remember Allah much.

22. When the Believers saw the Confederate forces, they said: "This is what Allah and His Messenger had promised us, and Allah and His Messenger told us what was true." And it only added to their faith and their zeal in obedience.

23. Among the Believers are men who have been true to their covenant with Allah: of them some have died and some (still) wait: but they have never changed (their determination) in the least:

24. That Allah may reward the men of Truth for their Truth, and punish the

Hypocrites if that be His Will, or turn to them in Mercy: for Allah is Oft-Forgiving, Most Merciful.

25. And Allah turned back the Unbelievers for (all) their fury: no advantage did they gain; and enough is Allah for the Believers in their fight. And Allah is full of Strength, Exalted in might.

26. And those of the people of the Book who aided them—Allah did take them down from their strongholds and cast terror into their hearts, (so that) some ye slew, and some ye made captives.

27. And He made you heirs of their lands, their houses, and their goods, and of a land which ye had not frequented (before). And Allah has power over all things.

28. O Prophet! say to thy Consorts: "If it be that ye desire the life of this world, and its glitter,—then come! I will provide for your enjoyment and set you free in a handsome manner.

29. But if ye seek Allah and His Messenger, and the Home of the Hereafter, Verily Allah has prepared for the well-doers amongst you a great reward.

30. O Consorts of the Prophet! If any of you were guilty of evident unseemly conduct, the Punishment would be doubled to her, and that is easy for Allah.

31. But any of you that is devout in the service of Allah and His Messenger, and works righteousness,— to her shall We grant her reward twice: and We have prepared for her a generous Sustenance.

32. O Consorts of the Prophet! Ye are not like any of the (other) women: if ye do fear (Allah), be not too complaisant of speech, lest one in whose heart is a disease should be moved with desire: but speak ye a speech (that is) just.

يٰنِسَآءَ النَّبِيِّ لَسْتُنَّ كَاَحَدٍ مِّنَ النِّسَاءِ اِنِ اتَّقَيْتُنَّ فَلَا تَخْضَعْنَ بِالْقَوْلِ فَيَطْمَعَ الَّذِىْ فِىْ قَلْبِهٖ مَرَضٌ وَّقُلْنَ قَوْلًا مَّعْرُوْفًا ۞

33. And stay quietly in your houses, and make not a dazzling display, like that of the former Times of Ignorance; and establish regular Prayer, and give zakat and obey Allah and His Messenger. And Allah only wishes to remove all abomination from you, ye Members of the Family, and to make you pure and spotless.

وَقَرْنَ فِىْ بُيُوْتِكُنَّ وَلَا تَبَرَّجْنَ تَبَرُّجَ الْجَاهِلِيَّةِ الْاُوْلٰى وَاَقِمْنَ الصَّلٰوةَ وَاٰتِيْنَ الزَّكٰوةَ وَاَطِعْنَ اللّٰهَ وَرَسُوْلَهٗ اِنَّمَا يُرِيْدُ اللّٰهُ لِيُذْهِبَ عَنْكُمُ الرِّجْسَ اَهْلَ الْبَيْتِ وَيُطَهِّرَكُمْ تَطْهِيْرًا ۞

34. And recite what is rehearsed to you in your homes, of the Signs of Allah and His Wisdom: for Allah is All-Subtle, All-Aware.

وَاذْكُرْنَ مَا يُتْلٰى فِىْ بُيُوْتِكُنَّ مِنْ اٰيٰتِ اللّٰهِ وَالْحِكْمَةِ اِنَّ اللّٰهَ كَانَ لَطِيْفًا خَبِيْرًا ۞

35. For Muslim men and women,—for believing men and women, for devout men and women, for true men and women, for men and women who are patient and constant, for men and women who humble themselves, for men and women who give in charity, for men and women who fast for men and women who guard their chastity, and for men and women who engage much in Allah's remembrance for them has Allah prepared forgiveness and great reward.

اِنَّ الْمُسْلِمِيْنَ وَالْمُسْلِمٰتِ وَالْمُؤْمِنِيْنَ وَالْمُؤْمِنٰتِ وَالْقٰنِتِيْنَ وَالْقٰنِتٰتِ وَالصّٰدِقِيْنَ وَالصّٰدِقٰتِ وَالصّٰبِرِيْنَ وَالصّٰبِرٰتِ وَالْخٰشِعِيْنَ وَالْخٰشِعٰتِ وَالْمُتَصَدِّقِيْنَ وَالْمُتَصَدِّقٰتِ وَالصَّآئِمِيْنَ وَالصّٰٓئِمٰتِ وَالْحٰفِظِيْنَ فُرُوْجَهُمْ وَالْحٰفِظٰتِ وَالذّٰكِرِيْنَ اللّٰهَ كَثِيْرًا وَّالذّٰكِرٰتِ اَعَدَّ اللّٰهُ لَهُمْ مَّغْفِرَةً وَّاَجْرًا عَظِيْمًا ۞

36. It is not fitting for a Believer, man or woman, when a matter has been decided by Allah and His Messenger, to have any option about their decision: if anyone disobeys Allah and His Messenger, he is indeed on a clearly wrong Path.

وَمَا كَانَ لِمُؤْمِنٍ وَّلَا مُؤْمِنَةٍ اِذَا قَضَى اللّٰهُ وَرَسُوْلُهٗٓ اَمْرًا اَنْ يَّكُوْنَ لَهُمُ الْخِيَرَةُ مِنْ اَمْرِهِمْ وَمَنْ يَّعْصِ اللّٰهَ وَرَسُوْلَهٗ فَقَدْ ضَلَّ ضَلٰلًا مُّبِيْنًا ۞

37. Behold! thou didst say to one who had received the grace of Allah and thy favour: "Retain thou (in wedlock) thy wife, and fear Allah." But thou didst hide in thy heart that which Allah was about to make manifest: thou didst fear the people, but it is more fitting that thou shouldst. Fear Allah.

وَاِذْ تَقُوْلُ لِلَّذِىْٓ اَنْعَمَ اللّٰهُ عَلَيْهِ وَاَنْعَمْتَ عَلَيْهِ اَمْسِكْ عَلَيْكَ زَوْجَكَ وَاتَّقِ اللّٰهَ وَتُخْفِىْ فِىْ نَفْسِكَ مَا اللّٰهُ مُبْدِيْهِ وَتَخْشَى النَّاسَ وَاللّٰهُ اَحَقُّ

Then when Zaid had dissolved (his marriage) with her We joined her in marriage to thee: in order that (in future) there may be no difficulty to the Believers in (the matter of) marriage with the wives of their adopted sons, when the latter have dissolved (their marriage) with them. And Allah's command must be fulfilled.

38. There can be no difficulty to the Prophet in what Allah has indicated to him as a duty: It was the practice (approved) of Allah amongst those of old that have passed away. And the command of Allah is a decree determined.

39. (It is the practice of those) who preach the Messages of Allah, and fear Him, and fear none but Allah. And enough is Allah to call (men) to account.

40. Muhammad is not the father of any of your men, but (he is) the Messenger of Allah, and the Seal of the Prophets: and Allah has full knowledge of all things.

41. O ye who believe! remember Allah, with much remembrance;

42. And glorify Him morning and evening.

43. He it is Who sends bessings on you, as do His angels, that He may bring you out from the depths of Darkness into Light: and He is Full of Mercy to the Believers.

44. Their salutation on the Day they meet Him will be "Peace!"; and He has prepared for them a generous Reward.

45. O Prophet! Truly We have sent thee as a Witness, a Bearer of Glad Tidings, and a Warner,—

46. And as one who invites to Allah's (Grace) by His leave, and as a Lamp spreading Light.

47. Then give the glad tidings to the Believers, that they shall have from Allah a very great Bounty.

48. And obey not (the behests) of the Unbelievers and the Hypocrites, and disregard their insolence but put thy trust in Allah. For enough is Allah as a Disposer of affairs.

49. O ye who believe! when ye marry believing women, and then divorce them before ye have touched them, no period of 'Iddat have ye to count in respect of them: so give them a present, and release them in a handsome manner.

50. O Prophet! We have made lawful to thee thy wives to whom thou hast paid their dowers; and those whom thy right hand possesses out of the captives of war whom Allah has assigned to thee; and daughters of thy paternal uncles and aunts, and daughters of thy maternal uncles and aunts, who migrated with thee; and any believing woman who gives herself to the Prophet if the Prophet wishes to wed her;—this only for thee, and not for the Believers (at large); We know what We have appointed for them as to their wives and the captives whom their right hands possess;—in order that there should be no difficulty for thee. And Allah is Oft-Forgiving, Most Merciful.

51. Thou mayest defer (the turn of) any of them that thou pleasest, and thou mayest receive any thou pleasest: and there is no blame on thee if thou invite one whose (turn) thou hadst set aside. This were nigher to the cooling of their eyes, the prevention of their grief, and their satisfaction—that of all of them—with that which thou hast to give them: and Allah knows (all) that is in your hearts: and Allah is All-Knowing, Most Forbearing.

52. It is not lawful for thee (to marry more) women after this, nor to change them for (other) wives, even though their beauty attract thee, except any thy right hand should possess (as handmaidens): and Allah doth watch over all things.

53. O ye who believe! enter not the Prophet's houses,—until leave is given

you,— for a meal, (and then) not (so early as) to wait for its preparation: but when ye are invited, enter; and when ye have taken your meal, disperse, without seeking familiar talk. Such (behaviour) annoys the Prophet he is shy to dismiss you, but Allah is not shy (to tell you) the truth.

And when ye ask (his ladies) for anything ye want, ask them from before a screen: that makes for greater purity for your hearts and for theirs.

Nor is it right for you that ye should annoy Allah's Messenger, or that ye should marry his widows after him at any time. Truly such a thing is in Allah's sight an enormity.

54. Whether ye reveal anything or conceal it, verily Allah has full knowledge of all things.

55. There is no blame (on those ladies if they appear) before their fathers or their sons, their brothers, or their brothers' sons, or their sisters' sons, or their women, or the (slaves) whom their right hands possess. And, (ladies), fear Allah; for Allah is Witness to all things.

56. Allah and His Angels, send blessings on the Prophet: O ye that believe! send ye blessings on him, and salute him with all respect.

57. Those who annoy Allah and His Messenger— Allah has cursed them in this world and in the Hereafter, and has prepared for them a humiliating Punishment.

58. And those who annoy believing men and women undeservedly, bear (on themselves) a calumny and a glaring sin.

59. O Prophet! tell thy wives and daughters, and the believing women, that

they should cast their outer garments over their persons (when out of doors): that is most convenient, that they should be known (as such) and not molested. And Allah is Oft-Forgiving, Most Merciful.

60. Truly, if the Hypocrites, and those in whose heart is a disease, and those who stir up sedition in the City, desist not, We shall certainly stir thee up against them: then will they not be able to stay in it as thy neighbours for any length of time:

61. They shall have a curse on them: wherever they are found, they shall be seized and slain.

62. (Such was) the practice (appro-ved) of Allah among those who lived aforetime: no change wilt thou find in the practice (approved) of Allah.

63. Men ask thee concerning the Hour: say, "The knowledge thereof is with Allah (alone)": and what will make thee understand?—perchance the Hour is nigh!

64. Verily Allah has cursed the Unbelievers and prepared for them a Blazing Fire,—

65. To dwell therein for ever: no protector will they find, nor helper.

66. The Day that their faces will be turned over in the Fire, they will say: "Woe to us! would that we had obeyed Allah and obeyed the Messenger!"

67. And they would say: "Our Lord! We obeyed our chiefs and our great ones, and they misled us as to the (right) path.

68. "Our Lord! Give Them double Chastiement and cure them with a very great Curse!"

69. O ye who believe! be ye not like those who hurt Moses, but Allah cleared him of the (calumnies) they had uttered:

SÛRA–34
SABĀ
(INTRODUCTION)

Now we begin a series of the Sûras, S. 34 to S. 39, which recapitulate some of the features of the spiritual world. This Sûra leads off with emphasis on Allah's Mercy and Power and Truth. Then (in S. 35) we are told how angles manifest the Power of Allah, and how different is Good from Evil and Truth from Falsehood. S. 34 is devoted to the Holy Prophet and the Qur-ān that came through him. In S. 37 the emphasis is on the snares of the Evil One; in S. 38, on the conquest of evil by wisdom and power as in the case of David and Solomon, and by Patience and Constancy as in the case of Job: and in S. 39 on the Final Judgment, which will sort out Faith from Unfaith and give to each its due.

The chronology has here no significance. This Sûra belongs to the early Makkan period.

and he was honourable in Allah's sight.

كَانَ عِنْدَ اللَّهِ وَجِيهًا ۞

70. O ye who believe! fear Allah, and make your utterance straight forward:

يَأَيُّهَا الَّذِينَ اٰمَنُوا اتَّقُوا اللَّهَ وَقُولُوا قَوْلًا سَدِيدًا ۞

71. That He may make your conduct whole and sound and forgive you your sins: he that obeys Allah and His Messenger, has already attained the great victory.

يُصْلِحْ لَكُمْ اَعْمَالَكُمْ وَيَغْفِرْ لَكُمْ ذُنُوبَكُمْ وَمَنْ يُّطِعِ اللَّهَ وَرَسُولَهُ فَقَدْ فَازَ فَوْزًا عَظِيمًا ۞

72. We did indeed offer the Trust to the Heavens and the Earth and the Mountians; but they refused to undertake it, being afraid thereof: but man undertook it:— he was indeed unjust and foolish,—

إِنَّا عَرَضْنَا الْاَمَانَةَ عَلَى السَّمٰوٰتِ وَالْاَرْضِ وَالْجِبَالِ فَاَبَيْنَ اَنْ يَّحْمِلْنَهَا وَاَشْفَقْنَ مِنْهَا وَحَمَلَهَا الْاِنْسَانُ ط اِنَّهُ كَانَ ظَلُومًا جَهُولًا ۞

73. (With the result) that Allah has to punish the Hypocrites, men and women, and the Unbelievers, men and women, and Allah turns in Mercy to the Believers, men and women: for Allah is Oft-Forgiving, Most merciful.

لِيُعَذِّبَ اللَّهُ الْمُنٰفِقِينَ وَالْمُنٰفِقٰتِ وَالْمُشْرِكِينَ وَالْمُشْرِكٰتِ وَيَتُوبَ اللَّهُ عَلَى الْمُؤْمِنِينَ وَالْمُؤْمِنٰتِ وَكَانَ اللَّهُ غَفُورًا رَّحِيمًا ۞

Sabā, or the City of Sabā

سُورَةُ سَبَأٍ مَكِّيَّةٌ وَهِيَ اَرْبَعٌ وَّخَمْسُونَ اٰيَةً وَسِتُّ رُكُوعَاتٍ

In the name of Allah, Most Gracious, Most Merciful.

بِسْمِ اللَّهِ الرَّحْمٰنِ الرَّحِيمِ ۞

1. Praise be to Allah, to whom belong all things in the heavens and on earth: to Him be Praise in the Hereafter: and He is All-Wise, All-Aware.

اَلْحَمْدُ لِلَّهِ الَّذِي لَهُ مَا فِي السَّمٰوٰتِ وَمَا فِي الْاَرْضِ وَلَهُ الْحَمْدُ فِي الْاٰخِرَةِ ط وَهُوَ الْحَكِيمُ الْخَبِيرُ ۞

2. He knows all that goes into the earth, and all that comes out thereof; all that comes down from the sky and all that ascends thereto and He is the Most Merciful, the Oft-Forgiving.

يَعْلَمُ مَا يَلِجُ فِي الْاَرْضِ وَمَا يَخْرُجُ مِنْهَا وَمَا يَنْزِلُ مِنَ السَّمَاءِ وَمَا يَعْرُجُ فِيهَا ط وَهُوَ الرَّحِيمُ الْغَفُورُ ۞

3. The Unbelievers say, "Never to us will come the Hour": say, "Nay! but most surely, by my Lord, it will come upon you;—by Him Who knows the unseen,— from Whom is not hidden the least little atom in the Heavens or on earth: nor is there anything less than that, or greater, but is in the Record

وَقَالَ الَّذِينَ كَفَرُوا لَا تَأْتِينَا السَّاعَةُ قُلْ بَلٰى وَرَبِّي لَتَأْتِيَنَّكُمْ عٰلِمِ الْغَيْبِ لَا يَعْزُبُ عَنْهُ مِثْقَالُ ذَرَّةٍ فِي السَّمٰوٰتِ وَلَا فِي الْاَرْضِ وَلَا اَصْغَرُ مِنْ ذٰلِكَ وَلَا اَكْبَرُ اِلَّا فِي كِتٰبٍ

Perspicuous:

4. That He may reward those who believe and work deeds of righteousness: for such is Forgiveness and a Sustenance Most Generous."

5. But those who strive against Our Signs, to frustrate them,—for such will be a Chastisement of painful wrath.

6. And those to whom knowledge has come see that the (Revelation) sent down to thee from thy Lord— that is the Truth, and that it guides to the Path of the Exalted (in Might), Worthy of all praise.

7. The Unbelievers say (in ridicule): "Shall we point out to you a man that will tell you, when ye are all scattered to pieces in disintegration, that ye shall (then be raised) in a New Creation?

8. "Has he invented a falsehood against Allah, or is he afflicted with madness". Nay, it is those who believe not in the Hereafter, that are in (real) Chastisement, and in farthest Error.

9. See they not what is before them and behind them, of the sky and the earth? If We wished, We could cause the earth to swallow them up, or cause a piece of the sky to fall upon them. Verily in this is a Sign for every devotee that turns to Allah (in repentance).

10. We bestowed Grace aforetime on David from Us "O ye Mountains! echo ye back the Praise of Allah with him! and ye birds (also)! And We made the iron soft for him;—

11. (Commanding), "Make thou coats of mail, balancing well the rings of chain armour, and work ye righteousness; for be sure I see (clearly) all that ye do."

12. And to Solomon (We made) the Wind (obedient): its early morning (stride) was a month's (journey), and its evening (stride) was a month's (journey): and We made a Font of molten brass to flow for him; and

there were Jinns that worked in front of
him, by the leave of his Lord, and if any of
them turned aside from Our command, We
made him taste of the Chastisement of the
Blazing Fire.

13. They worked for him as he desired,
(making) Arches, Images, Basons as large
as wells, and (cooking) Cauldrons fixed (in
their places): "Exercise thanks sons of
David, but few of My servants are grateful!"

14. Then, when We decreed (Solomon's)
death, nothing showed them his death
except a little worm of the earth, which kept
(slowly) gnawing away at his staff: so when
he fell down, the Jinns saw plainly that if
they had known the unseen, they would
not have tarried in the humiliating
Chastisement (of their Task).

15. There was, for Sabā, aforetime, a Sign
in their home-land—two Gardens to the
right and to the left. "Eat of the Sustenance
(provided) by your Lord, and be grateful to
Him: a territory fair and happy, and a Lord
Oft-Forgiving!"

16. But they turned away (from Allah), and
We sent against them the flood (released)
from the Dams, and We converted their
two garden (rows) into "gardens" producing
bitter fruit, and tamarisks, and some few
(stunted) Lote-trees.

17. That was the Requital We gave them
because they ungratefully rejected Faith:
and never do We give (such) requital except
to such as are ungrateful rejecters.

18. Between them and the Cities on which
We had poured Our blessings, We had
placed Cities in prominent positions, and
between them We had appointed stages of
journey in due proportion: "Travel therein,
secure, by night and by day."

19. But they said: "Our Lord! place longer
distances between our journey-stages": but
they wronged themselves (therein). At
length We made them as a tale (that is
told), and We dispersed them all in scattered
fragments. Verily in this are Signs for every
(soul that is) patiently constant and grateful.

بِإِذۡنِ رَبِّهٖ ۖ وَمَن يَزِغۡ مِنۡهُمۡ عَنۡ أَمۡرِنَا
نُذِقۡهُ مِنۡ عَذَابِ السَّعِيرِ ۝

يَعۡمَلُونَ لَهٗ مَا يَشَآءُ مِن مَّحَارِيبَ
وَتَمَاثِيلَ وَجِفَانٍ كَالۡجَوَابِ وَقُدُورٍ
رَّاسِيَاتٍ ۚ اعۡمَلُوٓا آلَ دَاوُۥدَ شُكۡرًا ۚ وَ
قَلِيلٌ مِّنۡ عِبَادِيَ الشَّكُورُ ۝

فَلَمَّا قَضَيۡنَا عَلَيۡهِ الۡمَوۡتَ مَا دَلَّهُمۡ
عَلَىٰ مَوۡتِهٖٓ إِلَّا دَآبَّةُ الۡأَرۡضِ تَأۡكُلُ
مِنسَأَتَهٗ ۖ فَلَمَّا خَرَّ تَبَيَّنَتِ الۡجِنُّ أَن
لَّوۡ كَانُوا يَعۡلَمُونَ الۡغَيۡبَ مَا لَبِثُوا فِى
الۡعَذَابِ الۡمُهِينِ ۝

لَقَدۡ كَانَ لِسَبَإٍ فِى مَسۡكَنِهِمۡ ءَايَةٌ ۖ جَنَّتَانِ
عَن يَمِينٍ وَشِمَالٍ ۖ كُلُوا مِن رِّزۡقِ
رَبِّكُمۡ وَاشۡكُرُوا لَهٗ ۚ بَلۡدَةٌ طَيِّبَةٌ
وَرَبٌّ غَفُورٌ ۝

فَأَعۡرَضُوا فَأَرۡسَلۡنَا عَلَيۡهِمۡ سَيۡلَ الۡعَرِمِ
وَبَدَّلۡنَاهُم بِجَنَّتَيۡهِمۡ جَنَّتَيۡنِ ذَوَاتَىۡ
أُكُلٍ خَمۡطٍ وَأَثۡلٍ وَشَىۡءٍ مِّن
سِدۡرٍ قَلِيلٍ ۝

ذَٰلِكَ جَزَيۡنَاهُم بِمَا كَفَرُوا ۖ وَهَلۡ نُجَٰزِىٓ إِلَّا الۡكَفُورَ
وَجَعَلۡنَا بَيۡنَهُمۡ وَبَيۡنَ الۡقُرَى الَّتِى
بَٰرَكۡنَا فِيهَا قُرًى ظَاهِرَةً وَقَدَّرۡنَا فِيهَا
السَّيۡرَ ۖ سِيرُوا فِيهَا لَيَالِىَ وَأَيَّامًا ءَامِنِينَ ۝

فَقَالُوا رَبَّنَا بَاعِدۡ بَيۡنَ أَسۡفَارِنَا وَ
ظَلَمُوٓا أَنفُسَهُمۡ فَجَعَلۡنَاهُمۡ أَحَادِيثَ
وَمَزَّقۡنَاهُمۡ كُلَّ مُمَزَّقٍ ۚ إِنَّ فِى ذَٰلِكَ
لَآيَاتٍ لِّكُلِّ صَبَّارٍ شَكُورٍ ۝

20. And on them did Satan prove true his idea, and they followed him, all but a Party that believed.

21. But he had no authority over them,— except that We might test the man who believes in the Hereafter from him who is in doubt concerning it: and thy Lord doth watch over all things.

22. Say: "Call upon other (gods) whom ye fancy, besides Allah: they have no power,— not the weight of an atom,— in the heavens or on earth: no (sort of) share have they therein, nor is any of them a helper to Allah.

23. "No intercession can avail with Him, except for those for whom He has granted permission. So far (is this the case) that, when terror is removed from their hearts (at the Day of Judgment, then) will they say, 'What is it that your Lord commanded?' They will say, 'That which is true and just; and He is the Most High, Most Great'."

24. Say: "Who gives you sustenance, from the heavens and the earth?" Say: "It is Allah; and certain it is that either we or ye are on right guidance or in manifest error!"

25. Say: "Ye shall not be questioned as to our sins, nor shall we be questioned as to what ye do."

26. Say: "Our Lord will gather us together and will in the end decide the matter between us (and you) in truth and justice: and He is the One to decide, the One Who knows all."

27. Say: "Show me those whom ye have joined with Him as partners: by no means (can ye). Nay, He is Allah, the Exalted in Power, the Wise."

28. We have not sent thee but as a (Messenger) to all mankind, giving them Glad tidings, and warning them (against sin), but most men know not.

29. They say: "When will this promise (come to pass) if ye are telling the truth?"

30. Say: "The appointment to you is for a Day, which ye cannot put back for an hour

nor put forward."

31. The Unbelievers say: "We shall neither believe in this scripture nor in (any) that (came) before it." Couldst thou but see when the wrong-doers will be made to stand before their Lord, throwing back the word (of blame) on one another! Those who were deemed weak will say to the arrogant ones: "Had it not been for you, we should certainly have been believers!"

32. The arrogant ones will say to those who had been deemed weak: "Was it we who kept you back from Guidance after it reached you? Nay, rather, it was ye who transgressed."

33. Those who had been deemed weak will say to the arrogant ones: "Nay! it was a plot (of yours) by day and by night: behold! ye (constantly) ordered us to be ungrateful to Allah and to attribute equals to Him!" They are filled with remorse. When they see the Chastisement: We shall put yokes on the necks of the Unbelievers: it would only be a requital for their (ill) Deeds.

34. Never did We send a Warner to a population, but the wealthy ones among them said: "We believe not in the (Message) with which ye have been sent."

35. They said: "We have more in wealth and in sons, and we cannot be chastised".

36. Say: "Verily my Lord enlarges and restricts the Provision to whom He pleases, but most men know not."

37. It is not your wealth nor your sons, that will bring you nearer to Us in degree: but only those who believe and work righteousness—these are the ones for whom there is a multiplied Reward for their

deeds, while secure they (reside) in the dwellings on high!

38. Those who strive against Our Signs, to frustrate them, will be given over into Chastisement.

39. Say: "Verily my Lord enlarges and restricts the Sustenance to such of His servants as He pleases: and nothing do ye spend in the least (in His Cause) but He replaces it: for He is the Best of those who grant Sustenance.

40. On the Day He will gather them all together, and say to the angels, "Was it you that these men used to worship?"

41. They will say, "Glory to Thee! Thou art our Protector —not them. Nay, but they worshipped the Jinns: most of them believed in them."

42. So on that Day no power shall they have over each other, for profit or harm: and We shall say to the wrong-doers. "Taste ye the Chastisement of the Fire,— the which ye were wont to deny!"

43. When Our Clear Signs are rehearsed to them, they say, "This is only a man who wishes to hinder you from the (worship) which your fathers practised." And they say, "This is only a falsehood invented!" And the Unbelievers say of the Truth when it comes to them, "This is nothing but evident magic!"

44. But We had not given them Books which they could study, nor sent messengers to them before thee as Warners.

45. And their predecessors rejected (the Truth); these have not received a tenth of what We had granted to those: yet when they rejected my messengers, how (terrible) was My punishment!

46. Say: "I do admonish you on one point: that ye do stand up before Allah,— (it may be) in pairs, or (it may be) singly,— and

See Introduction to the last Sûra.

This Sûra deals with the mystery of Creation and its maintenance, with various forces typified by the wings of Angels. Whether we look to outer nature or to man, Allah's Grace proclaims His Glory, and protects His votaries from Evil.

It is an early Makkan Sûra, but its chronology has no significance.

reflect (within yourselves): your Companion is not possessed: he is no less than a Warner to you, in face of a terrible Chastisement".

47. Say: "Whatever reward do I ask of you: it is yours: my reward is only due from Allah: and He is Witness to all things."

48. Say: "Verily my Lord doth cast the Truth,—he that has full knowledge of (all) that is hidden."

49. Say: "The Truth has arrived, and Falsehood showeth not its face and will not return."

50. Say: "If I am astray, I only stray to the loss of my own soul: but if I receive guidance, it is because of the inspiration of my Lord to me: it is He Who hears all things, and is (ever) near."

51. If thou couldst but see when they will quake with terror; but then there will be no escape (for them), and they will be seized from a position (quite) near.

52. And they will say, "We do believe (now) in the (Truth)"; but how could they receive (Faith) from a position (so) far off,—

53. Seeing that they did reject Faith (entirely) before, and that they cast (conjectures) with regard to the unseen from a position far off?

54. And between them and their desires, is placed a barrier, as was done in the past with their partisans: for they were indeed in suspicious (disquieting) doubt.

Fāṭir, or The Originator of Creation; or Malāîka, or The Angels

In the name of Allah, Most Gracious, Most Merciful.

1. Praise be to Allah, the Originator of the heavens and the earth, Who made the angels Messengers with wings,— two, or three, or four (Pairs): He adds to Creation as He pleases: for Allah has power over all things.

2. What Allah out of His Mercy doth bestow on mankind none can withhold: what He doth withhold, none can grant, apart from Him: and He is the Exalted in Power, Full of Wisdom.

3. O men! Remember the grace of Allah unto you! Is there a Creator, other than Allah, to give you sustenance from heaven or earth? There is no god but He: how then are ye perverted?

4. And if they reject thee, so were messengers rejected before thee: to Allah all affairs are returned.

5. O men! certainly the promise of Allah is true, let not then this present life deceive you, nor let the Chief Deceiver deceive you about Allah.

6. Verily Satan is an enemy to you: so treat him as an enemy. He only invites his adherents, that they may become companions of the Blazing Fire.

7. For those who reject Allah, is a terrible Chastisement but for those who believe and work righteous deeds, is Forgiveness, and a magnificent Reward.

8. Is he, then, to whom the evil of his conduct is made alluring, so that he looks upon it as good, (equal to one who is rightly guided)? For Allah leaves to stray whom He wills, and guides whom He wills. So let not thy soul be vested in regret for them for Allah knows well all that they do!

9. It is Allah Who sends forth the Winds, so that they raise up the Clouds, and We drive them to a land that is dead, and revive the earth therewith after its death: even so (will be) the Resurrection!

10. If any do seek for glory and power,— to Allah belong all glory and power. To Him mount up (all) Words of Purity: it is He Who exalts each Deed of Righteousness. Those that lay Plots of Evil,—for them is a Chastisement terrible; and the plotting of such will be void (of result).

11. And Allah did create you from dust; then from a sperm-drop; then He made you in pairs. And no female conceives, or lays down (her load), but with His knowledge. Nor is a man long-lived granted length of days, nor is a part cut off from his life, but is in a Book (ordained). All this is easy to Allah.

12. Nor are the two seas alike,— the one palatable, sweet, and pleasant to drink, and the other, salt and bitter. Yet from each (kind of water) do ye eat flesh fresh and tender, and ye extract ornaments to wear; and thou seest the ships therein that plough the waves, that ye may seek (thus) of the Bounty of Allah that ye may be grateful.

13. He merges Night into Day, and He merges Day into Night, and He has subjected the sun and the moon (to His Law): each one runs its course for a term appointed. Such is Allah your Lord: to Him belongs all Dominion. And those whom ye invoke besides Him own not a straw.

14. If ye invoke them, they will not listen to your call, and if they were to listen, they cannot answer your (prayer). On the Day of Judgment they will reject your "Partnership". And none, (O man!) can inform you like Him who is All-Aware.

15. O ye men! It is ye that have need of Allah: but Allah is the One Free of all wants, Worthy of all praise.

16. If He so pleased, He could blot you out and bring in a New Creation.

17. Nor is that (at all) difficult for Allah.

18. Nor can a bearer of burdens bear another's burden. If one heavily laden should call another to (bear) his load, not the least portion of it can be carried (by the other) even though he be nearly related. Thou canst but warn such as fear their Lord unseen and establish regular Prayer. And whoever purifies himself does so for the

benefit of his own soul; and the destination (of all) is to Allah.

19. The blind and the seeing are not alike;

20. Nor are the depths of Darkness and the Light;

21. Nor are the (chilly) shade and the (genial) heat of the sun:

22. Nor are alike those that are living and those that are dead. Allah can make any that He wills to hear; but thou canst not make those to hear who are (burried) in graves.

23. Thou art no other than a warner.

24. Verily We have sent thee with truth, as a bearer of glad tidings. and as a warner: and there never was a people, without a warner having lived among them (in the past).

25. And if they reject thee, so did their predecessors, to whom came their messengers with Clear Signs, Scriptures and the illuminating Book.

26. In the end did I punish those who rejected Faith: and how (terrible) was My punishment.

27. Seest thou not that Allah sends down rain from the sky? With it We then bring out produce of various colours. And in the mountains are tracts white and red, of various shades of colour, and black intense in hue.

28. And so amongst men and beasts and cattle, are they of various colours. Those truly fear Allah, among His Servants Who have knowledge: for Allah is Exalted in Might, Oft-Forgiving.

29. Those who rehearse the Book of Allah, establish regular Prayer, and spend (in Charity) out of what We have provided for them, secretly and openly, hope for a Commerce that will never fail:

30. For He will pay them their meed, nay, He will give them (even) more out of His

Bounty: for He is Oft-Forgiving, Most Ready to appreciate (service).

31. That which We have revealed to thee of the Book is the Truth,—confirming what was (revealed) before it: for Allah is assuredly— with respect to His servants— well acquainted and fully Observant.

32. Then We have given the Book for inheritance to such of Our servants as We have chosen: but there are among them some who wrong their own souls; some who follow a middle course; and some who are, by Allah's leave, foremost in good deeds; that is the highest Grace.

33. Gardens of Eternity will they enter: therein will they be adorned with bracelets of gold and pearls; and their garments there will be of silk.

34. And they will say: "Praise be to Allah, Who has removed from us (all) sorrow: for our Lord is indeed Oft-Forgiving ready to appreciate (service):

35. "Who has, out of His Bounty, settled us in a Home that will last: no toil nor sense of weariness shall touch us therein."

36. But those who reject (Allah)—for them will be the Fire of Hell: no term shall be determined for them, so they should die, nor shall its Chastisement be lightened for them. Thus do We reward every ungrateful one!

37. Therein will they cry aloud (for assistance): "Our Lord! Bring us out: we shall work righteousness, not the (deeds) we used to do!"—"Did we not give you long enough life so that he that would should receive admonition? And (moreover) the warner came to you. So taste ye (the fruits of your deeds): for the Wrong-doers there is no helper."

38. Verily Allah knows (all) the hidden things of the heavens and the earth: verily He has full knowledge of all that is in (men's) hearts.

39. He it is that has made you inheritors in

the earth: so, he who disbelieves his disbelief be on his own self their disbelief: but adds to the odium for the Unbelievers in the sight of their Lord: their disbelief but adds to (their own) loss.

40. Say: "Have ye seen (these) 'Partners' of yours whom ye call upon besides Allah? Show me what it is they have created in the (wide) earth. Or have they a share in the heavens? Or have We given them a Book from which they (can derive) clear (evidence)?—Nay, the wrong-doers promise each other nothing but delusions.

41. It is Allah Who sustains the heavens and the earth, lest they cease (to function): and if they should fail. There is none—not one— can sustain them thereafter: verily He is Most Forbearing, Oft-Forgiving.

42. They swore their strongest oaths by Allah that if a warner came to them, they would be more rightly guided than anyone of the nations: but when a warner came to them, it has only increased their aversion.

43. On account of their arrogance in the land and their plotting of Evil. But the plotting of Evil will hem in only the authors thereof. Now are they but looking for the way the ancients were dealt with? But no change wilt thou find in Allah's way (of dealing): no turning off wilt thou find in Allah's way (of dealing).

44. Do they not travel through the earth, and see what was the End of those before them,— though they were superior to them in strength? Nor is Allah to be frustrated by anything whatever in the heavens or on earth: for He is All-Knowing, All-Powerful.

45. If Allah were to punish men according to what they deserve

SÛRA–36
YĀSÎN
(INTRODUCTION)

See Introduction to S. 34. This particular Sûra is devoted to the Holy Prophet and the Revelation which he brought. The Abbreviated Letters *Yā-Sîn* are usually construed as a title of the Holy Prophet. But it is not permissible to be dogmatic about the meaning of Abbreviated Letters. This Sûra is considered to be "the heart of the Qur-ān," as it concerns the central figure in the teaching of Islam and central doctrine of Revelation and the Hereafter. As referring to the Hereafter, it is apropriately read in solemn ceremonies after death.

In chronology it belongs to the middle or early Makkan period.

In S. 37: 130 (a cognate Sûra) occurs the word *Il-yā-sîn*.

He would not leave on the back of the (earth) a single living creature: but He gives them respite for a stated Term: when their Term expires, verily Allah has in His sight all His servants.

Yā-Sîn (being Abbreviated Letters)

In the name of Allah, Most Gracious, Most Merciful.

1.   Yā-Sîn.

2.   By the Qur'an, full of Wisdom,—

3.   Thou art indeed one of the messengers,

4.   On a Straight Way.

5.   (It is a Revelation) sent down by (Him), the Exalted in Might, Most Merciful,

6.   In order that thou mayest warn a people, whose fathers were not warned, and who therefore remain heedless (of the Signs of Allah).

7.   The Word is proved true against the greater part of them: for they do not believe.

8.   We have put yokes round their necks right up to their chins, so that they cannot bow their heads.

9.   And We have put a bar in front of them and a bar behind them, and further, We have covered them up; so that they cannot see.

10.   The same is to them whether thou admonish them or thou do not admonish them: they will not believe.

11.   Thou canst but admonish such a one as follows the Message and fears the Most Gracious, unseen: give such a one, therefore, good tidings, of Forgiveness and a Reward most generous.

12.   Verily We shall give life to the dead, and We record that which they send before and that which they leave behind, and of all things have We taken account. In a clear Book (of evidence).

13.   Set forth to them, by way of a parable, the (story of) the Companions of the City. Behold, there came messengers to it.

14. When We (first) sent to them two messengers, they rejected them: but We strengthened them with a third: they said, "Truly, we have been sent on a mission to you."

15. The (people) said: "Ye are only men like ourselves; and The Most Gracious sends no sort of revelation: ye do nothing but lie."

16. They said: "Our Lord doth know that we have been sent on a mission to you:

17. "And our duty is only to deliver the clear Message."

18. The (people) said: "For us, we augur an evil omen from you: if ye desist not, we will certainly stone you, and a grievous punishment indeed will be inflicted on you by us."

19. They said: "Your evil omens are with yourselves: (Deem ye this an evil omen). If ye are admonished? Nay, but ye are a people transgressing all bounds!"

20. Then there came running, from the farthest part of the City, a man, saying, "O my People! obey the messengers:

21. "Obey those who ask no reward of you (for themselves), and who are themselves guided.

22. "Why should not I serve Him Who created me, and to Whom ye shall (all) be brought back.

23. "Shall I take (other) gods besides Him? If The Most Gracious should intend some adversity for me, of no use whatever will be their intercession for me, nor can they deliver me.

24. "I would indeed, then be in manifest Error.

25. "For me, I have faith in the Lord of you (all): listen, then, to me!"

26. It was said: "Enter thou the Garden." He said: "Ah me! Would that my People knew (what I know)!

27. "From That my Lord has gran-ted me Forgiveness and has enrolled me among those held in honour!"

28. And We sent not down against his

People, after him, any hosts from heaven,
nor was it needful for Us so to do.

29. It was no more than a single mighty
Blast, and behold! they were (like ashes)
quenched and silent.

30. Ah! alas for the servants! there comes
not a messenger to them but they mock
him!

31. See they not how many generations
before them We destroyed? Not to them
will they return:

32. But each one of them all—will be
brought before Us (for judgment).

33. A Sign for them is the earth that is
dead: We do give it life, and produce grain
therefrom, of which ye do eat.

34. And We produce therein orchards with
date-palms and vines, and We cause
springs to gush forth therein:

35. That they may enjoy the fruits of this
(artistry): it was not their hands that made
this: will they not then give thanks?

36. Glory to Allah, Who created in pairs all
things that the earth produces, as well as
their own (human) kind and (other) things
of which they have no knowledge.

37. And a Sign for them is the Night: We
withdraw therefrom the Day, and behold
they are plunged in darkness;

38. And the Sun runs unto a resting place,
for him: that is the decree of (Him), the
Exalted in Might, the All-Knowing.

39. And the Moon,—We have measured
for her stations (to traverse) till she returns
like the old (and withered) lower part of a
date-stalk.

40. It is not permitted to the Sun to catch
up the Moon, nor can the Night outstrip the
Day: each (just) swims along in (its own)
orbit (according to Law).

41. And a Sign for them is that We bore
their race (through the Flood) in the

جُنْدٍ مِّنَ السَّمَاءِ وَمَا كُنَّا مُنْزِلِيْنَ ۝

اِنْ كَانَتْ اِلَّا صَيْحَةً وَّاحِدَةً فَاِذَا
هُمْ خَامِدُوْنَ ۝

يٰحَسْرَةً عَلَى الْعِبَادِ مَا يَاْتِيْهِمْ مِّنْ
رَّسُوْلٍ اِلَّا كَانُوْا بِهٖ يَسْتَهْزِءُوْنَ ۝

اَلَمْ يَرَوْا كَمْ اَهْلَكْنَا قَبْلَهُمْ مِّنَ الْقُرُوْنِ
اَنَّهُمْ اِلَيْهِمْ لَا يَرْجِعُوْنَ ۝

وَاِنْ كُلٌّ لَّمَّا جَمِيْعٌ لَّدَيْنَا مُحْضَرُوْنَ ۝

وَاٰيَةٌ لَّهُمُ الْاَرْضُ الْمَيْتَةُ ۚ اَحْيَيْنٰهَا
وَاَخْرَجْنَا مِنْهَا حَبًّا فَمِنْهُ يَاْكُلُوْنَ ۝

وَجَعَلْنَا فِيْهَا جَنّٰتٍ مِّنْ نَّخِيْلٍ وَّاَعْنَابٍ
وَّفَجَّرْنَا فِيْهَا مِنَ الْعُيُوْنِ ۝

لِيَاْكُلُوْا مِنْ ثَمَرِهٖ ۙ وَمَا عَمِلَتْهُ اَيْدِيْهِمْ
اَفَلَا يَشْكُرُوْنَ ۝

سُبْحٰنَ الَّذِيْ خَلَقَ الْاَزْوَاجَ كُلَّهَا
مِمَّا تُنْبِتُ الْاَرْضُ وَمِنْ اَنْفُسِهِمْ
وَمِمَّا لَا يَعْلَمُوْنَ ۝

وَاٰيَةٌ لَّهُمُ الَّيْلُ �ۚ نَسْلَخُ مِنْهُ النَّهَارَ
فَاِذَا هُمْ مُّظْلِمُوْنَ ۝

وَالشَّمْسُ تَجْرِيْ لِمُسْتَقَرٍّ لَّهَا ۚ ذٰلِكَ
تَقْدِيْرُ الْعَزِيْزِ الْعَلِيْمِ ۝

وَالْقَمَرَ قَدَّرْنٰهُ مَنَازِلَ حَتّٰى عَادَ
كَالْعُرْجُوْنِ الْقَدِيْمِ ۝

لَا الشَّمْسُ يَنْۢبَغِيْ لَهَا اَنْ تُدْرِكَ الْقَمَرَ
وَلَا الَّيْلُ سَابِقُ النَّهَارِ ۚ وَكُلٌّ فِيْ فَلَكٍ
يَّسْبَحُوْنَ ۝

وَاٰيَةٌ لَّهُمْ اَنَّا حَمَلْنَا ذُرِّيَّتَهُمْ فِي الْفُلْكِ

loaded Ark;

42. And We have created for them similar (vessels) on which they ride.

43. If it were Our Will, We could drown them: then would there be no helper (to hear their cry), nor could they be delivered,

44. Except by way of Mercy from Us, and by way of (worldly) convenience (to serve them) for a time.

45. When they are told, "Fear ye that which is before you and that wh·ich will be after you. in order that ye may receive Mercy," (they turn back).

46. Not a Sign comes to them from among the Signs of their Lord, but they turn away therefrom.

47. And when they are told, "Spend ye of (the bounties) with which Allah has provided you," the Unbelievers say to those who believe: "Shall we then feed those whom, if Allah had so willed, He would have fed, (Himself)?—Ye are in nothing but manifest error."

48. Further, they say, "When will this promise (come to pass), if what ye say is true?"

49. They will not (have to) wait for aught but a single Blast: it will seize them while they are yet disputing among themselves!

50. No (chance) will they then have, by will, to dispose (of their affairs), nor to return to their own people!

51. The trumpet shall be sounded, when behold! from the sepulchres (men) will rush forth to their Lord!

52. They will say: "Ah! woe unto us! Who hath raised us up from our beds of repose?"...(A voice will say:) "This is what The Most Gracious had promised. And true was the word of the messengers!"

53. It will be no more than a single Blast, when lo! they will all be brought up before Us!

54. Then, on that Day, not a soul will be wronged in the least, and ye shall but be repaid the meeds of your past Deeds.

55. Verily the Companions of the Garden shall that Day have joy in all that they do;

اِنَّ اَصْحٰبَ الْجَنَّةِ الْيَوْمَ فِيْ شُغُلٍ فٰكِهُوْنَ ۝

56. They and their associates will be in pleasant shade, reclining on raised couches;

هُمْ وَاَزْوَاجُهُمْ فِيْ ظِلٰلٍ عَلَى الْاَرَآئِكِ مُتَّكِئُوْنَ ۝

57. (Every) fruit will be there for them; they shall have whatever they call for;

لَهُمْ فِيْهَا فَاكِهَةٌ وَّلَهُمْ مَّا يَدَّعُوْنَ ۝

58. "Peace!—a Word (of salu-tation) from a Lord Most Merciful!

سَلٰمٌ ۚ قَوْلًا مِّنْ رَّبٍّ رَّحِيْمٍ ۝

59. "And O ye in sin! Get ye apart this Day!

وَامْتَازُوا الْيَوْمَ اَيُّهَا الْمُجْرِمُوْنَ ۝

60. "Did I not enjoin on you, O ye children of Adam, that ye should not worship Satan; for that he was to you an enemy avowed?—

اَلَمْ اَعْهَدْ اِلَيْكُمْ يٰبَنِيْۤ اٰدَمَ اَنْ لَّا تَعْبُدُوا الشَّيْطٰنَ ۚ اِنَّهٗ لَكُمْ عَدُوٌّ مُّبِيْنٌ ۝

61. "And that ye should worship Me, (for that) this was the Straight Way?

وَّاَنِ اعْبُدُوْنِيْ ۚ هٰذَا صِرَاطٌ مُّسْتَقِيْمٌ ۝

62. "But he did lead astray a great multitude of you. Did ye not, then, understand?

وَلَقَدْ اَضَلَّ مِنْكُمْ جِبِلًّا كَثِيْرًا ۚ اَفَلَمْ تَكُوْنُوْا تَعْقِلُوْنَ ۝

63. "This is the Hell of which ye were promised

هٰذِهٖ جَهَنَّمُ الَّتِيْ كُنْتُمْ تُوْعَدُوْنَ ۝

64. "Embrace ye the (Fire) this Day, for that ye (persistently) rejected (Truth)."

اِصْلَوْهَا الْيَوْمَ بِمَا كُنْتُمْ تَكْفُرُوْنَ ۝

65. That Day shall We set a seal on their mouths. But their hands will speak to Us, and their feet bear witness, to all that they did.

اَلْيَوْمَ نَخْتِمُ عَلٰۤى اَفْوَاهِهِمْ وَتُكَلِّمُنَاۤ اَيْدِيْهِمْ وَتَشْهَدُ اَرْجُلُهُمْ بِمَا كَانُوْا يَكْسِبُوْنَ ۝

66. If it had been Our Will, We co-uld surely have blotted out their eyes; then they should have raced to the Path, but how could they have seen?

وَلَوْ نَشَآءُ لَطَمَسْنَا عَلٰۤى اَعْيُنِهِمْ فَاسْتَبَقُوا الصِّرَاطَ فَاَنّٰى يُبْصِرُوْنَ ۝

67. And if it had been Our Will, We could have transformed them in their places; then should they have been unable to move about, nor could they have returned (after error).

وَلَوْ نَشَآءُ لَمَسَخْنٰهُمْ عَلٰى مَكَانَتِهِمْ فَمَا اسْتَطَاعُوْا مُضِيًّا وَّلَا يَرْجِعُوْنَ ۝

68. If We grant long life to any, We cause him to be reversed in nature: will they not then understand?

وَمَنْ نُّعَمِّرْهُ نُنَكِّسْهُ فِى الْخَلْقِ ۚ اَفَلَا يَعْقِلُوْنَ ۝

69. We have not instructed the (Prophet) in Poetry, nor is it meet for him: this is no less than a Message and a Qur'an making things clear:

وَمَا عَلَّمْنٰهُ الشِّعْرَ وَمَا يَنْۢبَغِيْ لَهٗ ۚ اِنْ هُوَ اِلَّا ذِكْرٌ وَّقُرْاٰنٌ مُّبِيْنٌ ۝

70. That it may give admonition to any (who are) alive, and that the word may be proved true against those who reject (Truth).

لِّيُنْذِرَ مَنْ كَانَ حَيًّا وَّيَحِقَّ الْقَوْلُ عَلَى الْكٰفِرِيْنَ ۝

71. See they not that it is We Who have created for them—among the things which our hands have fashioned— cattle, which are under their dominion?—

أَوَلَمْ يَرَوْا أَنَّا خَلَقْنَا لَهُمْ مِّمَّا عَمِلَتْ أَيْدِيْنَا أَنْعَامًا فَهُمْ لَهَا مَالِكُوْنَ ۝

72. And that We have subjected them to their (use)? Of them some do carry them and some they eat:

وَذَلَّلْنَاهَا لَهُمْ فَمِنْهَا رَكُوْبُهُمْ وَمِنْهَا يَأْكُلُوْنَ ۝

73. And they have (other) profits from them (besides), and they get (milk) to drink. Will they not then be grateful?

وَلَهُمْ فِيْهَا مَنَافِعُ وَمَشَارِبُ أَفَلَا يَشْكُرُوْنَ ۝

74. Yet they take (for worship) Gods other than Allah, (hoping) that they might be helped!

وَاتَّخَذُوْا مِنْ دُوْنِ اللهِ آلِهَةً لَّعَلَّهُمْ يُنْصَرُوْنَ ۝

75. They have not the power to help them: and they are a host brought up before them.

لَا يَسْتَطِيْعُوْنَ نَصْرَهُمْ وَهُمْ لَهُمْ جُنْدٌ مُّحْضَرُوْنَ ۝

76. Let not their speech, then, grieve thee. Verily We know what they hide as well as what they disclose.

فَلَا يَحْزُنْكَ قَوْلُهُمْ إِنَّا نَعْلَمُ مَا يُسِرُّوْنَ وَمَا يُعْلِنُوْنَ ۝

77. Doth not man see that it is We Who created him from sperm? Yet behold! he (stands forth) as an open adversary!

أَوَلَمْ يَرَ الْإِنْسَانُ أَنَّا خَلَقْنَاهُ مِنْ نُّطْفَةٍ فَإِذَا هُوَ خَصِيْمٌ مُّبِيْنٌ ۝

78. And he makes comparisons for Us, and forgets his own (origin and) Creation: He says, "Who can give life to (dry) bones and decomposed ones (at that)?"

وَضَرَبَ لَنَا مَثَلًا وَّنَسِيَ خَلْقَهُ قَالَ مَنْ يُّحْيِ الْعِظَامَ وَهِيَ رَمِيْمٌ ۝

79. Say, "He will give them life Who created them for the first time! For He fully knows all creation.

قُلْ يُحْيِيْهَا الَّذِيْ أَنْشَأَهَا أَوَّلَ مَرَّةٍ وَهُوَ بِكُلِّ خَلْقٍ عَلِيْمٌ ۝

80. "The same Who produces for you fire out of the green tree, when behold! Ye kindle therewith (your own fires)!

الَّذِيْ جَعَلَ لَكُمْ مِّنَ الشَّجَرِ الْأَخْضَرِ نَارًا فَإِذَا أَنْتُمْ مِّنْهُ تُوْقِدُوْنَ ۝

81. "Is not He Who created the heavens and the earth able to create the like thereof?"— Yea, indeed! For He is the Creator Supreme, of skill and knowledge (infinite)!

أَوَلَيْسَ الَّذِيْ خَلَقَ السَّمَاوَاتِ وَالْأَرْضَ بِقَادِرٍ عَلَى أَنْ يَّخْلُقَ مِثْلَهُمْ بَلَى وَهُوَ الْخَلَّاقُ الْعَلِيْمُ ۝

82. Verily, when He intends a thing, His Command is, "Be", and it is!

إِنَّمَا أَمْرُهُ إِذَا أَرَادَ شَيْئًا أَنْ يَّقُوْلَ لَهُ كُنْ فَيَكُوْنُ ۝

83. So glory to Him in Whose Hands is the dominion of all things: and to Him will ye be all brought back.

فَسُبْحَانَ الَّذِيْ بِيَدِهِ مَلَكُوْتُ كُلِّ شَيْءٍ وَإِلَيْهِ تُرْجَعُوْنَ ۝

SÛRA–37
AṢ-ṢĀFFĀT
(INTRODUCTION)

As explained in the Introduction to S. 34. this is the fourth of a series of Sûras in which the mystries of the spiritual world are manifested in different ways, tending to the defeat and final extirpation of Evil. The defeat of Evil is throughout connected with Revelation, and here the ranged fight is illustrated by a reference to the angels in heaven and to the earlier Prophets in our earthly history, from Noah to Jonah. In chronology this Sûra belongs to the early middle Makkan period.

Aṣ-Ṣāffāt, or Those Ranged in Ranks

In the name of Allah, Most Gracious, Most Merciful.

1. By those who range themselves in ranks,

2. Those who so are strong in repelling (evil),

3. Those who thus proclaim the Message (of Allah)!

4. Verily, verily, your God is One!—

5. Lord of the heavens and of the earth, and all between them, and Lord of every point at the rising of the sun!

6. We have indeed decked the lower heaven with beauty (in) the stars,—

7. (For beauty) and for guard aga-inst all obstinate rebellious Satans.

8. (So) they should not listen their ears in the direction of the Exalted Assembly and they are cast away from every side,

9. Repulsed. And for them is a perpetual chastisement,

10. Except such as snatch away something by stealth, and they are pursued by a flaming Fire, of piercing brightness.

11. Just ask their opinion: are they the more difficult to create, or the (ot-her) beings We have created? Them have We created out of a sticky clay!

12. Truly dost thou marvel, while they ridicule,

13. And, when they are admonished, pay no heed,—

14. And, when they see a Sign, turn it to mockery,

15. And say, "This is nothing but evident sorcery!

16. "What! when we die, and become dust and bones, shall we (then) be raised up (again)?

17. "And also our fathers of old?"

18. Say thou: "Yea, and ye shall then be humiliated (on account of your evil)."

19. Then it will be a single (compelling) cry; and behold, they will begin to see!

20. They will say, "Ah! woe to us! this is the Day of Judgment!"

21. (A voice will say,) "This is the Day of Sorting Out, whose truth ye (once) denied!"

هٰذَا يَوْمُ الْفَصْلِ الَّذِىْ كُنْتُمْ بِهٖ تُكَذِّبُوْنَ ۞

22. "Bring ye up", it shall be said, "The wrong-doers and their wives, and the things they worshipped—

اُحْشُرُوا الَّذِيْنَ ظَلَمُوْا وَاَزْوَاجَهُمْ وَمَا كَانُوْا يَعْبُدُوْنَ ۞

23. "Besides Allah, and lead them to the Way to the (Fierce) Fire!

مِنْ دُوْنِ اللّٰهِ فَاهْدُوْهُمْ اِلٰى صِرَاطِ الْجَحِيْمِ ۞

24 "But stop them, for they must be asked:

وَقِفُوْهُمْ اِنَّهُمْ مَّسْئُوْلُوْنَ ۞

25. " 'What is the matter with you that ye help not each other?" '

مَا لَكُمْ لَا تَنَاصَرُوْنَ ۞

26. Nay, but that day they shall submit (to Judgment);

بَلْ هُمُ الْيَوْمَ مُسْتَسْلِمُوْنَ ۞

27. And they will turn to one another, and question one another.

وَاَقْبَلَ بَعْضُهُمْ عَلٰى بَعْضٍ يَّتَسَآءَلُوْنَ ۞

23. They will say: "It was ye who used to come to us from the right hand."

قَالُوْۤا اِنَّكُمْ كُنْتُمْ تَاْتُوْنَنَا عَنِ الْيَمِيْنِ ۞

29. They will reply: "Nay, ye yourselves had no Faith!

قَالُوْا بَلْ لَّمْ تَكُوْنُوْا مُؤْمِنِيْنَ ۞

30. "Nor had we any authority over you. Nay, it was ye who were a people in obstinate rebellion!

وَمَا كَانَ لَنَا عَلَيْكُمْ مِّنْ سُلْطٰنٍ ۚ بَلْ كُنْتُمْ قَوْمًا طٰغِيْنَ ۞

31. "So now has been proved true, against us, the Word of our Lord that we shall indeed (have to) taste (the punishment of our sins):

فَحَقَّ عَلَيْنَا قَوْلُ رَبِّنَآ ۖ اِنَّا لَذَآئِقُوْنَ ۞

32. "We led you astray: for truly we were ourselves astray."

فَاَغْوَيْنٰكُمْ اِنَّا كُنَّا غٰوِيْنَ ۞

33. Truly, that Day, they will (all) share in the Chastisement.

فَاِنَّهُمْ يَوْمَئِذٍ فِى الْعَذَابِ مُشْتَرِكُوْنَ ۞

34. Verily that is how We shall deal with Sinners.

اِنَّا كَذٰلِكَ نَفْعَلُ بِالْمُجْرِمِيْنَ ۞

?5. For they, when they were told that there is no god except Allah, would puff themselves up with Pride,

اِنَّهُمْ كَانُوْۤا اِذَا قِيْلَ لَهُمْ لَاۤ اِلٰهَ اِلَّا اللّٰهُ يَسْتَكْبِرُوْنَ ۞

36. And say: "What! Shall we give up our gods for the sake of a Poet possessed?"

وَيَقُوْلُوْنَ اَئِنَّا لَتَارِكُوْۤا اٰلِهَتِنَا لِشَاعِرٍ مَّجْنُوْنٍ ۞

37. Nay! he has come with the (very) Truth and he confirms (the Message of) the messengers (before him).

بَلْ جَآءَ بِالْحَقِّ وَصَدَّقَ الْمُرْسَلِيْنَ ۞

38. Ye shall indeed taste of the Grievous Chastisement;—

اِنَّكُمْ لَذَآئِقُوا الْعَذَابِ الْاَلِيْمِ ۞

39. And you are requited naught save what ye did.

وَمَا تُجْزَوْنَ اِلَّا مَا كُنْتُمْ تَعْمَلُوْنَ ۞

40. But the chosen servants of Allah,—

اِلَّا عِبَادَ اللّٰهِ الْمُخْلَصِيْنَ ۞

41. For them is a Sustenance determined,

اُولٰٓئِكَ لَهُمْ رِزْقٌ مَّعْلُوْمٌ ۞

42. Fruits; and they (shall enjoy) honour and dignity.

فَوَاكِهُ ۚ وَهُمْ مُّكْرَمُوْنَ ۞

43. In Gardens of delight.

44. Facing each other on raised couches.

45. Round will be passed to them a Cup from a clear-flowing fountain.

46. Crystal-white, of a taste delicious to those who drink (thereof),

47. Free from headiness; nor will they suffer intoxication therefrom.

48. And besides them will be cha-ste women; restraining their glances, with big eyes (of wonder and beauty).

49. As if they were (delicate) eggs closely guarded.

50. Then they will turn to one another and question one another.

51. One of them will say: "I had an intimate companion (on the earth),

52. "Who used to say, do you really believe?

53. " 'When we die and become dust and bones, shall we indeed receive rewards and punishments?'"

54. He said: "Would ye like to look down?"

55. He looked down and saw him in the midst of the Fire.

56. He said: "By Allah! thou wast little short of bringing me to perdition!

57. "Had it not been for the Grace of my Lord, I should certainly have been among those brought (there)!

58. "Is it (the case) that we shall not die,

59. "Except our first death, and that we Shall not be punished?"

60. Verily this is the supreme triumph.

61. For the like of this let all strive, who wish to strive.

62. Is that the better entertainment or the Tree of Zaqqum?

63. For We have truly made it (as) a trial for the wrong-doers.

64. For it is a tree that springs out of the bottom of Hell-fire:

65. The shoots of its fruit-stalks are like the heads of devils:

66. Truly they will eat thereof and fill their bellies therewith.

67. Then on top of that they will be given a mixture made of boiling water.

68. Then shall their return be to the (Blazing) Fire.

69. Truly they found their fathers on the wrong Path;

70. So they (too) were rushed down on their footsteps!

71. And truly before them, many of the ancients went astray;—

72. But We sent aforetime, among them, warners.

73. Then see what was the End of those who were warned

74. Except the chosen Servants of Allah.

75. (In the days of old), Noah cried to Us, and We are the Best to hear prayer.

76. And We delivered him and his people from the Great Calamity,

77. And made his progeny to endure (on this earth);

78. And We left (this blessing) for him among generations to come in later times:

79. "Peace and salutation to Noah among the nations!"

80. Thus indeed do We reward those who do right.

81. For he was one of Our believing Servants.

82. Then the rest We overwhelmed in the Flood.

83. Verily from his party was Abraham.

84. Behold, he approached his Lord with a sound heart.

85. Behold, he said to his father and to his people, "What is that which ye worship?

86. "Is it a Falsehood— gods other than Allah that ye desire?

87. "Then what is your idea about the Lord of the Worlds?"

88. Then did he cast a glance at the Stars,

89. And he said, "I am indeed sick (at heart)!"

90. So they turned away from him, and departed.

91. Then did he turn to their gods and said, "Will ye not eat (of the offerings before you)?

92. "What is the matter with you that ye speak not?"

93. Then did he turn upon them, striking (them) with the right hand.

94. Then came (the worshippers with hurried steps, to him.

95. He said: "Worship ye that which ye have (yourselves) carved?

96. "But Allah has created you and your handiwork!"

97. They said, "Build him a furnace, and throw him into the blazing fire!"

98. (This failing), they then plotted against him, but We made them the ones most humiliated!

99. He said: "I will go to my Lord! He will surely guide me!

100. "O my Lord! grant me a righteous (son)!"

101. So We gave him the good news of a forbearing son.

102. Then, when (the son) reached (the age of) (serious) work with him, he said: "O my son! I have seen in a dream that I offer thee in sacrifice: now see what is thy view!" (The son) said: "O my father! Do as thou art commanded: thou will find me, if Allah so wills one of the steadfast."

103. So when they had both submitted (to Allah), and he had laid him prostrate on his forehead (for sacrifice),

104. We called out to him, "O Abraham!

105. "Thou hast already fulfilled the dream!"—thus indeed do We reward those who do right.

106. For this was a clear trial—

107. And We ransomed him with a momentous sacrifice:

108. And We left for him among generations (to come) in later times:

109. "Peace and salutation to Abraham!"

110. Thus indeed do We reward those who do right

111. For he was one of Our believing Servants.

112. And We gave him the good news of Isaac—a prophet,— one of the Righteous.

113. We blessed him and Isaac: but of their progeny are (some) that do right, and (some) that obviously do wrong, to themselves.

114. Again, (of old.) We bestowed Our favour on Moses and Aaron,

115. And We delivered them and th-eir people from (their) Great distress.

116. And We helped them, so they were victorious;

117. And We gave them the Book which helps to make things clear;

118. And We guided them to the Straight Way.

119. And We left for them among generations (to come) in later times:

120. "Peace and salutation to Moses and Aaron!"

121. Thus indeed do We reward those who do right.

122. For they were two of Our believing Servants.

123. So also was Elias among those sent (by Us).

124. Behold, he said to his people, "Will ye not fear (Allah)?

125. "Will ye call upon Baal and forsake the Best of Creators,—

126. "Allah, your Lord and Cherisher and the Lord and Cherisher of your fathers of old?"

127. But they rejected him, and they will certainly be called up (for punishment),

128. Except the chosen servants of Allah (among them).

129. And We left for him among generations (to come) in later times:

130. "Peace and salutation to such as Elias!"

131. Thus indeed do We reward those who do right.

132. For he was one of Our believing Servants.

133. So also was Lût among those sent (by Us).

134. Behold, We delivered him and his adherents, all

135. Except an old woman who was among those who lagged behind:

136. Then We destroyed the rest.

137. Verily, ye pass by their (sites), by day—

138. And by night: will ye not understand?

139. So also was Jonah among those sent (by Us).

140. When he ran away (like a slave from captivity) to the ship (fully) laden,

143. Had it not been that he (repented and) glorified Allah,

144. He would certainly have remained inside the Fish till the Day of Resurrection.

145. But We cast him forth on the naked shore in a state of sickness,

146. And We caused to grow, over him, a spreading plant of the Gourd kind.

147. And We sent him (on a mission) to a hundred thousand (men) or more.

148. And they believed; so We permitted them to enjoy (their life) for a while.

149. Now ask them their opinion: is it that thy Lord has (only) daughters, and they have sons?—

150. Or that We created the angels female, and they are witnesses (thereto)?

151. Behold they say, out of their own invention,

152. "Allah has begotten children"? But they are liars!

153. Did He (then) choose daughters rather than sons?

154. What is the matter with you? How judge ye?

155. Will ye not then receive admonition?

156. Or have ye an authority manifest?

157. Then bring ye your Book (of authority) if ye be Truthful!

158. And they have invented a kinship between Him and the Jinns: but the Jinns know (Quite well) that they will be brought before Him.

159. Glory to Allah! (He is free) from the things they ascribe (to Him)!

160. Not (so do) the Servants of Allah, the chosen ones.

161. For, verily, neither ye nor those ye worship

162. Can lead (any) into temptation concerning Allah,

163. Except such as are (themselves) going to the blazing Fire!

164. (The angels) "Not one of us but has a place appointed;

165. "And we are verily ranged in ranks (for service);

166. "And we are verily those who declare (Allah's) glory!"

167. And there were those who said,

SÛRA–38
ṢĀD
(INTRODUCTION)

For the place of this Sûra in the series of six, dealing with some of the mysteries of the spiritual world, see Introduction to S. 34.

This Sûra, both in chronology and subject-matter, is cognate to S. 37, and carries forward the same argument. But here the emphasis is laid on the working of earthly power when combined with spiritual power, and it is pointed out how much more significant (and real) spiritual power is. For this reason the illustrative stories are mainly those of David and Solomon who were kings as well as prophets, and a parallel is suggested with the unfolding public life of our Holy Prophet.

168. "If only we had had before us a Message from those of old,

169. "We should certainly have been Servants of Allah, sincere (and devoted)!"

170. But (now that the Qur'an has come), they reject it: but soon will they know!

171. Already has Our Word been passed before (this) to Our Servants sent (by Us),

172. That they would certainly be assisted,

173. And that Our forces,— they surely must conquer.

174. So turn thou away from them for a little while,

175. And watch them (how they fare), and they soon shall see (how thou farest)!

176. Do they wish (indeed) to hurry on our Punishment?

177. But when it descends upon their courtyards before them, Evil will be the morning for those who were warned (and heeded not)!

178. So turn thou away from them for a little while,

179. And watch (how they fare) and they soon shall see (how thou farest)!

180. Glory to thy Lord, the Lord of Honour and Power! (He is free) from what they ascribe (to Him)!

181. And Peace on the messengers!

182. And Praise to Allah, the Lord and Cherisher of the Worlds.

Ṣād (being one of the Abbreviated Letters)

In the name of Allah, Most Gracious, Most Merciful.

1. Ṣād: by the Qur-ān, full of Admonition: (this is the Truth).

2. But the Unbelievers (are steeped) in Self-glory and opposition.

3. How many generations before them did We destroy? In the end they cried (for mercy)—when there was no longer time for being saved!

4. So they wonder that a Warner has come to them from among themselves! And the Unbelievers say, "This is a scorcerer telling lies!

5. "Has he made gods (all) into one God? Truly this is a strange thing!"

6. And the leaders among them go away (impatiently), (saying), "Walk ye away, and remain constant to your gods! For this is truly a thing designed (against you)!

7. "We never heard (the like) of this in the last religion this is nothing but a made-up tale!"

8. "What! Has the Message been sent to him— (of all persons) among us?... But they are in doubt concerning My (own) Message! Nay, they have not yet tasted My Punishment!

9. Or have they the Treasures of the Mercy of thy Lord,—the Exalted in Power, the Grantor of Bounties without measure?

10. Or have they the dominion of the heavens and the earth and all between? If so, let them mount up with the ropes and means (to reach that end)!

11. They are but a host of confederates and they will be put to flight.

12. Before them (were many who) rejected messengers,— the People of Noah, and 'Ād, and Pharaoh the Lord of Stakes,

13. And Thamūd, and the People of Lūt, and the Companions of the Wood;—such were the Confederates.

14. Not one (of them) but rejected the messengers, but My Punishment came justly and inevitably (on them).

15. These (to-day) only wait for a single mighty Blast, which (when it comes) will brook no delay.

16. They say: "Our Lord! Hasten to us our sentence (even) before the Day of Account!"

17. Have patience at what they say, and remember Our Servant David, the man of strength: for he ever turned (in repentance to Allah).

18. It was We that made the hills declare, in unison with him, our Praises, at eventide and at break of day,

19. And the birds gathered (in assemblies): all with him did turn (to Allah).

20. We strengthened his kingdom, and

gave him wisdom and sound judgment in speech and decision.

21. Has the Story of the Disputants reached thee? Behold, they climbed over the wall of the private chamber;

22. When they entered to David, and he was terrified of them, they said: "Fear not: we are two disputants, one of whom has wronged the other: decide now between us with truth, and treat us not with injustice, but guide us to the even Path.

23. "This man is my brother: He has nine and ninety ewes, and I have (but) one: yet he says, 'Commit her to my care,' and he overcame me in the argument.

24. (David) said: "He has undoubtedly wronged thee in demanding thy (single) ewe to be added to his (flock of) ewes: truly many are the Partners (in business) who wrong each other: not so do those who believe and work deeds of righteousness, and how few are they?"... And David gathered that We had tried him: he asked forgiveness of his Lord, fell down, bowing (in prostration), and turned (to Allah in repentance).

25. So We forgave him this (lapse): he enjoyed, indeed, a Near Approach to Us, and a beautiful Place of (final) Return.

26. O David! We did indeed make thee a vicegerent on earth: so judge thou between men in truth (and justice): nor follow thou the lust (of thy heart), for it will mislead thee from the Path of Allah: for those who wander astray from the Path of Allah, is a Chastisement Grevious, for that they forget the Day of Account.

27. Not without purpose did We create heaven and earth and all between! That were the thought of Unbelievers! But woe to the Unbelivers because of the Fire (of Hell)!

28. Shall We treat those who believe and work deeds of righteousness, the same as those who do mischief on earth? Shall We treat those who guard against evil, the same as those who trun aside from the right?

29. (Here is) a Book which we have sent down unto thee, full of blessings, that they may meditate on its Signs, and that men of understanding may receive admonition.

30. To David We bestowed Solomon (for a son),— how excellent is the servant! ever did he turn (to Us in repentance)!

31. Behold, there were brought before him, at eventide, coursers of the highest breeding, and swift of foot;

32. And he siad, "Truly do I prefer wealth to the remembrance of my Lord." Until (the sun) was hidden in the veil (of Night):

33. "Bring them back to me." Then began he to pass his hand over (their) legs and their necks.

34. And We did try Solomon: We placed on his throne a body but he did turn (to Us in true devotion):

35. He said, "O my Lord! forgive me, and grant me a Kingdom which, will not belong to another after me: for Thou art the Grantor of Bounties (without measure).

36. Then We subjected the Wind to his power, to flow gently to his order, whithersoever he willed,—

37. As also the Satans, (including) every kind of builder and diver,—

38. As also others bound together in fetters.

39. "Such are Our Bounties: whether thou bestow them (on others) or withhold them, no account will be asked."

40. And he enjoyed, indeed, a Near Approach to Us, and a beautiful Place of (final) Return.

41. Commemorate Our Servant Job, behold he cried to his Lord: "Satan has afflicted me with distress and suffering!"

42. "Strike with thy foot: here is (water) wherein to wash, cool and refreshing, and (water) to drink."

43. And We gave him (back) his people and doubled their number,—as a Grace from Us, and a thing for commemoration, for all who have Understanding.

44. "And take in thy hand a little grass, and strike therewith: and break not (thy oath)." Truly We found him full of patience and constancy. How excellent is the servant! Ever did he turn (to Us)!

45. And commemorate Our Servants Abraham, Isaac, and Jacob, possessors of Power and Vision.

46. Verily We did choose them for a special (purpose)— the remembrance of the Hereafter.

47. They were, in Our sight, truly, of the company of the Elect and the Good.

48. And commemorate Isma'il, Elisha, and Zul-Kifl: each of them was of the company of the Good.

49. This is a Message (of admonition): and verily, for the Righteous, is a beautiful place of (final) Return,—

50. Gardens of Eternity, whose doors will (ever) be open to them;

51. Therein will they recline (at ease); therein can they call (at pleasure) for fruit in abundance, and (delicious) drink;

52. And beside them will be chaste women restraining their glances, (companions) of equal age.

53. Such is the Promise made to you for the Day of Account!

54. Truly such will be Our Bounty (to you); it will never fail;—

55. Yea, such! But— for the wrong-doers will be an evil place of (final) Return!—

56. Hell!— they will burn therein,—an evil bed (indeed, to lie on)!—

57. Yea, such!—Then shall they taste it,— a boiling fluid, and a fluid dark, murky, intensely cold!—

58. And other Penalties of a similar kind, to match them!

59. Here is a troop rushing headlong with you! No welcome for them! Truly, they shall burn in the Fire!

60. (The followers shall cry to the misleaders:) "Nay, ye (too)! No welcome for you! It is ye who have brought this upon us! Now evil is (this) place to stay in!"

61. They will say: "Our Lord! whoever brought this upon us,—add to him a double Chastisement in the Fire!"

62. And they will say: how is it with us that we see not men who we used to number among the bad ones?

63. "Did we treat them (as such) in ridicule, or have (our) eyes failed to perceive them?"

64. That is true,— the mutual recriminations of the People of the Fire!

65. Say: "Truly am I a Warner: no god is there but Allah, the One, Supreme and Irresistible,—

66. "The Lord of the heavens and the earth, and all between,—Exalted in Might, Ever-Forgiving.

67. Say: "That is a Tremendous Tidings.

68. "From which ye do turn away!

69. "No knowledge have I of the Exalted Chiefs when they discuss (matters) among themselves.

70. "Only this has been revealed to me: that I am to give warning plainly and publicly."

71. Behold, thy Lord said to the angels: "I am about to create man from clay:

72. "When I have fashioned him and breathed into him of My spirit, fall ye down in prostration unto him."

73. So the angels prostrated themselves, all of them together:

74. Not so Iblîs: he was haughty, and became one of those who reject Faith.

75. (Allah) said: "O Iblîs! what prevents thee from prostrating thyself to one whom I have created with My hands? Art thou haughty? Or art thou one of the high (and mighty) ones?

SÛRA-39
AZ-ZUMAR
(INTRODUCTION)

This is the last of the series of six Sûras beginning with S. 34, which deal with the mysteries of the spiritual world, as leading up to the *Ma'ād*, or the Hereafter. See Introductrion to S. 34.

Its subject-matter is how Creation in its great variety is yet sorted out in Groups or Classes, all governed by one Plan, and created and sustained by One Allah, Who will separate Good from Evil at the last Day. The word *zumar* occurs in verses 71 and 73.

Its chronology has no significance. It belongs to the late Makkan period.

76. (Iblîs) said: "I am better than he: Thou createdst me from fire, and him Thou createdst from clay."

77. (Allah) said: "Then get thee out from here: for thou art rejected, accursed.

78. "And My Curse shall be on thee till the Day of Judgment."

79. (Iblîs) said: "O my Lord! give me then respite till the Day the (dead) are raised."

80. (Allah) said: "Respite then is granted thee—

81. "Till the Day of the Time Appointed."

82. (Iblîs) said: "Then, by Thy Power, I will lead them all astray.

83. "Except Thy Servants amongst them, sincere and purified (by Thy grace)."

84. (Allah) said: "This is the Truth, and the Truth I say.

85. "That I will certainly fill Hell with thee and those that follow thee,—every one."

86. Say: "No reward do I ask of you for this (Qur'an), nor am I a pretender.

87. "This is no less than a Reminder to (all) the Worlds.

88. "And ye shall certainly know the truth of it (all) after a while."

Az-Zumar, or the Groups

In the name of Allah, Most Gracious, Most Merciful.

1. The revelation of this Book is from Allah, the Exalted in Power, Full of Wisdom.

2. Verily it is We Who have revealed the Book to thee in Truth: so serve Allah, offering Him sincere devotion.

3. Is it not to Allah that sincere devotion is due? But those who take for protectors others than Allah (say): "We only serve them in order that they may bring us nearer to Allah." Truly Allah will judge between them in that wherein they differ. But Allah guides not such as are false and ungrateful.

4.   Had Allah wished to take to Himself a
son, He could have chosen whom He
pleased out of those whom He doth create:
but Glory be to Him! (He is above such
things.) He is Allah, the One, the
Overpowering.

5.   He created the heavens and the earth
in true (proportions): He makes the Night
overlap the Day, and the Day overlap the
Night: He has subjected the sun and the
moon (to His law): each one follows a
course for a time appointed. Is not He the
Exalted in Power—He Who forgives again
and again?

6.   He created you (all) from a single
Person: then created, of like nature, his
mate; and He sent down for you eight head
of cattle in pairs: He creates you, in the
wombs of your mothers, in stages, one
after another, in three veils of darkness.
Such is Allah, your Lord and Cherisher: to
Him belongs (all) dominion. There is no
god but He: then how are ye turned away
(from your true Lord)?

7.   If ye reject (Allah), truly Allah hath no
need of you; but He liketh not ingratitude
from His servants: if ye are grateful, He is
pleased with you. No bearer of burdens
can bear of burden of another. In the End,
to your Lord is your Return. when He will
tell you the truth of all that ye did (in this
life). For He knoweth well all that is in
(men's) hearts.

8.   When some trouble toucheth man He
crieth unto his Lord, turning to Him in
repentance: But when He bestoweth a
favour upon him as from Himself, (man)
doth forget what he cried and prayed for
before. and he doth set up rivals unto Allah,
thus misleading others from Allah's Path.
Say, "Enjoy thy disbelief for a little while.
verily thou art (one) of the Companions of
the Fire!"

9.   Is one who worships devoutly during
the hours of the night prostrating himself or
standing (in adoration), who takes heed of
the Hereafter. and who Places his hope in
the Mercy of his Lord—(like one who does

not)? Say: "Are those equal, those who know and those who do not know?" It is those who are endued with understanding that receive admonition.

10. Say: "O ye My servants who believe! fear your Lord. Good is (the reward) for those who do good in this world. Spacious is Allah's earth! Those who patiently persevere will truly receive a reward without measure!"

11. Say: "Verily, i am commanded to serve Allah with sincere devotion;

12. "And I am commanded to be the first of those who submit to Allah in Islam."

13. Say: "I would, if I disobeyed my Lord, indeed have fear of the Chastisement of a Mighty Day."

14. Say: "It is Allah I serve, with my sincere (and exclusive) devotion:

15. "Serve ye what ye will besides Him." Say: "Truly, those in loss are those who lose their own souls and their people on the Day of Judgment: ah! that is indeed the (real and) evident Loss!

16. They shall have Layers of Fire above them, and Layers (of Fire) below them: with this doth Allah warn off His servants: "O My Servants! then fear ye Me!"

17. Those who eschew Taghut and fall not into its worship,—and turn to Allah (in repentance),— for them is Good News: so announce the Good News to My Servants,—

18. Those who listen to the Word, and follow the best of it: those are the ones who Allah has guided, and those are the ones endued with understanding.

19. Is, then, one against whom the decree of Punishment is justly due (equal to one who eschews evil)? Wouldst thou, then, deliver one (who is) in the Fire?

20. But it is for those who fear their Lord, that lofty mansions, one above another,

have been built: beneath them flow rivers:
(such is) the Promise of Allah: never doth
Allah fail in (His) promise.

21. Seest thou not that Allah sends down
rain from the sky, and leads it through
springs in the earth? Then He causes to
grow, therewith, produce of various colours:
then it withers; thou wilt see it grow yellow;
then He makes it dry up and crumble away.
Truly, in this, is a Message of remembrance
to men of understanding.

22. Is one whose heart Allah has opened
to Islam, so that he has received Light from
Allah, (no better than one hard-hearted)?
Woe to those whose hearts are hardened
against the remembrance of Allah! They
are manifestly wandering (in error)!

23. Allah has revealed (from time to time)
the most beautiful Message in the form of a
Book, consistent with itself, (yet) repeating
(its teaching in various aspects): the skins
of those who fear their Lord tremble threat;
then their skins and their hearts do soften
to the remembrance of Allah. Such is the
guidance of Allah; He guides therewith
whom He pleases, but such as Allah leaves
to stray, can have none to guide.

24. Is, then, one who has to ward off the
brunt of the Chastisement on the Day of
Judgment (and receive it) by his face, (like
one guarded therefrom)? It will be said to
the wrong-doers: "Taste ye (the fruits of)
what ye earned!"

25. Those before them (also) rejected
(revelation), and so the Punishment came to
them from directions they did not perceive.

26. So Allah gave them a taste of humiliation in the present life, but greater is the
Punishment of the Hereafter, if they only knew!

27. We have put forth for men, in the
Qur-ān every kind of Parable, in order that
they may receive admonition.

28. (It is) a Qur-ān in Arabic, without any
crookedness (therein): in order that

they may guard against Evil.

29. Allah puts forth a Parable— a man belonging to many partners at variance with each other, and a man belonging entirely to one master: are those two equal in comparison? Praise be to Allah! but most of them have no knowledge.

30. Truly thou wilt die (one day), and truly they (too) will die (one day).

31. In the End will ye (all) dispute on the Day of Judgment, in the presence of your Lord.

32. Who, then, doth more wrong than one who utters a lie concerning Allah and rejects the Truth when it comes to him! Is there not in Hell an abode for the unbelievers?

33. And he who brings the Truth and he who confirms (and supports) it—such are the men who do right.

34. They shall have all that they wish for, with their Lord: such is the reward of those who do good:

35. So that Allah will remit from them (even) the worst in their deeds and give them their reward according to the best of what they have done.

36. Is not Allah enough for His servant? But they try to frighten thee with other (gods) besides Him! for such as Allah leaves to stray, there can be no guide.

37. And such as Allah doth guide there can be none to lead astray. Is not Allah Exalted in Power, Lord of Retribution?

38. If indeed thou ask them who it is that created the heavens and the earth, they would be sure to say, "Allah". Say: "See ye then? The things that ye invoke besides Allah,—can they, if Allah wills some affliction for me, remove His affliction or if He wills

some Mercy for me, can they keep back
His Mercy" Say: "Sufficient is Allah for me!
In Him trust those who put their trust."

39. Say: "O my people! do whatever ye
can: I will do (my part): but soon will ye
know—

40. "Who it is to whom comes a
Chastisement or ignominy, and on whom
Descends a Chastisement that abides."

41. Verily We have revealed the Book to
thee in Truth, for (instructing) mankind. He,
then, that receives guidance benefits his own
soul: but he that strays injures his own soul.
Nor art thou set a Custodian over them.

42. It is Allah that takes the souls (of men)
at death; and those that die not (He takes)
during their sleep: those on whom He has
passed the decree of death, He keeps back
(from returning to life), but the rest He sends
(to their bodies) for a term appointed. Verily
in this are Signs for those who reflect.

43. What! Do they take for intercessors
others besides Allah? Say: "Even if they have
no power whatever and no intelligence?"

44. Say: "To Allah belongs exclusively (the
right to) grant) Intercession: to Him belongs
the dominion of the heavens and the earth:
in the End, it is to Him that ye shall be
brought back."

45. When Allah, Alone is mentioned, the
hearts of those who believe not in the
Hereafter are filled with disgust; but when
(gods) other than He are mentioned, behold,
they are filled with joy!

46. Say: "O Allah! Creator of the heavens
and the earth! Knower of all that is hidden
and open! It is Thou that wilt judge between
Thy Servants in those matters about which
they have differed."

47. Even if the wrong-doers had all that
there is on earth, and as much more, (in
vain) would they offer it for ransom from the
pain of the Chastisement on the Day of

Judgment: but something will confront them from Allah, which they could never have counted upon!

48. For the evils of their Deeds will confront them, and they will be (completely) encircled by that which they used to mock at!

49. Now, when trouble touches man, he cries to Us: but when We bestow a favour upon him as from Us, he says, "This has been given to me because of a certain knowledge (I have)! Nay, but this is but a trial, but most of them understand not!

50. Thus did the (generations) before them say! But all that they did was of no profit to them.

51. Nay, the evil results of their deeds overtook them. And the wrong-doers of this (generation)—the evil results of their deeds will soon overtake them (too), and they shall not escape!

52. Know they not that Allah enlarges the provision or restricts it, for any He pleases? Verily, in this are Signs for those who believe!

53. Say: "O my Servants who have transgressed against their souls! despair not of the Mercy of Allah: for Allah forgives all sins: for He is Oft-Forgiving, Most Merciful.

54. "Turn ye to your Lord (in repentance) and submit to Him, before the Chastisement comes on you: after that ye shall not be helped.

55. "And follow the Best that which was revealed to you from your Lord, before the Chastisement comes on you—of a sudden, while ye perceive not!—

56. "Lest the soul should (then) say: 'Ah! woe is me!— In that I neglected (my Duty) towards Allah, and was but among those who mocked!'—

57. "Or (lest) it should say: 'If only Allah had guided me, I should certainly have

been among the righteous!'—

58. "Or (lest) it should say when it (actually) sees the Chastisement: 'If only I had another chance, I should certainly be among those who do good!'

59. "(The reply will be:) 'Nay, but there came to thee My Signs, and thou didst reject them: thou wast Haughty, and became one of those who reject Faith!'"

60. On the Day of Judgment wilt thou see those who told lies against Allah;— their faces will be turned black; is there not in Hell an abode for the Haughty?

61. But Allah will deliver the righteous for they have earned salvation: no evil shall touch them, nor shall they grieve.

62. Allah is the Creator of all things, and He is the Guardian and Disposer of all affairs.

63. To Him belong the keys of the heavens and the earth: and those who reject the Signs of Allah,—it is they who will be in loss.

64. Say: "Is it some one other than Allah that ye order me to worship, O ye ignorant ones?"

65. But it has already been revealed to thee,— as it was to those before thee,— "If thou wert to join (gods with Allah), truly fruitless will be thy work (in life), and thou wilt surely be among the losers."

66. Nay, but worship Allah, and be of those who give thanks.

67. No just estimate have they made of Allah, such as is due to Him: on the Day of Judgment the whole of the earth will be but His handful, and the heavens will be rolled up in His right hand: glory to Him! High is He above the Partners they attribute to Him!

68. The Trumpet will (just) be sounded, when all that are in the heavens and on earth will swoon, except such as it will please Allah (to exempt). Then will a second one be sounded, when, behold, they will be

standing and looking on!

69. And the Earth will shine with the light of its Lord: the Record (of Deeds) will be placed (open); the prophets and the witnesses will be brought forward; and a just decision pronounced between them; and they will not be wronged (in the least).

70. And to every soul will be paid in full (the fruit) of its deeds; and (Allah) knoweth best all that they do.

71. The Unbelievers will be led to Hell in groups: until, when they arrive there, its gates will be opened. And its Keepers will say, "Did not messengers come to you from among yourselves, rehearsing to you the Signs of your Lord, and warning you of the Meeting of this Day of yours?" The answer will be: "True: but the Decree of Chastisement has been proved true against the Unbelievers!"

72. (To them) will be said: "Enter ye the gates of Hell, to dwell therein: and evil is (this) abode of the arrogant!"

73. And those who feared their Lord will be led to the Garden in groups: until behold, they arrive there; its gates will be opened; and its Keepers will say: "Peace be upon you! Well have ye done! Enter ye here, to dwell therein."

74. They will say: "Praise be to Allah, Who has truly fulfilled His promise to us, and has given us (this) land in heritage: we can dwell in the Garden as we will: how excellent a reward for those who work (righteousness)!"

75. And thou wilt see the angels surrounding the Throne (Divine) on all sides, singing Glory and Praise to their Lord. The Decision between them (at Judgment) will be in (perfect) justice, and the cry (on all sides) will be, "Praise be to Allah, the Lord of the Worlds!"

تَنظُرُونَ ۝

وَأَشْرَقَتِ الْأَرْضُ بِنُورِ رَبِّهَا وَوُضِعَ الْكِتَابُ وَجِاْىءَ بِالنَّبِيِّنَ وَالشُّهَدَآءِ وَقُضِيَ بَيْنَهُم بِالْحَقِّ وَهُمْ لَا يُظْلَمُونَ ۝

وَوُفِّيَتْ كُلُّ نَفْسٍ مَّا عَمِلَتْ وَهُوَ أَعْلَمُ بِمَا يَفْعَلُونَ ۝

وَسِيقَ الَّذِينَ كَفَرُوا إِلَى جَهَنَّمَ زُمَرًا حَتَّى إِذَا جَاءُوهَا فُتِحَتْ أَبْوَابُهَا وَقَالَ لَهُمْ خَزَنَتُهَا أَلَمْ يَأْتِكُمْ رُسُلٌ مِّنكُمْ يَتْلُونَ عَلَيْكُمْ ءَايَاتِ رَبِّكُمْ وَيُنذِرُونَكُمْ لِقَاءَ يَوْمِكُمْ هَذَا قَالُوا بَلَى وَلَكِنْ حَقَّتْ كَلِمَةُ الْعَذَابِ عَلَى الْكَافِرِينَ ۝

قِيلَ ادْخُلُوا أَبْوَابَ جَهَنَّمَ خَالِدِينَ فِيهَا فَبِئْسَ مَثْوَى الْمُتَكَبِّرِينَ ۝

وَسِيقَ الَّذِينَ اتَّقَوْا رَبَّهُمْ إِلَى الْجَنَّةِ زُمَرًا حَتَّى إِذَا جَاءُوهَا وَفُتِحَتْ أَبْوَابُهَا وَقَالَ لَهُمْ خَزَنَتُهَا سَلَامٌ عَلَيْكُمْ طِبْتُمْ فَادْخُلُوهَا خَالِدِينَ ۝

وَقَالُوا الْحَمْدُ لِلَّهِ الَّذِي صَدَقَنَا وَعْدَهُ وَأَوْرَثَنَا الْأَرْضَ نَتَبَوَّأُ مِنَ الْجَنَّةِ حَيْثُ نَشَاءُ فَنِعْمَ أَجْرُ الْعَامِلِينَ ۝

وَتَرَى الْمَلَائِكَةَ حَافِّينَ مِنْ حَوْلِ الْعَرْشِ يُسَبِّحُونَ بِحَمْدِ رَبِّهِمْ وَقُضِيَ بَيْنَهُم بِالْحَقِّ وَقِيلَ الْحَمْدُ لِلَّهِ رَبِّ الْعَالَمِينَ ۝

SÛRA–40
AL-MÛ-MIN
(INTRODUCTION)

This Sûra is called "The Believer" (*Mû-min*) from the story of the individual Believer among the people of Pharaoh, who declares his faith and looks to the Future (verses 28-45). It is also called *Gâfir* (He who forgives, see verse 3). In S. 23, called *The Believers (Mû-minûn)*, the argument was about the collective force of Faith and Virtue. Here it is about the Individual's witness to Faith and Virtue, and his triumph in the End.

We now begin a series of seven Sûras (40-46) to which are affixed the abbreviated Letters *Ha-Mîm*. Chronologically they all belong to the same period, the later Makkan Period, and they immediately follow the last Sûra in time. As to the precise meaning of *Ha-Mîm* no authoritative explanation is available. If *Mîm* here has a signification similar to *Mîm* in A.L.M. it means the End of things, the Last Day, and all these Sûras direct our special attention to that. *Hâ*, the emphatic guttural, in contrast with the softer breathing of *Alif*, may be meant to suggest that the Beginning is only for the End, the Present for the Future, and to emphasise the eschatological element in Faith. But this is mere conjecture, and should be taken, for no more than it is worth.

The general theme of the whole series is the relation of Faith to Unfaith, Revelation to Rejection, Goodness to Evil, Truth to Falsehood. It is shown that the first in each of these pairs is the real friend, helper, and protector of man, while the second is his enemy. The very word *Hamîm* in that sense is used in Sûras 40 and 41 (40: 18 and 41: 34), while in the other Sûras we have words of equivalent import, e.g. *walî* or *naṣir* (42: 8 and 31); *qarîn* (43: 36, 38); *maulā* (44: 41); *auliyāa* or *nāṣirîn* (45: 19, 34); and *auliyāa* (46: 32). Is it permissible to connect the Abbreviated Letters *Ha-Mîm* with these ideas as expressed in the word *Hamîm*?

Another suggestion worthy of consideration is that *Hā* stands for *Hāiy,* and *Mîm* for *Qaiyûm.* These are two attributes of Allah, meaning, (1) the Living, and (2) the Self-Subsisting, Eternal. The one points to Life and Revelation, and the other to the Hereafter and Eternity; and both these matters are specially dealt with in the seven *Ha-Mîm* Sûras. The first letter of *Hāiy* (*Hā*) is appropriate for life, and the last letter of *Qaiyûm* is appropriate for the last Days, the *Ma'ād*, the Hereafter. Again, this is mere conjecture, and should not be taken for more than it is worth.

Al-Mû-min, or The Believer

In the name of Allah, Most Gracious, Most Merciful.

بِسۡمِ اللهِ الرَّحۡمٰنِ الرَّحِيۡمِ

1. Hā-Mîm.

حٰمٓ ۚ

2. The revelation of this Book is from Allah, Exalted in Power, Full of Knowledge,—

تَنۡزِيۡلُ الۡكِتٰبِ مِنَ اللهِ الۡعَزِيۡزِ الۡعَلِيۡمِ ۙ

3. Who forgiveth Sin, accepteth Repentance, is Severe in Punishment, and is all-Bountiful. There is no god but He: to Him is the Final Goal.

غَافِرِ الذَّنۡبِ وَقَابِلِ التَّوۡبِ شَدِيۡدِ الۡعِقَابِ ذِى الطَّوۡلِ ۚ لَاۤ اِلٰهَ اِلَّا هُوَ ؕ اِلَيۡهِ الۡمَصِيۡرُ

4. None can dispute about the Signs of Allah but the Unbelievers. Let not, then their strutting about through the land deceive thee!

مَا يُجَادِلُ فِىۡۤ اٰيٰتِ اللهِ اِلَّا الَّذِيۡنَ كَفَرُوۡا فَلَا يَغۡرُرۡكَ تَقَلُّبُهُمۡ فِى الۡبِلَادِ

5. But (there were people) before them, who denied (the Signs), the People of Noah, and the Confe-derates after them; and every People plotted against their prophet, to seize him, and disputed by means of vanities, therewith to obliterate the Truth: but it was I that seized them! And how (terrible) was My Requital!

كَذَّبَتۡ قَبۡلَهُمۡ قَوۡمُ نُوۡحٍ وَّالۡاَحۡزَابُ مِنۡۢ بَعۡدِهِمۡ ۪ وَهَمَّتۡ كُلُّ اُمَّةٍۭ بِرَسُوۡلِهِمۡ لِيَاۡخُذُوۡهُ وَجَادَلُوۡا بِالۡبَاطِلِ لِيُدۡحِضُوۡا بِهِ الۡحَقَّ فَاَخَذۡتُهُمۡ ۫ فَكَيۡفَ كَانَ عِقَابِ

6. Thus was the Word of thy Lord proved true against the Unbelievers; that truly they are companions of the Fire!

وَكَذٰلِكَ حَقَّتۡ كَلِمَتُ رَبِّكَ عَلَى الَّذِيۡنَ كَفَرُوۡۤا اَنَّهُمۡ اَصۡحٰبُ النَّارِ ۘ

7. Those who bear the Throne (of Allah) and those around it sing Glory and Praise to their Lord; believe in Him; and implore Forgiveness for those who believe: "Our Lord! Thou embracest all things, in Mercy and Knowledge. Forgive, then, those who turn in Repentance, and follow Thy Path; and preserve them from the Chastisement of the Blazing Fire!

اَلَّذِيۡنَ يَحۡمِلُوۡنَ الۡعَرۡشَ وَمَنۡ حَوۡلَهٗ يُسَبِّحُوۡنَ بِحَمۡدِ رَبِّهِمۡ وَيُؤۡمِنُوۡنَ بِهٖ وَيَسۡتَغۡفِرُوۡنَ لِلَّذِيۡنَ اٰمَنُوۡا ۚ رَبَّنَا وَسِعۡتَ كُلَّ شَىۡءٍ رَّحۡمَةً وَّعِلۡمًا فَاغۡفِرۡ لِلَّذِيۡنَ تَابُوۡا وَاتَّبَعُوۡا سَبِيۡلَكَ وَقِهِمۡ عَذَابَ الۡجَحِيۡمِ

8. "And grant, our Lord! that they enter the Gardens of Eternity, which Thou hast promised to them, and to the righteous among their fathers, their wives, and their posterity! for Thou art (He), the Exalted in Might, Full of Wisdom.

رَبَّنَا وَاَدۡخِلۡهُمۡ جَنّٰتِ عَدۡنِ ِۣالَّتِىۡ وَعَدتَّهُمۡ وَمَنۡ صَلَحَ مِنۡ اٰبَآئِهِمۡ وَاَزۡوَاجِهِمۡ وَذُرِّيّٰتِهِمۡ ؕ اِنَّكَ اَنۡتَ الۡعَزِيۡزُ الۡحَكِيۡمُ ۙ

9. "And preserve them from (all) ills; and any whom Thou dost preserve from ills that Day,—on them wilt Thou have bestowed mercy indeed: and that will be truly the highest Achievement."

وَقِهِمُ السَّيِّاٰتِ ؕ وَمَنۡ تَقِ السَّيِّاٰتِ يَوۡمَئِذٍ فَقَدۡ رَحِمۡتَهٗ ؕ وَذٰلِكَ هُوَ الۡفَوۡزُ الۡعَظِيۡمُ

10. The Unbelievers will be addressed:

اِنَّ الَّذِيۡنَ كَفَرُوۡا يُنَادَوۡنَ لَمَقۡتُ اللهِ

"Greater was the aversion of Allah to you than (is) your aversion to yourselves, seeing that ye were called to the Faith and ye used to refuse."

11. They will say: "Our Lord! twice hast Thou made us to die, and twice Hast Thou given us Life! Now have we recognised our sins: is there any way out (of this)?"

12. (The answer will be:) "This is because, when Allah was invoked as the Only (object of worship), ye did reject Faith, but when partners were joined to Him, ye believed! The Command is with Allah, Most High, Most Great!"

13. He it is Who showeth you His Signs, and sendeth down Sustenance for you from the sky: but only those receive admonition who turn (to Allah).

14. Call ye, then, upon Allah with sincere devotion to Him, even though the Unbelievers may detest it.

15. Exalted is He in His attributes. (He is) the Lord of the Throne: by His Command doth He send the spirit (of inspiration) to any of His servants He pleases, that it may warn (men) of the Day of Mutual Meeting,—

16. The Day whereon they will (all) come forth: not a single thing concerning them is hidden from Allah. Whose will be the Dominion that Day? That of Allah, the One, the Overpowering!

17. That Day will every soul be requited for what it earned; no injustice will there be that Day, for Allah is Swift in taking account.

18. Warn them of the Day that is (ever) drawing near, when the Hearts will (come) right up to the Throats to choke (them); no intimate friend nor intercessors will the wrong-doers have, who could be listened to.

19. (Allah) knows the treachery of the eyes, and all that the hearts (of men) conceal.

20. And Allah will judge with (Justice and)

Truth: but those whom (men) invoke besides Him, will not (be in a position) to judge at all. Verily it is Allah (alone) Who hears and sees (all things).

21. Do they not travel through the earth and see what was the End of those before them? They were even superior to them in strength, and in the traces (they have left) in the land: but Allah did call them to account for their sins, and none had they to defend them against Allah.

22. That was because there came to them their messengers with Clear (Signs), but they rejected them: so Allah called them to account: for He is Full of Strength, Severe in Punishment.

23. Of old We sent Moses, with Our Signs and an Authority manifest,

24. To Pharaoh, Hāmān, and Qārūn; but they called (him) "a sorcerer telling lies!"...

25. Now, when he brought them the Truth, from Us, they said, "Slay the sons of those who believe with him, and keep alive their females," but the plots of unbelievers (end) in nothing but errors (and delusions)!...

26. Said Pharaoh: "Leave me to slay Moses; and let him call on his Lord! What I fear is lest He should change your religion, or lest he should cause mischief to appear in the land!"

27. Moses said: "I have indeed called upon my Lord and your Lord (for protection) from every arrogant one who believes not in the Day of Account!"

28. A Believer, a man from among the people of Pharaoh, who had concealed his faith, said: "Will ye slay a man because he says, 'My Lord is Allah'?—when he has indeed come to you with Clear (Signs) from your Lord? And if he be a liar, on him is (the sin of) his lie; but, if he is telling the Truth,

then will fall on you something of the (calamity) of which He warns you: truly Allah guides not one who transgresses and lies!

29. "O my People! yours is the dominion this day: Ye have the upper hand in the land: but who will help us from the Punishment of Allah, should it befall us?" Pharaoh said: "I but point out to you that which I see (myself); nor do I guide you but to the Path of Right!"

30. Then said the man who believed: "O my People! truly I do fear for you something like the Day (of disaster) of the Confederates (is sin)!—

31. "Something like the fate of the People of Noah, the 'Ad, and the Thamûd, and those who came after them: but Allah never wishes injustice to His Servants.

32. "And O my People! I fear for you a Day when there will be mutual calling (and wailing),—

33. "A Day when ye shall turn your backs and flee: no defender shall ye have from Allah: any whom Allah leaves to stray, there is none to guide...

34. "And to you there came Joseph in times gone by, with Clear Signs, but ye ceased not to doubt of the (mission) for which he had come: at length, when he died, ye said: 'No messenger will Allah send after him.' Thus doth Allah leave to stray such as transgress and live in doubt,—

35. "(Such) as dispute about the Signs of Allah, without any authority that hath reached them, very hateful (is such conduct) in the sight of Allah and of the Believers. Thus doth Allah seal up every heart—of arrogant tyrinical."

36. Pharaoh said: "O Haman! build me a lofty palace, that I may attain the ways and

means—

37. "The ways and means of (reaching) the heavens, and that I may look up to the God of Moses: but surely, I think (Moses) is a liar!" Thus was made alluring, in Pharaoh's eyes, the evil of his deeds, and he was hindered from the Path; and the plot of Pharaoh led to nothing but perdition (for him).

38. The man who believed said further: "O my People! follow me: I will lead you to the Path of Right.

39. "O my People! this life of the present is nothing but (temporary) enjoyment: it is the Hereafter that is the Home that will last.

40. "He that works evil will not be requited but by the like thereof: and he that works a righteous deed—whether man or woman—and is a Believer—such will enter the Garden (of Bliss): therein will they have abundance without measure.

41. "And O my People! how (strange) it is for me to call you to Salvation while ye call me to the Fire!

42. "Ye do call upon me to blaspheme against Allah, and to join with Him Partners of whom I have no knowledge; and I call you to the Exalted in Power, Who forgives again and again!

43. "Without doubt ye do call me to one who has no claim to be called to, whether in this world, or in the Hereafter: our Return will be to Allah; and the Transgressors will be Companions of the Fire!

44. "Soon will ye remember what I say to you (now). My (own) affair I commit to Allah: for Allah (ever) watches over His Servants".

صَرْحًا لَّعَلِّىٓ أَبْلُغُ الْأَسْبَابَ ۞ أَسْبَابَ السَّمٰوٰتِ فَأَطَّلِعَ إِلٰى إِلٰهِ مُوسٰى وَإِنِّى لَأَظُنُّهُ كَاذِبًا ۚ وَكَذٰلِكَ زُيِّنَ لِفِرْعَوْنَ سُوٓءُ عَمَلِهِ وَصُدَّ عَنِ السَّبِيلِ ۚ وَمَا كَيْدُ فِرْعَوْنَ إِلَّا فِى تَبَابٍ ۞

وَقَالَ الَّذِىٓ ءَامَنَ يٰقَوْمِ اتَّبِعُونِ أَهْدِكُمْ سَبِيلَ الرَّشَادِ ۞

يٰقَوْمِ إِنَّمَا هٰذِهِ الْحَيٰوةُ الدُّنْيَا مَتَاعٌ ۖ وَإِنَّ الْأَخِرَةَ هِىَ دَارُ الْقَرَارِ ۞

مَنْ عَمِلَ سَيِّئَةً فَلَا يُجْزٰىٓ إِلَّا مِثْلَهَا ۖ وَمَنْ عَمِلَ صَالِحًا مِّنْ ذَكَرٍ أَوْ أُنْثٰى وَهُوَ مُؤْمِنٌ فَأُولٰٓئِكَ يَدْخُلُونَ الْجَنَّةَ يُرْزَقُونَ فِيهَا بِغَيْرِ حِسَابٍ ۞

وَيٰقَوْمِ مَا لِىٓ أَدْعُوكُمْ إِلَى النَّجٰوةِ وَتَدْعُونَنِىٓ إِلَى النَّارِ ۞

تَدْعُونَنِى لِأَكْفُرَ بِاللّٰهِ وَأُشْرِكَ بِهِ مَا لَيْسَ لِى بِهِ عِلْمٌ ۖ وَأَنَا أَدْعُوكُمْ إِلَى الْعَزِيزِ الْغَفَّارِ ۞

لَا جَرَمَ أَنَّمَا تَدْعُونَنِىٓ إِلَيْهِ لَيْسَ لَهُ دَعْوَةٌ فِى الدُّنْيَا وَلَا فِى الْأَخِرَةِ وَأَنَّ مَرَدَّنَا إِلَى اللّٰهِ وَأَنَّ الْمُسْرِفِينَ هُمْ أَصْحَابُ النَّارِ ۞

فَسَتَذْكُرُونَ مَآ أَقُولُ لَكُمْ ۚ وَأُفَوِّضُ أَمْرِىٓ إِلَى اللّٰهِ ۚ إِنَّ اللّٰهَ بَصِيرٌۢ بِالْعِبَادِ ۞

45. Then Allah saved him from (every) evil that they plotted (against him), but the brunt of the Chastisement encompassed on all sides the People of Pharaoh.

46. In front of the Fire will they be brought, morning and evening: and (the Sentence will be) on the Day when the Hour comes to pass: "Cast ye the People of Pharaoh into the severest Penalty !"

47. Behold, they will dispute with each other in the Fire! The weak ones (who followed) will say to those who had been arrogant, "We but followed you: can ye then take (on yourselves) from us some share of the Fire?"

48. Those who had been arrogant will say: "We are all in this (Fire)! Truly, Allah has judged between (His) Servants!"

49. Those in the Fire will say to the Keepers of Hell: "Pray to your Lord to lighten us the Chastisement for a Day (at least)!"

50. They will say: "Did there not come to you your messengers with Clear Signs?" They will say, "Yes". They will reply, "Then pray (as ye like)! But the Prayer of those without Faith is nothing but (futile wandering) in (mazes of) error!"

51. We will, without doubt, help Our messengers and those who believe, (both) in this world's life and on the Day when the Witnesses will stand forth,—

52. The Day when no profit will it be to Wrong-doers to present their excuses, but they will (only) have the Curse and the Home of Misery.

53. We did aforetime give Moses the Guidance, and We gave the Book in inheritance to the Children of Israel,—

54. A Guide and a Reminder to men of understanding.

55. Patiently, then, persevere: for the Promise of Allah is true: and ask forgiveness for thy fault, and celebrate the Praises of thy Lord in the evening and in the morning.

56. Those who dispute about the Signs of

Allah without any authority bestowed on them,—there is nothing in their breasts but (the quest of) greatness, which they shall never attain to: seek refuge, then, in Allah: it is He Who hears and sees (all things).

57. Assuredly the creation of the heavens and the earth is a greater (matter) than the creation of men: yet most men know not.

58. Not equal are the blind and those who (clearly) see: nor are (equal) those who believe and work deeds of righteousness, and those who do evil. Little do ye learn by admonition!

59. The Hour will certainly come: therein is no doubt: yet most men believe not.

60. And your Lord says: "Call on Me; I will answer your (Prayer): but those who are too arrogant to serve Me will surely enter Hell abased."

61. It is Allah Who has made the Night for you, that ye may rest therein, and the Day, to give you light. Verily Allah is Full of Grace and Bounty to men: yet most men give no thanks.

62. Such is Allah, your Lord, the Creator of all things, there is no god but He: then how ye are deluded away from the Truth!

63. Thus are deluded those who are wont to reject the Signs of Allah.

64. It is Allah Who has made for you the earth as a resting place, and the sky as a canopy, and has given you shape— and made your shapes beautiful,—and has provided for you Sustenance, of things pure and good;— such is Allah your Lord. So Glory to Allah, the Lord of the Worlds!

65. He is the Living (One): there is no god but He: call upon Him, giving Him sincere devotion. Praise be to Allah, Lord of the

Worlds!

بِاللَّهِ رَبِّ الْعَلَمِينَ ۝

66. Say: "I have been forbidden to invoke those whom ye invoke besides Allah,— seeing that the Clear Signs have come to me from my Lord; and I have been commanded to submit (in Islam) to the Lord of the Worlds."

قُلْ إِنِّى نُهِيتُ أَنْ أَعْبُدَ الَّذِينَ تَدْعُونَ مِن دُونِ اللَّهِ لَمَّا جَآءَنِىَ الْبَيِّنَتُ مِن رَّبِّى وَأُمِرْتُ أَنْ أُسْلِمَ لِرَبِّ الْعَلَمِينَ ۝

67. It is He Who has created you from dust, then from a sperm-drop, then from a leech-like clot; then does He get you out (into the light) as a child: then lets you (grow and) reach your age of full strength; then lets you become old,— though of you there are some who die before;— and lets you reach a Term appointed; in order that ye may understand.

هُوَ الَّذِى خَلَقَكُم مِّن تُرَابٍ ثُمَّ مِن نُّطْفَةٍ ثُمَّ مِنْ عَلَقَةٍ ثُمَّ يُخْرِجُكُمْ طِفْلًا ثُمَّ لِتَبْلُغُوٓا أَشُدَّكُمْ ثُمَّ لِتَكُونُوا شُيُوخًا وَمِنكُم مَّن يُتَوَفَّى مِن قَبْلُ وَلِتَبْلُغُوٓا أَجَلًا مُّسَمًّى وَلَعَلَّكُمْ تَعْقِلُونَ ۝

68. It is He Who gives Life and Death; and when He decides upon an affair, He says to it, "Be", and it is.

هُوَ الَّذِى يُحْىِۦ وَيُمِيتُ فَإِذَا قَضَىٰٓ أَمْرًا فَإِنَّمَا يَقُولُ لَهُۥ كُن فَيَكُونُ ۝

69. Seest thou not those that dispute concerning the Signs of Allah? How are they turned away from Reality)?—

أَلَمْ تَرَ إِلَى الَّذِينَ يُجَٰدِلُونَ فِىٓ ءَايَٰتِ اللَّهِ أَنَّىٰ يُصْرَفُونَ ۝

70. Those who reject the Book and the (revelations) with which We sent Our messengers: but soon shall they know,—

الَّذِينَ كَذَّبُوا بِالْكِتَٰبِ وَبِمَآ أَرْسَلْنَا بِهِۦ رُسُلَنَا فَسَوْفَ يَعْلَمُونَ ۝

71. When the yokes (shall be) round their necks, and the chains; they shall be dragged along—

إِذِ الْأَغْلَٰلُ فِىٓ أَعْنَٰقِهِمْ وَالسَّلَٰسِلُ يُسْحَبُونَ ۝

72. In the boiling fetid fluid; then in the Fire shall they be burned;

فِى الْحَمِيمِ ثُمَّ فِى النَّارِ يُسْجَرُونَ ۝

73. Then shall it be said to them: "Where are the (deities) to which ye gave part-worship—

ثُمَّ قِيلَ لَهُمْ أَيْنَ مَا كُنتُمْ تُشْرِكُونَ ۝

74. "Besides Allah?" They will reply: "They have left us in the lurch: nay, we invoked not, of old, anything (that had real existence)." Thus does Allah leave the Unbelievers to stray.

مِن دُونِ اللَّهِ قَالُوا ضَلُّوا عَنَّا بَل لَّمْ نَكُن نَّدْعُوا مِن قَبْلُ شَيْـًٔا كَذَٰلِكَ يُضِلُّ اللَّهُ الْكَٰفِرِينَ ۝

75. "That was because ye were wont to rejoice on the earth in things other than the Truth, and that ye were wont to be insolent.

ذَٰلِكُم بِمَا كُنتُمْ تَفْرَحُونَ فِى الْأَرْضِ بِغَيْرِ الْحَقِّ وَبِمَا كُنتُمْ تَمْرَحُونَ ۝

76. "Enter ye the gates of Hell, to dwell therein: and evil is (this) abode of the arrogant!"

ادْخُلُوٓا أَبْوَٰبَ جَهَنَّمَ خَٰلِدِينَ فِيهَا فَبِئْسَ مَثْوَى الْمُتَكَبِّرِينَ ۝

77. So persevere in patience; for the Promise of Allah is true: and whether We show thee (in this life) some part of what We promise them,—or We take thy soul (to Our Mercy) (before that),—(in any case) it is to Us that they shall (all) return.

78. We did aforetime send Messengers before thee: of them there are some whose story We have related to thee, and some whose story We have not related to thee. It was not (possible) for any messenger to bring a Sign except by the leave of Allah: but when the Command of Allah issued, the matter was decided in truth and justice, and there perished, there and then, those who stood on Falsehoods.

79. It is Allah who made cattle for you, that ye may use some for riding and some for food;

80. And there are (other) advantages in them for you (besides); that ye may through them attain to any need (there may be) in your hearts; and on them and on ships ye are carried.

81. And He shows you (always) His Signs: then which of the Signs of Allah will ye deny?

82. Do they not travel through the earth and see what was the End of those before them? They were more numerous than these and superior in strength and in the traces (they have left) in the land: yet all that they accomplished was of no profit to them.

83. For when their messengers came to them with Clear Signs, they exulted in such knowledge (and skill) as they had; but that very (Wrath) at which they were wont to scoff hemmed them in.

84. But when they saw Our Might, they said: "We believe in Allah,—the One God—and we reject the partners we used to join with Him."

85. But their professing the Faith when they (actually) saw Our Punishment was not going to profit them. (Such has been)

فَاصْبِرْ اِنَّ وَعْدَاللّٰهِ حَقٌّ فَاِمَّا نُرِيَنَّكَ بَعْضَ الَّذِىْ نَعِدُهُمْ اَوْنَتَوَفَّيَنَّكَ فَاِلَيْنَا يُرْجَعُوْنَ ۝

وَلَقَدْ اَرْسَلْنَا رُسُلًا مِّنْ قَبْلِكَ مِنْهُمْ مَّنْ قَصَصْنَا عَلَيْكَ وَمِنْهُمْ مَّنْ لَّمْ نَقْصُصْ عَلَيْكَ وَمَا كَانَ لِرَسُوْلٍ اَنْ يَّأْتِىَ بِاٰيَةٍ اِلَّا بِاِذْنِ اللّٰهِ فَاِذَا جَآءَ اَمْرُ اللّٰهِ قُضِىَ بِالْحَقِّ وَخَسِرَ هُنَالِكَ الْمُبْطِلُوْنَ ۝

اَللّٰهُ الَّذِىْ جَعَلَ لَكُمُ الْاَنْعَامَ لِتَرْكَبُوْا مِنْهَا وَمِنْهَا تَأْكُلُوْنَ ۝

وَلَكُمْ فِيْهَا مَنَافِعُ وَلِتَبْلُغُوْا عَلَيْهَا حَاجَةً فِىْ صُدُوْرِكُمْ وَعَلَيْهَا وَعَلَى الْفُلْكِ تُحْمَلُوْنَ ۝

وَيُرِيْكُمْ اٰيٰتِهٖ ۖ فَاَىَّ اٰيٰتِ اللّٰهِ تُنْكِرُوْنَ ۝

اَفَلَمْ يَسِيْرُوْا فِى الْاَرْضِ فَيَنْظُرُوْا كَيْفَ كَانَ عَاقِبَةُ الَّذِيْنَ مِنْ قَبْلِهِمْ كَانُوْا اَكْثَرَ مِنْهُمْ وَاَشَدَّ قُوَّةً وَّ اٰثَارًا فِى الْاَرْضِ فَمَا اَغْنٰى عَنْهُمْ مَّا كَانُوْا يَكْسِبُوْنَ ۝

فَلَمَّا جَآءَتْهُمْ رُسُلُهُمْ بِالْبَيِّنٰتِ فَرِحُوْا بِمَا عِنْدَهُمْ مِّنَ الْعِلْمِ وَحَاقَ بِهِمْ مَّا كَانُوْا بِهٖ يَسْتَهْزِءُوْنَ ۝

فَلَمَّا رَاَوْا بَأْسَنَا قَالُوْا اٰمَنَّا بِاللّٰهِ وَحْدَهٗ وَكَفَرْنَا بِمَا كُنَّا بِهٖ مُشْرِكِيْنَ ۝

فَلَمْ يَكُ يَنْفَعُهُمْ اِيْمَانُهُمْ لَمَّا رَاَوْا

SÛRA–41
FUṢṢILAT
(INTRODUCTION)

This is the second of the series of seven Sûras bearing the Abbreviated Letters *Ḥā-Mîm*, as explained in the Introduction to S. 40. To prevent confusion with other Sûras of the *Ḥā-Mîm* series, the word *Sajda* is sometimes added to the title, making it *Ḥā-Mîm as-Sajda*, the double title being necessary as there is another Sûra called *Sajda* (S. 32). To avoid the double title it is sometimes called *Fuṣṣilat*, from the occurrence of the word in verse 3.

The meaning of *Ḥā-Mîm* has been explained in the Introduction to S. 40, where will also be found a note on the chronology and general theme of the seven *Ḥā-Mîm* Sûras.

For this particular Sûra the theme is that the basis of Faith and Revelation is Allah's Power and Goodness, and the fruit of both is man's righteousness and healing.

Allah's way of dealing with His servants (from the most ancient times). And even thus did the rejecters of Allah lose (utterly)!

بِأَسْنَآ سُنَّتَ اللهِ الَّتِيْ قَدْ خَلَتْ فِيْ عِبَادِهٖ ۚ وَخَسِرَ هُنَالِكَ الْكٰفِرُوْنَ ۞

Ḥā-Mīm (Abbreviated Letters), Or Ḥā-Mīm Sajda, or Fuṣṣilat

حٰمٓ التَّنْزِيْلُ مِنَ الرَّحْمٰنِ الرَّحِيْمِ

In the name of Allah, Most Gracious, Most Merciful.

بِسْمِ اللهِ الرَّحْمٰنِ الرَّحِيْمِ ۞

1. Ḥā-Mīm:

2. A revelation from The Most Gracious, Most Merciful;—

حٰمٓ ۚ تَنْزِيْلٌ مِّنَ الرَّحْمٰنِ الرَّحِيْمِ ۞

3. A Book, whereof the verses are explained in detail;— a Qur-ān in Arabic, for people who understand;—

كِتٰبٌ فُصِّلَتْ اٰيٰتُهٗ قُرْاٰنًا عَرَبِيًّا لِّقَوْمٍ يَّعْلَمُوْنَ ۞

4. Giving Good News and Admonition: yet most of them turn away, and so they hear not.

بَشِيْرًا وَّنَذِيْرًا ۚ فَأَعْرَضَ أَكْثَرُهُمْ فَهُمْ لَا يَسْمَعُوْنَ ۞

5. They say: "Our hearts are under veils, (concealed) from that to which thou dost invite us, and in our ears is a deafness, between us and thee is a screen: so do thou (what thou wilt); for us, we shall do (what we will!)"

وَقَالُوْا قُلُوْبُنَا فِيْ أَكِنَّةٍ مِّمَّا تَدْعُوْنَا إِلَيْهِ وَفِيْ اٰذَانِنَا وَقْرٌ وَّمِنْ بَيْنِنَا وَبَيْنِكَ حِجَابٌ فَاعْمَلْ إِنَّنَا عٰمِلُوْنَ ۞

6. Say thou: "I am but a man like you: it is revealed to me by inspiration, that your God is One God: so take the straight path unto Him and ask for His forgiveness." And woe to those who join gods with Allah,—

قُلْ إِنَّمَا أَنَا بَشَرٌ مِّثْلُكُمْ يُوْحٰى إِلَيَّ أَنَّمَا إِلٰهُكُمْ إِلٰهٌ وَّاحِدٌ فَاسْتَقِيْمُوْا إِلَيْهِ وَاسْتَغْفِرُوْهُ ۚ وَوَيْلٌ لِّلْمُشْرِكِيْنَ ۙ ۞

7. Those who pay not Zakat and who even deny the Hereafter.

الَّذِيْنَ لَا يُؤْتُوْنَ الزَّكٰوةَ وَهُمْ بِالْاٰخِرَةِ هُمْ كٰفِرُوْنَ ۞

8. For those who believe and work deeds of righteousness is a reward that will never fail.

إِنَّ الَّذِيْنَ اٰمَنُوْا وَعَمِلُوا الصّٰلِحٰتِ لَهُمْ أَجْرٌ غَيْرُ مَمْنُوْنٍ ۞

9. Say: Is it that ye deny Him Who created the earth in two Days? And do ye join equals with Him? He is the Lord of (all) the Worlds.

قُلْ أَئِنَّكُمْ لَتَكْفُرُوْنَ بِالَّذِيْ خَلَقَ الْأَرْضَ فِيْ يَوْمَيْنِ وَتَجْعَلُوْنَ لَهٗ أَنْدَادًا ۚ ذٰلِكَ رَبُّ الْعٰلَمِيْنَ ۞

10. He set on the (earth), mountains standing firm, high above it, and bestowed blessings on the earth, and measured therein its sustenance in four Days, alike for (all) who ask..

وَجَعَلَ فِيْهَا رَوَاسِيَ مِنْ فَوْقِهَا وَبٰرَكَ فِيْهَا وَقَدَّرَ فِيْهَا أَقْوَاتَهَا فِيْ أَرْبَعَةِ أَيَّامٍ ۚ سَوَآءً لِّلسَّآئِلِيْنَ ۞

11. Then He turned to the sky, and it had been (as) smoke: He said to it and to the

ثُمَّ اسْتَوٰى إِلَى السَّمَآءِ وَهِيَ دُخَانٌ

earth: "Come ye together, willingly or unwillingly." They said: "We do come (together), in willing obedience."

12. So He completed them as seven firmaments in two Days, and He assigned to each heaven its duty and command. And We adorned the lower heaven with lights, and (provided it) with guard. Such is the Decree of (Him) the Exalted in Might, Full of knowledge.

13. But if they turn away, say thou: "I have warned you of a thunderbolt like the thunderbolt of the 'Ād and the Thamūd!"

14. Behold, the messengers came to them, from before them and behind them, (preaching): "Serve none but Allah." They said, "If our Lord had so pleased, He would certainly have sent down angels: so we disbelieve in the Message you were sent with.

15. Now the 'Ād behaved arrogantly through the land, against (all) truth and reason, and said: "Who is superior to us in strength?" What! did they not see that Allah, Who created them, was superior to them in strength? But they continued to reject Our Signs!

16. So We sent against them a furious Wind through days of disaster, that We might give them a taste of a Chastisement of humiliation in this Life; but the Penalty of the Hereafter will be more humiliating still: and they will find no help.

17. As to the Thamūd, We gave them guidance, but they preferred blindness (of heart) to Guidance: so the thunderbolt of the Chastisement of humiliation seized them, because of what they had earned.

18. But We delivered those who believed and practised righteousness.

19. The Day that the enemies of Allah will be gathered together to the Fire, they will be marched in ranks.

20. At length, when they reach the (Fire), their hearing, their sight, and their skins will bear witness against them, as to (all) their deeds.

حَتّىٰٓ اِذَا مَا جَآءُوْهَا شَهِدَ عَلَيْهِمْ سَمْعُهُمْ وَاَبْصَارُهُمْ وَجُلُوْدُهُمْ بِمَا كَانُوْا يَعْمَلُوْنَ ۝

21. They will say to their skins: "Why bear ye witness against us?" They will say: "Allah hath given us speech, (He) Who giveth speech to everything: He created you for the first time, and unto Him were ye to return.

وَقَالُوْا لِجُلُوْدِهِمْ لِمَ شَهِدْتُّمْ عَلَيْنَا قَالُوْٓا اَنْطَقَنَا اللّٰهُ الَّذِيْٓ اَنْطَقَ كُلَّ شَيْءٍ وَّهُوَ خَلَقَكُمْ اَوَّلَ مَرَّةٍ وَّاِلَيْهِ تُرْجَعُوْنَ ۝

22. "Ye did not seek to hide yourselves, lest your hearing, your sight, and your skins should bear witness against you! But ye did think that Allah knew not many of the things that ye used to do!

وَمَا كُنْتُمْ تَسْتَتِرُوْنَ اَنْ يَّشْهَدَ عَلَيْكُمْ سَمْعُكُمْ وَلَاۤ اَبْصَارُكُمْ وَلَا جُلُوْدُكُمْ وَلٰكِنْ ظَنَنْتُمْ اَنَّ اللّٰهَ لَا يَعْلَمُ كَثِيْرًا مِّمَّا تَعْمَلُوْنَ ۝

23. "But this thought of yours which ye did entertain concerning your Lord, hath brought you to destruction, and (now) have ye become of those utterly lost!"

وَذٰلِكُمْ ظَنُّكُمُ الَّذِيْ ظَنَنْتُمْ بِرَبِّكُمْ اَرْدٰىكُمْ فَاَصْبَحْتُمْ مِّنَ الْخٰسِرِيْنَ ۝

24. If, then, they have patience, the Fire will be a Home for them! And if they beg for pardon, their suit shall not be granted.

فَاِنْ يَّصْبِرُوْا فَالنَّارُ مَثْوًى لَّهُمْ وَاِنْ يَّسْتَعْتِبُوْا فَمَا هُمْ مِّنَ الْمُعْتَبِيْنَ ۝

25. And We have destined for them intimate companions (of like nature), who made alluring to them what was before them and behind them; and the word among the previous generations of Jinns and men, who have passed away, is proved against them; for they are utterly lost.

وَقَيَّضْنَا لَهُمْ قُرَنَآءَ فَزَيَّنُوْا لَهُمْ مَّا بَيْنَ اَيْدِيْهِمْ وَمَا خَلْفَهُمْ وَحَقَّ عَلَيْهِمُ الْقَوْلُ فِيْٓ اُمَمٍ قَدْ خَلَتْ مِنْ قَبْلِهِمْ مِّنَ الْجِنِّ وَالْاِنْسِ اِنَّهُمْ كَانُوْا خٰسِرِيْنَ ۝

26. The Unbelievers say: "Listen not to this Qur-ān, but talk at random in the midst of its (reading), that ye may gain the upper hand!"

وَقَالَ الَّذِيْنَ كَفَرُوْا لَا تَسْمَعُوْا لِهٰذَا الْقُرْاٰنِ وَالْغَوْا فِيْهِ لَعَلَّكُمْ تَغْلِبُوْنَ ۝

27. But We will certainly give the Unbelievers a taste of a severe Chastisement, and We will requite them for the worst of their deeds.

فَلَنُذِيْقَنَّ الَّذِيْنَ كَفَرُوْا عَذَابًا شَدِيْدًا وَّلَنَجْزِيَنَّهُمْ اَسْوَاَ الَّذِيْ كَانُوْا يَعْمَلُوْنَ ۝

28. Such is the requital of the enemies of Allah,— the Fire: therein will be for them the Eternal Home: a (fit) requital, for that they were wont to reject Our Signs.

ذٰلِكَ جَزَآءُ اَعْدَآءِ اللّٰهِ النَّارُ لَهُمْ فِيْهَا دَارُ الْخُلْدِ جَزَآءًۢ بِمَا كَانُوْا بِاٰيٰتِنَا يَجْحَدُوْنَ ۝

29. And the Unbelievers will say: "Our Lord! Show us those, among Jinns and men, who misled us: we shall crush them beneath our feet, so that they become the vilest."

وَقَالَ الَّذِيْنَ كَفَرُوْا رَبَّنَآ اَرِنَا الَّذَيْنِ اَضَلّٰنَا مِنَ الْجِنِّ وَالْاِنْسِ نَجْعَلْهُمَا تَحْتَ اَقْدَامِنَا لِيَكُوْنَا مِنَ الْاَسْفَلِيْنَ ۝

30. In the case of those who say, "Our Lord is Allah", and, further, stand straight and steadfast, the angels descend on them (from time to time): "Fear ye not!" (they suggest), "Nor grieve! But receive the Glad Tidings of the Garden (of Bliss), the which ye were promised!

31. "We are your protectors in this life and in the Hereafter: therein shall ye have all that you shall desire; therein shall ye have all that ye ask for!—

32. "A hospitable gift from One Oft-Forgiving, Most Merciful!"

33. Who is better in speech than one who calls (men) to Allah, works righteousness, and says, "I am of those who bow in Islam"?

34. Nor can Goodness and Evil be equal. Repel (Evil) with what is better: then will he between whom and thee was hatred become as it were thy friend and intimate!

35. And no one will be granted such goodness except those who exercise patience and self-restraint,—none but persons of the greatest good fortune.

36. And if (at any time) an incitement to discord is made to thee by the Satan, seek refuge in Allah. He is the One Who hears and knows all things.

37. Among His Signs are the Night and the Day, and the Sun and the Moon. Prostrate not to the sun and the moon, but prostrate to Allah, Who created them, if it is Him ye wish to serve.

38. But if the (Unbelievers) are arrogant, (no matter): for in the presence of thy Lord are those who celebrate His praises by night and by day. And they never flag (nor feel themselves above it).

39. And among His Signs is this: thou seest the earth humble; but when We send down rain to it, it is stirred to life and yields increase. Truly, He Who gives life to the (dead) earth can surely give life to (men)

who are dead. For He has power over all things.

40. Those who pervert the Truth in Our Signs are not hidden from Us. Which is better?—he that is cast into the Fire, or he that comes safe through, on the Day of Judgment? Do what ye will: verily He seeth (clearly) all that ye do.

41. Those who reject the Message when it comes to them (are not hidden from Us). And indeed it is a Book of exalted power.

42. No falsehood can approach it from before or behind it: it is sent down by One Full of Wisdom, Worthy of all Praise.

43. Nothing is said to thee that was not said to the messengers before thee: surely thy Lord has at His command (all) Forgiveness as well as a most grievous Chastisement.

44. Had We sent this as a Qur'ān (in a language) other than Arabic, they would Have said: "Why are not its verses explained in detail? What! a foreign (tongue) and (a Messenger) an Arab?" Say: "It is a guide and a healing to those who believe; and for those who believe not, there is a deafness in their ears, and it is blindness in their (eyes): they are (as it were) being called from a place far distant!"

45. We certainly gave Moses the Book aforetime: but disputes arose therein. Had it not been for a Word that went forth before from thy Lord, (their differences) would have been settled between them: but they remained in suspicious disquieting doubt thereon.

46. Whoever works righteousness benefits his own soul; whoever works evil, it is against his own soul: nor is thy Lord ever unjust (in the least) to His servants.

47. To Him is referred the Knowledge of the Hour (of Judgment: He knows all): no fruit comes out of its sheath, nor does a female conceive (within her womb) nor bring forth (young), but by His Knowledge. The Day that (Allah) will propound to them the (question), "Where are the Partners (ye attributed) to Me?" They will say, "We do assure Thee not one of us can bear witness!"

48. The (deities) they used to invoke aforetime will leave them in the lurch, and they will perceive that they have no way of escape.

49. Man does not weary of asking for good (things), but if ill touches him, he gives up all hope (and) is lost in despair.

50. When We give him a taste of some mercy from Us, after some adversity has touched him, he is sure to say, "This is due to my (merit): I think not that the Hour (of Judgment) will (ever) be established; but if I am brought back to my Lord, I have (much) good (stored) in His sight!" But We will show the Unbelievers the truth of all that they did, and We shall give them the taste of a severe Chastisement.

51. When We bestow favours on man, he turns away, and gets himself remote on his side (instead of coming to Us); and when evil seizes him, (he comes) full of prolonged prayer!

52. Say: "See ye if the (Revelation) is (really) from Allah, and yet do ye Reject it? Who is more astray than one who is in a schism far (from any purpose)?"

53. Soon will We show them Our Signs in the (furthest) regions (of the earth), and in their own souls, until it becomes manifest to them that this is the Truth. Is it not enough that thy Lord doth witness all things?

54. Ah indeed! are they in doubt concerning the Meeting with their Lord? Ah indeed! it is He that doth encompass all things!

SÛRA–42
ASH-SHÛRA
(INTRODUCTION)

This is the third Sûra of the *Ḥā-Mîm* series of seven Sûras, for which see the Introduction to S. 40.

The theme is how evil and blasphemy can be cured by the Mercy and Guidance of Allah, which come through His Revelation. Men are asked to settle their differences in patience by mutual Consultation (42: 38), which explains the title of the Sûra.

Ash-Shūrā, or Consultation

In the name of Allah, Most Gracious Most Merciful.

1. Hā-Mīm;

2. 'Ain. Sîn. Qāf.

3. Thus doth (He) send inspiration to thee as (He did) to those before thee,— Allah, Exalted in Power, Full of Wisdom.

4. To Him belongs all that is in the heavens and on earth: and He is Most High, Most Great.

5. The heavens are almost rent asunder from above them (by His Glory): and the angels celebrate the Praises of their Lord, and pray for forgiveness for all beings on earth: behold! Verily Allah is He, the Oft-Forgiving, Most Merciful.

6. And those who take as protectors others besides Him,— Allah doth watch over them; and thou art not the disposer of their affairs.

7. Thus have We sent by inspiration to thee an Arabic Qur-ān: that thou mayest warn the Mother of Cities and all around her,— and warn (them) of the Day of Assembly, of which there is no doubt: (when) some will be in the Garden, and some in the Blazing Fire.—

8. If Allah had so willed, he could have made them a single people; but He admits whom He will to His Mercy; and the wrong-doers will have no protector nor helper.

9. What! Have they taken (for worship) protectors besides Him? But it is Allah,— He is the Protector, and it is He Who gives life to the dead: it is He Who has power over all things.

10. Whatever it be wherein ye differ, the decision thereof is with Allah: such is Allah

my Lord: in Him I trust, and to Him I turn.

وَإِلَيْهِ أُنِيبُ ۞

11. (He is) the Creator of the heavens and the earth: He has made for you pairs from among yourselves, and pairs among cattle: by this means does He multiply you: there is nothing whatever like unto Him, and He is the One that hears and sees.

فَاطِرُ السَّمَوَٰتِ وَالْأَرْضِ جَعَلَ لَكُم مِّنْ أَنفُسِكُمْ أَزْوَٰجًا وَمِنَ الْأَنْعَٰمِ أَزْوَٰجًا يَذْرَؤُكُمْ فِيهِ لَيْسَ كَمِثْلِهِۦ شَىْءٌ وَهُوَ السَّمِيعُ الْبَصِيرُ ۞

12. To Him belong the keys of the heavens and the earth: he enlarges and restricts the Sustenance to whom he will: for He knows full well all things.

لَهُۥ مَقَالِيدُ السَّمَوَٰتِ وَالْأَرْضِ يَبْسُطُ الرِّزْقَ لِمَن يَشَآءُ وَيَقْدِرُ إِنَّهُۥ بِكُلِّ شَىْءٍ عَلِيمٌ ۞

13. The same religion has He established for you as that which He enjoined on Noah— the which We have sent by inspiration to thee— and that which We enjoined on Abraham, Moses, and Jesus: namely, that ye should remain steadfast in Religion, and make no divisions therein: to those who worship other things than Allah, hard is the (way) to which thou callest them. Allah chooses to Himself those whom He pleases, and guides to Himself those who turn (to Him).

شَرَعَ لَكُم مِّنَ الدِّينِ مَا وَصَّىٰ بِهِۦ نُوحًا وَالَّذِىٓ أَوْحَيْنَآ إِلَيْكَ وَمَا وَصَّيْنَا بِهِۦٓ إِبْرَٰهِيمَ وَمُوسَىٰ وَعِيسَىٰٓ أَنْ أَقِيمُوا الدِّينَ وَلَا تَتَفَرَّقُوا فِيهِ كَبُرَ عَلَى الْمُشْرِكِينَ مَا تَدْعُوهُمْ إِلَيْهِ اللَّهُ يَجْتَبِىٓ إِلَيْهِ مَن يَشَآءُ وَيَهْدِىٓ إِلَيْهِ مَن يُنِيبُ ۞

14. And they became divided only after knowledge reached them,—being insolent to one another. Had it not been for a Word that went forth before from thy Lord, (tending) to a Term appointed, the matter would have been settled between them: but truly those who have inherited the Book after them are in suspicious (disquieting) doubt concerning it.

وَمَا تَفَرَّقُوٓا إِلَّا مِنۢ بَعْدِ مَا جَآءَهُمُ الْعِلْمُ بَغْيًۢا بَيْنَهُمْ وَلَوْلَا كَلِمَةٌ سَبَقَتْ مِن رَّبِّكَ إِلَىٰٓ أَجَلٍ مُّسَمًّى لَّقُضِىَ بَيْنَهُمْ وَإِنَّ الَّذِينَ أُورِثُوا الْكِتَٰبَ مِنۢ بَعْدِهِمْ لَفِى شَكٍّ مِّنْهُ مُرِيبٍ ۞

15. Now then, for that (reason), call (them to the Faith), and stand steadfast as thou art commanded, nor follow thou their vain desires; but say: "I believe in whatever Book Allah has sent down; and I am commanded to judge justly between you. Allah is our Lord and your Lord! For us (is the responsibility for) our deeds, and for you for your deeds. There is no contention between us and you. Allah will bring us together, and to Him is (our) final goal."

فَلِذَٰلِكَ فَادْعُ وَاسْتَقِمْ كَمَآ أُمِرْتَ وَلَا تَتَّبِعْ أَهْوَآءَهُمْ وَقُلْ ءَامَنتُ بِمَآ أَنزَلَ اللَّهُ مِن كِتَٰبٍ وَأُمِرْتُ لِأَعْدِلَ بَيْنَكُمُ اللَّهُ رَبُّنَا وَرَبُّكُمْ لَنَآ أَعْمَٰلُنَا وَلَكُمْ أَعْمَٰلُكُمْ لَا حُجَّةَ بَيْنَنَا وَبَيْنَكُمُ اللَّهُ يَجْمَعُ بَيْنَنَا وَإِلَيْهِ الْمَصِيرُ ۞

16. But those who dispute concerning Allah after He has been accepted,— futile is their argument in the sight of their Lord: on them is Wrath, and for them will be a Chastisement terrible.

وَالَّذِیۡنَ یُحَآجُّوۡنَ فِی اللّٰهِ مِنۡۢ بَعۡدِ مَا اسۡتُجِیۡبَ لَهٗ حُجَّتُهُمۡ دَاحِضَةٌ عِنۡدَ رَبِّهِمۡ وَعَلَیۡهِمۡ غَضَبٌ وَّلَهُمۡ عَذَابٌ شَدِیۡدٌ ۟

17. It is Allah Who has sent down the Book in truth, and the Balance and what will make thee realise that perhaps the Hour is close at hand?

اَللّٰهُ الَّذِیۡۤ اَنۡزَلَ الۡکِتٰبَ بِالۡحَقِّ وَالۡمِیۡزَانَ وَمَا یُدۡرِیۡکَ لَعَلَّ السَّاعَةَ قَرِیۡبٌ ۟

18. Only those wish to hasten it who believe not in it: those who believe hold it in awe, and know that it is the Truth. Behold, verily those that dispute concerning the Hour are far astray.

یَسۡتَعۡجِلُ بِهَا الَّذِیۡنَ لَا یُؤۡمِنُوۡنَ بِهَا وَالَّذِیۡنَ اٰمَنُوۡا مُشۡفِقُوۡنَ مِنۡهَا وَ یَعۡلَمُوۡنَ اَنَّهَا الۡحَقُّ اَلَاۤ اِنَّ الَّذِیۡنَ یُمَارُوۡنَ فِی السَّاعَةِ لَفِیۡ ضَلٰلٍۭ بَعِیۡدٍ ۟

19. Gracious is Allah to His servants: he gives Sustenance to whom He pleases: and He is the Strong, the Mighty.

اَللّٰهُ لَطِیۡفٌۢ بِعِبَادِهٖ یَرۡزُقُ مَنۡ یَّشَآءُ وَهُوَ الۡقَوِیُّ الۡعَزِیۡزُ ۟

20. To any that desires the tilth of the Hereafter, We give increase in his tilth; and to any that desires the tilth of this world, We grant somewhat thereof, but he has no share or lot in the Hereafter.

مَنۡ کَانَ یُرِیۡدُ حَرۡثَ الۡاٰخِرَةِ نَزِدۡ لَهٗ فِیۡ حَرۡثِهٖ وَمَنۡ کَانَ یُرِیۡدُ حَرۡثَ الدُّنۡیَا نُؤۡتِهٖ مِنۡهَا وَمَا لَهٗ فِی الۡاٰخِرَةِ مِنۡ نَّصِیۡبٍ ۟

21. What! Have they partners (in godhead), who have established for them some religion without the permission of Allah? Had it not been for the Decree of Judgment, the matter would have been decided between them (at once). But verily the wrong-doers will have a grievous Chastisement.

اَمۡ لَهُمۡ شُرَکٰٓؤُا شَرَعُوۡا لَهُمۡ مِّنَ الدِّیۡنِ مَا لَمۡ یَاۡذَنۡۢ بِهِ اللّٰهُ وَلَوۡ لَا کَلِمَةُ الۡفَصۡلِ لَقُضِیَ بَیۡنَهُمۡ وَاِنَّ الظّٰلِمِیۡنَ لَهُمۡ عَذَابٌ اَلِیۡمٌ ۟

22. Thou wilt see the wrong-doers in fear on account of what they have earned, and (the burden of) that must (necessarily) fall on them. But those who believe and work righteous deeds will be in the Meadows of the Gardens: they shall have, before their Lord, all that they wish for. That will indeed be the magnificent Bounty (of Allah).

تَرَی الظّٰلِمِیۡنَ مُشۡفِقِیۡنَ مِمَّا کَسَبُوۡا وَهُوَ وَاقِعٌۢ بِهِمۡ وَالَّذِیۡنَ اٰمَنُوۡا وَ عَمِلُوا الصّٰلِحٰتِ فِیۡ رَوۡضَاتِ الۡجَنّٰتِ لَهُمۡ مَّا یَشَآءُوۡنَ عِنۡدَ رَبِّهِمۡ ذٰلِکَ هُوَ الۡفَضۡلُ الۡکَبِیۡرُ ۟

23. That is (the Bounty) whereof Allah gives Glad Tidings to His Servants who believe and do righteous deeds. Say: "No

ذٰلِکَ الَّذِیۡ یُبَشِّرُ اللّٰهُ عِبَادَهُ الَّذِیۡنَ اٰمَنُوۡا وَعَمِلُوا الصّٰلِحٰتِ قُلۡ لَّاۤ اَسۡـَٔلُکُمۡ

reward do I ask of you for this except the love of those near of kin." And if anyone earns any good, We shall give him an increase of good in respect thereof: for Allah is Oft-Forgiving, Grateful.

24. What! Do they say, "He has forged a falsehood against Allah"? But if Allah willed, He could seal up thy heart. And Allah blots out falsehood, and proves the Truth by His Words. For He knows well the secrets of all hearts.

25. He is the One that accepts repentance from His Servants and forgives sins: and He knows all that ye do.

26. And He listens to those who believe and do deeds of righteousness, and gives them increase of His Bounty: but for the Unbelievers there is a terrible Chastisement.

27. If Allah were to enlarge the provision for His Servants, they would indeed transgress beyond all bounds through the earth: but He sends (it) down in due measure as He pleases. For He is with His Servants well-acquainted, Watchful.

28. He is the One that sends down rain (even) after (men) have given up all hope, and scatters His Mercy (far and wide). And He is the Protector, Worthy of all Praise.

29. And among His Signs is the creation of the heavens and the earth, and the living creatures that He has scattered through them: and He has power to gather them together when He wills.

30. Whatever misfortune happens to you, is because of the things your hands have wrought, and for many (a sin) He grants forgiveness.

31. Nor can ye escape through the earth; nor have ye, besides Allah, anyone to protect or to help.

32. And among His Signs are the ships, smooth-running through the ocean. (tall) as mountains.

33. If it be His Will, He can still the Wind: then would they become motionless on the

عَلَيۡهِ أَجۡرًا إِلَّا ٱلۡمَوَدَّةَ فِي ٱلۡقُرۡبَىٰ ۗ وَمَن يَقۡتَرِفۡ حَسَنَةً نَّزِدۡ لَهُۥ فِيهَا حُسۡنًا ۚ إِنَّ ٱللَّهَ غَفُورٌ شَكُورٌ ٢٣

أَمۡ يَقُولُونَ ٱفۡتَرَىٰ عَلَى ٱللَّهِ كَذِبًا ۖ فَإِن يَشَإِ ٱللَّهُ يَخۡتِمۡ عَلَىٰ قَلۡبِكَ ۗ وَيَمۡحُ ٱللَّهُ ٱلۡبَٰطِلَ وَيُحِقُّ ٱلۡحَقَّ بِكَلِمَٰتِهِۦٓ ۚ إِنَّهُۥ عَلِيمٌۢ بِذَاتِ ٱلصُّدُورِ ٢٤

وَهُوَ ٱلَّذِي يَقۡبَلُ ٱلتَّوۡبَةَ عَنۡ عِبَادِهِۦ وَيَعۡفُواْ عَنِ ٱلسَّيِّـَٔاتِ وَيَعۡلَمُ مَا تَفۡعَلُونَ ٢٥

وَيَسۡتَجِيبُ ٱلَّذِينَ ءَامَنُواْ وَعَمِلُواْ ٱلصَّٰلِحَٰتِ وَيَزِيدُهُم مِّن فَضۡلِهِۦ ۚ وَٱلۡكَٰفِرُونَ لَهُمۡ عَذَابٌ شَدِيدٌ ٢٦

وَلَوۡ بَسَطَ ٱللَّهُ ٱلرِّزۡقَ لِعِبَادِهِۦ لَبَغَوۡاْ فِي ٱلۡأَرۡضِ وَلَٰكِن يُنَزِّلُ بِقَدَرٍ مَّا يَشَآءُ ۚ إِنَّهُۥ بِعِبَادِهِۦ خَبِيرٌۢ بَصِيرٌ ٢٧

وَهُوَ ٱلَّذِي يُنَزِّلُ ٱلۡغَيۡثَ مِنۢ بَعۡدِ مَا قَنَطُواْ وَيَنشُرُ رَحۡمَتَهُۥ ۚ وَهُوَ ٱلۡوَلِيُّ ٱلۡحَمِيدُ ٢٨

وَمِنۡ ءَايَٰتِهِۦ خَلۡقُ ٱلسَّمَٰوَٰتِ وَٱلۡأَرۡضِ وَمَا بَثَّ فِيهِمَا مِن دَآبَّةٍ ۚ وَهُوَ عَلَىٰ جَمۡعِهِمۡ إِذَا يَشَآءُ قَدِيرٌ ٢٩

وَمَآ أَصَٰبَكُم مِّن مُّصِيبَةٍ فَبِمَا كَسَبَتۡ أَيۡدِيكُمۡ وَيَعۡفُواْ عَن كَثِيرٍ ٣٠

وَمَآ أَنتُم بِمُعۡجِزِينَ فِي ٱلۡأَرۡضِ ۖ وَمَا لَكُم مِّن دُونِ ٱللَّهِ مِن وَلِيٍّ وَلَا نَصِيرٍ ٣١

وَمِنۡ ءَايَٰتِهِ ٱلۡجَوَارِ فِي ٱلۡبَحۡرِ كَٱلۡأَعۡلَٰمِ ٣٢

إِن يَشَأۡ يُسۡكِنِ ٱلرِّيحَ فَيَظۡلَلۡنَ رَوَاكِدَ

back of the (ocean). Verily in this are Signs for everyone who patiently perseveres and is grateful.

34. Or He can cause them to perish because of the (evil) which (the men) have earned; but much doth He forgive.

35. But let those know, who dispute about Our Signs, that there is for them no way of escape.

36. Whatever ye are given (here) is (but) the enjoyment of this Life: but that which is with Allah is better and more lasting: (it is) for those who believe and put their trust in their Lord:

37. Those who avoid the greater sins and indecencies and, when they are angry even then forgive;

38. Those who respond to their Lord, and establish regular prayer; who (conduct) their affairs by mutual Consultation; who spend out of what We bestow on them for Sustenance;

39. And those who, when an oppressive wrong is inflicted on them, (are not cowed but) help and defend themselves.

40. The recompense for an injury is an injury equal thereto (in degree): but if a person forgives and makes reconciliation, his reward is due from Allah: for (Allah) loveth not those who do wrong.

41. But indeed if any do help and defend himself after a wrong (done) to him, against such there is no cause of blame.

42. The blame is only against those who oppress men with wrong-doing and insolently transgress beyond bounds through the land, defying right and justice: for such there will be a Chastisement grievous.

43. But indeed if any show patience and forgive, that would truly be an affair of great Resolution.

44. For any whom Allah leaves astray, there is no protector thereafter. And thou wilt see the wrong-doers, when in sight of the Chastisement, say: "Is there any way

(to effect) a return?"

قِنْ سَبِيْلٍ ۞

45.   And thou wilt see them brought forward to the (Penalty), abject in humbleness (and) looking with a stealthy glance. And the Believers will say: "Those are indeed in loss who lose themselves and their families. On the Day of Judgment. Behold! Truly the wrong-doers are in a lasting Chastisement!"

وَتَرٰىهُمْ يُعْرَضُوْنَ عَلَيْهَا خٰشِعِيْنَ مِنَ الذُّلِّ يَنْظُرُوْنَ مِنْ طَرْفٍ خَفِيٍّ ۗ وَقَالَ الَّذِيْنَ اٰمَنُوْۤا اِنَّ الْخٰسِرِيْنَ الَّذِيْنَ خَسِرُوْۤا اَنْفُسَهُمْ وَاَهْلِيْهِمْ يَوْمَ الْقِيٰمَةِ ۗ اَلَاۤ اِنَّ الظّٰلِمِيْنَ فِيْ عَذَابٍ مُّقِيْمٍ ۞

46.   And no protectors have they to help them, other than Allah. And for any whom Allah leaves to stray, there is no way (to the Goal).

وَمَا كَانَ لَهُمْ مِّنْ اَوْلِيَآءَ يَنْصُرُوْنَهُمْ مِّنْ دُوْنِ اللّٰهِ ۗ وَمَنْ يُّضْلِلِ اللّٰهُ فَمَا لَهٗ مِنْ سَبِيْلٍ ۞

47.   Respond ye to your Lord, before there come a Day which there will be no putting back, because of (the ordainment of) Allah! That Day there will be for you no place of refuge nor will there be for you any room for denial (of your sins)!

اِسْتَجِيْبُوْا لِرَبِّكُمْ مِّنْ قَبْلِ اَنْ يَّاْتِيَ يَوْمٌ لَّا مَرَدَّ لَهٗ مِنَ اللّٰهِ ۗ مَا لَكُمْ مِّنْ مَّلْجَاٍ يَّوْمَئِذٍ وَّمَا لَكُمْ مِّنْ نَّكِيْرٍ ۞

48.   If then they turn away, We have not sent thee as a guard over them. Thy duty is but to convey (the Message). And truly, when We give man a taste of a Mercy from Us, he doth exult thereat, but when some ill happens to him, on account of the deeds which his hands have sent forth, truly then is man ungrateful!

فَاِنْ اَعْرَضُوْا فَمَاۤ اَرْسَلْنٰكَ عَلَيْهِمْ حَفِيْظًا ۗ اِنْ عَلَيْكَ اِلَّا الْبَلٰغُ ۗ وَاِنَّاۤ اِذَاۤ اَذَقْنَا الْاِنْسَانَ مِنَّا رَحْمَةً فَرِحَ بِهَا ۚ وَاِنْ تُصِبْهُمْ سَيِّئَةٌ ۢ بِمَا قَدَّمَتْ اَيْدِيْهِمْ فَاِنَّ الْاِنْسَانَ كَفُوْرٌ ۞

49.   To Allah belongs the dominion of the heavens and the earth. He creates what He wills. He bestows (children) male or female according to His Will,

لِلّٰهِ مُلْكُ السَّمٰوٰتِ وَالْاَرْضِ ۗ يَخْلُقُ مَا يَشَآءُ ۗ يَهَبُ لِمَنْ يَّشَآءُ اِنَاثًا وَّ يَهَبُ لِمَنْ يَّشَآءُ الذُّكُوْرَ ۞

50.   Or He bestows both males and females, and He leaves barren whom He will: for He is full of Knowledge and Power.

اَوْ يُزَوِّجُهُمْ ذُكْرَانًا وَّاِنَاثًا ۚ وَيَجْعَلُ مَنْ يَّشَآءُ عَقِيْمًا ۗ اِنَّهٗ عَلِيْمٌ قَدِيْرٌ ۞

51.   It is not fitting for a man that Allah should speak to him except by inspiration, or from behind a veil, or by the sending of a Messenger to reveal. with Allah's permission. what Allah wills: for He is Most High, Most Wise.

وَمَا كَانَ لِبَشَرٍ اَنْ يُّكَلِّمَهُ اللّٰهُ اِلَّا وَحْيًا اَوْ مِنْ وَّرَآئِ حِجَابٍ اَوْ يُرْسِلَ رَسُوْلًا فَيُوْحِيَ بِاِذْنِهٖ مَا يَشَآءُ ۗ اِنَّهٗ عَلِيٌّ حَكِيْمٌ ۞

SÛRA–43
AZ-ZUKHRUF
(INTRODUCTION)

This is the fourth Sûra of the *Hā-Mîm* series of seven Sûras. For their chronology and general theme see the Introduction to S. 40.

This Sûra deals with the contrasts between the real glory of Truth and Revelation and the false glitter of what people like to believe and worship. It cites tha examples of Abraham, Moses, and Jesus, as exposing the False holding up the Truth. The key-word *Zukhruf* (Gold Adornments) occurs in verse 38, but the idea occurs all through the Sûra.

52. And thus have We, by Our command, sent inspiration to thee: thou knewest not (before) what was Revelation, and what was Faith; but We have made the (Qur'ān) a Light, wherewith We guide such of Our servants as We will; and verily thou dost guide (men) to the Straight Way,—

وَكَذَلِكَ أَوْحَيْنَا إِلَيْكَ رُوحًا مِّنْ أَمْرِنَا مَا كُنْتَ تَدْرِي مَا الْكِتَابُ وَلَا الْإِيمَانُ وَلَكِنْ جَعَلْنَاهُ نُورًا نَّهْدِي بِهِ مَنْ نَّشَاءُ مِنْ عِبَادِنَا وَإِنَّكَ لَتَهْدِي إِلَى صِرَاطٍ مُّسْتَقِيمٍ ۝

53. The Way of Allah, to Whom belongs whatever is in the heavens and whatever is on earth. Behold (how) all affairs tend towards Allah!

صِرَاطِ اللَّهِ الَّذِي لَهُ مَا فِي السَّمَوَاتِ وَمَا فِي الْأَرْضِ أَلَا إِلَى اللَّهِ تَصِيرُ الْأُمُورُ ۝

Az-Zukhruf, or Gold Adornments

In the name of Allah, Most Gracious, Most Merciful.

بِسْمِ اللَّهِ الرَّحْمَنِ الرَّحِيمِ

1. Hā-Mīm.

2. By the Book that makes things clear,—

3. We have made it a Qur'ān in Arabic, that ye may be able to understand.

4. And verily, it is in the Mother of the Book, with Us, high (in dignity), full of wisdom.

حم ۝ وَالْكِتَابِ الْمُبِينِ ۝ إِنَّا جَعَلْنَاهُ قُرْآنًا عَرَبِيًّا لَّعَلَّكُمْ تَعْقِلُونَ ۝ وَإِنَّهُ فِي أُمِّ الْكِتَابِ لَدَيْنَا لَعَلِيٌّ حَكِيمٌ ۝

5. Shall We then turn away the Reminder from you altogether, for that ye are a people transgressing beyond bounds?

أَفَنَضْرِبُ عَنكُمُ الذِّكْرَ صَفْحًا أَن كُنتُمْ قَوْمًا مُّسْرِفِينَ ۝

6. But how many were the prophets We sent amongst the peoples of old?

وَكَمْ أَرْسَلْنَا مِن نَّبِيٍّ فِي الْأَوَّلِينَ ۝

7. And never came there a prophet to them but they mocked him.

وَمَا يَأْتِيهِم مِّن نَّبِيٍّ إِلَّا كَانُوا بِهِ يَسْتَهْزِئُونَ ۝

8. So We destroyed men—stronger in power than these; and (thus) has passed on the example of the peoples of old.

فَأَهْلَكْنَا أَشَدَّ مِنْهُم بَطْشًا وَمَضَى مَثَلُ الْأَوَّلِينَ ۝

9. If thou wert to question them, 'Who created the heavens and the earth?' they would be sure to reply, 'They were created by (Him), the Exalted in Power, full of Knowledge';–

وَلَئِن سَأَلْتَهُم مَّنْ خَلَقَ السَّمَوَاتِ وَالْأَرْضَ لَيَقُولُنَّ خَلَقَهُنَّ الْعَزِيزُ الْعَلِيمُ ۝

10. (Yea, the same that) has made for you the earth spread out, and has made for you roads (and channels) therein, in order that ye may find guidance (on the way);

الَّذِي جَعَلَ لَكُمُ الْأَرْضَ مَهْدًا وَجَعَلَ لَكُمْ فِيهَا سُبُلًا لَّعَلَّكُمْ تَهْتَدُونَ ۝

11. That sends down (from time to time) rain from the sky in due measure;— and We raise to life therewith a land that is dead; even so will ye be raised (from the dead);—

وَالَّذِي نَزَّلَ مِنَ السَّمَاءِ مَاءً بِقَدَرٍ فَأَنشَرْنَا بِهِ بَلْدَةً مَّيْتًا كَذَلِكَ تُخْرَجُونَ ۝

12. That has created pairs in all things,

وَالَّذِي خَلَقَ الْأَزْوَاجَ كُلَّهَا وَجَعَلَ

and has made for you ships and cattle on which ye ride,

13. In order that ye may sit firm and square on their backs, and when so seated, ye may remember the (kind) favour of your Lord, and say, "Glory to Him Who has subjected these to our (use), for we could never be able to do it.

14. "And to our Lord, surely, must we turn back!"

15. Yet they attribute to some of His servants a share with Him truly is man clearly unthankful.

16. What! Has He taken daughter out of what He himself creates, and granted to you sons for choice?

17. When news is brought to one of them of (the birth of) what he sets up as a likeness to (Allah) Most Gracious, his face darkens, and he is filled with inward grief!

18. Is then one brought up among trinkets, and unable to give a clear account in a dispute (to be associated with Allah)?

19. And they make into females angels who themselves serve Allah. Did they witness their creation? Their evidence will be recorded, and they will be called to account!

20. ("Ah!") they say, "If it had been the Will of The Most Gracious, we should not have worshipped such (deities)!" Of that they have no knowledge! They do nothing but lie!

21. What! have We given them a Book before this, to which they are holding fast?

22. Nay! they say: "We found our fathers following a certain religion, and we do guide ourselves by their footsteps."

23. Just in the same way, whenever We sent a Warner before thee to any people, the wealthy ones among them said: "We found our fathers following a certain religion,

and we will certainly follow in their footsteps."

24. He said "What! even if I brought you better guidance than that which ye found your fathers following?" They said: "For us, we deny that which ye (prophets) are sent with."

25. So We exacted retribution from them: now see what was the end of those who rejected (Truth)!

26. Behold! Abraham said to his father and his people: "I do indeed clear myself of what ye worship:

27. "(I worship) only Him Who originated me, and He will certainly guide me."

28. And he left it as a Word to endure among those who came after him, that they may turn back (to Allah).

29. Yea, I have given the good things of this life to these (men) and their fathers, until the Truth has come to them, and a Messenger making things clear.

30. But when the Truth came to them, they said: "This is sorcery, and we do reject it."

31. Also, they say: "Why is not this Qur'ān sent down to some leading man in either of the two (chief) cities?"

32. Is it they who would portion out the Mercy of thy Lord? It is We Who portion out between them their livelihood in the life of this world: and We raise some of them above others in ranks, so that some may command work from others. But the Mercy of thy Lord is better than the (wealth) which they amass.

33. And were it not that (all) men might become one community We would provide, for everyone that blasphemes against The Most Gracious, silver roofs for their houses, and (silver) stairways on which to go up,

34. And (silver) doors to their houses, and couches (of silver) on which they could recline,

35. And also adornments of gold. But all this was nothing but enjoyment of the

اَثَرِهِمْ مُقْتَدُوْنَ ۝

قُلْ اَوَلَوْجِئْتُكُمْ بِاَهْدٰى مِمَّا وَجَدْتُّمْ عَلَيْهِ اٰبَآءَكُمْ قَالُوْآ اِنَّا بِمَآ اُرْسِلْتُمْ بِهٖ كٰفِرُوْنَ ۝

فَانْتَقَمْنَا مِنْهُمْ فَانْظُرْ كَيْفَ كَانَ عَاقِبَةُ الْمُكَذِّبِيْنَ ۝

وَاِذْ قَالَ اِبْرٰهِيْمُ لِاَبِيْهِ وَقَوْمِهٖٓ اِنَّنِيْ بَرَآءٌ مِّمَّا تَعْبُدُوْنَ ۝

اِلَّا الَّذِيْ فَطَرَنِيْ فَاِنَّهٗ سَيَهْدِيْنِ ۝

وَجَعَلَهَا كَلِمَةً بَاقِيَةً فِيْ عَقِبِهٖ لَعَلَّهُمْ يَرْجِعُوْنَ ۝

بَلْ مَتَّعْتُ هٰٓؤُلَآءِ وَاٰبَآءَهُمْ حَتّٰى جَآءَهُمُ الْحَقُّ وَرَسُوْلٌ مُّبِيْنٌ ۝

وَلَمَّا جَآءَهُمُ الْحَقُّ قَالُوْا هٰذَا سِحْرٌ وَّاِنَّا بِهٖ كٰفِرُوْنَ ۝

وَقَالُوْا لَوْلَا نُزِّلَ هٰذَا الْقُرْاٰنُ عَلٰى رَجُلٍ مِّنَ الْقَرْيَتَيْنِ عَظِيْمٍ ۝

اَهُمْ يَقْسِمُوْنَ رَحْمَتَ رَبِّكَ نَحْنُ قَسَمْنَا بَيْنَهُمْ مَّعِيْشَتَهُمْ فِي الْحَيٰوةِ الدُّنْيَا وَ رَفَعْنَا بَعْضَهُمْ فَوْقَ بَعْضٍ دَرَجٰتٍ لِّيَتَّخِذَ بَعْضُهُمْ بَعْضًا سُخْرِيًّا وَرَحْمَتُ رَبِّكَ خَيْرٌ مِّمَّا يَجْمَعُوْنَ ۝

وَلَوْلَآ اَنْ يَّكُوْنَ النَّاسُ اُمَّةً وَّاحِدَةً لَّجَعَلْنَا لِمَنْ يَّكْفُرُ بِالرَّحْمٰنِ لِبُيُوْتِهِمْ سُقُفًا مِّنْ فِضَّةٍ وَّمَعَارِجَ عَلَيْهَا يَظْهَرُوْنَ ۝

وَلِبُيُوْتِهِمْ اَبْوَابًا وَّسُرُرًا عَلَيْهَا يَتَّكِئُوْنَ ۝

وَزُخْرُفًا وَاِنْ كُلُّ ذٰلِكَ لَمَّا مَتَاعُ

present life: the Hereafter, in the sight of thy Lord, is for the Righteous.

36. If anyone withdraws himself from remembrance of The Most Gracious, We appoint for him a Satan, to be an intimate companion to him.

37. Such (Satans) really hinder them from the Path, but they think that they are being guided aright!

38. At length, when (such a one) comes to Us, he says (to his evil companion): "Would that between me and thee were the distance of East and West!" Ah! evil is the companion (indeed)!

39. When ye have done wrong, it will avail you nothing, that day, that ye shall be partners in punishment!

40. Canst thou then make the deaf to hear, or give direction to the blind or to such as (wander) in manifest error?

41. Even if We take thee away, We shall be sure to exact retribution from them,

42. Or We shall show thee that (accomplished) which We have promised them: for verily We have power over them.

43. So hold thou fast to the Revelation sent down to thee: verily thou art on a Straight Way.

44. The (Qur-ān) is indeed a Reminder for thee and for thy people; and soon shall ye (all) be brought to account.

45. And question thou our messengers whom We sent before thee; did We appoint any deities other than The Most Gracious, to be worshipped?

46. We did send Moses aforetime, with Our Signs, to Pharaoh and his Chiefs: he said, "I am a messenger of the Lord of the Worlds."

47. But when he came to them with Our Signs, behold, they laughed at them.

48. We showed them Sign after Sign, each greater than its fellow, and We seized them with Punishment, in order that they might turn (to Us).

49. And they said, "O thou sorcerer! Invoke thy Lord for us according to His covenant with thee; for we shall truly accept guidance."—

وَقَالُوْا يَا يُهَ السّٰحِرُ ادْعُ لَنَا رَبَّكَ بِمَا عَهِدَ عِنْدَكَ اِنَّنَا لَمُهْتَدُوْنَ ۝

50. But when We removed the Chastisement from them, behold, they broke their word.

فَلَمَّا كَشَفْنَا عَنْهُمُ الْعَذَابَ اِذَا هُمْ يَنْكُثُوْنَ ۝

51. And Pharaoh proclaimed among his people, saying: "O my people! Does not the dominion of Egypt belong to me, (witness) these streams flowing underneath my (palace)? What! See ye not then?

وَنَادٰى فِرْعَوْنُ فِيْ قَوْمِهٖ قَالَ يٰقَوْمِ اَلَيْسَ لِيْ مُلْكُ مِصْرَ وَهٰذِهِ الْاَنْهٰرُ تَجْرِيْ مِنْ تَحْتِيْ ۚ اَفَلَا تُبْصِرُوْنَ ۝

52. "Am I not better than this (Moses), who is a contemptible wretch and can scarcely express himself clearly?

اَمْ اَنَا خَيْرٌ مِّنْ هٰذَا الَّذِيْ هُوَ مَهِيْنٌ ۙ وَّلَا يَكَادُ يُبِيْنُ ۝

53. "Then why are not gold bracelets bestowed on him, or (why) come (not) with him angels accompanying him in procession?"

فَلَوْلَا اُلْقِيَ عَلَيْهِ اَسْوِرَةٌ مِّنْ ذَهَبٍ اَوْ جَآءَ مَعَهُ الْمَلٰٓئِكَةُ مُقْتَرِنِيْنَ ۝

54. Thus did he make fools of his people, and they obeyed him: truly were they a people rebellious (against Allah).

فَاسْتَخَفَّ قَوْمَهٗ فَاَطَاعُوْهُ ۚ اِنَّهُمْ كَانُوْا قَوْمًا فٰسِقِيْنَ ۝

55. When at length they provoked Us, We exacted retribution from them, and We drowned them all.

فَلَمَّا اٰسَفُوْنَا انْتَقَمْنَا مِنْهُمْ فَاَغْرَقْنٰهُمْ اَجْمَعِيْنَ ۙ

56. And We made them (a People) of the Past and an Example to later ages.

فَجَعَلْنٰهُمْ سَلَفًا وَّمَثَلًا لِّلْاٰخِرِيْنَ ۝

57. When (Jesus) the son of Mary is held up as an example, behold, thy people raise a clamour threat (in ridicule)!

وَلَمَّا ضُرِبَ ابْنُ مَرْيَمَ مَثَلًا اِذَا قَوْمُكَ مِنْهُ يَصِدُّوْنَ ۝

58. And they say, "Are our gods best, or he?" This they set forth to thee, only by way of disputation: yea, they are a contentious people.

وَقَالُوْا ءَاٰلِهَتُنَا خَيْرٌ اَمْ هُوَ ۭ مَا ضَرَبُوْهُ لَكَ اِلَّا جَدَلًا ۭ بَلْ هُمْ قَوْمٌ خَصِمُوْنَ ۝

59. He was no more than a servant: We granted Our favour to him, and We made him an example to the Children of Israel.

اِنْ هُوَ اِلَّا عَبْدٌ اَنْعَمْنَا عَلَيْهِ وَجَعَلْنٰهُ مَثَلًا لِّبَنِيْ اِسْرَآءِيْلَ ۝

60. And if it were Our Will, We could make angels from amongst you, succeeding each other on the earth.

وَلَوْ نَشَآءُ لَجَعَلْنَا مِنْكُمْ مَّلٰٓئِكَةً فِي الْاَرْضِ يَخْلُفُوْنَ ۝

61. And (Jesus) shall be a Sign (for the coming of) the Hour (Of Judgment): therefore have no doubt about the (Hour), but follow ye Me: this is a Straight Way.

وَاِنَّهٗ لَعِلْمٌ لِّلسَّاعَةِ فَلَا تَمْتَرُنَّ بِهَا وَاتَّبِعُوْنِ ۭ هٰذَا صِرَاطٌ مُّسْتَقِيْمٌ ۝

62. Let not Satan hinder you: for he is to you an enemy avowed.

وَلَا يَصُدَّنَّكُمُ الشَّيْطٰنُ ۚ اِنَّهٗ لَكُمْ عَدُوٌّ مُّبِيْنٌ ۝

63. When Jesus came with Clear Signs, he said: "Now have I come to you with Wisdom, and in order to make clear to you some of the (points) on which ye dispute: therefore fear Allah and obey me.

وَلَمَّا جَآءَ عِيسَى بِالْبَيِّنَتِ قَالَ قَـدْ جِئْتُكُم بِالْحِكْمَةِ وَلِأُبَيِّنَ لَكُم بَعْضَ الَّذِى تَخْتَلِفُونَ فِيهِ فَاتَّقُوا اللَّهَ وَأَطِيعُونِ ۝

64. "For Allah, He is my Lord and your Lord: so worship ye Him: this is a Straight Way."

إِنَّ اللَّهَ هُوَ رَبِّى وَرَبُّكُمْ فَاعْبُدُوهُ هَذَا صِرَاطٌ مُّسْتَقِيمٌ ۝

65. But sects from among themselves fell into disagreement: then woe to the wrongdoers, from the Chastisement of a Grievous Day!

فَاخْتَلَفَ الْأَحْزَابُ مِنْ بَيْنِهِمْ فَوَيْلٌ لِّلَّذِينَ ظَلَمُوا مِنْ عَذَابِ يَوْمٍ أَلِيمٍ ۝

66. Do they only wait for the Hour—that it should come on them all of a sudden, while they perceive not?

هَلْ يَنظُرُونَ إِلَّا السَّاعَةَ أَن تَأْتِيَهُم بَغْتَةً وَهُمْ لَا يَشْعُرُونَ ۝

67. Friends on that Day will be foes, one to another,—except the Righteous.

الْأَخِلَّآءُ يَوْمَئِذٍ بَعْضُهُمْ لِبَعْضٍ عَدُوٌّ إِلَّا الْمُتَّقِينَ ۝

68. My devotees! no fear shall be on you today nor shall ye grieve,—

يَعِبَادِ لَا خَوْفٌ عَلَيْكُمُ الْيَوْمَ وَلَا أَنتُمْ تَحْزَنُونَ ۝

69. Those who have believed in Our Signs and submitted (to Us).

الَّذِينَ ءَامَنُوا بِآيَاتِنَا وَكَانُوا مُسْلِمِينَ ۝

70. Enter ye the Garden, ye and your wives, in (beauty and) rejoicing.

ادْخُلُوا الْجَنَّةَ أَنتُمْ وَأَزْوَاجُكُمْ تُحْبَرُونَ ۝

71. To them will be passed round, dishes and goblets of gold: there will be there all that the souls could desire, all that the eyes could delight in: and ye shall abide therein (for aye).

يُطَافُ عَلَيْهِم بِصِحَافٍ مِّن ذَهَبٍ وَأَكْوَابٍ وَفِيهَا مَا تَشْتَهِيهِ الْأَنفُسُ وَتَلَذُّ الْأَعْيُنُ وَأَنتُمْ فِيهَا خَالِدُونَ ۝

72. Such will be the Garden of which ye are made heirs for your (good) deeds (in life).

وَتِلْكَ الْجَنَّةُ الَّتِى أُورِثْتُمُوهَا بِمَا كُنتُمْ تَعْمَلُونَ ۝

73. Ye shall have therein abundance of fruit from which ye shall eat.

74. The Sinners will be in the Punishment of Hell, to dwell therein (for aye):

لَكُمْ فِيهَا فَاكِهَةٌ كَثِيرَةٌ مِّنْهَا تَأْكُلُونَ ۝

75. Nowise will the (punishment) be lightened for them, and in despair will they be there overwhelmed.

إِنَّ الْمُجْرِمِينَ فِى عَذَابِ جَهَنَّمَ خَالِدُونَ ۝ لَا يُفَتَّرُ عَنْهُمْ وَهُمْ فِيهِ مُبْلِسُونَ ۝

76. Nowise shall We be unjust to them: but it is they who have been unjust themselves.

وَمَا ظَلَمْنَاهُمْ وَلَكِن كَانُوا هُمُ الظَّالِمِينَ ۝

77. They will cry: "O Malik! would that thy Lord put an end to us!" He will say, "Nay, but ye shall abide!"

78. Verily We have brought the Truth to you: but most of you have a hatred for Truth.

79. What! Have they settled some Plan (among themselves)? But it is We Who settle things.

80. Or do they think that We hear not their secrets and their private counsels? Indeed (We do), and Our Messengers are by them, to record.

81. Say: "If The Most Gracious had a son, I would be the first to worship."

82. Glory to the Lord of the heavens and the earth, the Lord of the Throne ! he is free from the things they attribute (to Him)!

83. So leave them to babble and play (with vanities) until they meet that Day of theirs, which they have been promised.

84. It is He Who is God in heaven and God on earth; and He is Full of Wisdom and Knowledge.

85. And blessed is He to Whom belongs the dominion of the heavens and the earth, and all between them: with Him is the knowledge of the Hour (of Judgment): and to Him shall ye be brought back.

86. And those whom they invoke besides Allah have no power of intercession;—only he who bears witness to the Truth, and with full knowledge.

87. If thou ask them, who created them, they will certainly say, Allah: how then are they deluded away (from the Truth)?

88. (Allah has knowledge) of the (Prophet's) cry, "O my Lord! Truly these are a people who believe not!"

89. But turn away from them, and say "Peace!" But soon shall they know!

SÛRA–44
AD-DUKHĀN
(INTRODUCTION)

For the chronology and the general theme of the Sûras of the *Ḥā-Mîm* series, of which this is the fifth, see the Introduction to S. 40.

The theme of this particular Sûra is how worldly pride and power are humbled in the dust if they resist spiritual forces, and how Evil and Good find their true setting in the Hereafter.

The title-word *Dukhān* occurs in verse 10. It means smoke or mist, and may refer to a drought or famine.

Ad-Dukhān, or Smoke (or Mist)

In the name of Allah, Most Gracious, Most Merciful.

1. Ḥā Mīm.

2. By the Book that makes things clear;—

3. We sent it down during a blessed night: for We (ever) wish to warn (against Evil).

4. In that (night) is made distinct every affair of wisdom,

5. By command, from Us. For We (ever) send (revelations),

6. As a Mercy from thy Lord; for He hears and knows (all things);

7. The Lord of the heavens and the earth and all between them, if ye (but) have an assured faith.

8. There is no god but He: it is He Who gives life and gives death,— the Lord and Cherisher to you and your earliest ancestors.

9. Yet they play about in doubt.

10. Then watch thou for the Day that the sky will bring forth a kind of smoke (or mist) plainly visible.

11. Enveloping the people: this will be a Chastisement grievous.

12. (They will say:) "Our Lord! Remove the Chastisement from us, for we do really believe!"

13. How should they have the Reminder. Seeing that a Messenger explaining things clearly has (already) come to them,—

14. Yet they turn away from him and say: "Tutored (by others), a man possessed!"

15. We shall indeed remove the Chastisement for a while, (but) truly ye will revert (to your ways).

16. The day We shall seize you with a mighty onslaught: We will indeed (then) exact Retribution!

17. We did, before them, try the people of Pharaoh: there came to them a messenger most honourable,

18. Saying: "Restore to me the servants of Allah: I am to you a messenger worthy of all trust;

19. "And be not arrogant as against Allah:

for I come to you with authority manifest.

20. "For me, I have sought safety with my Lord and your Lord, against your injuring me.

21. "If ye believe me not, at least keep yourselves away from me."

22. (But they were aggressive:) then he cried to his Lord: "These are indeed a people given to sin."

23. (The reply came:) "March forth with my servants by night: for ye are sure to be pursued.

24. "And leave the sea as a furrow (divided): for they are a host (destined) to be drowned."

25. How many were the gardens and springs they left behind,

26. And corn-fields and noble buildings,

27. And pleasant things wherein they had taken such delight!

28. Thus (was their end)! and We made other people inherit (those things)!

29. And neither heaven nor earth shed a tear over them: nor were they given a respite (again).

30. We did deliver aforetime the Children of Israel from humiliating Punishment,

31. Inflicted by Pharaoh, for he was arrogant (even) among inordinate transgressors.

32. And We chose them afore-time above the nations, knowingly,

33. And granted them Signs in which there was a manifest trial.

34. As to these (Quraish), they say forsooth:

35. "There is nothing beyond our first death, and we shall not be raised again.

36. "Then bring (back) our forefathers, if what ye say is true!"

37. What! are they better than the people of Tubba' and those who were before them? We destroyed them because they were

guilty of sin.

مُجْرِمِينَ ۞

38. We created not the heavens, the earth, and all between them, merely in (idle) sport:

وَمَا خَلَقْنَا السَّمٰوٰتِ وَالْأَرْضَ وَمَا بَيْنَهُمَا لٰعِبِينَ ۞

39. We created them not except for just ends: but most of them do not know.

مَا خَلَقْنٰهُمَا إِلَّا بِالْحَقِّ وَلٰكِنَّ أَكْثَرَهُمْ لَا يَعْلَمُونَ ۞

40. Verily the Day of sorting Out is the time appointed for all of them,—

إِنَّ يَوْمَ الْفَصْلِ مِيقَاتُهُمْ أَجْمَعِينَ ۙ۞

41. The Day when no protector can avail his client in aught, and no help can they receive,

يَوْمَ لَا يُغْنِي مَوْلًى عَنْ مَوْلًى شَيْئًا وَّلَا هُمْ يُنْصَرُونَ ۞

42. Except such as receive Allah's Mercy: for He is exalted in Might, Most Merciful.

إِلَّا مَنْ رَّحِمَ اللّٰهُ ۚ إِنَّهُ هُوَ الْعَزِيزُ الرَّحِيمُ ۞

43. Verily the tree of Zaqqum

إِنَّ شَجَرَتَ الزَّقُّومِ ۞

44. Will be the food of the Sinful,—

طَعَامُ الْأَثِيمِ ۞

45. Like molten brass; it will boil in their insides,
46. Like the boiling of scalding water.

كَالْمُهْلِ ۚ يَغْلِي فِي الْبُطُونِ ۞ كَغَلْيِ الْحَمِيمِ ۞

47. (A voice will cry:) "Seize ye him and drag him into the midst of the Blazing Fire!

خُذُوهُ فَاعْتِلُوهُ إِلٰى سَوَاءِ الْجَحِيمِ ۞

48. "Then pour over his head the Chastisement of Boiling Water;

ثُمَّ صُبُّوا فَوْقَ رَأْسِهِ مِنْ عَذَابِ الْحَمِيمِ ۞

49. "Taste thou (this)! Truly thou art mighty, full of honour!

ذُقْ ۚ إِنَّكَ أَنْتَ الْعَزِيزُ الْكَرِيمُ ۞

50. "Truly this is what ye used to doubt!"

إِنَّ هٰذَا مَا كُنْتُمْ بِهِ تَمْتَرُونَ ۞

51. As to the Righteous (they will be) in a position of Security,

إِنَّ الْمُتَّقِينَ فِي مَقَامٍ أَمِينٍ ۞

52. Among Gardens and Springs;

فِي جَنّٰتٍ وَّعُيُونٍ ۞

53. Dressed in fine silk and in rich brocade, they will face each other;

يَلْبَسُونَ مِنْ سُنْدُسٍ وَّإِسْتَبْرَقٍ مُّتَقَابِلِينَ ۞

54. So; and We shall wed them to maidens with beautiful, big, and lustrous eyes.

كَذٰلِكَ ۚ وَزَوَّجْنٰهُمْ بِحُورٍ عِينٍ ۞

55. There can they call for every kind of fruit in peace and security;

يَدْعُونَ فِيهَا بِكُلِّ فَاكِهَةٍ آمِنِينَ ۞

56. Nor will they there taste Death, except the first death; and He will preserve them from the Chastisement of the Blazing Fire.—

لَا يَذُوقُونَ فِيهَا الْمَوْتَ إِلَّا الْمَوْتَةَ الْأُولٰى ۚ وَوَقٰهُمْ عَذَابَ الْجَحِيمِ ۞

SÛRA–45
AL-JĀTHIYA
(INTRODUCTION)

This is the sixth Sûra of *Ḥā-Mîm* series: for their general theme and chronology, see the Introduction to S. 40.

57. As a Bounty from thy Lord! That will be the supreme achievement!

58. Verily, We have made this (Qur-ān) easy, in thy tongue, in order that they may give heed.

59. So wait thou and watch; for they (too) are waiting.

Al-Jāthiya, or Bowing the Knee

In the name of Allah, Most Gracious, Most Merciful.

1. Hā-Mîm.

2. The revelation of the Book is from Allah the Exalted in Power, full of Wisdom.

3. Verily in the heavens and the earth, are Signs for those who believe.

4. And in the creation of yourselves and the fact that animals are scattered (through the earth), are Signs for those of assured Faith.

5. And in the alternation of Night and Day, and the fact that Allah sends down Sustenance from the sky, and revives therewith the earth after its death, and in the change of the winds,— are Signs for those that are wise.

6. Such are the Signs of Allah, which We rehearse to thee in truth: then in what exposition will they believe after Allah and His Signs?

7. Woe to each sinful imposter.

8. He hears the Signs of Allah rehearsed to him, yet is obstinate and lofty, as if he had not heard them: then announce to him a Chastisement Grievous!

9. And when he learns something of Our Signs, He takes them in jest: for such there will be a humiliating Chastisement.

10. In front of them is Hell: and of no profit to them is anything they may have earned, nor any protectors they may have taken to themselves besides Allah: for them is a tremendous Chastisement.

فَضْلًا مِّن رَّبِّكَ ۚ ذَٰلِكَ هُوَ الْفَوْزُ الْعَظِيمُ ۝

فَإِنَّمَا يَسَّرْنَهُ بِلِسَانِكَ لَعَلَّهُمْ يَتَذَكَّرُونَ ۝

فَارْتَقِبْ إِنَّهُم مُّرْتَقِبُونَ ۝

بِسْمِ اللَّهِ الرَّحْمَٰنِ الرَّحِيمِ

حٰمٓ ۝ تَنزِيلُ الْكِتَٰبِ مِنَ اللَّهِ الْعَزِيزِ الْحَكِيمِ ۝

إِنَّ فِي السَّمَٰوَٰتِ وَالْأَرْضِ لَآيَٰتٍ لِّلْمُؤْمِنِينَ ۝

وَفِي خَلْقِكُمْ وَمَا يَبُثُّ مِن دَآبَّةٍ ءَايَٰتٌ لِّقَوْمٍ يُوقِنُونَ ۝

وَاخْتِلَٰفِ الَّيْلِ وَالنَّهَارِ وَمَآ أَنزَلَ اللَّهُ مِنَ السَّمَآءِ مِن رِّزْقٍ فَأَحْيَا بِهِ الْأَرْضَ بَعْدَ مَوْتِهَا وَتَصْرِيفِ الرِّيَٰحِ ءَايَٰتٌ لِّقَوْمٍ يَعْقِلُونَ ۝

تِلْكَ ءَايَٰتُ اللَّهِ نَتْلُوهَا عَلَيْكَ بِالْحَقِّ ۖ فَبِأَيِّ حَدِيثٍ بَعْدَ اللَّهِ وَءَايَٰتِهِ يُؤْمِنُونَ ۝

وَيْلٌ لِّكُلِّ أَفَّاكٍ أَثِيمٍ ۝

يَسْمَعُ ءَايَٰتِ اللَّهِ تُتْلَىٰ عَلَيْهِ ثُمَّ يُصِرُّ مُسْتَكْبِرًا كَأَن لَّمْ يَسْمَعْهَا ۖ فَبَشِّرْهُ بِعَذَابٍ أَلِيمٍ ۝

وَإِذَا عَلِمَ مِنْ ءَايَٰتِنَا شَيْئًا اتَّخَذَهَا هُزُوًا ۚ أُوْلَٰئِكَ لَهُمْ عَذَابٌ مُّهِينٌ ۝

مِّن وَرَآئِهِمْ جَهَنَّمُ ۖ وَلَا يُغْنِي عَنْهُم مَّا كَسَبُوا شَيْئًا وَلَا مَا اتَّخَذُوا مِن دُونِ اللَّهِ أَوْلِيَآءَ ۖ وَلَهُمْ عَذَابٌ عَظِيمٌ ۝

11. This is (true) Guidance: and for tho-se who reject the Signs of their Lord, is a grievous Chastisement of abomination.

12. It is Allah Who has subjected the sea to you, that ships may sail through it by His command, that ye may seek of His Bounty, and that ye may be grateful.

13. And He has subjected to you, as from Him, all that is in the heavens and on earth: behold, in that are Signs indeed for those who reflect.

14. Tell those who believe, to forgive those who do not hope for the Days of Allah; it is for Him to recompense (for good or ill) each People according to what they have earned.

15. If any one does a righteous deed, it is to his own benefit; if he does evil, it works against (his own soul). In the end will ye (all) be brought back to your Lord.

16. We did aforetime grant to the Children of Israel the Book, the Power of Command, and Prophethood; We gave them, for Sustenance, things good and pure; and We favoured them above the nations.

17. And We granted them Clear Signs in affairs (of Religion): it was only after knowledge had been granted to them that they fell into schisms, through insolent envy among themselves. Verily thy Lord will judge between them on the Day of Judgment as to those matters in which they set up differences.

18. Then We put thee on the (right) Way of Religion: so follow thou that (Way), and follow not the desires of those who know not.

19. They will be of no use to thee in the sight of Allah: it is only wrong-doers (that stand as) protectors, one to another: but Allah is the Protector of the Righteous.

20. These are clear evidences to men, and a Guidance and Mercy to those of assured Faith.

21. What! do those who do evil deeds think that We shall make them as equal with those who believe and do righteous deeds,—that equal will be their life and their death? Ill is the judgment that they make.

22. Allah created the heavens and the earth for just ends, and in order that each soul may find the recompense of what it has earned, and none of them shall be wronged.

23. Then seest thou such a one as takes as his god his own vain desire? Allah has, knowing (him as such), left him astray, and sealed his hearing and his heart (and understanding), and put a cover on his sight. Who, then, will guide him after Allah (has withdrawn guidance)? Will ye not then receive admonition?

24. And they say: "What is there but our life in this world? We shall die and we live, and nothing but Time can destroy us." But of that they have no knowledge: they merely conjecture:

25. And when Our Clear signs are rehearsed to them, their argument is nothing but this: they say, "Bring (back) our forefathers, if what ye say is true!"

26. Say: "It is Allah Who gives you life, then gives you death; then he will gather you together for the Day of Judgment about which there is no doubt": but most men do not know.

27. To Allah belongs the dominion of the heavens and the earth, and the Day that the Hour of Judgment is established,— that Day will the followers of Falsehood perish!

28. And thou wilt see every nation bowing the knee: every nation will be called to its Record: "This Day shall ye be recompensed for all that ye did!

29. "This Our Record speaks about you with truth: for We were wont to put on record all that ye did."

SÛRA–46
AL-AḤQĀF
(INTRODUCTION)

This is the seventh and last Sûra of the *Ḥā-Mîm* series. For the general theme and chronological place of these Sûras see the Introduction to S. 40.

The *Aḥqāf* (mentioned in verse 21) are the long and winding crooked tracts of sand-hills, characteristic of the country of the 'Ād people, adjoining Ḥaḍhramaut and Yaman: See 7: 65. These people had, at that time, probably a fertile irrigated country, but their sins brought on the calamity, mentioned in 46: 24-25. The lesson of this Sûra is that if the Truth is challenged, the challenge will be duly answered, and Truth vindicated.

30. Then, as to those who beli-eved and did righteous deeds, their Lord will admit them to His Mercy: that will be the manifest triumph.

31. But as to those who rejected Allah, (to them will be said): "Were not Our Signs rehearsed to you? But ye were arrogant, and were a people given to sin!

32. "And when it was said that the promise of Allah was true, and that the Hour— there was no doubt about its (coming), ye used to say, 'We know not what is the Hour: we only think it a conjecture, and we have no firm assurance.'"

33. Then will appear to them the evil (fruits) of what they did, and they will be completely encircled by that which they used to mock at!

34. It will also be said: "This Day We will forget you as ye forgot the meeting of this Day of yours! And your abode is the Fire, and no helpers have ye!

35. "This, because ye used to take the Signs of Allah in jest, and the life of the world deceived you:" (from) that Day, therefore, they shall not be taken out thence, nor can they make amends.

36. Then Praise be to Allah, Lord of the heavens and Lord of the earth, Lord and Cherisher of all the worlds!

37. And unto Him (alone) belongeth Majesty in the heavens and the earth: and He is Exalted in Power, Full of Wisdom!

Al-Aḥqāf, or Winding Sand-tracts

In the name of Allah, Most Gracious, Most Merciful.

1. Ḥā-Mîm.

2. The revelation of the Book is from Allah the Exalted in Power, Full of Wisdom.

3. We created not the heavens and the earth and all between them but for just ends, and for a term appointed: but those who reject Faith turn away from that whereof they are warned.

4.   Say: "Do ye see what it is ye invoke besides Allah? Show me what it is they have created on earth, or have they a share in the heavens? Bring me a Book (revealed) before this, or any remnant of knowledge (ye may have), if ye are telling the truth!

5.   And who is more astray than one who invokes, besides Allah, such as will not answer him to the Day of Judgment, and who (in fact) are unconscious of their call (to them)?

6.   And when mankind are gathered together (at the Resurrection), they will be hostile to them and deny that (men) had worshipped them.

7.   When Our Clear Signs are rehearsed to them, the Unbelievers say, of the Truth when it comes to them: "This is evident sorcery!"

8.   Or do they say, "He has forged it"? Say: "Had I forged it, then ye have no power to help me against Allah. He knows best of that whereof ye talk (so glibly)! Enough is He for a witness between me and you! And He is oft-Forgiving, Most Merciful."

9.   Say: "I am not an innovation among the messengers, nor do I know what will be done with me or with you. I follow but that which is revealed to me by inspiration; I am but a Warner open and clear."

10.   Say: "See ye? If (this teaching) be from Allah, and ye reject it, and a witness from among the Children of Israel testifies to its similarity (with earlier scripture), and has believed while ye are arrogant, (how unjust ye are!) Truly, Allah guides not a people unjust."

11.   The Unbelievers say of those who believe: "If (this Message) were a good thing, (such men) would not have gone to it first, before us!" and seeing that they guide not themselves thereby, they will say, "This is an (old,) old falsehood!"

12. And before this, was the Book of Moses as a guide and a mercy: and this Book confirms (it) in the Arabic tongue; to admonish the unjust, and as Glad Tidings to those who do right.

13. Verily those who say, "Our Lord is Allah", and remain firm (on that Path),— on them shall be no fear, nor shall they grieve.

14. Such shall be Companions of the Garden, dwelling therein (for aye): a recompense for their (good) deeds.

15. We have enjoined on man kindness to his parents: in pain did his mother bear him, and in pain did she give him birth. The carrying of the (child) to his weaning is (a period of) thirty months. At length, when he reaches the age of full strength and attains forty years, he says, "O my Lord! grant me that I may be grateful for Thy favour which Thou hast bestowed upon me, and upon both my parents, and that I may work righteousness such as Thou mayest approve; and be gracious to me in my issue. Truly have I turned to Thee and truly do I submit (to Thee) in Islam."

16. Such are they from whom We shall accept the best of their deeds and pass by their ill deeds: (they shall be) among the Companions of the Garden: a promise of truth, which was made to them (in this life).

17. But (there is one) who says to his parents, "Fie on you! Do ye hold out the promise to me that I shall be raised up, even though generations have passed before me (without rising again)?" And they two seek Allah's aid, (and rebuke the son): "Woe to thee! Have Faith! For the promise of Allah is true." But he says, "This is nothing but tales of the ancients!"

18. Such are they against whom the word proved true among the previous generations of Jinns and men, that have passed away;

وَمِنْ قَبْلِهٖ كِتٰبُ مُوْسٰٓى اِمَامًا وَّرَحْمَةً ۖ وَّهٰذَا كِتٰبٌ مُّصَدِّقٌ لِّسَانًا عَرَبِيًّا لِّيُنْذِرَ الَّذِيْنَ ظَلَمُوْا ۖ وَبُشْرٰى لِلْمُحْسِنِيْنَ ۝

اِنَّ الَّذِيْنَ قَالُوْا رَبُّنَا اللّٰهُ ثُمَّ اسْتَقَامُوْا فَلَا خَوْفٌ عَلَيْهِمْ وَلَا هُمْ يَحْزَنُوْنَ ۝

اُولٰٓئِكَ اَصْحٰبُ الْجَنَّةِ خٰلِدِيْنَ فِيْهَا ۚ جَزَآءً بِمَا كَانُوْا يَعْمَلُوْنَ ۝

وَوَصَّيْنَا الْاِنْسَانَ بِوَالِدَيْهِ اِحْسٰنًا ۖ حَمَلَتْهُ اُمُّهٗ كُرْهًا وَّوَضَعَتْهُ كُرْهًا ۖ وَحَمْلُهٗ وَفِصٰلُهٗ ثَلٰثُوْنَ شَهْرًا ۚ حَتّٰٓى اِذَا بَلَغَ اَشُدَّهٗ وَبَلَغَ اَرْبَعِيْنَ سَنَةً ۙ قَالَ رَبِّ اَوْزِعْنِيْٓ اَنْ اَشْكُرَ نِعْمَتَكَ الَّتِيْٓ اَنْعَمْتَ عَلَيَّ وَعَلٰى وَالِدَيَّ وَاَنْ اَعْمَلَ صَالِحًا تَرْضٰهُ وَاَصْلِحْ لِيْ فِيْ ذُرِّيَّتِيْ ۚ اِنِّيْ تُبْتُ اِلَيْكَ وَاِنِّيْ مِنَ الْمُسْلِمِيْنَ ۝

اُولٰٓئِكَ الَّذِيْنَ نَتَقَبَّلُ عَنْهُمْ اَحْسَنَ مَا عَمِلُوْا وَنَتَجَاوَزُ عَنْ سَيِّاٰتِهِمْ فِيْٓ اَصْحٰبِ الْجَنَّةِ ۖ وَعْدَ الصِّدْقِ الَّذِيْ كَانُوْا يُوْعَدُوْنَ ۝

وَالَّذِيْ قَالَ لِوَالِدَيْهِ اُفٍّ لَّكُمَآ اَتَعِدٰنِنِيْٓ اَنْ اُخْرَجَ وَقَدْ خَلَتِ الْقُرُوْنُ مِنْ قَبْلِيْ ۚ وَهُمَا يَسْتَغِيْثٰنِ اللّٰهَ وَيْلَكَ اٰمِنْ ۖ اِنَّ وَعْدَ اللّٰهِ حَقٌّ ۖ فَيَقُوْلُ مَا هٰذَآ اِلَّآ اَسَاطِيْرُ الْاَوَّلِيْنَ ۝

اُولٰٓئِكَ الَّذِيْنَ حَقَّ عَلَيْهِمُ الْقَوْلُ فِيْٓ اُمَمٍ قَدْ خَلَتْ مِنْ قَبْلِهِمْ مِّنَ الْجِنِّ وَالْاِنْسِ ۚ اِنَّهُمْ كَانُوْا

for they will be (utterly) lost.

19. And to all are (assigned) degrees according to the deeds which they (have done), and in order that (Allah) may recompense their deeds; and no injustice will be done to them.

20. And on the Day that the Unbelievers will be placed before the Fire, (it will be said to them): "Ye squandered your good things in the life of the world, and ye took your pleasure out of them: but to-day shall ye be recompensed with a Chastisement of humiliation: for that ye were arrogant on earth without just cause, and that ye (ever) transgressed."

21. Mention (Hûd) one of 'Âd's (own) brethren: behold, he warned his people beside the winding Sand-tracts: but there have been Warners before him and after him: "Worship ye none other than Allah: truly I fear for you the Chastisement of a Mighty Day."

22. They said: "Hast thou come in order to turn us aside from our gods? Then bring upon us the (calamity) with which thou dost threaten us, if thou art telling the truth!"

23. He said: "The Knowledge (of when it will come) is only with Allah: I proclaim to you the mission on which I have been sent: but I see that ye are a people in ignorance!"...

24. Then, when they saw a cloud advancing towards their valleys, they said, "This cloud will give us rain!" "Nay, it is the (calamity) ye are asking to be hastened!— a wind wherein is a Grievous Chastisement!

25. "Everything will it destroy by the command of its Lord!" then by the morning they— nothing was to be seen but (the ruins of) their houses! Thus do We recompense those given to sin!

26. And We had firmly established them in a (prosperity and) power which We have not given to you (ye Quraish!) and We had endowed them with (faculties of) hearing,

seeing, heart and intellect: but of no profit to them were their (faculties of) hearing, sight, and heart and intellect, when they went on rejecting the Signs of Allah: and they were (completely) encircled by that which they used to mock at!

27. We destroyed aforetime towns round about you; and We have shown the Signs in various ways, that they may turn (to Us).

28. Why then was no help forthcoming to them from those whom they worshipped as gods, besides Allah, as a means of access (to Allah)? Nay, they left them in the lurch: but that was their falsehood and their invention.

29. Behold, We turned towards thee a company of Jinns (quietly) listening to the Qur'ān: when they stood in the presence thereof, they said, "Listen in silence!" When the (reading) was finished, they returned to their people, to warn them.

30. They said, "O our people! we have heard a Book revealed after Moses, confirming what came before it: it guides to the Truth and to a Straight Path.

31. "O our people, hearken to the one who invites (you) to Allah, and believe in him: He will forgive you your faults, and deliver you from a Chastisement Grievous.

32. "If any does not hearken to the one who invites (us) to Allah, he cannot escape in the earth, and no protectors can he have besides Allah: such are in manifest error."

33. See they not that Allah, Who created the heavens and the earth, and never wearied with their creation, is able to give life to the dead? Yea, verily He has power over all things.

34. And on the Day that the Unbelievers will be placed before the Fire, (they will be asked,) "Is this not the Truth?"

SÛRA–47
MUHAMMAD
(INTRODUCTION)

We have examined and followed the current arrangement of the Sûras according to subject-matter and independently of Chronology, and we have found that a logical thread runs through them. We have now finished more than five-sixths of the Qur-ān. The remaining sixth consists of short Sûras, but these are again grouped according to subject-matter.

We begin the first of such groups with a group of three Sûras (47 to 49), which deal with the organisation of the Muslim Ummat or community both for external defence and in internal relations. The present Sûra deals with the necessity of defence against external foes by courage and strenous fighting, and dates from about the first of the Hijra, when the Muslims were under threat of extinction by invasion from Makkah.

They will say, "Yea, by our Lord" (he will say:) "Then taste ye the Chastisement, for that ye were wont to deny (Truth)!"

35. Therefore patiently persevere, as did (all) messengers of firm resolution; and be in no haste about the (Unbelievers). On the Day that they see the (Punishment) promised them, (it will be) as if they had not tarried more than an hour in a single day. (Thine but) to deliver the Message: but shall any be destroyed except those who transgress?

Muḥammad (the Prophet)

In the name of Allah, Most Gracious Most Merciful.

1. Those who reject Allah and hinder (men) from the Path of Allah,—their deeds will Allah bring to naught.

2. But those who believe and work deeds of righteousness, and believe in the (Revelation) sent down to Muḥammad—for it is the Truth from their Lord,— he will remove from them their ills and improve their condition.

3. This because those who reject Allah follow falsehood. While those who believe follow the Truth from their Lord: thus does Allah set forth for men their lessons by similitudes.

4. Therefore, when ye meet the Unbelievers (in fight), smite at their necks; at length, when ye have thoroughly subdued them, bind (the captives) firmly: therefore (is the time for) either generosity or ransom: until the war lays down its burdens. Thus (are ye commanded): but if it had been Allah's Will, he could certainly have exacted retribution from them (Himself); but (He lets you fight) in order to test you, some with others. But those who are slain in the way of Allah,— he will never let their deeds be lost.

5. Soon will He guide them and improve their condition,

6. And admit them to the Garden which He has made known to them.

7. O ye who believe! if ye will help (the cause of) Allah, he will help you, and plant your feet firmly.

8.   But those who reject (Allah),—for them is destruction, and (Allah) will bring their deeds to naught.

9.   That is because they hate the Revelation of Allah; so He has made their deeds fruitless.

10.   Do they not travel through the earth, and see what was the End of those before them (who did evil)? Allah brought utter destruction on them, and similar (fates await) those who reject Allah.

11.   That is because Allah is the Protector of those who believe, but those who reject Allah have no protector.

12.   Verily Allah will admit those who believe and do righteous deeds, to Gardens beneath which rivers flow; while those who reject Allah will enjoy (this world) and eat as cattle eat; and the Fire will be their abode.

13.   And how many cities, with more power than thy city which has driven thee out, have We destroyed (for their sins)? And there was none to aid them.

14.   Is then one who is on a clear (Path) from his Lord, no better than one to whom the evil of his conduct seems pleasing, and such as follow their own lusts?

15.   (Here is) the description of the Garden which the righteous are promised: in it are rivers of water unstaling; rivers of milk of which the taste never changes; rivers of wine, a joy to those who drink; and rivers of honey pure and clear. In it there are for them all kinds of fruits; and Forgiveness from their Lord, (can those in such Bliss) be compared to such as shall dwell for ever in the Fire, and be given, to drink, boiling water, so that it cuts up their bowels (to pieces)?

16.   And among them are men who listen to thee, till when they go out from thee, they say to those who have received

Knowledge, "What is it he said just then?"
Such are men whose hearts Allah has
sealed, and who follow their own lusts.

17. But to those who receive guidance, He
increases their Guidance, and bestows on
them their Piety and Restraint (from evil).

18. Do they then only wait for the Hour,—
that it should come on them of a sudden?
But already have come some tokens
thereof, and when it comes to them, how
shall they have their Reminder?

19. Know, therefore, that there is no god
but Allah, and ask forgiveness for thy fault,
and for the men and women who believe:
for Allah knows how ye move about and
how ye dwell in your homes.

20. Those who believe say, "Why is not a
Sûra sent down (for us)?" But when a Sûra
of decisive meaning is revealed, and fighting
is mentioned therein, thou wilt see those in
whose hearts is a disease looking at thee
with a look of one in swoon at the approach
of death. But more fitting for them—

21. Were it to obey and say what is just,
and when a matter is resolved on, it were
best for them if they were true to Allah.

22. Then, is it to be expected of you, if ye
were put in authority, that ye will do mischief
in the land, and break your ties of kith and
kin?

23. Such are the men whom Allah has
cursed, for He has made them deaf and
blinded their sight.

24. Do they not then earnestly seek to
understand the Qur-ān, or is that there are
locks upon their hearts?

25. Those who turn back as apostates
after Guidance was clearly shown to
them,— Satan has instigated them and
buoyed them up with false hopes.

26. This, because they said to those who
hate what Allah has revealed, "We will obey

you in part of (this) matter"; but Allah knows their (inner) secrets.

27. But how (will it be) when the angels take their souls at death, and smite their faces and their backs?

28. This because they followed that which displeased Allah, and they hated Allah's good pleasure; so He made their deeds of no effect.

29. Or do those in whose hearts is a disease, think that Allah will not bring to light all their rancour?

30. Had We so willed, We could have shown them up to thee, and thou shouldst have known them by their marks: but surely thou wilt know them by the tone of their speech! And Allah knows all that ye do.

31. And We shall try you until We test those among you who strive their utmost and persevere in patience; and We shall try your reported (mettle).

32. Those who disbelieve, hinder (men) from the Path of Allah, and resist the Messenger, after Guidance has been clearly shown to them, will not harm Allah in the least, but He will make their deeds of no effect.

33. O ye who believe! obey Allah, and obey the Messenger, and make not vain your deeds!

34. Those who disbelieve, and hinder (men) from the Path of Allah, then die disbelieving,— Allah will not forgive them.

35. Be not weary and faint-hearted, crying for peace, when ye are the Uppermost: for Allah is with you, and will never put you in loss for your (good) deeds.

36. The life of this world is but play and amusement: and if ye believe and guard against evil, he will grant you your recompense, and will not ask you (to give up) your possessions.

1. This is the second of the group of three Madinah Sûras described in the Introduction to S. 47. Its date is fixed by the mention of the Treaty of Ḥudaibîya, Ẓul-qa'd A.H. 6=Feb. 628.

2. Ḥudaibîya is a plain, a short day's march to the north of Makkah, a little to the west of the Madinah-Makkah road, as used in the Prophet's time. Six years had passed since the Prophet had left his beloved City, and it had been in the hands of the Pagan autocracy. But Islam had grown during these six years. Its Qibla was towards the Ka'ba. The Pagans had tried to attack Islam at various times and had been foiled. By Arab custom every Arab was entitled to visit the Sacred Enclosure unarmed, and fighting of any kind was prohibited during the Sacred Months which included the month of Ẓul-qa'd. In Ẓul-qa'd A.H. 6, therefore, the Prophet desired to perform the 'Umra or lesser Pilgrimage, unarmed but accompanied with his followers. A large following joined him, to the number of fourteen to fiften hundred.

3. This was not to the liking of the Pagan autocracy at Makkah, which took alarm, and in breach of all Arab tradition and usage, prepared to prevent the peaceful party from performing the rites of Pilgrimage. They marched out to fight the unarmed party. The Prophet turned a little to the west of the road, and encamped at Ḥudaibîya, where negotiations took place. On the one hand the Prophet was unwilling to give the Quraish any pretended excuse for violence in the Sacred Territory; on the other, the Quraish had learnt, by six years' bitter experience, that their power was crumbling on all sides, and Islam was growing with its moral aud spiritual forces, which were also reflected in its powers of organisation and resistance. The enthusiasm with which the Covenant of Fealty was entered into under a tree in Ḥudaibîya (48: 18) by that great multitude united in devotion to their great leader, was evidence of the great power which he commanded even

in a worldly sense if the Quraish had chosen to try conclusions with him.

4. A peaceful Treaty was therefore concluded, known as the Treaty of Ḥudaibîya. It stipulated: (1) that there was to be peace between the parties for ten years; (2) that any tribe or person was free to join either party or make an alliance with it; (3) that if a Quraish person from Makkah, under guardianship, should join the Prophet without the guardian's permission, he (or she) should be sent back to the guardian, but in the contrary case, they should not be sent back; and (4) that the Prophet and his party were not to enter Makkah that year, but that they could enter unarmed the following year.

5. Item (3), not being reciprocal was objected to in the Muslim camp, but it really was of little importance. Muslims under guardianship, sent back to Makkah, were not likely to renounce the blessings of Islam: on the other hand, Muslims going to Makkah would be centers of influence for Islam, and it was more important that they should be allowed to remain there than that they should be sent back to Madinah. It was impossible to think that there whould be apostates or renegades to Paganism! "Look on this picture, and on that!"

6. The Muslims faithfully observed the terms of the Treaty. The following year (A.H. 7) they performed the lesser Pilgrimage in great state for three days. It is true that the Makkans later on broke the Peace in the attack which one of their allied tribes (the Banû Bakr) made on the Muslim Banû Khuzā'a (who were in alliance with the Prophet), but this led to the conquest of Makkah and the sweeping away of the autocracy. Meanwhile Ḥudaibîya was a great victory, moral and social, as well as political, and its lessons are expounded in this Sûra, as the lessons of Badr were expounded in 8: 42-48, and of Uḥud in 3: 121-129, 149-180.

37. If He were to ask you for all of them, and press you, ye would covetously withhold, and He would bring out all your ill-feeling.

38. Behold, ye are those invited to spend (of your substance) in the Way of Allah: but among you are some that are niggardly. But any who are niggardly are so at the expense of their own souls. But Allah is free of all wants, and it is ye that are needy. If ye turn back (from the Path), He will substitute in your stead another people; then they would not be like you!

Al-Fat-ḥ or Victory

In the name of Allah, Most Gracious Most Merciful.

1. Verily We have granted thee a manifest Victory:

2. That Allah may forgive thee thy faults of the past and those to follow; fulfil His favour to thee; and guide thee on the Straight Way;

3. And that Allah may help thee with powerful help.

4. It is He Who sent down Tranquillity into the hearts of the Believers, that they may add Faith to their Faith;— for to Allah belong the Forces of the heavens and the earth; and Allah is Full of Knowledge and Wisdom;—

5. That He may admit the men and women who believe, to Gardens beneath which rivers flow, to dwell therein for a ve, and remove their sins from them;—and that is, in the sight of Allah, the grand triumph,

6. And that He may punish the Hypocrites, men and women, and the Polytheists, men and women, who think an evil thought of Allah. On them is a round of Evil: the Wrath of Allah is on them: He has cursed them and got Hell ready for them: and evil is it for a destination.

7.   For to Allah belong the Forces of the heavens and the earth; and Allah is exalted in Power, Full of Wisdom.

8.   We have truly sent thee as a witness, as a bringer of Glad Tidings, and as a Warner:

9.   In order that ye (O men) may believe in Allah and His Messenger, that ye may assist and honour him, and celebrate His praises morning and evening.

10.   Verily those who plight their fealty to thee plight their fealty in truth to Allah: the Hand of Allah is over their hands: then anyone who violates his oath, does so to the harm of his own soul, and anyone who fulfils what he has covenanted with Allah,— Allah will soon grant him a great Reward.

11.   The desert Arabs who lagged behind will say to thee: "We were engaged in (looking after) our flocks and herds, and our families: do thou then ask forgiveness for us." They say with their tongues what is not in their hearts. Say: "Who then has any power at all (to intervene) on your behalf with Allah, if His Will is to give you some loss or to give you some profit? But Allah is well acquainted with all that ye do.

12.   'Nay ye thought that the Messenger and the Believers would never return to their families; this seemed pleasing in your hearts, and ye conceived an evil thought, for ye are a people doomed to perish."

13.   And if any believe not in Allah and His Messenger, We have prepared, for those who reject Allah, a Blazing Fire!

14.   To Allah belongs the dominion of the heavens and the earth: He forgives whom He wills, and He punishes whom He wills: but Allah is Oft-Forgiving, Most Merciful.

15.   Those who lagged behind (will say), when ye set forth to acquire booty (in war):

"Permit us to follow you." They wish to change Allah's word: say: "Not thus will ye follow us: Allah has already declared (this) beforehand": then they will say, "But ye are jealous of us." Nay, but little do they understand (such things).

16. Say to the desert Arabs who lagged behind: "Ye shall be summoned (to fight) against a people given to vehement war: then shall ye fight, or they shall submit. Then if ye show obedience, Allah will grant you a goodly reward, but if ye turn back as ye did before, He will punish you with a grievous Chastisement."

17. No blame is there on the blind, nor is there blame on the lame, nor on one ill (if he joins not the war): but he that obeys Allah and His Messenger,—(Allah) will admit him to Gardens beneath which rivers flow; and he who turns back, (Allah) will punish him with a grievous Chastisement.

18. Allah's Good Pleasure was on the Believers when they swore Fealty to thee under the Tree: He knew what was in their hearts, and He sent down Tranquillity to them; and He rewarded them with a speedy Victory;

19. And many gains will they acquire (besides): and Allah is Exalted in Power, Full of Wisdom.

20. Allah has promised you many gains that ye shall acquire, and He has given you these beforehand; and He has restrained the hands of men from you; that it may be a Sign for the Believers, and that He may guide you to a Straight Path;

21. And other gains (there are), which are not within your power, but which Allah has compassed: and Allah has power over all things.

22. If the Unbelievers should fight you, they would certainly turn their backs; then would they find neither protector nor helper.

23. (Such has been) the practice of Allah already in the past: no change wilt thou find in the practice of Allah.

24. And it is He Who has restrained their hands from you and your hands from them in the valley of Makkah, after that He gave you the victory over them. And Allah sees well all that ye do.

25. They are the ones who disbelieved and hindered you from the Sacred Mosque and the sacrificial animals, detained from reaching their place of sacrifice. Had there not been believing men and believing women whom ye did not know that ye were trampling down and on whose account a guilt would have accrued to you without (your) knowledge, (Allah would have allowed you to force your way, but He held back your hands) that He may admit to His Mercy whom He will. If they had been apart. We should certainly have punished the Unbelievers among them with a grievous Punishment.

26. While the Unbelievers got up in their hearts heat and cant—the heat and cant of Ignorance,— Allah sent down His Tranquillity to His Messenger and to the Believers, and made them stick close to the command of self-restraint; and well were they entitled to it and worthy of it. And Allah has full knowledge of all things.

27. Truly did Allah fulfil the vision for His Messenger: ye shall enter the Sacred Mosque, if Allah wills, with minds secure, heads shaved, hair cut short, and without fear. For He knew what ye knew not, and He granted, besides this, a speedy victory.

SÛRA–49
AL-ḤUJURÂT
(INTRODUCTION)

This is the third of the group of three Madinah Sûras, which began with S. 47. See the Introduction to that Sûra.

Its subject-matter is the manners to be observed by the members of the rapidly-growing Muslim community, among themselves and towards its Leader. The key-word "*Ḥujurāt*" (Inner Apartments) occurs in verse 4.

Its date is referred to the Year of Deputations, A.H. 9, when a large number of deputations of all kinds visited Madinah to offer their allegiance to Islam.

28. It is He Who has sent His Messenger with Guidance and the Religion of Truth, to make it prevail over all religion: and enough is Allah for a Witness.

هُوَ الَّذِىٓ أَرْسَلَ رَسُولَهُ بِالْهُدَىٰ وَدِينِ الْحَقِّ لِيُظْهِرَهُ عَلَى الدِّينِ كُلِّهِ ۚ وَكَفَىٰ بِاللَّهِ شَهِيدًا ۞

29. Muhammad is the Messenger of Allah; and those who are with him are strong against Unbelievers, (but) compassionate amongst each other. Thou wilt see them bow and prostrate themselves (in prayer), seeking Grace from Allah and (His) Good Pleasure. On their faces are their marks, (being) the traces of their prostration. This is their similitude in the Taurāt; and their similitude in the Gospel is: Like a seed which sends forth its blade, then makes it strong; it then becomes thick, and it stands on its own stem, (filling) the sowers with wonder and delight. As a result, it fills the Unbelievers with rage at them. Allah has promised those among them who believe and do righteous deeds forgiveness, and a great Reward.

مُحَمَّدٌ رَسُولُ اللَّهِ ۚ وَالَّذِينَ مَعَهُ أَشِدَّآءُ عَلَى الْكُفَّارِ رُحَمَآءُ بَيْنَهُمْ ۖ تَرَىٰهُمْ رُكَّعًا سُجَّدًا يَبْتَغُونَ فَضْلًا مِّنَ اللَّهِ وَرِضْوَانًا ۖ سِيمَاهُمْ فِى وُجُوهِهِم مِّنْ أَثَرِ السُّجُودِ ۚ ذَٰلِكَ مَثَلُهُمْ فِى التَّوْرَىٰةِ ۚ وَمَثَلُهُمْ فِى الْإِنجِيلِ كَزَرْعٍ أَخْرَجَ شَطْأَهُ فَآزَرَهُ فَاسْتَغْلَظَ فَاسْتَوَىٰ عَلَىٰ سُوقِهِ يُعْجِبُ الزُّرَّاعَ لِيَغِيظَ بِهِمُ الْكُفَّارَ ۗ وَعَدَ اللَّهُ الَّذِينَ ءَامَنُوا وَعَمِلُوا الصَّٰلِحَٰتِ مِنْهُم مَّغْفِرَةً وَأَجْرًا عَظِيمًا ۞

Al-Ḥujurāt, or the Inner Apartments

In the name of Allah, Most Gracious, Most Merciful.

بِسْمِ اللَّهِ الرَّحْمَٰنِ الرَّحِيمِ

1. O ye who believe! put not yourselves forward before Allah and His Messenger; but fear Allah: for Allah is He Who hears and knows all things.

يَٰٓأَيُّهَا الَّذِينَ ءَامَنُوا لَا تُقَدِّمُوا بَيْنَ يَدَىِ اللَّهِ وَرَسُولِهِ ۖ وَاتَّقُوا اللَّهَ ۚ إِنَّ اللَّهَ سَمِيعٌ عَلِيمٌ ۞

2. O ye who believe! raise not your voices above the voice of the Prophet, nor speak aloud to him in talk, as ye may speak aloud to one another, lest your deeds become vain and ye perceive not.

يَٰٓأَيُّهَا الَّذِينَ ءَامَنُوا لَا تَرْفَعُوٓا أَصْوَٰتَكُمْ فَوْقَ صَوْتِ النَّبِىِّ وَلَا تَجْهَرُوا لَهُ بِالْقَوْلِ كَجَهْرِ بَعْضِكُمْ لِبَعْضٍ أَن تَحْبَطَ أَعْمَٰلُكُمْ وَأَنتُمْ لَا تَشْعُرُونَ ۞

3. Those that lower their voice in the Presence of Allah's Messenger,—their hearts has Allah tested for piety: for them is Forgiveness and a great Reward.

إِنَّ الَّذِينَ يَغُضُّونَ أَصْوَٰتَهُمْ عِندَ رَسُولِ اللَّهِ أُولَٰٓئِكَ الَّذِينَ امْتَحَنَ اللَّهُ قُلُوبَهُمْ لِلتَّقْوَىٰ ۚ لَهُم مَّغْفِرَةٌ وَأَجْرٌ عَظِيمٌ ۞

4. Those who shout out to thee from without the Inner Apartments— most of

إِنَّ الَّذِينَ يُنَادُونَكَ مِن وَرَآءِ الْحُجُرَٰتِ

them lack understanding.

5. If only they had patience until thou couldst come out to them, it would be best for them: but Allah is Oft-Forgiving, Most Merciful.

6. O ye who believe! if a sinner comes to you with any news, ascertain the truth, lest ye harm people unwittingly, and afterwards become full of repentance for what ye have done.

7. And know that among you is Allah's Messenger: were he, in many matters, to follow your (wishes), ye would certainly suffer: but Allah has endeared the Faith to you, and has made it beautiful in your hearts, and He has made hateful to you unbelief, wrongdoing, and rebellion: such indeed are those who walk in righteousness;—

8. A grace and favour from Allah; and Allah is Full of Knowledge and Wisdom.

9. If two parties among the Believers fall into a fight, make ye peace between them: but if one of them transgresses beyond bounds against the other, then fight ye (all) against the one that transgresses until it complies with the command of Allah; but if it complies, then make peace between them with justice, and be fair: for Allah loves those who are fair (and just).

10. The Believers are but a single Brotherhood: So make peace and reconciliation between your two (contending) brothers; and fear Allah, that ye may receive Mercy.

11. O ye who believe! Let not some men among you laugh at others: it may be that the (latter) are better than the (former): nor let some women laugh at others: it may be that the (latter) are better than the (former): nor defame nor be sarcastic to each other, nor call each other by (offensive) nicknames: ill-seeming is a name connoting

wickedness, (to be used of one) after he has believed: and those who do not desist are (indeed) doing wrong.

12. O ye who believe! avoid suspicion as much (as possible): for suspicion in some cases is a sin: and spy not on each other, nor speak ill of each other behind their backs. Would any of you like to eat the flesh of his dead brother? Nay, ye would abhor it... But fear Allah: for Allah is Oft-Returning, Most Merciful.

13. O mankind! We created you from a single (pair) of a male and a female, and made you into nations and tribes, that ye may know each other (not that ye may despise (each other). Verily the most honoured of you in the sight of Allah is (he who is) the most righteous of you. And Allah has full knowledge and is well acquainted (with all things).

14. The desert Arabs say, "We believe." Say, "Ye have no faith; but ye (only) say, 'We have submitted our wills to Allah,' for not yet has Faith entered your hearts. But if ye obey Allah and His Messenger, He will not belittle aught of your deeds: for Allah is Oft-Forgiving, Most Merciful."

15. Only those are Believers who have believed in Allah and His Messenger, and have never since doubted, but have striven with their belongings and their persons in the Cause of Allah: such are the sincere ones.

16. Say: "What! Will ye tell Allah about your religion? But Allah knows all that is in the heavens and on earth: He has full knowledge of all things.

17. They impress on thee as a favour that they have embraced Islam. Say, "Count not your Islam as a favour upon me: nay, Allah has conferred a favour upon you that He has guided you to the Faith, if ye be true and sincere.

18. "Verily Allah knows the Unseen of the heavens and the earth: and Allah

SÛRA–50
QĀF
(INTRODUCTION)

We now come to a group of seven Makkan Sûras (50-56) dealing with Allah's revelation through nature, through history, and through the mouths of the prophets, and pointing to the Hereafter. We saw that the last group of three (47-49) dealt with the external and internal relations of the Ummat when formed. In the present group our attention is more particularly directed to aspects eschatological,—the Future before us when this life is done.

This particular Sûra belongs to the early Makkan period. After an appeal to nature and to the fate of wicked peoples in history, it removes as it were the evil (verse 22) from the Future after death.

sees well all that ye do."

QĀF

In the name of Allah, Most Gracious, Most Merciful.

1.   Qaf: By the Glorious Qur'ān (thou art Allah's Messenger).

2.   But they wonder that there has come to them a Warner from among themselves. So the Unbelievers say:" "This is a wonderful thing!"

3.   "What! When we die and become dust, (shall we live again?) That is a (sort of) Return far (from our understanding)."

4.   We already know how much of them the earth takes away: with Us is a Record guarding (the full account).

5.   But they deny the truth when it comes to them: so they are in a confused state.

6.   Do they not look at the sky above them?—How We have made it and adorned it, and there are no flaws in it?

7.   And the earth—We have spread it out, and set thereon mountains standing firm, and produced therein every kind of beautiful growth (in pairs)—

8.   For an insight and Reminder to every servant turning (to Allah).

9.   And We send down from the sky Rain charged with blessing, and We produce therewith Gardens and Grain for harvests;

10.   And tall (and stately) Palm-trees, with shoots of fruit-stalks, piled one over another;—

11.   As sustenance for (Allah's) Servants;— and We give (new) life therewith to land that is dead: thus will be the Resurrection.

12.   Before them was denied (the Hereafter) by the People of Noah, the Companions of the Rass, the Thamūd,

13.   The 'Ād, Pharaoh, the Brethren of Lût,

14.   The Companions of the Wood, and the People of Tubba'; each one (of them) rejected the messengers, and My warning was duly fulfilled (in them).

15. Were We then weary with the first Creation, that they should be in confused doubt about a new Creation?

16. It was We Who created man, and We know what suggestions his soul makes to him: for We are nearer to him than (his) jugular vein.

17. Behold, two (guardian angels) appointed to learn (his doings) learn (and note them), one sitting on the right and one on the left.

18. Not a word does he utter but there is a vigilant Guardian.

19. And the stupor of death comes in truth. "This was the thing which thou wast trying to escape!"

20. And the Trumpet shall be blown: that will be the Day whereof Warning (had been given).

21. And there will come forth every soul: with each will be an (angel) to drive, and an (angel) to bear witness.

22. (It will be said:) "Thou wast heedless of this; now have We removed thy veil, and sharp is thy sight this Day!"

23. And his Companion will say: "Here is (his Record) ready with me!"

24. (The sentence will be:) "Throw, both of you, into Hell every contumacious Rejecter (of Allah)!—

25. "Who forbade what was good, transgressed all bounds, cast doubts and suspicions;

26. "Who set up another god beside Allah: throw him into a severe Chastisement."

27. His Companion will say: "Our Lord! I did not make him transgress, but he was (himself) far astray."

28. He will say: "Dispute not with each other in My Presence: I had already in advance sent you Warning.

29. "The Word changes not with Me, and I do not the least injustice to My Servants."

30. The Day We will ask Hell, "Art thou filled to the full?" It will say, "Are there any more (to come)?"

أَفَعَيِينَا بِالْخَلْقِ الْأَوَّلِ ۚ بَلْ هُمْ فِى لَبْسٍ مِّنْ خَلْقٍ جَدِيدٍ ۞

وَلَقَدْ خَلَقْنَا الْإِنسَانَ وَنَعْلَمُ مَا تُوَسْوِسُ بِهِۦ نَفْسُهُۥ ۖ وَنَحْنُ أَقْرَبُ إِلَيْهِ مِنْ حَبْلِ الْوَرِيدِ ۞

إِذْ يَتَلَقَّى الْمُتَلَقِّيَانِ عَنِ الْيَمِينِ وَعَنِ الشِّمَالِ قَعِيدٌ ۞

مَّا يَلْفِظُ مِن قَوْلٍ إِلَّا لَدَيْهِ رَقِيبٌ عَتِيدٌ ۞

وَجَآءَتْ سَكْرَةُ الْمَوْتِ بِالْحَقِّ ۖ ذَٰلِكَ مَا كُنتَ مِنْهُ تَحِيدُ ۞

وَنُفِخَ فِى الصُّورِ ۚ ذَٰلِكَ يَوْمُ الْوَعِيدِ ۞ وَجَآءَتْ كُلُّ نَفْسٍ مَّعَهَا سَآئِقٌ وَشَهِيدٌ ۞

لَّقَدْ كُنتَ فِى غَفْلَةٍ مِّنْ هَٰذَا فَكَشَفْنَا عَنكَ غِطَآءَكَ فَبَصَرُكَ الْيَوْمَ حَدِيدٌ ۞ وَقَالَ قَرِينُهُۥ هَٰذَا مَا لَدَىَّ عَتِيدٌ ۞

أَلْقِيَا فِى جَهَنَّمَ كُلَّ كَفَّارٍ عَنِيدٍ ۞ مَّنَّاعٍ لِّلْخَيْرِ مُعْتَدٍ مُّرِيبٍ ۞

الَّذِى جَعَلَ مَعَ اللَّهِ إِلَٰهًا ءَاخَرَ فَأَلْقِيَاهُ فِى الْعَذَابِ الشَّدِيدِ ۞ قَالَ قَرِينُهُۥ رَبَّنَا مَآ أَطْغَيْتُهُۥ وَلَٰكِن كَانَ فِى ضَلَٰلٍ بَعِيدٍ ۞

قَالَ لَا تَخْتَصِمُوا لَدَىَّ وَقَدْ قَدَّمْتُ إِلَيْكُم بِالْوَعِيدِ ۞

مَا يُبَدَّلُ الْقَوْلُ لَدَىَّ وَمَآ أَنَا بِظَلَّٰمٍ لِّلْعَبِيدِ ۞

يَوْمَ نَقُولُ لِجَهَنَّمَ هَلِ امْتَلَأْتِ وَتَقُولُ هَلْ مِن مَّزِيدٍ ۞

31. And the Garden will be brought nigh to the Righteous,—no more a thing distant.

32. (A voice will say:) "This is what was promised for you,—for every penitent heedful one,

33. "Who feared the Most Gracious unseen, and brought a heart turned in devotion (to Him):

34. "Enter ye therein in Peace and Security; this is a Day of Eternal Life!"

35. There will be for them therein all that they wish,—and there is more with us.

36. But how many generations before them did We destroy (for their sins),— stronger in power than they? Then did they wander through the land: was there any place of escape (for them)?

37. Verily in this is a Message for any that has a heart and understanding or who gives ear and is a witness.

38. We created the heavens and the earth and all between them in Six Days, nor did any sense of weariness touch Us.

39. Bear, then, with patience, all that they say, and celebrate the praises of thy Lord, before the rising of the sun and before (its) setting,

40. And during part of the night, (also,) celebrate His praises, and (so likewise) after the prostration.

41. And listen the Day when the Caller will call out from a place quite near,—

42. The Day when they will hear a (mighty) Blast in (very) truth: that will be the Day of Resurrection.

43. Verily it is We Who give Life and Death; and to Us is the Final Return—

44. The Day when the Earth will be rent asunder, letting them hurrying out: that will be a gathering together,—quite easy for Us.

45. We know best what they say; and thou art not one to compel them by force. So admonish with the Qur'ān such as fear My Warning!

SÛRA–51
AZ-ZĀRIYĀT
(INTRODUCTION)

This is an early Makkan Sûra, with a highly mystic meaning.
It is the second of the seven Sûras forming a group dealing
with Revelation and the Hereafter. See Introduction to S. 50.
This Sûra deals with the varying ways in which Truth prevails
irresistibly even against all human probabilities.

Az-Zāriyāt, or the
Winds That Scatter

بِسْمِ اللهِ الرَّحْمٰنِ الرَّحِيْمِ ۟

In the name of Allah, Most Gracious, Most Merciful.

1. By the (Winds) that scatter broadcast;

2. And those that lift and bear away heavy weights;

3. And those that flow with ease and gentleness;

4. And those that distribute the affair;—

5. Verily that which ye are promised is true;

6. And verily Judgment and Justice will surely come to pass.

7. By the Sky with (its) numerous Paths,

8. Truly ye are of varying opinion.

9. Through which are deluded (away from the Truth) such as would be deluded.

10. Cursed be the conjecturers.

11. Those who (flounder) heedless in a flood of confusion:

12. They ask, "When will be the Day of Judgment and Justice?"

13. (It will be) a Day when they will be tried (and tested) over the Fire!

14. "Taste ye your trial! This is what ye used to ask to be hastened!"

15. As to the Righteous, they will be in the midst of Gardens and Springs,

16. Taking joy in the things which their Lord gives them, because, before then, they have done good deeds.

17. They were in the habit of sleeping but little by night,

18. And in the hours of early dawn, they (were found) praying for Forgiveness;

19. And in their wealth there is a due share for the beggar and the deprived.

20. On the earth are Signs for those of assured Faith,

21. As also in your own selves: will ye not then see?

22. And in heaven is your Sustenance, as (also) that which ye are promised.

23. Then, by the Lord of heaven and earth, this is the very Truth, as much as

the fact that ye can speak intelligently to each other.

24. Has the story reached thee, of the honoured Guests of Abraham?

25. Behold, they entered His presence, and said: "Peace!" He said, "Peace!" (and thought), "These seem unknown people."

26. Then he turned quickly to his household, brought out a fatted calf,

27. And placed it before them... He said, "Will ye not Eat?"

28. (When they did not eat), he conceived a fear of them. They said, "Fear not," and they gave him glad tidings of a son endowed with knowledge.

29. But his wife came forward clamouring: she smote her forehead and said: "A barren old woman!"

30. They said, "Even so has thy Lord spoken: and He is Full of Wisdom and Knowledge."

31. (Abraham) said: "And what, O ye Messengers, is your errand (now)?

32. They said, "We have been sent to a people (deep) in sin;—

33. "To bring on, on them, (a sho-wer of) stones of clay (brimstone),

34. "Marked as from thy Lord for those who trespass beyond bounds."

35. Then We evacuated those of the Believers who were there,

36. But We found not there any except one Muslim household:

37. And We left there a Sign for such as fear the Grievous Chastisement.

38. And in Moses (was another Sign): behold, We sent him to Pharaoh, with authority manifest.

39. But (Pharaoh) turned back on account of his might, and said, "A sorcerer, or one possessed!"

40. So We took him and his forces, and threw them into the sea: and his was the blame.

41. And in the 'Ād (people) (was another Sign): behold, We sent against them the devastating Wind:

42. It left nothing whatever that it came up against, but reduced it to ruin and rottenness.

43. And in the <u>Th</u>amūd (was another Sign): behold, they were told, "Enjoy (your brief day) for a little while!"

44. But they insolently defied the Command of their Lord: so the thunderbolt seized them, even while they were looking on.

45. Then they could not even stand (on their feet), nor could they help themselves.

46. So were the People of Noah before them: for they wickedly transgressed.

47. We have built the Firmament with might: and We indeed have vast power.

48. And We have spread out the (spacious) earth: how excellently We do spread out!

49. And of every thing We have created pairs: that ye may reflect.

50. Therefore flee unto Allah: I am from Him a Warner to you, clear and open!

51. And make not another an object of worship with Allah: I am from Him a Warner to you, clear and open!

52. Similarly, no messenger came to the Peoples before them, but they said (of him) in like manner, "A sorcerer, or one possessed"!

53. Is this the legacy they have transmitted, one to another? Nay, they are themselves a people transgressing beyond bounds!

54. So turn away from them: not thine is the blame.

55. But remind: for reminding benefits the Believers.

56. I have only created Jinns and men, that they may serve Me.

57. No Sustenance do I require of them,

SÛRA–52
AṬ-ṬÛR
(INTRODUCTION)

This is the third of the group of seven Makkan Sûras described in the Introduction to S. 50.

It is, like its predecessor, an early Makkan Sûra. The points here emphasised are: that Revelation is in accord with all Allah's Signs, including previous Revelations, and that the Hereafter is inevitable, and we must prepare for it.

do I require that they should feed Me.

58. For Allah is He Who gives (all) Sustenance,— Lord of Power,— Steadfast (for ever).

59. For the wrong-doers, their portion is like unto the portion of their fellows (of earlier generations): then let them not ask Me to hasten (that portion)!

60. Woe, then, to the Unbelievers, from that Day of theirs which they have been promised!

Aṭ-Ṭûr, or the Mount

In the name of Allah, Most Gracious, Most Merciful.

1. By the Mount (of Revelation);

2. By a Book Inscribed

3. In a parchment unfolded;

4. By the much-frequented House;

5. By the Conopy Raised High;

6. And by the Ocean filled with Swell:—

7. Verily, the Chastisement of thy Lord will indeed come to pass;—

8. There is none can avert it;—

9. On the Day when the firmament will be in dreadful commotion.

10. And the mountains will move.

11. Then woe that Day to the rejecters (of Truth);—

12. That play (and paddle) in shallow trifles.

13. That Day shall they be thrust down to the Fire of Hell, irresistibly.

14. "This", it will be said, "Is the Fire,— which ye were wont to deny!

15. "Is this then a magic, or is it ye that do not see?

16. "Burn ye therein: the same is it to you whether ye bear it with patience, or not: ye but receive the recompense of your (own) deeds."

17. As to the Righteous, they will be in Gardens, and in Happiness,—

18. Enjoying the (Bliss) which their Lord hath bestowed on them, and their Lord shall deliver them from the Chastisement of the Fire.

19. (To them will be said:) "Eat and drink ye, with profit and health, because of your (good) deeds."

كُلُوا وَاشْرَبُوا هَنِيئًا بِمَا كُنتُمْ تَعْمَلُونَ ۞

20. They will recline (with ease) upon couches arranged in ranks; and We shall wed them to maidens, with beautiful big and lustrous eyes.

مُتَّكِئِينَ عَلَىٰ سُرُرٍ مَّصْفُوفَةٍ ۖ وَزَوَّجْنَاهُم بِحُورٍ عِينٍ ۞

21. And those who believe and whose seeds follow them in Faith,—to them shall We join their families: nor shall We deprive them (of the fruit) of aught of their works: (yet) is each individual in pledge for his deeds.

وَالَّذِينَ آمَنُوا وَاتَّبَعَتْهُمْ ذُرِّيَّتُهُم بِإِيمَانٍ أَلْحَقْنَا بِهِمْ ذُرِّيَّتَهُمْ وَمَا أَلَتْنَاهُم مِّنْ عَمَلِهِم مِّن شَيْءٍ ۚ كُلُّ امْرِئٍ بِمَا كَسَبَ رَهِينٌ ۞

22. And We shall bestow on them, of fruit and meat, anything they shall desire.

وَأَمْدَدْنَاهُم بِفَاكِهَةٍ وَلَحْمٍ مِّمَّا يَشْتَهُونَ ۞

23. They shall there exchange, one with another, a cup free of frivolity, free of sin.

يَتَنَازَعُونَ فِيهَا كَأْسًا لَّا لَغْوٌ فِيهَا وَلَا تَأْثِيمٌ ۞

24. Round about them will serve, (devoted) to them, youths (handsome) as Pearls well-guarded.

وَيَطُوفُ عَلَيْهِمْ غِلْمَانٌ لَّهُمْ كَأَنَّهُمْ لُؤْلُؤٌ مَّكْنُونٌ ۞

25. They will advance to each other, engaging in mutual enquiry.

وَأَقْبَلَ بَعْضُهُمْ عَلَىٰ بَعْضٍ يَتَسَاءَلُونَ ۞

26. They will say: "Aforetime, we were not without fear for the sake of our people.

قَالُوا إِنَّا كُنَّا قَبْلُ فِي أَهْلِنَا مُشْفِقِينَ ۞

27. "But Allah has been good to us, and has delivered us from the Chastisement of the Scorching Wind.

فَمَنَّ اللَّهُ عَلَيْنَا وَوَقَانَا عَذَابَ السَّمُومِ ۞

28. "Truly, we did call unto Him from of old: truly it is He, the Beneficent, the Merciful!"

إِنَّا كُنَّا مِن قَبْلُ نَدْعُوهُ ۖ إِنَّهُ هُوَ الْبَرُّ الرَّحِيمُ ۞

29. Therefore Remind for by the Grace of thy Lord, thou art no soothsayer, nor possessed.

فَذَكِّرْ فَمَا أَنتَ بِنِعْمَتِ رَبِّكَ بِكَاهِنٍ وَلَا مَجْنُونٍ ۞

30. Or do they say: "A Poet! we await for him some calamity (hatched) by Time!"

أَمْ يَقُولُونَ شَاعِرٌ نَّتَرَبَّصُ بِهِ رَيْبَ الْمَنُونِ ۞

31. Say thou: "Await ye!— I too will wait along with you!"

قُلْ تَرَبَّصُوا فَإِنِّي مَعَكُم مِّنَ الْمُتَرَبِّصِينَ ۞

32. Is it that their intellects urges them to this, or are they but a people transgressing beyond bounds?

أَمْ تَأْمُرُهُمْ أَحْلَامُهُم بِهَٰذَا ۚ أَمْ هُمْ قَوْمٌ طَاغُونَ ۞

33. Or do they say, "He fabricated the (Message)"? Nay, they have no faith!

أَمْ يَقُولُونَ تَقَوَّلَهُ ۚ بَل لَّا يُؤْمِنُونَ ۞

34. Let them then produce a saying like unto it,— If (it be) they speak the Truth!

35. Were they created of nothing, or were they themselves the creators?

36. Or did they create the heavens and the earth? Nay, they have no firm belief.

37. Or are the Treasures of thy Lord with them, or have they control over them.

38. Or have they a ladder, by which they can (climb up to heaven and) listen (to its secrets)? Then let (such a) listener of theirs produce a manifest proof.

39. Or has He only daughters and ye have sons?

40. Or is it that thou dost ask for a reward, so that they are burdened with a load of debt?—

41. Or that the Unseen is in their hands, and they write it down?

42. Or do they intend a plot (against thee)? But those who disbelieve are themselves ensnared in a Plot.

43. Or have they a god other than Allah? Exalted is Allah far above the things they associate with Him!

44. Were they to see a piece of the sky falling (on them), they would (only) say: "Clouds gathered in heaps!"

45. So leave them alone until they encounter that Day of theirs, wherein they shall be thunderstruck.

46. The Day when their plotting will avail them nothing and no help shall be given them.

47. And verily, for those who do wrong, there is another punishment besides this: but most of them know not.

48. Now await in patience the command of thy Lord: for verily thou art in Our eyes: and celebrate the praises of thy Lord the while thou standest forth,

SÛRA–53
AN-NAJM
(INTRODUCTION)

This is an early Makkan Sûra, and is the fourth of the series of seven which were described in the Introduction to S. 50.

The particular theme of this Sûra is that Revelation is not an illusion: the illusion is in the minds of those who doubt and have false ideas of Allah: Allah is the source and goal of all things.

In some Sûras the consecutive arrangement is shown or suggested by a cue-word. Here the cue-word is "star," corresponding to "stars" in the last verse of the last Sûra. So in 46: 1, the words: "Exalted in Power, Full of Wisdom": are carried forward from the last verse of S. 45, and indeed the same words occur in the first verse of S. 45. So, again the words: "Most Merciful, Oft-Forgiving": in 34: 2, refer back to the words: "Oft-Forgiving, Most Merciful": in the last line of S. 33. In S. 54: 1, the nearness of Judgment recalls the same idea at the end of the previous Sûra (53: 57). Other examples will also be found.

49. And for part of the night also praise thou Him,— and at the setting of the stars!

An-Najm, or the Star

In the name of Allah, Most Gracious, Most Merciful.

1. By the Star when it goes down,—

2. Your Companion is neither astray nor being misled,

3. Nor does he say (aught) of (his own) Desire.

4. It is no less than inspiration sent down to him:

5. He was taught by one Mighty in Power,

6. Endued with Wisdom: for he appeared (in stately form)

7. While he was in the highest part of the horizon:

8. Then he approached and came closer,

9. And was at a distance of but two bow-lengths or (even) nearer;

10. So did (Allah) convey the inspiration to His Servant (conveyed) what He (meant) to convey.

11. The (Prophet's) (mind and) heart in no way falsified that which he saw.

12. Will ye then dispute with him concerning what he saw?

13. For indeed he saw him at a second descent,

14. Near the Lote-tree of the utmost boundary.

15. Near it is the Garden of Abode.

16. Behold, the Lote-tree was shrouded with what shrouds.

17. (His) sight never swerved, nor did it go wrong!

18. For truly did he see, of the Signs of his Lord, the Greatest!

19. Have ye seen Lāt, and 'Uzzā,

20. And another, the third (goddess), Manāt?

21. What! For you the male sex, and for Him, the female?

22. Behold, such would be indeed a division most unfair!

23. These are nothing but names which ye have devised,— ye and your fathers,— for which Allah has sent down no authority

(whatever). They follow nothing but; conjecture and what the souls desire ! — even though there has already come to them Guidance from their Lord!

24. Nay, shall man have (just) anything he hankers after?

25. But to Allah belongeth the Hereafter and the Former life.

26. How many-so-ever be the angels in the heavens, their intercession will avail nothing except after Allah has given leave for whom He pleases and that he is acceptable to Him.

27. Those who believe not in the Hereafter, name the angels with female names.

28. But they have no knowledge therein. They follow nothing but conjecture: and conjecture avails nothing against Truth.

29. Therefore shun those who turn away from Our Message and desire nothing but the life of this world.

30. That is their attainment of Knowledge. Verily thy Lord knoweth best those who stray from His path, and He knoweth best those who receive guidance.

31. Yea, to Allah belongs all that is in the heavens and on earth: so that He rewards those who do evil, according to their deeds, and He rewards those who do good, with what is best.

32. Those who avoid great sins and indecent deeds, save lesser offences,— verily thy Lord is ample in forgiveness. He knows you well when He brings you out of the earth, and when ye are hidden in your mothers' wombs. Therefore hold not yourselves purified: He knows best who it is that guards against evil.

33. Seest thou one who turns back,
34. Gives a little, then hardens (his heart)?
35. What! Has he knowledge of the unseen so that he can see?
36. Nay, is he not acquainted with what is in the books of Moses—
37. And of Abraham who fulfilled his (commandments)
38. Namely, that no bearer of burdens can bear the burden of another;
39. That man can have nothing but what he strives for;
40. That (the fruit of) his striving will soon come in sight;
41. Then will he be rewarded with a reward complete;
42. That to thy Lord is the final Goal;
43. That it is He Who granteth Laughter and Tears;
44. That it is He Who granteth Death and Life;
45. That He did create the pairs,—male and female,
46. From a sperm-drop when lodged (in its place);
47. That He hath promised a Second Creation (raising of the Dead);
48. That it is He Who giveth wealth and satisfaction;
49. That He is the Lord of Sirius (the Mighty Star);
50. And that it is He Who destroyed the (powerful) ancient 'Ad (people),
51. And the Thamūd, He left no trace of them.
52. And before them, the people of Noah, for that they were (all) most unjust and most insolent transgressors,
53. And He destroyed the Overthrown Cities (of Sodom and Gomorrah),
54. So that there covered it that which covered.
55. Then which of the favours of thy Lord, (O man,) wilt thou dispute about?
56. This is a Warner, of the (series of) Warners of old!
57. The (Hour) ever approaching draws nigh:
58. No one but Allah can disclose it.
59. Do ye then wonder at this recital?

SÛRA–54
AL-QAMAR
(INTRODUCTION)

This is an early Makkan Sûra, the fifth in the series dealing with Judgment, and the truth of Revelation, as explained in the Introduction to S. 50.

The theme of the Sûra is explained by the refrain: "Is there any that will receive admonition?" which occurs six times, at the end of each reference to a past story of sin and rejection of warnings and in the appeal to the simplicity of the Qur-ān (verses 15, 17, 22, 32, 40, and 51). There is an invitation to listen to the Message and turn to Truth and Righteousness.

60. And will ye laugh and not weep,—

61. Wasting your time in vanities?

62. But fall ye down in prostration to Allah and adore (Him)!

Al-Qamar, or the Moon

In the name of Allah, Most Gracious Most Merciful.

1. The Hour (of Judgment) is nigh, and the moon was cleft asunder.

2. But if they see a Sign, they turn away, and say, "This is (but) continuous magic."

3. They reject (the warning) and follow their (own) lusts but every matter has its appointed time.

4. There have already come to them such tidings as contain a deterrent,

5. A wisdom far-reaching:—but (the preaching of) Warners Profits them not.

6. Therefore, (O Prophet,) turn away from them. (And wait for) the Day that the Caller will call (them) to a terrible affair,

7. They will come forth,—their eyes humbled—from (their) graves, (torpid) like locusts scattered abroad,

8. Hastening, with eyes transfixed, towards the Caller!—"Hard is this Day!" the Unbelievers will say.

9. Before them the People of Noah rejected (their messenger): they rejected Our servant and said, "Here is one possessed!", and he was driven out.

10. Then he called on his Lord: "I am one overcome: do Thou then help (me)!"

11. So We opened the gates of heaven, with water pouring forth.

12. And We caused the earth to gush forth with springs. So the waters met (and rose) to the extent decreed.

13. But We bore him on an (Ark) made of broad planks and caulked with palm-fibre:

14. She floats under Our eyes (and care): a recompense to one who had been rejected (with scorn)!

15　And We have left this as a Sign (for all time): then is there any that will receive admonition?

16.　But how (terrible) was My Chastisement and My Warning?

17.　And We have indeed made the Qur'ān easy to understand and remember: then is there any that will receive admonition?

18.　The 'Ād (people) (too) rejected (Truth): then how terrible was My Chastisement and My Warning?

19.　For We sent against them a furious wind, on a Day of bitter ill-luck,

20.　Plucking out men as if they were roots of palm-trees torn up (from the ground).

21.　Yea, how (terrible) was My Chastisement and My Warning!

22.　But We have indeed made the Qur'an easy to understand and remember: then is there any that will receive admonition?

23.　The Thamūd (also) rejected (their) Warners.

24.　For they said: "What! a man! a solitary one from among ourselves! Shall we follow such a one? Truly should we then be in error and madness.

25.　"Is it that the Message is sent to *him*, of all people amongst us? Nay, he is a liar, an insolent one!"

26.　Ah! they will know on the morrow, which is the liar the insolent one!

27.　For We will send the she-camel by way of trial for them. So watch them, (O Sālih), and possess thyself in patience!

28.　And tell them that the water is to be divided between them: each one's right to drink being brought forward (by suitable turns).

29.　But they called to their companion, and he took a sword in hand, and hamstrung (her).

30.　Ah! how (terrible) was My Chastisement and My Warning!

31.　For We sent against them a single Mighty Blast, and they became like the dry stubble used by one who pens cattle.

32.　And We have indeed made the Qur'an easy to understand and remember: then is there any that will receive admonition?

33.　The People of Lūt rejected (his) Warning.

34. We sent against them a violent tornado with showers of stones, (which destroyed them), except Lût's household: them We delivered by early Dawn,—

35. As a Grace from Us: thus do We reward those who give thanks.

36. And (Lût) did warn them of Our violent Seizure but they disputed about the Warning.

37. And they even sought to snatch away his guests from him, but We blinded their eyes. (They heard:) "Now taste ye My Wrath and My Warning."

38. Early on the morrow an abiding Chastisement seized them:

39. "So taste ye My Chastisement and my Warning."

40. And We have indeed made the Qur'ān easy to understand and remember: then is there any that will receive admonition?

41. To the People of Pharaoh, too, aforetime, came Warners (from Allah).

42. The (people) rejected all Our Signs; but We seized them with the Seizure of a Mighty, Powerful.

43. Are your Unbelievers, (O Quraish), better than they? Or have ye an immunity in the Sacred Books?

44. Or do they say: "We acting together can defend ourselves"?

45. Soon will their multitude be put to flight, and they will show their backs.

46. Nay, the Hour (of Judgment) is the time promised them (for their full recompense): and that Hour will be most grievous and most bitter.

47. Truly those in sin are the ones in error and madness.

48. The Day they will be dragged through the Fire on their faces, (they will hear:) "Taste ye the touch of Hell!"

49. Verily, all things have We created in proportion and measure.

50. And Our Command is but a single Word,— like the twinkling of an eye.

51. And (oft) in the past, have We destroyed gangs like unto you: then is there any that will receive admonition?

SÛRA–55
AR-RAHMĀN
(INTRODUCTION)

The majority of Commentators consider this an early Makkan Sûra, though some consider at least a part of it as dating from Madinah. The graeater part of it is undoubtedly early Makkan.

It is highly poetical and mystical, and the refrain "Then which of the favours of your Lord will ye deny?" is interspersed 31 times among its 78 verses.

It is the sixth of the series of seven dealing with Revelation, the favours of Allah, and the Hereafter: see Introduction to S. 50.

Here the special theme is indicated by the refrain. The rhyme in most cases is in the Dual grammatical form and the Argument implies that though things are created in pairs, there is an underlying Unity, through the Creator, in the favours which He bestows, and in the goal to which they are marching.

52. All that they do is noted in (their) Books (of Deeds):

53. Every matter, small and great, is on record.

54. As to the Righteous, they will be in the midst of Gardens and Rivers,

55. In a sure abode with a Sovereign Omnipotent.

Ar-Raḥmān, or (Allah) Most Gracious

In the name of Allah, Most Gracious, Most Merciful.

1. The Most Gracious!

2. It is He Who has taught the Qur'ān.

3. He has created man:

4. He has taught him an intelligent speech.

5. The sun and the moon follow courses (exactly) computed;

6. And the herbs and the trees— both (alike) bow in adoration.

7. And the Firmament has He raised high, and He has set up the Balance (of Justice),

8. In order that ye may not transgress (due) balance.

9. So establish weight with justice and fall not short in the balance.

10. It is He Who has spread out the earth for (His) creatures:

11. Therein is fruit and date-palms, producing spathes (enclosing dates);

12. Also corn, with (its) leaves and stalk for fodder, and sweet-smelling plants.

13. Then which of the favours of your Lord will ye deny?

14. He created man from sounding clay like unto pottery,

15. And He created Jinns from fire free of smoke:

16. Then which of the favours of your Lord will ye deny?

17. (He is) Lord of the two Easts and Lord of the two Wests:

18. Then which of the favours of your Lord will ye deny?

19. He has let free the two Seas meeting together:

20. Between them is a Barrier which they do not transgress:

21. Then which of the favours of your Lord will ye deny?

22. Out of them come Pearls and Coral:

23. Then which of the favours of your Lord will ye deny?

24. And His are the Ships sailing smoothly through the seas, lofty as mountains:

25. Then which of the favours of your Lord will ye deny?

26. All that is on earth will perish:

27. But will abide (for ever) the Face of thy Lord,— full of Majesty, Bounty and Honour.

28. Then which of the favours of your Lord will ye deny?

29. Of Him seeks (its need) every creature in the heavens and on earth: every day in (new) Splendour doth He (shine)!

30. Then which of the favours of your Lord will ye deny?

31. Soon shall We settle your affairs, O both ye worlds!

32. Then which of the favours of your Lord will ye deny?

33. O ye assembly of Jinns and men! If it be ye can pass beyond the zones of the heavens and the earth, pass ye! Not without authority shall ye be able to pass!

34. Then which of the favours of your Lord will ye deny?

35. On you will be sent (O ye evil ones twain!) a flame of fire (to burn) and a (flash of) molten brass no defence will ye have:

36. Then which of the favours of your Lord will ye deny?

37. When the sky is rent asunder, and it becomes red like ointment:

38. Then which of the favours of your Lord will ye deny?

39. On that Day no question will be asked of man or Jinn as to his sin,

40. Then which of the favours of your Lord will ye deny?

41. (For) the sinners will be known by their Marks: and they will be seized by their forelocks and their feet.

42. Then which of the favours of your Lord will ye deny?

43. This is the Hell which the Sinners deny:
44. In its midst and in the midst of boiling hot water will they wander round!
45. Then which of the favours of your Lord will ye deny?
46. But for such as fear the time when they will stand before (the Judgment Seat of) their Lord, there will be two Gardens—
47. Then which of the favours of your Lord will ye deny?—
48. Abounding in branches,—
49. Then which of the favours of your Lord will ye deny?
50. In them (each) will be two Springs flowing (free);
51. Then which of the favours of your Lord will ye deny?
52. In them will be Fruits of every kind, two and two.
53. Then which of the favours of your Lord will ye deny?
54. They will recline on Carpets, whose inner linings will be of rich brocade: the Fruit of the Gardens will be near (and easy of reach).
55. Then which of the favours of your Lord will ye deny?
56. In them will be (Maidens), chaste, restraining their glances, whom no man or Jinn before them has touched;—
57. Then which of the favours of your Lord will ye deny?
58. Like unto rubies and coral.
59. Then which of the favours of your Lord will ye deny?
60. Is there any Reward for Good-other than Good?
61. Then which of the favours of your Lord will ye deny?
62. And besides these two, there are two other Gardens,—
63. Then which of the favours of your Lord will ye deny?—
64. Dark-green in colour (from plentiful watering).
65. Then which of the favours of your Lord will ye deny?
66. In them (each) will be two Springs pouring forth water in continuous abundance:
67. Then which of the favours of your Lord will ye deny?

SÛRA–56
AL-WĀQI'A
(INTRODUCTION)

This is the seventh and last Sûra of the series devoted to Revelation and the Hereafter, as explained in the Introduction to S. 50.

It belongs to the early Makkan period, with the possible exception of one or two verses.

The theme is the certainty of the Day of Judgment and its adjustment of true Values (56: 1-56); Allah's Power, Goodness and Glory (56: 57-74); and the truth of Revelation (56: 75-96).

68. In them will be Fruits, and dates and pomegranates.

فِيهِمَا فَاكِهَةٌ وَّنَخْلٌ وَّرُمَّانٌ ۞

69. Then which of the favours of your Lord will ye deny?

فَبِأَيِّ اٰلَاءِ رَبِّكُمَا تُكَذِّبٰنِ ۞

70. In them will be fair (Maidens), good, beautiful;—

فِيهِنَّ خَيْرٰتٌ حِسَانٌ ۞

71. Then which of the favours of your Lord will ye deny?—

فَبِأَيِّ اٰلَاءِ رَبِّكُمَا تُكَذِّبٰنِ ۞

72. Maidens restrained (as to their glances), in (goodly) pavilions:—

حُوْرٌ مَّقْصُوْرٰتٌ فِي الْخِيَامِ ۞

73. Then which of the favours of your Lord will ye deny?—

فَبِأَيِّ اٰلَاءِ رَبِّكُمَا تُكَذِّبٰنِ ۞

74. Whom no man or Jinn before them has touched;—

لَمْ يَطْمِثْهُنَّ اِنْسٌ قَبْلَهُمْ وَلَا جَآنٌّ ۞

75. Then which of the favours of your Lord will ye deny?—

فَبِأَيِّ اٰلَاءِ رَبِّكُمَا تُكَذِّبٰنِ ۞

76. Reclining on green Cushions and rich Carpets of beauty.

مُتَّكِـِٕيْنَ عَلٰى رَفْرَفٍ خُضْرٍ وَّعَبْقَرِيٍّ حِسَانٍ ۞

77. Then which of the favours of your Lord will ye deny?

فَبِأَيِّ اٰلَاءِ رَبِّكُمَا تُكَذِّبٰنِ ۞

78. Blessed be the name of thy Lord, Full of Majesty, Bounty and Honour.

تَبٰرَكَ اسْمُ رَبِّكَ ذِي الْجَلٰلِ وَالْاِكْرَامِ ۞

Al-Wāqi'a, or The Inevitable Event

سُوْرَةُ الْوَاقِعَةِ مَكِّيَّةٌ وَّهِيَ سِتٌّ وَّتِسْعُوْنَ اٰيَةً وَّتِسْعُ رُكُوْعَاتٍ

In the name of Allah, Most Gracious, Most Merciful.

بِسْمِ اللهِ الرَّحْمٰنِ الرَّحِيْمِ

1. When the Event Inevitable cometh to pass,

اِذَا وَقَعَتِ الْوَاقِعَةُ ۞

2. Then will no (soul) deny its coming.

لَيْسَ لِوَقْعَتِهَا كَاذِبَةٌ ۞

3. (Many) will it bring low; (many) will it exalt;

خَافِضَةٌ رَّافِعَةٌ ۞

4. When the earth shall be shaken to its depths,

اِذَا رُجَّتِ الْاَرْضُ رَجًّا ۞

5. And the mountains shall be crumbled to atoms,

وَّبُسَّتِ الْجِبَالُ بَسًّا ۞

6. Becoming dust scattered abroad,

فَكَانَتْ هَبَآءً مُّنْبَثًّا ۞

7. And ye shall be sorted out into three classes.

وَّكُنْتُمْ اَزْوَاجًا ثَلٰثَةً ۞

8. Then (there will be) the Companions of the Right Hand;— what will be the Companions of the Right Hand?

فَاَصْحٰبُ الْمَيْمَنَةِ مَآ اَصْحٰبُ الْمَيْمَنَةِ ۞

9. And the Companions of the Left Hand,— what will be the Companions of the Left Hand!

وَاَصْحٰبُ الْمَشْـَٔمَةِ مَآ اَصْحٰبُ الْمَشْـَٔمَةِ ۞

10. And those Foremost (in Faith) will be foremost (in the Hereafter).

وَالسّٰبِقُوْنَ السّٰبِقُوْنَ ۞

11. These will be those Nearest to Allah:

اُولٰٓئِكَ الْمُقَرَّبُوْنَ ۞

12. In Gardens of Bliss:

فِيْ جَنّٰتِ النَّعِيْمِ ۞

13. A number of people from those of old,

ثُلَّةٌ مِّنَ الْاَوَّلِيْنَ ۞

14. And a few from those of later times.

15. (They will be) on couches encrusted (with gold and precious stones),

16. Reclining on them, facing each other.

17. Round about them will (serve) youths of perpetual (freshness),

18. With goblets, (shining) beakers, and cups (filled) out of clear-flowing fountains:

19. No after-ache will they receive therefrom, nor will they suffer intoxication:

20. And with fruits, any that they may select;

21. And the flesh of fowls, any that they may desire.

22. And (there will be) Companions with beautiful, big, and lustrous eyes,—

23. Like unto Pearls well-guarded.

24. A Reward for the Deeds of their past (Life).

25. No frivolity will they hear therein, nor any Mischief,—

26. Only the Saying, "Peace! Peace" 27. The Companions of the Right Hand,— what will be the Companions of the Right Hand!

28. (They will be) among Lote-trees without thorns,

29. Among Talh trees with flowers (or fruits) piled one above another,—

30. In shade long-extended,

31. By water flowing constantly,

32. And fruit in abundance.

33. Whose season is not limited, nor (supply) forbidden,

34. And on couches raised high.

35. We have created them of special creation.

36. And made them virgin-pure (and undefiled),—

37. Full of love (for their mates) equal in age,—

38. For the Companions of the Right Hand.

39. A (goodly) number from those of old,

40. And a (goodly) number from those of later times.

41. The Companions of the Left Hand,—what will be the Companions of the Left Hand!

42. (They will be) in the midst of a fierce Blast of Fire and in Boiling Water.

43. And in the shades of Black Smoke:

44. Neither cool nor refreshing:

45. For that they were wont to be indulged, before that, in sinful luxury,

46. And persisted obstinately in wickedness supreme!

47. And they used to say, "What! when we die and become dust and bones, shall we then indeed be raised up again?—

48. "(We) and our fathers of old?"

49. Say: "Yea, those of old and those of later times,

50. "All will certainly be gathered together for the meeting appointed for a Day well-known.

51. "Then will ye truly,— O ye that go wrong, and deny (the truth);

52. "Ye will surely taste of the Tree of Zaqqūm.

53. "Then will ye fill your insides therewith,

54. "And drink Boiling Water on top of it:

55. "Indeed ye shall drink Like diseased camels raging with thirst!"

56. Such will be their entertainment on the Day of Requital!

57. It is We Who have created you: why will ye not admit the Truth?

58. Do ye then see? the (human Seed) that ye emit,—

59. Is it ye who create it, or are We the Creators?

60. We have decreed Death to be your common lot, and We are not to be frustrated

61. From changing your Forms and creating you (again) in (Forms) that ye know not.

62. And ye certainly know already the first form of creation: why then do ye not take heed?

63. See ye the seed that ye sow in the ground?

64. Is it ye that cause it to grow, or are We the Cause?

65. Were it Our Will, We could make it broken orts. And ye would be left in wonderment,

66. (Saying), "We are indeed Left with debts (for nothing):

67. "Indeed we are deprived".

68. See ye the water which ye drink?

69. Do ye bring it Down (in rain) from the Cloud or do We?

70. Were it Our Will, We could make it Saltish (and unpalatable): then why do ye not give thanks?

71. See ye the Fire which ye kindle?

72. Is it ye who grow the tree which feeds the fire, or do We grow it?

73. We have made it a reminder and an article of comfort and convenience for the denizens of deserts.

74. Then glorify the name of thy Lord, the Supreme!

75. Furthermore I swear by the setting of the Stars,—

76. And that is indeed a mighty adjuration if ye but knew,—

77. That this is indeed a Qur'ān most honourable,

78. In a Book well-guarded,

79. Which none shall touch but those who are clean:

80. A Revelation from the Lord of the Worlds.

81. Is it such a Message that ye would hold in light esteem?

82. And have ye made it your livelihood that ye should declare it false?

83. Then why do ye not (intervene) when (the soul of the dying man) reaches the throat,—

84. And ye the while (sit) looking on—

85. But We are nearer to him than ye, and yet see not,—

86. Then why do ye not,— if you are exempt from (future) account,—

87. Call back the soul, if ye are tr-ue (in your claim of independence)?

88. Thus then, if he be of those Nearest to Allah.

SÛRA–57
AL-ḤADÎD
(INTRODUCTION)

We have now studied the contents of nearly nine-tenths of the Qur-ān. We have found that the arrangement of the Sûras in the present Text is not haphazard, but that they follow a distinct logical order more helpful for study than the chronological order. The comprehensive scheme of building up the new *Ummat* or Brotherhood and its spiritual implications is now complete. The remaining tenth of the Qur-ān may be roughly considered in two parts. The first contains ten Sûras (S. 57 to 66), all revealed in Madinah, and each dealing with some special point which needs emphasis in the social life of the Ummat. The second (S. 67 to S. 114) contains short Makkan lyrics, each dealing with some aspect of spiritual life, expressed in language of great mystic beauty.

The present Madinah Sûra is chiefly concerned with spiritual humility and the avoidance of arrogance, and a warning that retirement from the world may not be the best way of seeking the good pleasure of Allah. Its probable date is after the Conquest of Makkah, A.H. 8.

89. (There is for him) Rest and Satisfaction, and a Garden of Delights.

90. And if he be of the Companions of the Right Hand,

91. (For him is the salutation), "Peace be unto thee," from the Companions of the Right Hand.

92. And if he be of those who deny (the truth) who go wrong,

93. For him is Entertainment with Boiling Water,

94. And burning in Hell-Fire.

95. Verily, this is the very Truth of assured Certainty.

96. So glorify the name of thy Lord, the Supreme.

Al-Ḥadîd, or Iron,

In the name of Allah, Most Gracious, Most Merciful.

1. Whatever is in the heavens and on earth,— declares the Praises and Glory of Allah: for He is the Exalted in Might, the Wise.

2. To Him belongs the dominion of the heavens and the earth: it is He Who gives Life and Death; and He has Power over all things.

3. He is the First and the Last, the Evident and the Hidden: and He has full knowledge of all things.

4. He it is Who created the heavens and the earth in six Days, then He established Himself on the Throne. He knows what enters within the earth and what comes forth out of it, what comes down from heaven and what mounts up to it. And He is with you wheresoever ye may be. And Allah sees well all that ye do.

5. To Him belongs the dominion of the heavens and the earth: and all affairs go back to Allah.

6. He merges Night into Day, and He merges Day into Night; and He has full knowledge of the secrets of (all) hearts.

7. Believe in Allah and His Messenger, and spend (in charity) out of the (substance)

whereof He has made you heirs. For, those of you who believe and spend (in charity),— for them is a great Reward.

8. How is it with you that you believe not in Allah?—And the Messenger invites you to believe in your Lord and has indeed taken your Covenant, if ye are men of faith.

9. He is the One Who sends to His Servant Manifest Signs, that He may lead you from the depths of Darkness into the Light and verily, Allah is to you Most Kind and Merciful.

10. How is it with you that you spend not in the cause of Allah?— For to Allah belongs the heritage of the heavens and the earth. Not equal among you are those who spent (freely) and fought, before the Victory, (with those who did so later). Those are higher in rank than those who spent (freely) and fought afterwards. But to all has Allah promised a goodly (reward). And Allah is well acquainted with all that ye do.

11. Who is he that will loan to Allah a beautiful loan? For (Allah) will increase it manifold to his credit, and he will have (besides) a generous reward.

12. The Day shalt thou see the believing men and the believing women— how their Light runs forward before them and by their right hands: (their greeting will be): "Good News for you this Day! Gardens beneath which flow rivers! To dwell therein for aye! This is indeed the highest Triumph."

13. The Day will the Hypocrites— men and women—say to the Believers: "Wait for us! Let us borrow (a light) from your Light!" It will be said: "Turn ye back to your rear! Then seek a light (where ye can)!" So a wall will be put up betwixt them, with a gate therein. Within it will be Mercy throughout, and without it, all alongside, will be (Wrath and) Punishment!

14. (Those without) will call out, "Were we not with you?" (The others) will reply, "True!

but ye led yourselves into temptation; ye waited (to our ruin); ye doubted (Allah's Promise); and (your false) desires deceived you; until there issued the Command of Allah. And the Deceiver deceived you in respect of Allah.

15. "This Day shall no ransom be accepted of you, nor of those who rejected Allah. Your abode is the Fire: that is the proper place to claim you: and an evil refuge it is!"

16. Has not the time arrived for the Believers that their hearts in all humility should engage in the remembrance of Allah and of the Truth which has been revealed (to them), and that they should not become like those to whom was given the Book aforetime, but long ages passed over them and their hearts grew hard? For many among them are rebellious transgressors.

17. Know ye (all) that Allah giveth life to the earth after its death! Alrea-dy have We shown the Signs plainly to you, that ye may understand.

18. For those who give in Charity, men and women, and loan to Allah a Beautiful Loan, it shall be increased manifold (to their credit), and they shall have (besides) a generous reward.

19. And those who believe in Allah and His messengers—they are the Truthful and the martyrs, in the eye of their Lord: they shall have their Reward and their Light. But those who reject Allah and deny Our Signs,—they are the Companions of Hell-Fire.

20. Know ye (all), that the life of this world is but play and a pastime, adornment and mutual boasting and multiplying, (in rivalry) among yourselves, riches and children. Here is a similitude: how rain and the growth which it brings forth, delight (the hearts of) the tillers; soon it withers; thou wilt see it grow yellow; then it becomes dry and crumbles away. But in the Hereafter is a Chastisement severe (for the devotees of wrong). And Forgiveness from Allah and (His) Good Pleasure (for the devotees of Allah). And what is the life of this world, but goods and chattels of deception?

21. Be ye foremost (in seeking) Forgiveness from your Lord, and a Garden (of Bliss), the width whereof is as the width of Heaven and earth, prepared for those who believe in Allah and His messengers: that is the Grace of Allah, which He bestows on whom He pleases: and Allah is the Lord of Grace abounding.

22. No misfortune can happen on earth or in your souls but is recorded in a Book before We bring it into existence: that is truly easy for Allah:

23. In order that ye may not despair over matters that pass you by, nor exult over favours bestowed upon you. For Allah loveth not any vainglorious boaster,—

24. Such persons as are covetous and commend covetousness to men. And if any turn back (from Allah's Way), verily Allah is free of all needs, worthy of all praise.

25. We sent aforetime Our messengers with Clear Signs and sent down with them the Book and the Balance (of Right and Wrong), that men may stand forth in justice: and We sent down Iron, in which is great might, as well as many benefits for mankind, that Allah may test who it is that will help, unseen, Him and His messengers: for Allah is Full of Strength, Exalted in Might.

26. And We sent Noah and Abraham, and established in their line Prophethood and Revelation: and some of them were on right guidance, but many of them became rebellious transgressors.

27. Then, in their wake, We followed them up with (others of) Our messengers: We sent after them Jesus the son of Mary, and bestowed on him the Gospel: and We ordained in the hearts of those who followed him Compassion and Mercy. But the Monasticism which they invented for themselves. We did not prescribe for them: (we commanded) only the seeking for the

SÛRA–58
AL-MUJĀDILA
(INTRODUCTION)

This is the second of the ten Madinah Sûras referred to in the Introduction to the last Sûra. Its subject-matter is the acceptance of a women's Plea on behalf of herself and her children and a condemnation of all secret counsels and intrigues in the Muslim Brotherhood.

The date is somewhat close to that of S. 33, say between A.H. 5. and A.H. 7.

Good Pleasure of Allah; but that they did not foster as they should have done. Yet We bestowed, on those among them who believed, their (due) reward, but many of them are rebellious transgressors.

28. O ye that believe! fear Allah, and believe in His Messenger, and He will bestow on you a double portion of His Mercy: He will provide for you a Light by which ye shall walk (straight in your path), and He will forgive you (your past): for Allah is Oft-Forgiving, Most Merciful:

29. That the People of the Book may know that they have no power whatever over the Grace of Allah, that (His) Grace is (entirely) in His Hand, to bestow it on whomsoever He wills. For Allah is the Lord of Grace abounding.

Al-Mujādila, or The Woman who Pleads

In the name of Allah, Most Gracious, Most Merciful.

1. Allah has indeed heard (and accepted) the statement of the woman who pleads with thee concerning her husband and carries her complaint (in prayer) to Allah: and Allah (always) hears the arguments between both of you: for Allah hears and sees (all things).

2. If any men among you divorce their wives by *Zihār* (calling them mothers), they cannot be their mothers: none can be their mothers except those who gave them birth. And in fact they use words (both) iniquitous and false: but truly Allah is All-Pardoning, All-Forgiving.

3. But those who pronounce the word "*Zihār*" to their wives then wish to go back on the words they uttered,— (it is ordained that such a one) should free a slave before they touch each other: this are ye admonished to perform: and Allah is well-acquainted with (all) that ye do.

4. And if any has not (the means), he should fast for two months consecutively before they touch each other, but if any is unable to do so, he should feed sixty indigent ones. This, that ye may show your faith in Allah and His Messenger. Those are limits (set by) Allah. For those who reject (Him),

there is a grievous Chastisement.

5. Those who oppose (the commands of) Allah and His Messenger will be humbled to dust, as were those before them: for We have already sent down Clear Signs. And the Unbelievers (will have) a humiliating Chastisement,

6. On the Day that Allah will raise them all up (again) and tell them of their deeds (which) Allah has reckoned and which they forgot, for Allah is Witness to all things.

7. Seest thou not that Allah doth know (all) that is in the heavens and on earth? There is not a secret consultation between three, but He is the fourth of them,— nor between five but he is the sixth,— nor between fewer nor more, but He is with them, wheresoever they be: in the end will He tell them what they did on the Day of Judgment. For Allah Has full knowledge of all things.

8. Seest thou not those who were forbidden secret counsels yet revert to that which they were forbidden (to do)? And they hold secret counsels among themselves for iniquity and hostility, and disobedience to the Messenger. And when they come to thee, they salute thee, not as Allah salutes thee, (but in crooked ways): and they say to themselves, "Why does not Allah punish us for our words?" Enough for them is Hell: in it will they burn, and evil is that destination!

9. O ye who believe! when ye hold secret counsel, do it not for iniquity and hostility, and disobedience to the Messenger; but do it for righteousness and self-restraint; and fear Allah, to Whom ye shall be brought back.

10. Secret counsels are only (inspired) by Satan, in order that he may cause grief to the Believers; but he cannot harm them in the least, except as Allah permits; and on

وَلِلْكٰفِرِيْنَ عَذَابٌ اَلِيْمٌ ۞

اِنَّ الَّذِيْنَ يُحَآدُّوْنَ اللهَ وَرَسُوْلَهٗ كُبِتُوْا كَمَا كُبِتَ الَّذِيْنَ مِنْ قَبْلِهِمْ وَقَدْ اَنْزَلْنَآ اٰيٰتٍۭ بَيِّنٰتٍ ؕ وَلِلْكٰفِرِيْنَ عَذَابٌ مُّهِيْنٌ ۞

يَّوْمَ يَبْعَثُهُمُ اللهُ جَمِيْعًا فَيُنَبِّئُهُمْ بِمَا عَمِلُوْا ؕ اَحْصٰهُ اللهُ وَنَسُوْهُ ؕ وَاللهُ عَلٰى كُلِّ شَيْءٍ شَهِيْدٌ ۞

اَلَمْ تَرَ اَنَّ اللهَ يَعْلَمُ مَا فِى السَّمٰوٰتِ وَ مَا فِى الْاَرْضِ ؕ مَا يَكُوْنُ مِنْ نَّجْوٰى ثَلٰثَةٍ اِلَّا هُوَ رَابِعُهُمْ وَلَا خَمْسَةٍ اِلَّا هُوَ سَادِسُهُمْ وَلَاۤ اَدْنٰى مِنْ ذٰلِكَ وَلَاۤ اَكْثَرَ اِلَّا هُوَ مَعَهُمْ اَيْنَ مَا كَانُوْا ۚ ثُمَّ يُنَبِّئُهُمْ بِمَا عَمِلُوْا يَوْمَ الْقِيٰمَةِ ؕ اِنَّ اللهَ بِكُلِّ شَيْءٍ عَلِيْمٌ ۞

اَلَمْ تَرَ اِلَى الَّذِيْنَ نُهُوْا عَنِ النَّجْوٰى ثُمَّ يَعُوْدُوْنَ لِمَا نُهُوْا عَنْهُ وَيَتَنَاجَوْنَ بِالْاِثْمِ وَالْعُدْوَانِ وَمَعْصِيَتِ الرَّسُوْلِ ؗ وَاِذَا جَآءُوْكَ حَيَّوْكَ بِمَا لَمْ يُحَيِّكَ بِهِ اللهُ ۙ وَيَقُوْلُوْنَ فِىْٓ اَنْفُسِهِمْ لَوْلَا يُعَذِّبُنَا اللهُ بِمَا نَقُوْلُ ؕ حَسْبُهُمْ جَهَنَّمُ ۚ يَصْلَوْنَهَا ۚ فَبِئْسَ الْمَصِيْرُ ۞

يٰۤاَيُّهَا الَّذِيْنَ اٰمَنُوْۤا اِذَا تَنَاجَيْتُمْ فَلَا تَتَنَاجَوْا بِالْاِثْمِ وَالْعُدْوَانِ وَمَعْصِيَتِ الرَّسُوْلِ وَتَنَاجَوْا بِالْبِرِّ وَالتَّقْوٰى ؕ وَ اتَّقُوا اللهَ الَّذِىْٓ اِلَيْهِ تُحْشَرُوْنَ ۞

اِنَّمَا النَّجْوٰى مِنَ الشَّيْطٰنِ لِيَحْزُنَ الَّذِيْنَ اٰمَنُوْا وَلَيْسَ بِضَآرِّهِمْ شَيْئًا اِلَّا بِاِذْنِ اللهِ ؕ وَعَلَى اللهِ فَلْيَتَوَكَّلِ

Allah let the Believers put their trust.

11. O ye who believe! when ye are told to make room in the assemblies, (spread out and) make room: (ample) room will Allah provide for you. And when ye are told to rise up, rise up: Allah will raise up, to (suitable) ranks (and degrees), those of you who believe and who have been granted Knowledge. And Allah is well-acquainted with all ye do.

12. O ye who believe ! when ye consult the Messenger in private, spend something in charity before your private consultation. That will be best for you, and most conducive to purity (of conduct). But if ye find not (the wherewithal), Allah is Oft-Forgiving, Most Merciful.

13. Is it that ye are afraid of spending sums in charity before your private consultation (with him)? If, then, ye do not so, and Allah forgives you, then (at least) establish regular prayer; give Zakat and obey Allah and His Messenger. And Allah is well-acquainted with all that ye do.

14. Seest thou not those who turn (in friendship) to such as have the Wrath of Allah upon them? They are neither of you nor of them, and they swear to falsehood knowingly.

15. Allah has prepared for them a severe Chastisement: evil indeed are their deeds.

16. They have made their oaths a screen (for their misdeeds): thus they obstruct (men) from the Path of Allah: therefore shall they have a humiliating Chastisement.

17. Of no profit whatever to them, against Allah, will be their riches nor their sons: they will be Companions of the Fire, to dwell therein (for aye)!

18. The Day will Allah raise them all up (for Judgment): then will they swear to Him as they swear to you: and they think that they have something (to stand upon).

SÛRA–59
AL-ḤASHR
(INTRODUCTION)

This is the third of the series of ten short Madinah   Sûras, dealing each with a special point in the life of the Ummat: see Introduction to S. 57. The special theme here is how treachery to the Ummat on the part of its enemies recoils on the enemies themselves, while it strengthens the bond between the different sections of the Ummat itself, and this is illustrated by the story of the expulsion of the Jewish tribe of the Banû Naḍhîr in Rabî' I A.H. 4.

This fixes the date of the Sûra.

No, indeed ! they are but liars !

19. Satan has got the better of them: so he has made them forgot the remembrance of Allah. They are the Party of Satan. Truly, it is the Party of Satan that will lose.

20. Those who oppose (the commands of) Allah and His Messenger will be among those most humiliated.

21. Allah has decreed: "It is I and My messengers who must prevail": for Allah is Strong, Mighty.

22. Thou wilt not find any people who believe in Allah and the Last Day, loving those who oppose Allah and His Messenger, even though they were their fathers or their sons, or their brothers, or their kindred. For such he has written Faith in their hearts, and strengthened them with a spirit from Himself. And He will admit them to Gardens beneath which Rivers flow, to dwell therein (for ever). Allah will be well pleased with them, and they with Him. They are the Party of Allah. Truly it is the Party of Allah that will achieve Success.

Al-Ḥashr, or The Gathering (or Banishment,)

In the name of Allah, Most Gracious, Most Merciful.

1. Whatever is in the heavens and on earth, declares the Praises and Glory of Allah: for He is the Exalted in Might, the Wise.

2. It is He Who got out the Unbelievers among the People of the Book from their homes at the first gathering (of the forces). Little did ye think that they would get out: and they thought that their fortresses would defend them from Allah! But the (Wrath of) Allah came to them from quarters from which they little expected (it), and cast terror into their hearts, so that they destroyed their dwellings by their own hands and the hands of the Believers. Take warning, then,

O ye with eyes (to see) !

يَاأُولِى الْأَبْصَارِ ۞

3. And had it not been that Allah had decreed banishment for them, he would certainly have punished them in this world: and in the Hereafter they shall (certainly) have the Punishment of the Fire.

وَلَوْلَا أَن كَتَبَ اللهُ عَلَيْهِمُ الْجَلَاءَ لَعَذَّبَهُمْ فِى الدُّنْيَا وَلَهُمْ فِى الْآخِرَةِ عَذَابُ النَّارِ ۞

4. That is because they resisted Allah and His Messenger and if anyone resists Allah, verily Allah is severe in Punishment.

ذَلِكَ بِأَنَّهُمْ شَاقُّوا اللهَ وَرَسُولَهُ وَمَن يُشَاقِّ اللهَ فَإِنَّ اللهَ شَدِيدُ الْعِقَابِ ۞

5. Whatever ye cut down (O ye Muslims!) of the tender palm-trees, or ye left them standing on their roots, it was by leave of Allah, and in order that He might cover with shame the rebellious transgressors.

مَا قَطَعْتُم مِّن لِّينَةٍ أَوْ تَرَكْتُمُوهَا قَائِمَةً عَلَى أُصُولِهَا فَبِإِذْنِ اللهِ وَلِيُخْزِىَ الْفَاسِقِينَ ۞

6. What Allah has bestowed on His Messenger (and taken away) from them—for this ye made no expedition with either cavalry or camelry: but Allah gives power to His messengers over any He pleases: and Allah has power over all things.

وَمَا أَفَاءَ اللهُ عَلَى رَسُولِهِ مِنْهُمْ فَمَا أَوْجَفْتُمْ عَلَيْهِ مِنْ خَيْلٍ وَلَا رِكَابٍ وَلَكِنَّ اللهَ يُسَلِّطُ رُسُلَهُ عَلَى مَن يَشَاءُ وَاللهُ عَلَى كُلِّ شَيْءٍ قَدِيرٌ ۞

7. What Allah has bestowed on His Messenger (and taken away) from the people of the townships,—belongs to Allah,—to His Messenger and to kindred and orphans, the needy and the wayfarer; in order that it may not (Merely) make a circuit between the wealthy among you. So take what the Messenger gives you, and refrain from what he prohibits you. And fear Allah; for Allah is strict in Punishment.

مَا أَفَاءَ اللهُ عَلَى رَسُولِهِ مِنْ أَهْلِ الْقُرَى فَلِلَّهِ وَلِلرَّسُولِ وَلِذِى الْقُرْبَى وَالْيَتَامَى وَالْمَسَاكِينِ وَابْنِ السَّبِيلِ كَىْ لَا يَكُونَ دُولَةً بَيْنَ الْأَغْنِيَاءِ مِنكُمْ وَمَا آتَاكُمُ الرَّسُولُ فَخُذُوهُ وَمَا نَهَاكُمْ عَنْهُ فَانتَهُوا وَاتَّقُوا اللهَ إِنَّ اللهَ شَدِيدُ الْعِقَابِ ۞

8. (Some part is due) to the indigent Muhājirs, those who were expelled from their homes and their property. while seeking Grace from Allah and (His) Good Pleasure, and aiding Allah and His Messenger: such are indeed the truthful;—

لِلْفُقَرَاءِ الْمُهَاجِرِينَ الَّذِينَ أُخْرِجُوا مِن دِيَارِهِمْ وَأَمْوَالِهِمْ يَبْتَغُونَ فَضْلًا مِّنَ اللهِ وَرِضْوَانًا وَيَنصُرُونَ اللهَ وَرَسُولَهُ أُولَئِكَ هُمُ الصَّادِقُونَ ۞

9. And those who before them. had homes (in Madinah) and had adopted the Faith,—show their affection to such as came to them for refuge, and entertain no desire in their hearts for things given to the (latter), but give them preference over themselves.

وَالَّذِينَ تَبَوَّءُوا الدَّارَ وَالْإِيمَانَ مِن قَبْلِهِمْ يُحِبُّونَ مَنْ هَاجَرَ إِلَيْهِمْ وَلَا يَجِدُونَ فِى صُدُورِهِمْ حَاجَةً مِّمَّا أُوتُوا وَيُؤْثِرُونَ

even though poverty was their (own lot).
And those saved from the covetousness of
their own souls,—they are the ones that
achieve prosperity.

10. And those who came after them say:
"Our Lord ! forgive us, and our brethren
who came before us into the Faith, and
leave not, in our hearts, rancour (or sense
of injury) against those who have believed.
Our Lord ! Thou art indeed Full of Kindness,
Most Merciful."

11. Hast thou not observed the Hypocrites
say to their misbelieving brethren among
the People of the Book?— "If ye are
expelled, we too will go out with you, and
we will never hearken to anyone in your
affair; and if ye are attacked (in fight) we
will help you". But Allah is witness that they
are indeed liars.

12. If they are expelled, never will they go
out with them; and if they are attacked (in
fight), they will never help them: and if they
do help them, they will turn their backs; so
they will receive no help.

13. Of a truth ye arouse greater fear in
their hearts, than Allah. This is because
they are men devoid of understanding.

14. They will not fight you (even) together,
except in fortified townships, or from behind
walls. Strong is their fighting (spirit) amongst
themselves: thou wouldst think they were
united, but their hearts are divided: that is
because they are a people devoid of
wisdom.

15. Like those who lately preceded them,
they have tasted the evil result of their
conduct; and (in the Hereafter there is) for
them a grievous Chastisement;—

16. (Their allies deceived them), like Satan
when he says to man, "Disbelieve": but
when (man) disbelieves, Satan says, "I am
free of thee: I do fear Allah, the Lord of the
Worlds !"

17. The end of both will be that they will
go into the Fire, dwelling therein for ever.
Such is the reward of the wrong-doers.

SÛRA-60
AL-MUMTAHANA
(INTRODUCTION)

This is the fourth of the ten Madinah Sûras, each dealing with a special point in the life of the Ummat.

Here the point is: what social relations are possible with the Unbelievers? A distinction is made between those who persecute you for your Faith and want to destroy you and your Faith, and those who have shown no such rancour. For the latter there is hope of mercy and forgiveness. The question of women and cross-marriages is equitably dealt with.

The date is after the Pagans had broken the treaty of Hudaibîya, for which see Introduction to S. 47— say about A.H. 8, not long before the conquest of Makkah.

18. O ye who believe ! fear Allah and let every soul look to what (provision) he has sent forth for the morrow. Yea, fear Allah: for Allah is well-acquainted with (all) that ye do.

يَأَيُّهَا الَّذِينَ اٰمَنُوا اتَّقُوا اللهَ وَلْتَنْظُرْ نَفْسٌ مَّا قَدَّمَتْ لِغَدٍ ۚ وَاتَّقُوا اللهَ ۚ إِنَّ اللهَ خَبِيرٌ بِمَا تَعْمَلُونَ ۞

19. And be ye not like those who forgot Allah; and He made them forget themselves ! Such are the rebellious transgressors !

وَلَا تَكُونُوا كَالَّذِينَ نَسُوا اللهَ فَأَنْسَاهُمْ أَنْفُسَهُمْ ۚ أُولَئِكَ هُمُ الْفَاسِقُونَ ۞

20. Not equal are the Companions of the Fire and the Companions of the Garden: it is the Companions of the Garden, that will achieve Felicity.

لَا يَسْتَوِي أَصْحَابُ النَّارِ وَأَصْحَابُ الْجَنَّةِ ۚ أَصْحَابُ الْجَنَّةِ هُمُ الْفَائِزُونَ ۞

21. Had We sent down this Qur-ān on a mountain, verily, thou wouldst have seen it humble itself and cleave asunder for fear of Allah. Such are the similitudes which We propound to men, that they may reflect.

لَوْ أَنْزَلْنَا هَذَا الْقُرْآنَ عَلَى جَبَلٍ لَّرَأَيْتَهُ خَاشِعًا مُتَصَدِّعًا مِّنْ خَشْيَةِ اللهِ ۚ وَتِلْكَ الْأَمْثَالُ نَضْرِبُهَا لِلنَّاسِ لَعَلَّهُمْ يَتَفَكَّرُونَ ۞

22. Allah is He, than Whom there is no other god;— Who knows (all things) both secret and open; He, Most Gracious, Most Merciful.

هُوَ اللهُ الَّذِي لَا إِلَهَ إِلَّا هُوَ ۖ عَالِمُ الْغَيْبِ وَالشَّهَادَةِ ۖ هُوَ الرَّحْمَنُ الرَّحِيمُ ۞

23. Allah is He, than Whom there is no other god;— the Sovereign, the Holy One, the Source of Peace (and Perfection), the Guardian of Faith, the Preserver of Safety. the Exalted in Might, the Irresistible, the justly Proud glory to Allah ! (High is He) above the partners they attribute to Him.

هُوَ اللهُ الَّذِي لَا إِلَهَ إِلَّا هُوَ ۚ الْمَلِكُ الْقُدُّوسُ السَّلَامُ الْمُؤْمِنُ الْمُهَيْمِنُ الْعَزِيزُ الْجَبَّارُ الْمُتَكَبِّرُ ۚ سُبْحَانَ اللهِ عَمَّا يُشْرِكُونَ ۞

24. He is Allah, the Creator the Originator, the Fashioner. To Him belong the Most Beautiful Names: whatever is in the heavens and on earth. doth declare His Praises and Glory: and He is the Exalted in Might, the Wise.

هُوَ اللهُ الْخَالِقُ الْبَارِئُ الْمُصَوِّرُ ۖ لَهُ الْأَسْمَاءُ الْحُسْنَى ۚ يُسَبِّحُ لَهُ مَا فِي السَّمَوَاتِ وَالْأَرْضِ ۖ وَهُوَ الْعَزِيزُ الْحَكِيمُ ۞

Al-Mumtaḥana, or the Woman to be Examined

سُورَةُ الْمُمْتَحِنَةِ مَدَنِيَّةٌ وَهِيَ ثَلَاثَ عَشَرَةَ آيَةً وَفِيهَا رُكُوعَانِ

In the name of Allah, Most Gracious, Most Merciful.

بِسْمِ اللهِ الرَّحْمَنِ الرَّحِيمِ

1. O ye who believe ! take not My enemies and yours as friends (or protectors),—offering them (your) love, even though they have rejected the Truth that has come to you, and have (on the contrary) driven out the Messenger and yourselves (from your homes), (simply) because ye believe in Allah

يَأَيُّهَا الَّذِينَ اٰمَنُوا لَا تَتَّخِذُوا عَدُوِّي وَعَدُوَّكُمْ أَوْلِيَاءَ تُلْقُونَ إِلَيْهِمْ بِالْمَوَدَّةِ وَقَدْ كَفَرُوا بِمَا جَاءَكُمْ مِّنَ الْحَقِّ يُخْرِجُونَ الرَّسُولَ وَإِيَّاكُمْ ۙ أَنْ تُؤْمِنُوا بِاللهِ رَبِّكُمْ ۚ إِنْ كُنْتُمْ خَرَجْتُمْ جِهَادًا فِي سَبِيلِي وَ

your Lord ! If ye have come out to strive in My Way and to seek My Good Pleasure, showing friendship unto them in secret: for I know full well all that ye conceal and all that ye reveal. And any of you that does this has strayed from the Straight Path.

2. If they overcome you they would behave to you as enemies, and stretch forth their hands and their tongues against you for evil; and they desire that ye should reject the Truth.

3. Of no profit to you will be your relatives and your children on the Day of Judgment: He will judge between you: for Allah sees well all that ye do.

4. There is for you an excellent example (to follow) in Abraham and those with him, when they said to their people: "We are clear of you and of whatever ye worship besides Allah: we have rejected you, and there has arisen, between us and you, enmity and hatred for ever,—unless ye believe in Allah and Him alone": but not when Abraham said to his father: "I will pray for forgiveness for thee, though I have no power (to get) aught on thy behalf from Allah." (They prayed): "Our Lord ! in Thee do we trust, and to Thee do we turn in repentance: to Thee is (our) final Return.

5. "Our Lord ! Make us not a (test and) trial for the Unbelievers, but forgive us, our Lord ! For Thou art the Exalted in Might, the Wise."

6. There was indeed in them an excellent example for you to follow,—for those whose hope is in Allah and in the last Day. But if any turn away, truly Allah is Free of all wants, Worthy of all Praise.

7. It may be that Allah will Establish friendship between you and those whom ye (now) hold as enemies. For Allah has power (Over all things); and Allah is Oft-Forgiving, Most Merciful.

8. Allah forbids you not, with regard to those who fight you not for (your) Faith nor

drive you out of your homes, from dealing kindly and justly with them: for Allah loveth those who are just.

9.   Allah only forbids you, with regard to those who fight you for (your) Faith, and drive you out of your homes, and support (others) in driving you out, from turning to them (for friendship and protection). It is such as turn to them (in these circumstances), that do wrong.

10.   O ye who believe ! when there come to you believing women refugees, examine (and test) them: Allah knows best as to their Faith: if ye ascertain that they are Believers, then send them not back to the Unbelievers. They are not lawful (wives) for the Unbelievers, nor are the (Unbelievers) lawful (husbands) for them. But pay the Unbelievers what they have spent (on their dower). And there will be no blame on you if ye marry them on payment of their dower to them. But hold not to the ties (marriage contract) of Unbelieving women: ask for what ye have spent on their dowers, and let the (Unbelievers) ask for what they have spent (on the dowers of women who come over to you). Such is the command of Allah: He judges (with justice) between you. And Allah is Full of Knowledge and Wisdom.

11.   And if any of your wives deserts you to the Unbelievers, and ye have your turn (by the coming over of a woman from the other side). Then pay to those whose wives have deserted the equivalent of what they had spent (on their dower). And fear Allah, in whom ye believe.

12.   O Prophet ! when believing women come to thee to take the oath of fealty to thee, that they will not associate in worship any other thing whatever with Allah, that they will not steal, that they will not commit adultery (or fornication), that they will not kill their children, that they will not utter slander, intentionally forging falsehood and that they will not

SÛRA–61
AṢ-ṢAFF
(INTRODUCTION)

This is the fifth Sûra of the series of short Madinah Sûras beginning with S. 57. Its subject-matter is the need for discipline, practical work, and self-sacrifice in the cause of the Ummat. Its date is uncertain, but it was probably shortly after the battle of Uḥud, which was fought in Shawwal, A.H. 3.

disobey thee in any just matter,— then do thou receive their fealty, and pray to Allah for the forgiveness (of their sins): for Allah is Oft-Forgiving, Most Merciful.

13.   O ye who believe ! turn not (for friendship) to people on whom is the Wrath of Allah. Of the Hereafter they are already in despair, just as the Unbelievers are in despair about those (buried) in graves.

Aṣ-Ṣaff, or Battle Array

In the name of Allah, Most Gracious, Most Merciful.

1.   Whatever is in the heavens and on earth, declares the Praises and Glory of Allah: for He is the Exalted in Might, the Wise.

2.   O ye who believe ! why say ye that which ye do not?

3.   Grievously hateful is it in the sight of Allah that ye say that which ye do not.

4.   Truly Allah loves those who fight in His Cause in battle array, as if they were a solid cemented structure.

5.   And remember, Moses said to his people: "O my people ! why do ye vex and insult me, though ye know that I am the messenger of Allah (sent) to you?" Then when they went wrong, Allah let their hearts go wrong. For Allah guides not those who are rebellious transgressors.

6.   And remember, Jesus, the son of Mary, said: "O Children of Israel ! I am the messenger of Allah (sent) to you, confirming the Taurat (which came) before me, and giving glad Tidings of a messenger to come after me, whose name shall be Ahmad." But when he came to them with Clear Signs they said, "This is Evident sorcery !"

7.   Who doth greater wrong than one who forges falsehood against Allah, even as he is being invited to Islam? And Allah Guides not those who do wrong.

8.   Their intention is to extinguish Allah's Light (by blowing) with their mouths: but Allah will complete His Light, even though the Unbelievers may detest (it).

9.   It is He Who has sent His Messenger with Guidance and the Religion of Truth. That He make it prevail over all religion, even though the Pagans may detest (it).

10.   O ye who believe ! shall I lead you to a bargain that will save you from a grievous Chastisement ?—

11.   That ye believe in Allah and His Messenger, and that ye strive (your utmost) in the Cause of Allah, with your wealth and your persons: that will be best for you, if ye but knew !

12.   He will forgive you your sins, and admit you to Gardens beneath which rivers flow, and to beautiful Mansions in Gardens of Eternity: that is indeed the Supreme Triumph.

13.   And another (favour will He bestow), which ye do love .—help from Allah and a speedy victory. So give the Glad Tidings to the Believers.

14.   O ye who believe ! be ye helpers of Allah: as said Jesus the son of Mary to the Disciples, "Who will be my helpers to (the work of) Allah ?" Said the Disciples, "We are Allah's helpers !" Then a portion of the Children of Israel believed, and a portion disbelieved: but We gave power to those who believed against their enemies. and they became the ones that prevailed.

يُرِيْدُوْنَ لِيُطْفِـُٔوْا نُوْرَ اللّٰهِ بِاَفْوَاهِهِمْ وَاللّٰهُ مُتِمُّ نُوْرِهٖ وَلَوْ كَرِهَ الْكٰفِرُوْنَ ۝

هُوَ الَّذِيْٓ اَرْسَلَ رَسُوْلَهٗ بِالْهُدٰى وَ دِيْنِ الْحَقِّ لِيُظْهِرَهٗ عَلَى الدِّيْنِ كُلِّهٖ وَلَوْ كَرِهَ الْمُشْرِكُوْنَ ۝

يٰٓاَيُّهَا الَّذِيْنَ اٰمَنُوْا هَلْ اَدُلُّكُمْ عَلٰى تِجَارَةٍ تُنْجِيْكُمْ مِّنْ عَذَابٍ اَلِيْمٍ ۝

تُؤْمِنُوْنَ بِاللّٰهِ وَرَسُوْلِهٖ وَتُجَاهِدُوْنَ فِيْ سَبِيْلِ اللّٰهِ بِاَمْوَالِكُمْ وَاَنْفُسِكُمْ ذٰلِكُمْ خَيْرٌ لَّكُمْ اِنْ كُنْتُمْ تَعْلَمُوْنَ ۝

يَغْفِرْ لَكُمْ ذُنُوْبَكُمْ وَيُدْخِلْكُمْ جَنّٰتٍ تَجْرِيْ مِنْ تَحْتِهَا الْاَنْهٰرُ وَمَسٰكِنَ طَيِّبَةً فِيْ جَنّٰتِ عَدْنٍ ذٰلِكَ الْفَوْزُ الْعَظِيْمُ ۝

وَاُخْرٰى تُحِبُّوْنَهَا نَصْرٌ مِّنَ اللّٰهِ وَ فَتْحٌ قَرِيْبٌ وَبَشِّرِ الْمُؤْمِنِيْنَ ۝

يٰٓاَيُّهَا الَّذِيْنَ اٰمَنُوْا كُوْنُوْٓا اَنْصَارَ اللّٰهِ كَمَا قَالَ عِيْسَى ابْنُ مَرْيَمَ لِلْحَوَارِيّٖنَ مَنْ اَنْصَارِيْٓ اِلَى اللّٰهِ قَالَ الْحَوَارِيُّوْنَ نَحْنُ اَنْصَارُ اللّٰهِ فَاٰمَنَتْ طَّائِفَةٌ مِّنْ بَنِيْٓ اِسْرَآءِيْلَ وَكَفَرَتْ طَّائِفَةٌ فَاَيَّدْنَا الَّذِيْنَ اٰمَنُوْا عَلٰى عَدُوِّهِمْ فَاَصْبَحُوْا ظَاهِرِيْنَ ۝

SÛRA–62
AL-JUMU'A
(INTRODUCTION)

This is the sixth Sûra in the Madinah series of short Sûras which began with S. 57.

The special theme here is the need for mutual contact in the Community for worship and understanding: for the spirit of the Message is for all, ignorant and learned, in order that they may be purified and may learn wisdom.

The date has no special significance: it may be placed in the early Madinah period, say, between A.H. 2 and 5.

Al-Jumu'a, or the Assembly (Friday) Prayer

In the name of Allah, Most Gracious, Most Merciful.

1. Whatever is in the heavens and on earth, doth declare the Praises and Glory of Allah,—the Sovereign, the Holy One, the Exalted in Might, the Wise.

2. It is He Who has sent amongst the Unlettered a messenger from among themselves, to rehearse to them His Signs, to purify them, and to instruct them in The Book and Wisdom,—although they had been, before, in manifest error;—

3. Alongwith others of them, who have not already joined them: and He is Exalted in Might, Wise.

4. Such is the Bounty of Allah, which He bestows on whom He will: and Allah is the Lord of the highest bounty.

5. The similitude of those who were entrusted with the (obligations of) Taurat, but who subsequently failed in those (obligations), is that of a donkey which carries huge tomes (but understands them not). Evil is the similitude of people who falsify the Signs of Allah: and Allah guides not people who do wrong.

6. Say: O ye of Jewry ! if ye think that ye are friends to Allah, to the exclusion of (other) men, then express your desire for Death, if ye are truthful!"

7. But never will they express their desire (for Death), because of the (deeds) their hands have sent on before them ! And Allah knows well those that do wrong !

8. Say: "The Death from which ye flee will truly overtake you: then will ye be sent back to the Knower of things secret and open: and He will tell you the things that ye did !"

9. O ye who believe ! when the call is proclaimed to prayer on Friday

SÛRA–63
AL-MUNÃFÎQÛN
(INTRODUCTION)

This is the seventh of the ten short Madinah Sûras dealing with a special feature in the social life of the Brotherhood.

The special feature here dealt with is the wiles and mischief of the Hypocrite element in any community, and the need of guarding against it and against the temptation it throws in the way of the Believers.

The battle of Uḥud (Shawwãl A.H. 3) unmasked the Hypocrites in Madinah: see 3: 167. This Sûra may be referred to sometime after that event, say about 4 A.H. or possibly 5 A.H. if the words reported in verse 8 were uttered in the expedition against the Banu Muṣṭaliq, A.H. 5.

(the Day of Assembly), hasten earnestly to the Remembrance of Allah, and leave off business (and traffic): that is best for you if ye but knew !

10. And when the Prayer is finished, then may ye Disperse through the land, and seek of the Bounty of Allah: and remember Allah frequently that ye may prosper.

11. But when they see some bargain or some pastime, they disperse headlong to it, and leave thee standing. Say: "That which Allah has is better than any pastime or bargain ! And Allah is the Best to provide (for all needs)."

Al-Munāfiqūn, or the Hypocrites

In the name of Allah, Most Gracious, Most Merciful.

1. When the Hypocrites come to thee, they say, "We bear witness that thou art indeed the Messenger of Allah." Yea, Allah knoweth that thou art indeed His Messenger. And Allah beareth witness that the Hypocrites are indeed liars.

2. They have made their oaths a screen (for their misdeeds): thus they obstruct (men) from the Path of Allah: truly evil are their deeds.

3. That is because they believed, then they rejected Faith: so a seal was set on their hearts: therefore they understand not.

4. When thou lookest at them, their bodies please thee; and when they speak, thou listenest to their words. They are as (worthless as hollow) pieces of timber propped up, (unable to stand on their own). They think that every cry is against them. They are the enemies; so beware of them. The curse of Allah be on them ! How are they deluded (away from the Truth) !

5. And when it is said to them, "Come, the Messenger of Allah will pray for your Forgiveness", they turn aside their heads, and thou wouldst see them turning away their faces in arrogance.

SÛRA–64
AT-TAGĀBUN
(INTRODUCTION)

This is the eighth of the ten short Madinah Sûras, each dealing with a special aspect of the life of the Community.

The special aspect spoken of here is the mutual gain and loss of Good and Evil, contrasted in this life and in the Hereafter.

It is an early Madinah Sûra, of the year 1 of the Hijra or possibly even of the Makkan period just before the Hijrat.

6. It is equal to them whether thou pray for their forgiveness or not. Allah will not forgive them. Truly Allah guides not rebellious transgressors.

7. They are the ones who say, "Spend nothing on those who are with Allah's Messenger till they disperse (and quit Madinah)." But to Allah belong the treasures of the heavens and the earth; but the Hypocrites understand not.

8. They say, "If we return to Madinah, surely the more honourable (element) will expel therefrom the meaner". But honour belongs to Allah and His Messenger, and to the Believers; but the Hypocrites know not.

9. O ye who believe ! let not your riches or your children divert you from the remembrance of Allah. If any act thus, surely they are the losers.

10. And spend something (in charity) out of the substance which We have bestowed on you, before Death should come to any of you and he should say, "O my Lord ! Why didst Thou not give me respite for a little while? I should then have given (largely) in charity, and I should have been one of the doers of good".

11. But to no soul will Allah grant respite when the time appointed (for it) has come; and Allah is well acquainted with (all) that ye do.

Tagābun, or Mutual Loss and Gain

In the name of Allah, Most Gracious, Most Merciful.

1. Whatever is in the heavens and on earth, doth declare the Praises and Glory of Allah: to Him belongs dominion, and to Him belongs Praise: and He has power over all things.

2. It is He Who has Created you; and of you are some that are Unbelievers, and

some that are Believers: and Allah sees well all that ye do.

3.   He has created the heavens and the earth with the truth, and has given you shape and made your shapes beautiful: and to Him is the final Return.

4.   He knows what is in the heavens and on earth; and He knows what ye conceal and what ye reveal: yea, Allah knows well the (secrets) of (all) hearts.

5.   Has not the story reached you, of those who rejected Faith aforetime? So they tasted the evil result of their conduct; and they had a grievous Chastisement.

6.   That was because there came to them messengers with Clear Signs, but they said: "Shall (mere) human beings direct us?" So they rejected (the Message) and turned away. But Allah can do without (them): and Allah is free of all needs worthy of all praise.

7.   The Unbelievers think that they will not be raised up (for Judgment). Say: "Yea, by my Lord, ye shall surely be raised up: then shall ye be told (the truth) of all that ye did. And that is easy for Allah."

8.   Believe, therefore, in Allah and His Messenger, and in the Light which We have sent down. And Allah is well acquainted with all that ye do.

9.   The Day that He assembles you (all) for a Day of Assembly,—that will be a day of mutual loss and gain (among you). And those who believe in Allah and work righteousness,—He will remove from them their ill, and He will admit them to gardens beneath which rivers flow, to dwell therein for ever: that will be the Supreme Triumph.

10. But those who reject Faith and treat Our Signs as falsehoods, they will be Companions of the Fire, to dwell therein for aye: and evil is that Goal.

11. No kind of calamity can occur, except by the leave of Allah: and if anyone believes in Allah, (Allah) guides his heart (aright): for Allah knows all things.

مُّؤۡمِنُ ۚ وَاللّٰهُ بِمَا تَعۡمَلُوۡنَ بَصِيۡرٌ ۞

خَلَقَ السَّمٰوٰتِ وَالۡاَرۡضَ بِالۡحَقِّ وَصَوَّرَكُمۡ فَاَحۡسَنَ صُوَرَكُمۡ ۚ وَاِلَيۡهِ الۡمَصِيۡرُ ۞

يَعۡلَمُ مَا فِى السَّمٰوٰتِ وَالۡاَرۡضِ وَيَعۡلَمُ مَا تُسِرُّوۡنَ وَمَا تُعۡلِنُوۡنَ ۚ وَاللّٰهُ عَلِيۡمٌۢ بِذَاتِ الصُّدُوۡرِ ۞

اَلَمۡ يَاۡتِكُمۡ نَبَؤُا الَّذِيۡنَ كَفَرُوۡا مِنۡ قَبۡلُ ۫ فَذَاقُوۡا وَبَالَ اَمۡرِهِمۡ وَلَهُمۡ عَذَابٌ اَلِيۡمٌ ۞

ذٰلِكَ بِاَنَّهٗ كَانَتۡ تَّاۡتِيۡهِمۡ رُسُلُهُمۡ بِالۡبَيِّنٰتِ فَقَالُوۡۤا اَبَشَرٌ يَّهۡدُوۡنَنَا ۫ فَكَفَرُوۡا وَتَوَلَّوۡا ۚ وَّاسۡتَغۡنَى اللّٰهُ ۚ وَاللّٰهُ غَنِيٌّ حَمِيۡدٌ ۞

زَعَمَ الَّذِيۡنَ كَفَرُوۡۤا اَنۡ لَّنۡ يُّبۡعَثُوۡا ۫ قُلۡ بَلٰى وَرَبِّىۡ لَتُبۡعَثُنَّ ثُمَّ لَتُنَبَّؤُنَّ بِمَا عَمِلۡتُمۡ ۚ وَذٰلِكَ عَلَى اللّٰهِ يَسِيۡرٌ ۞

فَاٰمِنُوۡا بِاللّٰهِ وَرَسُوۡلِهٖ وَالنُّوۡرِ الَّذِىۡۤ اَنۡزَلۡنَا ۚ وَاللّٰهُ بِمَا تَعۡمَلُوۡنَ خَبِيۡرٌ ۞

يَوۡمَ يَجۡمَعُكُمۡ لِيَوۡمِ الۡجَمۡعِ ۫ ذٰلِكَ يَوۡمُ التَّغَابُنِ ۚ وَمَنۡ يُّؤۡمِنۡۢ بِاللّٰهِ وَيَعۡمَلۡ صَالِحًا يُّكَفِّرۡ عَنۡهُ سَيِّاٰتِهٖ وَيُدۡخِلۡهُ جَنّٰتٍ تَجۡرِىۡ مِنۡ تَحۡتِهَا الۡاَنۡهٰرُ خٰلِدِيۡنَ فِيۡهَاۤ اَبَدًا ۚ ذٰلِكَ الۡفَوۡزُ الۡعَظِيۡمُ ۞

وَالَّذِيۡنَ كَفَرُوۡا وَكَذَّبُوۡا بِاٰيٰتِنَاۤ اُولٰٓئِكَ اَصۡحٰبُ النَّارِ خٰلِدِيۡنَ فِيۡهَا ۫ وَبِئۡسَ الۡمَصِيۡرُ ۞

مَاۤ اَصَابَ مِنۡ مُّصِيۡبَةٍ اِلَّا بِاِذۡنِ اللّٰهِ ۫ وَمَنۡ يُّؤۡمِنۡۢ بِاللّٰهِ يَهۡدِ قَلۡبَهٗ ۚ وَاللّٰهُ بِكُلِّ شَىۡءٍ عَلِيۡمٌ ۞

SÛRA–65
AṬ-ṬALĀQ
(INTRODUCTION)

This is the ninth of the ten short Madinah Sûras dealing with the social life of the Community. The aspect dealt with here is Divorce and the necessity of precautions to guard against its abuse. The relations of the sexes are an important factor in the social life of the Community, and this and the following Sûra deal with certain aspects of it. "Of all things permitted by law," said the Prophet, "divorce is the most hateful in the sight of Allah" (Abû Dā-ûd, *Sunan,* 13: 3). While the sanctity of marriage is the essential basis of family life, the incompatibility of individuals and the weaknesses of human nature require certain outlets and safeguards if that sanctity is not to be made into a fetish at the expense of human life. That is why the question of Divorce is in the Sûra linked with the question of insolent impiety and its punishment.

The date is somewhere about A.H. 6, but the chronology has no significance.

12. So obey Allah, and obey his Messenger: but if ye turn back, the duty of Our Messenger is but to deliver (the Message) clearly and openly.

13. Allah ! There is no god but He: and on Allah, therefore, let the Believers put their trust.

14. O ye who believe ! truly, among your wives and your children are (some that are) enemies to yourselves: so beware of them ! But if ye forgive and overlook and cover up (their faults), verily Allah is Oft-Forgiving, Most Merciful.

15. Your riches and your children may be but a trial: whereas Allah, with Him is the highest Reward.

16. So fear Allah as much as ye can; listen and obey; and spend in charity for the benefit of your own souls. And those saved from the covetousness of their own souls,— they are the ones that achieve prosperity.

17. If ye loan to Allah a beautiful loan, He will double it to your (credit), and He will grant you Forgiveness: for Allah is All-Thankful Most Forbearing,

18. Knower of what is hidden and what is open, Exalted in Might, Full of Wisdom.

At-Ṭalāq, or Divorce

In the name of Allah, Most Gracious, Most Merciful.

1. O Prophet ! When ye do divorce women, divorce them at their prescribed periods, and count (accurately) their prescribed periods: and fear Allah your Lord: and turn them not out of their houses, nor shall they (themselves) leave, except in case they are guilty of some open lewdness, those are limits set by Allah: and any who transgresses the limits of Allah, does verily wrong his (own) soul: thou knowest not if perchance Allah will being about thereafter some new situation.

2.   Thus when they fulfil their term appointed, either take them back on equitable terms or part with them on equitable terms; and take for witness two persons from among you, endued with justice, and establish the evidence for the sake of Allah. Such is the admonition given to him who believes in Allah and the Last Day. And for those who fear Allah, He (ever) prepares a way out,

3.   And He provides for him from (sources) he never could expect. And if anyone puts his trust in Allah, sufficient is (Allah) for him. For Allah will surely accomplish His purpose: verily, for all things has Allah appointed a due proportion.

4.   Such of your women as have passed the age of monthly courses, for them the prescribed period, if ye have any doubts, is three months, and for those who have no courses (it is the same): for those who are pregnant, their period is until they deliver their burdens: and for those who fear Allah, He will make things easy for them.

5.   That is the Command of Allah, which He has sent down to you: And if any one fears Allah, He will remove his evil deeds from him, and will enlarge his reward.

6.   Let the women live (in *'iddat*) in the same style as ye live, according to your means: annoy them not, so as to restrict them. And if they are pregnant, then spend (your substance) on them until they deliver their burden: and if they suckle your (offspring), give them their recompense: and take mutual counsel together, according to what is just and reasonable. And if ye find yourselves in difficulties, let another woman suckle (the child) on the (father's) behalf.

7.   Let the man of means spend according to his means: and the man whose resources are restricted, let him spend according to what Allah has given him. Allah puts no burden on any person beyond what He has given him. After a difficulty, Allah will soon grant relief.

8.   How many populations that insolently opposed the command of their Lord and of His messengers, did   We not then call to

SÛRA–66
AT-TAḤRÎM
(INTRODUCTION)

This is the tenth and last of the series of ten short Madinah Sûras which began with S. 57: see Introduction to that Sûra. The point dealt with here is: how far the turning away from sex or the opposition of one sex against another or a want of harmony between the sexes may injure the higher interests of society.

The date may be taken to be somewhere about A.H. 7.

account,— to severe account?—And We chastised them with a horrible Chastisement.

9. Then did they taste the evil result of their conduct, and the End of their conduct was Perdition.

10. Allah has prepared for them a severe Punishment (in the Hereafter). Therefore fear Allah, O ye men of understanding–who have believed !—for Allah hath indeed sent down to you a Message,—

11. A Messenger, who rehearses to you the Signs of Allah containing clear explanations, that he may lead forth those who believe and do righteous deeds from the depths of Darknesss into Light. And those who believe in Allah and work righteousness, He will admit to Gardens beneath which rivers flow, to dwell therein for ever: Allah has indeed granted for them a most excellent provision.

12. Allah is He Who created seven Firmaments and of the earth a similar number through the midst of them (all) descends his Command: that ye may know that Allah has power over all things, and that Allah comprehends all things in (His) Knowledge.

At-Taḥrim, or Holding (something) to be Forbidden

In the name of Allah, Most Gracious, Most Merciful.

1. O Prophet ! Why holdest thou to be forbidden that which Allah has made lawful to thee, thou seekest to please thy consorts? But Allah is Oft-Forgiving, Most Merciful.

2. Allah has already ordained for you, the expiation of your oaths (in some cases): and Allah is your Protector, and He is Full of Knowledge and Wisdom.

3. When the Prophet disclosed a matter in confidence to one of his consorts, and she then divulged it (to another), and Allah made it known to him, he confirmed part thereof and passed over a part. Then when he told her thereof, she said, "Who told thee this?" He said, "He told me Who is the Knower, The Aware."

4. If ye two turn in repentance to Allah, your hearts are indeed so inclined; but if ye back up each other against him, truly Allah is his Protector, and Gabriel, and (every) righteous one among those who believe,—and furthermore, the angels—will back (him) up.

5. It may be, if he divorced you (all), that Allah will give him in exchange Consorts better than you,—who submit (their wills), who believe, who are devout; who turn to Allah in repentance, who worship (in humility), who fast,— previously married or virgins.

6. O ye who believe ! save yourselves and your families from a Fire whose fuel is Men and Stones, over which are (appointed) angels stern (and) severe who flinch not (from executing) the Commands they receive from Allah, but do (precisely) what they are commanded.

7. (It will be said) "O ye Unbelievers! makes no excuses this Day ! Ye are being but requited for all that ye did !"

8. O ye who believe ! turn to Allah with sincere repentance: in the hope that your Lord will remove from you your evil deeds, and admit you to Gardens beneath which Rivers flow,—the Day that Allah will not permit to be humiliated the Prophet and those who believe with him. Their Light will run forward before them and by their right hands, while they say, "Our Lord ! perfect our Light for us, and grant us Forgiveness: for Thou hast power over all things."

9. O Prophet ! Strive hard against the Unbelievers and the Hypocrites, and be harsh with them. Their abode is Hell,—an evil refuge (indeed).

10. Allah sets forth, for an example to the Unbelievers, the wife of Noah and the wife of Lût: they were (respectively) under two of our righteous servants but they betrayed their (husbands), and they profited

SÛRA–67
AL-MULK
(INTRODUCTION)

We have now done fourteen-fifteenths of the Qur-ān, and have followed step by step the development of its argument establishing the *Ummat* or Brotherhood of Islam.

There is a logical break here. The remaining fifteenth consists of short spiritual Lyrics, mostly of the Makkan period, dealing mainly with the inner life of man, and in its individual aspects. They may be compared to Hymns or Psalms in other religious literature. But these short Quranic Sûras have a grandeur, a beauty, a mystic meaning, and a force of earnestness under persecution, all their own. With their sources in the sublimest regions of the Empyrean, their light penetrates into the darkest recesses of Life, into the concrete facts which are often mistaken for the whole of Reality, though they are but an insignificant portion and on the surface and fleeting. There is much symbolism in language and thought, in describing the spiritual in terms of the things we see and understand.

It is the contrast between the shadows of Reality here and the eternal Reality, between the surface world and the profound inner World, that is urged on our attention here.

This Sûra of 30 verses belongs to the middle Makkan period, just before S. 69 and S. 70. Allah is mentioned here by the name *Rahmān* (Most Gracious), as He is mentioned by the names of *Rabb* (Lord and Cherisher) and *Rahmān* (Most Gracious) in S. 19.

nothing before Allah on their account, but were told: "Enter ye the Fire along with (others) that enter !"

11. And Allah sets forth, as an example to those who believe the wife of Pharaoh: behold she said: "O my Lord ! build for me, in nearness to Thee, a mansion in the Garden, and save me from Pharaoh and his doings, and save me from those that do wrong";

12. And Mary the daughter of 'Imrān, who guarded her chastity and We breathed into (her body) of Our spirit; and she testified to the truth of the words of her Lord and of His Revelations, and was one of the devout (servants).

Al-Mulk, or Dominion

In the name of Allah, Most Gracious, Most Merciful.

1. Blessed be He in Whose hands is Dominion; and He over all things hath Power;—

2. He Who created Death and Life, that He may try which of you is best in deed: and He is the Exalted in Might, Oft-Forgiving;—

3. He Who created the seven heavens one above another: no want of proportion wilt thou see in the Creation of The Most Gracious. So turn thy vision again: seest thou any flaw?

4. Again turn thy vision a second time: (thy) vision will come back to thee dull and discomfited, in a state worn out.

5. And We have, (from of old), adorned the lowest heaven with Lamps, and We have made such (Lamps) (as) missiles to drive away Satans, and have prepared for them the Chastisement of the Blazing Fire.

6. For those who reject their Lord (and Cherisher) is the Chastisement of Hell: and evil is (such) destination.

7. When they are cast therein, they will hear the (terrible) drawing in of its breath

even as it blazes forth.

8. Almost bursting with fury: every time a Group will ask, is cast therein, its Keepers will ask, "Did no Warner come to you?"

9. They will say: "Yes indeed; a Warner did come to us, but we rejected him and said, 'Allah never sent down any (Message): ye are in nothing but a grave error' !"

10. They will further say: "Had we but listened or used our intelligence we should not (now) be among the Companions of the Blazing Fire!"

11. They will then confess their sins: but far from Allah's mercy are the Companions of the Blazing Fire!

12. As for those who fear their Lord unseen for them is Forgiveness and a great Reward.

13. And whether ye hide your word or make it known, He certainly has (full) knowledge, of the secrets of (all) hearts.

14. Should He not know,—He that created? And He is the Subtle the Aware.

15. It is He Who has made the earth manageable for you, so traverse ye through its tracts and enjoy of the Sustenance which He furnishes: but unto Him is the Resurrection.

16. Do ye feel secure that He Who is in Heaven will not cause you to be swallowed up by the earth when it shakes (as in an earthquake) ?

17. Or do ye feel secure that He Who is in Heaven will not send aga-inst you a violent tornado (with showers of stones), so that ye shall know how (terrible) was My warning?

18. But indeed men before them rejected (My warning): then how (terrible) was My punishment (of them)?

19. Do they not observe the birds above them, spreading their wings and folding them in ? None can uphold them except The Most Gracious: truly it is He that

watches over all things.

20. Nay, who is there that can help you, (even as) an army, besides The Most Merciful ? In nothing but delusion are the Unbelievers.

إِنَّهُ بِكُلِّ شَىْءٍ بَصِيرٌ ۞

أَمَّنْ هٰذَا الَّذِى هُوَ جُنْدٌ لَّكُمْ يَنْصُرُكُمْ مِّنْ دُونِ الرَّحْمٰنِ ۖ إِنِ الْكٰفِرُونَ إِلَّا فِى غُرُورٍ ۞

21. Or who is there that can provide you with Sustenance if He were to withhold His provision? Nay, they obstinately persist in insolent impiety and flight (from the Truth).

22. Is then one who walks headlong, with his face grovelling, better guided,—or one who walks evenly on a Straight Way ?

23. Say: "It is He Who has created you, and made for you the faculties of hearing, seeing, and understanding: little thanks it is ye give.

24. Say: "It is He Who has multiplied you through the earth, and to Him shall ye be gathered together."

25. They ask: When will this promise be (fulfilled)? If ye are telling the truth.

26. Say: "As to the knowledge of the time, it is with Allah alone: I am a plain warner."

أَمَّنْ هٰذَا الَّذِى يَرْزُقُكُمْ إِنْ أَمْسَكَ رِزْقَهُ ۚ بَلْ لَّجُّوا فِى عُتُوٍّ وَنُفُورٍ ۞

أَفَمَنْ يَمْشِى مُكِبًّا عَلَىٰ وَجْهِهِ أَهْدَىٰ أَمَّنْ يَمْشِى سَوِيًّا عَلَىٰ صِرَاطٍ مُّسْتَقِيمٍ ۞

قُلْ هُوَ الَّذِى أَنْشَأَكُمْ وَجَعَلَ لَكُمُ السَّمْعَ وَالْأَبْصَارَ وَالْأَفْئِدَةَ ۖ قَلِيلًا مَّا تَشْكُرُونَ ۞

قُلْ هُوَ الَّذِى ذَرَأَكُمْ فِى الْأَرْضِ وَإِلَيْهِ تُحْشَرُونَ ۞

وَيَقُولُونَ مَتَىٰ هٰذَا الْوَعْدُ إِنْ كُنْتُمْ صٰدِقِينَ ۞

قُلْ إِنَّمَا الْعِلْمُ عِنْدَ اللّٰهِ وَإِنَّمَا أَنَا نَذِيرٌ مُّبِينٌ ۞

27. At length, when they see it close at hand, grieved will be the faces of the Unbelievers, and it will be said (to them): "This is (the promise fulfilled) which ye were calling for !"

28. Say: "See ye ?—If Allah were to destroy me, and those with me, or if He bestows his Mercy on us,— yet who can deliver the Unbelievers from a grievous Chastisement ?

29. Say: "He is The most Gracious: we have believed in Him, and on Him have we put our trust: so, soon will ye know which (of us) it is that is in manifest error."

30. Say. "See ye ?— If your stream be some morning lost (in the underground earth), who then can supply you with clear-flowing water?"

فَلَمَّا رَأَوْهُ زُلْفَةً سِيئَتْ وُجُوهُ الَّذِينَ كَفَرُوا وَقِيلَ هٰذَا الَّذِى كُنْتُمْ بِهِ تَدَّعُونَ ۞

قُلْ أَرَأَيْتُمْ إِنْ أَهْلَكَنِيَ اللّٰهُ وَمَنْ مَّعِىَ أَوْ رَحِمَنَا فَمَنْ يُجِيرُ الْكٰفِرِينَ مِنْ عَذَابٍ أَلِيمٍ ۞

قُلْ هُوَ الرَّحْمٰنُ آمَنَّا بِهِ وَعَلَيْهِ تَوَكَّلْنَا ۖ فَسَتَعْلَمُونَ مَنْ هُوَ فِى ضَلٰلٍ مُّبِينٍ ۞

قُلْ أَرَأَيْتُمْ إِنْ أَصْبَحَ مَاؤُكُمْ غَوْرًا فَمَنْ يَأْتِيكُمْ بِمَاءٍ مَّعِينٍ ۞

SÛRA–68
AL-QALAM
(INTRODUCTION)

This is a very early Makkan revelation. The general Muslim opinion is that a great part of it was second in order of revelation, the first being S. 96. (*Iqraa*), verses 1-5: see *Itqān*, Chapter 7.

The last Sûra having defined the true Reality in contrast with the false standards set up by men, this illustrates the theme by an actual historical example. Our Holy Prophet was the sanest and wisest of man: those who could not understand him called him mad or possessed. So, in every age, it is the habit of the world to call Truth Falsehood and Wisdom Madness, and, on the other hand, to exalt Selfishness as Planning, and Arrogance as Power. The contrast is shown up between the two kinds of men and their inner worth.

Al-Qalam, or the Pen, or Nûn

سورة القلم مكية وهي ثنتان وخمسون اثة وهيارفراكمان

بِسْمِ اللهِ الرَّحْمٰنِ الرَّحِيْمِ ۟

In the name of Allah, Most Gracious, Most Merciful.

1. Nûn. By the Pen and by the (Record) which (men) write,—

نّ وَالْقَلَمِ وَمَا يَسْطُرُوْنَ ۟ۙ

2. Thou art not, by the grace of thy Lord, mad or possessed.

مَا أَنْتَ بِنِعْمَةِ رَبِّكَ بِمَجْنُوْنٍ ۟ۚ

3. Nay, verily for thee is a Reward unfailing;

وَإِنَّ لَكَ لَأَجْرًا غَيْرَ مَمْنُوْنٍ ۟ۚ

4. And surely thou hast sublime morals.

وَإِنَّكَ لَعَلٰى خُلُقٍ عَظِيْمٍ ۟

5. Soon wilt thou see, and they will see,

6. Which of you is afflicted with madness.

فَسَتُبْصِرُ وَيُبْصِرُوْنَ ۟ۙ

بِأَيِّكُمُ الْمَفْتُوْنُ ۟

7. Verily it is thy Lord that knoweth best, which (among men) hath strayed from His Path: and He knoweth best those who receive (true) Guidance.

إِنَّ رَبَّكَ هُوَ أَعْلَمُ بِمَنْ ضَلَّ عَنْ سَبِيْلِهِ ۟ وَهُوَ أَعْلَمُ بِالْمُهْتَدِيْنَ ۟

8. So obey not to those who deny (the Truth).

فَلَا تُطِعِ الْمُكَذِّبِيْنَ ۟

9. Their desire is that thou shouldst be pliant: so would they be pliant.

وَدُّوْا لَوْ تُدْهِنُ فَيُدْهِنُوْنَ ۟

10. Obey not every mean,— swearer

وَلَا تُطِعْ كُلَّ حَلَّافٍ مَهِيْنٍ ۟ۙ

11. A slanderer, going about with calumnies,

هَمَّازٍ مَشَّاءٍ بِنَمِيْمٍ ۟ۙ

12. (Habitually) hindering (all) good, transgressing beyond bounds, deep in sin,

مَنَّاعٍ لِلْخَيْرِ مُعْتَدٍ أَثِيْمٍ ۟ۙ

13. Violent (and cruel),— with all that, of a doubtful birth,—

عُتُلٍّ بَعْدَ ذٰلِكَ زَنِيْمٍ ۟ۙ

14. Because he possesses wealth and (numerous) sons.

أَنْ كَانَ ذَا مَالٍ وَبَنِيْنَ ۟

15. When to him are rehearsed Our Signs, "Tales of the Ancients", he cries !

إِذَا تُتْلٰى عَلَيْهِ اٰيٰتُنَا قَالَ أَسَاطِيْرُ الْأَوَّلِيْنَ ۟

16. Soon shall We brand (the beast) on the snout!

سَنَسِمُهُ عَلَى الْخُرْطُوْمِ ۟

17. Verily We have tried them as We tried the People of the Garden, when they resolved to gather the fruits of the (garden) in the morning,

إِنَّا بَلَوْنٰهُمْ كَمَا بَلَوْنَا أَصْحٰبَ الْجَنَّةِ ۟ إِذْ أَقْسَمُوْا لَيَصْرِمُنَّهَا مُصْبِحِيْنَ ۟ۙ

18. But made no reservation, ("if it be Allah's Will").

وَلَا يَسْتَثْنُوْنَ ۟

19. Then there came on the (garden) a visitation from thy Lord, (which swept away) all around, while they were asleep.

فَطَافَ عَلَيْهَا طَائِفٌ مِنْ رَبِّكَ وَهُمْ نَائِمُوْنَ ۟

20. So the (garden) became, by the morning, like a dark and desolate spot, (whose fruit had been gathered).

فَأَصْبَحَتْ كَالصَّرِيْمِ ۟ۙ

21. As the morning broke, they called out, one to another,—

فَتَنَادَوْا مُصْبِحِيْنَ ۟ۙ

22. "Go ye to your tilth (betimes) in the morning, if ye would gather the fruits."

23. So they departed, conversing in secret low tones, (saying)—

24. "Let not a single indigent person break in upon you into the (garden) this day."

25. And they opened the morning, strong in an (unjust) resolve.

26. But when they saw the (garden), they said: "We have surely lost our way:

27. "Indeed we are deprived (of the fruits of our labour) !"

28. Said one of them, more just (than the rest): "Did I not say to you, 'Why not glorify (Allah)?' "

29. They said: "Glory to our Lord! Verily we have been doing wrong!"

30. Then they turned, one against another, in reproach.

31. They said: "Alas for us ! We have indeed transgressed !

32. "It may be that our Lord will give us in exchange a better (garden) than this: for we do turn to Him (in repentance) !"

33. Such is the Punishment (in this life); but greater is the Punishment in the Hereafter,— if only they knew !

34. Verily, for the Righteous, are Gardens of Delight, with their Lord.

35. Shall We then treat the People of Faith like the People of Sin ?

36. What is the matter with you ? How judge ye?

37. Or have ye a Book through which ye learn—

38. That ye shall have, through it whatever ye choose ?

39. Or have ye Covenants with Us on oath, reaching to the Day of Judgment, (providing) that ye shall have whatever ye shall demand ?

40. Ask thou of them, which of them will stand surety for that !

41. Or have they some "partners" (in Godhead)? Then let them produce their "partners" if they are truthful !

SÛRA–69
AL-ḤĀQQA
(INTRODUCTION)

This Sûra belongs to the early middle period of Makkan Revelation. The eschatological argument is pressed home: "the absolute Truth cannot fail; it must prevail; therefore, be not lured by false appearances in this life; it is Revelation that points to the sure and certain Reality."

42. The Day that the Shin shall be laid bare, to prostrate, but they shall not be able,—

43. Their eyes will be cast down, ignominy will cover them; seeing that they had been summoned aforetime to bow in adoration, while they were whole, (and had refused).

44. Then leave Me alone with such as reject this Message: by degrees shall We draw them on little by little from directions they perceive not.

45. A (long) respite will I grant them: truly powerful is My Plan.

46. Or is it that thou dost ask them for a reward, so that they are burdened with a load of debt?—

47. Or that the Unseen is in their hands, so that they can write it down?

48. So wait with patience for the Command of thy Lord, and be not like the Companion of the Fish,—when he cried out in agony.

49. Had not Grace from His Lord reached him, he would indeed have been cast off on the naked shore, in disgrace.

50. Thus did his Lord choose him and make him of the company of the Righteous.

51. And the Unbelievers would almost trip thee up with their eyes when they hear the Message; and they say: "Surely he is possessed!"

52. But it is nothing less than a Message to all the worlds.

Al-Ḥāqqa, or the Sure Reality

In the name of Allah, Most Gracious, Most Merciful.

1. The Sure Reality !

2. What is the Sure Reality ?

3. And what will make thee realise what the Sure Reality is ?

4. The Thamūd and the 'Ād people disbelieved in the day of Noise and Clamour!

5. But the Thamūd,—they were destroyed by a terrible Storm of thunder and lightning !

6. And the 'Ād,— they were destroyed by a furious Wind, exceedingly violent;

7. He made it rage against them seven nights and eight days in succession: so that thou couldst see the (whole) people lying

overthrown in its (path), as if they had been roots of hollow palm-trees tumbled down !

8. Then seest thou any of them left surviving?

9. And Pharaoh, and those before him, and the Cities Overthrown committed habitual Sin,

10. And disobeyed (each) the messenger of their Lord; so He punis-hed them with an abundant Penalty.

11. We, when the water (of Noah's Flood) overflowed beyond its limits, carried you (mankind), in the floating (Ark),

12. That We might make it a Reminder unto you, and that ears (that should hear the tale and) retain its memory should bear its (lessons) in remembrance.

13. Then, when one blast is sounded on the Trumpet,

14. And the earth is moved, and its mountains, and they are crushed at one stroke,—

15. On that Day shall the (Great) Event come to pass,

16. And the sky will be rent asunder, for it will that Day be flimsy,

17. And the angels will be on its sides and eight will, that Day, bear the Throne of thy Lord above them.

18. That Day shall ye be brought to Judgment: not an act of yours that ye hide will be hidden.

19. Then he that will be given his Record in his right hand will say: "Ah here ! Read ye my Record!

20. "I did really think that my Account would (one Day) reach me!"

21. And he will be in a life of Bliss,

22. In a Garden on high,

23. The Fruits whereof (will hang in bunches) low and near.

24. "Eat ye and drink ye, with full satisfaction; because of the (good) that ye sent before you, in the days that are gone !"

25. And he that will be given his Record in his left hand, will say: "Ah ! would that my record had not been given to me !

كَأَنَّهُمْ أَعْجَازُ نَخْلٍ خَاوِيَةٍ ۝

فَهَلْ تَرٰى لَهُمْ مِّنْ بَاقِيَةٍ ۝

وَجَاۤءَ فِرْعَوْنُ وَمَنْ قَبْلَهٗ وَالْمُؤْتَفِكٰتُ بِالْخَاطِئَةِ ۝

فَعَصَوْا رَسُوْلَ رَبِّهِمْ فَأَخَذَهُمْ أَخْذَةً رَّابِيَةً ۝

إِنَّا لَمَّا طَغَا الْمَاۤءُ حَمَلْنٰكُمْ فِى الْجَارِيَةِ ۝

لِنَجْعَلَهَا لَكُمْ تَذْكِرَةً وَّتَعِيَهَاۤ أُذُنٌ وَّاعِيَةٌ ۝

فَإِذَا نُفِخَ فِى الصُّوْرِ نَفْخَةٌ وَّاحِدَةٌ ۝

وَّحُمِلَتِ الْأَرْضُ وَالْجِبَالُ فَدُكَّتَا دَكَّةً وَّاحِدَةً ۝

فَيَوْمَئِذٍ وَّقَعَتِ الْوَاقِعَةُ ۝

وَانْشَقَّتِ السَّمَاۤءُ فَهِىَ يَوْمَئِذٍ وَّاهِيَةٌ ۝

وَّالْمَلَكُ عَلٰۤى أَرْجَاۤئِهَا ۚ وَيَحْمِلُ عَرْشَ رَبِّكَ فَوْقَهُمْ يَوْمَئِذٍ ثَمٰنِيَةٌ ۝

يَوْمَئِذٍ تُعْرَضُوْنَ لَا تَخْفٰى مِنْكُمْ خَافِيَةٌ ۝

فَأَمَّا مَنْ أُوْتِىَ كِتٰبَهٗ بِيَمِيْنِهٖ فَيَقُوْلُ هَاۤؤُمُ اقْرَءُوْا كِتٰبِيَهْ ۝

إِنِّى ظَنَنْتُ أَنِّى مُلٰقٍ حِسَابِيَهْ ۝

فَهُوَ فِىْ عِيْشَةٍ رَّاضِيَةٍ ۝

فِىْ جَنَّةٍ عَالِيَةٍ ۝

قُطُوْفُهَا دَانِيَةٌ ۝

كُلُوْا وَاشْرَبُوْا هَنِيۤئًا بِمَاۤ أَسْلَفْتُمْ فِى الْأَيَّامِ الْخَالِيَةِ ۝

وَأَمَّا مَنْ أُوْتِىَ كِتٰبَهٗ بِشِمَالِهٖ فَيَقُوْلُ يٰلَيْتَنِىْ لَمْ أُوْتَ كِتٰبِيَهْ ۝

26. "And that I had never realised how my account (stood) !

وَلَمْ أَدْرِ مَا حِسَابِيَهْ ۟

27. "Ah ! would that (Death) had made an end of me !

يٰلَيْتَهَا كَانَتِ الْقَاضِيَةَ ۟

28. "Of no profit to me has been my wealth!

مَآ أَغْنٰى عَنِّى مَالِيَهْ ۟

29. "My power has perished from me !"...

هَلَكَ عَنِّى سُلْطٰنِيَهْ ۟

30. (The stern command will say): "Seize ye him, and bind ye him,

خُذُوهُ فَغُلُّوهُ ۟

31. "And burn ye him in the Blazing Fire.

ثُمَّ الْجَحِيمَ صَلُّوهُ ۟

32. "Further, insert him in a chain, whereof the length is seventy cubits!

ثُمَّ فِى سِلْسِلَةٍ ذَرْعُهَا سَبْعُونَ ذِرَاعًا فَاسْلُكُوهُ ۟

33. "This was he that would not believe in Allah Most High,

إِنَّهُ كَانَ لَا يُؤْمِنُ بِاللّٰهِ الْعَظِيمِ ۟

34. "And would not encourage the feeding of the indigent !

وَلَا يَحُضُّ عَلٰى طَعَامِ الْمِسْكِينِ ۟

35. "So no friend hath he here this Day.

فَلَيْسَ لَهُ الْيَوْمَ هٰهُنَا حَمِيمٌ ۟

36. "Nor hath he any food except the foul pus from the washing of wounds,

وَلَا طَعَامٌ إِلَّا مِنْ غِسْلِينٍ ۟

37. "Which none do eat but those in sin."

لَا يَأْكُلُهُ إِلَّا الْخَاطِئُونَ ۟

38. So I do call to witness what ye see

فَلَا أُقْسِمُ بِمَا تُبْصِرُونَ ۟

39. And what ye see not,

وَمَا لَا تُبْصِرُونَ ۟

40. That this is verily the word of an honoured messenger;

إِنَّهُ لَقَوْلُ رَسُولٍ كَرِيمٍ ۟

41. It is not the word of a poet: little it is ye believe!

وَمَا هُوَ بِقَوْلِ شَاعِرٍ قَلِيلًا مَا تُؤْمِنُونَ ۟

42. Nor is it the word of a soothsayer: little admonition it is ye receive.

وَلَا بِقَوْلِ كَاهِنٍ قَلِيلًا مَا تَذَكَّرُونَ ۟

43. (This is) a Message sent down from the Lord of the Worlds.

تَنْزِيلٌ مِنْ رَبِّ الْعٰلَمِينَ ۟

44. And if the messenger were to invent any sayings in Our name,

وَلَوْ تَقَوَّلَ عَلَيْنَا بَعْضَ الْأَقَاوِيلِ ۟

45. We should certainly seize him by his right hand

لَأَخَذْنَا مِنْهُ بِالْيَمِينِ ۟

46. And We should certainly then cut off the artery of his heart:

ثُمَّ لَقَطَعْنَا مِنْهُ الْوَتِينَ ۟

47. Nor could any of you withhold him (from Our wrath).

فَمَا مِنْكُمْ مِنْ أَحَدٍ عَنْهُ حَاجِزِينَ ۟

48. But verily this is a Message for the God-fearing.

وَإِنَّهُ لَتَذْكِرَةٌ لِلْمُتَّقِينَ ۟

49. And We certainly know that there are amongst you those that reject (it).

وَإِنَّا لَنَعْلَمُ أَنَّ مِنْكُمْ مُكَذِّبِينَ ۟

50. But truly (Revelation) is a cause of sorrow for the Unbelievers.

وَإِنَّهُ لَحَسْرَةٌ عَلَى الْكٰفِرِينَ ۟

51. But verily it is Truth of assured certainty.

وَإِنَّهُ لَحَقُّ الْيَقِينِ ۟

SÛRA-70
AL-MA'ÂRIJ
(INTRODUCTION)

This is another eschatological Sûra closely connected in subject-matter with the last one. Patience and the mystery of Time will show the ways that climb to Heaven. Sin and Goodness must each eventually come to its own.

Chronologically it belongs to the late early or early middle Makkan period, possibly soon after S. 69.

52. So glorify the name of thy Lord Most High.

Al-Ma'ārij, or the Ways of Ascent.

In the name of Allah, Most Gracious, Most Merciful.

1. A questioner asked about a Chastisement to befall—

2. The Unbelievers, the which there is none to ward off,—

3. (A Penalty) from Allah, Lord of the Ways of Ascent.

4. The angels and the Spirit ascend unto Him in a Day the measure whereof is (as) fifty thousand years:

5. Therefore do thou hold Patience,—a Patience of beautiful (contentment).

6. They see the (Day) indeed as a far-off (event):

7. But We see it (quite) near.

8. The Day that the sky will be like molten brass,

9. And the mountains will be like wool,

10. And no friend will ask after a friend,

11. Though they will be put in sight of each other,—the sinner's desire will be: would that he could redeem himself from the Chastisement of that Day by his children,

12. His wife and his brother,

13. His kindred who sheltered him,

14. And all, all that is on earth,—so it could deliver him:

15. By no means! for it would be the Blazing Fire—

16. Plucking out (his being) right to the skull!—

17. Inviting (all) such as turn their backs and turn away their faces (from the Right).

18. And collect (wealth) and hide it (from use)!

19. Truly man was created, very impatient;

20. Fretful when evil touches him;

21. And niggardly when good reaches him,—

22. Not so those devoted to Prayer:—

23. Those who remain steadfast to their prayer;

24. And those in whose wealth is a recognised right

25. For the (needy) who asks and him who is deprived (for some reason from asking);

26. And those who hold to the truth of the Day of Judgment:

27. And those who fear the punishment of their Lord,--

28. For their Lord's punishment is not a thing to feel secure from:—

29. And those who guard their chastity,

30. Except with their wives and the (captives) whom their right hands possess.— for (then) they are no to be blamed.

31. But those who trespass beyond this are transgressors;—

32. And those who respect their trusts and covenants.

33. And those who stand firm in their testimonies;

34. And those who (strictly) guard their worship;—

35. Such will be the honoured ones in the Gardens (of Bliss).

36. Now what is the matter with the Unbelievers that they rush madly before thee—

37. From the right and from the left, in crowds?

38. Does every man of them long to enter the Garden of Bliss ?

39. By no means ! for We have created them out of the (base matter) they know!

40. Now I do call to witness the Lord of all points in the East and the West that We can certainly—

41. Substitute for them better (men) than they; and We are not to be defeated (in Our Plan).

42. So leave them to plunge in vain talk and play about, until they encounter that Day of theirs which they have been promised!

43. The Day whereon they will issue from their sepulchres in sudden haste

SÛRA-71

NÛḤ

(INTRODUCTION)

This is another early Makkan Sûra, of which the date has no significance. The theme is that while Good must uphold the standard of Truth and Righteousness, a stage is reached when it must definitely part company with Evil, lest Evil should spread its corruption abroad. This theme is embodied in the prayer of Noah just before the Flood. The story of Noah's agony is almost a Parable for the Holy Prophet's persecution in the Makkan period.

as if they were rushing to a goal-post (fixed for them),—

44. Their eyes lowered in dejection,— ignominy covering them (all over) ! Such is the Day the which they are promised!

Nûḥ, or Noah

In the name of Allah, Most Gracious. Most Merciful.

1. We sent Noah to his People (with the Command): "Do thou warn thy People before there comes to them a grievous Chastisement."

2. He said: "O my People ! I am to you a Warner, clear and open:

3. "That ye should worship Allah, fear Him, and obey me:

4. "So He may forgive you your sins and give you respite for a stated Term: for when the Term given by Allah is accomplished, it cannot be put forward: if ye only knew."

5. He said: "O my Lord ! I have called to my People night and day:

6. "But my call only increases (their) flight (from the Right).

7. "And every time I have called to them, that Thou mightest forgive them, they have (only) thrust their fingers into their ears, covered themselves up with their garments, grown obstinate, and given themselves up to arrogance.

8. "So I have called to them aloud:

9. "Further I have spoken to them in public and secretly in private,

10. "Saying, 'Ask forgiveness from your Lord, for He is Oft-Forgiving;

11. " 'He will send rain to you in abundance;

12. " 'Give you increase in wealth and sons; and bestow on you gardens and bestow on you rivers (of flowing water).

13. " 'What is the matter with you, that ye are not conscious of Allah's majesty,—

14. " 'Seeing that it is He that has created you in diverse stages ?

15. " 'See ye not how Allah has created the seven heavens one above another,

اَلَمْ تَرَوْا كَيْفَ خَلَقَ اللّٰهُ سَبْعَ سَمٰوٰتٍ طِبَاقًا ۞

16. " 'And made the moon a light in their midst, and made the sun as a (Glorious) Lamp?

وَّجَعَلَ الْقَمَرَ فِيهِنَّ نُوْرًا وَّجَعَلَ الشَّمْسَ سِرَاجًا ۞

17. " 'And Allah has produced you from the earth, growing (gradually),

وَاللّٰهُ اَنْبَتَكُمْ مِّنَ الْاَرْضِ نَبَاتًا ۞

18. " 'And in the End He will return you into the (earth), and raise you forth (again at the Resurrection) ?

ثُمَّ يُعِيْدُكُمْ فِيهَا وَيُخْرِجُكُمْ اِخْرَاجًا ۞

19. " 'And Allah has made the earth for you as a carpet (spread out),

وَاللّٰهُ جَعَلَ لَكُمُ الْاَرْضَ بِسَاطًا ۞

20. " 'That ye may go about therein, in spacious roads.'

لِّتَسْلُكُوْا مِنْهَا سُبُلًا فِجَاجًا ۞

21. Noah said: "O my Lord! they have disobeyed me, but they follow (men) whose wealth and children give them no Increase but only Loss.

قَالَ نُوْحٌ رَّبِّ اِنَّهُمْ عَصَوْنِيْ وَاتَّبَعُوْا مَنْ لَّمْ يَزِدْهُ مَالُهُ وَوَلَدُهُ اِلَّا خَسَارًا ۞

22. "And they have devised a tremendous Plot.

وَمَكَرُوْا مَكْرًا كُبَّارًا ۞

23. "And they have said (to each other), 'Abandon not your gods: abandon neither Wadd nor Suwa', neither Yagûth nor Ya'ûq, nor Nasr';—

وَقَالُوْا لَا تَذَرُنَّ اٰلِهَتَكُمْ وَلَا تَذَرُنَّ وَدًّا وَّلَا سُوَاعًا ەۙ وَّلَا يَغُوْثَ وَيَعُوْقَ وَنَسْرًا ۞

24. "They have already misled many; and grant Thou no increase to the wrong-doers but in straying (from their mark)."

وَقَدْ اَضَلُّوْا كَثِيْرًا ەۚ وَلَا تَزِدِ الظّٰلِمِيْنَ اِلَّا ضَلٰلًا ۞

25. Because of their sins they were drowned (in the flood), and were made to enter the Fire and they found— in lieu of Allah— none to help them.

مِمَّا خَطِيْٓئٰتِهِمْ اُغْرِقُوْا فَاُدْخِلُوْا نَارًا ەۙ فَلَمْ يَجِدُوْا لَهُمْ مِّنْ دُوْنِ اللّٰهِ اَنْصَارًا ۞

26. And Noah said: "O my Lord ! Leave not of the Unbelievers, a single one on earth !

وَقَالَ نُوْحٌ رَّبِّ لَا تَذَرْ عَلَى الْاَرْضِ مِنَ الْكٰفِرِيْنَ دَيَّارًا ۞

27. "For, if Thou dost leave (any of) them, they will but mislead Thy devotees, and they will breed none but wicked ungrateful ones.

اِنَّكَ اِنْ تَذَرْهُمْ يُضِلُّوْا عِبَادَكَ وَلَا يَلِدُوْٓا اِلَّا فَاجِرًا كَفَّارًا ۞

28. "O my Lord ! Forgive me, my parents, all who enter my house in Faith, and (all) believing men and believing women: and to the wrong-doers grant Thou no increase but in Perdition !"

رَبِّ اغْفِرْ لِيْ وَلِوَالِدَيَّ وَلِمَنْ دَخَلَ بَيْتِيَ مُؤْمِنًا وَّلِلْمُؤْمِنِيْنَ وَالْمُؤْمِنٰتِ ەۭ وَلَا تَزِدِ الظّٰلِمِيْنَ اِلَّا تَبَارًا ۞

SÛRA-72
AL-JINN
(INTRODUCTION)

This is a late Makkan Sûra, of which we can be tolerably certain of the date. It was two years before the Hijrat, when the Prophet, despised and rejected in his native city of Makkah, went to evangelise the lordly men of Ṭaif. They maltreated him and nearly killed him; what caused him even greater pain was the maltreatment of the humble and lowly men who went with him. Ṭabarî has handed down that memorable Prayer of faith and humility which he offered in the midst of his suffering. On his return journey to Makkah, a glorious vision was revealed to him, —hidden spiritual forces working for him, —people not known to him accepting his mission while his own people were still rejecting him. Within two months some strangers from Madinah had privately met him and laid the faundations of that Hijrat which was to change the fate of Arabia and the course of world history.

Al-Jinn, The Jinn

In the name of Allah, Most Gracious, Most Merciful.

1. Say: It has been revealed to me that a company of Jinns listened (to the Qur-ān). They said, 'We have really heard a wonderful Recital!

2. 'It gives guidance to the Right, and we have believed therein: we shall not join (in worship) any (gods) with our Lord,

3. 'And exalted is the Majesty of our Lord: He has taken neither a wife nor a son.

4. 'There were some foolish ones among us, who used to utter extravagant lies against Allah;

5. 'But we do think that no man or jinn should say aught that is untrue against Allah.

6. 'True, there were persons among mankind who took shelter with persons among the Jinns, but they increased them into further error.

7. 'And they (came to) think as ye thought, that Allah would not raise up anyone (to Judgment).

8. 'And we pried into the (secrets of) heaven; but we found it filled with stern guards and flaming fires.

9. 'We used, indeed, to sit there in (hidden) stations, to (steal) a hearing; but any who listens now will find a flaming fire watching him in ambush.

10. 'And we understand not whether ill is intended to those on earth on whether their Lord (really) intends to guide them to right conduct.

11. 'There are among us some that are righteous, and some the contrary: we follow divergent paths.

12. 'But we think that we can by no means frustrate Allah throughout the earth, nor can we escape Him by flight.

13. 'And as for us, since we have listened to the Guidance, we have accepted it: and any who believes in his Lord has no fear,

either of a short (account) or of any injustice.

14. 'Amongst us are some that submit their wills (to Allah), and some that swerve from justice. Now those who submit their wills— they have sought out (the path) of right conduct:

15. 'But those who swerve,— they are (but) fuel for Hell-fire'—

16. (And Allah's Message is): "If they (the Pagans) had (only) remained on the (right) Way, We should certainly have bestowed on them Rain in abundance.

17. "That We might try them by that (means). But if any turns away from the remembrance of his Lord, He will cause him to undergo ever-growing Chastisement.

18. "And the places of worship are for Allah (alone): so invoke not anyone along with Allah;

19. "Yet when the Devotees of Allah stood up to invoke Him, they just make round him a dense crowd."

20. Say: "I do no more than invoke my Lord, and I join not with Him any (false god)."

21. Say: "It is not in my power to cause you harm, or to bring you to right conduct."

22. Say: "No one can deliver me from Allah (if I were to disobey Him), nor should I find refuge except in Him.

23. "Unless I deliver what I receive from Allah and His Messages: for any that disobey Allah and His Messenger,—for them is Hell: they shall dwell therein for ever."

24. At length, when they see (with their own eyes) that which they are promised,— then will they know who it is that is weakest in (his) helper and least important in point of numbers.

25. Say: "I know not whether the (Punishment) which ye are promised is near, or whether my Lord will appoint for it a distant term.

26. "He (alone) knows the Unseen, nor does He make anyone acquainted with His Secrets,—

27. "Except a messenger whom He has chosen: and then He makes a band of

SÛRA–73
AL-MUZZAMMIL
(INTRODUCTION)

This is one of the earliest Sûras to have been revealed. The first was S. 96: 1-5 (*Iqraa*), in the fortieth year of the Prophet's life, say about 12 years before the Hijra. Then there was an interruption (*Fatra*), of which the duration cannot be exactly ascertained, as there was no external history connected with it. The usual estimate puts it at about six months, but it may have been a year or two years. The years were then counted by the lunisolar calendar: The second Sûra in chronological order was probably a great portion of S. 68 (*Qalam*), which came after the *Fatra* was over. About the same time came this Sûra (say third) and S. 74, which follows (say fourth), and the remainder of 96. We may roughly put the date of this Sûra at about 11 to 10 years before the Hijra.

The subject-matter is the significance of Prayer and Humility in spiritual life and the terrible fate of those who reject Faith and Revelation.

watchers march before him and behind him. مِنْۢ بَيْنِ يَدَيْهِ وَمِنْ خَلْفِهٖ رَصَدًا ۞

28. "That He may know that they have (truly) brought and delivered the Messages of their Lord and He encompasses all that is with them, and takes account of every single thing." لِّيَعْلَمَ اَنْ قَدْ اَبْلَغُوْا رِسٰلٰتِ رَبِّهِمْ وَ اَحَاطَ بِمَا لَدَيْهِمْ وَاَحْصٰى كُلَّ شَىْءٍ عَدَدًا ۞

Al-Muzzammil, or Folded in Garments

سُوْرَةُ الْمُزَّمِّلِ مَكِّيَّةٌ وَهِىَ خَمْسٌ وَعِشْرُوْنَ اٰيَةً

In the name of Allah, Most Gracious, Most Merciful. بِسْمِ اللهِ الرَّحْمٰنِ الرَّحِيْمِ

1. O thou folded in garments ! يٰۤاَيُّهَا الْمُزَّمِّلُ ۞

2. Stand (to prayer) by night, but not all night— قُمِ الَّيْلَ اِلَّا قَلِيْلًا ۞

3. Half of it,— or a little less. نِّصْفَهٗۤ اَوِ انْقُصْ مِنْهُ قَلِيْلًا ۞

4. Or a little more; and recite the Qur-ān in slow, measured rhythmic tones. اَوْ زِدْ عَلَيْهِ وَرَتِّلِ الْقُرْاٰنَ تَرْتِيْلًا ۞

5. Soon shall We send down to thee a weighty Word. اِنَّا سَنُلْقِيْ عَلَيْكَ قَوْلًا ثَقِيْلًا ۞

6. Truly the rising by night is a time when impression is more keen and speech more certain. اِنَّ نَاشِئَةَ الَّيْلِ هِىَ اَشَدُّ وَطْأً وَّاَقْوَمُ قِيْلًا ۞

7. True, there is for thee by day prolonged occupation with ordinary duties: اِنَّ لَكَ فِى النَّهَارِ سَبْحًا طَوِيْلًا ۞

8. But keep in remembrance the name of thy Lord, and devote thyself to Him whole-heartedly. وَاذْكُرِ اسْمَ رَبِّكَ وَتَبَتَّلْ اِلَيْهِ تَبْتِيْلًا ۞

9. (He is) Lord of the East and the West: there is no god but He: take Him therefore for (thy) Disposer of Affairs. رَبُّ الْمَشْرِقِ وَالْمَغْرِبِ لَاۤ اِلٰهَ اِلَّا هُوَ فَاتَّخِذْهُ وَكِيْلًا ۞

10. And have patience with what they say, and leave them with noble (dignity). وَاصْبِرْ عَلٰى مَا يَقُوْلُوْنَ وَاهْجُرْهُمْ هَجْرًا جَمِيْلًا ۞

11. And leave Me (alone to deal with) those in possession of the good things of life (who yet deny the Truth;) and bear with them for a little while. وَذَرْنِيْ وَالْمُكَذِّبِيْنَ اُولِى النَّعْمَةِ وَمَهِّلْهُمْ قَلِيْلًا ۞

12. With Us are Fetters (to bind them), and a Fire (to burn them). اِنَّ لَدَيْنَاۤ اَنْكَالًا وَّجَحِيْمًا ۞

13. And a Food that chokes and a Chastisement Grievous. وَّطَعَامًا ذَا غُصَّةٍ وَّعَذَابًا اَلِيْمًا ۞

14. The Day the earth and the mountains will be in violent commotion. And the mountains will be as a heap of sand poured out and flowing down. يَوْمَ تَرْجُفُ الْاَرْضُ وَالْجِبَالُ وَكَانَتِ الْجِبَالُ كَثِيْبًا مَّهِيْلًا ۞

15. We have sent to you. (O men!) a Messenger, to be a witness concerning you even as We sent a messenger to Pharaoh. اِنَّاۤ اَرْسَلْنَاۤ اِلَيْكُمْ رَسُوْلًا ۙ شَاهِدًا عَلَيْكُمْ كَمَاۤ اَرْسَلْنَاۤ اِلٰى فِرْعَوْنَ رَسُوْلًا ۞

SÛRA–74
AL-MUDDATHTHIR
(INTRODUCTION)

This Sûra dates from about the same time as the last one. Its subject-matter is also similar: Prayer, and Praise, and the need of patience in a period of great spiritual stress; the unjust who cause sorrow and suffering now will themselves experience agony in the Hereafter.

16. But Pharaoh disobeyed the messenger;
so We seized him with a heavy Punishment.

17. Then how shall ye, if ye deny (Allah),
guard yourselves against a Day that will
make children hoary-headed?—

18. Whereon the sky will be cleft asunder?
His Promise needs must be accomplished.

19. Verily this is an Admonition: therefore,
whoso will, let him take a (straight) path to
his Lord !

20. Thy Lord doth know that thou standest
forth (to prayer) nigh two-thirds of the night,
or half the night, or a third of the night, and
so doth a party of those with thee. But Allah
doth appoint Night and Day in due measure.
He knoweth that ye are unable to keep
count thereof. So He hath turned to you (in
mercy): read ye, therefore, of the Qur'ān as
much as may be easy for you. He knoweth
that there may be (some) among you in ill-
health; others travelling through the land,
seeking of Allah's bounty; yet others fighting
in Allah's Cause. Read ye, therefore, as
much of the Qur'ān as may be easy (for
you); and establish regular Prayer and give
zakat; and loan to Allah a Beautiful Loan.
And whatever good ye send forth for
yourselves, ye shall find it with Allah. Yea,
better and greater, in Reward, and seek ye
the Grace of Allah: for Allah is Oft-Forgiving,
Most Merciful.

Al-Muddaththir, or One Wrapped Up.

In the name of Allah, Most Gracious, Most
Merciful.

1. O thou wrapped up (in a mantle) !

2. Arise and deliver thy warning!

3. And thy Lord do thou magnify!

4. And thy garments keep free from stain!

5. And all abomination shun !

6. Nor expect, in giving, any increase (for thyself) !

وَلَا تَمْنُنْ تَسْتَكْثِرُ ۝

7. But, for thy Lord's (Cause) be patient and constant !

وَلِرَبِّكَ فَاصْبِرْ ۝

8. Finally, when the Trumpet is sounded,

فَإِذَا نُقِرَ فِي النَّاقُورِ ۝

9. That will be—that Day— a Day of Distress—

فَذَٰلِكَ يَوْمَئِذٍ يَوْمٌ عَسِيرٌ ۝

10. Far from easy for those without Faith.

عَلَى الْكَافِرِينَ غَيْرُ يَسِيرٍ ۝

11. Leave Me alone, (to deal) with the (creature) whom I created (bare and) alone!—

ذَرْنِي وَمَنْ خَلَقْتُ وَحِيدًا ۝

12. To whom I granted resources in abundance,

وَجَعَلْتُ لَهُ مَالًا مَّمْدُودًا ۝

13. And sons to be by his side !—

وَبَنِينَ شُهُودًا ۝

14. To whom I made (life) smooth and comfortable !

وَمَهَّدْتُ لَهُ تَمْهِيدًا ۝

15. Yet is he greedy— that I should add (yet more);

ثُمَّ يَطْمَعُ أَنْ أَزِيدَ ۝

16. By no means ! for to Our Signs He has been refractory !

كَلَّا إِنَّهُ كَانَ لِآيَاتِنَا عَنِيدًا ۝

17. Soon will I visit him with a mount of calamities¹

سَأُرْهِقُهُ صَعُودًا ۝

18. For he thought and he determined:—

إِنَّهُ فَكَّرَ وَقَدَّرَ ۝

19. And woe to him ! how he determined!—

فَقُتِلَ كَيْفَ قَدَّرَ ۝

20. Yea, woe to him: how he determined!—

ثُمَّ قُتِلَ كَيْفَ قَدَّرَ ۝

21. Then he reflected;

ثُمَّ نَظَرَ ۝

22. Then he frowned and he scowled:

ثُمَّ عَبَسَ وَبَسَرَ ۝

23. Then he turned back and was haughty;

ثُمَّ أَدْبَرَ وَاسْتَكْبَرَ ۝

24. Then said he; "This is nothing but magic, derived from of old;

فَقَالَ إِنْ هَٰذَا إِلَّا سِحْرٌ يُؤْثَرُ ۝

25. "This is nothing but the word of a mortal!"

إِنْ هَٰذَا إِلَّا قَوْلُ الْبَشَرِ ۝

26. Soon will I cast him into Hell-Fire !

سَأُصْلِيهِ سَقَرَ ۝

27. And what will explain to thee what Hell-Fire is?

وَمَا أَدْرَاكَ مَا سَقَرُ ۝

28. Naught doth it permit to endure, and naught doth it leave alone!—

لَا تُبْقِي وَلَا تَذَرُ ۝

29. Darkening and changing the colour of man!

لَوَّاحَةٌ لِلْبَشَرِ ۝

30. Over it are Nineteen.

عَلَيْهَا تِسْعَةَ عَشَرَ ۝

31. And We have set none but angels as guardians of the Fire; and We have fixed their number only as a trial for

وَمَا جَعَلْنَا أَصْحَابَ النَّارِ إِلَّا مَلَائِكَةً ۚ وَمَا جَعَلْنَا عِدَّتَهُمْ إِلَّا فِتْنَةً لِّلَّذِينَ

Unbelievers,—in order that the People of
the Book may arrive at certainty, and the
Believers may increase in Faith,—and that
no doubts may be left for the People of the
Book and the Believers, and that those in
whose hearts is a disease and the
Unbelievers may say, "What doth Allah
intend by this?" Thus doth Allah leave to
stray whom He pleaseth, and guide whom
He pleaseth: and none can know the forces
of thy Lord, except He, and this is no other
than a Reminder to mankind.

32. Nay, verily: by the Moon

33. And by the Night as it retreateth,

34. And by the Dawn as it shineth forth,—

35. This is but one of the mighty (Portents),

36. A warning to mankind,—

37. To any of you that chooses to press
forward, or to follow behind;—

38. Every soul will be (held) in pledge for
its deeds,

39. Except the Companions of the Right
Hand,

40. (They will be) in Gardens (of Delight):
they will question each other,

41. And (ask) of the Sinners:

42. "What led you into Hell-Fire?"

43. They will say: "We were not of those
who prayed;

44. "Nor were we of those who fed the
indigent;

45. "But we used to talk vanities with vain
talkers;

46. "And we used to deny the Day of
Judgment,

47. "Until there came to us (the Hour) that
is certain."

48. Then will no intercession of (any)
intercessors profit them.

49. Then what is the matter with them that
they turn away from admonition?—

50. As if they were affrighted asses,

51. Fleeing from a lion !

SÛRA-75
AL-QIYĀMAT
(INTRODUCTION)

This Sûra belongs to the early Makkan period, but comes chronologically a good deal later than the last two Sûras.

Its subject-matter is the Resurrection, viewed from the point of view of Man, especially unregenerate Man, as he is now, and as he will be then,—his inner and psychological history.

52. Forsooth, each one of them wants to be given Scrolls (of revelation) spread out !

بَلْ يُرِيدُ كُلُّ امْرِئٍ مِّنْهُمْ اَنْ يُّؤْتٰى صُحُفًا مُّنَشَّرَةً ۞

53. By no means ! But they fear not the Hereafter.

كَلَّا بَلْ لَّا يَخَافُوْنَ الْاٰخِرَةَ ۞

54. Nay, this surely is an admonition:

كَلَّا اِنَّهُ تَذْكِرَةٌ ۚ۞

55. Let any who will, keep it in remembrance !

فَمَنْ شَاءَ ذَكَرَهُ ۞

56. But none will keep it in remembrance except as Allah wills: He is the Lord of Righteousness, and the Lord of Forgiveness.

وَمَا يَذْكُرُوْنَ اِلَّا اَنْ يَّشَاءَ اللّٰهُ ۚ هُوَ اَهْلُ التَّقْوٰى وَاَهْلُ الْمَغْفِرَةِ ۞

Al-Qiyāmat, or the Resurrection

In the name of Allah, Most Gracious, Most Merciful.

بِسْمِ اللّٰهِ الرَّحْمٰنِ الرَّحِيْمِ ۞

1. I do swear by the Resurrection Day:

لَا اُقْسِمُ بِيَوْمِ الْقِيٰمَةِ ۙ۞

2. And I do swear by the self-reproaching soul.

وَلَا اُقْسِمُ بِالنَّفْسِ اللَّوَّامَةِ ۞

3. Does man think that We cannot assemble his bones ?

اَيَحْسَبُ الْاِنْسَانُ اَلَّنْ نَّجْمَعَ عِظَامَهُ ۞

4. Nay, We are able to put together in perfect order the very tips of his fingers.

بَلٰى قَادِرِيْنَ عَلٰى اَنْ نُّسَوِّيَ بَنَانَهُ ۞

5. But man wishes to do wrong (even) in the time in front of him.

بَلْ يُرِيدُ الْاِنْسَانُ لِيَفْجُرَ اَمَامَهُ ۞

6. He questions: "When is the Day of Resurrection ?"

يَسْئَلُ اَيَّانَ يَوْمُ الْقِيٰمَةِ ۞

7. At length, when the Sight is dazed.

فَاِذَا بَرِقَ الْبَصَرُ ۞

8. And the moon is buried in darkness.

وَخَسَفَ الْقَمَرُ ۞

9. And the sun and moon are joined together,—

وَجُمِعَ الشَّمْسُ وَالْقَمَرُ ۞

10. That Day will Man say: "Where is the refuge?"

يَقُوْلُ الْاِنْسَانُ يَوْمَئِذٍ اَيْنَ الْمَفَرُّ ۞

11. By no means ! no place of safety !

كَلَّا لَا وَزَرَ ۞

12. Before thy Lord (alone), that Day will be the place of rest.

اِلٰى رَبِّكَ يَوْمَئِذِ الْمُسْتَقَرُّ ۞

13. That Day will Man be told (all) that he put forward, and all that he put back.

يُنَبَّؤُا الْاِنْسَانُ يَوْمَئِذٍ بِمَا قَدَّمَ وَاَخَّرَ ۞

14. Nay, man will be evidence against himself,

بَلِ الْاِنْسَانُ عَلٰى نَفْسِهِ بَصِيْرَةٌ ۞

15. Even though he were to put up his excuses.

وَلَوْ اَلْقٰى مَعَاذِيْرَهُ ۞

16. Move not thy tongue concerning the (Qur-ān) to make haste therewith.

لَا تُحَرِّكْ بِهِ لِسَانَكَ لِتَعْجَلَ بِهِ ۞

17. It is for Us to collect it and to recite it:

اِنَّ عَلَيْنَا جَمْعَهُ وَقُرْاٰنَهُ ۞

18. But when We have recited it. follow thou its recital (as promulgated).

فَاِذَا قَرَاْنَاهُ فَاتَّبِعْ قُرْاٰنَهُ ۞

The revelation of this Sûra was probably in the early Makkan period, with the possible exception of some veres, but its date has no significance.

Its theme is the contrast between the two classes of men, those who choose good and those who choose evil, with special reference to the former.

The title of the Sûra recalls a Pagan Arab idea, which personified Time as existing spontaneously from eternity to enternity and responsible for the misery or the happiness of mankind. In 45: 24 we read: "They say,... 'nothing but Time can destroy us.'" This attitude is of course wrong. Time is a created thing: it has its mysteries, but it is no more eternal than matter. It is also relative to our conceptions and not absolute, as Einstein has proved. It is only Allah Who is Self-Subsisting, Eternal from the beginning and Eternal to the end, the absolute Existence and Reality. We must not transfer His attributes to any figments of our imagination.

This deification of Time (*Dahr*) as against a living personal Allah has given rise to the term *dahrîya*, as applied to an atheist or a materialist.

The whole of the Sûra is full of the highest symbolism, as s generally the case with Makkan Sûras, and this should always by remembered in their interpretation.

19. Nay more, it is for Us to explain it (and make it clear):

ثُمَّ إِنَّ عَلَيْنَا بَيَانَهُ ۞

20. Nay, (ye men !) but ye love the fleeting life.

كَلَّا بَلْ تُحِبُّونَ الْعَاجِلَةَ ۞

21. And leave alone the Hereafter.

وَتَذَرُونَ الْآخِرَةَ ۞

22. Some faces, that Day, will beam (in brightnesss and beauty):—

وُجُوهٌ يَوْمَئِذٍ نَاضِرَةٌ ۞

23. Looking towards their Lord;

إِلَى رَبِّهَا نَاظِرَةٌ ۞

24. And some faces, that Day, will be sad and dismal,

وَوُجُوهٌ يَوْمَئِذٍ بَاسِرَةٌ ۞

25. In the thought that some back-breaking calamity was about to be inflicted on them;

تَظُنُّ أَنْ يُفْعَلَ بِهَا فَاقِرَةٌ ۞

26. Yea, when (the soul) reaches to the collar-bone (in its exit),

كَلَّا إِذَا بَلَغَتِ التَّرَاقِيَ ۞

27. And there will be a cry, "Who is an enchanter (to restore him)?

وَقِيلَ مَنْ رَاقٍ ۞

28. And he will think that it was (the time) of Parting;

وَظَنَّ أَنَّهُ الْفِرَاقُ ۞

29. And one leg will be joined with another:

وَالْتَفَّتِ السَّاقُ بِالسَّاقِ ۞

30. That Day the Drive will be (all) to thy Lord !

إِلَى رَبِّكَ يَوْمَئِذٍ الْمَسَاقُ ۞

31. So he gave nothing in charity, nor did he pray!—

فَلَا صَدَّقَ وَلَا صَلَّى ۞

32. But on the contrary, he rejected Truth and turned away !

وَلَكِنْ كَذَّبَ وَتَوَلَّى ۞

33. Then did he stalk to his family in full conceit!

ثُمَّ ذَهَبَ إِلَى أَهْلِهِ يَتَمَطَّى ۞

34. Woe to thee, (O man !), yea, woe!

أَوْلَى لَكَ فَأَوْلَى ۞

35. Again, woe to thee, (O man!), yea, woe !

ثُمَّ أَوْلَى لَكَ فَأَوْلَى ۞

36. Does Man think that he will be left uncontrolled, (without purpose) ?

أَيَحْسَبُ الْإِنْسَانُ أَنْ يُتْرَكَ سُدًى ۞

37. Was he not a drop of sperm emitted (in lowly form) ?

أَلَمْ يَكُ نُطْفَةً مِنْ مَنِيٍّ يُمْنَى ۞

38. Then did he become a leach-like clot; then did (Allah) make and fashion (him) in due proportion.

ثُمَّ كَانَ عَلَقَةً فَخَلَقَ فَسَوَّى ۞

39. And of him He made two sexes, male and female.

فَجَعَلَ مِنْهُ الزَّوْجَيْنِ الذَّكَرَ وَالْأُنْثَى ۞

40. Has not He, (the same), the power to give life to the dead ?

أَلَيْسَ ذَلِكَ بِقَادِرٍ عَلَى أَنْ يُحْيِيَ الْمَوْتَى ۞

Ad-Dahr, or Time or Insān, or Man

In the name of Allah, Most Gracious, Most Merciful.

بِسْمِ اللَّهِ الرَّحْمَنِ الرَّحِيمِ

1. Has there not been over Man a long period of Time, when he was nothing—(not even) mentioned—?

هَلْ أَتَى عَلَى الْإِنْسَانِ حِينٌ مِنَ الدَّهْرِ لَمْ يَكُنْ شَيْئًا مَذْكُورًا ۞

2. Verily We created man from a drop of mingled sperm, in order to try him: so We

إِنَّا خَلَقْنَا الْإِنْسَانَ مِنْ نُطْفَةٍ أَمْشَاجٍ

gave him (the gifts), of Hearing and Sight.

تَبْتَلِيهِ فَجَعَلْنٰهُ سَمِيْعًۢا بَصِيْرًا ۞

3.   We showed him the Way: whether he be grateful or ungrateful.

اِنَّا هَدَيْنٰهُ السَّبِيْلَ اِمَّا شَاكِرًا وَّاِمَّا كَفُوْرًا ۞

4.   For the Rejecters We have prepared Chains, Yokes, and a Blazing Fire.

اِنَّاۤ اَعْتَدْنَا لِلْكٰفِرِيْنَ سَلٰسِلَا۠ وَاَغْلٰلًا وَّسَعِيْرًا ۞

5.   As to the Righteous, they shall drink of a Cup mixed with *Kāfūr,*—

اِنَّ الْاَبْرَارَ يَشْرَبُوْنَ مِنْ كَاْسٍ كَانَ مِزَاجُهَا كَافُوْرًا ۞

6.   A Fountain where the Devotees of Allah do drink, making it flow in unstinted abundance.

عَيْنًا يَّشْرَبُ بِهَا عِبَادُ اللهِ يُفَجِّرُوْنَهَا تَفْجِيْرًا ۞

7.   They perform (their) vows, and they fear a Day whose evil flies far and wide.

يُوْفُوْنَ بِالنَّذْرِ وَيَخَافُوْنَ يَوْمًا كَانَ شَرُّهٗ مُسْتَطِيْرًا ۞

8.   And they feed, for the love of Allah, the indigent, the orphan, and the captive,—

وَيُطْعِمُوْنَ الطَّعَامَ عَلٰى حُبِّهٖ مِسْكِيْنًا وَّيَتِيْمًا وَّاَسِيْرًا ۞

9.   (Saying), "We feed you for the sake of Allah alone: no reward do we desire from you, nor thanks.

اِنَّمَا نُطْعِمُكُمْ لِوَجْهِ اللهِ لَا نُرِيْدُ مِنْكُمْ جَزَآءً وَّلَا شُكُوْرًا ۞

10.   "We only fear a Day of frowning and distress from the side of our Lord".

اِنَّا نَخَافُ مِنْ رَّبِّنَا يَوْمًا عَبُوْسًا قَمْطَرِيْرًا ۞

11.   But Allah will deliver them from the evil of that Day, and will shed over them brightness and a (blissful) Joy.

فَوَقٰىهُمُ اللهُ شَرَّ ذٰلِكَ الْيَوْمِ وَلَقّٰىهُمْ نَضْرَةً وَّسُرُوْرًا ۞

12.   And because they were Patient and constant, He will reward them with a Garden and (garments of) silk.

وَجَزٰىهُمْ بِمَا صَبَرُوْا جَنَّةً وَّحَرِيْرًا ۞

13.   Reclining in the (Garden) on raised couches, they will see there neither the sun's (excessive heat) nor excessive cold.

مُّتَّكِئِيْنَ فِيْهَا عَلَى الْاَرَآئِكِ ۚ لَا يَرَوْنَ فِيْهَا شَمْسًا وَّلَا زَمْهَرِيْرًا ۞

14.   And the shades of the (Garden) will come low over them, and the bunches (of fruit), there, will hang low easy to reach.

وَدَانِيَةً عَلَيْهِمْ ظِلٰلُهَا وَذُلِّلَتْ قُطُوْفُهَا تَذْلِيْلًا ۞

15.   And amongst them will be passed round vessels of silver and goblets of crystal,—

وَيُطَافُ عَلَيْهِمْ بِاٰنِيَةٍ مِّنْ فِضَّةٍ وَّاَكْوَابٍ كَانَتْ قَوَارِيْرَا ۞

16.   Crystal-clear, made of silver: they will determine the measure thereof (according to their wishes).

قَوَارِيْرَا۟ مِنْ فِضَّةٍ قَدَّرُوْهَا تَقْدِيْرًا ۞

17. And they will be given to drink there of a Cup mixed with Zanjabîl,—

وَيُسْقَوْنَ فِيهَا كَأْسًا كَانَ مِزَاجُهَا زَنْجَبِيلًا ۞

18. A fountain there, called Salsabîl.

عَيْنًا فِيهَا تُسَمَّىٰ سَلْسَبِيلًا ۞

19. And round about them will (serve) youths of perpetual (freshness): if thou seest them, thou wouldst think them scattered Pearls.

وَيَطُوفُ عَلَيْهِمْ وِلْدَانٌ مُّخَلَّدُونَ إِذَا رَأَيْتَهُمْ حَسِبْتَهُمْ لُؤْلُؤًا مَّنْثُورًا ۞

20. And when thou lookest, it is there thou wilt see a Bliss and a Realm Magnificent.

وَإِذَا رَأَيْتَ ثَمَّ رَأَيْتَ نَعِيمًا وَمُلْكًا كَبِيرًا ۞

21. Upon them will be Green Garments of fine silk and heavy brocade, and they will be adorned with Bracelets of silver; and their Lord will give to them to drink a pure drink.

عَالِيَهُمْ ثِيَابُ سُنْدُسٍ خُضْرٌ وَإِسْتَبْرَقٌ وَحُلُّوا أَسَاوِرَ مِن فِضَّةٍ وَسَقَاهُمْ رَبُّهُمْ شَرَابًا طَهُورًا ۞

22. "Verily this is a Reward for you, and your Endeavour is accepted and recognised."

إِنَّ هَٰذَا كَانَ لَكُمْ جَزَاءً وَكَانَ سَعْيُكُم مَّشْكُورًا ۞

23. It is We Who have sent down the Qur-ān to thee by stages.

إِنَّا نَحْنُ نَزَّلْنَا عَلَيْكَ الْقُرْآنَ تَنزِيلًا ۞

24. Therefore be patient with constancy to the Command of thy Lord, and obey not to the sinner or the ingrate among them.

فَاصْبِرْ لِحُكْمِ رَبِّكَ وَلَا تُطِعْ مِنْهُمْ آثِمًا أَوْ كَفُورًا ۞

25. And celebrate the name of thy Lord morning and evening,

وَاذْكُرِ اسْمَ رَبِّكَ بُكْرَةً وَأَصِيلًا ۞

26. And part of the night, prostrate thyself to Him; and glorify Him a long night through.

وَمِنَ اللَّيْلِ فَاسْجُدْ لَهُ وَسَبِّحْهُ لَيْلًا طَوِيلًا ۞

27. As to these, they love the fleeting life, and put away behind them a Day (that will be) hard.

إِنَّ هَٰؤُلَاءِ يُحِبُّونَ الْعَاجِلَةَ وَيَذَرُونَ وَرَاءَهُمْ يَوْمًا ثَقِيلًا ۞

28. It is We Who created them, and We have made their frame strong; but, when We will, We shall exchange their likes.

نَحْنُ خَلَقْنَاهُمْ وَشَدَدْنَا أَسْرَهُمْ وَإِذَا شِئْنَا بَدَّلْنَا أَمْثَالَهُمْ تَبْدِيلًا ۞

29. This is an admonition: whosoever will, let him take a (straight) Path to his Lord.

إِنَّ هَٰذِهِ تَذْكِرَةٌ فَمَن شَاءَ اتَّخَذَ إِلَىٰ رَبِّهِ سَبِيلًا ۞

30. But ye will not, except as Allah wills; for Allah is full of Knowledge and Wisdom.

وَمَا تَشَاءُونَ إِلَّا أَن يَشَاءَ اللَّهُ ۚ إِنَّ اللَّهَ كَانَ عَلِيمًا حَكِيمًا ۞

31. He will admit to His Mercy Whom He will; but the wrong-doers,—

يُدْخِلُ مَن يَشَاءُ فِي رَحْمَتِهِ وَ

SÛRA–77
AL-MURSALÃT
(INTRODUCTION)

This Sûra belongs to the early Makkan period, somewhere near to S. 75 (*Qiyâmat*). The theme is some what similar. It denounces the horrors of the Hereafter, for those who rejected Truth. The refrain, "Ah woe, that Day, to the Rejecters of Truth!" which occurs ten times in its fifty verses, or on an average, once in every five verses, indicates the *leitmotif*.

for them has He prepared a grievous Chastisement.

Al-Mursalāt, or
Those Sent Forth

In the name of Allah, Most Gracious, Most Merciful.

1. By the (Winds) Sent Forth one after another (to man's profit);

2. Which then blow voilently in tempestuous Gusts,

3. And scatter (things) far and wide;

4. Then separate them, one from another,

5. Then spread abroad a Reminder,

6. Whether of Justification or of Warning;—

7. Assuredly, what ye are promised must come to pass.

8. Then when the stars become dim;

9. When the heaven is cleft asunder;

10. When the mountains are scattered (to the winds) as dust;

11. And when the messengers are (all) appointed a time (to collect);—

12. For what Day are these (portents) deferred?

13. For the Day of Sorting out.

14. And what will explain to thee what is the Day of Sorting out ?

15. Ah woe, that Day, to the Rejecters of Truth!

16. Did We not destroy the men of old (for their evil) ?

17. So shall We make later (generations) follow them.

18. Thus do We deal with men of sin.

19. Ah woe, that Day to the Rejecters of Truth!

20. Have We not created you from a fluid (held) despicable?—

21. The which We placed in a place of rest, firmly fixed,

22. For a period (of gestation), determined?

23. For We do determine for We are the Best to determine (things).

24. Ah woe, that Day ! to the Rejecters of Truth!

25. Have We not made the earth (as a place) to draw together

اَلَمْ نَجْعَلِ الْاَرْضَ كِفَاتًا ۞

26. The living and the dead,

اَحْيَآءً وَّاَمْوَاتًا ۞

27. And made therein mountains standing firm, lofty (in stature); and provided for you water sweet (and wholesome) ?

وَّجَعَلْنَا فِيْهَا رَوَاسِيَ شٰمِخٰتٍ وَّاَسْقَيْنٰكُمْ مَّآءً فُرَاتًا ۞

28. Ah woe, that Day, to the Rejecters of Truth!

وَيْلٌ يَّوْمَئِذٍ لِّلْمُكَذِّبِيْنَ ۞

29. (It will be said:) "Depart ye to that which ye used to reject as false!

اِنْطَلِقُوْا اِلٰى مَا كُنْتُمْ بِهٖ تُكَذِّبُوْنَ ۞

30. "Depart ye to a Shadow (of smoke ascending) in three columns,

اِنْطَلِقُوْا اِلٰى ظِلٍّ ذِيْ ثَلٰثِ شُعَبٍ ۞

31. "(Which yields) no shade of coolness, and is of no use against the fierce Blaze.

لَّا ظَلِيْلٍ وَّلَا يُغْنِيْ مِنَ اللَّهَبِ ۞

32. "Indeed it throws about sparks (huge) as Forts,

اِنَّهَا تَرْمِيْ بِشَرَرٍ كَالْقَصْرِ ۞

33. "As if there were (a string of) yellow camels (marching swiftly)."

كَاَنَّهٗ جِمٰلَتٌ صُفْرٌ ۞

34. Ah woe, that Day, to the Rejecters of Truth!

وَيْلٌ يَّوْمَئِذٍ لِّلْمُكَذِّبِيْنَ ۞

35. That will be a Day when they shall not be able to speak,

هٰذَا يَوْمُ لَا يَنْطِقُوْنَ ۞

36. Nor will it be open to them to put forth pleas.

وَلَا يُؤْذَنُ لَهُمْ فَيَعْتَذِرُوْنَ ۞

37. Ah woe, that Day, to the Rejecters of Truth!

وَيْلٌ يَّوْمَئِذٍ لِّلْمُكَذِّبِيْنَ ۞

38. That will be a Day of Sorting out ! We shall gather you together and those before (you) !

هٰذَا يَوْمُ الْفَصْلِ جَمَعْنٰكُمْ وَالْاَوَّلِيْنَ ۞

39. Now, if ye have a trick (or plot), use it against Me !

فَاِنْ كَانَ لَكُمْ كَيْدٌ فَكِيْدُوْنِ ۞

40. Ah woe, that Day, to the Rejecters of Truth!

وَيْلٌ يَّوْمَئِذٍ لِّلْمُكَذِّبِيْنَ ۞

41. As to the Righteous, they shall be amidst (cool) shades and springs (of water).

اِنَّ الْمُتَّقِيْنَ فِيْ ظِلٰلٍ وَّعُيُوْنٍ ۞

42. And (they shall have) fruits,—all they desire.

وَّفَوَاكِهَ مِمَّا يَشْتَهُوْنَ ۞

43. "Eat ye and drink ye to your heart's content: for that ye worked (righteousness).

كُلُوْا وَاشْرَبُوْا هَنِيْئًا بِمَا كُنْتُمْ تَعْمَلُوْنَ ۞

44. Thus do We certainly reward the Doers of Good.

اِنَّا كَذٰلِكَ نَجْزِي الْمُحْسِنِيْنَ ۞

45. Ah woe, that Day, to the Rejecters of Truth!

وَيْلٌ يَّوْمَئِذٍ لِّلْمُكَذِّبِيْنَ ۞

46. (O ye Unjust !) eat ye and enjoy yourselves (but) a little while, for that ye are Sinners.

كُلُوْا وَتَمَتَّعُوْا قَلِيْلًا اِنَّكُمْ مُّجْرِمُوْنَ ۞

47. Ah woe, that Day, to the Rejecters of Truth!

وَيْلٌ يَّوْمَئِذٍ لِّلْمُكَذِّبِيْنَ ۞

48. And when it is said to them, "Pro-strate yourselves !" they do not so.

وَاِذَا قِيْلَ لَهُمُ ارْكَعُوْا لَا يَرْكَعُوْنَ ۞

49. Ah woe, that Day, to the Rejecters of Truth!

وَيْلٌ يَّوْمَئِذٍ لِّلْمُكَذِّبِيْنَ ۞

50. Then what Message, after that, will they believe in ?

فَبِاَيِّ حَدِيْثٍ بَعْدَهٗ يُؤْمِنُوْنَ ۞

SÛRA–78
AN-NABAA
(INTRODUCTION)

This beautiful Makkan Sûra is not quite so early as the last (S. 77), nor quite so late as S. 76, but nearer in time to the latter.

It sets forth Allah's loving care in a fine nature-passage, and deduces from it the Promise of the Future, when Evil will be destroyed and Good will come to its own; and invites all who have the will, to seek refuge with their Lord.

An-Nabaa, or
The (Great) News

بِسْمِ اللهِ الرَّحْمٰنِ الرَّحِيمِ ۞

In the name of Allah, Most Gracious, Most Merciful.

1. Concerning what are they disputing ?

عَمَّ يَتَسَآءَلُوْنَ ۞

2. Concerning the Great News,

عَنِ النَّبَاِ الْعَظِيْمِ ۞

3. About which they cannot agree.

الَّذِيْ هُمْ فِيْهِ مُخْتَلِفُوْنَ ۞

4. Verily, they shall soon (come to) know!

كَلَّا سَيَعْلَمُوْنَ ۞

5. Verily, verily they shall soon (come to) know!

ثُمَّ كَلَّا سَيَعْلَمُوْنَ ۞

6. Have We not made the earth as a wide Expanse,

اَلَمْ نَجْعَلِ الْاَرْضَ مِهٰدًا ۞

7. And the mountains as pegs ?

وَّالْجِبَالَ اَوْتَادًا ۞

8. And (have We not) created you in pairs,

وَخَلَقْنٰكُمْ اَزْوَاجًا ۞

9. And made your sleep for rest,

وَّجَعَلْنَا نَوْمَكُمْ سُبَاتًا ۞

10. And made the night as a covering,

وَّجَعَلْنَا الَّيْلَ لِبَاسًا ۞

11. And made the day as a means of subsistence?

وَّجَعَلْنَا النَّهَارَ مَعَاشًا ۞

12. And (have We not) built over you the seven firmaments,

وَبَنَيْنَا فَوْقَكُمْ سَبْعًا شِدَادًا ۞

13. And placed (therein) a blazing lamp,

وَّجَعَلْنَا سِرَاجًا وَّهَّاجًا ۞

14. And do We not send down from the clouds water in abundance,

وَّاَنْزَلْنَا مِنَ الْمُعْصِرٰتِ مَآءً ثَجَّاجًا ۞

15. That We may produce therewith grain and vegetables,

لِّنُخْرِجَ بِهٖ حَبًّا وَّنَبَاتًا ۞

16. And gardens of luxurious growth?

وَّجَنّٰتٍ اَلْفَافًا ۞

17. Verily the Day of Sorting Out is a thing appointed,—

اِنَّ يَوْمَ الْفَصْلِ كَانَ مِيْقَاتًا ۞

18. The Day that the Trumpet shall be sounded, and ye shall come forth in crowds;

يَّوْمَ يُنْفَخُ فِي الصُّوْرِ فَتَأْتُوْنَ اَفْوَاجًا ۞

19. And the heavens shall be opened as if there were doors,

وَّفُتِحَتِ السَّمَآءُ فَكَانَتْ اَبْوَابًا ۞

20. And the mountains shall vanish, as if they were a mirage.

وَّسُيِّرَتِ الْجِبَالُ فَكَانَتْ سَرَابًا ۞

21. Truly Hell is as a place of ambush

اِنَّ جَهَنَّمَ كَانَتْ مِرْصَادًا ۞

22. For the transgressors a place of destination:

لِّلطّٰاغِيْنَ مَاٰبًا ۞

23. They will dwell therein for ages.

لّٰبِثِيْنَ فِيْهَا اَحْقَابًا ۞

24. Nothing cool shall they taste therein, nor any drink,

لَا يَذُوْقُوْنَ فِيْهَا بَرْدًا وَّلَا شَرَابًا ۞

25. Save a boiling fluid and a fluid, dark, murky, intensely cold,—

اِلَّا حَمِيْمًا وَّغَسَّاقًا ۞

SÛRA–79
AN-NÃZI'ÃT
(INTRODUCTION)

This is also an early Makkan Sûra, of about the same date as the last, and deals with the mystic theme of Judgment from the point of view of Pride and its Fall. The parable of Pharaoh occupies a central place in the argument: for he said, "I am your Lord Most High," and perished with his followers.

26. A fitting recompense (for them).

27. For that they used not to look for any account (for their deeds),

28. But they (impudently) treated our Signs as false

29. And all things have We preserved on record.

30. "So taste ye (the fruits of your deeds); for no increase shall We grant you, except in Chastisement.'

31. Verily for the Righteous there will be an Achievement,

32. Gardens enclosed, and Grape-vines;

33. Maidens of Equal Age;

34. And a Cup full (to the Brim).

35. No Vanity shall they hear therein, nor Untruth;—

36. Recompense from thy Lord, a Gift, (amply) sufficient,—

37. (From) the Lord of the heavens and the earth, and all between,— the Most Gracious: none shall have power to argue with Him.

38. The Day that the Spirit and the angels will stand forth in ranks, none shall speak except any who is permitted by The Most Gracious, and he will say what is right.

39. That is the True Day: therefore, whoso will, let him take a (straight) Return to his Lord !

40. Verily, We have warned you of a Chastisement near,— the Day when man will see (the Deeds) which his hands have sent forth, and the Unbeliever will say, "Woe unto me ! Would that I were (mere) dust !"

An-Nāzi'āt, or Those Who Tear Out

In the name of Allah, Most Gracious, Most Merciful.

1. By the (angels) who tear out (the souls of the wicked) with violence;

2. By those who gently draw out (the souls of the blessed);

3. And by those who glide along (on errands of mercy),

4. Then press forward as in a race.

5. Then arrange to do (the Commands of their Lord),—

فَالْمُدَبِّرٰتِ أَمْرًا ۗ

6. The Day everything that can be in commotion, will be in violent commotion,

يَوْمَ تَرْجُفُ الرَّاجِفَةُ ۙ

7. Followed by oft-repeated (commotions):

تَتْبَعُهَا الرَّادِفَةُ ۙ

8. Hearts that Day will be in agitation;

قُلُوبٌ يَّوْمَئِذٍ وَّاجِفَةٌ ۙ

9. Cast down will be (their owners') eyes.

اَبْصَارُهَا خَاشِعَةٌ ۘ

10. They say (now): "What! shall we indeed be returned to (our) former state?—

يَقُوْلُوْنَ ءَاِنَّا لَمَرْدُوْدُوْنَ فِى الْحَافِرَةِ ؕ

11. "What!—when we shall have become rotten bones?"

ءَاِذَا كُنَّا عِظَامًا نَّخِرَةً ؕ

12. They say: "It would, in that case, be a return with loss!"

قَالُوْا تِلْكَ اِذًا كَرَّةٌ خَاسِرَةٌ ۘ

13. But verily, it will be but a single (compelling) Cry,

فَاِنَّمَا هِيَ زَجْرَةٌ وَّاحِدَةٌ ۙ

14. When, behold, they will be brought out to the open.

فَاِذَا هُمْ بِالسَّاهِرَةِ ؕ

15. Has the story of Moses reached thee?

هَلْ اَتٰىكَ حَدِيْثُ مُوْسٰى ۘ

16. Behold, thy Lord did call to him in the sacred valley of Tuwā:—

اِذْ نَادٰىهُ رَبُّهٗ بِالْوَادِ الْمُقَدَّسِ طُوًى ۚ

17. "Go thou to Pharaoh, for he has indeed transgressed all bounds:

اِذْهَبْ اِلٰى فِرْعَوْنَ اِنَّهٗ طَغٰى ۖ

18. "And say to him, 'Wouldst thou that thou shouldst be purified (from sin)?—

فَقُلْ هَلْ لَّكَ اِلٰٓى اَنْ تَزَكّٰى ۙ

19. " 'And that I guide thee to thy Lord, so thou shouldst fear Him?' "

وَاَهْدِيَكَ اِلٰى رَبِّكَ فَتَخْشٰى ۚ

20. Then did (Moses) show him the Great Sign.

فَاَرٰىهُ الْاٰيَةَ الْكُبْرٰى ۫

21. But (Pharaoh) rejected it and disobeyed (guidance);

فَكَذَّبَ وَعَصٰى ۙ

22. Further, he turned his back, striving hard (against Allah).

ثُمَّ اَدْبَرَ يَسْعٰى ۙ

23. Then he collected (his men) and made a proclamation,

فَحَشَرَ فَنَادٰى ۙ

24. Saying, "I am your Lord, Most High".

فَقَالَ اَنَا رَبُّكُمُ الْاَعْلٰى ۙ

25. But Allah did punish him, (and made an) example of him,—in the Hereafter, as in this life.

فَاَخَذَهُ اللّٰهُ نَكَالَ الْاٰخِرَةِ وَالْاُوْلٰى ؕ

26. Verily in this is a lesson for whosoever feareth (Allah).

اِنَّ فِيْ ذٰلِكَ لَعِبْرَةً لِّمَنْ يَّخْشٰى ؕ

27. What! Are ye the more difficult to create or the heaven (above)? (Allah) hath constructed it:

ءَاَنْتُمْ اَشَدُّ خَلْقًا اَمِ السَّمَآءُ ؕ بَنٰىهَا ۙ

28. On high hath He raised its canopy, and He hath given it order and perfection.

رَفَعَ سَمْكَهَا فَسَوّٰىهَا ۙ

29. Its night doth He endow with darkness, and its splendour doth He bring out (with light).

وَاَغْطَشَ لَيْلَهَا وَاَخْرَجَ ضُحٰىهَا ۪

30. And the earth, moreover, hath He extended (to a wide expanse);

وَالْاَرْضَ بَعْدَ ذٰلِكَ دَحٰىهَا ؕ

31. He draweth out therefrom its water and its pasture,

اَخْرَجَ مِنْهَا مَآءَهَا وَمَرْعٰىهَا ۪

SÛRA–80
'ABASA
(INTRODUCTION)

This is an early Makkan Sûra, and is connected with an incident which reflects the highest honour on the Prophet's sincerity in the Revelations that were vouchsafed to him even if they seemed to reprove him for some natural and human zeal that led him to a false step in his mission according to his own high standards.

He was once deeply and earnestly engaged in trying to explain the Holy Qur-ān to Pagan Quraish leaders, when he was interrupted by blind man, 'Abdullah Umm Maktûm, one who was also poor, so that no one took any notice of him. He wanted to learn the Qur-ān. The Holy Prophet naturally disliked the interruption and showed impatience. Perhaps the poor man's feelings were hurt. But he whose gentle heart ever sympathised with the poor and the afflicted got new Light from above, and without the least hesitation published this revelation, which forms part of the sacred scripture of Islam, as described in verses 13-16. And the Prophet always afterwards held the man in high honour.

The incident was only a passing incident, but after explaining the eternal principles of revelation, the Sûra recapitulates the Mercies of Allah to man, and the consequences of a good or a wicked life here, as seen in the spiritual world to come, in the Hereafter.

32. And the mountains hath He firmly fixed;—

وَالْجِبَالَ اَرْسٰهَا ۞

33. A provision for you and your cattle.

مَتَاعًا لَّكُمْ وَلِاَنْعَامِكُمْ ۞

34. Therefore, when there comes the great, overwhelming (Event),—

فَاِذَا جَآءَتِ الطَّآمَّةُ الْكُبْرٰى ۞

35. The Day when Man shall remember (all) that he strove for.

يَوْمَ يَتَذَكَّرُ الْاِنْسَانُ مَا سَعٰى ۞

36. And Hell-Fire shall be placed in full view for him who sees.—

وَبُرِّزَتِ الْجَحِيْمُ لِمَنْ يَّرٰى ۞

37. Then, for such as had transgressed all bounds,

فَاَمَّا مَنْ طَغٰى ۞

38. And had preferred the life of this world,

وَاٰثَرَ الْحَيٰوةَ الدُّنْيَا ۞

39. The Abode will be Hell-Fire:

فَاِنَّ الْجَحِيْمَ هِيَ الْمَأْوٰى ۞

40. And for such as had entertained the fear of standing before their Lord's (tribunal) and had restrained (their) soul from lower Desires,

وَاَمَّا مَنْ خَافَ مَقَامَ رَبِّهِ وَنَهَى النَّفْسَ عَنِ الْهَوٰى ۞

41. Their Abode will be the Garden.

فَاِنَّ الْجَنَّةَ هِيَ الْمَأْوٰى ۞

42. They ask thee about the Hour,—'When will be its appointed time?'

يَسْـَٔلُوْنَكَ عَنِ السَّاعَةِ اَيَّانَ مُرْسٰهَا ۞

43. Wherein art thou (concerned) with the declaration thereof?

فِيْمَ اَنْتَ مِنْ ذِكْرٰهَا ۞

44. With thy Lord is the final end of it.

اِلٰى رَبِّكَ مُنْتَهٰىهَا ۞

45. Thou art but a Warner for such as fear it.

اِنَّمَآ اَنْتَ مُنْذِرُ مَنْ يَّخْشٰهَا ۞

46. The Day they see it, (it will be) as if they had tarried but a single evening, or (at most till) the following morn!

كَاَنَّهُمْ يَوْمَ يَرَوْنَهَا لَمْ يَلْبَثُوْٓا اِلَّا عَشِيَّةً اَوْ ضُحٰهَا ۞

'Abasa, or He Frowned

In the name of Allah, Most Gracious, Most Merciful.

بِسْمِ اللهِ الرَّحْمٰنِ الرَّحِيْمِ

1. (The Prophet) frowned and turned away,

عَبَسَ وَتَوَلّٰى ۞

2. Because there came to him the blind man (interrupting).

اَنْ جَآءَهُ الْاَعْمٰى ۞

3. But what could tell thee but that perchance he might grow in purity?

وَمَا يُدْرِيْكَ لَعَلَّهٗ يَزَّكّٰى ۞

4. Or that he might receive admoniton, and the Reminder might profit him?

اَوْ يَذَّكَّرُ فَتَنْفَعَهُ الذِّكْرٰى ۞

5. As to one who regards himself as self-sufficient,

اَمَّا مَنِ اسْتَغْنٰى ۞

6. To him dost thou attend;

فَاَنْتَ لَهٗ تَصَدّٰى ۞

7. Though it is no blame to thee if he grow not in purity.

وَمَا عَلَيْكَ اَلَّا يَزَّكّٰى ۞

8. But as to him who came to thee striving earnestly,

وَاَمَّا مَنْ جَآءَكَ يَسْعٰى ۞

9. And with fear (in his heart),

10. Of him wast thou unmindful.

11. By no means (should it be so)! for it is indeed a Message of remembrance.

12. Therefore let whose will, keep it in remembrance.

13. (It is) in Books held (greatly) in honour,

14. Exalted (in dignity), kept pure and holy,

15. (Written) by the hands of scribes—

16. Honourable and Pious and Just.

17. Woe to man ! What hath made him reject Allah?

18. From what stuff hath He created him ?

19. From a sperm-drop: He hath created him, and then mouldeth him in due Proportions;

20. Then doth He make His path smooth for him;

21. Then He causeth him to die, and putteth him in his Grave;

22. Then, when it is His Will, He will raise him up (again).

23. By no means hath he fulfilled what Allah hath commanded him.

24. Then let man look at his Food. (and now We provide it):

25. For that We pour forth water in abundance,

26. And We split the earth in fragments,

27. And produce therein grain,

28. And Grapes and the fresh vegetation,

29. And Olives and Dates,

30. And enclosed Gardens, dense with lofty trees,

31. And Fruits and Fodder,—

32. A provision for you and your cattle.

33. At length, when there comes the Deafening Noise,—

34. That Day shall a man flee from his own brother,

35. And from his mother and his father.

SÛRA–81
AT-TAKWÎR
(INTRODUCTION)

This is quite an early Makkan Sûra, perhaps the sixth or seventh in chronological order. It opens with a series of highly mystical metaphors suggesting the break-up of the world as we know it (verses 1-13) and the enforcement of complete personal responsibility for each soul (verse 14). Then there is a mystical passage showing how the Quranic Revelation was true, and revealed through the angel Gabriel, and not merely a rhepsody from one possessed. Revelation is given for man's spiritual guidance (verses 14-29).

Comparable with this Sûra are the Sûras 82 and 84 which may be read with this.

36. And from his wife and his children.

37. Each one of them, that Day, will have enough concern (of his own) to make him indifferent to the others.

وَصَاحِبَتِهِ وَبَنِيهِ ۞

لِكُلِّ امْرِئٍ مِّنْهُمْ يَوْمَئِذٍ شَأْنٌ يُّغْنِيهِ ۞

38. Some Faces that Day will be beaming,

39. Laughing, rejoicing.

وُجُوهٌ يَّوْمَئِذٍ مُّسْفِرَةٌ ۞

ضَاحِكَةٌ مُّسْتَبْشِرَةٌ ۞

40. And other faces that Day will be dust-stained;

41. Darkness will cover them:

وَوُجُوهٌ يَّوْمَئِذٍ عَلَيْهَا غَبَرَةٌ ۞

تَرْهَقُهَا قَتَرَةٌ ۞

42. Such will be the Rejecters of Allah the Doers of Iniquity.

أُولَئِكَ هُمُ الْكَفَرَةُ الْفَجَرَةُ ۞

At-Takwir, or the Folding Up

سُورَةُ التَّكْوِيرِ مَكِّيَّةٌ وَهِيَ تِسْعٌ وَعِشْرُونَ آيَةً

In the name of Allah, Most Gracious, Most Merciful.

بِسْمِ اللَّهِ الرَّحْمَنِ الرَّحِيمِ

1. When the sun (with its spacious light) is folded up;

إِذَا الشَّمْسُ كُوِّرَتْ ۞

2. When the stars fall, losing their lustre;

وَإِذَا النُّجُومُ انْكَدَرَتْ ۞

3. When the mountains vanish (like a mirage);

وَإِذَا الْجِبَالُ سُيِّرَتْ ۞

4. When the she-camels, ten mo-nths with young, are left untended:

وَإِذَا الْعِشَارُ عُطِّلَتْ ۞

5. When the wild beasts are herded together (in human habitations);

وَإِذَا الْوُحُوشُ حُشِرَتْ ۞

6. When the oceans boil over with a swell;

وَإِذَا الْبِحَارُ سُجِّرَتْ ۞

7. When the souls are sorted out, (being joined, like with like);

وَإِذَا النُّفُوسُ زُوِّجَتْ ۞

8. When the female (infant), buried alive, is questioned—

وَإِذَا الْمَوْءُودَةُ سُئِلَتْ ۞

9. For what crime she was killed,

بِأَيِّ ذَنْبٍ قُتِلَتْ ۞

10. When the Scrolls are laid open;

وَإِذَا الصُّحُفُ نُشِرَتْ ۞

11. When the sky is unveiled;

وَإِذَا السَّمَاءُ كُشِطَتْ ۞

12. When the Blazing Fire is kindled to fierce heat;

وَإِذَا الْجَحِيمُ سُعِّرَتْ ۞

13. And when the Garden is brought near—

وَإِذَا الْجَنَّةُ أُزْلِفَتْ ۞

14. (Then) shall each soul know what it has put forward.

عَلِمَتْ نَفْسٌ مَّا أَحْضَرَتْ ۞

15. So verily I call to witness the Planets—that recede,

فَلَا أُقْسِمُ بِالْخُنَّسِ ۞

16. Go straight, or hide;

الْجَوَارِ الْكُنَّسِ ۞

17. And the Night as it dissipates;

وَالَّيْلِ إِذَا عَسْعَسَ ۞

18. And the Dawn as it breathes away the darkness;—

وَالصُّبْحِ إِذَا تَنَفَّسَ ۞

SÛRA–82
AL-INFÎṬĀR
(INTRODUCTION)

In subject-matter this Sûra is cognate to the last, though the best authorities consider it a good deal later in chronology in the early Makkan period.

Its argument is subject to the threefold interpretation referring (1) to the final Day of Judgment, (2) to the Lesser Judgment, on an individual's death, and (3) to the awakening of the Inner Light in the soul at any time, that being considered as Death to the Falsities of this life and a Rebirth to the true spiritual Reality.

19. Verily this is the word of a most honourable Messenger,

اِنَّهُ لَقَوْلُ رَسُوْلٍ كَرِيْمٍ ۙ۞

20. Endued with Power, held in honour by the Lord of the Throne,

ذِيْ قُوَّةٍ عِنْدَ ذِى الْعَرْشِ مَكِيْنٍ ۙ۞

21. With authority there, (and) faithful to his trust.

مُّطَاعٍ ثَمَّ اَمِيْنٍ ۙ۞

22. And (O people) ! your Companion is not one possessed;

وَمَا صَاحِبُكُمْ بِمَجْنُوْنٍ ۚ۞

23. And without doubt he saw him in the clear horizon.

وَلَقَدْ رَاٰهُ بِالْاُفُقِ الْمُبِيْنِ ۚ۞

24. Neither doth he withhold grudgingly a knowledge of the Unseen.

وَمَا هُوَ عَلَى الْغَيْبِ بِضَنِيْنٍ ۚ۞

25. Nor is it the word of a Satan accursed.

وَمَا هُوَ بِقَوْلِ شَيْطٰنٍ رَّجِيْمٍ ۙ۞

26. Then whither go ye ?

فَاَيْنَ تَذْهَبُوْنَ ۞

27. Verily this is no less than a Message to (all) the Worlds:

اِنْ هُوَ اِلَّا ذِكْرٌ لِّلْعٰلَمِيْنَ ۙ۞

28. (With profit) to whoever among you wills to go straight:

لِمَنْ شَاءَ مِنْكُمْ اَنْ يَّسْتَقِيْمَ ۞

29. But ye shall not will except as Allah wills,— the Cherisher of the Worlds.

وَمَا تَشَاءُوْنَ اِلَّا اَنْ يَّشَاءَ اللّٰهُ رَبُّ الْعٰلَمِيْنَ ۞

Al-Infiṭār, or The Cleaving Asunder

In the name of Allah, Most Gracious, Most Merciful.

سُوْرَةُ الْإنْفِطَارِ مَكِّيَّةٌ وَهِيَ تِسْعَ عَشْرَةَ أٰيَةً

بِسْمِ اللّٰهِ الرَّحْمٰنِ الرَّحِيْمِ

1. When the Sky is cleft asunder;

اِذَا السَّمَاءُ انْفَطَرَتْ ۙ۞

2. When the Stars are scattered;

وَاِذَا الْكَوَاكِبُ انْتَثَرَتْ ۙ۞

3. When the Oceans are suffered to burst forth;

وَاِذَا الْبِحَارُ فُجِّرَتْ ۙ۞

4. And when the Graves are turned upside down;—

وَاِذَا الْقُبُوْرُ بُعْثِرَتْ ۙ۞

5. (Then) shall each soul know what it hath sent forward and (what it hath) kept back.

عَلِمَتْ نَفْسٌ مَّا قَدَّمَتْ وَاَخَّرَتْ ۞

6. O man ! what has seduced thee from thy Lord Most Beneficent?

يٰۤاَيُّهَا الْاِنْسَانُ مَا غَرَّكَ بِرَبِّكَ الْكَرِيْمِ ۙ۞

7. Him Who created thee, fashioned thee in due proportion, and gave thee a just bias;

الَّذِيْ خَلَقَكَ فَسَوّٰىكَ فَعَدَلَكَ ۙ۞

8. In whatever Form He wills, does He put thee together.

فِيْۤ اَيِّ صُوْرَةٍ مَّا شَاءَ رَكَّبَكَ ۞

9. Nay ! but ye do reject The Judgment !

كَلَّا بَلْ تُكَذِّبُوْنَ بِالدِّيْنِ ۙ۞

10. But verily over you (are appointed angels) to protect you,—

وَاِنَّ عَلَيْكُمْ لَحٰفِظِيْنَ ۙ۞

11. Kind and honourable,—writing down (your deeds).

كِرَامًا كَاتِبِيْنَ ۙ۞

12. They know all that ye do.

يَعْلَمُوْنَ مَا تَفْعَلُوْنَ ۞

13. As for the Righteous, they will be in Bliss;

اِنَّ الْاَبْرَارَ لَفِيْ نَعِيْمٍ ۚ۞

SÛRA–83
AL-MUŢAFFIFEEN
(INTRODUCTION)

This Sûra is close in time to the last one and the next one.

It condemns all fraud—in daily dealings, as well as and especially in matters of Religion and the higher spiritual Life.

14. And the Wicked—they will be in the Fire,

15. Which they will enter on the Day of Judgment,

16. And they will not be able to keep away therefrom.

17. And what will explain to thee what the Day of Judgment is?

18. Again, what will explain to thee what the Day of Judgment is?

19. (It will be) the Day when no soul shall have power (to do) aught for another: for the Command, that Day, will be (wholly) with Allah.

At-Taṭfif, or Al-Muṭaffifeen or Dealing in Fraud

In the name of Allah, Most Gracious, Most Merciful.

1. Woe to those that deal in fraud,—

2. Those who, when they have to receive by measure from men, exact full measure,

3. But when they have to give by measure or weight to men, give less than due.

4. Do they not think that they will be raised up?—

5. On a Mighty Day,

6. A Day when (all) mankind will stand before the Lord of the Worlds?

7. Nay ! Surely the Record of the Wicked is (preserved) in *Sijjin*.

8. And what will explain to thee what *Sijjin* is?

9. (There is) a Register (fully) inscribed.

10. Woe, that Day, to those that deny—

11. Those that deny the Day of Judgment.

12. And none can deny it but the Transgressor beyond bounds, the Sinner!

13. When Our Signs are rehearsed to him, he says, "Tales of the Ancients !"

14. By no means ! But on their hearts is the stain of the (ill) which they do !

15. Verily, from (the Light of) their Lord, that Day, will they be veiled.

16. Further, they will enter the Fire of Hell.

SÛRA–84
AL-INSHIQÃQ
(INTRODUCTION)

Chronologically this Sûra is closely connected with the last one. In subject-matter it resembles more S. 82, and 81 with which it may be compared.

By a number of mystic metaphors it is shown that the present phenomenal order will not last, and Allah's full Judgment will certainly be established: man should therefore strive for that World of Eternity and True Values.

17. Further, it will be said to them: "This is the (reality) which ye rejected as false!"

18. Nay, verily the Record of the Righteous is (preserved) in *'Illīyīn.*

19. And what will explain to thee what *'Illiyūn* is?

20. (There is) a Register (fully) inscribed,

21. To which bear witness those Nearest (to Allah).

22. Truly the Righteous will be in Bliss:

23. On raised couches will they command a sight (of all things):

24. Thou wilt recognise in their Fac-es the beaming brightness of Bliss.

25. Their thirst will be slaked with Pure Wine sealed:

26. The seal thereof will be musk: and for this let those aspire, who have aspirations:

27. With it will be (given) a mixture of *Tasnīm:*

28. A spring, from (the waters) whereof drink those Nearest to Allah.

29. Those in sin used to laugh at those who believed,

30. And whenever they passed by them, used to wink at each other (in mockery);

31. And when they returned to their own people, they would return jesting;

32. And whenever they saw them, they would say, "Behold! these are the people truly astray!"

33. But they had not been sent as Keepers over them!

34. But on this Day the Believers will laugh at the Unbelievers:

35. On raised couches they will command (a sight) (of all things).

36. Will not the Unbelievers have been paid back for what they did?

Al-Inshiqāq, or The Rending Asunder

In the name of Allah, Most Gracious, Most Merciful.

1. When the Sky is rent asunder,

2. And hearkens to (the Command of) its Lord,— and it must needs (do so);—

3. And when the Earth is flattened out,

ثُمَّ يُقَالُ هَٰذَا الَّذِى كُنْتُمْ بِهِ تُكَذِّبُونَ ﴿١٧﴾

كَلَّا إِنَّ كِتَٰبَ الْأَبْرَارِ لَفِى عِلِّيِّينَ ﴿١٨﴾

وَمَا أَدْرَاكَ مَا عِلِّيُّونَ ﴿١٩﴾

كِتَٰبٌ مَّرْقُومٌ ﴿٢٠﴾

يَشْهَدُهُ الْمُقَرَّبُونَ ﴿٢١﴾

إِنَّ الْأَبْرَارَ لَفِى نَعِيمٍ ﴿٢٢﴾

عَلَى الْأَرَائِكِ يَنْظُرُونَ ﴿٢٣﴾

تَعْرِفُ فِى وُجُوهِهِمْ نَضْرَةَ النَّعِيمِ ﴿٢٤﴾

يُسْقَوْنَ مِنْ رَّحِيقٍ مَّخْتُومٍ ﴿٢٥﴾

خِتَٰمُهُ مِسْكٌ وَفِى ذَٰلِكَ فَلْيَتَنَافَسِ الْمُتَنَافِسُونَ ﴿٢٦﴾

وَمِزَاجُهُ مِنْ تَسْنِيمٍ ﴿٢٧﴾

عَيْنًا يَشْرَبُ بِهَا الْمُقَرَّبُونَ ﴿٢٨﴾

إِنَّ الَّذِينَ أَجْرَمُوا كَانُوا مِنَ الَّذِينَ آمَنُوا يَضْحَكُونَ ﴿٢٩﴾

وَإِذَا مَرُّوا بِهِمْ يَتَغَامَزُونَ ﴿٣٠﴾

وَإِذَا انْقَلَبُوا إِلَىٰ أَهْلِهِمُ انْقَلَبُوا فَكِهِينَ ﴿٣١﴾

وَإِذَا رَأَوْهُمْ قَالُوا إِنَّ هَٰؤُلَاءِ لَضَالُّونَ ﴿٣٢﴾

وَمَا أُرْسِلُوا عَلَيْهِمْ حَافِظِينَ ﴿٣٣﴾

فَالْيَوْمَ الَّذِينَ آمَنُوا مِنَ الْكُفَّارِ يَضْحَكُونَ ﴿٣٤﴾

عَلَى الْأَرَائِكِ يَنْظُرُونَ ﴿٣٥﴾

هَلْ ثُوِّبَ الْكُفَّارُ مَا كَانُوا يَفْعَلُونَ ﴿٣٦﴾

سُورَةُ الْإِنْشِقَاقِ مَكِّيَّةٌ وَهِىَ خَمْسٌ وَعِشْرُونَ آيَةً

بِسْمِ اللَّهِ الرَّحْمَٰنِ الرَّحِيمِ

إِذَا السَّمَاءُ انْشَقَّتْ ﴿١﴾

وَأَذِنَتْ لِرَبِّهَا وَحُقَّتْ ﴿٢﴾

وَإِذَا الْأَرْضُ مُدَّتْ ﴿٣﴾

4.   And casts forth what is within it and becomes (clean) empty,

5.   And hearkens to (the Command of) its Lord,— and it must needs (do so); —(then will come home the full Reality).

6.   O thou man ! verily thou art ever toiling on towards thy Lord— painfully toiling,— but thou shalt meet Him.

7.   Then he who is given his Record in his right hand,

8.   Soon will his account be taken by an easy reckoning,

9.   And he will turn to his people, rejoicing!

10. But he who is given his Record behind his back,—

11. Soon will he cry for Perdition,

12. And he will enter a Blazing Fire.

13. Truly, did he go about among his people, rejoicing !

14. Truly, did he think that he would not have to return (to Us) !

15. Nay, nay ! for his Lord was (ever) watchful of him !

16. So I do call to witness the ruddy glow of Sunset;

17. The Night and its Homing;

18. And the Moon in her Fulness:

19. Ye shall surely travel from stage to stage.

20. What then is the matter with them, that they believe not?—

21. And when the Qur'ān is read to them, they fall not prostrate,

22. But on the contrary the Unbelievers reject (it).

23. But Allah has full Knowledge of what they secrete (in their breasts).

24. So announce to them a Chastisement Grievous.

25. Except to those who believe and work righteous deeds: for them is a Reward that will never fail.

وَأَلْقَتْ مَا فِيهَا وَتَخَلَّتْ ۞

وَأَذِنَتْ لِرَبِّهَا وَحُقَّتْ ۞

يَأَيُّهَا الْإِنْسَانُ إِنَّكَ كَادِحٌ إِلَى رَبِّكَ كَدْحًا فَمُلَقِيهِ ۞

فَأَمَّا مَنْ أُوتِيَ كِتَبَهُ بِيَمِينِهِ ۞

فَسَوْفَ يُحَاسَبُ حِسَابًا يَّسِيرًا ۞

وَيَنْقَلِبُ إِلَى أَهْلِهِ مَسْرُورًا ۞

وَأَمَّا مَنْ أُوتِيَ كِتَبَهُ وَرَاءَ ظَهْرِهِ ۞

فَسَوْفَ يَدْعُواْ ثُبُورًا ۞

وَيَصْلَى سَعِيرًا ۞

إِنَّهُ كَانَ فِى أَهْلِهِ مَسْرُورًا ۞

إِنَّهُ ظَنَّ أَنْ لَّنْ يَّحُورَ ۞

بَلَى إِنَّ رَبَّهُ كَانَ بِهِ بَصِيرًا ۞

فَلَا أُقْسِمُ بِالشَّفَقِ ۞

وَالَّيْلِ وَمَا وَسَقَ ۞

وَالْقَمَرِ إِذَا اتَّسَقَ ۞

لَتَرْكَبُنَّ طَبَقًا عَنْ طَبَقٍ ۞

فَمَا لَهُمْ لَا يُؤْمِنُونَ ۞

وَإِذَا قُرِئَ عَلَيْهِمُ الْقُرْآنُ لَا يَسْجُدُونَ ۩

بَلِ الَّذِينَ كَفَرُوا يُكَذِّبُونَ ۞

وَاللّٰهُ أَعْلَمُ بِمَا يُوعُونَ ۞

فَبَشِّرْهُمْ بِعَذَابٍ أَلِيمٍ ۞

إِلَّا الَّذِينَ آمَنُوا وَعَمِلُوا الصَّلِحَتِ لَهُمْ أَجْرٌ غَيْرُ مَمْنُونٍ ۞

SÛRA–85
AL-BURÛJ
(INTRODUCTION)

This is one of the earlier Makkan Sûras, chronologically cognate with S. 91. The subject-matter is the persecution of Allah's votaries. Allah watches over His own, and will deal with the enemies of Truth as He dealt with them in the past.

Al-Burûj, or The Zodiacal Signs

سورة البروج مكية وهي ثمان وعشرون آية

In the name of Allah, Most Gracious, Most Merciful.

بِسْمِ اللهِ الرَّحْمٰنِ الرَّحِيْمِ ۞

1.　By the Sky, with its constellations;

وَالسَّمَآءِ ذَاتِ الْبُرُوْجِ ۞

2.　By the promised Day (of Judgment);

وَالْيَوْمِ الْمَوْعُوْدِ ۞

3.　By one that witnesses, and the subject of the witness;—

وَشَاهِدٍ وَّمَشْهُوْدٍ ۞

4.　Woe to the makers of the pit (of fire),

قُتِلَ اَصْحٰبُ الْاُخْدُوْدِ ۞

5.　Fire supplied (abundantly) with Fuel:

النَّارِ ذَاتِ الْوَقُوْدِ ۞

6.　Behold! they sat over against the (fire),

اِذْ هُمْ عَلَيْهَا قُعُوْدٌ ۞

7.　And they witnessed (all) that they were doing against the Believers.

وَّهُمْ عَلٰى مَا يَفْعَلُوْنَ بِالْمُؤْمِنِيْنَ شُهُوْدٌ ۞

8.　And they ill-treated them for no other reason than that they believed in Allah, exalted in Power, Worthy of all Praise !—

وَمَا نَقَمُوْا مِنْهُمْ اِلَّا اَنْ يُّؤْمِنُوْا بِاللهِ الْعَزِيْزِ الْحَمِيْدِ ۞

9.　Him to Whom belongs the dominion of the heavens and the earth! And Allah is Witness to all things.

الَّذِيْ لَهٗ مُلْكُ السَّمٰوٰتِ وَالْاَرْضِ ۚ وَاللهُ عَلٰى كُلِّ شَيْءٍ شَهِيْدٌ ۞

10.　Those who persecute the Believers, men and women, and do not turn in repentance, will have the Chastisement of Hell: they will have the Chastisement of the Burning Fire.

اِنَّ الَّذِيْنَ فَتَنُوا الْمُؤْمِنِيْنَ وَالْمُؤْمِنٰتِ ثُمَّ لَمْ يَتُوْبُوْا فَلَهُمْ عَذَابُ جَهَنَّمَ وَلَهُمْ عَذَابُ الْحَرِيْقِ ۞

11.　For those who believe and do righteous deeds, will be Gardens. Beneath which Rivers flow: that is the great Triumph.

اِنَّ الَّذِيْنَ اٰمَنُوْا وَعَمِلُوا الصّٰلِحٰتِ لَهُمْ جَنّٰتٌ تَجْرِيْ مِنْ تَحْتِهَا الْاَنْهٰرُ ۚ ذٰلِكَ الْفَوْزُ الْكَبِيْرُ ۞

12.　Truly strong is the Grip of thy Lord.

اِنَّ بَطْشَ رَبِّكَ لَشَدِيْدٌ ۞

13.　It is He Who creates from the very beginning, and He can restore (life).

اِنَّهٗ هُوَ يُبْدِئُ وَيُعِيْدُ ۞

14.　And He is the Oft-Forgiving, full of loving-kindness,

وَهُوَ الْغَفُوْرُ الْوَدُوْدُ ۞

15.　Lord of the Throne, full of all glory,

ذُو الْعَرْشِ الْمَجِيْدُ ۞

16.　Doer (without let) of all that He intends.

فَعَّالٌ لِّمَا يُرِيْدُ ۞

17.　Has the story reached thee, of the Forces—

هَلْ اَتٰىكَ حَدِيْثُ الْجُنُوْدِ ۞

18.　Of Pharaoh and the Thamûd?

فِرْعَوْنَ وَثَمُوْدَ ۞

19.　And yet the Unbelievers (persist) in rejecting (the Truth) !

بَلِ الَّذِيْنَ كَفَرُوْا فِيْ تَكْذِيْبٍ ۞

SÛRA–86
AT-TARIQ
(INTRODUCTION)

This Sûra also belongs to the early Makkan period, perhaps not far removed from the last Sûra.

Its subject-matter is the protection afforded to every soul in the darkest period of its spiritual hisroty. The physical nature of man may be insignificant, but the soul given to him by Allah must win a glorious Future in the end.

SÛRA–87
AL-A'LÃ
(INTRODUCTION)

This is one of the earliest of the Makkan Sûras, being usually placed eighth in chronological order, and immediately after S. 81.

The argument is that Allah has made man capable of progress by ordered steps, and by His Revelation will lead him still higher to purification and perfection.

20. But Allah doth encompass them from behind!

21. Nay, this is a Glorious Qur-ān,

22. (Inscribed) in a Tablet Preserved!

Aṭ-Ṭāriq, or The Night-Visitant

In the name of Allah, Most Gracious, Most Merciful.

1. By the Sky and the Night-Visitant (therein);

2. And what will explain to thee what the Night-Visitant is?—

3. (It is) the Star of piercing brightness;—

4. There is no soul but has a protector over it.

5. Now let man but think from what he is created !

6. He is created from a drop emitted—

7. Proceeding from between the backbone and the ribs:

8. Surely (Allah) is able to bring him back (to life) !

9. The Day that (all) things secret will be tested,

10. (Man) will have no power, and no helper.

11. By the Firmament which giveth the returning rain,

12. And by the Earth which opens out (for the gushing of springs or the sprouting of vegetation),—

13. Behold this is the Word that distinguishes (Good from Evil):

14. It is not a thing for amusement.

15. As for them, they are but plotting a scheme,

16. And I am planning a scheme.

17. Therefore grant a delay to the Unbelievers: give respite to them gently (for awhile).

Al-A'lā, or The Most High

In the name of Allah, Most Gracious, Most Merciful.

1. Glorify the name of thy Guardian-Lord Most High,

2. Who hath created, and further, given order and proportion;

3. Who hath measured. And granted guidance:

This is a late Sûra of the early Makkan period, perhaps close in date to S. 52. Its subject-matter is the contrast between the destinies of the Good and the Evil in the Hereafter,—on the Day when the true balance will be restored: the Signs of Allah even in this life should remind us of the Day of Account, for Allah is good and just, and His creation is for a just Purpose.

4. And Who bringeth out the (green and luscious) pasture,

وَالَّذِىٓ اَخْرَجَ الْمَرْعٰى ۝

5. And then doth make it (but) swarthy stubble.

فَجَعَلَهٗ غُثَآءً اَحْوٰى ۝

6. By degrees shall We teach thee (the Message), so thou shalt not forget,

سَنُقْرِئُكَ فَلَا تَنْسٰىٓ ۝

7. Except as Allah wills: for He knoweth what is manifest and what is hidden.

اِلَّا مَا شَآءَ اللّٰهُ ۗ اِنَّهٗ يَعْلَمُ الْجَهْرَ وَمَا يَخْفٰى ۝

8. And We will make it easy for thee (to follow) the simple (Path).

وَنُيَسِّرُكَ لِلْيُسْرٰى ۝

9. Therefore give admonition in case the admonition profits (the hearer).

فَذَكِّرْ اِنْ نَّفَعَتِ الذِّكْرٰى ۝

10. He will heed who fears:

سَيَذَّكَّرُ مَنْ يَّخْشٰى ۝

11. But it will be avoided by the most unfortunate one,

وَيَتَجَنَّبُهَا الْاَشْقَى ۝

12. Who will enter the Great Fire,

الَّذِىْ يَصْلَى النَّارَ الْكُبْرٰى ۝

13. In which he will then neither die nor live.

ثُمَّ لَا يَمُوْتُ فِيْهَا وَلَا يَحْيٰى ۝

14. But he will prosper who purifies himself.

قَدْ اَفْلَحَ مَنْ تَزَكّٰى ۝

15. And remembers the name of his Guardian-Lord, and prays.

وَذَكَرَ اسْمَ رَبِّهٖ فَصَلّٰى ۝

16. Nay (behold), ye prefer the life of this world;

بَلْ تُؤْثِرُوْنَ الْحَيٰوةَ الدُّنْيَا ۝

17. But the Hereafter is better and more enduring.

وَالْاٰخِرَةُ خَيْرٌ وَّاَبْقٰى ۝

18. And this is in the Books of the earliest (Revelations),—

اِنَّ هٰذَا لَفِى الصُّحُفِ الْاُوْلٰى ۝

19. The Books of Abraham and Moses.

صُحُفِ اِبْرٰهِيْمَ وَمُوْسٰى ۝

Al-Gāshiya, or The Overwhelming Event

سُوْرَةُ الْغَاشِيَةِ مَكِّيَّةٌ وَهِىَ سِتٌّ وَّعِشْرُوْنَ اٰيَةً

In the name of Allah, Most Gracious, Most Merciful.

بِسْمِ اللّٰهِ الرَّحْمٰنِ الرَّحِيْمِ

1. Has the story reached thee, of the Overwhelming (Event)?

هَلْ اَتٰىكَ حَدِيْثُ الْغَاشِيَةِ ۝

2. Some faces, that Day, will be humiliated,

وُجُوْهٌ يَّوْمَئِذٍ خَاشِعَةٌ ۝

3. Labouring (hard), weary,—

عَامِلَةٌ نَّاصِبَةٌ ۝

4. The while they enter the Blazing Fire,—

تَصْلٰى نَارًا حَامِيَةً ۝

5. The while they are given, to drink, of a boiling hot spring,

تُسْقٰى مِنْ عَيْنٍ اٰنِيَةٍ ۝

6. No food will there be for them but a bitter *Dharī*

لَيْسَ لَهُمْ طَعَامٌ اِلَّا مِنْ ضَرِيْعٍ ۝

7. Which will neither nourish nor satisfy hunger.

لَا يُسْمِنُ وَلَا يُغْنِىْ مِنْ جُوْعٍ ۝

8. (Other) faces that Day will be joyful,

وُجُوْهٌ يَّوْمَئِذٍ نَّاعِمَةٌ ۝

SÛRA–89
AL-FAJR
(INTRODUCTION)

This is one of the earliest of the Sûras to be revealed,—probably within the first ten in chronologial order.

Its mystic meaning is suggested by contrasts,—contrasts in nature and in man's long history. Thus does it enforce the lesson of Faith in the Hereafter to "those who understand". Man's history and legendary lore show that greatness does not last and the proudest are brought low. For enforcing moral and spiritual truths, the strictest history is no better than legend. Indeed all artistic history is legend, for it is writen from a special point of view.

Man is easily cowed by contrasts in his own fortunes, and yet he does not learn from them the lesson of forbearance and kindness to others, and the final elevation of goodness in the Hereafter. When all the things on which his mind and heart are set on this earth shall be crushed to nothingness, he will see the real glory and power, love and beauty, of Allah, for these are the light of the Garden of Paradise.

9.   Pleased with their Striving,—

لِسَعْيِهَا رَاضِيَةٌ ۞

10.   In a Garden on high,

فِيْ جَنَّةٍ عَالِيَةٍ ۞

11.   Where they shall hear no (word) of vanity:

لَّا تَسْمَعُ فِيْهَا لَاغِيَةً ۞

12.   Therein will be a bubbling spring:

فِيْهَا عَيْنٌ جَارِيَةٌ ۞

13.   Therein will be couches (of dignity), raised on high,

فِيْهَا سُرُرٌ مَّرْفُوْعَةٌ ۞

14.   Goblets placed (ready),

وَّاَكْوَابٌ مَّوْضُوْعَةٌ ۞

15.   And Cushions set in rows,

وَّنَمَارِقُ مَصْفُوْفَةٌ ۞

16.   And rich carpets (all) spread out.

وَّزَرَابِيُّ مَبْثُوْثَةٌ ۞

17.   Do they not look at the Camels, how they are made ?—

اَفَلَا يَنْظُرُوْنَ اِلَى الْاِبِلِ كَيْفَ خُلِقَتْ ۞

18.   And at the Sky, how it is raised high?—

وَاِلَى السَّمَآءِ كَيْفَ رُفِعَتْ ۞

19.   And at the Mountains, how they are fixed firm?—

وَاِلَى الْجِبَالِ كَيْفَ نُصِبَتْ ۞

20.   And at the Earth, how it is spread out ?

وَاِلَى الْاَرْضِ كَيْفَ سُطِحَتْ ۞

21.   Therefore do thou remind for thou art one to remind.

فَذَكِّرْ اِنَّمَآ اَنْتَ مُذَكِّرٌ ۞

22.   Thou art not one to manage (their) affairs.

لَسْتَ عَلَيْهِمْ بِمُصَيْطِرٍ ۞

23.   But if any turn away and disbelieve,—

اِلَّا مَنْ تَوَلّٰى وَكَفَرَ ۞

24.   Allah will chastise him with a mighty Chastisement.

فَيُعَذِّبُهُ اللّٰهُ الْعَذَابَ الْاَكْبَرَ ۞

25.   For to Us will be their Return;

اِنَّ اِلَيْنَآ اِيَابَهُمْ ۞

26.   Then it will be for Us to call them to account.

ثُمَّ اِنَّ عَلَيْنَا حِسَابَهُمْ ۞

Al-Fajr, or The Dawn

In the name of Allah, Most Gracious, Most Merciful.

سُوْرَةُ الْفَجْرِ مَكِّيَّةٌ وَّهِيَ ثَلَاثُوْنَ اٰيَةً

بِسْمِ اللّٰهِ الرَّحْمٰنِ الرَّحِيْمِ ۞

1.   By the Dawn;

وَالْفَجْرِ ۞

2.   By the ten Nights;

وَلَيَالٍ عَشْرٍ ۞

3.   By the Even and Odd (contrasted);

وَّالشَّفْعِ وَالْوَتْرِ ۞

4.   And by the Night when it passeth away;—

وَالَّيْلِ اِذَا يَسْرِ ۞

5.   Is there (not) in these an adjuration (or evidence) for those who understand?

هَلْ فِيْ ذٰلِكَ قَسَمٌ لِّذِيْ حِجْرٍ ۞

6.   Seest thou not now thy Lord dealt with the 'Ad (people),—

اَلَمْ تَرَ كَيْفَ فَعَلَ رَبُّكَ بِعَادٍ ۞

7.   Of the (city of) Iram, with lofty pillars,

اِرَمَ ذَاتِ الْعِمَادِ ۞

8.   The like of which were not produced in (all) the land ?

9.   And with the <u>Thamūd</u> (people), who cut out (huge) rocks in the valley?—

10.   And with Pharaoh, lord of Stakes?

11.   (All) these transgressed beyond bounds in the lands.

12.   And heaped therein mischief (on mischief).

13.   Therefore did thy Lord pour on them a scourge of diverse chastisements:

14.   For thy Lord is watchful.

15.   Now, as for man, when his Lord trieth him, giving him honour and gifts, then saith he, (puffed up), "My Lord hath honoured me."

16.   But when He trieth him, restricting his subsistence for him, then saith he (in despair), "My Lord hath humiliated me !"

17.   Nay, nay ! But ye honour not the orphans !

18.   Nor do ye encourage one another to feed the poor !—

19.   And ye devour Inheritance—all with greed,

20.   And ye love wealth with inordinate love!

21.   Nay ! When the earth is pounded to powder,

22.   And thy Lord cometh, and His angels, rank upon rank,

23.   And Hell,—that Day, is brought (face to face), on that Day will man remember, but how will that remembrance profit him ?

24.   He will say: "Ah ! would that I had sent forth (Good Deeds) for (this) my (Future) Life !"

25.   For, that Day, His Chastisement will be such as none (else) can inflict,

26.   And His bonds will be such as none (other) can bind.

27.   (To the righteous soul will be said:) "O (thou) soul, in (complete) rest and satisfaction !

28.   "Come back thou to thy Lord,— well pleased (thyself), and well-pleasing unto Him!

29.   "Enter thou, then, among My Devotees!

30.   "Yea, enter thou My Heaven!"

SÛRA–90
AL-BALAD
(INTRODUCTION)

This is an early Makkan revelation, and refers to the mystic relation (by divine sanction) of the Holy Prophet with the city of Makkah. He was born in that City, which had already been sacred for ages before. He was nurtured in that City and had (to use a modern phrase) the freedom of that City, belonging, as he did, to the noble family which held the government of its sacred precincts in its hands. But he was an orphan, and orphans in his day had a poor time. But his mind was turned to things divine. He protested against the prevailing idolatry and sin, and his parent City persecuted him and cast him out. He made another City Yathrib, his own: it became the *Madinat un-Nabî*, the City of the Prophet, and it has ever since been Madinah. We can speak of Madinah as the Prophet's child. But the Prophet ever cherished in his heart the love of his parent City of Makkah, and in the fulness of time was received in triumph there. He purified it from all idols and abominations, re-established the worship of the One True Allah, overthrew the purse-proud selfish autocracy, restored the sway of the righteous (people of the Right Hand), the liberty of the slave, and the rights of the poor and downtrodden. What a wonderful career centring round a City! It becomes a symbol of the world's spiritual history.

Al-Balad, or The City

سُوۡرَةُ الۡبَلَدِ مَکِّیَّةٌ وَّ هِیَ عِشۡرُوۡنَ اٰیَةً

In the name of Allah, Most Gracious, Most Merciful.

بِسۡمِ اللّٰهِ الرَّحۡمٰنِ الرَّحِیۡمِ ۟

1. Nay I do swear by this City;—

لَاۤ اُقۡسِمُ بِهٰذَا الۡبَلَدِ ۙ

2. And, thou art an inhabitant of this City;—

وَ اَنۡتَ حِلٌّ بِهٰذَا الۡبَلَدِ ۙ

3. And the begetter and that he begot;—

وَ وَالِدٍ وَّ مَا وَلَدَ ۙ

4. Verily We have created man into toil and struggle.

لَقَدۡ خَلَقۡنَا الۡاِنۡسَانَ فِیۡ کَبَدٍ ؕ

5. Thinketh he, that none hath power over him?

اَیَحۡسَبُ اَنۡ لَّنۡ یَّقۡدِرَ عَلَیۡهِ اَحَدٌ ۘ

6. He may say (boastfully): "Wealth have I squandered in abundance !"

یَقُوۡلُ اَهۡلَکۡتُ مَالًا لُّبَدًا ؕ

7. Thinketh he that none beholdeth him?

اَیَحۡسَبُ اَنۡ لَّمۡ یَرَهٗۤ اَحَدٌ ؕ

8. Have We not made for him a pair of eyes ?

اَلَمۡ نَجۡعَلۡ لَّهٗ عَیۡنَیۡنِ ۙ

9. And a tongue, and a pair of lips ?

وَ لِسَانًا وَّ شَفَتَیۡنِ ۙ

10. And shown him the two highways?

وَ هَدَیۡنٰهُ النَّجۡدَیۡنِ ۚ

11. But he hath made not haste on the path that is steep.

فَلَا اقۡتَحَمَ الۡعَقَبَةَ ۫

12. And what will explain to thee the path that is steep ?—

وَ مَاۤ اَدۡرٰىکَ مَا الۡعَقَبَةُ ؕ

13. (It is:) freeing the bondman;

فَکُّ رَقَبَةٍ ۙ

14. Or the giving of food in a day of privation

اَوۡ اِطۡعٰمٌ فِیۡ یَوۡمٍ ذِیۡ مَسۡغَبَةٍ ۙ

15. To the orphan with claims of relationship,

یَّتِیۡمًا ذَا مَقۡرَبَةٍ ۙ

16. Or to the indigent (down) in the dust.

اَوۡ مِسۡکِیۡنًا ذَا مَتۡرَبَةٍ ؕ

17. Then will he be of those who believe, and enjoin patience, (constancy, and self-restraint), and enjoin deeds of kindness and compassion.

ثُمَّ کَانَ مِنَ الَّذِیۡنَ اٰمَنُوۡا وَ تَوَاصَوۡا بِالصَّبۡرِ وَ تَوَاصَوۡا بِالۡمَرۡحَمَةِ ؕ

18. Such are the Companions of the Right Hand.

اُولٰٓئِکَ اَصۡحٰبُ الۡمَیۡمَنَةِ ؕ

19. But those who reject Our Signs, they are the (unhappy) Companions of the Left Hand.

وَ الَّذِیۡنَ کَفَرُوۡا بِاٰیٰتِنَا هُمۡ اَصۡحٰبُ الۡمَشۡـَٔمَةِ ؕ

20. On them will be Fire vaulted over (all round).

عَلَیۡهِمۡ نَارٌ مُّؤۡصَدَةٌ ۟

SÛRA–91
ASH-SHAMS
(INTRODUCTION)

This is one of the early Makkan revelations. Beginning with a fine nature passage, and leading up to man's need of realising his spiritual responsibility, it ends with a warning of the terrible consequences for those who fear not the Hereafter.

SÛRA–92
AL-LAIL
(INTRODUCTION)

This was one of the first Sûras to be revealed,—within the first ten; and may be placed in date close to S. 89 and S. 93. Note that in all these Sûras the mystery and the contrast as between Night and Day are appealed to for the consolation of man in his spiritual yearning. Here we are told to strive our utmost towards Allah, and He will give us every help and satisfaction.

Ash-Shams,
or The Sun

سورة الشمس مكية وهي ثلث عشرة آية

In the name of Allah, Most Gracious, Most Merciful.

بسم الله الرحمن الرحيم

1. By the Sun and his (glorious) splendour;

والشمس وضحها ١

2. By the Moon as she follows him;

والقمر إذا تلها ٢

3. By the Day as it shows up (the Sun's) glory;

والنهار إذا جلها ٣

4. By the Night as it conceals it;

والليل إذا يغشها ٤

5. By the Firmament and its (wonderful) structure;

والسماء وما بنها ٥

6. By the Earth and its (wide) expanse:

والأرض وما طحها ٦

7. By the Soul, and the proportion and order given to it;

ونفس وما سوها ٧

8. And its inspiration as to its wrong and its right;—

فألهمها فجورها وتقوها ٨

9. Truly he succeeds that purifies it,

قد أفلح من زكها ٩

10. And he fails that corrupts it !

وقد خاب من دسها ١٠

11. The Thamûd (people) rejected (their prophet) through their inordinate wrong-doing,

كذبت ثمود بطغوها ١١

12. Behold, the most wicked man among them was deputed (for impiety).

إذ انبعث أشقها ١٢

13. But the messenger of Allah said to them: "It is a She-camel of Allah ! And (bar her not from) having her drink !"

فقال لهم رسول الله ناقة الله و سقيها ١٣

14. Then they rejected him (as a false prophet), and they hamstrung her. So their Lord, crushed them for their sin and levelled them.

فكذبوه فعقروها فدمدم عليهم ربهم بذنبهم فسوها ١٤

15. And for Him is no fear of its consequences.

ولا يخاف عقبها ١٥

Al-Lail, or The Night

سورة الليل مكية وهي إحدى وعشرون آية

In the name of Allah, Most Gracious, Most Merciful.

بسم الله الرحمن الرحيم

1. By the Night as it conceals (the light);

والليل إذا يغشى ١

2. By the Day as it appears in glory;

والنهار إذا تجلى ٢

3. By the creation of male and female;—

وما خلق الذكر والأنثى ٣

4. Verily, (the ends) ye strive for are diverse.

إن سعيكم لشتى ٤

5. So he who gives (in charity) and fears (Allah),

فأما من أعطى واتقى ٥

6. And (in all sincerity) testifies to the Best,—

وصدق بالحسنى ٦

SÛRA–93
ADH-DHUḤĀ
(INTRODUCTION)

This Sûra is close in date to Sûras 89 and 92, and the imagery drawn from the contrast of Night and Day is common to all three. In this Sûra the vicissitudes of human life are referred to, and a massage of hope and consolation is given to man's soul from Allah's past mercies, and he is bidden to pursue the path of goodness and proclaim the bounties of Allah. This is the general meaning. In particular, the Sûra seems to have been revealed in a dark period in the outer life of the Holy Prophet, when a man of less resolute will might have been discouraged. But the Prophet is told to hold the present of less account that the glorious Hereafter which awaited him like the glorious morning after a night of stillness and gloom. The Hereafter was, not only in the Future Life, but in his later life on this earth, full of victory and satisfaction.

7. We will indeed make smooth for him the path to Ease.

8. But he who is a greedy miser and thinks himself self-sufficient,

9. And gives the lie to the Best,–

10. We will indeed make smooth for him the Path to Misery;

11. Nor will his wealth profit him when he falls headlong (into the Pit).

12. Verily We take upon Us to guide,

13. And verily unto Us (belong) the End and the Beginning.

14. Therefore do I warn you of a Fire blazing fiercely;

15. None shall burn therein but those most unfortunate ones

16. Who give the lie to Truth and turn their backs.

17. But those most devoted to Allah shall be removed far from it,–

18. Those who spend their wealth for increase in self-purification,

19. And have in their minds no favour from anyone for which a reward is expected in return,

20. But only the desire to seek for the Countenance of their Lord Most High;

21. And soon will they attain (complete) satisfaction.

Ad-Dhuḥā, or The Glorious Morning Light

In the name of Allah, Most Gracious, Most Merciful.

1. By the Glorious Morning Light,

2. And by the Night when it is still,—

3. The Guardian-Lord hath not forsaken thee, nor is He displeased.

4. And verily the Hereafter will be better for thee than the present.

5. And soon will thy Guardian-Lord give thee (that wherewith) thou shalt be well-pleased.

6. Did He not find thee an orphan and give thee shelter (and care)?

7. And He found thee wandering, and He gave thee guidance.

8. And He found thee in need, and made thee independent.

9. Therefore, treat not the orphan with harshness,

10. Nor repulse him who asks;

SÛRA–94
AL-SHARḤ
(INTRODUCTION)

This short Sûra gives a message of hope and encouragement in a time of darkness and difficulty. It was revealed to the Holy Prophet soon after the last Sûra *(Dhuḥā)*, whose argument it supplements.

SÛRA–95
AT-TÎN
(INTRODUCTION)

This is also a very early Sûra. It appeals to the most sacred symbols to show that Allah created man in the best of moulds, but that man is capable of the utmost degradation unless he has Faith and leads a good life. In subject-matter this Sûra closely resembles S. 103.

SÛRA–96
AL-'ALAQ
(INTRODUCTION)

Verses 1-5 of this Sûra were the first direct Revelation to the Holy Prophet.

After that there was an interval or break *(Fatra)*, extending over some months or perhaps over a year. S. 68 is usually considered to have been the next revelation in point of time. But the remainder of the Sûra (96: 6-19) came soon after the *Fatra*, and that portion is joined on to the first five verses containing the command to preach, because it explains the chief obstacle to the delivery of the message to man, viz. man's own obstinacy, vanity, and insolence.

11.   But the Bounty of thy Lord— rehearse and proclaim !

Al-sharḥ, or The Expansion

In the name of Allah, Most Gracious, Most Merciful.

1.   Have We not expanded thee thy breast?—

2.   And removed from thee thy burden

3.   The which did gall thy back?—

4.   And raised high the esteem (in which) thou (art held) ?

5.   So, verily, with every difficulty, there is relief.

6.   Verily, with every difficulty there is relief.

7.   Therefore, when thou art free (from thine immediate task), still labour hard,

8.   And to thy Lord turn (all) thy attention.

At-Tīn, or The Fig

In the name of Allah, Most Gracious, Most Merciful.

1.   By the Fig and the Olive,

2.   And the Mount of Sinai,

3.   And this City of Security,—

4.   We have indeed created man in the best of moulds,

5.   Then do We abase him (to be) the lowest of the low,—

6.   Except such as believe and do righteous deeds: for they shall have a reward unfailing.

7.   What then, can after this make you deny the Last Judgment?

8.   Is not Allah the wisest of Judges ?

Iqraa, or Read ! or Proclaim ! Or Al-'Alaq, or The leech-like clot

In the name of Allah, Most Gracious, Most Merciful.

1.   Proclaim ! (or Read !) in the name of thy Lord and Cherisher, Who created—

2.   Created man, out of a leech-like clot:

3.   Proclaim ! And thy Lord is Most Bountiful,—

SÛRA–97
AL-QADR
(INTRODUCTION)

The chronology of this Sûra has no significance. It is probably Makkan, though some hold that it was revealed in Madinah.

The subject-matter as the mystic Night of Power (or Honour), in which Revelation comes down to a benighted world,—it may be to the wonderful Cosmos of an individual—and transforms the conflict of wrong-doing into Peace and Harmony—through the agency of the angelic host, representing the spiritual powers of the Mercy of Allah.

4.   He Who taught (the use of) the Pen,—

الَّذِي عَلَّمَ بِالْقَلَمِ ۞

5.   Taught man that which he knew not.

عَلَّمَ الْإِنْسَانَ مَا لَمْ يَعْلَمْ ۞

6.   Nay, but man doth transgress all bounds,

كَلَّا إِنَّ الْإِنْسَانَ لَيَطْغَى ۞

7.   In that he looketh upon himself as self-sufficient.

أَنْ رَآهُ اسْتَغْنَى ۞

8.   Verily, to thy Lord is the return (of all).

إِنَّ إِلَى رَبِّكَ الرُّجْعَى ۞

9.   Seest thou one who forbids—

أَرَأَيْتَ الَّذِي يَنْهَى ۞

10.   A votary when he (turns) to pray ?

عَبْدًا إِذَا صَلَّى ۞

11.   Seest thou if he is on (the road of) Guidance?—

أَرَأَيْتَ إِنْ كَانَ عَلَى الْهُدَى ۞

12.   Or enjoins Righteousness ?

أَوْ أَمَرَ بِالتَّقْوَى ۞

13.   Seest thou if he denies (Truth) and turns away ?

أَرَأَيْتَ إِنْ كَذَّبَ وَتَوَلَّى ۞

14.   Knoweth he not that Allah doth see ?

أَلَمْ يَعْلَمْ بِأَنَّ اللَّهَ يَرَى ۞

15.   Let him beware ! If he desist not, We will drag him by the forelock,—

كَلَّا لَئِنْ لَمْ يَنْتَهِ لَنَسْفَعًا بِالنَّاصِيَةِ ۞

16.   A lying, sinful forelock !

نَاصِيَةٍ كَاذِبَةٍ خَاطِئَةٍ ۞

17.   Then, let him call (for help) to his council (of comrades):

فَلْيَدْعُ نَادِيَهُ ۞

18.   We will call on the angels of punishment (to deal with him) !

سَنَدْعُ الزَّبَانِيَةَ ۞

19.   Nay, heed him not: but prostrate in adoration, and bring thyself the closer (to Allah) !

كَلَّا لَا تُطِعْهُ وَاسْجُدْ وَاقْتَرِبْ ۩

Al-Qadr, or The Night of Power (or Honour)

سُورَةُ الْقَدْرِ مَكِّيَّةٌ وَهِيَ خَمْسُ آيَاتٍ

In the name of Allah, Most Gracious, Most Merciful.

بِسْمِ اللَّهِ الرَّحْمَٰنِ الرَّحِيمِ

1.   We have indeed revealed this (Message) in the Night of Power:

إِنَّا أَنْزَلْنَاهُ فِي لَيْلَةِ الْقَدْرِ ۞

2.   And what will explain to thee what the Night of Power is ?

وَمَا أَدْرَاكَ مَا لَيْلَةُ الْقَدْرِ ۞

3.   The Night of Power is better than a thousand Months.

لَيْلَةُ الْقَدْرِ خَيْرٌ مِنْ أَلْفِ شَهْرٍ ۞

4.   Therein come down the angels and the Spirit by Allah's permission, on every errand.

تَنَزَّلُ الْمَلَائِكَةُ وَالرُّوحُ فِيهَا بِإِذْنِ رَبِّهِمْ مِنْ كُلِّ أَمْرٍ ۞

5.   Peace ! . . . This until the rise of Morn !

سَلَامٌ هِيَ حَتَّى مَطْلَعِ الْفَجْرِ ۞

SÛRA–98
AL-BAIYINA
(INTRODUCTION)

This Sûra was probably an early Madinah Sûra, or possibly a late Makkan Sûra.

In subject-matter it carries forward the argument of the last Sûra. The mystic night of revelation is indeed blessed: but those who reject Truth are impervious to Allah's Message, however clear may be the evidence in support of it.

SÛRA–99
AL-ZALZALAH
(INTRODUCTION)

This Sûra is close in date to the last: it is generally referred to the early Madinah period, though it may possibly be of the late Makkan period.

It refers to the tremendous convulsion and uprooting which will take place when the present order of the world is dissolved and the new spiritual world of Justice and Truth takes its place. The symbol used is that of an earthquake which will shake our present material and phenomenal world to its very foundations. The mystic words in which the earthquake is described are remarkable for both power and graphic aptness. With that shaking all hidden mysteries will be brought to light.

Al-Baiyina, or The Clear Evidence

In the name of Allah, Most Gracious, Most Merciful.

1. Those who disbelieve, among the People of the Book and among the Polytheists, were not going to depart (from their ways) until there should come to them clear Evidence,—

2. Messenger from Allah, rehe-arsing scriptures kept pure and holy:

3. Wherein are books right and straight.

4. Nor did the People of the Book make schisms, until after there came to them Clear Evidence.

5. And they have been commanded no more than this: to worship Allah, offering Him sincere devotion, being True (in faith); to establish regular Prayer; and to give zakat; and that is the Religion right and Straight.

6. Those who disbelieve, among the People of the Book and among the Polytheists, will be in Hell-Fire, to dwell therein (for aye). They are the worst of creatures.

7. Those who have faith and do righteous deeds,—they are the best of creatures.

8. Their reward is with Allah: Gardens of Eternity, beneath which rivers flow; they will dwell therein for ever; Allah well pleased with them, and they with Him: all this for such as fear their Lord and Cherisher.

Al-Zilzāl, or The Convulsion

In the name of Allah, Most Gracious, Most Merciful.

1. When the Earth is shaken to her (utmost) convulsion,

2. And the Earth throws up her burdens (from within),

3. And man cries (distressed); 'What is the matter with her ?—

4. On that Day will she declare her tidings:

SÛRA–100
AL-'ĀDIYĀT
(INTRODUCTION)

This is one of the earlier Makkan Sûras. In the depth of its mystery and the rhythm and sublimity of its language and sybolism, it may be compared with S. 79. Its subject-matter is the irresistible nature of spiritual power and knowledge, contrasted with unregenerate man's ingratitude, pettiness, helplessness, and ignorance.

SÛRA–101
AL-QĀRI'A
(INTRODUCTION)

This Makkan Sûra describes the Judgment Day as the Day of Clamour, when men will be distracted and the landmarks of this world will be lost, but every deed will be weighed in a just balance, and find its real value and setting.

5.   For that thy Lord will have given her inspiration.

6.   On that Day will men proceed in groups sorted out, to be shown the Deeds that they (had done).

7.   Then shall anyone who has done an atom's weight of good, see it !

8.   And anyone who has done an atom's weight of evil, shall see it.

بِأَنَّ رَبَّكَ أَوْحَى لَهَا ۞

يَوْمَئِذٍ يَصْدُرُ النَّاسُ أَشْتَاتًا ۞ لِّيُرَوْا أَعْمَالَهُمْ ۞

فَمَن يَعْمَلْ مِثْقَالَ ذَرَّةٍ خَيْرًا يَرَهُ ۞

وَمَن يَعْمَلْ مِثْقَالَ ذَرَّةٍ شَرًّا يَرَهُ ۞

Al-'Ādiyāt, or Those that run

In the name of Allah, Most Gracious, Most Merciful.

1.   By the (Steeds) that run, with panting (breath).

2.   And strike sparks of fire.

3.   And pusn home the charge in the morning,

4.   And raise the dust in clouds the while,

5.   And penetrate forthwith into the midst (of the foe) *en masse;*—

6.   Truly Man is, to his Lord, ungrateful;

7.   And to that (fact) he bears witness (by his deeds);

8.   And violent is he in his love of wealth.

9.   Does he not know,—when that which is in the graves is scattered abroad

10.   And that which is (locked up) in (numan) breasts is made manifest—

11.   That their Lord had been well-acquainted with them, (even to) that Day?

سُورَةُ الْعَادِيَاتِ مَكِّيَّةٌ وَهِيَ إِحْدَى عَشَرَةَ آيَةً

بِسْمِ اللهِ الرَّحْمَنِ الرَّحِيمِ

وَالْعَادِيَاتِ ضَبْحًا ۞

فَالْمُورِيَاتِ قَدْحًا ۞

فَالْمُغِيرَاتِ صُبْحًا ۞

فَأَثَرْنَ بِهِ نَقْعًا ۞

فَوَسَطْنَ بِهِ جَمْعًا ۞

إِنَّ الْإِنسَانَ لِرَبِّهِ لَكَنُودٌ ۞

وَإِنَّهُ عَلَى ذَلِكَ لَشَهِيدٌ ۞

وَإِنَّهُ لِحُبِّ الْخَيْرِ لَشَدِيدٌ ۞

أَفَلَا يَعْلَمُ إِذَا بُعْثِرَ مَا فِي الْقُبُورِ ۞

وَحُصِّلَ مَا فِي الصُّدُورِ ۞

إِنَّ رَبَّهُم بِهِمْ يَوْمَئِذٍ لَّخَبِيرٌ ۞

Al-Qāri'a, or The Day of Clamour

In the name of Allah, Most Gracious, Most Merciful.

1.   The (Day) of Clamour:

2.   What is the (Day) of Clamour?

3.   And what will explain to thee what the (Day) of Clamour is ?

4.   (It is) a Day whereon Men will be like moths scattered about.

5.   And the mountains will be like carded wooi.

سُورَةُ الْقَارِعَةِ مَكِّيَّةٌ وَهِيَ إِحْدَى عَشَرَةَ آيَةً

بِسْمِ اللهِ الرَّحْمَنِ الرَّحِيمِ

الْقَارِعَةُ ۞

مَا الْقَارِعَةُ ۞

وَمَا أَدْرَاكَ مَا الْقَارِعَةُ ۞

يَوْمَ يَكُونُ النَّاسُ كَالْفَرَاشِ الْمَبْثُوثِ ۞

وَتَكُونُ الْجِبَالُ كَالْعِهْنِ الْمَنفُوشِ ۞

SÛRA–102
AT-TAKĀTHUR
(INTRODUCTION)

This probably early Makkan Sûra gives a warning against acquisitveness, i.e., the passion for piling up quantities or numbers, whether in the good things of this world, or in man-power or in other forms of megalomania, which leave no time or opportunity for pursuing the higher things of life.

SÛRA–103
AL-'AṢR
(INTRODUCTION)

This early Makkan Sûra refers to the testimony of Time through the Ages. All history shows that Evil came to an evil end. But Time is always in favour of those who have Faith, live clean and pure lives, and know how to wait, in patience and constancy. Cf. the theme of S. 95.

SÛRA–104
AL-HUMAZA
(INTRODUCTION)

This Makkan Sûra condemns all sorts of scandal, backbiting, and selfish hoarding of wealth, as destroying the hearts and affections of men.

6. Then, he whose balance (of good deeds) will be (found) heavy,

7. Will be in a Life of good pleasure and satisfaction.

8. But he whose balance (of good deeds) will be (found) light,—

9. Will have his home in a (bottomless) Pit.

10. And what will explain to thee what this is ?

11. (It is) a Fire blazing fiercely !

At-Takāthur or Piling Up

In the name of Allah, Most Gracious, Most Merciful.

1. The mutual rivalry for piling up (the good things of this world) diverts you (from the more serious things),

2. Until ye visit the graves.

3. But nay, ye soon shall know (the reality).

4. Again, ye soon shall know !

5. Nay, were ye to know with certainty of mind, (ye would beware!)

6. Ye shall certainly see Hell-Fire !

7. Again, ye shall see it with certainty of sight!

8. Then, shall ye be questioned that Day about the joy (ye indulged in !)

Al-'Asr, or Time through the Ages

In the name of Allah, Most Gracious, Most Merciful.

1. By the time,

2. Verily Man is in loss,

3. Except such as have Faith, and do righteous deeds, and (join toge-ther) in the mutual enjoining of Truth, and of Patience and Constancy.

Al-Humaza, or the Scandal-monger

In the name of Allah, Most Gracious, Most Merciful.

1. Woe to every (kind of) scandal-monger and backbiter,

2. Who pileth up wealth and layeth it by,

3. Thinking that his wealth would make him last for ever !

4. By no means ! He will be sure to be thrown into that which Breaks to Pieces.

SÛRA–105
AL-FÎL
(INTRODUCTION)

This early Makkan Sûra refers to an event that happened in the year of the birth of our Holy Prophet, say, about 570 A.D. Yaman was then under the rule of the Abyssinians (Christians), who had driven out the Jewish Himyar rulers. Abraha Ashram was the Abyssinian governor or viceroy. Intoxicated with power and fired by religious fanaticism, he led a big expedition against Makkah, intending to destroy the Ka'ba. He had an elephant or elephants in his train. But his sacrilegious intentions were defeated by a miracle. No defence was offered by the custodians of the Ka'ba as the army was too strong for them, but it was believed that a shower of stones, thrown by flocks of birds, destroyed the invading army almost to a man. The stones produced sores and pustules on the skin, which spread like a pestilence.

SÛRA–106
QURAISH
(INTRODUCTION)

This Makkan Sûra may well be considered as a pendant to the last. If the Quraish were fond of Makkah and proud of it, if they profited, by its central position and its guaranteed security, from their caravans of trade and commerce, let them be grateful, adore the One True Allah, and accept His Message.

SÛRA–107
AL-MĀ'ÛN
(INTRODUCTION)

This Sûra—at least the first half of it—belongs to the early Makkan period. The subject-matter is the meaning of true worship, which requires Faith, the practical and helpful love of those in need, and sincerity rather than show in devotion and charity.

5. And what will explain to thee that which Breaks to Pieces ?

وَمَاۤ اَدْرٰىكَ مَا الْحُطَمَةُ ۝

6. (It is) the Fire of Allah kindled (to a blaze),

نَارُ اللّٰهِ الْمُوْقَدَةُ ۝

7. The which doth mount (right) to the Hearts:

الَّتِیْ تَطَّلِعُ عَلَی الْاَفْئِدَةِ ۝

8. It shall be made into a vault over them,

اِنَّهَا عَلَیْهِمْ مُّؤْصَدَةٌ ۝

9. In columns outstretched.

فِیْ عَمَدٍ مُّمَدَّدَةٍ ۝

Al-Fīl, or The Elephant

سُوْرَةُ الْفِیْلِ مَکِّیَّةٌ وَہِیَ خَمْسُ اٰیَاتٍ

In the name of Allah, Most Gracious, Most Merciful.

بِسْمِ اللّٰهِ الرَّحْمٰنِ الرَّحِیْمِ

1. Seest thou not how thy Lord dealt with the Companions of the Elephant ?

اَلَمْ تَرَ کَیْفَ فَعَلَ رَبُّكَ بِاَصْحٰبِ الْفِیْلِ ۝

2. Did He not make their treacherous plan go astray ?

اَلَمْ یَجْعَلْ کَیْدَہُمْ فِیْ تَضْلِیْلٍ ۝

3. And He sent against them Flights of Birds,

وَّاَرْسَلَ عَلَیْهِمْ طَیْرًا اَبَابِیْلَ ۝

4. Striking them with stones of baked clay.

تَرْمِیْهِمْ بِحِجَارَةٍ مِّنْ سِجِّیْلٍ ۝

5. Then did He make them like an empty field of stalks and straw, (of which the corn) has been eaten up.

فَجَعَلَہُمْ کَعَصْفٍ مَّاْکُوْلٍ ۝

Quraish or The Quraish, (Custodians of the Ka'ba)

سُوْرَةُ الْقُرَیْشِ مَکِّیَّةٌ وَہِیَ اَرْبَعُ اٰیَاتٍ

In the name of Allah, Most Gracious, Most Merciful.

بِسْمِ اللّٰهِ الرَّحْمٰنِ الرَّحِیْمِ

1. For the familiarity of the Quraish,

لِاِیْلٰفِ قُرَیْشٍ ۝

2. Their familiarity with the journeys by winter and summer,—

اٖلٰفِهِمْ رِحْلَةَ الشِّتَآءِ وَالصَّیْفِ ۝

3. Let them worship the Lord of this House,

فَلْیَعْبُدُوْا رَبَّ هٰذَا الْبَیْتِ ۝

4. Who provides them with food against hunger, and with security against fear (of danger).

الَّذِیْۤ اَطْعَمَهُمْ مِّنْ جُوْعٍ وَّاٰمَنَهُمْ مِّنْ خَوْفٍ ۝

Al-Mā'ūn or Neighbourly Needs.

سُوْرَةُ الْمَاعُوْنِ مَکِّیَّةٌ وَہِیَ سَبْعُ اٰیَاتٍ

In the name of Allah, Most Gracious, Most Merciful.

بِسْمِ اللّٰهِ الرَّحْمٰنِ الرَّحِیْمِ

1. Seest thou one who denies the Judgment (to come) ?

اَرَءَیْتَ الَّذِیْ یُکَذِّبُ بِالدِّیْنِ ۝

2. Then such is the one who repulses the orphan,

فَذٰلِكَ الَّذِیْ یَدُعُّ الْیَتِیْمَ ۝

3. And encourages not the feeding of the indigent.

وَلَا یَحُضُّ عَلٰی طَعَامِ الْمِسْکِیْنِ ۝

4. So woe to the worshippers

فَوَیْلٌ لِّلْمُصَلِّیْنَ ۝

5. Who are neglectful of their Prayers,

الَّذِیْنَ ہُمْ عَنْ صَلَاتِهِمْ سَاهُوْنَ ۝

6. Those who (want but) to be seen,

الَّذِیْنَ ہُمْ یُرَآءُوْنَ ۝

SÛRA–108
AL-KAUTHAR
(INTRODUCTION)

This very brief early Makkan Sûra sums up in the single mystic word *Kauthar* (Abundance) the doctrine of spiritual Riches through devotion and sacrifice. The converse also follows: indulgence in hatred means the cutting off of all hope of this life and the Hereafter.

SÛRA–109
AL-KÃFIRÛN
(INTRODUCTION)

This is another early Makkan Sûra. It defines the right attitude to those who reject Faith: in matters of Truth we can make no compromise, but there is no need to persecute or abuse anyone for his faith or belief.

SÛRA–110
AN-NASR
(INTRODUCTION)

This beautiful Sûra was the last of the Sûras to be revealed *as a whole,* though the portion of the verse v. 4, "This day have I perfected your religion for you," etc., contains probably the last *words* of the Qur-ān to be revealed.

The date of this Sûra was only a few months before the passing away of the Holy Prophet from this world, Rabi' I,

A.H. 11. The place was either the precincts of Makkah at the Farewell Pilgrimage, Zulḥijja, A.H. 10, or Madinah after his return from the Farewell Pilgrimage.

Victory is the crown of service, not an occasion for exultation. All victory comes from the help of Allah.

SÛRA-111
AL-MASAD OR AL-LAHAB
(INTRODUCTION)

This very early Makkan Sûra, though it referred in the first instance to a particular incident in a cruel and relentless persecution, carries the general lesson that cruelty ultimately ruins itself. The man who rages against holy things is burnt up in his own rage. His hands, which are the instruments of his action, perish, and he perishes him self. No boasted wealth or position will save him. The women, who are made for nobler emotions, may, if they go wrong, feed unholy rage with fiercer fuel—to their own loss. For they may twist the torturing rope round their own neck. It is a common experience that people perish by the very means by which they seek to destroy others.

7. But refuse (to supply) (even) neighbourly needs.

غ وَيَمْنَعُونَ الْمَاعُونَ ۞

Al-Kauthar, or Abundance

سُوۡرَةُ الۡکَوۡثَرِ مَکِّیَّۃٌ وَّ هِیَ ثَلٰثُ اٰیَاتٍ

In the name of Allah, Most Gracious, Most Merciful.

بِسۡمِ اللهِ الرَّحۡمٰنِ الرَّحِیۡمِ ۞

1. To thee have We granted the Abundance.

اِنَّاۤ اَعۡطَیۡنٰکَ الۡکَوۡثَرَ ۞

2. Therefore to thy Lord turn in Prayer and Sacrifice.

فَصَلِّ لِرَبِّکَ وَ انۡحَرۡ ۞

3. For he who hateth thee,—He will be cut off (from Future Hope).

غ اِنَّ شَانِئَکَ هُوَ الۡاَبۡتَرُ ۞

Al-Kāfirūn, or Those who reject Faith

سُوۡرَةُ الۡکٰفِرُوۡنَ مَکِّیَّۃٌ وَّ هِیَ سِتُّ اٰیَاتٍ

In the name of Allah, Most Gracious, Most Merciful.

بِسۡمِ اللهِ الرَّحۡمٰنِ الرَّحِیۡمِ ۞

1. Say: O ye that reject Faith !

قُلۡ یٰۤاَیُّهَا الۡکٰفِرُوۡنَ ۞

2. I worship not that which ye worship,

لَاۤ اَعۡبُدُ مَا تَعۡبُدُوۡنَ ۞

3. Nor will ye worship that which I worship.

وَ لَاۤ اَنۡتُمۡ عٰبِدُوۡنَ مَاۤ اَعۡبُدُ ۞

4. And I will not worship that which ye have been wont to worship

وَ لَاۤ اَنَا عَابِدٌ مَّا عَبَدۡتُّمۡ ۞

5. Nor will ye worship that which I worship.

وَ لَاۤ اَنۡتُمۡ عٰبِدُوۡنَ مَاۤ اَعۡبُدُ ۞

6. To you be your Way, and to me mine.

غ لَکُمۡ دِیۡنُکُمۡ وَ لِیَ دِیۡنِ ۞

An-Naṣr, or Help

سُوۡرَةُ النَّصۡرِ مَدَنِیَّۃٌ وَّ هِیَ ثَلٰثُ اٰیَاتٍ

In the name of Allah, Most Gracious, Most Merciful.

بِسۡمِ اللهِ الرَّحۡمٰنِ الرَّحِیۡمِ ۞

1. When comes the Help of Allah, and Victory,

اِذَا جَآءَ نَصۡرُ اللهِ وَ الۡفَتۡحُ ۞

2. And thou dost see the People enter Allah's Religion in crowds,

وَ رَاَیۡتَ النَّاسَ یَدۡخُلُوۡنَ فِیۡ دِیۡنِ اللهِ اَفۡوَاجًا ۞

3. Celebrate the Praises of thy Lord, and pray for His Forgiveness: for He is Oft-Returning (in forgiveness).

فَسَبِّحۡ بِحَمۡدِ رَبِّکَ وَ اسۡتَغۡفِرۡهُ غ اِنَّهٗ کَانَ تَوَّابًا ۞

Al-Lahab, or Al-Masad, or The Flame

سُوۡرَةُ اللَّهَبِ مَکِّیَّۃٌ وَّ هِیَ خَمۡسُ اٰیَاتٍ

In the name of Allah, Most Gracious, Most Merciful.

بِسۡمِ اللهِ الرَّحۡمٰنِ الرَّحِیۡمِ ۞

1. Perish the hands of the Father of Flame! Perish he !

تَبَّتۡ یَدَاۤ اَبِیۡ لَهَبٍ وَّ تَبَّ ۞

2. No profit to him from all his wealth, and all his gains !

مَاۤ اَغۡنٰی عَنۡهُ مَالُهٗ وَ مَا کَسَبَ ۞

3. Burnt soon will he be in a Fire of blazing Flame !

سَیَصۡلٰی نَارًا ذَاتَ لَهَبٍ ۞

4. His wife shall carry the (crackling) wood —as fuel !—

وَّ امۡرَاَتُهٗ حَمَّالَةَ الۡحَطَبِ ۞

SÛRA–112
AL-IKHLÂṢ
(INTRODUCTION)

This early Makkan Sûra sums up in a few terse words the Unity of the Godhead—often professed, but frequently mixed up in the popular mind with debasing superstitions.

SÛRA–113
AL-FALAQ
(INTRODUCTION)

This early Makkan Sûra provides the antidote to superstition and fear by teaching us to seek refuge in Allah from every kind of ill arising from outer nature and from dark and evil plottings and envy on the part of others.

SÛRA–114
AN-NÂS
(INTRODUCTION)

This early Makkan Sûra is a pendant to the last Sûra, and concludes the Holy Qur-ân with an appeal to us to trust in Allah, rather than man, as our sure shield and protection. It warns us specially against the secret whispers of evil within our own hearts.

5. A twisted rope of palm-leaf fibre round her (own) neck !

فِىْ جِيْدِهَا حَبْلٌ مِّنْ مَّسَدٍ ۝

Al-Ikhlās, or Purity (of Faith)

In the name of Allah, Most Gracious, Most Merciful.

بِسْمِ اللهِ الرَّحْمٰنِ الرَّحِيْمِ

1. Say: He is Allah the One;

قُلْ هُوَ اللهُ أَحَدٌ ۝

2. Allah, the Eternal, Absolute;

اللهُ الصَّمَدُ ۝

3. He begetteth not, nor is He begotten;

لَمْ يَلِدْ ۙ وَلَمْ يُوْلَدْ ۝

4. And there is none like unto Him.

وَلَمْ يَكُنْ لَّهٗ كُفُوًا أَحَدٌ ۝

Al-Falaq, or The Dawn

In the name of Allah, Most Gracious, Most Merciful.

بِسْمِ اللهِ الرَّحْمٰنِ الرَّحِيْمِ

1. Say: I seek refuge with the Lord of the Dawn,

قُلْ أَعُوْذُ بِرَبِّ الْفَلَقِ ۝

2. From the mischief of created things;

مِنْ شَرِّ مَا خَلَقَ ۝

3. From the mischief of Darkness as it overspreads;

وَمِنْ شَرِّ غَاسِقٍ إِذَا وَقَبَ ۝

4. From the mischief of those who blow on knots;

وَمِنْ شَرِّ النَّفّٰثٰتِ فِى الْعُقَدِ ۝

5. And from the mischief of the envious one as he practises envy.

وَمِنْ شَرِّ حَاسِدٍ إِذَا حَسَدَ ۝

An-Nās, or Mankind

In the name of Allah, Most Gracious, Most Merciful.

بِسْمِ اللهِ الرَّحْمٰنِ الرَّحِيْمِ

1. Say: I seek refuge with the Lord and Cherisher of Mankind,

قُلْ أَعُوْذُ بِرَبِّ النَّاسِ ۝

2. The King (or Ruler) of Mankind,

مَلِكِ النَّاسِ ۝

3. The God (or Judge) of Mankind,—

إِلٰهِ النَّاسِ ۝

4. From the mischief of the Whisperer (of Evil), who withdraws (after his whisper),—

مِنْ شَرِّ الْوَسْوَاسِ ۙ الْخَنَّاسِ ۝

5. Who whispers into the hearts of Mankind,—

الَّذِىْ يُوَسْوِسُ فِىْ صُدُوْرِ النَّاسِ ۝

6. Among Jinns and among Men.

مِنَ الْجِنَّةِ وَالنَّاسِ ۝

O Allah! Confer Thy grace on me through the Magnificent Qur-ān; make it for me a Book of instruction and evidence, light, guidance and mercy; Grant me the honour of reciting it day and night and make it an argument and proof for me, O Lord and Sustainer of all the worlds, through the gracious instrumentality of Muhammad, Thy Prophet, –May Allah shower blessings and peace on him!

اَللّٰهُمَّ عَلِّمْنِىْ مَا أَنْتَ وَرَّثَنِىْ ۔ اَللّٰهُمَّ ارْحَمْنِىْ بِالْقُرْآنِ الْعَظِيْمِ وَاجْعَلْهُ لِىْ إِمَامًا وَّنُوْرًا وَّهُدًى وَّرَحْمَةً ۔ وَارْزُقْنِىْ تِلَاوَتَهٗ آنَاءَ اللَّيْلِ وَآنَاءَ النَّهَارِ وَاجْعَلْهُ لِىْ حُجَّةً يَا رَبَّ الْعٰلَمِيْنَ ۔ بِحَقِّ نَبِيِّكَ مُحَمَّدٍ صَلَّى اللهُ عَلَيْهِ وَسَلَّمَ

INDEX